Corporate Bonds and Structured Financial Products

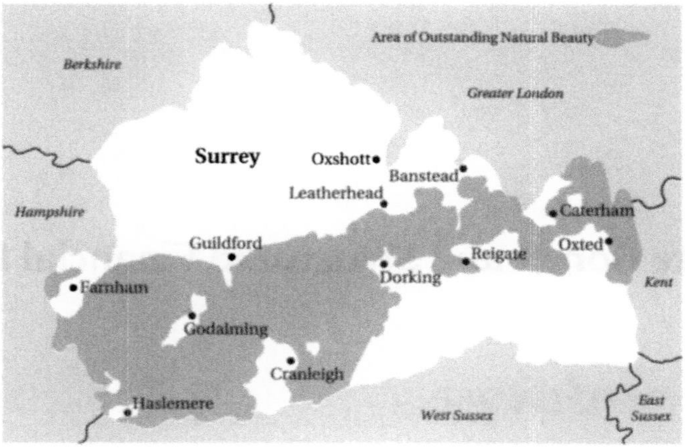

Map of Surrey, showing area of Outstanding Natural Beauty. Drawn from information supplied by The Surrey Hills Partnership. Reproduced with permission.

Moorad Choudhry lives in Surrey, England.

Corporate Bonds and Structured Financial Products

Moorad Choudhry

ELSEVIER
BUTTERWORTH
HEINEMANN

AMSTERDAM BOSTON HEIDELBERG LONDON NEW YORK OXFORD
PARIS SAN DIEGO SAN FRANCISCO SINGAPORE SYDNEY TOKYO

Elsevier Butterworth-Heinemann
Linacre House, Jordan Hill, Oxford OX2 8DP
30 Corporate Drive, Burlington, MA 01803

First published 2004
Reprinted 2005

British Library Cataloguing in Publication Data
A catalogue record for this book is available from the British Library

Library of Congress Cataloguing in Publication Data
A catalogue record for this book is available from the Library of Congress

ISBN 978-0-7506-6261-1

Transferred To Digital Printing 2010

To Derek Taylor, a market expert and a true gent...

Contents

Foreword

The fixed income markets have always been centres of innovation and creativity. This much is apparent from even a cursory glance at developments in recent and not-so-recent history. However, it is only in the last twenty years or so that such innovation has really been required, as markets changed significantly and capital started to move freely. The bond market has been the vital conduit through which capital has been raised; continuing product development in the markets has made a significant, and irreplaceable, contribution to global economic progress. The range of products available is vast and growing, as the needs of both providers and users of capital continually alters in response to changing conditions. This economic dynamic means that market participants observe a state of constant learning, as they must if they are to remain effective in their work. Consider, for instance, the new instruments and techniques that we have had to become familiar with in just the last few years: new instruments for hedging credit risk, new techniques for raising capital through synthetic securitisation of the most esoteric 'reference' assets, and new models for fitting the term structure of interest rates – there is much for market participants to keep in touch with. Inevitably practitioners are required to become specialists, as each segment of the debt markets demands increasingly complex approaches in addressing its problems and requirements.

Of course, users of capital are not limited to existing products for raising finance or hedging market risk exposure. They can ask an investment bank to design an instrument to meet their individual requirements, and target it at specific groups of customers. For example, it is arguable whether the growth of the 'credit-card banks' in the United States (such as MBNA) could have occurred so rapidly without the securitisation mechanism that enabled them to raise lower-cost funding. Witness also the introduction of exotic structured credit products, such as the synthetic collateralised debt obligation (CDO), which uses credit derivatives in its construction and followed rapidly on the development of more conventional CDO structures. The so-called 'CSO' was designed to meet regulatory capital and credit risk management requirements, as opposed to funding requirements. The increasing depth and complexity of the markets requires participants to be completely up-to-date on the latest analytical and valuation techniques if they are not to risk being left behind. It is clear that we operate in an environment in which there exists a long-term interest in the application of ever more sophisticated valuation and analytical techniques. The level of mathematical sophistication in use in financial markets today is phenomenal, not to mention very specialised.

That is why this book, from one of the leading researchers and writers on fixed income today, is such a welcome publication. I should of course say 'books', as we have a series here that forms part of a handsome Library. The antecedents of the author promise that these books will make a high-quality contribution to the field. But it is the books' clarity of approach and focus that I am most excited about. The books are welcome because they are part of the continuing need to remain, as Alan Greenspan would have said, ahead of the curve. They contain insights into practical techniques and applications used in the fixed income markets today, with a hint at what one might expect in the future. They also indicate the scope and significance of these techniques in the world of finance. Readers will notice that the text is fairly technical at many points. This reflects the level of mathematical sophistication one encounters in the markets.

If the author will indulge me, I would like to highlight those parts of the books I was particularly interested in.

The treatment of yield curve analysis in *Advanced Fixed Income Analysis* is first rate. For instance, I liked the comprehensive description of the 'variable roughness penalty' approach to cubic spline estimation of the term structure (Chapter 6). The author rightly points out that most market practitioners can have their analytical needs met by the simpler techniques of yield curve fitting, and only exotic option traders, who wish to model the volatility surface, really need to resort to multi-factor term structure models. That is why the practical demonstration of the cubic spline technique is so welcome in this book. Portfolio managers using this technique will get a good understanding of recent movements in the yield curve as well as good interpretive information for the future. Elsewhere we have a comprehensive treatment of the main single-factor and multi-factor yield curve models in use, with useful comment on the efficacies of using both. The practical implications of using the different interest-rate models are well handled and Chapters 4 and 5 will be of value to practitioners. There is also accessible coverage of the Heath–Jarrow–Morton interest-rate model, described and explained here in its single-factor and multi-factor forms. The author cleverly draws out the link between academic research and market applications by showing how financial institutions are able to continue meeting their clients' ever more complex requirements by incorporating insights from research into their product development.

I am very enthusiastic about the book *Corporate Bonds and Structured Financial Products*. The author captures all the key capital raising instruments. I was fascinated to learn about the synthetic asset-backed CP structure or 'conduit'. Distinct from conventional AB-CP programmes, I was very interested to read about this. Of course, one might (in hindsight!) easily have predicted its development, mirroring as it did the practice seen in the bonds and note market when credit derivatives were allied with traditional securitisation techniques to produce the synthetic CDO. The author presents a new look at established and new products, and both venerable and brand-new techniques. As such the book should be practical interest to fund managers and traders, as well as corporate treasurers.

It is a privilege to be asked to write this foreword. By drawing on both his practical experience of financial markets and research for his PhD at Birkbeck, University of London, Moorad Choudhry successfully combines insights from theory and practice to make a genuinely worthwhile contribution to the financial economics literature. I do hope that this exciting and interesting new Library spurs readers on to their own research and investigation; if they follow the application and dedication evident in this work, they will not be going far wrong.

Professor Christine Oughton
School of Management and Organizational Psychology
Birkbeck, University of London
March 2004

About the Author

Moorad Choudhry is Head of Treasury at KBC Financial Products in London. He previously worked in structured finance services at JPMorgan Chase Bank, and as a government bond trader at Hambros Bank Limited and ABN Amro Hoare Govett Sterling Bonds Limited.

Dr Choudhry is a Visiting Professor at the Department of Economics, London Metropolitan University, a Senior Fellow at the Centre for Mathematical Trading and Finance, CASS Business School, and a Fellow of the Securities Institute.

JP Morgan Chase ITS 1st XI
September 2002

Preface

This book is about the corporate bond markets. Although a large number of bonds issued by corporate entities are conventional or 'plain vanilla' bonds, meaning they have a fixed coupon and a fixed term to maturity, there is also a very large and significant market in structured bonds, or structured financial products, which is an all-encompassing term for securitised bonds, hybrid securities, credit-linked securities and so on. We describe the various forms of bond instrument that are encountered in the markets, always remembering that they are very dynamic and new instruments are being introduced all the time. As part of our description we discuss the yield curve, the main information tool of market participants.

Corporate borrowers wishing to finance long-term investment can raise capital in various ways. The main methods are:

- continued re-investment of the profits generated by a company's current operations;
- selling shares in the company, known as equity capital, equity securities or *equity*, which confirm on buyers a share in ownership of the company. The shareholders as owners have the right to vote at general meetings of the company, as well as the right to share in the company's profits by receiving dividends;
- borrowing money from a bank, via a bank loan. This can be a short-term loan such as an overdraft, or a longer term loan over two, three, five, years or even longer. Bank loans can be at either a fixed or more usually, variable rate of interest;
- borrowing money by issuing debt securities, in the form of *bonds* that subsequently trade in the debt capital market.

The first method may not generate sufficient funds, especially if a company is seeking to expand by growth or acquisition of other companies. In any case a proportion of annual after-tax profits will need to be paid out as dividends to shareholders. Selling further shares is not always popular amongst existing shareholders as it dilutes the extent of their ownership; there are also a host of other factors to consider including if there is any appetite in the market for that company's shares. A bank loan is often inflexible, and the interest rate charged by the bank may be comparatively high for all but the highest quality companies. We say comparatively, because there is often a cheaper way for corporates to borrow money: by tapping the bond markets. An issue of bonds will fix the rate of interest payable by the company for a long-term period, and the chief characteristic of bonds – that they are *tradeable* – makes investors more willing to lend a company funds.

Bond markets play a vital and essential role in raising finance for both governments and corporations. In 2002 the market in dollar-denominated bonds alone was worth over $13 trillion, which gives some idea of its importance. The basic bond instrument, which is a loan of funds by the buyer to the issuer of the bond, in return for regular interest payments up to the termination date of the loan, is still the most commonly issued instrument in the debt markets. Nowadays there is a large variety of bond instruments, issued by a variety of institutions. An almost exclusively corporate instrument, the international bond or Eurobond, is a large and diverse market. In 2002 the size of the Eurobond market was over $2 trillion. This book is intended to be an introduction to the extremely diverse and complex world of the corporate debt markets.

Intended audience

This book is aimed at anyone with an interest in the corporate bond markets. The material is deliberately made very accessible; more experienced practitioners may wish also to refer to the companion book in the Fixed Income Markets Library, *Advanced Fixed Income Analysis*.

The book is primarily aimed at people who work in the markets, including front office, middle office and back office banking and fund management staff who are involved to any extent in fixed interest markets. This includes traders, salespersons, arbitrageurs, money markets dealers, fund managers, stockbrokers and research analysts. Others including corporate and local authority treasurers, risk management personnel and operations staff will also find the contents useful, as will professionals who work in structured finance and other market sectors, such as accountants, lawyers and corporate financiers. For students wishing to enter a career in the financial services industry this book has been written to provide sufficient knowledge and understanding to be useful in their first job and beyond, thus enabling anyone to hit the ground running. It is also hoped that the book remains useful as a reference handbook.

Comments on the text are welcome and should be sent to the author care of Butterworth-Heinemann.

Organisation of the book

This book is organised into twenty-three chapters. The corporate debt markets are extremely diverse, and it is often in corporate markets that the latest and most exciting innovations are found. Some of the instruments used in the corporate markets demand their own particular type of analysis; to this end we review the pricing and analytics of callable bonds, asset-backed bonds and convertibles, among others. There is also a chapter on credit analysis. The latest development in corporate markets, the synthetic structured credit product, is considered in Chapter 22.

Further material on the fixed income markets generally can be obtained from the dedicated website at

www.YieldCurve.com

Moorad Choudhry
Surrey, England
August 2003

Acknowledgements

No thanks to anybody.

--- Felt, *Gold Mine Trash*
Cherry Red Records 1987

Memories of years gone by,
Dashed hopes of a dream that died...
Spirit pulled us through.

--- Redskins, *Lean On Me!*
CNT Records 1983

Part I

Fixed Income Securities

We begin by describing the main instruments that go to make up the bond markets. So in Part I we explain the structure of bonds, and the variety of instruments available. This includes bond pricing and yield, and an initial look at the yield curve. Chapter 2 on the yield curve is a fairly long one and looks not only at the different types of yield curve that may be encountered, but also the issue of spot and forward interest rates, and how to interpret the shape of the yield curve. The remaining two chapters introduce non-vanilla bonds.

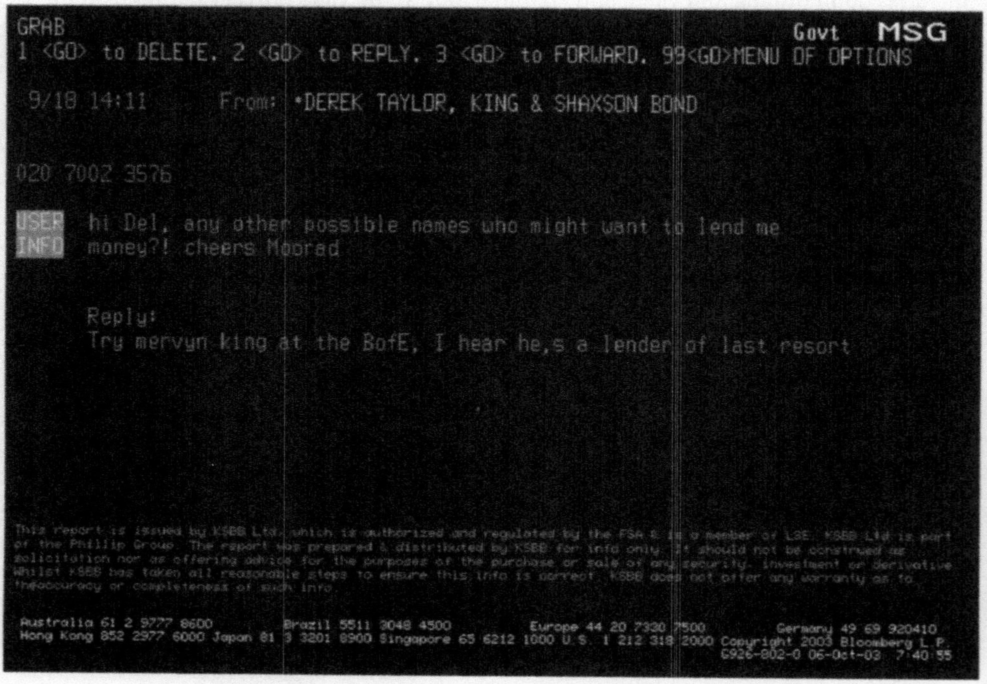
GRAB
Govt MSG
1 <GO> to DELETE. 2 <GO> to REPLY. 3 <GO> to FORWARD. 99<GO>MENU OF OPTIONS
9/18 14:11 From: *DEREK TAYLOR, KING & SHAXSON BOND
020 7002 3576
USER INFO
hi Del, any other possible names who might want to lend me money?! cheers Moorad
Reply:
Try mervyn king at the BofE, I hear he,s a lender of last resort
This report is issued by KSBB Ltd. which is authorized and regulated by the FSA & is a member of LSE. KSBB Ltd is part of the Phillip Group. The report was prepared & distributed by KSBB for info only. It should not be construed as solicitation nor as offering advice for the purposes of the purchase or sale of any security, investment or derivative Whilst KSBB has taken all reasonable steps to ensure this info is correct, KSBB does not offer any warranty as to theaccuracy or completeness of such info.
Australia 61 2 9777 8600 Brazil 5511 3048 4500 Europe 44 20 7330 7500 Germany 49 69 920410
Hong Kong 852 2977 6000 Japan 81 3 3201 8900 Singapore 65 6212 1000 U.S. 1 212 318 2000 Copyright 2003 Bloomberg L.P.
G926-802-0 06-Oct-03 7:40:55

1 A Primer on Bond Basics

Before we begin our look at specific instruments issued by corporate entities, we review the key features of conventional or plain vanilla bond instruments.

1.1 Description

We have said that a bond is a debt instrument, usually paying a fixed rate of interest over a fixed period of time. Therefore a bond is a collection of cash flows and this is illustrated at Figure 1.1. In our hypothetical example the bond is a six-year issue that pays fixed interest payments of C% of the *nominal* value on an annual basis. In the sixth year there is a final interest payment and the loan proceeds represented by the bond are also paid back, known as the maturity proceeds. The amount raised by the bond issuer is a function of the price of the bond at issue, which we have labelled here as the issue proceeds.

The upward facing arrow represents the cash flow paid and the downward facing arrows are the cash flows received by the bond investor. The cash flow diagram for a six-year bond that had a 5% fixed interest rate, known as a 5% *coupon*, would show interest payments of £5 per every £100 of bonds, with a final payment of £105 in the sixth year, representing the last coupon payment and the redemption payment. Again, the amount of funds raised per £100 of bonds depends on the price of the bond on the day it is first issued, and we will look further into this later. If our example bond paid its coupon on a semi-annual basis, the cash flows would be £2.50 every six months until the final redemption payment of £102.50.

Let us examine some of the key features of bonds.

1.1.1 *Type of issuer*

A primary distinguishing feature of a bond is its issuer. The nature of the issuer will affect the way the bond is viewed in the market. There are four issuers of bonds: sovereign governments and their agencies, local government authorities, supranational bodies such as the World Bank, and corporations. Within the corporate bond market there is a wide range of issuers, each with differing abilities to satisfy their contractual obligations to investors. The largest bond markets are those of sovereign borrowers, the government bond markets. The United Kingdom government issues *gilts*. In the United States government bonds are known as *Treasury Notes* and *Treasury Bonds*, or simply *Treasuries*.

1.1.2 *Term to maturity*

The *term to maturity* of a bond is the number of years after which the issuer will repay the obligation. During the term the issuer will also make periodic interest payments on the debt. The *maturity* of a bond refers to the date that the debt will cease to exist, at which time the issuer will redeem the bond by paying the principal. The practice in the market is often to refer simply to a bond's 'term' or 'maturity'. The provisions under which a bond is issued may allow either the issuer or investor to alter a bond's term to

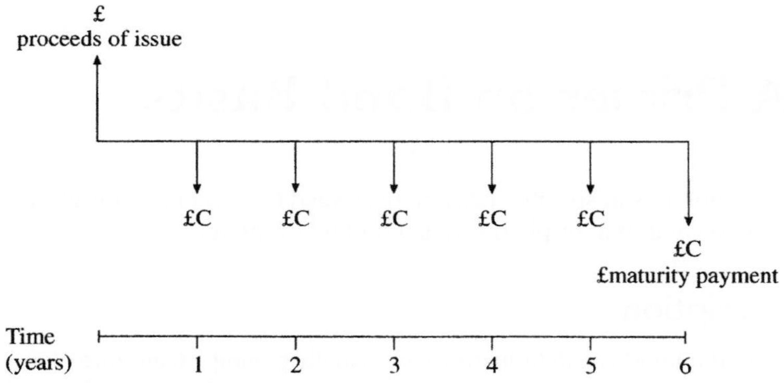

Figure 1.1: Cash flows associated with a six-year annual coupon bond.

maturity after a set notice period, and such bonds need to be analysed in a different way. The term to maturity is an important consideration in the make-up of a bond. It indicates the time period over which the bondholder can expect to receive the coupon payments and the number of years before the principal will be paid in full. The bond's *yield* also depends on the term to maturity. Finally, the price of a bond will fluctuate over its life as yields in the market change and as it approaches maturity. As we will discover later, the *volatility* of a bond's price is dependent on its maturity; assuming other factors constant, the longer a bond's maturity the greater the price volatility resulting from a change in market yields.

1.1.3 *Principal and coupon rate*

The *principal* of a bond is the amount that the issuer agrees to repay the bondholder on the maturity date. This amount is also referred to as the *redemption value, maturity value, par value* or *face amount,* or simply *par.* The *coupon rate* or *nominal rate* is the interest rate that the issuer agrees to pay each year. The annual amount of the interest payment made is called the *coupon.* The coupon rate multiplied by the principal of the bond provides the cash amount of the coupon. For example a bond with a 7% coupon rate and a principal of £1,000,000 will pay annual interest of £70,000. In the United Kingdom, United States and Japan the usual practice is for the issuer to pay the coupon in two semi-annual instalments. For bonds issued in European markets and the Eurobond market coupon payments are made annually. On rare occasions one will encounter bonds that pay interest on a quarterly basis. All bonds make periodic interest payments except for *zero-coupon bonds.* These bonds allow a holder to realise interest by being sold substantially below their principal value. The bonds are redeemed at par, with the interest amount then being the difference between the principal value and the price at which the bond was sold. We will explore zero-coupon bonds in greater detail later.

1.1.4 *Currency*

Bonds can be issued in virtually any currency. The largest volume of bonds in the global markets is denominated in US dollars; other major bond markets are denominated in euros, Japanese yen and sterling, and liquid markets also exist in Australian, New Zealand and

Canadian dollars, Swiss francs and other major currencies. The currency of issue may impact on a bond's attractiveness and liquidity which is why borrowers in developing countries often elect to issue in a currency other than their home currency, for example dollars, as this will make it easier to place the bond with investors. If a bond is aimed solely at a country's domestic investors it is more likely that the borrower will issue in the home currency.

1.2 Bond issuers

1.2.1 *Issuers and participants*

In most countries government expenditure exceeds the level of government income received through taxation. This shortfall is made up by government borrowing and bonds are issued to finance the government's debt. The core of any domestic capital market is usually the government bond market, which also forms the benchmark for all other borrowing.

In the United Kingdom, gilts are identified by their coupon rate and year of maturity; they are also given names such as *Treasury* or *Exchequer*. There is no significance attached to any particular name – all gilts are equivalent irrespective of their name. If a bond has a price of 106.77, this means £106.77 of par value. (Remember that par is the lump sum paid at maturity.) This price represents a *gross redemption yield* of 4.65%. If we pay £106.77 per £100 of stock today, we will receive £100 per £100 of stock on maturity. At first sight this appears to imply we will lose money, however we also receive coupon payments every six months.

Government agencies also issue bonds. Such bonds are virtually as secure as government bonds. In the United States agencies include the Federal National Mortgage Association. Local authorities issue bonds as part of financing for roads, schools, hospitals and other capital projects.

Corporate borrowers issue bonds both to raise finance for major projects and also to cover ongoing and operational expenses. Corporate finance is a mixture of debt and equity and a specific capital project will often be financed as a mixture of both.

1.2.2 *Capital market participants*

The debt capital markets exist because of the financing requirements of governments and corporates. The source of capital is varied, but the total supply of funds in a market is made up of personal or household savings, business savings and increases in the overall money supply. Growth in the money supply is a function of the overall state of the economy, and interested readers may wish to consult the reference list at the end of this chapter which includes several standard economic texts. Individuals save out of their current income for future consumption, while business savings represent retained earnings. The entire savings stock represents the capital available in a market. However, the requirements of savers and borrowers differ significantly, in that savers have a short-term investment horizon while borrowers prefer to take a longer-term view. The 'constitutional weakness' of what would otherwise be unintermediated financial markets led, from an early stage, to the development of financial intermediaries.

Financial intermediaries

In its simplest form a financial intermediary is a *broker* or *agent*. Today we would classify the broker as someone who acts on behalf of the borrower or lender, buying or selling a bond as instructed. However intermediaries originally acted between borrowers and lenders in placing funds as required. A broker would not simply on-lend funds that have been placed with it, but would accept deposits and make loans as required by its customers. This resulted in the first banks.

A *retail bank* deals mainly with the personal financial sector and small businesses, and in addition to loans and deposits also provides cash transmission services. A retail bank is required to maintain a minimum cash reserve, to meet potential withdrawals, but the remainder of its deposit base can be used to make loans. This does not mean that the total size of its loan book is restricted to what it has taken in deposits: loans can also be funded in the wholesale market.

An *investment bank* will deal with governments, corporates and institutional investors. Investment banks perform an agency role for their customers and are the primary vehicle through which a corporate will borrow funds in the bond markets. This is part of the bank's corporate finance function. It will also act as wholesaler in the bond markets, a function known as *market making*. The bond issuing function of an investment bank, by which the bank will issue bonds on behalf of a customer and pass the funds raised to this customer, is known as *origination*. Investment banks will also carry out a range of other functions for institutional customers, including export finance, corporate advisory and fund management. Other financial intermediaries will trade not on behalf of clients but for their own *book*. These include *arbitrageurs* and speculators. Usually such market participants form part of investment banks.

Investors

There is a large variety of players in the bond markets, each trading some or all of the different instruments available to suit their own purposes. We can group the main types of investors according to the time horizon of their investment activity.

Short-term institutional investors

These include banks and building societies, money market fund managers, central banks and the treasury desks of some types of corporates. Such bodies are driven by short-term investment views, often subject to close guidelines, and will be driven by the total return available on their investments. Banks will have an additional requirement to maintain *liquidity*, often in fulfilment of regulatory authority rules, by holding a proportion of their assets in the form of easily-tradeable short-term instruments.

Long-term institutional investors

Typically these types of investors include pension funds and life assurance companies. Their investment horizon is long-term, reflecting the nature of their liabilities. Often they will seek to match these liabilities by holding long-dated bonds.

Mixed horizon institutional investors

This is possibly the largest category of investors and will include general insurance companies and most corporate bodies. Like banks and financial sector companies, they are also very active in the primary market, issuing bonds to finance their operations.

Market professionals

This category includes the banks and specialist financial intermediaries mentioned above, firms that one would not automatically classify as 'investors' although they will also have an investment objective. Their time horizon will range from one day to the very long-term. They include the proprietary trading desks of investment banks, as well as bond market makers in securities houses and banks who are providing a service to their customers. Proprietary traders will actively position themselves in the market in order to gain trading profit, for example in response to their view on where they think interest rate levels are headed. These participants will trade direct with other market professionals and investors, or via brokers. Market makers or *traders* (also called *dealers* in the United States) are wholesalers in the bond markets; they make two-way prices in selected bonds. Firms will not necessarily be active market makers in all types of bonds; smaller firms often specialise in certain sectors. In a two-way quote the *bid price* is the price at which the market maker will buy stock, so it is the price the investor will receive when selling stock. The *offer price* or *ask price* is the price at which investors can buy stock from the market maker. As one might expect the bid price is always higher than the offer price, and it is this *spread* that represents the theoretical profit to the market maker. The bid-offer spread set by the market maker is determined by several factors, including supply and demand, and liquidity considerations for that particular stock, the trader's view on market direction and *volatility*, as well as that of the stock itself and the presence of any market intelligence. A large bid-offer spread reflects low liquidity in the stock, as well as low demand.

Markets

Markets are that part of the financial system where capital market transactions, including the buying and selling of securities, takes place. A market can describe a traditional stock exchange, a physical trading floor where securities trading occurs. Many financial instruments are traded over the telephone or electronically over computer links; these markets are known as *over-the-counter* (OTC) markets. A distinction is made between financial instruments of up to one year's maturity and instruments of over one year's maturity. Short-term instruments make up the *money market* while all other instruments are deemed to be part of the *capital market*. There is also a distinction made between the *primary market* and the *secondary market*. A new issue of bonds made by an investment bank on behalf of its client is made in the primary market. Such an issue can be a *public* offer, in which anyone can apply to buy the bonds, or a *private* offer where the customers of the investment bank are offered the stock. The secondary market is the market in which existing bonds and shares are subsequently traded.

1.3 World bond markets

The origin of the spectacular increase in the size of global financial markets was the rise in oil prices in the early 1970s. Higher oil prices stimulated the development of a sophisticated international banking system, as they resulted in large capital inflows to developed country banks from the oil-producing countries. A significant proportion of these capital flows were placed in *Eurodollar* deposits in major banks. The growing trade deficit and level of public borrowing in the United States also contributed. The last twenty years has seen tremendous growth in capital markets' volumes and trading. As capital controls were eased and exchange rates moved from fixed to floating, domestic capital markets became internationalised. Growth was assisted by the rapid advance in information technology and the widespread use of financial engineering techniques. Today we would think nothing of dealing in virtually any liquid currency bond in financial centres around the world, often at the touch of a button. Global bond issues, underwritten by the subsidiaries of the same banks, are commonplace. The ease with which transactions can be undertaken has also contributed to a very competitive market in liquid currency assets. The world bond market has increased in size more than fifteen times in the last thirty years. As at the end of 2002 outstanding volume stood at over $21 trillion.

The market in US Treasury securities is the largest bond market in the world. Like the government bond markets in the UK, Germany, France and other developed economies, it is also very liquid and transparent. Table 1.1 lists the major government bond markets in the world; the US market makes up nearly half of the total. The Japanese market is second in size, followed by the German market. A large part of the government bond market is concentrated therefore in just a few countries. Government bonds are traded on major exchanges as well as over-the-counter. Generally OTC refers to trades that are not carried out on an exchange but directly between the counterparties. Bonds are also listed on exchanges, for example the NYSE had over 600 government issues listed on it at the end of 1998, with a total par value of $2.6 billion.

The corporate bond market varies in liquidity, depending on the currency and type of issuer of any particular bond. Outstanding volume as at the end of 2001 was over $7.5 trillion. Corporate bonds are also traded on exchanges and OTC. One of the most liquid corporate bond types is the *Eurobond*, which is an international bond issued and traded across national boundaries.

Companies finance their operations in a number of ways, from equity to short-term debt such as bank overdrafts. It is often advantageous for companies to fix longer-term finance, which is why bonds are so popular. Bonds are also attractive as a means of raising finance because the interest payable on them to investors is tax deductible for the company. Dividends on equity are not tax deductible. A corporate needs to get a reasonable mix of debt versus equity in its funding however, as a high level of interest payments will be difficult to service in times of recession or general market downturn. For this reason the market views unfavourably companies that have a high level of debt.

Country	**Nominal value ($ billion)**	**Percentage (rounded)**
United States	5,490	48.5
Japan	2,980	26.3
Germany	1,236	10.9
France	513	4.5
Canada	335	3.0
United Kingdom	331	2.9
Netherlands	253	2.2
Australia	82	0.7
Denmark	72	0.6
Switzerland	37	0.3
Total	11,329	100

Table 1.1: Major government bond markets, December 2002. Source: IFC 2003.

1.4 Non-conventional bonds

The definition of bonds given earlier in this chapter referred to conventional or *plain vanilla* bonds. There are many variations on vanilla bonds and we can introduce a few of them here.

Floating rate notes

The bond market is often referred to as the *fixed income* market, or the *fixed interest* market in the UK. Floating rate notes (FRNs) do not have a fixed coupon at all but instead link their interest payments to an external reference, such as the three-month bank lending rate. Bank interest rates will fluctuate constantly during the life of the bond and so an FRN's cash flows are not known with certainty. Usually FRNs pay a fixed margin or *spread* over the specified reference rate; occasionally the spread is not fixed and such a bond is known as a *variable rate note*. Because FRNs pay coupons based on the three-month or six-month bank rate they trade essentially as money market instruments.

Index-linked bonds

An index-linked bond has its coupon and redemption payment, or possibly just either one of these, linked to a specified index. When governments issue index-linked bonds the cash flows are linked to a price index such as consumer or commodity prices. Corporates have issued index-linked bonds that are connected to inflation or a stock market index.

Zero-coupon bonds

Certain bonds do not make any coupon payments at all and these are known as *zero-coupon bonds*. A zero-coupon bond or *strip* only has cash flow, the redemption payment, on maturity. If we assume that the maturity payment is say, £100 per cent or *par* the issue price will be at a discount to par. Such bonds are also known therefore as *discounted* bonds. The difference between the price paid on issue and the redemption payment is the interest realised by the bondholder. As we will discover when we look at strips this has certain advantages for investors, the main one being that there are no coupon payments to be invested during the bond's life. Both governments and corporates issue zero-coupon bonds. Conventional coupon-bearing bonds can be *stripped* into a series of individual cash flows, which would then trade as separate zero-coupon bonds. This is a common practice in government bond markets such as Treasuries or gilts where the borrowing authority does not actually issue strips, and they have to be created via the stripping process.

Securitised bonds

There is a large market in bonds whose interest and principal liability payments are backed by an underlying cash flow from another asset. By securitising the asset, a borrower can provide an element of cash flow backing to investors. For instance, a mortgage bank can use the cash inflows it receives on its mortgage book as asset backing for an issue of bonds. Such an issue would be known as a mortgage-backed security (MBS). Because residential mortgages rarely run to their full term, but are usually paid off earlier by homeowners, the notes that are backed by mortgages are also prepaid ahead of their legal final maturity. This feature means that MBS securities are not bullet bonds like vanilla securities, but are instead known as *amortising* bonds. Other asset classes that can be securitised include credit card balances, car loans, equipment lease receivables, nursing home receipts, museum or leisure park receipts, and so on.

Bonds with embedded options

Some bonds include a provision in their offer particulars that gives either the bondholder and/or the issuer an option to enforce early redemption of the bond. The most common type of option embedded in a bond is a *call feature*. A call provision grants the issuer the right to redeem all or part of the debt before the specified maturity date. An issuing company may wish to include such a feature as it allows it to replace an old bond issue with a lower coupon rate issue if interest rates in the market have declined. As a call feature allows the issuer to change the maturity date of a bond it is considered harmful to the bondholder's interests; therefore the market price of the bond at any time will reflect this. A call option is included in all asset-backed securities based on mortgages, for obvious reasons (asset-backed bonds are considered in a later chapter). A bond issue may also include a provision that allows the investor to change the maturity of the bond. This is known as a *put feature* and gives the bondholder the right to sell the bond back to the issuer at par on specified dates. The advantage to the bondholder is that if interest rates rise after the issue date, thus depressing the bond's value, the investor can realise par value by *putting* the bond back to the issuer. A *convertible* bond is an issue giving the bondholder the right to exchange the bond for a specified amount of shares (equity) in the issuing company. This feature allows the investor to take advantage of favourable movements in the price of the issuer's shares. The presence of embedded options in a bond makes valuation more complex compared to plain vanilla bonds.

1.5 Pricing a conventional bond

The principles of pricing in the bond market are exactly the same as those in other financial markets, which states that the price of any financial instrument is equal to the net present value today of all the future cash flows from the instrument. A bond price is expressed as per 100 nominal of the bond, or 'per cent'. So for example if the all-in price of a US dollar denominated bond is quoted as '98.00', this means that for every $100 nominal of the bond a buyer would pay $98. The interest rate or discount rate used as part of the present value (price) calculation is key to everything, as it reflects where the bond is trading in the market and how it is perceived by the market. All the determining factors that identify the bond – those discussed in this chapter and including the type of issuer, the maturity, the coupon and the currency – influence the interest rate at which a bond's cash flows are discounted, which will be roughly similar to the rate used for comparable bonds.

Since the price of a bond is equal to the present value of its cash flows, first we need to know the bond's cash flows before then determining the appropriate interest rate at which to discount the cash flows. We can then compute the price of the bond.

1.5.1 *Bond cash flows*

A vanilla bond's cash flows are the interest payments or coupons that are paid during the life of the bond, together with the final redemption payment. It is possible to determine the cash flows with certainty only for conventional bonds of a fixed maturity. So for example, we do not know with certainty what the cash flows are for bonds that have embedded options and can be redeemed early. The coupon payments for conventional bonds are made annually, semi-annually or quarterly. Some bonds pay monthly interest.

Therefore a conventional bond of fixed redemption date is made up of an annuity (its coupon payments) and the maturity payment. If the coupon is paid semi-annually, this means exactly half the coupon is paid as interest every six months. Both gilts and US Treasuries pay semi-annual coupons. For example, the 5% 2012 gilt has the following cash flows:

$$\begin{aligned}\text{Semi-annual coupon} &= £100 \times 0.025\\ &= £2.50\\ \text{Redumption payment} &= £100\end{aligned}$$

The bond was issued on 23 June 1999 and is redeemed on 7 March 2012, and pays coupon on 7 March and 7 September each year. So in 2002 the bond is made up of 20 cash flows of £2.50 and one of £100. The time between coupon payments for any bond is counted as 1 period, so there are 20 periods between the first and last cash flows for the gilt in our example. The maturity payment is received 20 periods from today.

1.5.2 *The discount rate*

The interest rate that is used to discount a bond's cash flows (therefore called the *discount* rate) is the rate required by the bondholder. It is therefore known as the bond's *yield*. The yield on the bond will be determined by the market and is the price demanded by investors for buying it, which is why it is sometimes called the bond's *return*. The required yield for any bond will depend on a number of political and economic factors, including what yield is being earned by other bonds of the same class. Yield is always quoted as an annualised interest rate, so that for a semi-annually paying bond exactly half of the annual rate is used to discount the cash flows.

1.5.3 *Bond pricing*

The *fair price* of a bond is the present value of all its cash flows. Therefore when pricing a bond we need to calculate the present value of all the coupon interest payments and the present value of the redemption payment, and sum these. The price of a conventional bond that pays annual coupons can therefore be given by (1.1).

$$\begin{aligned}P &= \frac{C}{(1+r)} + \frac{C}{(1+r)^2} + \frac{C}{(1+r)^3} + \cdots + \frac{C}{(1+r)^N} + \frac{M}{(1+r)^N}\\ &= \sum_{n=1}^{N} \frac{C}{(1+r)^N} + \frac{M}{(1+r)^N}\end{aligned} \tag{1.1}$$

where

- P is the price
- C is the annual coupon payment
- r is the discount rate (therefore, the required yield)
- N is the number of years to maturity (therefore, the number of interest periods in an annually-paying bond; for a semi-annual bond the number of interest periods is $N \times 2$)
- M is the maturity payment or par value (usually 100 per cent of currency).

For long-hand calculation purposes the first half of (1.1) is usually simplified and in fact can be expressed in two ways as shown by (1.2) below.

$$P = C\frac{1 - \left[\frac{1}{(1+r)^N}\right]}{r}$$

or

$$P = \frac{C}{r}\left[1 - \frac{1}{(1+r)^N}\right] \tag{1.2}$$

The price of a bond that pays semi-annual coupons is given by the expression at (1.3), which is our earlier expression modified to allow for the twice-yearly discounting:

$$\begin{aligned} P &= \frac{\frac{C}{2}}{\left(1+\frac{1}{2}r\right)} + \frac{\frac{C}{2}}{\left(1+\frac{1}{2}r\right)^2} + \frac{\frac{C}{2}}{\left(1+\frac{1}{2}r\right)^3} + \cdots + \frac{\frac{C}{2}}{\left(1+\frac{1}{2}r\right)^{2N}} + \frac{M}{\left(1+\frac{1}{2}r\right)^{2N}} \\ &= \sum_{t=1}^{2T} \frac{\frac{C}{2}}{\left(1+\frac{1}{2}r\right)^N} + \frac{M}{\left(1+\frac{1}{2}r\right)^{2N}} \\ &= \frac{C}{r}\left[1 - \frac{1}{\left(1+\frac{1}{2}r\right)^{2N}}\right] + \frac{M}{\left(1+\frac{1}{2}r\right)^{2N}} \end{aligned} \tag{1.3}$$

Note how we set $2N$ as the power to which to raise the discount factor, as there are two interest payments every year for a bond that pays semi-annually. Therefore a more convenient function to use might be the number of interest periods in the life of the bond, as opposed to the number of years to maturity, which we could set as n, allowing us to alter the equation for a semi-annually paying bond as:

$$P = \frac{C}{r}\left[1 - \frac{1}{\left(1+\frac{1}{2}r\right)^n}\right] + \frac{M}{\left(1+\frac{1}{2}r\right)^n} \tag{1.4}$$

The formula at (1.4) calculates the fair price on a coupon payment date, so that there is no *accrued interest* incorporated into the price. It also assumes that there is an even number of coupon payment dates remaining before maturity.

The date used as the point for calculation is the *settlement date* for the bond, the date on which a bond will change hands after it is traded. For a new issue of bonds the settlement date is the day when the stock is delivered to investors and payment is received by the bond issuer. The settlement date for a bond traded in the *secondary market* is the day that the buyer transfers payment to the seller of the bond and when the seller transfers the bond to the buyer. Different markets will have different settlement conventions, for example UK gilts normally settle one business day after the trade date (the notation used in bond markets is 'T + 1') whereas Eurobonds settle on T + 3. The term *value date* is sometimes used in place of settlement date, however the two terms are not strictly synonymous. A settlement date can only fall on a business date, so that a gilt traded on a Friday will settle on a Monday. However a value date can sometimes fall on a non-business day, for example when accrued interest is being calculated.

The standard price formula also assumes that the bond is traded for price settlement on a day that is precisely one interest period before the next coupon payment. The price formula is adjusted if dealing takes place between coupon dates. If we take the value date (almost always the settlement date, although unlike the settlement date the value date can fall on a non-working day) for any transaction, we then need to calculate the number of calendar days from this day to the next coupon date. We then use the following ratio i when adjusting the exponent for the discount factor:

$$i = \frac{\text{Days from value date to next coupon date}}{\text{Days in the interest period}}$$

The number of days in the interest period is the number of calendar days between the last coupon date and the next one, and it will depend on the day count basis used for that specific bond; this is covered in the section on day counts. The price formula is then modified as shown at (1.5),

$$P = \frac{C}{(1+r)^i} + \frac{C}{(1+r)^{1+i}} + \frac{C}{(1+r)^{2+i}} + \cdots + \frac{C}{(1+r)^{n-1+i}} + \frac{M}{(1+r)^{n-1+i}} \tag{1.5}$$

where the variables C, M, n and r are as before. Note that (1.5) assumes r for an annually-paying bond and is adjusted to $r/2$ for a semi-annually paying bond.

Example 1.1

In these examples we illustrate the long-hand price calculation, using both expressions for the calculation of the present value of the annuity stream of a bond's cash flows.

1.1(a)
Calculate the fair pricing of a UK gilt, the 9% Treasury 2008, which pays semi-annual coupons, with the following terms:

$C = £9.00$ per £100 nominal
$M = £100$
$N = 10$ years (that is, the calculation is for value on 13 October 1998)
$r = 4.98\%$

$$\begin{aligned} P &= \frac{£9.00}{0.0498}\left\{1 - \frac{1}{\left[1+\frac{1}{2}(0.0498)\right]^{20}}\right\} + \frac{£100}{\left[1+\frac{1}{2}(0.0498)\right]^{20}} \\ &= £70.2175 + £61.1463 \\ &= £131.3638 \end{aligned}$$

The fair price of the gilt is £131.3638, which is composed of the present value of the stream of coupon payments (£70.2175) and the present value of the return of the principal (£61.1463).

1.1(b)
What is the price of a 5% coupon sterling bond with precisely 5 years to maturity, with semi-annual coupon payments, if the yield required is 5.40%? As the cash flows for this bond are 10 semi-annual coupons of £2.50 and a redemption payment of £100 in 10 six-month periods from now, the price of the bond can be obtained by solving the following expression, where we substitute $C = 2.5$, $n = 10$ and $r = 0.027$ into the price equation (the values for C and r reflect the adjustments necessary for a semi-annual paying bond).

$$P = 2.5\left[\frac{1-\left[\frac{1}{(1.027)^{10}}\right]}{0.027}\right] + \frac{100}{(1.027)^{10}}$$
$$= £21.65574 + £76.61178$$
$$= £98.26752$$

The price of the bond is £98.2675 per £100 nominal.

1.1(c)
What is the price of a 5% coupon euro bond with five years to maturity paying annual coupons, again with a required yield of 5.40%?

In this case there are five periods of interest, so we may set $C=5$, $n=5$, with $r=0.05$.

$$P = 5\left[\frac{1-\left[\frac{1}{(1.054)^{5}}\right]}{0.054}\right] + \frac{100}{(1.054)^{5}}$$
$$= £21.410121 + £76.877092$$
$$= £98.287213$$

Note how the annual-paying bond has a slightly higher price for the same required annualised yield. This is because the semi-annual paying sterling bond has a higher effective yield than the euro bond, resulting in a lower price.

1.1(d)
Consider our 5% sterling bond again, but this time the required yield has risen and is now 6%. This makes $C=2.5$, $n=10$ and $r=0.03$.

$$P = 2.5\left[\frac{1-\left[\frac{1}{(1.03)^{10}}\right]}{0.03}\right] + \frac{100}{(1.03)^{10}}$$
$$= £21.325507 + £74.409391$$
$$= £95.734898$$

As the required yield has risen, the discount rate used in the price calculation is now higher, and the result of the higher discount is a lower present value (price).

1.1(e)
Calculate the price of our sterling bond, still with five years to maturity but offering a yield of 5.10%.

$$P = 2.5\left[\frac{1-\left[\frac{1}{(1.0255)^{10}}\right]}{0.0255}\right] + \frac{100}{(1.0255)^{10}}$$
$$= £21.823737 + £77.739788$$
$$= £99.563525$$

To satisfy the lower required yield of 5.10% the price of the bond has fallen to £99.56 per £100.

1.1(f)

Calculate the price of the 5% sterling bond one year later, with precisely four years left to maturity and with the required yield still at the original 5.40%. This sets the terms in 1.1(a) unchanged, except now $n=8$.

$$P = 2.5\left[\frac{1-\left[\frac{1}{(1.027)^8}\right]}{0.027}\right] + \frac{100}{(1.027)^8}$$

$$= £17.773458 + £80.804668$$

$$= £98.578126$$

The price of the bond is £98.58. Compared to 1.1(b) this illustrates how, other things being equal, the price of a bond will approach par (£100 per cent) as it approaches maturity.

1.5.4 *Pricing undated bonds*

There also exist *perpetual* or *irredeemable* bonds which have no redemption date, so that interest on them is paid indefinitely. They are also known as *undated* bonds. An example of an undated bond is the 3 1/2% War Loan, a gilt formed out of issues in 1916 to help pay for the 1914–1918 war effort. Most undated bonds date from a long time in the past and it is unusual to see them issued today. In structure the cash flow from an undated bond can be viewed as a continuous annuity. The fair price of such a bond is given from (1.1) by setting $N=\infty$, such that:

$$P = \frac{C}{r} \qquad (1.6)$$

where the inputs C and r are as before.

1.5.5 *Bond price quotations*

The convention in most bond markets is to quote prices as a percentage of par. The value of par is assumed to be 100 units of currency unless otherwise stated. A sterling bond quoted at an *offer* price of £98.45 means that £100 nominal of the bond will cost a buyer £98.45. A bond selling at below par is considered to be trading at a *discount*, while a price above par means the bond is trading at a *premium* to par. Do not confuse the term trading at a discount with a discount instrument however, which generally refers to a zero-coupon bond.

In most markets bond prices are quoted in decimals, in minimum increments of 1/100ths. This is the case for example with Eurobonds, euro denominated bonds and gilts. Certain markets including the US Treasury market for example, and certain Commonwealth markets such as South African and Indian government bonds quote prices in *ticks*, where the minimum increment is 1/32nd. One tick is therefore equal to 0.03125. A US Treasury might be priced at '98–05' which means '98 and 5 ticks'. This is equal to 98 and 5/32nds which is 98.15625.

Example 1.2

- What is the total consideration for £5 million nominal of a gilt, where the price is 114.50?

The price of the gilt is £114.50 per £100, so the consideration is:

$$1.145 \times 5,000,000 = £5,725,000$$

- What consideration is payable for $5 million nominal of a US Treasury, quoted at an all-in price of 99–16?

The US Treasury price is 99–16, which is equal to 99 and 16/32, or 99.50 per $100. The consideration is therefore:

$$0.9950 \times 5,000,000 = \$4,975,000$$

If the price of a bond is below par the total consideration is below the nominal amount, whereas if it is priced above par the consideration will be above the nominal amount.

1.6 Clean and dirty bond prices

1.6.1 *Accrued interest*

Our discussion of bond pricing up to now has ignored coupon interest. All bonds (except zero-coupon bonds) accrue interest on a daily basis, and this is then paid out on the coupon date. The calculation of bond prices using present value analysis does not account for coupon interest or *accrued interest*. In all major bond markets the convention is to quote price as a *clean price*. This is the price of the bond as given by the net present value of its cash flows, but excluding coupon interest that has accrued on the bond since the last dividend payment. As all bonds accrue interest on a daily basis, even if a bond is held for only one day, interest will have been earned by the bondholder. However we have referred already to a bond's *all-in* price, which is the price that is actually paid for the bond in the market. This is also known as the *dirty price* (or *gross price*), which is the clean price of a bond plus accrued interest. In other words the accrued interest must be added to the quoted price to get the total consideration for the bond.

Accruing interest compensates the seller of the bond for giving up all of the next coupon payment even though they will have held the bond for part of the period since the last coupon payment. The clean price for a bond will move with changes in market interest rates; assuming that this is constant in a coupon period, the clean price will be constant for this period. However the dirty price for the same bond will increase steadily from one interest payment date until the next one. On the coupon date the clean and dirty prices are the same and the accrued interest is zero. Between the coupon payment date and the next *ex-dividend* date the bond is traded *cum dividend*, so that the buyer gets the next coupon payment. The seller is compensated for not receiving the next coupon payment by receiving accrued interest instead. This is positive and increases up to the next ex-dividend date, at which point the dirty price falls by the present value of the amount of the coupon payment. The dirty price at this point is below the clean price, reflecting the fact that accrued interest is now negative. This is because after the ex-dividend date the bond is traded 'ex-dividend'; the seller not the buyer receives the next coupon and the buyer has to be compensated for not receiving the next coupon by means of a lower price for holding the bond.

The net interest accrued since the last ex-dividend date is determined as follows:

$$AI = C \times \left[\frac{N_{xt} - N_{xc}}{\text{Day Base}}\right] \tag{1.7}$$

where

AI	is the next accrued interest
C	is the bond coupon
N_{xc}	is the number of days between the ex-dividend date and the coupon payment date (7 business days for UK gilts)
N_{xt}	is the number of days between the ex-dividend date and the date for the calculation
Day Base	is the day count base (usually 365 or 360).

Interest accrues on a bond from and including the last coupon date up to and excluding what is called the *value date*. The value date is almost always the *settlement* date for the bond, or the date when a bond is passed to the buyer and the seller receives payment. Interest does not accrue on bonds whose issuer has subsequently gone into default. Bonds that trade without accrued interest are said to be trading *flat* or *clean*. By definition therefore,

$$\text{Clean price of a bond} = \text{Dirty price} - AI$$

For bonds that are trading ex-dividend, the accrued coupon is negative and would be subtracted from the clean price. The calculation is given by (1.8) below.

$$AI = -C \times \frac{\text{Days to next coupon}}{\text{Day Base}} \tag{1.8}$$

Certain classes of bonds, for example US Treasuries and Eurobonds, do not have an ex-dividend period and therefore trade cum dividend right up to the coupon date.

1.6.2 *Accrual day count conventions*

The accrued interest calculation for a bond is dependent on the day-count basis specified for the bond in question. We have already seen that when bonds are traded in the market the actual consideration that changes hands is made up of the clean price of the bond together with the accrued interest that has accumulated on the bond since the last coupon payment; these two components make up the dirty price of the bond. When calculating the accrued interest, the market will use the appropriate day-count convention for that bond. A particular market will apply one of five different methods to calculate accrued interest; these are:

actual/365	Accrued = Coupon × days/365
actual/360	Accrued = Coupon × days/360
actual/actual	Accrued = Coupon × days/actual number of days in the interest period
30/360	See below
30E/360	See below

When determining the number of days in between two dates, include the first date but not the second; thus, under the actual/365 convention, there are 37 days between 4 August and 10 September. The last two conventions assume 30 days in each month, so for example there are '30 days' between 10 February and 10 March. Under the 30/360 convention, if the first date falls on the 31st, it is changed to the 30th of the month, and if the second date falls on the 31st and the first date is on the 30th or 31st, the second date is changed to the 30th. The difference under the 30E/360 method is that if the second date falls on the 31st of the month it is automatically changed to the 30th.

The day count basis, together with the coupon frequency, of selected major government bond markets around the world is given in Table 1.2.

Bloomberg users can select screen DCX to check the day-count for a particular market and also the impact of any public holidays. The screen is of some use when dealing in bonds traded on a 30/360 basis, which international securities such as Eurobonds and many corporate bonds are. Figure 1.2 Bloomberg below shows the three-month period beginning 15 August 2003 in the UK market; we see that for a 30/360 day-count bond this is 93 days and also note that there is a public holiday in the UK market during this period.

Example 1.3

Accrual calculation for 7% Treasury 2002

This gilt has coupon dates of 7 June and 7 December each year. £100 nominal of the bond is traded for value on 27 August 1998. What is the accrued interest on the value date?

On the value date 81 days have passed since the last coupon date. Under the old system for gilts, act/365, the calculation was:

$$7 \times \frac{81}{365} = 1.55342.$$

Under the current system of act/act, which came into effect for gilts in November 1998, the accrued calculation uses the actual number of days between the two coupon dates, giving us:

$$7 \times \frac{81}{183} \times 0.5 = 1.54918.$$

Example 1.4

Mansur buys £25,000 nominal of the 7% 2002 gilt for value on 27 August 1998, at a price of 102.4375. How much does he actually pay for the bond?

The clean price of the bond is 102.4375. The dirty price of the bond is:

$$102.4375 + 1.55342 = 103.99092$$

The total consideration is therefore 1.0399092 × 25,000 = £25,997.73.

Example 1.5

A Norwegian government bond with a coupon of 8% is purchased for settlement on 30 July 1999 at a price of 99.50. Assume that this is 7 days before the coupon date and therefore the bond trades ex-dividend. What is the all-in price?

$$\text{The accrued interest} = -8 \times \frac{7}{365} = -0.153424$$

The all-in price is therefore 99.50 − 0.1534 = 99.3466.

Market	Coupon frequency	Day count basis	Ex-dividend period
Australia	Semi-annual	actual/actual	Yes
Austria	Annual	actual/actual	No
Belgium	Annual	actual/actual	No
Canada	Semi-annual	actual/actual	No
Denmark	Annual	actual/actual	Yes
Eurobonds	Annual	30/360	No
France	Annual	actual/actual	No
Germany	Annual	actual/actual	No
Eire	Annual	actual/actual	No
Italy	Annual	actual/actual	No
New Zealand	Semi-annual	actual/actual	Yes
Norway	Annual	actual/365	Yes
Spain	Annual	actual/actual	No
Sweden	Annual	30E/360	Yes
Switzerland	Annual	30E/360	No
United Kingdom	Semi-annual	actual/actual	Yes
United States	Semi-annual	actual/actual	No

Table 1.2: Government bond market conventions.

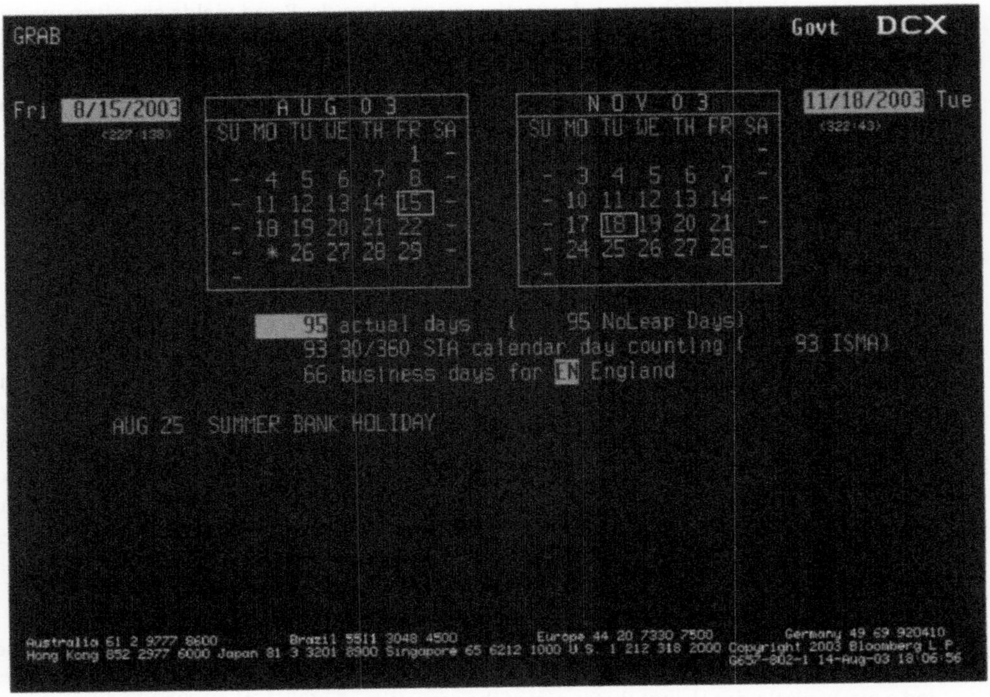

Figure 1.2: Bloomberg screen DCX. © Bloomberg L.P. Used with permission.

1.7 Market yield

We referred in Section 1.5.2 to the yield that is 'required' by the market at any one time. Just as there are many different types of bond and many different types of borrower, so there are different types of yield. The price of any bond will change in line with changes in required yield, so that straight away we can see that it is not price changes that we are really interested in, but yields. It is a change in required yield that will drive a change in price.[1] So in the bond market we are concerned with examining the determinants of market yields.

The main quoted yield in any market is the government bond yield. This is the yield on a domestic market's government bonds. The required yield on these bonds is mainly a function of the central bank's *base rate* or *minimum lending rate*, set by the government or central bank. Other factors will also impact the yield, including the relative size of the public sector budget deficit and national debt as a percentage of the national product (usually measured as Gross Domestic Product or Gross National Product), the economic policies that are adopted, and of course supply and demand for government bonds themselves. A change in any of these factors can and does affect government bond prices. While it is common to view government bonds as the safest credit for investors, this really only applies to the largest developed country markets. Certain countries within the Organisation for Economic Co-operation and Development (OECD), for example, Greece, South Korea and Mexico, do not have their government debt given the highest possible rating by credit analysts.

Bonds issued by non-sovereign borrowers will be priced off government bonds, which means that the yields required on them will be at some level above their respective government bond yields, if they are domestic currency bonds. Bond yields are often quoted as a *yield spread* over the equivalent government bond. This is known as the *credit spread* on a bond. A change in the required credit spread for any bond will affect the bond's price. Credit spreads will fluctuate for a variety of reasons, including when there is a change in the way the borrower is perceived in the market (such as a poor set of financial results by a corporate), which will affect the rate at which the borrower can raise funds. Credit spreads can sometimes change because comparable bonds' yields change, as well as due to supply and demand factors and liquidity factors.

1.7.1 *Yield measurement*

Bonds are generally traded on the basis of their prices but because of the complicated patterns of cash flows that different bonds can have, they are generally compared in terms of their yields. This means that a market-maker will usually quote a two-way price at which they will buy or sell a particular bond, but it is the yield at which the bond is trading that is important to the market-maker's customer. This is because a bond's price does not actually tell us anything useful about what we are getting. Remember that in any market there will be a number of bonds with different issuers, coupons and terms to maturity. Even in a homogeneous market such as the gilt market, different gilts will trade according to their own specific characteristics. To compare bonds in the market therefore we need the yield on any bond and it is yields that

1 We have observed how the price of a bond will gradually converge towards par as it approaches maturity, irrespective of the price it trades at during its life. However this is an automatic process and a mechanical price change that is part of the properties of a bond. As such it need not concern us unduly.

we compare, not prices. A fund manager quoted a price at which they can buy a bond will be instantly aware of what yield that price represents, and whether this yield represents fair value. So it is the yield represented by the price that is the important figure for bond traders.

The yield on any investment is the interest rate that will make the present value of the cash flows from the investment equal to the initial cost (price) of the investment. So mathematically the yield on any investment is the interest rate that satisfies our basic bond price equation introduced earlier as equation (1.1).

But as we have noted there are other types of yield measure used in the market for different purposes. The most important of these are bond redemption yields, *spot* rates and *forward* rates. We will now discuss each type of yield measure and show how it is computed, followed by a discussion of the relative usefulness of each measure.

1.7.2 *Current yield*

The simplest measure of the yield on a bond is the *current yield,* also known as the *flat yield, interest yield* or *running yield.* The running yield is given by (1.9).

$$rc = \frac{C}{P} \times 100 \tag{1.9}$$

where

rc	is the current yield
C	is the bond coupon
P	is the clean price of the bond.

In (1.9) C is not expressed as a decimal. Current yield ignores any capital gain or loss that might arise from holding and trading a bond and does not consider the time value of money. It essentially calculates the bond coupon income as a proportion of the price paid for the bond, and to be accurate would have to assume that the bond was more like an annuity rather than a fixed-term instrument.

The current yield is useful as a 'rough-and-ready' interest rate calculation; it is often used to estimate the cost of or profit from a short-term holding of a bond. For example if other short-term interest rates such as the one-week or three-month rates are higher than the current yield, holding the bond is said to involve a *running cost.* This is also known as *negative carry* or *negative funding.* The term is used by bond traders and market makers and *leveraged* investors. The *carry* on a bond is a useful measure for all market practitioners as it illustrates the cost of holding or funding a bond. The funding rate is the bondholder's short-term cost of funds. A private investor could also apply this to a short-term holding of bonds.

Example 1.6

Running yield

A bond with a coupon of 6% is trading at a clean price of 97.89. What is the current yield of the bond?

$$\begin{aligned} rc &= \frac{6.00}{97.89} \times 100 \\ &= 6.129\% \end{aligned}$$

Example 1.7

What is the current yield of a bond with 7% coupon and a clean price of 103.49?

$$rc = \frac{7}{103.49} \times 100$$
$$= 6.76\%$$

Note from examples 1.6 and 1.7 that the current yield of a bond will lie above the coupon rate if the price of the bond is below par, and vice-versa if the price is above par.

1.7.3 *Yield to maturity*

The *yield to maturity* (YTM) or *gross redemption yield* is the most frequently used measure of return from holding a bond.[2] Yield to maturity takes into account the pattern of coupon payments, the bond's term to maturity and the capital gain (or loss) arising over the remaining life of the bond. We saw from our bond price in equation (1.1) that these elements were all related and were important components determining a bond's price. If we set the IRR for a set of cash flows to be the rate that applies from a start date to an end date we can assume the IRR to be the YTM for those cash flows. The YTM therefore is equivalent to the *internal rate of return* (IRR) on the bond, the rate that equates the value of the discounted cash flows on the bond to its current price. The calculation assumes that the bond is held until maturity and therefore it is the cash flows to maturity that are discounted in the calculation. It also employs the concept of the time value of money.

As we would expect the formula for YTM is essentially that for calculating the price of a bond. For a bond paying annual coupons the YTM is calculated by solving equation (1.10), and we assume that the first coupon will be paid exactly one interest period from now (which, for an annual coupon bond is exactly one year from now).

$$P_d = \frac{C}{(1+rm)^1} + \frac{C}{(1+rm)^2} + \frac{C}{(1+rm)^3} + \cdots + \frac{C}{(1+rm)^n} + \frac{M}{(1+rm)^n} \tag{1.10}$$

where

P_d	is the bond dirty price
C	is the coupon rate
M	is the par or redemption payment (100)
rm	is the annual yield to maturity (the YTM)
n	is the number of interest periods.

Note that the number of interest periods in an annual-coupon bond is equal to the number of years to maturity, and so for these bonds n is equal to the number of years to maturity.

---

2 In this book the terms *yield to maturity* and *gross redemption yield* are used synonymously. The latter term is encountered in sterling markets.

We can simplify (1.10) using $\sum$ where '$\sum$' means 'is the sum of'.

$$P_d = \sum_{n=1}^{N} \frac{C}{(1+rm)^n} + \frac{M}{(1+rm)^n} \tag{1.11}$$

Note that the expression at (1.11) has two variable parameters, the price *Pd* and yield *rm*. It cannot be re-arranged to solve for yield *rm* explicitly and in fact the only way to solve for the yield is to use the process of numerical iteration. The process involves estimating a value for *rm* and calculating the price associated with the estimated yield. If the calculated price is higher than the price of the bond at the time, the yield estimate is lower than the actual yield, and so it must be adjusted until it converges to the level that corresponds with the bond price.[3] For YTM for a semi-annual coupon bond we have to adjust the formula to allow for the semi-annual payments. Equation (1.11) is modified as shown by (1.12), again assuming there are precisely six months to the next coupon payment.

$$P_d = \sum_{n=1}^{N} \frac{\frac{C}{2}}{\left(1+\frac{1}{2}rm\right)^n} + \frac{M}{\left(1+\frac{1}{2}rm\right)^n} \tag{1.12}$$

where *n* is now the number of interest periods in the life of the bond and therefore equal to the number of years to maturity multiplied by 2.

All the YTM equations above use *rm* to discount a bond's cash flows back to the next coupon payment and then discount the value at that date back to the date of the calculation. In other words *rm* is the internal rate of return that equates the value of the discounted cash flows on the bond to the current dirty price of the bond (at the current date). The internal rate of return is the discount rate which, if applied to all of the cash flows will solve for a number that is equal to the dirty price of the bond (its present value). By assuming that this rate will be unchanged for the reinvestment of all the coupon cash flows, and that the instrument will be held to maturity, the IRR can then be seen as the yield to maturity. In effect both measures are identical; the assumption of uniform reinvestment rate allows us to calculate the IRR as equivalent to the redemption yield. It is common for the IRR measure to be used by corporate financiers for project appraisal, while the redemption yield measure is used in bond markets. The solution to the equation for *rm* cannot be found analytically and has to be solved through numerical iteration, that is, by estimating the yield from two trial values for *rm*, then solving by using the formula for linear interpolation. It is more common nowadays to use a spreadsheet programme or programmable calculator such as a Hewlett-Packard calculator.

Note that the redemption yield as discussed in this section is the gross redemption yield, the yield that results from payment of coupons without deduction of any withholding tax. The *net redemption yield* is obtained by multiplying the coupon rate *C* by (1 – marginal tax rate). The net yield is what will be received if the bond is traded in a market where bonds pay coupon net, which means net of a withholding tax. The net redemption yield is always lower than the gross redemption yield.

---

3 Bloomberg® also uses the term yield-to-workout where 'workout' refers to the maturity date for the bond.

1.7.4 *Using the redemption yield calculation*

We have already alluded to the key assumption behind the YTM calculation, namely that the rate *rm* remains stable for the entire period of the life of the bond. By assuming the same yield we can say that all coupons are reinvested at the same yield *rm*. For the bond in example 1.8 this means that if all the cash flows are discounted at 6.5% they will have a total present value or NPV of 97.89. At the same time if all the cash flows received during the life of the bond are reinvested at 6.5% until the maturity of the bond, the final redemption yield will be 6.5%. This is patently unrealistic since we can predict with virtual certainty that interest rates for instruments of similar maturity to the bond at each coupon date will not remain at 6.5% for five years.

In practice, however, investors require a rate of return that is equivalent to the price that they are paying for a bond and the redemption yield is, to put it simply, as good a measurement as any. A more accurate measurement might be to calculate present values of future cash flows using the discount rate that is equal to the market's view on where interest rates will be at that point, known as the *forward* interest rate. However forward rates are *implied* interest rates, and a YTM measurement calculated using forward rates can be as speculative as one calculated using the conventional formula. This is because the actual market interest rate at any time is invariably different from the rate implied earlier in the forward markets. So a YTM calculation made using forward rates would not be realised in practice either.[4] We shall see later in this chapter how the *zero-coupon* interest rate is the true interest rate for any term to maturity. However the YTM is, despite the limitations presented by its assumptions, the main measure of return used in the markets.

Example 1.8

Comparing the different yield measures

The examples in this section illustrated a five-year bond with a coupon of 6% trading at a price of 97.89. Using the three common measures of return we have:

Running yield = 6.129%
Simple yield = 6.560%
Redemption yield = 6.50%

1.8 Bond pricing and yield

The approach we have described is very much the traditional one. Academic texts express bond prices and yields in different terms, which we consider briefly now. The terminology is that used in leading texts including Jarrow (1996), Neftci (1996), Baxter and Rennie (1996) and Hull (1997).

Consider a zero-coupon bond that has a maturity date at time *T*. The price of this bond today (at time *t*) is denoted by *P*(*t*, *T*) and given by (1.13) below,

$$P(t,T) = \frac{1}{[r(t,T)]^{(T-t)}} \tag{1.13}$$

[4] Such an approach is used to price interest-rate swaps, however.

where $r(t, T)$ is the yield of the T-maturity bond at time t. Expression (1.13) above can be re-written as follows, in terms of the bond yield.

$$r(t,T) = \left[\frac{1}{P(t,T)}\right]^{1/(T,t)} \tag{1.14}$$

This states that the yield on the zero-coupon bond is the percentage return earned in the period from the time the bond is held (t) to its maturity date T. We can then derive an expression for the bond price in terms of a *forward rate*. The forward rate $rf(t, T)$ is the rate that applies at time t for the period $(T, T+1)$ and is given by (1.15) below,

$$rf(t,T) = \frac{P(t,T)}{P(t,T+1)} \tag{1.15}$$

and is the interest-rate that is earned on a deposit over the time period $(T, T+1)$ that has been put on at time t. Expression (1.1) above may be used to obtain a formula for the price of a bond, given below.

$$P(T,t) = \frac{1}{\prod_{j=1}^{T-1} rf(t,j)} \tag{1.16}$$

Expression (1.16) states the price of a bond in terms of the forward rates for maturity periods up to the maturity of the bond itself. For a zero-coupon bond the price is the present value of 1 that is received at time T, discounted at the forward rates that apply to each interest period from t to the maturity date. This is the bond price expression found in later texts. In fact the bond price is usually given in terms of an *integral* of forward rates, because rates are analysed as occurring in a *continuous time* environment. This is an advanced area of bond mathematics and interested readers should consult the texts listed in the bibliography. The derivation of (1.16) is given in Jarrow (1996) and other texts.

1.9 The price/yield relationship

This chapter has illustrated a fundamental property of bonds, namely that an upward change in the price results in a downward move in the yield, and vice-versa. This is of course immediately apparent since the price is the present value of the cash flows; as the required yield for a bond say decreases, the present value and hence the price of the cash flow for the bond will increase. It also reflects the fact that for plain vanilla bonds the coupon is fixed, therefore it is the price of the bond that will need to fluctuate to reflect changes in market yields. It is useful sometimes to plot the relationship between yield and price for a bond. A typical price/yield profile is represented graphically at Figure 1.3, which shows a *convex* curve.

To reiterate, for a plain vanilla bond with a fixed coupon, the price is the only variable that can change to reflect changes in the market environment. When the coupon rate of a bond is equal to the market rate, the bond price will be par (100). If the required interest rate in the market moves above a bond's coupon rate at any point in time, the price of the bond will adjust downward in order for the bondholder to realise the additional return required. Similarly if the required yield moves below the coupon rate, the price will move up to equate the yield on the bond to the market rate. As a bond will redeem at par, the capital appreciation realised on maturity acts as compensation when the coupon rate is lower than the market yield.

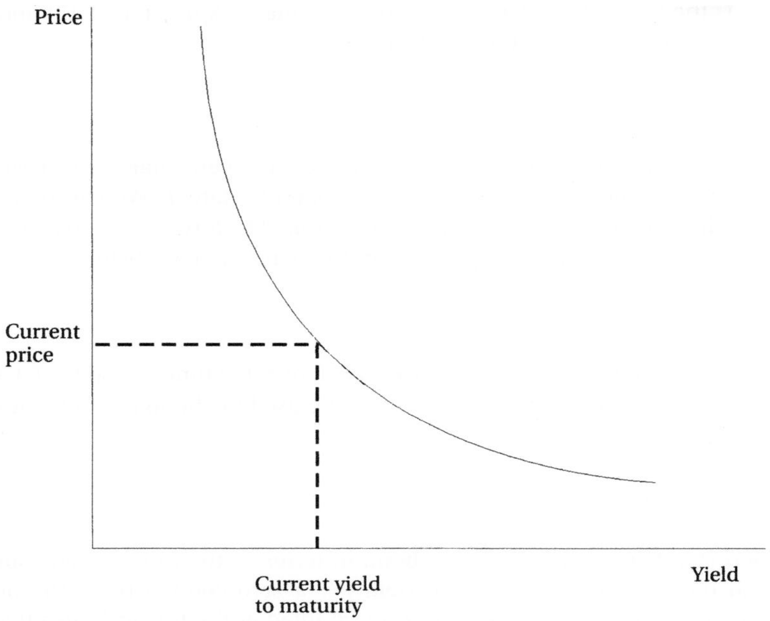

Figure 1.3: Diagrammatic representation of the bond price/yield relationship.

The price of a bond will move for a variety of reasons, including the market-related ones noted here:

- when there is a change in the yield required by the market, either because of changes in the base rate or a perceived change in credit quality of the bond issuer (credit considerations do not affect developed country government bonds);
- when there is a change because as the bond is approaching maturity, its price moves gradually towards par;
- when there is a change in the market-required yield due to a change in the yield on comparable bonds.

Bond prices also move for liquidity reasons and normal supply-and-demand reasons, for example if there is a large amount of a particular bond in issue it is easier to trade the bond; also if there is demand due to a large customer base for the bond. Liquidity is a general term used here to mean the ease with which a market participant can trade in or out of a position. If there is always a ready buyer or seller for a particular bond, it will be easier to trade in the market.

Table 1.3 shows the prices for a hypothetical 7% coupon, quoted for settlement on 10 August 1999 and maturing on 10 August 2004. The bond pays annual coupons on a 30/360 basis. The prices are calculated by inserting the required yield values into the standard formulae for a set of cash flows. We can calculate the present value of the annuity stream represented by the bond and the present value of the final maturity payment. Note that when the required yield is at the same level as the bond's fixed coupon (in this case 7%) the price of the bond is 100 per cent, or *par*.

Yield (%)	Price
4.0	113.3555
4.5	110.9750
5.0	108.6590
5.5	106.4054
6.0	104.2124
6.5	102.0778
7.0	**100.0000**
7.5	97.9770
8.0	96.0073
8.5	94.0890
9.0	92.2207
9.5	90.4007
10.0	88.6276

Table 1.3: Prices and yields for a 7% five-year bond.

1.9.1 *Coupon, yield and price relationship*

The bond markets are also known as the 'fixed income' or 'fixed interest' markets. This reflects the fact that the coupon for conventional bonds is fixed, and in most cases the maturity date is also fixed. Therefore when required yield levels in the market change, the price is the only factor that can change to reflect the new market yield levels. We saw in Table 1.3 how the price of our hypothetical 7% five-year bond changed as the required yield changed. This is an important result. Let us consider the situation – if the required yield in the market for our 7% bond is fixed, investors will be happy to hold the bond. What if required yields subsequently rise above the 7% level? Bondholders will be unhappy as they are now being paid 7% when elsewhere in the market higher yields are available. The market price of the bond will therefore change so that the yield on the bond changes, to compensate bondholders. If the required yield for the bond changes to 8%, we see from Table 1.3 that the price has fallen from par to 96.00. If this did not happen bondholders would sell the 7% issue and buy a bond that was yielding 8%; the market price mechanism ensures that this does not happen. If the situation is reversed the price mechanism will again operate to equalise the yield on the bond with those prevalent in the marketplace. If required yields drop to 6% the bond price rises to 104.21, because bondholders would now be receiving 7% when yields available in the market are now only 6%. We can see then that when required yield in the market is equal to a bond's coupon, the bond price will be par; the price will move respectively above or below par if required yields are below or above the coupon rate.

If a bond is priced at below its par value it is said to be trading at a *discount*, while if it is trading above par value it is said to be trading at a *premium* to its par value.

When merchant banks issue bonds on behalf of borrowers, they will set a bond's coupon at the level that would make the bond price equal to par. This means that the bond coupon will be equal to the yield required by the market at the time of issue. The bond's price would then fluctuate as market yields changed, as we showed in Table 1.3. Investors generally prefer to pay par or just under par when they buy a new issue of bonds, which is why a merchant bank will set the coupon that equates the bond price to par or in a range between

99.00 and par. The reason behind this preference to pay no more than par is often purely cosmetic, since an issue price above par would simply indicate a coupon higher than the market rate. However, as many fund managers and investors buy a bond and hold it until maturity, one often finds this prejudice against paying over par for a new issue.

What will happen if market yields remain unchanged during the life of a bond from when it was issued? In this unlikely scenario the price of a conventional bond will remain unchanged at par. The price of any bond will ultimately equal its redemption value, which is par. Therefore a bond that is priced at a premium or a discount will gradually converge to par as it approaches maturity.

As a bond approaches maturity there are fewer and fewer coupon payments, so that progressively more of the bond's price is made up of the present value of the final redemption payment. The present value of this payment will steadily increase as the maturity date is approached, since it is being discounted over a shorter period of time. The present value of the annuity cash flows of the bond steadily declines as we get fewer of them, and this is not offset by the increase in value of the maturity payment. Hence the price of the bond steadily declines. The opposite happens when the bond price starts off at a discount, where the increase in the value of the maturity payment outweighs the decrease in the price of the coupons, so that the bond price steadily converges to par.

Example 1.9

Illustration of price/yield changes for two selected gilts

Prices of selected gilts on 14 July 1999 for next-day settlement

UK Treasury stock 5% 2004

Price	Yield %
98.61750	5.324
98.64875	5.317
98.68000	5.309 (actual quoted price at the time of asking)
98.71100	5.302
98.74200	5.295

UK Treasury stock 5 3/4% 2009

Price	Yield %
104.73750	5.155
104.76875	5.151
104.80000	5.147 (actual quoted price at the time of asking)
104.83125	5.143
104.86250	5.140

1.10 Duration, modified duration and convexity

Bonds pay a part of their total return during their lifetime, in the form of coupon interest, so that the term to maturity does not reflect the true period over which the bond's return is earned. Additionally if we wish to gain an idea of the trading characteristics of a bond, and compare this to other bonds of say, similar maturity, term to maturity is insufficient and so we need a more accurate measure. A plain vanilla coupon bond pays out a proportion of its return during the course of its life, in the form of coupon interest. If we were to analyse the properties of a bond, we should conclude quite quickly that its maturity gives us little indication of how much of its return is paid out during its life, nor any idea of the timing or size of its cash flows, and hence its sensitivity to moves in market interest rates. For example, if comparing two bonds with the same maturity date but different coupons, the higher coupon bond provides a larger proportion of its return in the form of coupon income than does the lower coupon bond. The higher coupon bond provides its return at a faster rate; its value is theoretically therefore less subject to subsequent fluctuations in interest rates.

We may wish to calculate an average of the time to receipt of a bond's cash flows, and use this measure as a more realistic indication of maturity. However, cash flows during the life of a bond are not all equal in value, so a more accurate measure would be to take the average time to receipt of a bond's cash flows, but weighted in the form of the cash flows' present value. This is, in effect, *duration*. We can measure the speed of payment of a bond, and hence its price risk relative to other bonds of the same maturity by measuring the average maturity of the bond's cash flow stream. Bond analysts use duration to measure this property (it is sometimes known as *Macaulay's duration*, after its inventor, who first introduced it in 1938).[5] Duration is the weighted average time until the receipt of cash flows from a bond, where the weights are the present values of the cash flows, measured in years. At the time that he introduced the concept, Macaulay used the duration measure as an alternative for the length of time that a bond investment had remaining to maturity.

1.10.1 *Duration*

Recall that the price/yield formula for a plain vanilla bond is as given at (1.17) below, assuming complete years to maturity paying annual coupons, and with no accrued interest at the calculation date. The yield to maturity reverts to the symbol r in this section.

$$P = \frac{C}{(1+r)} + \frac{C}{(1+r)^2} + \frac{C}{(1+r)^3} + \cdots + \frac{C}{(1+r)^n} + \frac{M}{(1+r)^n} \tag{1.17}$$

If we take the first derivative of this expression we obtain (1.18).

$$\frac{dP}{dr} = \frac{-1C}{(1+r)^2} + \frac{-2C}{(1+r)^3} + \cdots + \frac{(-n)C}{(1+r)^{n+1}} + \frac{(-n)M}{(1+r)^{n+1}} \tag{1.18}$$

If we re-arrange (1.18) we will obtain the expression at (1.19), which is our equation to calculate the approximate change in price for a small change in yield.

$$\frac{dP}{dr} = -\frac{1}{(1+r)}\left[\frac{1C}{(1+r)} + \frac{2C}{(1+r)^2} + \cdots + \frac{nC}{(1+r)^n} + \frac{nM}{(1+r)^n}\right] \tag{1.19}$$

5 Macaulay, F., *Some theoretical problems suggested by the movements of interest rates, bond yields and stock prices in the United States since 1865*, National Bureau of Economic Research, NY 1938. This remains a fascinating read and is available from Risk Classics publishing, under the title *Interest rates, bond yields and stock prices in the United States since 1856.*

Readers may feel a sense of familiarity regarding the expression in brackets in equation (1.19) as this is the weighted average time to maturity of the cash flows from a bond, where the weights are the present values of each cash flow. The expression at (1.19) gives us the approximate measure of the change in price for a small change in yield. If we divide both sides of (1.19) by P we obtain the expression for the approximate percentage price change, given at (1.20).

$$\frac{dP}{dr}\frac{1}{P} = -\frac{1}{(1+r)}\left[\frac{1C}{(1+r)} + \frac{2C}{(1+r)^2} + \cdots + \frac{nC}{(1+r)^n} + \frac{nM}{(1+r)^n}\right]\frac{1}{P} \tag{1.20}$$

If we divide the bracketed expression in (1.20) by the current price of the bond P we obtain the definition of Macaulay duration, given at (1.21).

$$D = \frac{\frac{1C}{(1+r)} + \frac{2C}{(1+r)^2} + \cdots + \frac{nC}{(1+r)^n} + \frac{nM}{(1+r)^n}}{P} \tag{1.21}$$

Equation (1.21) is simplified using E notation as shown by (1.22).

$$D = \frac{\sum_{n=1}^{N} \frac{nC_n}{(1+r)^n}}{P} \tag{1.22}$$

where C represents the bond cash flow at time n.

Example 1.10 calculates the Macaulay duration for a hypothetical bond, an 8% 2009 annual coupon bond.

Example 1.10

Calculating the Macaulay duration for an 8% 2009 annual coupon bond

Issued	30 September 1999
Maturity	30 September 2009
Price	102.497
Yield	7.634%

Period (n)	Cash flow	PV at current yield*	n × PV
1	8	7.43260	7.4326
2	8	6.90543	13.81086
3	8	6.41566	19.24698
4	8	5.96063	23.84252
5	8	5.53787	27.68935
6	8	5.14509	30.87054
7	8	4.78017	33.46119
8	8	4.44114	35.529096
9	8	4.12615	37.13535
10	108	51.75222	517.5222
Total		102.49696	746.540686

*Calculated as $C/(1+r)n$.

Macaulay Duration = 746.540686/102.497 = 7.283539998 years.

Modified Duration = 7.28354/1.07634 = 6.76695.

Table 1.4: Duration calculation for the 8% 2009 bond.

The Macaulay duration value given by (1.22) is measured in years. An interesting observation by Galen Burghardt in *The Treasury Bond Basis* is that, 'measured in years, Macaulay's duration is of no particular use to anyone' (Burghardt 1994, page 90). This is essentially correct. However, as a risk measure and hedge calculation measure, duration transformed into *modified duration* was the primary measure of interest rate risk used in the markets, and is still widely used despite the advent of the *value-at-risk* measure for market risk.

If we substitute the expression for Macaulay duration (1.21) into equation (1.20) for the approximate percentage change in price we obtain (1.23) below.

$$\frac{dP}{dr}\frac{1}{P} = -\frac{1}{(1+r)}D \tag{1.23}$$

This is the definition of modified duration, given as (1.24).

$$MD = \frac{D}{(1+r)} \tag{1.24}$$

Modified duration is clearly related to duration then, in fact we can use it to indicate that, for small changes in yield, a given change in yield results in an inverse change in bond price. We can illustrate this by substituting (1.24) into (1.23), giving us (1.25).

$$\frac{dP}{dr}\frac{1}{P} = -MD \tag{1.25}$$

If we are determining duration long-hand, there is another arrangement we can use to shorten the procedure. Instead of equation (1.17) we use (1.26) as the bond price formula, which calculates price based on a bond being comprised of an annuity stream and a redemption payment, and summing the present values of these two elements. Again we assume an annual coupon bond priced on a date that leaves a complete number of years to maturity and with no interest accrued.

$$P = C\left[\frac{1-\frac{1}{(1+r)^n}}{r}\right] + \frac{M}{(1+r)^n} \tag{1.26}$$

This expression calculates the price of a bond as the present value of the stream of coupon payments and the present value of the redemption payment. If we take the first derivative of (1.26) and then divide this by the current price of the bond P, the result is another expression for the modified duration formula, given at (1.27).

$$MD = \frac{\frac{C}{r^2}\left[1-\frac{1}{(1+r)^n}\right] + \frac{n\left(M-\frac{C}{r}\right)}{(1+r)^{n+1}}}{P} \tag{1.27}$$

We have already shown that modified duration and duration are related; to obtain the expression for Macaulay duration from (1.27) we multiply it by $(1+r)$. This short-hand formula is demonstrated in Example 1.11 for a hypothetical bond, the annual coupon 8% 2009.

Example 1.11

8% 2009 bond: using equation (1.27) for the modified duration calculation

Coupon	8%, annual basis
Yield	7.634%
N	10
Price	102.497

Substituting the above terms into the equation we obtain:

$$MD = \frac{\frac{8}{(0.07634^2)}\left[1 - \frac{1}{(1.07634)^{10}}\right] + \frac{10\left(100 - \frac{8}{0.07634}\right)}{(1.07634)}}{102.497}$$

$$= 6.076695$$

To obtain the Macaulay duration we multiply the modified duration by $(1 + r)$, in this case 1.07634, which gives us a value of 7.28354 years.

For an irredeemable bond duration is given by:

$$D = \frac{1}{rc} \tag{1.28}$$

where $rc = (C/P_d)$ is the *running yield* (or *current yield*) of the bond. This follows from equation (1.22) as $N \rightarrow \infty$, recognising that for an irredeemable bond $r = rc$. Equation (1.28) provides the limiting value to duration. For bonds trading at or above par duration increases with maturity and approaches this limit from below. For bonds trading at a discount to par duration increases to a maximum at around 20 years and then declines towards the limit given by (1.28). So in general, duration increases with maturity, with an upper bound given by (1.28).

1.10.2 *Properties of Macaulay duration*

A bond's duration is always less than its maturity. This is because some weight is given to the cash flows in the early years of the bond's life, which brings forward the average time at which cash flows are received. In the case of a zero-coupon bond, there is no present value weighting of the cash flows, for the simple reason that there are no cash flows, and so duration for a zero-coupon bond is equal to its term to maturity. Duration varies with coupon, yield and maturity. The following three factors imply higher duration for a bond:

- the lower the coupon;
- the lower the yield;
- broadly, the longer the maturity.

Duration increases as coupon and yield decrease. As the coupon falls, more of the relative weight of the cash flows is transferred to the maturity date and this causes duration to rise. Because the coupon on index-linked bonds is generally much lower than on vanilla bonds, this means that the duration of index-linked bonds will be much higher than for vanilla bonds of the same maturity. As yield increases, the present values of all future cash flows fall, but the present values of the more distant cash flows fall relatively more than those of the nearer cash flows. This has the effect of increasing the relative weight given to nearer cash flows and hence of reducing duration.

The effect of the coupon frequency

Certain bonds such as Eurobonds pay coupon annually compared to say, gilts which pay semi-annual coupons. If we imagine that every coupon is divided into two parts, with one part paid a half-period earlier than the other, this will represent a shift in weight to the left, as part of the coupon is paid earlier. Thus, increasing the coupon frequency shortens duration, and of course decreasing coupon frequency has the effect of lengthening duration.

Duration as maturity approaches

Using our definition of duration we can see that initially it will decline slowly, and then at a more rapid pace as a bond approaches maturity.

Duration of a portfolio

Portfolio duration is a weighted average of the duration of the individual bonds. The weights are the present values of the bonds divided by the full price of the entire portfolio, and the resulting duration calculation is often referred to as a 'market-weighted' duration. This approach is in effect the duration calculation for a single bond. Portfolio duration has the same application as duration for an individual bond, and can be used to structure an *immunised* portfolio.

1.10.3 *Modified duration*

Although it is common for newcomers to the market to think intuitively of duration much as Macaulay originally did, as a proxy measure for the time to maturity of a bond, such an interpretation is to miss the main point of duration, which is a measure of price volatility or interest rate risk.

Using the first term of a Taylor's expansion of the bond price function[6] we can show the following relationship between price volatility and the duration measure, which is expressed as (1.29) below.

$$\Delta P = -\left[\frac{1}{(1+r)}\right] \times \text{Macaulay duration} \times \text{Change in yield} \tag{1.29}$$

where r is the yield to maturity for an annual-paying bond (for a semi-annual coupon bond, we use $r/2$). If we combine the first two components of the right-hand side, we obtain the definition of modified duration. Equation (1.29) expresses the approximate percentage change in price as being equal to the modified duration multiplied by the change in yield. We saw in the previous section how the formula for Macaulay duration

6 For an accessible explanation of the Taylor expansion, see Butler, C., *Mastering Value-at-Risk*, FT Prentice Hall 1998, pp. 112–114.

could be modified to obtain the *modified duration* for a bond. There is a clear relationship between the two measures. From the Macaulay duration of a bond can be derived its modified duration, which gives a measure of the sensitivity of a bond's price to small changes in yield. As we have seen, the relationship between modified duration and duration is given by (1.30).

$$MD = \frac{D}{1+r} \tag{1.30}$$

where MD is the modified duration in years. However, it also measures the approximate change in bond price for a 1% change in bond yield. For a bond that pays semi-annual coupons, the equation becomes:

$$MD = \frac{D}{1+\frac{1}{2}r} \tag{1.31}$$

This means that the following relationship holds between modified duration and bond prices:

$$\Delta P = MD \times \Delta r \times P \tag{1.32}$$

In the UK markets the term *volatility* is sometimes used to refer to modified duration but this is becoming increasingly uncommon in order to avoid confusion with option markets' use of the same term, which there often refers to *implied volatility* and is something different.

Example 1.12

Using modified duration

An 8% annual coupon bond is trading at par with a duration of 2.74 years. If yields rise from 8% to 8.50%, then the price of the bond will fall by:

$$\begin{aligned}\Delta P &= -D \times \frac{\Delta r}{1+r} \times P \\ &= -(2.74) \times \left(\frac{0.005}{1.080}\right) \times 100 \\ &= -£1.2685\end{aligned}$$

That is, the price of the bond will now be £98.7315.

The modified duration of a bond with a duration of 2.74 years and yield of 8% is obviously:

$$MD = \frac{2.74}{1.08}$$

which gives us MD equal to 2.537 years.

This tells us that for a 1 per cent move in the yield to maturity, the price of the bond will move (in the opposite direction) by 2.54%.

We can use modified duration to approximate bond prices for a given yield change. This is illustrated with the following expression:

$$\Delta P = -MD \times (\Delta r) \times P \tag{1.33}$$

For a bond with a modified duration of 3.99, priced at par, an increase in yield of 1 basis point (100 basis = 1 per cent) leads to a fall in the bond's price of:

$$\Delta P = (-3.24/100) \times (+0.01) \times 100.00$$

$$\Delta P = £0.0399, \text{ or } 3.99 \text{ pence}$$

In this case 3.99 pence is the *basis point value* of the bond, which is the change in the bond price given a 1 basis point change in the bond's yield. The basis point value of a bond can be calculated using (1.34).

$$BPV = \frac{MD}{100} \times \frac{P}{100} \tag{1.34}$$

Basis point values are used in hedging bond positions. To hedge a bond position requires an opposite position to be taken in the hedging instrument. So if we are long a 10-year bond, we may wish to sell short a similar 10-year bond as a hedge against it. Similarly a short position in a bond will be hedged through a purchase of an equivalent amount of the hedging instrument. In fact there are a variety of hedging instruments available, both on and off-balance sheet. Once the hedge is put on, any loss in the primary position should in theory be offset by a gain in the hedge position, and vice-versa. The objective of a hedge is to ensure that the price change in the primary instrument is equal to the price change in the hedging instrument. If we are hedging a position with another bond, we use the BPVs of each bond to calculate the amount of the hedging instrument required. This is important because each bond will have different BPVs, so that to hedge a long position in say £1 million nominal of a 30-year bond does not mean we simply sell £1 million of another 30-year bond. This is because the BPVs of the two bonds will almost certainly be different. Also there may not be another 30-year bond in that particular bond. What if we have to hedge with a 10-year bond? How much nominal of this bond would be required? We need to know the ratio given at (1.35) to calculate the nominal hedge position.

$$\frac{BPV_p}{BPV_h} \tag{1.35}$$

where

BPV_p is the basis point value of the primary bond (the position to be hedged)
BPV_h is the basis point value of the hedging instrument.

The *hedge ratio* is used to calculate the size of the hedge position and is given at (1.36).

$$\frac{BPV_p}{BPV_h} \times \frac{\text{change in yield for primary bond position}}{\text{change in yield for hedge instrument}} \tag{1.36}$$

The second ratio in (1.36) is known as the *yield beta*.

Example 1.13 illustrates using the hedge ratio.

Example 1.13

Calculating hedge size using basis point value

A trader holds a long position of £1 million of the 8% 2019 bond. The modified duration of the bond is 11.14692 and its price is 129.87596. The basis point value of this bond is therefore 0.14477. The trader decides, to protect against a rise in interest rates, to hedge the position using the 0% 2009 bond, which has a BPV of 0.05549. If we assume that the yield beta is 1, what nominal value of the zero-coupon bond must be sold in order to hedge the position?

The hedge ratio is:

$$\frac{0.14477}{0.05549} \times 1 = 2.60894.$$

Therefore to hedge £1 million of the 20-year bond the trader shorts £2,608,940 of the zero-coupon bond. If we use the respective BPVs to see the net effect of a 1 basis point rise in yield, the loss on the long position is approximately equal to the gain in the hedge position.

Example 1.14

The nature of the modified duration approximation

Table 1.5 shows the change in price for one of our hypothetical bonds, the 8% 2009, for a selection of yields. We see that for a 1 basis point change in yield, the change in price given by the dollar duration figure, while not completely accurate, is a reasonable estimation of the actual change in price. For a large move however, say 200 basis points, the approximation is significantly in error and analysts would not use it. Notice also for our hypothetical bond how the dollar duration value, which is the suggested change in cash value resulting from the change in yields calculated from the modified duration measurement, underestimates the change in price resulting from a fall in yields but overestimates the price change for a rise in yields. This is a reflection of the price/yield relationship for this bond. Some bonds will have a more pronounced convex relationship between price and yield and the modified duration calculation will underestimate the price change resulting from both a fall or a rise in yields.

1.10.4 *Convexity*

Duration can be regarded as a first-order measure of interest rate risk: it measures the *slope* of the present value/yield profile. It is, however, only an approximation of the actual change in bond price given a small change in yield to maturity. Similarly for modified duration, which describes the price sensitivity of a bond to small changes in yield. However, as Figure 1.4 illustrates, the approximation is an underestimate of the actual price at the new yield. This is the weakness of the duration measure.

Convexity is a second-order measure of interest rate risk; it measures the *curvature* of the present value/yield profile. Convexity can be regarded as an indication of the error we make when using duration and modified duration, as it measures the degree to which the curvature of a bond's price/yield relationship diverges from the straight-line estimation. The convexity

Bond	Maturity (years)	Modified Duration	Price duration of basis point	Yield 6.00%	6.50%	7.00%	7.50%	7.99%	8.00%	8.01%	8.50%	9.00%	10.00%
8% 2009	10	6.76695	0.06936	114.72017	110.78325	107.02358	103.43204	100.0671	100.00000	99.932929	96.71933	93.58234	87.71087

Yield change	Price change	Estimate using price duration
down 1 bp	0.06713	0.06936
up 1 bp	0.06707	0.06936
down 200 bp	14.72017	13.872
up 200 bp	12.28913	13.872

Table 1.5: Nature of the modified duration approximation.

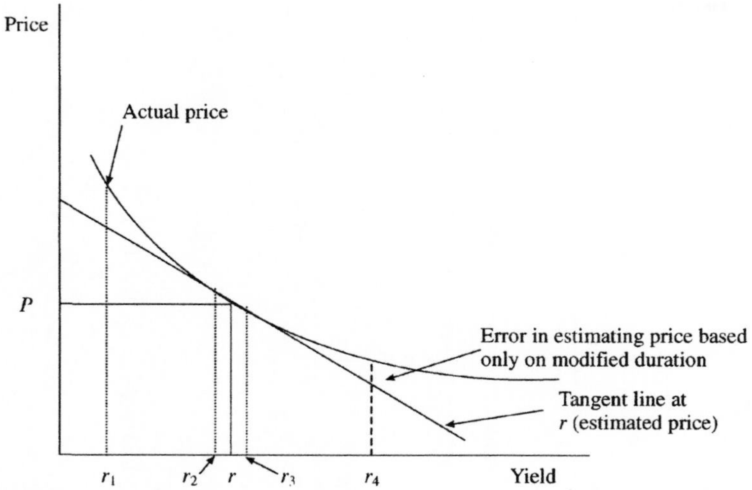

Figure 1.4: Approximation of the bond price change using modified duration. Reproduced with permission from Frank J Fabozzi, *Fixed Income Mathematics*, McGraw-Hill 1997.

of a bond is positively related to the dispersion of its cash flows thus, other things being equal, if one bond's cash flows are more spread out in time than another's, then it will have a higher *dispersion* and hence a higher convexity. Convexity is also positively related to duration.

The second-order differential of the bond price equation with respect to the redemption yield r is:

$$\begin{aligned}\frac{\Delta P}{P} &= \frac{1}{P}\frac{\Delta P}{\Delta r}(\Delta r) + \frac{1}{2P}\frac{\Delta^2 P}{\Delta r^2}(\Delta r^2) \\ &= -MD\left(\Delta r + \frac{CV}{2}\right)(\Delta r)^2\end{aligned} \tag{1.37}$$

where CV is the convexity.

From equation (1.37), convexity is the rate at which price variation to yield changes with respect to yield. That is, it describes a bond's modified duration changes with respect to changes in yield. It can be approximated by expression (1.38).

$$CV = 10^8\left(\frac{\Delta P'}{P} + \frac{\Delta P''}{P}\right) \tag{1.38}$$

where

$\Delta P'$ is the change in bond price if yield increases by 1 basis point (0.01)
$\Delta P''$ is the change in bond price if yield decreases by 1 basis point (0.01).

The unit of measurement for convexity using (1.38) is the number of interest periods. For annual coupon bonds this is equal to the number of years; for bonds paying coupon on a different frequency we use (1.39) to convert the convexity measure to years.

$$CV_{years} = \frac{CV}{C^2} \tag{1.39}$$

The convexity measure for a zero-coupon bond is given by (1.40).

$$CV = \frac{n(n+1)}{(1+r)^2} \tag{1.40}$$

Convexity is a second-order approximation of the change in price resulting from a change in yield. This is given by:

$$\Delta P = \frac{1}{2} \times CV \times (\Delta r)^2 \tag{1.41}$$

The reason we multiply the convexity by 1/2 to obtain the convexity adjustment is because the second term in the Taylor expansion contains the coefficient 1/2. The convexity approximation is obtained from a Taylor expansion of the bond price formula. An illustration of Taylor expansion of the bond price/yield equation is given in Appendix 39.3 of the author's book *The Bond and Money Markets*. The formula is the same for a semi-annual coupon bond.

Note that the value for convexity given by the expressions above will always be positive, that is the approximate price change due to convexity is positive for both yield increases and decreases.

Convexity is an attractive property for a bond to have. What level of premium will be attached to a bond's higher convexity? This is a function of the current yield levels in the market as well as market volatility. Remember that modified duration and convexity are functions of yield level, and that the effect of both is magnified at lower yield levels. As well as the relative level, investors will value convexity higher if the current market conditions are volatile. Remember that the cash effect of convexity is noticeable only for large moves in yield. If an investor expects market yields to move only by relatively small amounts, they will attach a lower value to convexity; and vice-versa for large movements in yield. Therefore the yield premium attached to a bond with higher convexity will vary according to market expectations of the future size of interest rate changes.

The convexity measure increases with the square of maturity, and it decreases with both coupon and yield. As the measure is a function of modified duration, index-linked bonds have greater convexity than conventional bonds. We discussed how the price/yield profile will be more convex for a bond of higher convexity, and that such a bond will outperform a bond of lower convexity whatever happens to market interest rates. High convexity is therefore a desirable property for bonds to have. In principle a more convex bond should fall in price less than a less convex one when yields rise, and rise in price more when yields fall. That is, convexity can be equated with the potential to outperform. Thus, other things being equal, the higher the convexity of a bond the more desirable it should, in principle, be to investors. In some cases investors may be prepared to accept a bond with a lower yield in order to gain convexity. We noted also that convexity is in principle of more value if uncertainty, and hence expected market volatility, is high, because the convexity effect of a bond is amplified for large changes in yield. The value of convexity is therefore greater in volatile market conditions.

For a conventional vanilla bond convexity is almost always positive. Negative convexity resulting from a bond with a concave price/yield profile would not be an attractive property for a bondholder; the most common occurrence of negative convexity in the cash markets is with callable bonds.

Selected references and bibliography

Baxter, M., Rennie, A., *Financial Calculus*, Cambridge University Press 1996

Bierwag, G.O., 'Immunization, duration and the term structure of interest rates,' *Journal of Financial and Quantitative Analysis*, December 1977, pp. 725–741

Bierwag, G.O., 'Measures of duration,' *Economic Inquiry 16*, October 1978, pp. 497–507

Burghardt, G., *The Treasury Bond Basis*, McGraw-Hill 1994

Choudhry, M., *The Bond and Money Markets: Strategy, Trading, Analysis*, Butterworth-Heinemann 2001, Chapters 2–10, 39

Fabozzi, F., *Bond Markets, Analysis and Strategies*, Prentice Hall 1989, Chapter 2

Garbade, K., *Fixed Income Analytics*, MIT Press 1996, Chapters 3, 4 and 12

Hull, J., *Options, Futures and Other Derivatives*, 3rd edition, Prentice Hall 1997

Jarrow, R., *Modelling Fixed Income Securities and Interest Rate Options*, McGraw-Hill 1996

Macaulay, F., *The Movements of Interest Rates, Bond Yields and Stock Prices in the United States Since 1856*, RISK Classics Library 1999

Neftci, S., *Mathematics of Financial Derivatives*, Academic Press 1996

Steiner, R., *Mastering Financial Calculations*, FT Pitman 1998

2 The Yield Curve

The main measure of return associated with holding bonds is the *yield to maturity* or *gross redemption yield*. In developed markets, as well as a fair number of developing ones, there is usually a large number of bonds trading at one time, at different yields and with varying terms to maturity. Investors and traders frequently examine the relationship between the yields on bonds that are in the same class; plotting yields of bonds that differ only in their term to maturity produces what is known as a *yield curve*. The yield curve is an important indicator and knowledge source of the state of a debt capital market. It is sometimes referred to as the *term structure of interest rates*, but strictly speaking this is not correct, as this term should be reserved for the zero-coupon yield curve only. We shall examine this in detail later.

Much of the analysis and pricing activity that takes place in the bond markets revolves around the yield curve. The yield curve describes the relationship between a particular redemption yield and a bond's maturity. Plotting the yields of bonds along the maturity term structure will give us our yield curve. It is very important that only bonds from the same class of issuer or with the same degree of liquidity are used when plotting the yield curve; for example a curve may be constructed for UK gilts or for AA-rated sterling Eurobonds, but not a mixture of both, because gilts and Eurobonds are bonds from different class issuers. The primary yield curve in any domestic capital market is the government bond yield curve, so for example in the US market it is the US Treasury yield curve. With the advent of the euro currency in the European Union, in theory any euro-currency government bond can be used to plot a default-free euro yield curve. In practice only bonds from the same government are used, as for various reasons different country bonds within euroland trade at different yields. Outside the government bond markets yield curves are plotted for Eurobonds, money market instruments, off-balance sheet instruments, in fact virtually all debt market instruments. So it is always important to remember to compare like-for-like when analysing yield curves across markets.

In this chapter we will consider the yield to maturity yield curve as well as other types of yield curve that may be constructed. Later in this chapter we will consider how to derive spot and forward yields from a current redemption yield curve.

2.1 Using the yield curve

Let us first consider the main uses of the yield curve. All participants in the debt capital markets have an interest in the current shape and level of the yield curve, as well as what this information implies for the future. The main uses are summarised below.

- **Setting the yield for all debt market instruments.** The yield curve essentially fixes the cost of money over the maturity term structure. The yields of government bonds from the shortest-maturity instrument to the longest set the benchmark for yields for all other debt instruments in the market, around which all debt instruments are analysed. Issuers of debt (and their underwriting banks) therefore use the yield curve to price bonds and all other debt instruments. Generally the zero-coupon yield curve is used to price new issue securities, rather than the redemption yield curve.

- **Acting as an indicator of future yield levels.** As we discuss later in this chapter, the yield curve assumes certain shapes in response to market expectations of the future interest rates. Bond market participants analyse the present shape of the yield curve in an effort to determine the implications regarding the future direction of market interest rates. This is perhaps one of the most important functions of the yield curve, and it is as much an art as a science. The yield curve is scrutinised for its information content not just by bond traders and fund managers but also by corporate financiers as part of project appraisal. Central banks and government treasury departments also analyse the yield curve for its information content, not just regarding forward interest rates but also with regard to expected inflation levels.
- **Measuring and comparing returns across the maturity spectrum.** Portfolio managers use the yield curve to assess the relative value of investments across the maturity spectrum. The yield curve indicates the returns that are available at different maturity points and is therefore very important to fixed-income fund managers, who can use it to assess which point of the curve offers the best return relative to other points.
- **Indicating relative value between different bonds of similar maturity.** The yield curve can be analysed to indicate which bonds are cheap or dear to the curve. Placing bonds relative to the zero-coupon yield curve helps to highlight which bonds should be bought or sold either outright or as part of a bond spread trade.
- **Pricing interest-rate derivative securities.** The price of derivative securities revolves around the yield curve. At the short-end, products such as Forward Rate Agreements are priced off the futures curve, but futures rates reflect the market's view on forward three-month cash deposit rates. At the longer end, interest-rate swaps are priced off the yield curve, while hybrid instruments that incorporate an option feature such as convertibles and callable bonds also reflect current yield curve levels. The 'risk-free' interest rate, which is one of the parameters used in option pricing, is the T-bill rate or short-term government repo rate, both constituents of the money market yield curve.

2.2 Yield to maturity yield curve

The most commonly occurring yield curve is the yield to maturity yield curve. The equation used to calculate the yield to maturity was shown in Chapter 1. The curve itself is constructed by plotting the yield to maturity against the term to maturity for a group of bonds of the same class. Three different examples are shown at Figure 2.1. Bonds used in constructing the curve will only rarely have an exact number of whole years to redemption; however it is often common to see yields plotted against whole years on the x-axis. This is because once a bond is designated the *benchmark* for that term, its yield is taken to be the representative yield. For example, the then ten-year benchmark bond in the UK gilt market, the 5 3/4% Treasury 2009, maintained its benchmark status throughout 1999 and into 2000, even as its term to maturity fell below ten years. The yield to maturity yield curve is the most

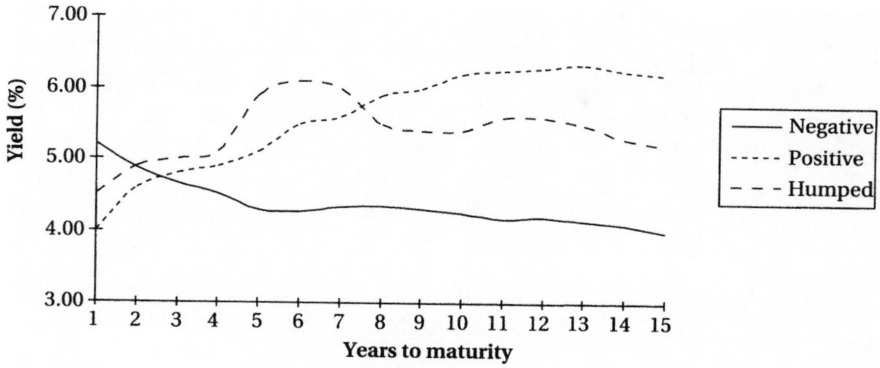

Figure 2.1: Yield to maturity yield curves.

commonly observed curve simply because yield to maturity is the most frequent measure of return used. The business sections of daily newspapers, where they quote bond yields at all, usually quote bond yields to maturity.

As we might expect, given the source data from which it is constructed, the yield to maturity yield curve contains some inaccuracies. We have already come across the main weakness of the yield to maturity measure, which is the assumption of a constant rate for coupon reinvestment during the bond's life at the redemption yield level. Since market rates will fluctuate over time, it will not be possible to achieve this (a feature known as *reinvestment risk*). Only zero-coupon bondholders avoid reinvestment risk as no coupon is paid during the life of a zero-coupon bond.

The yield to maturity yield curve does not distinguish between different payment patterns that may result from bonds with different coupons, that is, the fact that low-coupon bonds pay a higher portion of their cash flows at a later date than high-coupon bonds of the same maturity. The curve also assumes an even cash flow pattern for all bonds. Therefore in this case cash flows are not discounted at the appropriate rate for the bonds in the group being used to construct the curve. To get around this bond analysts may sometimes construct a *coupon yield curve*, which plots yield to maturity against term to maturity for a group of bonds with the same coupon. This may be useful when a group of bonds contains some with very high coupons; high coupon bonds often trade 'cheap to the curve', that is they have higher yields than corresponding bonds of same maturity but lower coupon. This is usually because of reinvestment risk and, in some markets (including the UK), for tax reasons.

For the reasons we have discussed the market often uses other types of yield curve for analysis when the yield to maturity yield curve is deemed unsuitable.

That there are a number of yield curves that can be plotted, each relevant to its own market, can be seen from Figure 2.2 below, which shows the curves that can be selected for the US dollar market, from screen IYC on Bloomberg. We see that curves can be selected for US Treasuries, US dollar swaps, strips, agency securities, and so on.

Figure 2.3 shows the yield-to-maturity curve for US Treasuries, the interest-rate swap curve and the zero-coupon yield curve during August 2003. We discuss next the various types of curve that can be plotted.

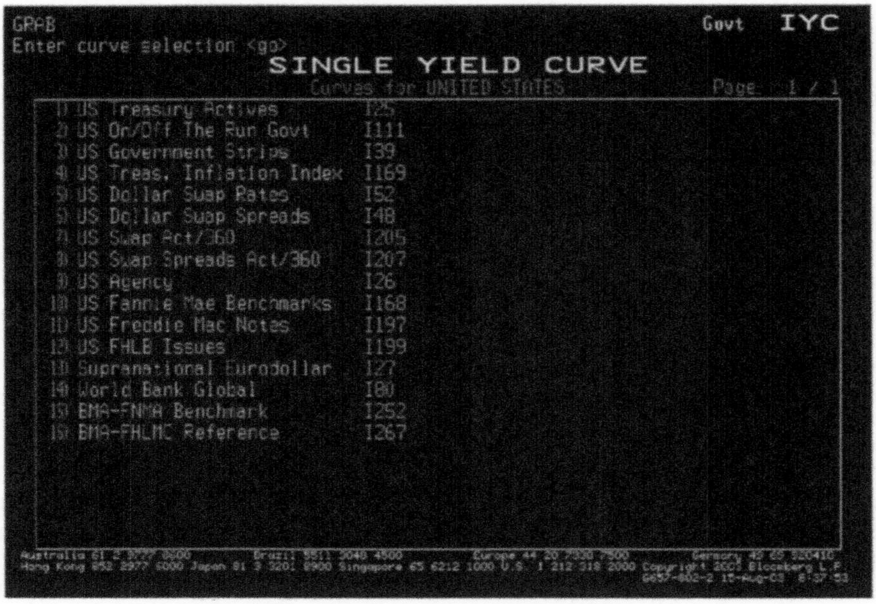

Figure 2.2: Yield curve menu for US dollar assets, on Bloomberg. © Bloomberg L.P. Used with permission.

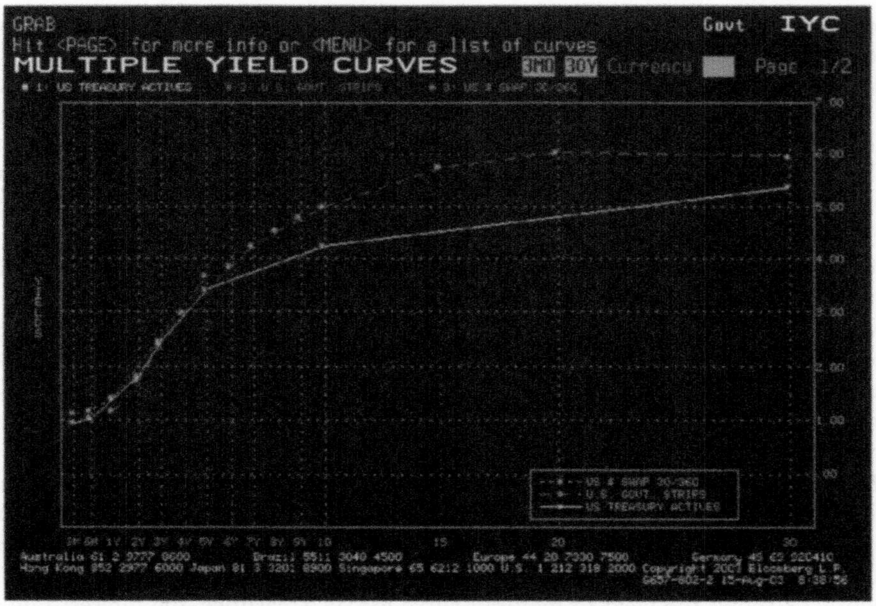

Figure 2.3: Treasury, USD swaps and Treasury strips yield curves, August 2003. © Bloomberg L.P. Used with permission.

2.3 The coupon yield curve

The *coupon yield curve* is a plot of the yield to maturity against term to maturity for a group of bonds with the same coupon. If we were to construct such a curve we would see that in general high-coupon bonds trade at a discount (have higher yields) relative to low-coupon bonds, because of reinvestment risk and for tax reasons (in the UK for example, on gilts the coupon is taxed as income tax, while any capital gain is exempt from capital gains tax; even in jurisdictions where capital gain on bonds is taxable, this can often be deferred whereas income tax cannot). It is frequently the case that yields vary considerably with coupons for the same term to maturity, and with term to maturity for different coupons. Put another way, usually we observe different coupon curves not only at different levels but also with different shapes. Distortions arise in the yield to maturity curve if no allowance is made for coupon differences. For this reason bond analysts frequently draw a line of 'best fit' through a plot of redemption yields, because the coupon effect in a group of bonds will produce a curve with humps and troughs. Figure 2.4 shows a hypothetical set of coupon yield curves, however since in any group of bonds it is unusual to observe bonds with the same coupon along the entire term structure this type of curve is relatively rare.

2.4 The par yield curve

The *par yield curve* is not usually encountered in secondary market trading, however it is often constructed for use by corporate financiers and others in the new issues or *primary* market. The par yield curve plots yield to maturity against term to maturity for current bonds trading at par.[1] The par yield is therefore equal to the coupon rate for bonds priced at par or near to par, as the yield to maturity for bonds priced exactly at par is equal to the coupon rate. Those involved in the primary market will use a par yield curve to determine

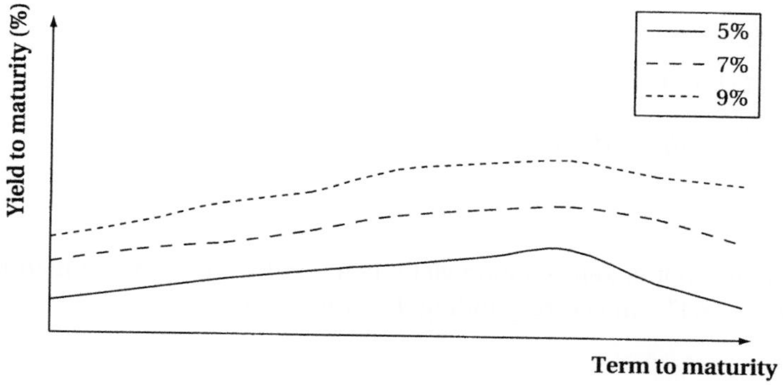

Figure 2.4: Coupon yield curves.

[1] Par price for a bond is almost invariably 100 per cent. Certain bonds have par defined as 1000 per 1000 nominal of paper.

the required coupon for a new bond that is to be issued at par. This is because investors prefer not to pay over par for a new-issue bond, so the bond requires a coupon that will result in a price at or slightly below par.

The par yield curve can be derived directly from bond yields when bonds are trading at or near par. If bonds in the market are trading substantially away from par then the resulting curve will be distorted. It is then necessary to derive it by iteration from the spot yield curve. As we would observe at almost any time, it is rare to encounter bonds trading at par for any particular maturity. The market therefore uses actual non-par vanilla bond yield curves to derive *zero-coupon yield curves* and then constructs hypothetical par yields that would be observed were there any par bonds being traded.

2.5 The zero-coupon (or spot) yield curve

The *zero-coupon* (or *spot*) *yield curve* plots zero-coupon yields (or spot yields) against term to maturity. A zero-coupon yield is the yield prevailing on a bond that has no coupons. In the first instance if there is a liquid zero-coupon bond market we can plot the yields from these bonds if we wish to construct this curve. However it is not necessary to have a set of zero-coupon bonds in order to construct the curve, as we can derive it from a coupon or par yield curve; in fact in many markets where no zero-coupon bonds are traded, a spot yield curve is derived from the conventional yield to maturity yield curve. This is of course a *theoretical* zero-coupon (spot) yield curve, as opposed to the *market* or *observed* spot curve that can be constructed using the yields of actual zero-coupon bonds trading in the market.[2]

2.5.1 *Basic concepts*

Spot yields must comply with equation (2.1). This equation assumes annual coupon payments and that the calculation is carried out on a coupon date so that accrued interest is zero.

$$\begin{aligned} P_d &= \sum_{n=1}^{N} \frac{C}{(1+rs_n)^n} + \frac{M}{(1+rs_N)^N} \\ &= \sum_{n=1}^{N} C \times df_n + M \times df_N \end{aligned} \tag{2.1}$$

where

rs_n is the spot or zero-coupon yield on a bond with n years to maturity
$df_n \equiv 1/(1+rs_n)^n =$ the corresponding *discount factor*.

---

2 It is common to see the terms spot rate and zero-coupon rate used synonymously. However the spot rate is a theoretical construct and cannot be observed in the market. The definition of the spot rate, which is the rate of return on a single cash flow that has been dealt today and is received at some point in the future, comes very close to that of the yield on a zero-coupon bond, which can be observed directly in the market. Zero-coupon rates can therefore be taken to be spot rates in practice, which is why the terms are frequently used interchangeably.

In (2.1) rs_1 is the current one-year spot yield, rs_2 the current two-year spot yield, and so on. Theoretically the spot yield for a particular term to maturity is the same as the yield on a zero-coupon bond of the same maturity, which is why spot yields are also known as zero-coupon yields.

This last is an important result, as spot yields can be derived from redemption yields that have been observed in the market.

As with the yield to redemption yield curve, the spot yield curve is commonly used in the market. It is viewed as the true term structure of interest rates because there is no reinvestment risk involved; the stated yield is equal to the actual annual return. That is, the yield on a zero-coupon bond of n years maturity is regarded as the true n-year interest rate. Because the observed government bond redemption yield curve is not considered to be the true interest rate, analysts often construct a theoretical spot yield curve. Essentially this is done by breaking down each coupon bond being observed into its constituent cash flows, which become a series of individual zero-coupon bonds. For example, £100 nominal of a 5% two-year bond (paying annual coupons) is considered equivalent to £5 nominal of a one-year zero-coupon bond and £105 nominal of a two-year zero-coupon bond.

Let us assume that in the market there are 30 bonds all paying annual coupons. The first bond has a maturity of one year, the second bond of two years, and so on out to thirty years. We know the price of each of these bonds, and we wish to determine what the prices imply about the market's estimate of future interest rates. We naturally expect interest rates to vary over time, but that all payments being made on the same date are valued using the same rate. For the one-year bond we know its current price and the amount of the payment (comprised of one coupon payment and the redemption proceeds) we will receive at the end of the year; therefore we can calculate the interest rate for the first year: assume the one-year bond has a coupon of 5%. If the bond is priced at par and we invest £100 today we will receive £105 in one year's time, hence the rate of interest is apparent and is 5%. For the two-year bond we use this interest rate to calculate the future value of its current price in one year's time: *this is how much we would receive if we had invested the same amount in the one-year bond.* However the two-year bond pays a coupon at the end of the first year; if we subtract this amount from the future value of the current price, the net amount is what we should be giving up in one year in return for the one remaining payment. From these numbers we can calculate the interest rate in year two.

Assume that the two-year bond pays a coupon of 6% and is priced at 99.00. If the 99.00 was invested at the rate we calculated for the one-year bond (5%), it would accumulate £103.95 in one year, made up of the £99 investment and interest of £4.95. On the payment date in one year's time, the one-year bond matures and the two-year bond pays a coupon of 6%. If everyone expected that at this time the two-year bond would be priced at more than 97.95 (which is 103.95 minus 6.00), then no investor would buy the one-year bond, since it would be more advantageous to buy the two-year bond and sell it after one year for a greater return. Similarly if the price was less than 97.95 no investor would buy the two-year bond, as it would be cheaper to buy the shorter bond and then buy the longer-dated bond with the proceeds received when the one-year bond matures. Therefore the two-year bond must be priced at exactly 97.95 in 12 months' time. For this £97.95 to grow to £106.00 (the maturity proceeds from the two-year bond, comprising the redemption payment and coupon interest), the interest rate in year two must be 8.20% We can check this using the present value formula covered earlier. At these two interest rates, the two bonds are said to be in equilibrium.

This is an important result and shows that (in theory) there can be no arbitrage opportunity along the yield curve; using interest rates available today the return from buying the two-year bond must equal the return from buying the one-year bond and rolling over the proceeds (or *reinvesting*) for another year. This is the known as the *breakeven principle*, a law of no-arbitrage.

Using the price and coupon of the three-year bond we can calculate the interest rate in year three in precisely the same way. Using each of the bonds in turn, we can link together the *implied one-year rates* for each year up to the maturity of the longest-dated bond. The process is known as *boot-strapping*. The 'average' of the rates over a given period is the spot yield for that term: in the example given above, the rate in year one is 5%, and in year two is 8.20%. An investment of £100 at these rates would grow to £113.61. This gives a total percentage increase of 13.61% over two years, or 6.588% per annum (the average rate is not obtained by simply dividing 13.61 by 2, but – using our present value relationship again – by calculating the square root of '1 plus the interest rate' and then subtracting 1 from this number). Thus the one-year yield is 5% and the two-year yield is 8.20%.

In real-world markets it is not necessarily as straightforward as this; for instance on some dates there may be several bonds maturing, with different coupons, and on some dates there may be no bonds maturing. It is most unlikely that there will be a regular spacing of bond redemptions exactly one year apart. For this reason it is common for analysts to use a software model to calculate the set of implied spot rates which best fits the market prices of the bonds that do exist in the market. For instance if there are several one-year bonds, each of their prices may imply a slightly different rate of interest. We choose the rate which gives the smallest average price error. In practice all bonds are used to find the rate in year one, all bonds with a term longer than one year are used to calculate the rate in year two, and so on. The zero-coupon curve can also be calculated directly from the coupon yield curve using a method similar to that described above; in this case the bonds would be priced at par and their coupons set to the par yield values.

The zero-coupon yield curve is ideal to use when deriving implied forward rates, which we consider next, and defining the term structure of interest rates. It is also the best curve to use when determining the *relative value*, whether cheap or dear, of bonds trading in the market, and when pricing new issues, irrespective of their coupons. However it is not an absolutely accurate indicator of average market yields because most bonds are not zero-coupon bonds.

2.5.2 *Zero-coupon discount factors*

Having introduced the concept of the zero-coupon curve in the previous paragraph, we can illustrate more formally the mathematics involved. When deriving spot yields from redemption yields, we view conventional bonds as being made up of an *annuity*, which is the stream of fixed coupon payments, and a zero-coupon bond, which is the redemption payment on maturity. To derive the rates we can use (2.1), setting $P_d = M = 100$ and

$C = rm_N$, as shown in (2.2) below. This has the coupon bonds trading at par, so that the coupon is equal to the yield.

$$\begin{aligned} 100 &= rm_N \times \sum_{n=1}^{N} df_n + 100 \times df_N \\ &= rm_N \times A_N + 100 \times df_N \end{aligned} \tag{2.2}$$

where rm_N is the par yield for a term to maturity of N years, where the discount factor df_N is the fair price of a zero-coupon bond with a par value of £1 and a term to maturity of N years, and where

$$A_N = \sum_{n=1}^{N} df_n = A_{N-1} + df_N \tag{2.3}$$

is the fair price of an annuity of £1 per year for N years (with $A_0 = 0$ by convention). Substituting (2.3) into (2.2) and rearranging will give us the expression below for the N-year discount factor, shown at (2.4):

$$df_N = \frac{1 - rm_N \times A_{N-1}}{1 + rm_N}. \tag{2.4}$$

If we assume one-year, two-year and three-year redemption yields for bonds priced at par to be 5%, 5.25% and 5.75% respectively, we will obtain the following solutions for the discount factors:

$$\begin{aligned} df_1 &= \frac{1}{1 + 0.05} = 0.95238 \\ df_2 &= \frac{1 - (0.0525)(0.95238)}{1 + 0.0525} = 0.90261 \\ df_3 &= \frac{1 - (0.0575)(0.95238 + 0.90261)}{1 + 0.0575} = 0.84476. \end{aligned}$$

We can confirm that these are the correct discount factors by substituting them back into equation (2.2); this gives us the following results for the one-year, two-year and three-year par value bonds (with coupons of 5%, 5.25% and 5.75% respectively):

$$\begin{aligned} 100 &= 105 \times 0.95238 \\ 100 &= 5.25 \times 0.95238 + 105.25 \times 0.90261 \\ 100 &= 5.75 \times 0.95238 + 5.75 \times 0.90261 + 105.75 \times 0.84476. \end{aligned}$$

Now that we have found the correct discount factors it is relatively straightforward to calculate the spot yields using equation (2.1), and this is shown below:

$$\begin{aligned} df_1 &= \frac{1}{(1 + rs_1)} = 0.95238 \text{ which gives } rs_1 = 5.0\% \\ df_2 &= \frac{1}{(1 + rs_2)^2} = 0.90261 \text{ which gives } rs_2 = 5.269\% \\ df_3 &= \frac{1}{(1 + rs_3)^3} = 0.84476 \text{ which gives } rs_3 = 5.778\%. \end{aligned}$$

Equation (2.1) discounts the n-year cash flow (comprising the coupon payment and/or principal repayment) by the corresponding n-year spot yield. In other words rs_n is the *time-weighted rate of return* on a n-year bond. Thus as we said in the previous section the spot yield curve is the correct method for pricing or valuing any cash flow, including an irregular cash flow, because it uses the appropriate discount factors. That is, it matches each cash flow to the discount rate that applies to the time period in which the cash flow is paid. Compare this to the approach for the yield-to-maturity procedure discussed earlier, which discounts all cash flows by the same yield to maturity. This illustrates neatly why the N-period zero-coupon interest rate is the true interest rate for an N-year bond.

The expressions above are solved algebraically in the conventional manner, although those wishing to use a spreadsheet application such as Microsoft Excel® can input the constituents of each equation into individual cells and solve using the 'Tools' and 'Goal Seek' functions.

Example 2.1: Zero-coupon yields

- Consider the following zero-coupon market rates:

One-year (1y)	5.000%
2y	5.271%
3y	5.598%
4y	6.675%
5y	7.213%

- Calculate the zero-coupon discount factors and the prices and yields of:

  (a) a 6% two-year bond, and
  (b) a 7% five-year bond.

Assume both are annual coupon bonds.

The zero-coupon discount factors are:

$$1y: \ 1/1.05 = 0.95238095$$
$$2y: \ 1/(1.05271)^2 = 0.90236554$$
$$3y: \ 1/(1.05598)^3 = 0.84924485$$
$$4y: \ 1/(1.06675)^4 = 0.77223484$$
$$5y: \ 1/(1.07213)^5 = 0.70593182$$

The price of the 6% two-year bond is then calculated in the normal fashion using present values of the cash flows:

$$(6 \times 0.95238095) + (106 \times 0.90236554) = 101.365.$$

The yield to maturity is 5.263%, obtained using the iterative method, with a spreadsheet function such as Microsoft Excel® 'Goal Seek' or a Hewlett Packard (HP) calculator.

The price of the 7% five-year bond is:

$$(7 \times 0.95238095) + (7 \times 0.90236554) + (7 \times 0.84924485) + (7 \times 0.77223484) + (107 \times 0.70593182) = 99.869.$$

The yield to maturity is 7.032%.

Formula Summary

Example 2.1 illustrates that if the zero-coupon discount factor for n years is df_n and the par yield for N years is rp, then the expression at (2.5) is always true.

$$(rp \times df_1) + (rp \times df_2) + \cdots + (rp \times df_N) + (1 \times df_N) = 1$$

$$\Rightarrow rp \times (df_1 + df_2 + \cdots + df_N) = 1 - df_N$$

$$\Rightarrow rp = \frac{1 - df_N}{\sum_{n=1}^{N} df_n}. \tag{2.5}$$

2.5.3 *Using spot rates in bond analysis*

The convention in the markets is to quote the yield on a non-government bond as a certain *spread* over the yield on the equivalent maturity government bond, usually using gross redemption yields. Traders and investment managers will assess the relative merits of holding the non-government bond based on the risk associated with the bond's issuer and the magnitude of its yield spread. For example, in the UK at the beginning of 1999 companies such as National Grid, Severn Trent Water, Abbey National plc and Tesco plc issued sterling denominated bonds, all of which paid a certain spread over the equivalent gilt bond.[3] Figure 2.5 shows the average yield spreads of corporate bonds over gilts in the UK market through 1998/99.

Traditionally investors will compare the redemption yield of the bond they are analysing with the redemption yield of the equivalent government bond. Just as with the redemption

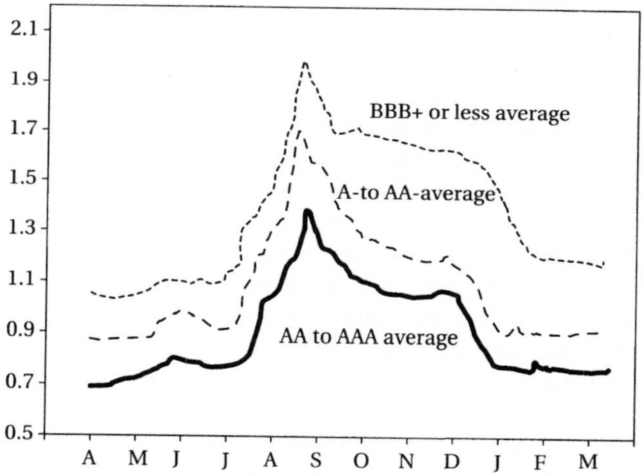

Figure 2.5: Average yield spreads of UK corporate bonds versus gilts, 2001/2002. Source: Bank of England

3 The spread is, of course, not fixed and fluctuates with market conditions and supply and demand.

yield measure however there is a flaw with this measure, in that the spread quoted is not really comparing like-for-like, as the yields do not reflect the true term structure given by the spot rate curve. There is an additional flaw if the cash flow stream of the two bonds do not match, which in practice they will do only rarely.

Therefore the correct method for assessing the yield spread of a corporate bond is to replicate its cash flows with those of a government bond, which can be done in theory by matching the cash flows of the corporate bond with a package of government zero-coupon bonds of the same nominal value. If no zero-coupon bond market exists, the cash flows can be matched synthetically by valuing a coupon bond's cash flows on a zero-coupon basis. The corporate bond's price is of course the sum of the present value of all its cash flows, which should be valued at the spot rates in place for each cash flow's maturity. It is the yield spread of each individual cash flow over the equivalent maturity government spot rate that is then taken to be the true yield spread.

This measure is known in US markets as the *zero-volatility spread* or *static spread*, and it is a measure of the spread that would be realised over the government spot rate yield curve if the corporate bond were to be held to maturity. It is therefore a different measure to the traditional spread, as it is not taken over one point on the (redemption yield) curve but over the whole term to maturity. The zero-volatility spread is that spread which equates the present value of the corporate bond's cash flows to its price, where the discount rates are each relevant government spot rate. The spread is found through an iterative process, and it is a more realistic yield spread measure than the traditional one.

2.6 The forward yield curve

2.6.1 *Forward yields*

Most transactions in the market are for immediate delivery, which is known as the *cash* market, although some markets also use the expression *spot* market, which is more common in foreign exchange. Cash market transactions are settled straight away, with the purchaser of a bond being entitled to interest from the settlement date onwards.[4] There is a large market in *forward* transactions, which are trades carried out today for a forward settlement date. For financial transactions that are forward transactions, the parties to the trade agree today to exchange a security for cash at a future date, but at a price agreed today. So the *forward rate* applicable to a bond is the spot bond yield as at the forward date. That is, it is the yield of a zero-coupon bond that is purchased for settlement at the forward date. It is derived today, using data from a present-day yield curve, so it is not correct to consider forward rates to be a prediction of the spot rates as at the forward date.

Forward rates can be derived from spot interest rates. Such rates are then known as *implied* forward rates, since they are implied by the current range of spot interest rates. The

[4] We refer to 'immediate' settlement, although of course there is a delay between trade date and settlement date, which can be anything from one day to seven days, or even longer in some markets. The most common settlement period is known as 'spot' and is two business days.

forward (or *forward-forward*) *yield curve* is a plot of forward rates against term to maturity. Forward rates satisfy expression (2.6):

$$P_d = \frac{C}{(1 + {}_0rf_1)} + \frac{C}{(1 + {}_0rf_1)(1 + {}_1rf_2)} + \cdots + \frac{M}{(1 + {}_0rf_1)\ldots(1 + {}_{N-1}rf_N)}$$
$$= \sum_{n=1}^{n} \frac{C}{\prod_{i=1}^{n}(1 + {}_{i-1}rf_i)} + \frac{M}{\prod_{i=1}^{N}(1 + {}_{i-1}rf_i)} \qquad (2.6)$$

where ${}_{n-1}rf_n$ is the implicit forward rate (or forward-forward rate) on a one-year bond maturing in year N.

As a forward or forward-forward yield is implied from spot rates, the forward rate is a forward zero-coupon rate. Comparing (2.1) and (2.6) we see that the spot yield is the *geometric mean* of the forward rates, as shown below:

$$(1 + rs_n)^n = (1 + {}_0rf_1)(1 + {}_1rf_2)\cdots(1 + {}_{n-1}rf_n). \qquad (2.7)$$

This implies the following relationship between spot and forward rates:

$$(1 + {}_{n-1}rf_n) = \frac{(1 + rs_n)^n}{(1 + rs_{n-1})^{n-1}} = \frac{df_{n-1}}{df_n}. \qquad (2.8)$$

Using the spot yields we calculated in the earlier paragraph we can derive the implied forward rates from (2.8). For example, the two-year and three-year forward rates are given by:

$$(1 + {}_1rf_2) = \frac{(1 + 0.05269)^2}{(1 + 0.05)} = 5.539\% \qquad (1 + {}_2rf_3) = \frac{(1 + 0.05778)^3}{(1 + 0.05269)^2} = 6.803\%.$$

Using our expression gives us ${}_0rf_1$ equal to 5%, ${}_1rf_2$ equal to 5.539% and ${}_2rf_3$ as 6.803%. This means for example that given current spot yields, which we calculated from the one-year, two-year and three-year bond redemption yields (which were priced at par), the market is expecting the yield on a bond with one year to mature in three years' time to be 6.803% (that is, the three year one-period forward-forward rate is 6.803%).

The relationship between the par yields, spot yields and forward rates is shown in Table 2.1.

Figure 2.6 highlights our results for all three yield curves graphically. This illustrates another important property of the relationship between the three curves, in

Year	Coupon yield (%)	Zero-coupon yield (%)	Forward rate (%)
1	5.000	5.000	5.000
2	5.250	5.269	5.539
3	5.750	5.778	6.803

Table 2.1: Coupon, spot and forward yields.

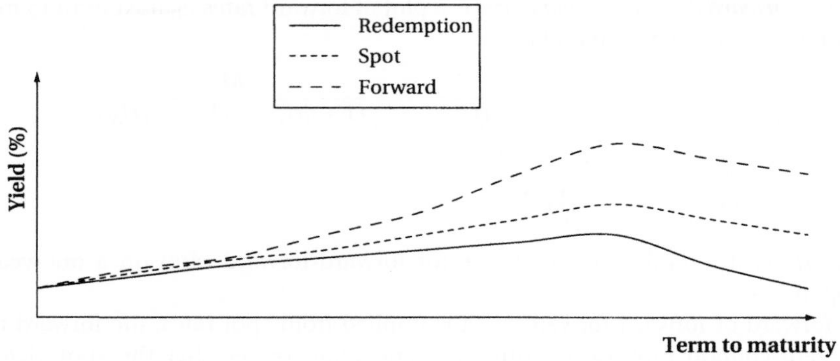

Figure 2.6: Redemption, spot and forward yield curves: traditional analysis.

that as the original coupon yield curve was positively sloping, so the spot and forward yield curves lie above it. The reasons behind this will be considered later in the chapter.

Let us now consider the following example. Suppose that a two-year bond with cash flows of £5.25 at the end of year 1 and £105.25 at the end of year 2 is trading at par, hence it has a redemption yield (indeed a par yield) of 5.25% (this is the bond in our table above). As we showed in the section on zero-coupon yields and the idea of the break-even principle, in order to be regarded as equivalent to this a pure zero-coupon bond or discount bond making a lump sum payment at the end of year 2 only (so with no cash flow at the end of year 1) would require a rate of return of 5.269%, which is the spot yield. That is, for the same investment of £100 the maturity value would have to be £110.82 (this figure is obtained by multiplying 100 by $(1+0.05269)^2$).

This illustrates why the zero-coupon curve is important to corporate financiers involved in new bond issues. If we know the spot yields then we can calculate the coupon required on a new three-year bond that is going to be issued at par in this interest-rate environment by making the following calculation:

$$100 = \frac{C}{(1.05)} + \frac{C}{(1.05269)^2} + \frac{C+100}{(1.05778)^3}.$$

This is solved in the conventional algebraic manner to give C equal to 5.75%.

The relationship between spot yields and forward rates was shown at (2.8). We can illustrate it as follows. If the spot yield is the *average return*, then the forward rate can be interpreted as the *marginal return*. If the marginal return between years 2 and 3 increases from 5.539% to 6.803%, then the average return increases from 5.269% up to the three-year spot yield of 5.778% as shown below:

$$\left((1.05269)^2(1.06803)\right)^{1/3} - 1 = 0.05777868$$

or 5.778%, as shown in Table 2.1.

Formula Summary

- The forward zero-coupon rate from interest period a to period b is given by (2.9).

$$_a rf_b = \left(\frac{(1+rs_b)^b}{(1+rs_a)^a}\right)^{1/(b-a)} - 1 \qquad (2.9)$$

where rs_a and rs_b are the a and b period spot rates respectively.

- The forward rate from interest period a to period $(a+1)$ is given by (2.10):

$$_a rf_{a+1} = \frac{(1+rs_{a+1})^{a+1}}{(1+rs_a)^a} - 1. \qquad (2.10)$$

2.6.2 *Calculating spot rates from forward rates*

The previous section showed the relationship between spot and forward rates. Just as we have derived forward rates from spot rates based on this mathematical relationship, it is possible to reverse this and calculate spot rates from forward rates. If we are presented with a forward yield curve, plotted from a set of one-period forward rates, we can use this to construct a spot yield curve. Equation (2.7) states the relationship between spot and forward rates, rearranged as (2.11) to solve for the spot rate:

$$rs_n = ((1 + {_1rf_1}) \times (1 + {_2rf_1}) \times (1 + {_3rf_1}) \times \cdots \times (1 + {_nrf_1}))^{1/n} - 1 \qquad (2.11)$$

where ${_1rf_1}$, ${_2rf_1}$, ${_3rf_1}$ are the one-period versus two-period, two-period versus three-period forward rates up to the $(n-1)$ period versus n-period forward rates.

Remember to adjust (2.11) as necessary if dealing with forward rates relating to a deposit of a different interest period. If we are dealing with the current six-month spot rate and implied six-month forward rates, the relationship between these and the n-period spot rate is given by (2.11) in the same way as if we were dealing with the current one-year spot rate and implied one-year forward rates.

Example 2.2(i)

- The one-year cash market yield is 5.00%. Market expectations have priced one-year rates in one year's time at 5.95% and in two years' time at 7.25%. What is the current three-year spot rate that would produce these forward rate views?

To calculate this we assume an investment strategy dealing today at forward rates, and calculate the return generated from this strategy. The return after a three-year period is given by the future value relationship, which in this case is $1.05 \times 1.0595 \times 1.0725 = 1.1931$.

The three-year spot rate is then obtained by:

$$\left(\frac{1.1931}{1}\right)^{\frac{1}{3}} - 1 = 6.062\%.$$

Example 2.2(ii)

- Consider the following six-month implied forward rates, when the six-month spot rate is 4.0000%:

$_1rf_1$ 4.0000%
$_2rf_1$ 4.4516%
$_3rf_1$ 5.1532%
$_4rf_1$ 5.6586%
$_5rf_1$ 6.0947%
$_6rf_1$ 7.1129%.

An investor is debating between purchasing a three-year zero-coupon bond at a price of £72.79481 per £100 nominal or buying a six-month zero-coupon bond and then rolling over her investment every six months for the three year term. If the investor was able to re-invest her proceeds every six months at the actual forward rates in place today, what would her proceeds be at the end of the three year term?

An investment of £72.79481 at the spot rate of 4% and then re-invested at the forward rates in our table over the next three years would yield a terminal value of:

$$72.79481 \times (1.04)(1.044516)(1.051532)(1.056586)(1.060947)(1.071129) = 100.$$

This merely reflects our spot and forward rates relationship, in that if all the forward rates are indeed realised, our investor's £72.79 will produce a terminal value that matches the investment in a three-year zero-coupon bond priced at the three-year spot rate. This illustrates the relationship between the three-year spot rate, the six-month spot rate and the implied six-month forward rates. So what is the three-year zero-coupon bond trading at? Using (2.11) the solution to this is given by:

$$rs_6 = ((1.04)(1.044516)(1.051532)(1.056586)(1.060947)(1.071129))^{\frac{1}{6}} - 1 = 5.4346\%$$

which solves our three-year spot rate rs_6 as 5.4346%. Of course we could have also solved for rs_6 using the conventional price/yield formula for zero-coupon bonds, however the calculation above illustrates the relationship between spot and forward rates.

2.6.3 *An important note on spot and forward rates*

Forward rates that exist at any one time reflect everything that is known in the market *up to that point.* Certain market participants may believe that the forward rate curve is a forecast of the future spot rate curve. This is implied by the *unbiased expectations hypothesis* that we consider below. In fact there is no direct relationship between the forward rate curve and the spot rate curve; for an excellent analysis of this see Jarrow (1996). It is possible for example for the forward rate curve to be upward sloping at the same time that short-dated spot rates are expected to decline.

To view the forward rate curve as a predictor of rates is a misuse of it. The derivation of forward rates reflects all currently known market information. Assuming that all developed country markets are at least semi-strong form, to preserve market equilibrium there can only be one set of forward rates from a given spot rate curve. However this does not mean that such rates are a prediction because the instant after they have been calculated, new market knowledge may become available that alters the markets' view of future interest rates. This will cause the forward rate curve to change.

Forward rates are important because they are required to make prices today for dealing at a future date. For example a bank's corporate customer may wish to fix today the interest rate payable on a loan that begins in one year from now; what rate does the bank quote? The forward rate is used by market makers to quote prices for dealing today, and is the best *expectation* of future interest rates given everything that is known in the market up to now, but it is not a prediction of future spot rates. What would happen if a bank was privy to insider information, for example it knew that central bank base rates would be changed very shortly? A bank in possession of such information (if we ignore the ethical implications) would not quote forward rates based on the spot rate curve, but would quote rates that reflected its insider knowledge.

2.6.4 *Bond valuation using forward rates*

That there is a relationship between spot rates and implied forward rates, although it is not necessarily a straightforward one, should tell us that, in theory there is no difference in valuing a conventional bond with either spot rates or forward rates. The present value of a cash flow C received in period n using forward rates is given by (2.12):

$$PV_C = \frac{C}{(1 + rs_1)(1 + {}_1rf_1)(1 + {}_2rf_1)\ldots(1 + {}_nrf_1)}. \tag{2.12}$$

Therefore we use (2.12) to assemble the expression for valuing an N-period term bond using implied forward rates, with coupon C, given at (2.13). Note that we use the six-month or one-year spot rates and the six-month or one-year implied forward rates for the forward dates according to whether the bond pays annual or semi-annual coupons. Equation (2.13) assumes an exact number of interest periods to maturity.

$$\begin{aligned} P_d = &\frac{C}{(1 + rs_1)} + \frac{C}{(1 + rs_1)(1 + {}_0rf_1)} + \frac{C}{(1 + rs_1)(1 + {}_1rf_1)(1 + {}_2rf_1)} + \cdots \\ &\cdots + \frac{C + M}{(1 + rs_1)(1 + {}_1rf_1)(1 + {}_2rf_1)\cdots(1 + {}_Nrf_1)}. \end{aligned} \tag{2.13}$$

Although bond analysts may use either spot or implied forward rates to present value cash flow streams, the final valuation will be the same regardless of whichever rates are used.

2.7 The annuity yield curve

Life assurance companies and other providers of personal pensions are users of the *annuity yield curve,* which is a plot of annuity yields against term to maturity. The *annuity yield* is the implied yield on an annuity where the annuity is valued using spot yields. In (2.2) above we decomposed a bond into an annuity and a zero-coupon discounted bond. We used the spot yield to price the discount bond component. Now we are concerned with the annuity or pure coupon component.

The value of the annuity component of a bond is given by (2.14):

$$\begin{aligned} A'_N &= \sum_{n=1}^{N} \frac{C}{(1+rs_n)^n} = \sum_{n=1}^{N} C \times df_n \\ &= C \times A_N \end{aligned} \tag{2.14}$$

where rs_n and df_n are the n-period spot rate and discount factor, as defined earlier, and A_N is the fair price of an N-year annuity of £1. However, A_N is also given by the standard formula (2.15):

$$A_N = \frac{1}{ra_N}\left(1 - \frac{1}{(1+ra_N)^N}\right) \tag{2.15}$$

where ra_N is the annuity yield on an N-year annuity.

Again using the same rates as before, consider a three-year bond with a coupon of 5.75%. To obtain the value of the annuity portion of the bond we would use (2.14) to give us:

$$\begin{aligned} A'_3 &= \frac{5.75}{1.05} + \frac{5.75}{(1.05269)^2} + \frac{5.75}{(1.05778)^3} \\ &= 15.52. \end{aligned}$$

This indicates a value for A_3 of £2.70, obtained by dividing 15.52 by 5.75. We can then use this value to solve for the annuity yield ra using (2.15) or using annuity tables; in this case the three-year annuity yield is 5.46%.

The relationship between the spot and annuity yield curves will depend on the level of market rates. With a positive-sloping spot yield curve, the annuity yield is below the end-of-period spot yield; with a negative sloping spot yield curve, the annuity yield curve lies above it. With a low-coupon bond the present value will be dominated by the terminal payment and the annuity curve will lie close to the spot curve; with a high-coupon bond the two curves will be further apart.

2.8 Analysing and interpreting the yield curve

From observing yield curves in different markets at any time, we notice that a yield curve can adopt one of four basic shapes, which are:

- *normal* or *conventional*: in which yields are at 'average' levels and the curve slopes gently upwards as maturity increases;
- *upward sloping* or *positive* or *rising*: in which yields are at historically low levels, with long rates substantially greater than short rates;
- *downward sloping* or *inverted* or *negative*: in which yield levels are very high by historical standards, but long-term yields are significantly lower than short rates;
- *humped*: where yields are high with the curve rising to a peak in the medium-term maturity area, and then sloping downwards at longer maturities.

Sometimes yield curves will incorporate a mixture of the above features.

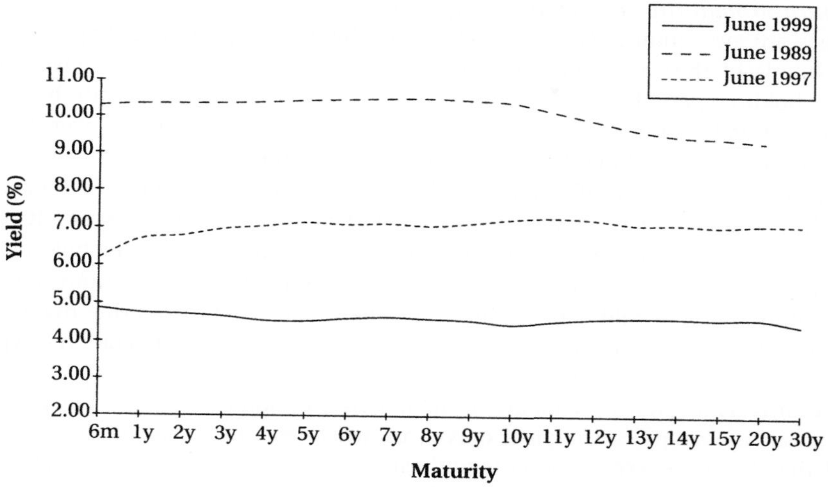

Figure 2.7: UK gilt redemption yield curves. Source: Bloomberg.

A great deal of effort is expended by bond analysts and economists analysing and interpreting yield curves. There is often a considerable information content associated with any curve at any time. For example Figure 2.7 shows the UK gilt redemption yield curve at three different times in the ten years from June 1989 to June 1999. What does the shape of each curve tell us about the UK debt market, and the UK economy at each particular time?

In this section we will consider the various explanations that have been put forward to explain the shape of the yield curve at any one time. None of the theories can adequately explain everything about yield curves and the shapes they assume at any time, so generally observers seek to explain specific curves using a combination of the accepted theories. This subject is a large one, indeed we could devote several books to it, so at this stage we will introduce the main ideas.

The existence of a yield curve itself indicates that there is a cost associated with funds of different maturities, otherwise we would observe a flat yield curve. The fact that we very rarely observe anything approaching a flat yield suggests that investors require different rates of return depending on the maturity of the instrument they are holding. In this section we review the main theories that have put forward to explain the shape of the yield curve, which all have fairly long-dated antecedents.

An excellent account of the term structure is given in *Theory of Financial Decision Making* by Jonathan Ingersoll (1987), Chapter 18. In fact it is worth purchasing this book just for Chapter 18 alone. Another quality account of the term structure is by Shiller (1990). In the following section we provide an introductory review of the research on this subject to date.

2.8.1 *The expectations hypothesis*

The expectations hypothesis suggests that bondholders' expectations determine the course of future interest rates. There are two main competing versions of this hypothesis, the *local expectations hypothesis* and the *unbiased expectations hypothesis.*

The *return-to-maturity expectations* hypothesis and *yield-to-maturity expectations* hypothesis are also quoted (see Ingersoll 1987). The local expectations hypothesis states that all bonds of the same class but differing in term to maturity will have the same expected holding period rate of return. This suggests that a six-month bond and a twenty-year bond will produce the same rate of return, on average, over the stated holding period. So if we intend to hold a bond for six months, we will receive the same return no matter what specific bond we buy. The author feels that this theory is not always the case nor relevant, despite being mathematically neat; however it is worth spending a few moments discussing it and related points. Generally holding period returns from longer-dated bonds are on average higher than those from short-dated bonds. Intuitively we would expect this, with longer-dated bonds offering higher returns to compensate for their higher price volatility (risk). The local expectations hypothesis would not agree with the conventional belief that investors, being risk averse, require higher returns as a reward for taking on higher risk; in addition it does not provide any insight about the shape of the yield curve. An article by Cox, Ingersoll and Ross (1981) showed that the local expectations hypothesis best reflected equilibrium between spot and forward yields. This was demonstrated using a feature known as Jensen's inequality, which is described in Appendix 2.2. Robert Jarrow (1996) states

> '... in an economic equilibrium, the returns on ... similar maturity zero-coupon binds cannot be too different. If they were too different, no investor would hold the bond with the smaller return. This difference could not persist in an economic equilibrium'.
>
> (Jarrow 1996, p. 50)

This reflects economic logic, but in practice other factors can impact on holding period returns between bonds that do not have similar maturities. For instance investors will have restrictions as to which bonds they can hold, for example banks and building societies are required to hold short-dated bonds for liquidity purposes. In an environment of economic dis-equilibrium, these investors would still have to hold shorter-dated bonds, even if the holding period return was lower.

So although it is economically neat to expect that the return on a long-dated bond is equivalent to rolling over a series of shorter-dated bonds, it is often observed that longer-term (default-free) returns exceed annualised short-term default-free returns. So an investor that continually rolled over a series of short-dated zero-coupon bonds would most likely receive a lower return than if she had invested in a long-dated zero-coupon bond. Rubinstein (1999) gives an excellent, accessible explanation of why this should be so. The reason is that compared to the theoretical model, in reality future spot rates are not known with certainty. This means that short-dated zero-coupon bonds are more attractive to investors for two reasons; first, they are more appropriate instruments to use for hedging purposes, and secondly they are more liquid instruments, in that they may be more readily converted back into cash than long-dated instruments. With regard to hedging, consider an exposure to rising interest rates. If the yield curve shifts upwards at some point in the future, the price of long-dated bonds will fall by a greater amount. This is a negative result for holders of such bonds, whereas the investor in short-dated bonds will benefit from rolling over his funds at the (new) higher rates. With regard to the second issue, Rubinstein (1999) states

> '... it can be shown that in an economy with risk-averse individuals, uncertainty concerning the timing of aggregate consumption, the partial irreversibility of real investments (longer-term physical investments cannot be converted into investments with earlier payouts without sacrifice), [and] ... real assets with shorter-term payouts will tend to have a 'liquidity' advantage.'
>
> (Rubinstein 1999, p. 84–85)

Therefore the demand for short-term instruments is frequently higher, and hence short-term returns are often lower than long-term returns.

The *pure* or *unbiased expectations hypothesis* is more commonly encountered and states that current implied forward rates are unbiased estimators of future spot interest rates.[5] It assumes that investors act in a way that eliminates any advantage of holding instruments of a particular maturity. Therefore if we have a positive-sloping yield curve, the unbiased expectations hypothesis states that the market expects spot interest rates to rise. Equally, an inverted yield curve is an indication that spot rates are expected to fall. If short-term interest rates are expected to rise, then longer yields should be higher than shorter ones to reflect this. If this were not the case, investors would only buy the shorter-dated bonds and roll over the investment when they matured. Likewise if rates are expected to fall then longer yields should be lower than short yields. The unbiased expectations hypothesis states that the long-term interest rate is a geometric average of expected future short-term rates. This was in fact the theory that was used to derive the forward yield curve using (2.5) and (2.7) previously. This gives us:

$$(1 + rs_N)^N = (1 + rs_1)(1 + {}_1rf_2) \cdots (1 + {}_{N-1}rf_N) \tag{2.16}$$

or

$$(1 + rs_N)^N = (1 + rs_{N-1})^{N-1}(1 + {}_{N-1}rf_N) \tag{2.17}$$

where rs_N is the spot yield on a N-year bond and ${}_{n-1}rf_n$ is the implied one-year rate n years ahead. For example if the current one-year spot rate is $rs_1 = 5.0\%$ and the market is expecting the one-year rate in a year's time to be ${}_1rf_2 = 5.539\%$, then the market is expecting a £100 investment in two one-year bonds to yield:

$$£100(1.05)(1.05539) = £110.82$$

after two years. To be equivalent to this an investment in a two-year bond has to yield the same amount, implying that the current two-year rate is $rs_2 = 5.7\%$, as shown below:

$$£100(1 + rs_2)^2 = £110.82$$

which gives us rs_2 equal to 5.27%, and gives us the correct future value as shown below:

$$£100(1.0527)^2 = £110.82.$$

This result must be so, to ensure no arbitrage opportunities exist in the market and in fact we showed as much earlier in the chapter when we considered forward rates. According

5 For original discussion, see Lutz (1940) and Fisher (1986, although he formulated his ideas earlier).

to the unbiased expectations hypothesis therefore the forward rate ${}_0rf_2$ is an unbiased predictor of the spot rate ${}_1rs_1$ observed one period later; on average the forward rate should equal the subsequent spot rate. The hypothesis can be used to explain any shape in the yield curve.

A rising yield curve is therefore explained by investors expecting short-term interest rates to rise, that is ${}_1rf_2 > rs_2$. A falling yield curve is explained by investors expecting short-term rates to be lower in the future. A humped yield curve is explained by investors expecting short-term interest rates to rise and long-term rates to fall. Expectations, or views on the future direction of the market, are a function mainly of the expected rate of inflation. If the market expects inflationary pressures in the future, the yield curve will be positively shaped, while if inflation expectations are inclined towards disinflation, then the yield curve will be negative. However, several empirical studies including one by Fama (1976) have shown that forward rates are essentially biased predictors of future spot interest rates, and often over-estimate future levels of spot rates. The unbiased hypothesis has also been criticised for suggesting that investors can forecast (or have a view on) very long-dated spot interest rates, which might be considered slightly unrealistic. As yield curves in most developed country markets exist to a maturity of up to thirty years or longer, such criticisms may have some substance. Are investors able to forecast interest rates 10, 20 or 30 years into the future? Perhaps not, nevertheless this is indeed the information content of say, a thirty-year bond; since the yield on the bond is set by the market, it is valid to suggest that the market has a view on inflation and future interest rates for up to thirty years forward.

The expectations hypothesis is stated in more than one way; we have already encountered the local expectations hypothesis. Other versions include the *return-to-maturity* expectations hypothesis, which states that the total return from holding a zero-coupon bond to maturity will be equal to the total return that is generated by holding a short-term instrument and continuously rolling it over the same maturity period. A related version, the *yield-to-maturity* hypothesis, states that the periodic return from holding a zero-coupon bond will be equal to the return from rolling over a series of coupon bonds, but refers to the annualised return earned each year rather than the total return earned over the life of the bond. This assumption enables a zero-coupon yield curve to be derived from the redemption yields of coupon bonds. The unbiased expectations hypothesis of course states that forward rates are equal to the spot rates expected by the market in the future. The Cox–Ingersoll–Ross article suggests that only the local expectations hypothesis describes a model that is purely arbitrage-free, as under the other scenarios it would be possible to employ certain investment strategies that would produce returns in excess of what was implied by today's yields. Although it has been suggested[6] that the differences between the local and the unbiased hypotheses are not material, a model that describes such a scenario would not reflect investors' beliefs, which is why further research is ongoing in this area.

The unbiased expectations hypothesis does not by itself explain all the shapes of the yield curve or the information content contained within it, so it is often tied in with other explanations, including the liquidity preference theory.

6 For example, see Campbell (1986) and Livingstone (1990).

2.8.2 *Liquidity preference theory*

Intuitively we might feel that longer maturity investments are more risky than shorter ones. An investor lending money for a five-year term will usually demand a higher rate of interest than if they were to lend the same customer money for a five-week term. This is because the borrower may not be able to repay the loan over the longer time period as they may for instance, have gone bankrupt in that period. For this reason longer-dated yields should be higher than short-dated yields, to recompense the lender for the higher risk exposure during the term of the loan.[7]

We can consider this theory in terms of inflation expectations as well. Where inflation is expected to remain roughly stable over time, the market would anticipate a positive yield curve. However the expectations hypothesis cannot by itself explain this phenomenon, as under stable inflationary conditions one would expect a flat yield curve. The risk inherent in longer-dated investments, or the *liquidity preference theory*, seeks to explain a positive shaped curve. Generally borrowers prefer to borrow over as long a term as possible, while lenders will wish to lend over as short a term as possible. Therefore, as we first stated, lenders have to be compensated for lending over the longer term; this compensation is considered a premium for a loss in *liquidity* for the lender. The premium is increased the further the investor lends across the term structure, so that the longest-dated investments will, all else being equal, have the highest yield. So the liquidity preference theory states that the yield curve should almost always be upward sloping, reflecting bondholders preference for the liquidity and lower risk of shorter-dated bonds. An inverted yield curve could still be explained by the liquidity preference theory when it is combined with the unbiased expectations hypothesis. A *humped* yield curve might be viewed as a combination of an inverted yield curve together with a positive-sloping liquidity preference curve.

The difference between a yield curve explained by unbiased expectations and an actual observed yield curve is sometimes referred to as the *liquidity premium*. This refers to the fact that in some cases short-dated bonds are easier to transact in the market than long-term bonds. It is difficult to quantify the effect of the liquidity premium, which in any case is not static and fluctuates over time. The liquidity premium is so-called because, in order to induce investors to hold longer-dated securities, the yields on such securities must be higher than those available on short-dated securities, which are more liquid and may be converted into cash more easily. The liquidity premium is the compensation required for holding less liquid instruments. If longer-dated securities then provide higher yields, as is suggested by the existence of the liquidity premium, they should generate on average higher total returns over an investment period. This is not consistent with the local expectations hypothesis. More formally we can write:

$$0 = L_1 < L_2 < L_3 < \cdots < L_n \text{ and } (L_2 - L_1) > (L_3 - L_2) > \cdots (L_n - L_{n-1})$$

where L is the premium for a bond with term to maturity of n years, which states that the premium increases as the term to maturity rises and that an otherwise flat yield curve will have a positively sloping curve, with the degree of slope steadily decreasing as we extend along the yield curve. This is consistent with observation of yield curves under 'normal' conditions.

---

7 For original discussion, see Hicks (1946).

The expectations hypothesis assumes that forward rates are equal to the expected future spot rates, that is as shown in (2.18):

$$_{n-1}rf_n = E(_{n-1}rs_n) \tag{2.18}$$

where $E()$ is the expectations operator for the current period. This assumption implies that the forward rate is an unbiased predictor of the future spot rate, as we suggested in the previous paragraph. Liquidity preference theory on the other hand, recognises the possibility that the forward rate may contain an element of liquidity premium which declines over time as the period approaches, given by (2.19):

$$_{n-1}rf_n > E(_{n-1}rs_n). \tag{2.19}$$

If there was uncertainty in the market about the future direction of spot rates and hence where the forward rate should lie, (2.19) is adjusted to give the reverse inequality.

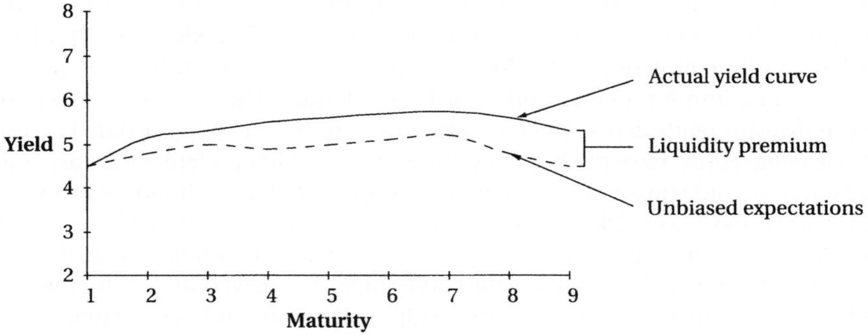

Figure 2.8: Yield curve explained by expectations hypothesis and liquidity preference.

2.8.3 *Money substitute hypothesis*

A particular explanation of short-dated bond yield curves has been attempted by Kessel (1965). In the *money substitute* theory short-dated bonds are regarded as substitutes for holding cash. Investors hold only short-dated market instruments because these are viewed as low or negligible risk. As a result the yields of short-dated bonds are depressed due to the increased demand and lie below longer-dated bonds. Borrowers on the other hand prefer to issue debt for longer maturities, and on as few occasions as possible to minimise costs. Therefore the yields of longer-dated paper are driven upwards due to a combination of increased supply and lower liquidity. In certain respects the money substitute theory is closely related to the liquidity preference theory, and by itself does not explain inverted or humped yield curves.

2.8.4 *Segmentation hypothesis*

The capital markets are made up of a wide variety of users, each with different requirements. Certain classes of investors will prefer dealing at the short-end of the yield curve, while others will concentrate on the longer end of the market. The *segmented markets* theory suggests that activity is concentrated in certain specific areas of the market, and that there are no inter-relationships between these parts of the market; the relative amounts of funds invested in each of the maturity spectrum causes differentials in supply and demand, which results in humps in the yield curve. That is, the shape of the yield curve is determined by supply and demand for certain specific maturity investments, each of which has no reference to any other part of the curve.

For example banks and building societies concentrate a large part of their activity at the short end of the curve, as part of daily cash management (known as *asset and liability management*) and for regulatory purposes (known as *liquidity* requirements). Fund managers such as pension funds and insurance companies are active at the long end of the market. Few institutional investors however have any preference for medium-dated bonds. This behaviour on the part of investors will lead to high prices (low yields) at both the short and long ends of the yield curve and lower prices (higher yields) in the middle of the term structure.

Since according to the segmented markets hypothesis a separate market exists for specific maturities along the term structure, interest rates for these maturities are set by supply and demand.[8] Where there is no demand for a particular maturity, the yield will lie above other segments. Market participants do not hold bonds in any other area of the curve outside their area of interest[9] so that short-dated and long-dated bond yields exist independently of each other. The segmented markets theory is usually illustrated by reference to banks and life companies. Banks and building societies hold their funds in short-dated instruments, usually no longer than five years in maturity. This is because of the nature of retail banking operations, with a large volume of instant access funds being deposited at banks, and also for regulatory purposes. Holding short-term, liquid bonds enables banks to meet any sudden or unexpected demand for funds from customers. The classic theory suggests that as banks invest their funds in short-dated bonds, the yields on these bonds is driven down. When they then liquidate part of their holding, perhaps to meet higher demand for loans, the yields are driven up and prices of the bonds fall. This affects the short end of the yield curve but not the long end.

The segmented markets theory can be used to explain any particular shape of the yield curve, although it fits best perhaps with positive sloping curves. However it cannot be used to interpret the yield curve whatever shape it may be, and therefore offers no information content during analysis. By definition the theory suggests that for investors bonds with different maturities are not perfect substitutes for each other. This is because different bonds would have different holding period returns, making them imperfect substitutes of one another.[10] As a result of bonds being imperfect substitutes, markets are segmented according to maturity.

The segmentations hypothesis is a reasonable explanation of certain features of a conventional positively-sloping yield curve, but by itself is not sufficient. There is no doubt that banks and building societies have a requirement to hold securities at the short end of the yield curve, as much for regulatory purposes as for yield considerations, however other investors are probably more flexible and will place funds where value is deemed to exist. Nonetheless the higher demand for benchmark securities does drive down yields along certain segments of the curve.

A slightly modified version of the market segmentation hypothesis is known as the *preferred habitat theory*. This suggests that different market participants have an interest in

---

8 See Culbertson (1957).

9 For example, retail and commercial banks hold bonds in the short dates, while life assurance companies hold long-dated bonds.

10 *Ibid.*

specified areas of the yield curve, but can be induced to hold bonds from other parts of the maturity spectrum if there is sufficient incentive. Hence banks may at certain times hold longer-dated bonds once the price of these bonds falls to a certain level, making the return on the bonds worth the risk involved in holding them. Similar considerations may persuade long-term investors to hold short-dated debt. So higher yields will be required to make bond holders shift out of their usual area of interest. This theory essentially recognises the flexibility that investors have, outside regulatory or legal requirements (such as the terms of an institutional fund's objectives), to invest in whatever part of the yield curve they identify value.

2.8.5 *Humped yield curves*

When plotting a yield curve of all the bonds in a certain class, it is common to observe humped yield curves. These usually occur for a variety of reasons. In line with the unbiased expectations hypothesis, humped curves will be observed when interest rates are expected to rise over the next several periods and then decline. On other occasions humped curves can result from skewed expectations of future interest rates. This is when the market believes that fairly constant future interest rates are likely, but also believes that there is a small probability for lower rates in the medium term. The other common explanation for humped curves is the preferred habitat theory.

2.8.6 *The combined theory*

The explanation for the shape of the yield curve at any time is more likely to be described by a combination of the pure expectations hypothesis and the liquidity preference theory, and possibly one or two other theories. Market analysts often combine the unbiased expectations hypothesis with the liquidity preference theory into an 'eclectic' theory. The result is fairly consistent with any shape of yield curve, and is also a predictor of rising interest rates. In the combined theory the forward interest rate is equal to the expected future spot rate, together with a quantified liquidity premium. This is shown at (2.20):

$$ {}_0rf_i = E({}_{i-1}rs_1) + L_i \tag{2.20} $$

where L_i is the liquidity premium for a term to maturity of i. The size of the liquidity premium is expected to increase with increasing maturity.[11] An illustration is given at Example 2.3.

Example 2.3: Positive yield curve with constant expected future interest rates

- Consider the interest rates structure in Table 2.2.

Period n	0	1	2	3	4	5
$E(rs)$		4.5%	4.5%	4.5%	4.5%	4.5%
Forward rate ${}_0rf_n$		5.00%	5.50%	6.00%	6.50%	7.50%
Spot rate rs_n	5%	5.30%	5.80%	6.20%	6.80%	7%

Table 2.2: Positive yield curve with constant expected future rates.

11 So that $L_i > L_{i-1}$.

The current term structure is positive sloping since the spot rates increase with increasing maturity. However the market expects future spot rates to be constant at 4.5%. The forward and spot rates are also shown, however the forward rate is a function of the expected spot rate and the liquidity premium. This premium is equal to 0.50% for the first year, 1.0% in the second and so on.

The combined theory is consistent with an inverted yield curve. This will apply even when the liquidity premium is increasing with maturity, for example where the expected future spot interest rate is declining. Typically this would be where there was a current term structure of falling yields along the term structure. The spot rates might be declining where the fall in the expected future spot rate exceeds the corresponding increase in the liquidity premium.

2.8.7 *The flat yield curve*

The conventional theories do not seek to explain a flat yield curve. Although it is rare to observe flat curves in a market, certainly for any length of time, at times they do emerge in response to peculiar economic circumstances. In the conventional thinking, a flat curve is not tenable because investors should in theory have no incentive to hold long-dated bonds over shorter-dated bonds when there is no yield premium, so that as they sell off long-dated paper the yield at the long end should rise, producing an upward sloping curve. In previous circumstances of a flat curve, analysts have produced different explanations for their existence. In November 1988 the US Treasury yield curve was flat relative to the recent past; researchers contended that this was the result of the market's view that long-dated yields would fall as bond prices rallied upwards.[12] One recommendation is to buy longer maturities when the yield curve is flat, in anticipation of lower long-term interest rates, which is the direct opposite to the view that a flat curve is a signal to sell long bonds. In the case of the US market in 1988, long bond yields did in fact fall by approximately 2% in the following 12 months. This would seem to indicate that one's view of future long-term rates should be behind the decision to buy or sell long bonds, rather than the shape of the yield curve itself. A flat curve may well be more heavily influenced by supply and demand factors than anything else, with the majority opinion eventually winning out and forcing a change in the curve to a more conventional shape.

2.8.8 *Yield curves as a function of the stochastic behaviour of interest rates*

As a result of research into the behaviour of asset prices more recent explanations for the shape of the yield curve have sought to describe it as reflecting the behaviour of interest rates and the process that interest rates follow. These explanations are termed *stochastic processes*. A stochastic process is one where random phenomena evolve over time, and

[12] See Levy (1999).

these may be asset prices, interest rates, returns on an investment portfolio and so on. Under these explanations then, yield curves reflect the following:

- bond yields follow a stochastic process over time, and hence the yield curve reflects this;
- bond yields at any one time satisfy the no-arbitrage pricing rule for spot and forward rates.

The model of the term structure as being an arbitrage-free stochastic process evolved with option pricing theory and was described separately.[13] Such models sought to describe the term structure in terms of the short-term interest rate only, more recent models describe the whole term structure as part of a stochastic process.[14] This subject is key to yield curve modelling.

2.8.9 *Further views on the yield curve*

In this chapter our discussion of present values, spot and forward interest rates has assumed an economist's world of the *perfect market* (also sometimes called the *frictionless* financial market). Such a perfect capital market is characterised by:

- perfect information;
- no taxes;
- bullet maturity bonds;
- no transaction costs.

Of course in practice markets are not completely perfect. However assuming perfect markets makes the discussion of spot and forward rates and the term structure easier to handle. When we analyse yield curves for their information content, we have to remember that the markets that they represent are not perfect, and that frequently we observe anomalies that are not explained by the conventional theories.

At any one time it is probably more realistic to suggest that a range of factors contributes to the yield curve being one particular shape. For instance short-term interest rates are greatly influenced by the availability of funds in the money market. The slope of the yield curve (usually defined as the 10-year yield minus the three-month interest rate) is also a measure of the degree of tightness of government monetary policy. A low, upward sloping curve is often thought to be a sign that an environment of cheap money, due to a more loose monetary policy, is to be followed by a period of higher inflation and higher bond yields. Equally a high downward sloping curve is taken to mean that a situation of tight credit, due to more strict monetary policy, will result in falling inflation and lower bond yields. Inverted yield curves have often preceded recessions; for instance *The Economist* in an article from April 1998 remarked that in the United States every recession since 1955 bar one had been preceded by a negative yield curve. The analysis is the same: if investors expect a recession they also expect inflation to fall, so the yields on long-term bonds will fall relative to short-term bonds. So the conventional explanation for an inverted yield curve is that the markets and the investment community expect

---

13 See Black and Scholes (1973) and Merton (1973).

14 For example, see Heath, Jarrow and Morton (1992).

either a slow-down of the economy, or an outright recession.[15] In this case one would expect the monetary authorities to ease the money supply by reducing the base interest rate in the near future: hence an inverted curve. At the same time, a reduction of short-term interest rates will affect short-dated bonds and these are sold off by investors, further raising their yield.

While the conventional explanation for negative yield curves is an expectation of economic slow-down, on occasion other factors will be involved. In the UK in the period July 1997–June 1999 the gilt yield curve was inverted.[16] There was no general view that the economy was heading for recession however, in fact the new Labour government led by Tony Blair inherited an economy believed to be in good health. Instead the explanation behind the inverted shape of the gilt yield curve focused on two other factors: first, the handing of responsibility for setting interest rates to the Monetary Policy Committee (MPC) of the Bank of England, and secondly the expectation that the UK would over the medium term, abandon sterling and join the euro currency. The yield curve in this time suggested that the market expected the MPC to be successful and keep inflation at a level around 2.5% over the long term (its target is actually a 1% range either side of 2.5%), and also that sterling interest rates would need to come down over the medium term as part of *convergence* with interest rates in euroland. These are both medium-term expectations however, and in the author's view not logical at the short-end of the yield curve. In fact the term structure moved to a positive-sloped shape up to the 6–7 year area, before inverting out to the long-end of the curve, in June 1999. This is a more logical shape for the curve to assume, but it was short-lived and returned to being inverted after the 2-year term.

There is therefore significant information content in the yield curve, and economists and bond analysts will consider the shape of the curve as part of their policy making and investment advice. The shape of parts of the curve, whether the short-end or long-end, as well as that of the entire curve, can serve as useful predictors of future market conditions. As part of an analysis it is also worthwhile considering the yield curves across several different markets and currencies. For instance the interest-rate swap curve, and its position relative to that of the government bond yield curve, is also regularly analysed for its information content. In developed country economies the swap market is invariably as liquid as the government bond market, if not more liquid, and so it is common to see the swap curve analysed when making predictions about say, the future level of short-term interest rates.

Government policy will influence the shape and level of the yield curve, including policy on public sector borrowing, debt management and open-market operations. The markets perception of the size of public sector debt will influence bond yields; for instance an increase in the level of debt can lead to an increase in bond yields across the maturity range. Open-market operations, which refers to the daily operation by the Bank of England to control the level of the money supply (to which end the Bank purchases short-term bills and also engages in repo dealing), can have a number of effects. In the short-term it can tilt

15 A recession is formally defined as two successive quarters of falling output in the domestic economy.

16 Although the curve briefly went positively sloped out to 7–8 years in July 1999, it very quickly reverted to being inverted throughout the term structure, and remained so at the time of writing.

the yield curve both upwards and downwards; longer term, changes in the level of the base rate will affect yield levels. An anticipated rise in base rates can lead to a drop in prices for short-term bonds, whose yields will be expected to rise; this can lead to a temporary inverted curve. Finally debt management policy will influence the yield curve. (In the United Kingdom this is now the responsibility of the Debt Management Office.) Much government debt is rolled over as it matures, but the maturity of the replacement debt can have a significant influence on the yield curve in the form of humps in the market segment in which the debt is placed, if the debt is priced by the market at a relatively low price and hence high yield.

2.9 Interpreting the yield curve

We illustrate some of the points we have raised here using yield curves from the United Kingdom gilt market during the 1990s. It is of course easier to analyse them for their information content in hindsight than it might have been at the time, but these observations illustrate the general conclusions that might be made.

To begin consider the observed yield curves for January and June 1990 in Figures 2.9 and 2.10.[17]

The yield curve for the first date suggests declining short-term rates and this is indicated by the yield curve for June 1990. The prediction is approximately accurate.

That the yield curves were inverted is not surprising given that the UK economy was shortly to enter an economic recession, however at that date – January 1990 – it had not yet begun. The evidence of GDP output data is that the recession took place during 1990–91. The markets were therefore expecting some loosening of monetary policy given the economic slow-down during 1989. There was an additional anomaly in that during 1988 the

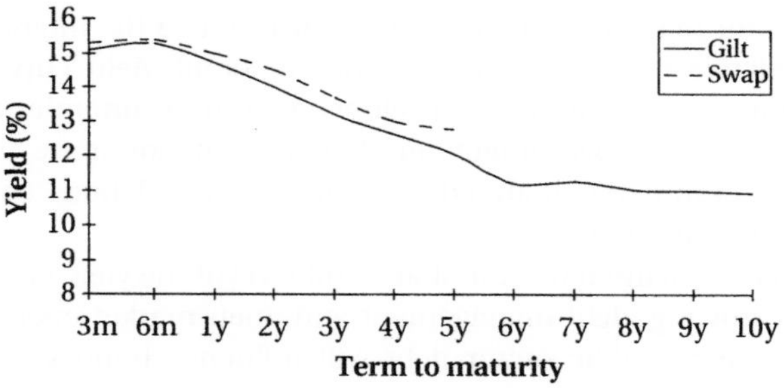

Figure 2.9: January 1990.

[17] All government yield curves shown are fitted par yield curves, using the Bank of England's internal model (see Mastronikola (1991) and Anderson and Sleath (1999)), except where indicated. Source data is the Bank of England. The other curve is the interest-rate swap curve, also called the Libor curve, for sterling swaps. In practice interest-rate swaps are priced off the government yield curve, and reflect the market's view of interbank credit risk, as the swap rate is payable by a bank (or corporate) viewed as having an element of credit risk. All swap curves are drawn using interest data from Bloomberg.

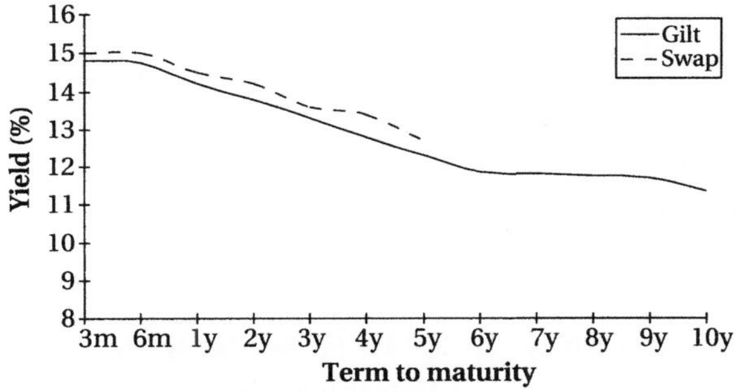

Figure 2.10: June 1990.

government had been paying off public sector debt, leading some commentators to suggest that gilt supply would be reduced in coming years. This may have contributed to the depressed yields at the long end in January 1990 but almost certainly had less influence in June 1990, when the recession was underway.

Consider the same curves for June 1991 and January 1992, shown as Figures 2.11 and 2.12 respectively. In this case the money market has priced swaps to give a different shape yield curve; does this mean that the money market has a different view of forward rates to government bond investors? Observing the yield curves for January 1992 suggests not: the divergence in the swap curve reflects credit considerations that price long maturity corporate rates at increasing yield spreads. This is common during recessions, and indeed the curves reflect recession conditions in the UK economy at the time, as predicted by the yield curves during 1990. Another indicator is the continuation of the wide swap spread as the term to maturity increases to ten years, rather than the conventional mirroring of the government curve. Note also that the short-term segment of the swap curve in June 1991 (Figure 2.11) matches the government yield curve, indicating that the market agreed with the short-term forward rate prediction of the government curve.

During 1992 as the UK economy came out of recession the government yield curve changed from inverted to steadily positive, while the swap curve mirrored the shape of

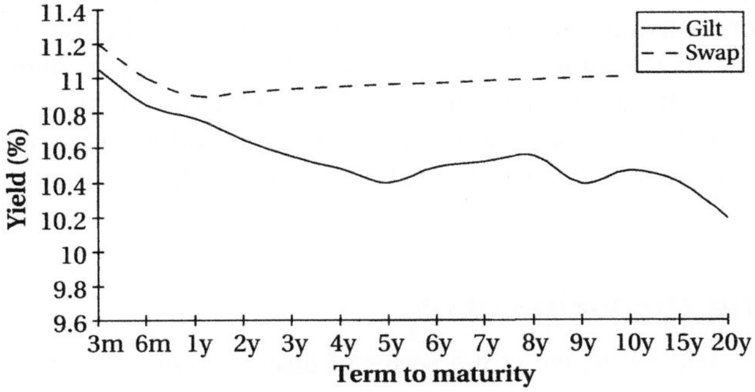

Figure 2.11: June 1991.

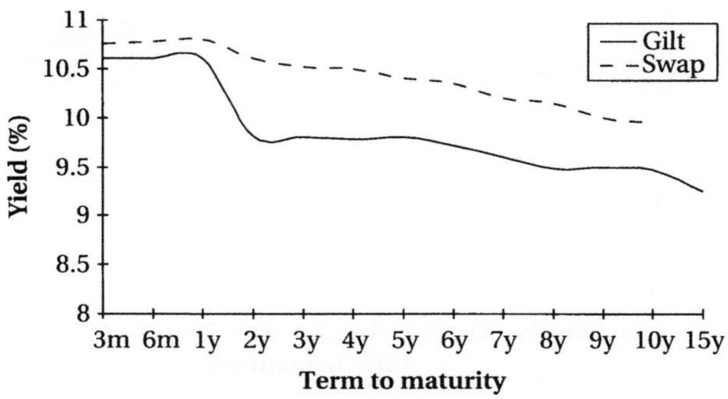

Figure 2.12: January 1992.

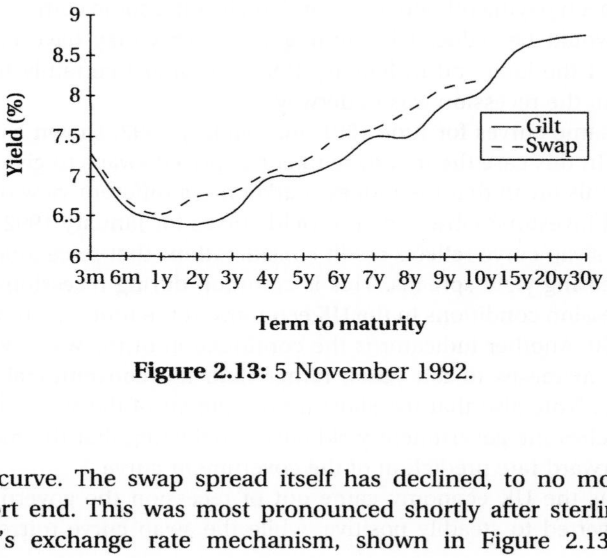

Figure 2.13: 5 November 1992.

the government curve. The swap spread itself has declined, to no more than 10 basis points at the short end. This was most pronounced shortly after sterling fell out of the European Union's exchange rate mechanism, shown in Figure 2.13, the curves for November 1992.

Both yield curves had reverted to being purely positive sloping by January 1993.

The illustrations used are examples where government yield curves were shown to be accurate predictors of the short-term rates that followed, more so than the swap curve. This is to be expected: the government or *benchmark* yield curve is the cornerstone of the debt markets, and is used by the market to price all other debt instruments, including interest-rate swaps. This reflects both the liquidity of the government market and its risk-free status.

2.10 Fitting the yield curve

When graphing a yield curve, we plot a series of discrete points of yield against maturity. Similarly for the term structure of interest rates, we plot spot rates for a fixed time period against that time period. The yield curve itself however is a smooth curve drawn through these points. Therefore we require a method that allows us to fit the curve as accurately as possible, known as *yield curve modelling* or *estimating the term structure.* There are several ways to model a yield curve, which we introduce in this section.

Ideally the fitted yield curve should be a continuous function, with no gaps in the curve, while passing through the observed yield vertices. The curve also needs to be 'smooth', as kinks in the curve will produce sudden sharp jumps in derived forward rates. We have stated how it is possible to calculate a set of discrete discount factors or a continuous discount function. It has been shown that the discount function, par yield curve, spot rate yield curve and forward rate curve are all related mathematically, such that if one knows any one of these, the other three can be derived. In practice in many markets it is not possible usually to observe the curves directly, hence they need to be derived from coupon bond prices and yields. In attempting to model a yield curve from bond yields we need to consider the two fundamental issues introduced above. First is the problem of gaps in the maturity spectrum, as in reality there will not be a bond maturing at regular intervals along the complete term structure. For example in the UK gilt market, currently there is no bond at all maturing between 2017 and 2021, or between 2021 and 2028. Secondly as we have seen the term structure is formally defined in terms of spot or zero-coupon interest rates, but in many markets there is no actual zero-coupon bond market. In such cases spot rates cannot be inferred directly but must be implied from coupon bonds. Where zero-coupon bonds are traded, for example in the US and UK government bond markets, we are able to observe zero-coupon yields directly in the market.

Further problems in fitting the curve arise from these two issues. How is the gap in maturities to be tackled? Analysts need to choose between 'smoothness' and 'responsiveness' of the curve estimate. Most models opt for a smooth fitting, however enough flexibility should be retained to allow for true movements in the term structure where indicated by the data. Should the yield curve be estimated from the discount function or say, the par yield curve? There are other practical factors to consider as well, such as the effect of withholding tax on coupons, and the size of bond coupons themselves. We will consider the issues connected with estimating the yield curve in a later chapter; at this point we confine ourselves to introducing the main methods.

2.10.1 *Interpolation*

The simplest method that is employed to fit a curve is *linear interpolation,* which involves drawing a straight line joining each pair of yield vertices. To calculate the yield for one vertex we use (2.21):

$$rm_t = rm_i + \frac{t - n_i}{n_{i+1} - n_i} \times (rm_{i+1} - rm_i) \tag{2.21}$$

where rm_t is the yield being estimated and n is the number of years to maturity for yields that are observed. For example consider the following redemption yields:

1 month:	4.00%
2 years:	5.00%
4 years:	6.50%
10 years:	6.75%

If we wish to estimate the six-year yield we calculate it using (2.21), which is:

$$rm_{6y} = 6.50\% + \frac{6-4}{10-6} \times 6.75\% - 6.50\%$$
$$= 6.5833\%$$

The limitations of using linear interpolation are that first, the curve can have sharp angles at the vertices where two straight lines meet, resulting in unreasonable jumps in the derived forward rates. Second and more fundamentally being a straight-line method, it assumes the yield between two vertices should automatically be rising (in a positive yield curve environment) or falling. This assumption can lead to gross inaccuracies in the fitted curve.

Another approach is to use *logarithmic interpolation*, which involves applying linear interpolation to the natural logarithms of the corresponding discount factors. Therefore given any two discount factors we can calculate an intermediate discount factor using (2.22):

$$ln(df_t) = ln(df_{n_i}) + \frac{t - n_i}{n_{i-1} - n_i} \times (ln(df_{n_{i+1}}) - ln(df_{n_i})). \qquad (2.22)$$

To calculate the six-year yield from the same yield structure above, we use the following procedure:

- calculate the discount factors for years 4 and 10 and then take the natural logarithms of these discount factors;
- perform a linear interpolation on these logarithms;
- take the anti-log of the result, to get the implied interpolated discount factor;
- calculate the implied yield in this discount factor.

Using (2.22) we obtain a six-year yield of 6.6388%. The logarithmic interpolation method reduces the sharpness of angles on the curve and so makes it smoother, but it retains the other drawbacks of the linear interpolation method.

2.10.2 *Polynomial models*[18]

The most straightforward method for estimating the yield curve involves fitting a single polynomial in time. For example a model might use an F-order polynomial, illustrated with (2.23):

$$rm_i = \alpha + \beta_1 N_i + \beta_2 N_i^2 + \cdots + \beta_F N_i^F + u_i \qquad (2.23)$$

where

rm_i	is the yield to maturity of the i-th bond
N_i	is the term to maturity of the i-th bond
α, β_F	are coefficients of the polynomial
u_i	is the residual error on the i-th bond

[18] These are standard econometric techniques. For an excellent account see Campbell *et al.* (1997).

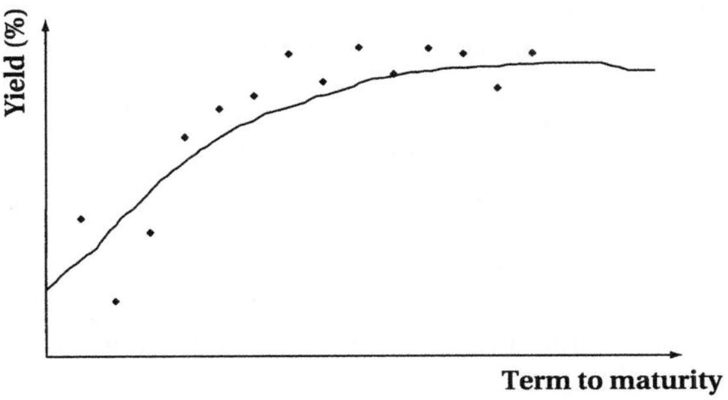

Figure 2.14: Polynomial curve fitting.

To determine the coefficients of the polynomial we minimise the sum of the squared residual errors, given by:

$$\sum_{i}^{T} u_i^2 \tag{2.24}$$

where T is the number of bonds used. This is represented graphically in Figure 2.14.

The type of curve that results is a function of the order of the polynomial F. If F is too large the curve will not be smooth but will be in effect too 'responsive', such that the curve runs through every point, known as being 'over-fitted'. The extreme of this is given when $F = T - 1$. If F is too small the curve will be an over-estimation.

The method described above has been supplanted by a more complex method, which fits different polynomials over different but overlapping terms to maturity. The fitted curves are then spliced together to produce a single smooth curve over the entire term structure. This is known as a *spline* curve and is the one most commonly encountered in the markets. For an accessible introduction to spline techniques see James and Webber (2000) and Choudhry *et al.* (2001).

The limitation of the polynomial method is that a blip in the observed series of vertices, for instance a vertex which is out of line with others in the series, produces a 'wobbled' shape, causing wild oscillations in the corresponding forward yields. This can result in the calculation of negative long-dated forward rates.

2.10.3 *Cubic splines*

The cubic spline method involves connecting each pair of yield vertices by fitting a unique cubic equation between them. This results in a yield curve where the whole curve is represented by a chain of cubic equations, instead of a single polynomial. This technique adds some 'stiffness' to the yield curve, while at the same time preserving its smoothness.[19]

Using the same example as before, we wish to fit the yield curve from 0 to 10 years.

19 In case you're wondering, a spline is a tool used by a carpenter to draw smooth curves.

There are four observed vertices, so we require three cubic equations, $rm_{(i,t)}$, each one connecting two adjacent vertices n_i and n_{i+1} as follows:

$$rm_{(0,t)} = a_0 n^3 + b_0 n^2 + c_0 n + d_0, \text{which connects vertex } n_0 \text{ with } n_1,$$
$$rm_{(1,t)} = a_1 n^3 + b_1 n^2 + c_1 n + d_1, \text{which connects vertex } n_1 \text{ with } n_2, \text{ and}$$
$$rm_{(2,t)} = a_2 n^3 + b_2 n^2 + c_2 n + d_2, \text{which connects vertex } n_2 \text{ with } n_3,$$

where *a, b, c,* and *d* are unknowns. The equations each contain four unknowns (the coefficients *a* to *d*), and there are three equations so we require twelve conditions in all to solve the system. The cubic spline method imposes certain conditions on the curves which makes it possible to solve the system.

The three cubic equations for the data in this example are:

$$rm_{(0,t)} = 0.022 \times n^3 + 0.413 \times n + 4.000 \text{ for vertices } n_0 - n_1,$$
$$rm_{(1,t)} = -0.047 \times n^3 + 0.411 \times n^2 - 0.410 \times n + 4.548 \text{ for vertices } n_1 - n_2, \text{ and}$$
$$rm_{(2,t)} = 0.008 \times n^3 - 0.249 \times n^2 + 2.230 \times n + 1.029 \text{ for vertices } n_2 - n_3.$$

Using a cubic spline produces a smoother curve for both the spot rates and the forward rates, while the derived forward curve will have fewer 'kinks' in it.

To calculate the estimated yield for the 6-year maturity we apply the third cubic equation, which spans the 4–10 year vertices, which is $rm_{(2,t)} = 0.008 \times 6^3 - 0.249 \times 6^2 + 2.230 \times 6 + 1.029 = 7.173\%$.

Simply to fit a 4-vertex spline requires the inversion of a fairly large matrix. In practice more efficient mathematical techniques, known as basis splines or *B-splines* are typically used when there are a larger number of observed yield vertices. This produces results that are very close to what we would obtain by simple matrix inversion.

2.10.4 *Regression models*

A variation on polynomial fitting is regression analysis. In this method bond prices are used as the dependent variable, with the coupon and maturity cash flows of the bonds being the independent variables. This is given by (2.25):

$$P_{di} = \beta_1 C_{1i} + \beta_2 C_{2i} + \cdots + \beta_n (C_{ni} + M) + u_i \tag{2.25}$$

where

P_{di}	is the dirty price of the *i*-th bond
C_{ni}	is the coupon of the *i*-th bond in period *n*
β_n	is the coefficient of the regression equation
u_i	is the residual error in the *i*-th bond

In fact, the coefficient in (2.25) is an estimate of the discount factor, as shown by (2.26) and can be used to generate the spot interest rate curve.

$$\beta_n = df_n = \frac{1}{(1 + rs_n)^n}. \tag{2.26}$$

In the form shown, (2.25) cannot be estimated directly. This is because individual coupon payment dates will differ across different bonds, and in a semi-annual coupon market there will be more coupons than bonds available. In practice therefore the term

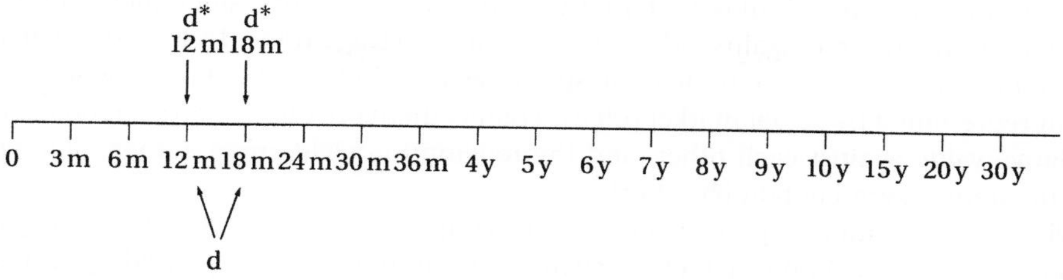

Figure 2.15: Grid point allocation in regression analysis.

structure is divided into specific dates, known as *grid points*, along the entire maturity term; coupon payments are then allocated between two grid points. The allocation between two points is done in such a way so that the present value of the coupon is not altered. This is shown in Figure 2.15.

Note how there are more grid points at the short end of the term structure, with progressively fewer points as we reach the longer end. This is because the preponderance of the data is invariably at the shorter end of the curve, which makes yield curve fitting more difficult. At the long end however the shortage of data, due to the relative lack of issues, makes curve estimation more inaccurate.

The actual regression equation that is used in the analysis is given at (2.27) where d^*_{ni} represents the grid points.

$$P_{di} = \beta_1 d^*_{1i} + \beta_2 d^*_{2i} + \cdots + \beta_n (d^*_{ni} + M) + u_i. \quad (2.27)$$

The two methodologies described above are the most commonly encountered in the market. Generally models used to estimate the term structure generally fall into two distinct categories, these being the ones that estimate the structure using the par yield curve and those that fit it using a discount function. We shall examine these in greater detail in a later chapter.

2.11 Spot and forward rates in the market

2.11.1 *Using spot rates*

The concepts discussed in this chapter are important and form a core part of debt markets analysis. It may appear that the content is largely theoretical, especially since many markets do not trade zero-coupon instruments and so spot rates are therefore not observable in practice; however the concept of the spot rate is an essential part of bond (and other instruments') pricing. In the first instance we are already aware that bond redemption yields do not reflect a true interest rate for that maturity, for which we use the spot rate. For relative value purposes, traders and portfolio managers frequently compare a bond's actual market price to its theoretical price, calculated using specific zero-coupon yields for each cash flow, and determine whether the bond is 'cheap' or 'dear'. Even where there is some misalignment between the theoretical price of a bond and the actual price, the decision to buy or sell may be based on judgemental factors, since there is often no zero-coupon instrument against which to effect an arbitrage trade. In a market where no zero-coupon instruments are traded, the spot rates used in the analysis are theoretical and are not represented by actual market prices. Traders therefore often analyse bonds in terms of relative value against each other, and the redemption yield curve, rather than against their theoretical zero-coupon based price.

What considerations apply where a zero-coupon bond market exists alongside a conventional coupon-bond market? In such a case, in theory arbitrage trading is possible if a bond is priced above or below the price suggested by zero-coupon rates. For example, a bond priced above its theoretical price could be sold, and zero-coupon bonds that equated its cash flow stream could be purchased; the difference in price is the arbitrage profit. Or a bond trading below its theoretical price could be purchased and its coupons 'stripped' and sold individually as zero-coupon bonds; the proceeds from the sale of the zero-coupon bonds would then exceed the purchase price of the coupon bond. In practice often the existence of both markets equalises prices between both markets so that arbitrage is no longer possible, although opportunities will still occasionally present themselves.

2.11.2 *Using forward rates*

Newcomers to the markets frequently experience confusion when first confronted with forward rates. Do they represent the market's expectation of where interest rates will actually be when the forward date arrives? If forward rates are a predictor of future interest rates, exactly how good are they at making this prediction? Empirical evidence[20] suggests that in fact forward rates are not accurate predictors of future interest rates, frequently over-stating them by a considerable margin. If this is the case, should we attach any value or importance to forward rates?

The value of forward rates does not lie however in its track record as a market predictor, but moreover in its use as a hedging tool. As we illustrate in Example 2.5 the forward rate is calculated on the basis that if we are to price say, a cash deposit with a forward starting date, but we wish to deal today, the return from the deposit will be exactly the same as if we invested for a start date today and rolled over the investment at the forward date. The forward rate allows us to lock in a dealing rate now. Once we have dealt today, it is irrelevant what the actual rate pertaining on the forward date is – we have already dealt. Therefore forward rates are often called *hedge* rates, as they allow us to lock in a dealing rate for a future period, thus removing uncertainty.

The existence of forward prices in the market also allows us to make an investment decision, based on our view compared to the market view. The forward rate implied by say, government bond prices is in effect the market's view of future interest rates. If we happen not to agree with this view, we will deal accordingly. In effect we are comparing our view on future interest rates with that of the market, and making our investment decision based on this comparison.

20 Including Fama (1976).

Example 2.4: Spot and forward rates calculation: bootstrapping from the par yield curve

◆ Zero-coupon rates

As we have seen, zero-coupon (or spot), par and forward rates are linked. The term 'zero-coupon' is a bond market term and describes a bond which has no coupons. The yield on a zero-coupon bond can be viewed as a true yield, if the paper is held to maturity as no reinvestment is involved and there are no interim cash flows vulnerable to a change in interest rates. Because zero-coupon rates can be derived from coupon rates, we can assume that:

- zero-coupon rates can be derived at any time where there is a liquid government bond market;
- these zero-coupon rates can then be used as the benchmark term structure.

Where zero-coupon bonds are traded the yield on a zero-coupon bond of a particular maturity is the zero-coupon rate for that maturity. However it is not necessary to have zero-coupon bonds in order to deduce zero-coupon rates. It is possible to calculate zero-coupon rates from a range of market rates and prices, including coupon bonds, interest-rate futures and currency deposits. The price of a zero-coupon bond of a particular maturity defines directly the value today of a cash flow due on the bond's redemption date, and indirectly the zero-coupon rate for that maturity. It is therefore that term to maturity's true interest rate.

◆ Discount factors and the discount function

As we have seen already it is possible to determine a set of *discount factors* from market rates. A discount factor is the number in the range zero to one which can be used to obtain the present value of some future value.

Because

$$PV = \frac{FV}{(1+r)^n} \tag{2.28}$$

where

PV	is the present value
r	is the required interest rate
FV	is the future value
n	is the number of interest rate periods

we know that

$$PV_n = df_n \times FV_n \tag{2.29}$$

where

PV_n is the present value of the future cash flow occurring at time n
FV_n is the future cash flow occurring at time n
df_n is the discount factor for cash flows occurring at time n.

Discount factors can be calculated most easily from zero-coupon rates; equations (2.30) and (2.31) apply to zero-coupon rates for periods up to one year (which would be money market terms) and over one year (bond market maturities) respectively.

$$df_n = \frac{1}{(1 + rs_n T_n)} \tag{2.30}$$

$$df_n = \frac{1}{(1 + rs_n)^{T_n}} \tag{2.31}$$

where

df_n is the discount factor for cash flows occurring at time n
rs_n is the zero-coupon or spot rate for the period to time n
T_n is the time from the value date to time n, expressed in years and fractions of a year.

Individual zero-coupon rates allow discount factors to be calculated at specific points along the maturity spectrum. As cash flows may occur at any time in the future, and not necessarily at convenient times like in three months or one year, discount factors often need to be calculated for every possible date in the future. The complete set of discount factors is called the *discount function.*

2.12 Case Study: Deriving a discount function[21]

In this example we present a traditional bootstrapping technique for deriving a discount function for yield curve fitting purposes. This technique has been called 'naïve' (for instance see James and Webber (2000), page 129) because it suffers from a number of drawbacks, for example it results in an unrealistic forward rate curve, which means that it is unlikely to be used in practice. We review the drawbacks at the end of the case study.

- Today is 14 July 2000. The following rates are observed in the market. We assume that the day-count basis for the cash instruments and swaps is act/365. Construct the money market discount function.

21 In this illustration, the discount function is derived using interest rate data from two off-balance instruments, futures and swaps, as well as money market deposit rates. Derivative instruments are covered in Eales and Choudhry (2003).

Money Market rates	Rate (%)	Expiry	Days
One month (1 m)	4 7/32	14/8/00	31
3 m	4 1/4	16/10/00	94
6 m	4 1/2	15/1/01	185
Future prices			
Sep-00	95.60	20/9/00	68
Dec-00	95.39	20/12/00	159
Mar-01	95.25	21/3/01	249
Jun-01	94.80	20/6/01	340
Swap rates			
One year (1y)	4.95	16/7/01	367
2y	5.125	15/7/02	731
3y	5.28	14/7/03	1095
4y	5.55	14/7/04	1461
5y	6.00	14/7/05	1826

Creating the discount function

Using the cash money market rates we can create discount factors up to a maturity of six months, using the expression at (2.32):

$$df = \frac{1}{\left(1 + r \times \frac{days}{365}\right)}. \tag{2.32}$$

The resulting discount factors are shown below.

From	To	Days	r%	df
14/7/00	14/8/00	31	4 7/32	0.99642974
	16/10/00	94	4 1/4	0.98917329
	15/1/01	185	4 1/2	0.97770040

We can also calculate forward discount factors from the rates implied in the futures prices, which are shown below.

From	To	Days	r%	df
20/9/00	20/12/00	91	4.40	0.98914917
20/12/00	21/3/01	91	4.61	0.98863717
21/3/01	20/6/01	91	4.75	0.98829614
20/6/01	19/9/00	91	5.20	0.98720154

In order to convert these values into zero-coupon discount factors, we need to first derive a cash 'stub' rate up to the expiry of the first futures contract. The most straightforward way to do this is by linear interpolation of the one-month and three-month rates, as shown in Figure 2.16 below.

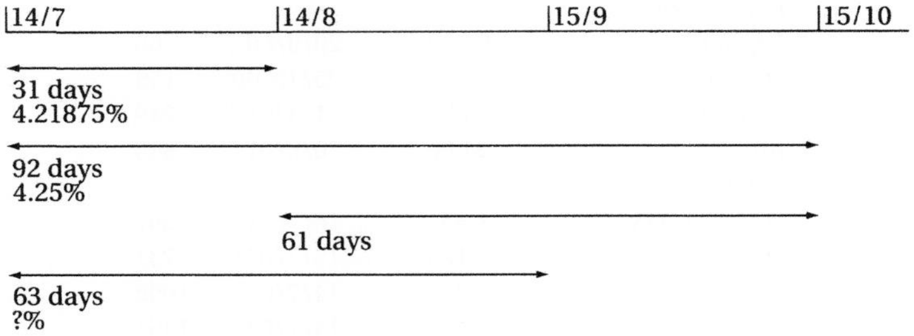

Figure 2.16: Linear interpolation of money and futures rates.

For instance, the calculation for the term marked is

$$4.21875 + \left((4.25 - 4.21875) \times \frac{32}{61}\right) = 4.235143\%.$$

To convert this to a discount factor:

$$\frac{1}{1 + (0.04235143 \times \frac{63}{365})} = 0.99274308.$$

From the futures implied forward rates, the zero-coupon discount factors are calculated by successive multiplication of the individual discount factors. These are shown below.

From	To	Days	df
14/7/00	0/9/00	68	0.99172819
	20/12/00	159	0.98172542
	21/3/01	250	0.96992763
	20/6/01	341	0.960231459
	19/9/01	432	0.948925494

For the interest-rate swap rates, to calculate discount factors for the relevant dates we use the boot-strapping technique.

- **1y swap:**

We assume a par swap, the present value is known to be 100, and as we know the future value as well, we are able to calculate the one-year zero-coupon rate as shown from the one-year swap rate,

$$df_1 = \frac{1}{1+r} = \frac{100}{104.95}$$
$$= 0.95283468.$$

- **2y swap:**

The coupon payment occurring at the end of period one can be discounted back using the one-year discount factor above, leaving a zero-coupon structure as before.

$$df_2 = \frac{100 - C \times Df_1}{105.125}.$$

This gives df_2 equal to 0.91379405.

The same process can be employed for the three, four and five-year par swap rates to calculate the appropriate discount factors.

$$df_3 = \frac{100 - C \times (df_1 + df_2)}{105.28}.$$

This gives df_3 equal to 0.87875624. The discount factors for the four-year and five-year maturities, calculated in the same way, are 0.82899694 and 0.77835621 respectively.

The full discount function is given in Table 2.3 and illustrated graphically at Figure 2.17.

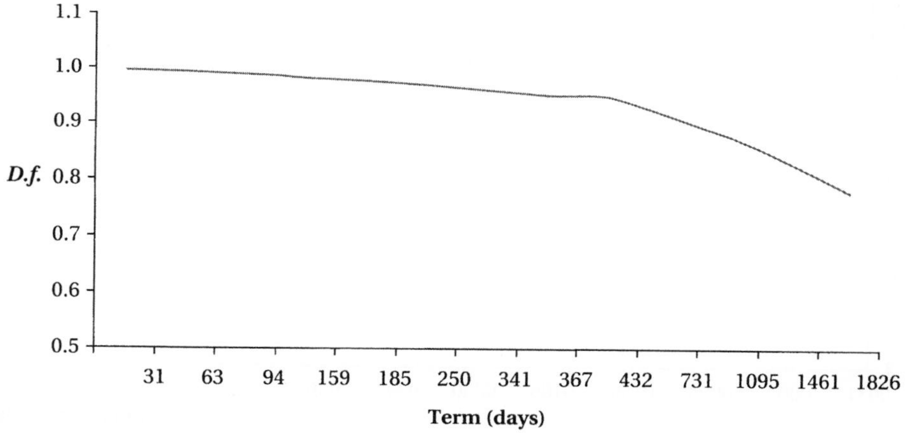

Figure 2.17: Discount function.

From	To	Days	Zero-coupon (%)	Discount factor	Source
14/07/2000	14/08/2000	31	4.21875	0.99642974	Money market
	20/09/2000	63	4.23500	0.99274308	Money market
	16/10/2000	94	4.25000	0.98917329	Money market
	20/12/2000	159	4.38000	0.98172542	Futures
	15/01/2001	185	4.50000	0.97777004	Money market
	21/03/2001	250	4.55000	0.96992763	Futures
	20/06/2001	341	4.73000	0.96023145	Futures
	16/07/2001	367	4.95000	0.95283468	Swap
	19/09/2001	432	5.01000	0.94892549	Futures
	15/07/2002	731	5.12500	0.91379405	Swap
	14/07/2003	1095	5.28000	0.87875624	Swap
	15/07/2004	1461	5.58000	0.82899694	Swap
	15/07/2005	1826	6.10000	0.77835621	Swap

Table 2.3: Discount factors.

2.12.1 *Critique of the traditional technique*

The method used to derive the discount function in the case study used three different price sources to produce an integrated function and hence yield curve. However there is no effective method by which the three separate curves, which are shown at Figure 2.18, can be integrated into one complete curve. The result is that a curve formed from the three separate curves will exhibit distinct kinks or steps at the points at which one data source is replaced by another data source.

The money market and swap rates incorporate a credit risk premium, reflecting the fact that interbank market counterparties carry an element of default risk. This means that

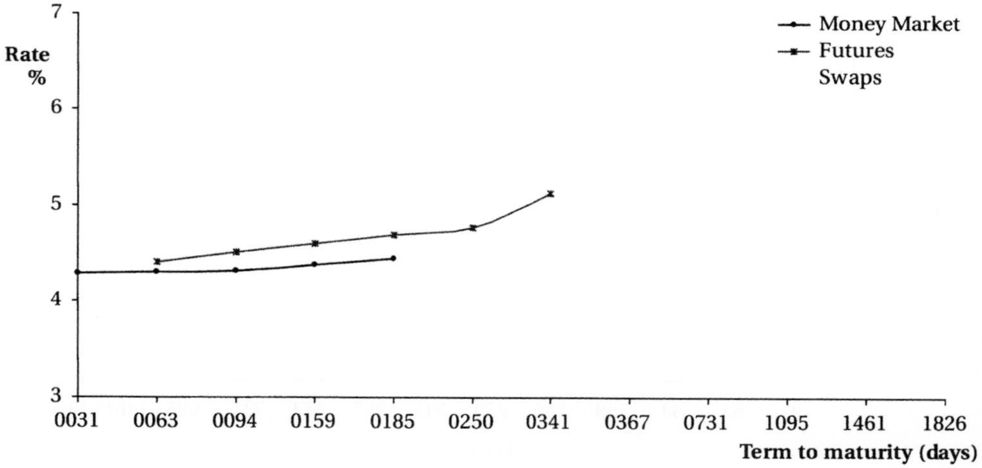

Figure 2.18: Comparison of money market curves.

money market rates lie above government repo rates. Futures rates do not reflect default risk, as they are exchange-traded contracts and the exchange clearing house takes on counterparty risk for each transaction. However futures rates are treated as one-point period rates, in effect making them equivalent to forward-rate agreement (FRA) rates. In practice, as the cash flow from FRAs is received as a discounted payoff at one point, whereas futures contract trades require a daily margin payment, a *convexity adjustment* is required to convert futures accurately to FRA rates.

Swap rates also incorporate an element of credit risk, although generally they are considered lower risk as they are off-balance sheet instruments and no principal is at risk. As liquid swap rates are only available for set maturity points, linear interpolation is used to plot points in between available rates. This results in an unstable forward rate curve calculated from the spot rate curve (see James and Webber, 2000), due to the interpolation effect. Nevertheless market makers in certain markets price intermediate-dated swaps based on this linear interpolation method. Another drawback is that the bootstrapping method uses near-maturity rates to build up the curve to far-maturity rates. One of the features of a spot curve derived in this way is that even small changes in short-term rates causes excessive changes in long-dated spot rates, and oscillations in the forward curve. Finally, money market rates beyond the 'stub' period are not considered once the discount factor to the stub date is calculated, so their impact is not felt.

For these reasons the traditional technique, while still encountered in textbooks and training courses (including this one), is not used very often in the markets.

2.13 Case Study exercise: Deriving the theoretical (spot) zero-coupon rate curve[22]

Here we construct a theoretical spot interest rate curve using the yields observed on coupon bonds. To illustrate the methodology, we will use a hypothetical set of bonds that are trading in a positive yield curve environment. The maturity, price and yield for ten bonds are shown in Table 2.4. The prices shown are for settlement on 1 March 1999, and all the bonds have precisely 1, 1.5, 2 and so on years to maturity, that is they mature on 1 March or 1 September of their maturity year. That means that the first bond has no intermediate coupon before it is redeemed, and we can assume it trades as a zero-coupon bond. All bonds have no accrued interest because the settlement date is a coupon date. Bonds pay semi-annual coupon.

According to the principle of no-arbitrage pricing, the value of any bond should be equal to the value of the sum of all its cash flows, should these be stripped into a series of zero-coupon bonds whose last bond matures at the same time as the coupon bond. Consider the first bond in Table 2.4. As it matures in precisely six months' time, it is effectively a zero-coupon bond; its yield of 6% is equal to the six-month spot rate. Given this spot rate we can derive the spot rate for a one-year zero-coupon gilt. The price of a one-year gilt strip must

22 This illustrates bootstrapping, as well as the principle behind stripping a coupon bond, and follows the approach described in Fabbozi (1993).

Maturity date	Years to maturity	Coupon (%)	Yield to maturity	Price
1-Sep-99	0.5	5.0	6.00	99.5146
1-Mar-00	1.0	10.0	6.30	103.5322
1-Sep-00	1.5	7.0	6.40	100.8453
1-Mar-01	2.0	6.5	6.70	99.6314
1-Sep-01	2.5	8.0	6.90	102.4868
1-Mar-02	3.0	10.5	7.30	108.4838
1-Sep-02	3.5	9.0	7.60	104.2327
1-Mar-03	4.0	7.3	7.80	98.1408
1-Sep-03	4.5	7.5	7.95	98.3251
1-Mar-04	5.0	8.0	8.00	100.0000

Table 2.4: Set of hypothetical bonds.

equal the present value of the two cash flows from the 10% one-year coupon gilt. If we use £100 as par, the cash flows from the one-year coupon bond are:

0.5 years 10% × £100 × 0.5 = £5
1.0 years 10% × £100 × 0.5 = £5 + £100 redemption payment

The present value of the total cash flow is $\frac{5}{(1+\frac{1}{2}r_1)} + \frac{105}{(1+\frac{1}{2}r_2)^2}$ where

r_1 is the six-month theoretical spot rate
r_2 is the one-year theoretical spot rate.

Therefore the present value of the one-year coupon gilt is $5/(1.03) + 105/(1+\frac{1}{2}r_2)^2$. As the price of the one-year gilt is 103.5322, from Table 2.4, the following relationship must be true:

$$103.5322 = \frac{5}{(1.03)} + \frac{105}{(1+\frac{1}{2}r_2)^2}.$$

Using this relationship we are now in a position to calculate the one-year theoretical spot rate as shown below.

$$103.5322 = 4.85437 + \frac{105}{(1+\frac{1}{2}r_2)^2}$$

$$98.67783 = 105/(1+\frac{1}{2}r_2)^2$$

$$(1+\frac{1}{2}r_2)^2 = 105/98.67783 = 1.064069\cdot$$

$$(1+\frac{1}{2}r_2) = \sqrt{1.064069}$$

$$\frac{1}{2}r_2 = 0.03154$$

Therefore r_2 is 0.06308, or 6.308%, which is the theoretical one-year spot rate. Now that we have obtained the theoretical one-year spot rate, we are in a position to calculate the theoretical 1.5-year spot rate. The cash flow for the 7% 1.5-year coupon gilt shown in the table is:

0.5 years $7\% \times £100 \times 0.5 = £3.5$
1.0 years $7\% \times £100 \times 0.5 = £3.5$
1.5 years $7\% \times £100 \times 0.5 = £3.5 + \text{redemption payment}(£100)$

The present value of this stream of cash flows is:

$$\frac{3.5}{(1+\frac{1}{2}r_1)} + \frac{3.5}{(1+\frac{1}{2}r_2)^2} + \frac{103.5}{(1+\frac{1}{2}r_3)^3}$$

where r_3 is the 1.5-year theoretical spot rate. We have established that the six-month and one-year spot rates are 6% and 6.308% respectively, so that r_1 is 0.06 and r_2 is 0.06308. Therefore the present value of the 7% 1.5-year coupon gilt is:

$$\frac{3.5}{(1.03)} + \frac{3.5}{(1.03154)^2} + \frac{103.5}{(1+\frac{1}{2}r_3)^3}.$$

From the table the price of the 7% 1.5-year gilt is 100.8453; therefore the following relationship must be true:

$$100.8453 = \frac{3.5}{(1.03)} + \frac{3.5}{(1.03154)^2} + \frac{103.5}{(1+\frac{1}{2}r_3)^3}.$$

This equation can then be solved to obtain r_3:

$$100.8453 = 3.39806 + 3.28924 + 103.5\Big/\left(1+\frac{1}{2}r_3\right)^3$$

$$94.158 = 103.5\Big/\left(1+\frac{1}{2}r_3\right)^3$$

$$(1+\frac{1}{2}r_3)^3 = 1.099216$$

$$\frac{1}{2}r_3 = 0.032035.$$

The theoretical 1.5-year spot rate bond equivalent yield is two times this result which is 6.407%.

2.13.1 *Mathematical relationship*

The relationship used to derive a theoretical spot rate can be generalised, so that in order to calculate the theoretical spot rate for the nth six-month period, we use the following expression:

$$P_n = \frac{C/2}{(1+\frac{1}{2}r)} + \frac{C/2}{(1+\frac{1}{2}r_2)^2} + \frac{C/2}{(1+\frac{1}{2}r_3)^3} + \cdots + \frac{C/2+100}{(1+\frac{1}{2}r_n)^n}$$

where

P_n	is the dirty price of the coupon bond with n periods to maturity
C	is the annual coupon rate for the coupon bond
r_n	is the theoretical n-year spot rate.

We can re-write this expression as

$$P_n = \frac{C}{2}\sum_{t=1}^{n-1}\frac{1}{(1+\frac{1}{2}r_t)^t} + \frac{C/2+100}{(1+\frac{1}{2}r_n)^n}$$

where r_t for $t = 1, 2, \ldots, n-1$ is the theoretical spot rates that are already known. This equation can be rearranged so that we may solve for r_n:

$$r_n = \left(\frac{C/2+100}{P_n - \frac{C}{2}\sum\limits_{t=1}^{n-1}\frac{1}{(1+\frac{1}{2}r_t)^t}}\right)^{\frac{1}{n}} - 1.$$

The methodology used here is the *bootstrapping* technique.

If we carry on the process for the bonds in the table we obtain the results shown in Table 2.5.

2.13.2 *Implied forward rates*

We now use the theoretical spot rate curve to infer the market's expectations of future interest rates. Consider the following, where an investor with a one-year time horizon has the following two investment options:

Maturity date	Years to maturity	Yield to maturity (%)	Theoretical spot rate (%)
1-Sep-99	0.5	6.00	6.000
1-Mar-00	1.0	6.30	6.308
1-Sep-00	1.5	6.40	6.407
1-Mar-01	2.0	6.70	6.720
1-Sep-01	2.5	6.90	6.936
1-Mar-02	3.0	7.30	7.394
1-Sep-02	3.5	7.60	7.712
1-Mar-03	4.0	7.80	7.908
1-Sep-03	4.5	7.95	8.069
1-Mar-04	5.0	8.00	8.147

Table 2.5: Theoretical spot rates.

- Option 1: Buy the one-year bond
- Option 2: Buy the six-month bond, and when it matures in six months buy another six-month bond

The investor will be indifferent between the two alternatives if they produce the same yield at the end of the one-year period. The investor knows the spot rate on the six-month bond and the one-year bond, but does not know what yield will be available on a six-month bond purchased six months from now. The yield on a six-month bond six months from now is the *forward rate*. Given the spot rate for the six-month bond and the one-year bond spot yield, the forward rate on a six-month bond that will make the investor indifferent to the two alternatives can be derived from the spot curve, shown below.

By investing in a one-year zero-coupon bond, the investor will receive the maturity value at the end of one year. The redemption proceeds of the one-year zero-coupon bond is £105. The price (cost) of this bond is:

$$105/(1+\frac{1}{2}r_2)^2$$

where r_2 is half the bond-equivalent yield of the theoretical one-year spot rate.

Suppose that the investor purchases a six-month gilt for P pounds. At the end of the six months the value of this investment would be $P(1+\frac{1}{2}r_1)$ where r_1 is the bond-equivalent yield of the theoretical six-month spot rate.

Let f be the forward rate on a six-month bond available six months from now. The future value of this bond in one year from the £P invested is given by $P(1+\frac{1}{2}r_1)(1+f)$.

How much would we need to invest to get £105 one year from now? This is found as follows,

$$P(1+\frac{1}{2}r_1)(1+f) = 105.$$

Solving this expression gives us:

$$P = \frac{105}{(1+\frac{1}{2}r_1)(1+f)}.$$

The investor is indifferent between the two methods if they receive £105 from both methods in one year's time. That is, the investor is indifferent if:

$$\frac{105}{(1+\frac{1}{2}r_2)^2} = \frac{105}{(1+\frac{1}{2}r_1)(1+f)}$$

Solving for f gives us $f = \frac{(1+\frac{1}{2}r_2)^2}{(1+\frac{1}{2}r_1)} - 1.$

Therefore f gives us the bond-equivalent rate for the six-month forward rate. We can illustrate this by using the spot rates from the bond table.

$$\text{Six-month bond spot rate} = 6\% \Rightarrow \frac{1}{2}r_1 = 0.03$$

$$\text{One-year bond spot rate} = 6.308\% \Rightarrow \frac{1}{2}r_2 = 0.03154.$$

Substituting these vales into the equation gives us $f = \dfrac{(1.03154)^2}{(1.03)} - 1 = 0.0330823.$

We double this result to give the forward rate on a six-month bond as 6.6165%. As we use theoretical spot rates in its calculation, the resulting forward rate is called the *implied forward rate*.

We can use the same methodology to determine the implied forward rate six months from now for an investment period longer than six months. We can also look at forward rates that start more than six months from now.

We use the following notation for forward rates: ${}_nf_t$ = the forward rate n periods from now for t periods. We can use the following equation when calculating forward rates where the final maturity is one year or more from now,

$${}_nf_t = \left(\frac{(1+\frac{1}{2}r_{n+1})^{n+1}}{(1+\frac{1}{2}r_n)^n}\right)^{1/t} - 1$$

where r_n is the spot rate. The result ${}_nf_t$ gives us the implied forward rate on a bond-equivalent basis.

Complete the six-month forward rates in the table below.

Maturity date	Years to maturity	Yield to maturity (%)	Theoretical spot rate (%)	Forward rate (%)
1-Sep-99	0.5	6.00	6.000	–
1-Mar-00	1.0	6.30	6.308	–
1-Sep-00	1.5	6.40	6.407	–
1-Mar-01	2.0	6.70	6.720	7.133%
1-Sep-01	2.5	6.90	6.936	–
1-Mar-02	3.0	7.30	7.394	8.755%
1-Sep-02	3.5	7.60	7.712	–
1-Mar-03	4.0	7.80	7.908	9.465%
1-Sep-03	4.5	7.95	8.069	–
1-Mar-04	5.0	8.00	8.147	9.108%

Table 2.6: Forward rates.

Appendices

Appendix 2.1: Testing the unbiased expectations hypothesis

For empirical studies testing the unbiased expectations hypothesis see Kessel (1965) and Fama (1976). If we consider the expectations hypothesis to be true then the forward rate ${}_0rf_2$ should be an accurate predictor of the spot rate in period 2. Put another way, the mean of ${}_0rf_2$ should be equal to the mean of ${}_1rs_1$. In previous studies (*ibid.*) it has been shown that forward rates are in fact biased upwards in their estimates of future spot rates. That is, ${}_0rf_2$ is usually higher than the mean of ${}_1rs_1$. This bias tends to be magnified the further one moves along the term structure. We can test the unbiased expectations hypothesis by determining if the following condition holds:

$$ {}_1rs_1 = p + q({}_0rf_2). \tag{2.33} $$

In an environment where we upheld the expectations hypothesis, then p should be equal to zero and q equal to one. Outside of the very short end of the yield curve, there is no evidence that this is true. Another approach, adopted by Fama (1984), involved subtracting the current spot rate rs_1 from both sides of equation (2.34) and testing whether:

$$ {}_1rs_1 - {}_0rs_1 = p + q({}_0rf_2 - {}_0rs_1). \tag{2.34} $$

If the hypothesis were accurate, we would again have p equal to zero and q equal to one. This is because ${}_1rs_1 - {}_0rs_1$ is the change in the spot rate predicted by the hypothesis. The left-hand side of (2.34) is the actual change in the spot rate, which must equal the right-hand side of the equation if the hypothesis is true. Evidence from the earlier studies mentioned has suggested that q is a positive number less than one. This of course is not consistent with the unbiased expectations hypothesis. However the studies indicate that the prediction of changes in future spot rates is linked to actual changes that occur. This suggests then that forward rates are indeed based on the market's view of future spot rates, but not in a completely unbiased manner.

An earlier study was conducted by Meiselman (1962), referred to as his error-learning model. According to this, if the unbiased expectations hypothesis is true, forward rates are not then completely accurate forecasts of future spot rates. The study tested whether (2.35) was true.

$$ {}_1rf_n - {}_0rf_n = p + q_1rs_1 - {}_0rf_2. \tag{2.35} $$

If the hypothesis is true then p should be equal to zero and q should be positive. The error-learning model suggests a positive correlation between forward rates, but this would hold in an environment where the unbiased expectations hypothesis did not apply.

The empirical evidence suggests that the predictions of future spot rates reflected in forward rates is related to subsequent actual spot rates. So forward rates do include an element of market interest rate forecasts. However this would indicate more a biased expectations theory, rather than the pure unbiased expectations hypothesis.

Appendix 2.2: Jensen's inequality and the shape of the yield curve

In Cox, Ingersoll and Ross (1981) an analysis on the shape of the term structure used a feature known as *Jensen's inequality* to illustrate that the expectations hypothesis was consistent with forward rates being an indicator of future spot rates. Jensen's inequality states that the expected value of the reciprocal of a variable is not identical to the reciprocal of the expected value of that variable. Following this, if the expected holding period returns on a set of bonds are all equal, the expected holding period returns on the bonds cannot then be equal over any other holding period. Applying this in practice, consider two zero-coupon bonds, a one-year bond with a yield of 11.11% and a two-year zero-coupon bond with a yield of 11.8034%. The prices of the bonds are as follows:

1 year: 90
2 year: 80

Assume that the price of the two-year bond in one year's time can be either 86.89 or 90.89, with identical probability. At the end of year 1, the total return generated by the two-year will be either (86.89/80)8.6125% or, (90.89/80) 13.6125% while at this point the (now) one-year bond will offer a return of either (100/86.89) 15.089% or (100/90.89) 10.023%. The two possible prices have been set deliberately so as to ensure that the expected return over one year for the two-year bond is equal to the return available today on the one-year bond, which is 11.11% as we noted at the start. The return expected on the two-year bond is indeed the same (provided either of the two prices is available), that is $((0.5) \times (86.89/80) + (0.5) \times (90.89/80))$ or 11.11%. Therefore it cannot also be true that the certain return over two years for the two-year bond is equal to the expected return for two years from rolling over the investment in the one-year bond. At the start of the period the two-year bond has a guaranteed return of [100/80] 25% over its lifetime. However investing in the one-year bond and then re-investing at the one-year period after the first year will produce a return that is higher than this, as shown:

$$11.11\% \times ((0.5) \times (100/86.89) + (0.5) \times (100/90.89))$$

or 25.063%. Under this scenario then investors cannot expect equality of returns for all bonds over all investment horizons.

Selected bibliography and references

Anderson, N., Sleath, J., *Bank of England Quarterly Bulletin*, November 1999
Campbell, J., 'A Defence of Traditional Hypotheses about the Term Structure of Interest Rates', *Journal of Finance*, March 1986, pp. 183–193
Campbell, J., Lo, A., MacKinlay, A., *The Econometrics of Financial Markets*. Princeton UP, 1997, Chapters 10–11
Choudhry, M., 'The information content of the United Kingdom gilt yield curve', unpublished MBA assignment, Henley Management College, 1998
Choudhry, M., Joannas, D., Pereira, R., Pienaar, R., *Capital Markets Instruments*, FT Prentice Hall, 2001
Cox, J., Ingersoll, J.E., Ross, S.A., 'A re-examination of traditional hypothesis about the term structure of interest rates', *Journal of Finance* 36, Sep 1981, pp. 769–99

Culbertson, J.M., 'The term structure of interest rates', *Quarterly Journal of Economics* 71, November 1957, pp. 485–517
Eales, B., Choudhry, M. *Derivative Instruments: A Guide to Theory and Practice*, Butterworth-Heinemann, 2003
The Economist, 'Admiring those shapely curves', 4 April 1998, p. 117
Fabozzi, F., *Bond Markets, Analysis and Strategies*, 2nd edition, Prentice Hall, 1993
Fama, E.F., 'Forward rates as predictors of future spot interest rates', *Journal of Financial Economics*, Vol. 3, No.4, Oct 1976, pp. 361–377
Fama, E.F., 'The information in the term structure', *Journal of Financial Economics* 13, Dec 1984, pp. 509–528
Fisher, I., 'Appreciation of Interest', *Publications of the American Economic Association*, August 1986, pp. 23–39
Heath, D., Jarrow, R., Morton, A., 'Bond pricing and the term structure of interest rates', *Journal of Financial and Quantitative Analysis* 25, 1990, pp. 419–440
Hicks, J., *Value and Capital*, OUP, 1946
Ingersoll, J., *Theory of Financial Decision Making*, Rowman & Littlefield 1987, Chapter 18
James, J., Webber, N., *Interest Rate Modelling*, John Wiley and Sons, 2000
Jarrow, R., 'Liquidity premiums and the expectations hypothesis', *Journal of Banking and Finance* 5(4), 1981, pp. 539–546
Jarrow, R., *Modelling Fixed Income Securities and Interest Rate Options*, McGraw-Hill, 1996
Kessel, R.A., 'The cyclical behaviour of the term structure of interest rates', *Essays in Applied Price Theory*, University of Chicago, 1965
Levy, H., *Introduction to Investments*, 2nd edition, South-Western College Publishing, 1999
Livingstone, M., *Money and Capital Markets*, Prentice-Hall, 1990, pp. 254–256
Lutz, F., 'The Structure of Interest Rates', *Quarterly Journal of Economics*, November 1940, pp. 36–63
Mastronikola, K., 'Yield curves for gilt-edged stocks: a new model', *Bank of England Discussion Paper (Technical Series)*, No. 49, 1991
McCulloch, J.H., 'An estimate of the liquidity premium', *Journal of Political Economy* 83, Jan–Feb 1975, pp. 95–119
Meiselman, D., *The Term Structure of Interest Rates*, Prentice Hall, 1962
Ryan, R. (ed.), *Yield Curve Dynamics*, Glenlake Publishing Company, 1997
Rubinstein, M., *Rubinstein on Derivatives*, RISK 1999, pp. 84–85
Shiller, R., 'The Term Structure of Interest Rates', in Friedman, B., Hahn, F. (eds.), *Handbook of Monetary Economics*, North-Holland 1990, Chapter 13
Windas, T., *An Introduction to Option-Adjusted Spread Analysis*, Bloomberg Publishing, 1993

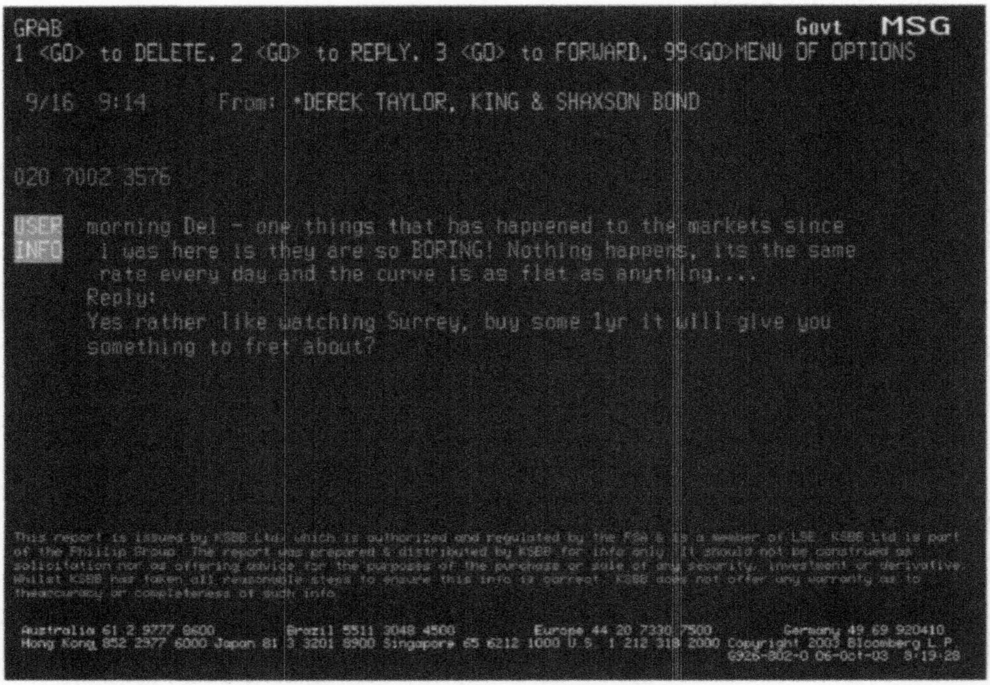

GRAB
Govt MSG
1 <GO> to DELETE, 2 <GO> to REPLY, 3 <GO> to FORWARD, 99<GO>MENU OF OPTIONS
9/16 9:14 From: *DEREK TAYLOR, KING & SHAXSON BOND
020 7002 3576
USER INFO
morning Del - one things that has happened to the markets since I was here is they are so BORING! Nothing happens, its the same rate every day and the curve is as flat as anything....
Reply:
Yes rather like watching Surrey, buy some 1yr it will give you something to fret about?
This report is issued by KSBB Ltd, which is authorized and regulated by the FSA & is a member of LSE. KSBB Ltd is part of the Phillip Group. The report was prepared & distributed by KSBB for info only. It should not be construed as solicitation nor as offering advice for the purposes of the purchase or sale of any security, investment or derivative. Whilst KSBB has taken all reasonable steps to ensure this info is correct, KSBB does not offer any warranty as to theaccuracy or completeness of such info.
Australia 61 2 9777 8600 Brazil 5511 3048 4500 Europe 44 20 7330 7500 Germany 49 69 920410
Hong Kong 852 2977 6000 Japan 81 3 3201 8900 Singapore 65 6212 1000 U.S. 1 212 318 2000 Copyright 2003 Bloomberg L.P.
6926-802-0 06-Oct-03 8:19:28

3 Review of Bond Market Instruments

The development of financial engineering techniques in banks around the world has resulted in a great variety of financial instruments being traded. The bond markets are no exception to this and there is a range of instruments in the debt market with special features. Such bonds require a variation of the basic tools we considered in chapter 1, which limited the discussion and analysis to conventional or plain vanilla bonds, that is, instruments with a fixed coupon and term to maturity. We will use this chapter to introduce in overview form some variations on the basic plain vanilla bond. This is to give readers some flavour of the other types of bonds that exist in the market, and which we will look at in greater detail later in this book.

3.1 Floating rate notes

Floating rate notes (FRNs) are bonds that have variable rates of interest; the coupon rate is linked to a specified index and changes periodically as the index changes. An FRN is usually issued with a coupon that pays a fixed spread over a reference index; for example the coupon may be 50 basis points over the six-month interbank rate. An FRN whose spread over the reference rate is not fixed is known as a *variable rate note*. Since the value for the reference benchmark index is not known, it is not possible to calculate the redemption yield for an FRN. Additional features have been added to FRNs, including *floors* (the coupon cannot fall below a specified minimum rate), *caps* (the coupon cannot rise above a maximum rate) and *callability*. There also exist perpetual FRNs. As in other markets borrowers frequently issue paper with specific or even esoteric terms in order to meet particular requirements or meet customer demand, for example a US bank recently issued US dollar-denominated FRNs with interest payments indexed to the uribor rate, and another FRN with its day count basis linked to a specified Libor range.

Generally the reference interest rate for FRNs is the London interbank rate; the *offered* rate, that is the rate at which a bank will lend funds to another bank is LIBOR. An FRN will pay interest at LIBOR plus a quoted margin (or spread). The interest rate is fixed for a three-month or six-month period and is reset in line with the LIBOR *fixing* at the end of the interest period. Hence at the coupon re-set date for a sterling FRN paying six-month Libor + 0.50%, if the Libor fix is 7.6875%, then the FRN will pay a coupon of 8.1875%. Interest therefore will accrue at a daily rate of £0.0224315.

On the coupon reset date an FRN will be priced precisely at par. Between reset dates it will trade very close to par because of the way in which the coupon is reset. If market rates rise between reset dates an FRN will trade slightly below par, similarly if rates fall the paper will trade slightly above. This makes FRNs very similar in behaviour to money market instruments traded on a yield basis, although of course FRNs have much longer maturities. Investors can opt to view FRNs as essentially money market instruments or as alternatives to conventional bonds. For this reason one can use two approaches in analysing FRNs. The first approach is known as the *margin method*. This calculates the difference between the return on an FRN and that on an equivalent money market security. There are two variations on this, simple margin and discounted margin.

The simple margin method is sometimes preferred because it does not require the forecasting of future interest rates and coupon values. *Simple margin* is defined as the average return on an FRN throughout its life compared with the reference interest rate. It has two components: a *quoted margin* either above or below the reference rate, and a capital gain or loss element which is calculated under the assumption that the difference between the current price of the FRN and the maturity value is spread evenly over the remaining life of the bond. Simple margin uses the expression at (3.1):

$$\text{Simple margin} = \frac{(M - P_d)}{(100 \times T)} + M_q \tag{3.1}$$

where

P_d	is P + AI, the dirty price
M	is the par value
T	is the number of years from settlement date to maturity
M_q	is the quoted margin.

A quoted margin that is positive reflects yield for an FRN that is offering a higher yield than the comparable money market security.

Example 3.1: Simple margin

- An FRN with a par value of £100, a quoted margin of 10 basis points over six-month Libor is currently trading at a clean price of 98.50. The previous LIBOR fixing was 5.375%. There are 90 days of accrued interest, 92 days until the next coupon payment and five years from the next coupon payment before maturity. Therefore we have:

$$P_d = 98.50 + \frac{90}{365} \times 5.375 = 99.825.$$

We obtain T as shown:

$$T = 10 + \frac{92}{365} = 10.252$$

Inserting these results into (3.1) we have the following simple margin:

$$\text{Simple margin} = \frac{100 - 98.825}{100 \times 10.252} + 0.0010 = 0.00117$$

or 11.7 basis points.

At certain times the simple margin formula is adjusted to take into account any change in the reference rate since the last coupon reset date. This is done by defining an adjusted price, which is either:

$$AP_d = P_d + (re + QM) \times \frac{N_{SC}}{365} \times 100 - \frac{C}{2} \times 100 \tag{3.2}$$

or

$$AP_d = P_d + (re + QM) \times \frac{N_{SC}}{365} \times P_d - \frac{C}{2} \times 100$$

where

AP_d	is the adjusted dirty price
re	is the current value of the reference interest rate (such as Libor)
$C/2$	is the next coupon payment (that is, C is the reference interest rate on the last coupon reset date plus M_q
N_{sc}	is the number of days between settlement and the next coupon date.

The upper equation in (3.2) above ignores the current yield effect: all payments are assumed to be received on the basis of par, and this understates the value of the coupon for FRNs trading below par and overstates the value when they are trading above par. The lower equation in (3.2) takes account of the current yield effect.

The adjusted price AP_d replaces the current price P_d in (3.1) to give an *adjusted simple margin*. The simple margin method has the disadvantage of amortising the discount or premium on the FRN in a straight line over the remaining life of the bond rather than at a constantly compounded rate. The discounted margin method uses the latter approach. The distinction between simple margin and discounted margin is exactly the same as that between simple yield to maturity and yield to maturity. The discounted margin method does have a disadvantage in that it requires a forecast of the reference interest rate over the remaining life of the bond.

The discounted margin is the solution to equation (3.3) shown below, given for an FRN that pays semi-annual coupons.

$$P_d = \left(\frac{1}{(1 + \frac{1}{2}(re + DM))^{days/year}} \right) \times \left(\frac{C}{2} + \sum_{t=1}^{N-1} \frac{(re^* + QM) \times 100/2}{(1 + \frac{1}{2}(re^* + DM))^t} + \frac{M}{(1 + \frac{1}{2}(re^* + DM))^{N-1}} \right) \tag{3.3}$$

where

DM	is the discounted margin
re	is the current value of the reference interest rate
re^*	is the assumed (or forecast) value of the reference rate over the remaining life of the bond
QM_q	is the quoted margin
N	is the number of coupon payments before redemption.
M	is the par value

Equation (3.3) may be stated in terms of discount factors instead of the reference rate. This version is given in Appendix 3.1. The *yield to maturity spread* method of evaluating FRNs is designed to allow direct comparison between FRNs and fixed-rate bonds. The yield to maturity on the FRN (rmf) is calculated using (3.3) with both $(re + DM)$ and $(re^* + DM)$ replaced with rmf. The yield to maturity on a reference bond (rmb) is calculated using the basic equation shown in chapter 1. The *yield to maturity spread* is defined as:

$$\text{yield to maturity spread} = rmf - rmb.$$

Name	Maturity	Price	d/m	Amount (£m)	Rating	Notes
Bradford & Bingley	Oct-99	100.00	6.5	4.0	A1	
Bradford & Bingley	Mar-01	100.14	7.5	3.0		
Bradford & Bingley	Nov-01	99.89	8.1	4.9	A2	
Britannia BS	Jan-00	100.12	6.0	3.0		
Britannia BS	Feb-01	99.89	8.7	1.5		
Bankers Trust	Feb-02	99.78	11.8	5.0		
Irish Permanent	Oct-98	100.374		10.0	A2	
Nationwide	Aug-01	99.78	5.7	5.0	A1	Callable Aug-00 at 99.93
Midland	Mar-02	99.97	0.5	5.0		
Midland	May-01	99.65	20.0	8.0		Sub-ordinated issue
Woolwich	Mar-99	100.14	6.1	0.930	A1	
Woolwich	Mar-01	99.87	6.8	0.600		
Royal Bank of Scotland	Jan-04	99.93	3.5	10.0	AA3/AA-	
Royal Bank of Scotland	Jun-05	100.05	36.5	4.5		Sub-ordinated issue; callable after Jun-00

Table 3.1: Market maker's FRN Offer Page.

If this is positive the FRN offers a higher yield than the reference bond.

Table 3.1 shows an extract from the screen of a market maker in sterling FRNs as at May 1997. The screen shows bonds at the price they are offered to investors, as well as the discount margin in basis points and the credit rating for the bond. The 'amount' is the amount of paper that the bank had to offer at that time.

In addition to plain vanilla FRNs, some of the other types of floating-rate bonds that have traded in the market are:

- **Collared FRNs:** these offer caps and floors on an instrument, thus establishing a maximum and minimum coupon on the deal. Effectively these securities contain two embedded options, the issuer buying a cap and selling a floor to the investor.
- **Step-up recovery FRNs:** where coupons are fixed against comparable longer maturity bonds, thus providing investors with the opportunity to maintain exposure to short-term assets while capitalising on a positive sloping yield curve.
- **Corridor FRNs:** these were introduced to capitalise on expectations of comparative interest rate inactivity. A high-risk/high-reward instrument, it offers investors a very substantial uplift over a chosen reference rate. But rates have to remain within a relatively narrow corridor if the interest payment is not to be forfeited entirely.

3.2 Inverse/reverse floating-rate bonds

3.2.1 *Introduction*

The coupon rate for some FRNs is set so that it does not change in the same direction as the reference interest rate, but rather in the opposite direction to the change in the reference rate. This means that if the reference rate increases from its level at the previous coupon reset date, the coupon rate on the bond will decline. These bonds are known as *inverse floating-rate notes*. Generally the coupon is calculated as a fixed rate, less a floating reference rate, implying that the product has an interest rate cap equal to the fixed rate element. Inverse FRNs originated in the US municipal and mortgage-backed bond markets. One of the first examples was a combined vanilla and inverse *collateralised mortgage obligation* FRN issued by Lehman Brothers in 1986, created by converting an existing fixed-rate bond issue into the combined FRN structure. They are common in the US corporate, municipal and collateralised mortgage obligation markets. The combined structure typically has an FRN with a coupon reset at a specified margin to an index such as Libor or (in the US market) the Federal Home Loan Cost of Funds Index or COFI. The coupon of the associated inverse FRN moves inversely with the specified index. Vanilla and inverse FRNs combination structures usually have caps and floors that set the maximum and minimum coupon payable on both bonds. The cap and floor may be explicit, in the form a specified maximum rate payable, or implicit, for example setting a floor equal to the margin if the index rate fell below say, 1%. Caps and floors may be fixed throughout the life of the bond or may be altered during its life. The inverse floater is sometimes issued with a set level from which the reference rate is subtracted, for example it may pay a rate of 10% – Libor. In some cases a *multiplier* is used, for example an inverse FRN paying a coupon of 20% – (2 × Libor) has a multiplier of two.

£200 m 10% bond, five-year maturity
Used to create:
  100 m FRN coupon set as Libor + 25 basis points, cap 9%
  100 m Inverse FRN coupon set as 9.75 – Libor, floor 1%

Where a combined structure has been created from an existing fixed coupon bond, the nominal amounts of the two new FRNs will add to the total size of the original issue. The sum of interest paid on the vanilla and inverse FRNs will also equal the coupon paid on the source bond. If a multiplier is used for the inverse FRN, its nominal size will need to be less than that of the vanilla FRN, in order to keep the combined interest payable at the same level as the original bond's coupon. The original conventional bond from which the floating-rate and inverse floater bonds are created is called the *collateral*.

Table 3.2 illustrates an hypothetical example for a combined vanilla and inverse FRN from a conventional 10% coupon bond. The two FRNs have their coupon set in line with Libor; the vanilla FRN coupon is fixed at Libor plus 25 basis points, with a cap at 9%, while the inverse FRN coupon is set as 9.75 – Libor. It has a floor of 1%. There is no multiplier so therefore the two bonds have equal nominal values.

3.2.2 *Modified duration*[1]

As we noted above an inverse floater is a security whose coupon rate changes inversely with the change in the specified reference rate. In many cases inverse floating-rate bonds are created from conventional bonds. The duration of such an inverse floater is a multiple of the duration of the collateral bond from which it was created. To illustrate this, consider a 25-year conventional bond with a market value of £100 million that is split into a floating-rate bond and an inverse floater security, which have market values of £80 million and

1 Duration and modified duration were reviewed in Chapter 2.

Libor	FRN coupon	Inverse FRN coupon	Total coupon
0.00	0.25	9.75	10
1.00	1.25	8.75	10
2.00	2.25	7.75	10
3.00	3.25	6.75	10
4.00	4.25	5.75	10
5.00	5.25	4.75	10
6.00	6.25	3.75	10
7.00	7.25	2.75	10
8.00	8.25	1.75	10
9.00	9.00	1.00	10
10.00	9.00	1.00	10
12.00	9.00	1.00	10
15.00	9.00	1.00	10

Table 3.2: Creation of FRN and inverse FRN from conventional coupon bond.

£20 million respectively. Assume that the conventional bond has a modified duration of 9.50; for a 1% change in yield, the value of this bond will change by approximately 9.5% or £9.5 million. Therefore, the two securities created by splitting the collateral bond must also change in value by a total of £9.5 million for the same change in rates. As we saw in Chapter 2, both the duration and the modified duration of an FRN are relatively small, due to the nature of the coupon re-set making the bond more of a money market security (that is, a semi-annually paying FRN has an interest-rate sensitivity similar to a six-month instrument). This means that the change in value of the new portfolio must come virtually entirely from the inverse floater bond. In our example, the modified duration of this bond must be 47.50. A modified duration of 47.50 means that there will be a 47.5% change in the value of the inverse floater for a 1% change in interest rates, a change in value of £9.5 million. Inverse floater securities have the highest modified duration measures of any instrument in the bond markets.

From the example given we see that the modified duration of the inverse floater bond is higher than the number of years to maturity of the collateral bond. This is an unexpected result for those who are more familiar with the duration measure referring to years, as originally defined by Macaulay, as the inverse floater bond has a duration higher than the bond from which it was created.

The general expression for the modified duration *MD* of an inverse floating rate security is given by (3.4), which assumes that the modified duration for the FRN is close to zero.

$$MD_{inverse} = (1 + l)(MD_{collateral}) \times \frac{P_{collateral}}{P_{inverse}} \tag{3.4}$$

where l is the leverage level of the inverse floating-rate security.

3.3 Introduction to asset-backed bonds

3.3.1 *Introduction*

There is a large group of bond instruments that trade under the overall heading of *asset-backed bonds*. These are bundled securities, so called because they are marketable instruments that result from the bundling or packaging together of a set of non-marketable assets. This process is known as *securitisation*, when an institution's assets or cash flow receivables are removed from its balance sheet and packaged together as one large loan, and then 'sold' on to an investor, or series of investors, who then receive the interest payments due on the assets until they are redeemed. The purchasers of the securitised assets often have no recourse to the original borrowers, in fact the original borrowers are not usually involved in the transaction or any of its processes. In this section we provide a brief overview of asset-backed bonds.

Securitisation was introduced in the US market and this market remains the largest for asset-backed bonds. The earliest examples of such bonds were in the US mortgage market, where residential mortgage loans made by a *thrift* (building society) were packaged together and sold on to investors who received the interest and principal payments made by the borrowers of the original loans. The process benefited the original lender in a number of ways. One key benefit was that removing assets from the balance sheet reduced risk exposure for the bank and enhanced its liquidity position.

The effect of these benefits is increased with the maturity of the original loans. For example in the case of mortgage loans, the term to maturity can be up to 25 years, perhaps longer. The bulk of these loans are financed out of deposits that can be withdrawn on demand, or at relatively short notice. In addition it is often the case that as a result of securitisation, the packaged loans are funded at a lower rate than that charged by the original lending institution. This implies that the bundled loans can be sold off at a higher value than the level at which the lending institution valued them. Put another way, securitising loans adds value to the loan book and it is the original lender that receives this value. Another benefit is that as a result of securitisation, the total funding available to the lending institution may well increase due to its access to capital markets; in other words, the firm becomes less dependent on its traditional deposit base. And finally by reducing the level of debt on the lending institution's balance sheet, it will improve the firm's gearing ratio.[2]

The main advantage to the investor of securitisation is that it offers a marketable asset-backed instrument to invest in. Often the instrument offers two levels of protection, the original assets and credit enhancement. The original assets will provide good security if they are well-diversified and equivalent in terms of quality, terms and conditions (for example the repayment structure and maturity of assets). A diversified asset base reduces the risk of a single drastic failure, while homogeneous assets make it more straightforward to analyse the loan base. If there is little or no liquidity in the original loans (no secondary market) then investors will often require *credit enhancement* in the form of an insurance contract, letters of credit, subordination of a second tranche which absorbs losses first[3], over-collateralisation or a reserve fund, for the instrument to be sold at a price acceptable to the original lender. Ironically, by implementing one or more of the protection features described, securitisation provides a better credit risk for the investor than the loans represented to the original lender.

Securitisation began in the US housing market in 1970 after the Government National Mortgage Association (GNMA or 'Ginnie Mae') began issuing *mortgage pass-through certificates*. A pass-through is a security representing ownership in a pool of mortgages.

---

2 Gearing is a firm's debt-to-equity ratio.

3 A second tranche of bonds that is junior to the first, so it would absorb any losses first.

The mortgages themselves were sold through a grantor trust and the certificates sold in the capital markets. As with standard mortgages the interest and amortised principal were paid monthly. Later on *mortgage-backed bonds* were issued with semi-annual payments and maturities of up to 15 years, which were terms familiar to domestic bondholders. In 1983 *collateralised mortgage obligations* were issued, the collateral provided by mortgages issued by the Federal Home Loans Mortgage Corporation. Being government agencies, the bonds that they issue are guaranteed and as such carry little additional risk compared to US Treasury securities. They can therefore be priced on the same basis as Treasuries. However they present an additional type of risk, that of *prepayment risk*. This is the risk that mortgages will be paid off early, ahead of their term, a risk that increases when mortgages have been taken out at high fixed interest rates and rates have subsequently fallen. The existence of this risk therefore dictates that these bonds pay a higher return than corresponding Treasury bonds. The term *average life* is used to describe the years to maturity for asset-backed bonds that have an element of prepayment risk about them, and is obviously an estimate used by bond analysts.

Securitisation was introduced in the UK market in 1985. A number of institutions were established for the purpose of securitising mortgages and other assets such as car loans and credit card debt. These included National Home Loans Corporation, Mortgage Funding Corporation and First Mortgage Securities.

3.3.2 *Credit rating*

In the sterling market all public mortgage-backed and asset-backed securities (MBS/ABS) are explicitly rated by one or both of two of the largest credit-rating agenices, Moody's and Standard & Poor's. In structured financings it is normal for the rating of the paper to be investment grade, with most issues at launch being rated Aaa and/or AAA. We can briefly touch on the issues involved in rating such paper. The rating of the issue is derived from a combination of factors. As it cannot generally be expected that investors will be sufficiently protected by the performance of the collateral alone, the rating agencies look to minimise the risk of principal default and ensure timely payment of interest coupons by requiring additional credit enhancement. The percentage of additional enhancement is determined by analysing the 'riskiness' of the collateral under a range of stress-tested environments which seek to quantify the effect of various interest rate, foreclosure and loss scenarios, which are largely based on the expected performance of the collateral base in a recession. Much of the analysis is based on performance in the US markets, and the rating agencies try to establish criteria for each market and collateral type that is rated. The amount of enhancement required depends on the rating required at launch, for instance less is required for a lower rated issue. In many cases issues will be backed by a larger nominal value of collateral, for example an issue size of £100 million is formed out of assets composed of say, £110 million or a higher amount.

Enhancement levels are also determined by the agencies reviewing the legal risks in the transaction. The legal analysis examines the competing rights and interests in the assets, including those of the bondholders and various third parties. Mortgage-backed securities (MBS) and asset-backed securities (ABS) are typically issued out of low capitalised 'special purpose vehicle' companies (SPV), established solely for the purpose of issuing the securities. The rating agencies need to be assured that there is no risk to the bondholders in the event of the originator, that is the seller of the assets to the SPV, becoming insolvent, and to be certain that a receiver or administrator cannot seize the assets or obtain rights to the SPV's cash flows. In addition the agencies need to be satisfied that the SPV will be able to meet its obligations to its investors in circumstances where the service body (the entity responsible for administering the collateral, usually the originator) becomes insolvent. Consequently significant emphasis is placed on ensuring that all primary and supporting documentation preserves the rights of investors in the security. An independent Trustee is appointed to represent the interests of investors. Providing Trustee services results in valuable fee-based income for banks.

A change in rating for an ABS or MBS issue may occur due to deterioration in performance of the collateral, heavy utilisation of credit enhancement, or downgrade of a supporting rating, for example an insurance company that was underwriting insurance on the pool of the assets.

3.3.3 *Credit enhancement*

Credit support enhancement for ABS and MBS issues is usually by either of the following methods:

- **Pool insurance:** an insurance policy provided by a composite insurance company to cover the risk of principal loss in the collateral pool. The claims paying rating of the insurance company is important in determining the overall rating of the issue. In many cases in the past the rating of the insurance company at launch proved to be insufficient to achieve the desired rating and a reinsurance policy was entered into with a higher rated company in order to achieve the desired rating.
- **Senior/Junior note classes:** credit enhancement is provided by subordinating a class of notes ('class B' notes) to the senior class notes ('class A' notes). The class B note's right to its proportional share of cash flows is subordinated to the rights of the senior noteholders. Class B notes do not receive payments of principal until certain rating agency requirements have been met, specifically satisfactory performance of the collateral pool over a pre-determined period, or in many cases until all of the senior note classes have been redeemed in full.
- **Margin step-up:** a number of ABS issues incorporate a step-up feature in the coupon structure, which typically coincides with a call date. Although the issuer is usually under no obligation to redeem the notes at this point, the step-up feature is an added incentive for investors, to convince them from the outset that the economic cost of paying a higher coupon would be unacceptable and that the issuer will seek to refinance by exercising its call option.
- **Substitution:** this feature enables the issuer to utilise principal cash flows from redemptions to purchase new collateral from the originator. This has the effect of lengthening the effective life of the transaction as the principal would otherwise have been used to redeem the notes. The issuer is usually under no obligation to substitute and it is an option granted by the investor.

3.3.4 *Redemption mechanism*

ABS and MBS issue terms usually incorporate one of two main methods through which redeeming principal can be passed back to investors.

- **Drawing by lot:** the available principal from the relevant interest period is repaid to investors by the international clearing agencies Euroclear and Clearstream drawing notes, at random, for cancellation. Notes will therefore trade at their nominal value.
- **Pro rata:** The available principal for the interest period is distributed among all investors, dependent upon their holding in the security. A *pool factor* is calculated, which is the remaining principal balance of the Note expressed as a factor of one. For instance if the pool factor is 0.62557, this means that for each Note of £10,000 nominal, £3,744.30 of principal has been repaid to date. A pool factor value is useful to investors since early repayment of say, mortgages reduces the level of asset backing available for an issue, the outstanding value of such an issue is reduced on a pro-rata basis, like early redemption, by a set percentage so that the remaining amount outstanding is adequately securitised.

3.3.5 *Additional features*

Some ABS structures will incorporate a *call option* feature. In some cases the terms of the issue prevent a call being exercised until a certain percentage of the issue remains outstanding, usually 10 per cent, and a certain date has been passed.

It is common for ABS issues to have an *average life* quoted for them. This says that based on the most recent principal balance for the security, it is assumed that a redemption rate is applied such that the resultant average life equals the number of months left from the last interest payment date until 50 per cent of the principal balance remains. Some issuers will announce the expected average life of their paper, and yield calculations are based on this average life.

3.4 PIBS

PIBS are a type of bond peculiar to the sterling market in London. The term comes from *P*ermanent *I*nterest *B*earing *S*hares, and they are issued exclusively by UK building societies. PIBS are very similar to preference shares issued by banks and other corporates, that is they are irredeemable (like preference shares and ordinary shares) and they are loss absorbing, again like preference and ordinary shares, in that a building society can elect not to pay the coupon (dividend) due on PIBS if by so doing it would leave the society insolvent. The principal difference between PIBS and bank preference shares is that PIBS coupon payments are tax deductible for a building society whereas a preference share dividend is not tax deductible for a bank. PIBS are thus very attractive to building societies and can therefore be issued at higher margins over gilts than bank preference shares and still appear relatively cheap to the issuer.

The first issue of PIBS was in 1991 when Hoare Govett Securities Limited raised £75 million for Leeds Permanent Building Society (subsequently merged with and now part of Halifax plc). Further issues followed and a list of current PIBS is shown at Table 3.3.

Further developments included the introduction of floating rate PIBS. Issuing such paper resulted in the building societies involved being rated for the first time. The highest rated societies such as Halifax and Cheltenham & Gloucester subsequently either converted into banks, with shares listed on the London Stock Exchange, or were taken over by banks. In theory PIBS offer no certainty as to capital value because the issuing building society is under no obligation to repay the principal. However no building society has ever gone out of

	Coupon	Current price	Yield %	Issue price	Minimum nominal amount (£)
Birmingham Midshires BS	9.375%	146.00	6.42	100.17	1,000
Bradford & Bingley BS	11.625%	187.00	6.22	100.13	10,000
Britannia BS	13.000%	197.00	6.60	100.42	1,000
Coventry BS	12.125%	195.00	6.22	100.75	1,000
Leeds & Holbeck BS	13.375%	200.00	6.69	100.23	1,000
Newcastle BS	10.750%	175.00	6.14	100.32	1,000
Skipton BS	12.875%	214.00	6.02	100.48	1,000
Bristol & West	13.375%	193.00	6.93	100.34	1,000
Cheltenham & Gloucester	11.750%	183.00	6.40	100.98	50,000
Halifax plc	12.000%	174.00	6.90	100.28	50,000
Northern Rock plc	12.625%	195.00	6.47	100.14	1,000

Table 3.3: PIBS and perpetual subordinated bonds of building societies and former building societies as at March 1999. Source: Barclays Capital.

business in the history of the movement (the oldest building society currently still in existence dates from 1845); where individual societies have found themselves in difficulties in the past, they have been taken over by another society. PIBS have delivered significant increases in capital gain for their holders, as sterling interest rates have fallen greatly from the levels that existed at the time most of the bonds were issued. They continue to trade in a liquid market.

The building society movement has contracted somewhat in recent years, as the largest societies converted to banks, with shares publicly listed on the Stock Exchange, or were taken over by banking groups.[4] This resulted in the PIBS sector experiencing a decline in recent years as no new issues were placed in the market. In October 1999 Manchester Building Society issued £5 million nominal of paper, this being the first new issue of PIBS since 1993. The bonds were placed by Barclays Capital, and the small size of the issue indicates that the paper was aimed largely at retail customers rather than institutions. The bonds had a coupon of 8% and were priced over the long-dated UK gilt, the 6% 2028.

3.5 Callable bonds

A callable bond is one that allows the issuer to *call* the issue before its stated maturity date, that is, redeem the bond early. This provision is sometimes referred to as a *call feature* and is widely used by corporate and local authority issuers of debt. A bond with a call provision carries two disadvantages for the bondholder. First an issuer will call a bond when the market interest rates are lower than the issue's coupon rate; for example if the coupon on a callable bond is 10 per cent and market interest rates are 8 per cent, it will be advantageous for the issuer to call the 10 per cent issue and refinance it with an 8 per cent issue. The

4 In 1980 there were nearly 200 building societies in the UK. At October 2003 this number had been reduced to 63. Many of the largest institutions, such as the Halifax, Woolwich and Alliance & Leicester building societies, had converted to banks. The oldest surviving building society, the Chesham Building Society, dates from 1845.

investor is faced with reinvesting the monies received as a result of the call at a lower interest rate. Thus callable bonds present investors with a higher level of reinvestment risk. Secondly the potential for the price of a callable bond to appreciate in a falling interest rate environment is less than that of a conventional bond. This is because the price of a callable bond will remain at or near its call price (the price above which it is economical for the issuer to redeem the bond) rather than rise to the higher price that would result for an otherwise comparable non-callable bond. Because callable bonds carry such disadvantages for the investor, the market also requires them to offer sufficient compensation for bondholders, in the form of higher yield compared to conventional bonds. The higher yield on callable bonds is the price they pay in return for asking investors to bear the associated call risk.

The *call price* for a callable bond is the price paid to bondholders when the bond is called. It is usually par, but it may be above par or set at different levels for different times. The prices and times at which a bond may be called are set out in the issue terms and form part of the *call schedule*. The most common reason why a bond is called is because the issuer can re-finance borrowing requirements at a lower interest rate, for example because it has achieved an improved credit rating. When lower borrowing costs are available an issuer will call an existing issue and replace it with a bond carrying a lower coupon. Another reason why a bond may be called is when the issuer can re-fund existing debt at a lower rate; in this case, following a drop in interest rates the current issue is called and replaced, again with a bond paying a lower coupon.

Investors in a callable bond are aware of the call feature attached to the bond, and the potential downside of holding the bond. For this reason, investors require a higher yield from holding callable bonds compared to non-callable bonds of similar maturity issued by the same or similar issuers. There is often a period of *call protection* built into the bond's terms, during which the bond may not be called. If we assume an efficient market mechanism, bondholders will have the same information about the market as the bond issuer, and the premium required by them when compared to the return from holding a non-callable bond is known at the time of issue of the callable bond. In an efficient market therefore there is no advantage to a borrower in issuing a callable bond compared to a non-callable one, since the advantages of the call feature are balanced by the higher funding cost associated with incorporating a call feature.

In certain cases callable bonds are issued with a period of *call protection* included in the terms. This is a period during which the bond cannot be called, for example a callable bond with a 10-year term to maturity that is not callable for the first five years of its life. Call protection is often provided by the issuer as an added incentive to investors to buy the bond.

3.5.1 *Analysis*

For callable bonds the market calculates a yield to maturity in the normal fashion but also calculates a *yield to call* for the bond. The yield to call is calculated on the assumption that the bond will be called at the first call date. The procedure is the same as for the normal yield calculation, that is, to determine the market interest rate of return that will equate the present value of all the cash flows to the current price. For yield to call the cash flows are those to the first call date. The normal practice for a bond trading above par is to calculate the yield to maturity and the yield to call and take the lower value as the bond's yield. In fact bond investors and analysts will usually calculate the yield to the first call date and also the yield to all possible call dates, and then use the lowest of these values as the bond's yield.

Bloomberg analysis refers to this value as the *yield to worst*. This yield calculation suffers from the same problems as yield to maturity, in that the figure computed assumes reinvestment of coupon at the same rate, and that bondholders will hold the bond to maturity. Yield to call also assumes that the issuer will call the bond on the assumed call date.

The price/yield relationship for a conventional bond is convex. For a bond with an option feature, such as a callable bond, the relationship differs at a certain yield point, such that the bond is said to then display *negative convexity*. This is discussed in greater detail in the chapter on duration and convexity.

3.5.2 *Constituents of a callable bond*

The best way to analyse a callable bond is to consider it as one for which the bondholder has sold the issuer an option that allows the issuer to redeem the bond, at his discretion, from the first call date until maturity. The bondholder has effectively entered into two separate transactions, first the purchase of a non-callable bond from the issuer at a price, and secondly the sale to the issuer of a *call option*, for which they receive a price (it is a call option as the issuer has the right, but not the obligation, to buy back the bond from the bondholder at a call date(s), which is in effect the expiry date(s) of the option). The position of the bondholder is therefore:

$$\text{Long position in callable bond} = \text{Long position in non-callable bond} + \text{short position in call option.}$$

The price of the callable bond is therefore equal to the net position of the two component parts.

$$\text{Price of callable bond} = \text{Price of non-callable bond} - \text{price of call option.}$$

If you think about it, the bondholder has sold the issuer a call option, therefore the 'proceeds' of this sale are subtracted from the price of the hypothetical non-callable bond. This is shown in Figure 3.1; at point *r* the price of the non-callable bond and the callable bond is the price of the call option on the bond.

As most callable bonds have a set of dates on which they can be called, or even a time period during which the bond can be called at any time after a requisite notice period, the

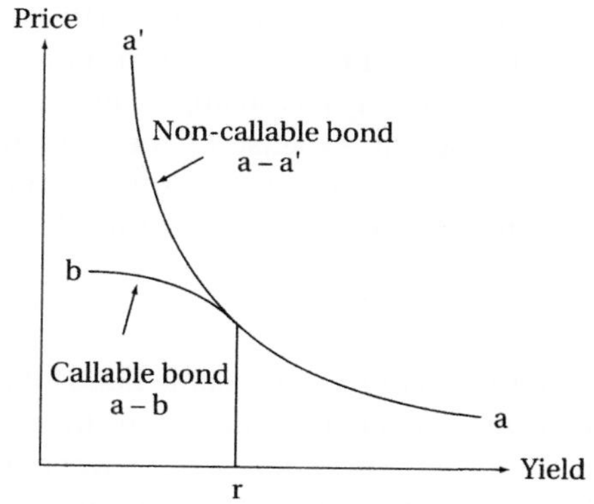

Figure 3.1: Price/yield relationship for callable bond. Reproduced with permission from Frank Fabozzi, *Fixed Income Mathematics*, McGraw Hill, 1997.

bondholder can be said to have sold not one call option on the bond, but a strip of options. The underlying asset for these call options is the set of cash flows that are not paid if the issuer exercises the call.

3.5.3 *Constituents of a putable bond*

The analysis we have applied to callable bonds can be repeated for bonds that have an embedded *put* feature. With a putable bond the bondholder has the right to sell the bond back to the issuer at a designated price and time. Again a putable bond can be viewed as representing two separate transactions; first the bondholder buys a non-putable bond, secondly the investor buys an option from the issuer that allows him to sell the bond to the issuer. This type of option is called a *put option.* The price of the putable bond is therefore:

$$\text{Price of putable bond} = \text{Price of non-putable bond} + \text{price of put option.}$$

3.5.4 *Refunding*

The term refunding is used to describe the process when a borrower calls an existing bond issue and replaces it with a new lower coupon bond issue. This is at the discretion of the issuer. A company that has borrowed funds via a callable bond will want to be aware of the best time at which to call the issue. The primary issues are if there is any net gain to be had from an immediate refinancing, and what the appropriate replacement bond should be.

On issue the yield of the callable bond will lie above a non-callable bond of the same maturity; this reflects the call premium benefit to the bondholder. At any point during the bond's life market interest rates may fall far enough below the coupon level such that it becomes attractive to the issuer to call in the bonds (before the stated maturity date) and replace the borrowing. The first issue for the borrower is what type of bond should be used to replace the called debt. If the replacement bond is non-callable and has the same maturity date as the original issue, it would have to offer the same yield as the existing issue in order to be attractive to investors. However the lower general level of interest rates may result in the issuer needing to offer a spread over, say, the government yield level that is lower than the spread offered on the original issue.

Borrowers also need to consider the timing of the refinancing and whether it is advantageous to delay calling the issue until a later date. However this is a judgement call based on the corporate treasurer's view of market interest rates. The decision to refinance after a material change in the general level of interest rates is an important one. If interest rates have fallen sufficiently an issuing company has an opportunity to refinance at a new (lower) borrowing rate, and this will be at the expense of the existing bondholders. Thus the existence of a call option provision as part of the bond's terms is an advantage to the borrower, and this option needs to be exercised in order for the borrower to gain from any fall in the level of interest rates.

3.5.5 *Advance refunding*

It is common for corporate borrowers to issue callable bonds that include a period of call protection. If there is a significant fall in interest rates during the period of this call protection, the borrower may consider an *advance refunding.* This is where the borrower offers to buy call-protected bonds at a price above the call price; when this happens bondholders are not obliged to respond to the call but may be tempted to do so because the terms of the call are attractive, while still enabling the borrower to achieve a funding gain.

Example 3.2

- A callable bond with a coupon of 8% has two years remaining on its call protection provision. The call price is £110 per cent once the bond becomes callable. Market interest rates are now at 5%. The firm may wish to refund immediately, rather than wait for two years and refund at an as yet unknown rate, providing it can offer a call price attractive enough to the bondholders whilst retaining an element of funding benefit for itself.

The fair value of the bond is the present value of the £8 coupon for the next two years together with the present value of the call price two years from now. This is given at (3.6):

$$P = \frac{8}{(1+r)} + \frac{8}{(1+r)^2} + \frac{110}{(1+r)^2}. \tag{3.6}$$

At a discount rate of 5% the price of the bond is 114.6485. If it wishes to advance refund, the issuer will have to set a call price above this level in order to induce bondholders to sell their bonds. However this allows it to gain a refunding advantage immediately instead of having to wait two years. Any funding gain must take into account the transaction costs associated with calling back the bonds and issuing new debt.

3.5.6 *Sinking funds*

In certain domestic markets including the UK and US markets, corporate bonds are issued with a *sinking fund* attached. This requires the borrower to redeem a part of the bond issue at regular intervals during the bond's life. An example of a sinking fund provision is illustrated at Figure 3.2.

In the example in Figure 3.2 a bond with a twenty-year maturity and a total issue size of £200 million has 5% of its outstanding issue size redeemed each year after ten years have elapsed, leaving £119.75 million to be paid back on maturity. At each anniversary of the sinking fund dates the borrowing firm can either purchase the required number of bonds in the open market or call the same number of bonds. The exact procedure will be set out in the bond issue terms, and the firm will elect the cheapest option.

	Year												
Time periods	**0**	**···**	**10**	**11**	**12**	**13**	**14**	**15**	**16**	**17**	**18**	**19**	**20**
Sinking fund payments as 5% of outstanding nominal (£m)			10	9.5	9.025	8.57375	8.14506	7.73781	7.35092	6.98337	6.63420	6.30249	
Final principal payment (£m)													119.7473867

Figure 3.2: £200 million 20-year bond issue: bond sinking fund payments.

The main reason why an issuer will include a sinking fund provision is to provide comfort to potential investors. A sinking fund will indicate a lower level of risk of default, since the availability of funds to repay a set proportion of the debt indicates a healthy cash flow state. However if the sinking fund is sourced from external funds this may not actually be the case. Nevertheless in theory a sinking fund signals favourable future prospects for the borrowing company, so as a result the yield required by investors from holding the bond consequently is lower.

3.5.7 *Analysing call provisions*

Callable bonds are very popular in corporate debt markets, significantly so in the United States. A study by Kish (1992) found that approximately 80% of corporate debt in the US market in the second half of the 1980s was issued with call provisions attached. It is often observed that only issuers whose paper is highly sought-after by investors raise funds without the existence of any call provision, and consequently at a lower yield.

In an economist's perfect market the increased yield available on a callable bond together with any period of call protection should take into account the probability of the call option being exercised. In theory therefore there should be no advantage either way to issuing a bond with a call provision attached. In practice however corporate issuers continue to issue a large volume of debt incorporating call features. Previous studies including the one by Kish have attempted to explain this phenomenon. These are summarised below.

- **Corporate management superior knowledge on direction of interest rates.** While an above-average forecasting ability on the direction of interest rates would indeed be a valuable skill, and would be advantageous to the issuers of callable bonds, it is highly unlikely that corporate managers possess such a skill. In any case the investors who purchase callable debt carry out their own market analysis and one would not expect their forecasting ability to be any poorer than that of corporate borrowers.
- **The risk averse nature of borrowers and lenders.** This premise suggests that borrowers do not favour locking in to high interest rates for anything more than short periods of time, while lenders wish to avoid large downward fluctuations in bond prices, and do not attach great value to the call feature. Again this is unrealistic with regard to the lenders' position, since the conventional preference for lenders is to lock in a fixed return over the complete term of a bond's life.
- **Corporate management knowledge of the firm's prospects.** In this analysis the suggestion is that managers possess superior knowledge of their firms' prospects over that of investors, who view the firm in less favourable light and therefore demand a higher yield on the debt. The managers expect the firm's circumstances to improve and refinance the borrowing at a better rate when this occurs. However this analysis does not explain why even well-rated firms issue callable bonds, or why firms issue both callable and non-callable debt.

Whatever the primary rationale behind the issue of callable debt, investors are frequently interested in increasing the yields on their investments and callable bonds provide one of the ways of achieving this. Therefore it is advantageous to both investors and borrowers for corporates to issue some callable debt as part of their overall funding requirement.

3.6 Index-linked bonds

In certain countries there is a market in bonds whose return, both coupon and final redemption payment, is linked to the consumer prices index. The exact design of such *index-linked bonds* varies across different markets. This of course makes the comparison of measures such as yield difficult and has in the past acted as a hindrance to arbitrageurs seeking to exploit real yield differentials. In this section we present an overview of indexed bonds and how they differ from the conventional market. Not all index-linked bonds link both coupon and maturity payments to a specified index; in some markets only the coupon payment is index-linked. Generally the most liquid market available will be the government bond market in index-linked instruments.

The structure of index-linked bond markets differs across the world, including in those areas noted below.

- **Choice of index.** In principle bonds can be indexed to any number of variables, including various price indices, earnings, output, specific commodities or foreign currencies. Although ideally the chosen index would reflect the hedging requirements of both parties, these may not coincide. In practice most bonds have been linked to an index of consumer prices such as the UK Retail Price Index, since this is usually widely circulated and well understood and issued on a regular basis.
- **Indexation lags.** In order to construct precise protection against inflation, interest payments for a given period would need to be corrected for actual inflation over the same period. However unavoidable lags between the movements in the price index and the adjustment to the bond cash flows distort the inflation-proofing properties of indexed bonds. The lags arise in two ways. First, inflation statistics can only be calculated and published with a delay. Secondly in some markets the size of the next coupon payment must be known before the start of the coupon period in order to calculate the accrued interest; this leads to a delay equal to the length of time between coupon payments.
- **Coupon frequency.** Index-linked bonds often pay interest on a semi-annual basis.
- **Indexing the cash flows.** There are four basic methods of linking the cash flows from a bond to an inflation index. These are:
    - **Interest-indexed bonds:** these pay a fixed real coupon and an indexation of the fixed principal every period; the principal repayment at maturity is not adjusted. In this case all the inflation adjustment is fully paid out as it occurs and does not accrue on the principal. These type of bonds have been issued in Australia, although the most recent issue was in 1987.
    - **Capital-indexed bonds:** the coupon rate is specified in real terms. Interest payments equal the coupon rate multiplied by the inflation-adjusted principal amount. At maturity the principal repayment is the product of the nominal value of the bond multiplied by the cumulative change in the index. Compared with interest-indexed bonds of similar maturity, these bonds have higher duration and lower reinvestment risk. These type of bonds have been issued in Australia, Canada, New Zealand, the UK and the USA.
    - **Zero-coupon indexed bonds:** as their name implies these pay no coupons but the principal repayment is scaled for inflation. These have the highest duration of all

indexed bonds and have no reinvestment risk. These bonds have been issued in Sweden.

- **Indexed-annuity bonds:** the payments consist of a fixed annuity payment and a varying element to compensate for inflation. These bonds have the lowest duration and highest reinvestment risk of all index-linked bonds. They have been issued in Australia, although not by the central government.

- **Coupon stripping feature.** Allowing market practitioners to strip indexed bonds enables them to create new inflation-linked products that are more specific to investors needs, such as indexed annuities or deferred payment indexed bonds. In markets which allow stripping of indexed government bonds, a strip is simply an individual uplifted cash flow. An exception to this is in New Zealand, where the cash flows are separated into three components: the principal, the principal inflation adjustment and the set of inflation-linked coupons (that is, an indexed annuity).

Country	**First issue date**	**Index used**	**Inflation in year before first issue**
Australia	1985	consumer prices	4.5%
Brazil	1991	wholesale prices	1477%
Canada	1991	consumer prices	4.8%
Chile	1967	consumer prices	17%
Colombia	1995	consumer prices	22.8%
Hungary	1995	consumer prices	22.1%
Iceland	1955	credit terms index	102.7%*
Israel	1955	consumer prices	12.3%
Mexico	1989	consumer prices	114.8%
New Zealand	1995	consumer prices	2.8%
Poland	1992	service price indices	60.4%
Sweden	1994	consumer prices	4.4%
Turkey	1997	consumer prices	84.9%
United Kingdom	1981	retail prices	14%
United States	1997	commodity prices	2.9%

* between 1949 and 1954.

Table 3.4: Current issuers of inflation-indexed government bonds.
Source: Bank of England.

Appendices

Appendix 3.1: Floating rate note discount margin equation using discount factor

The discounted margin for FRNs redeemed on a normal coupon date is given by (3.7):

$$P \cdot \left(1 + \frac{re + DM}{100} B\right) = C + \sum_{n=1}^{n-1} \frac{(re_2 + QM)}{m} \nu^n + M\nu^{n-1} \quad (3.7)$$

where

DM	is the required discounted margin %
P	is the dirty price
re	is the current market reference rate from the value date to the first coupon date
re_2	is the assumed market reference rate for subsequent coupon payments
B	is the number of days from the value date to the next coupon date, as a fraction of the day-count base (360, 365 or 365/366 days)
C	is the next coupon payment %
n	is the number of future coupon payments
QM	is the quoted margin %
m	is the number of coupon payments per year adjusted for the assumed number of days in the year
M	is the redemption value
ν	is the discount factor, that is $\nu = 1/(1 + (re_2 + DM)/100h)$.

The left-hand side of (3.7) represents the cost of the bond adjusted using current reference rates to the next coupon date.

For perpetual or undated FRNs (3.7) is simplified as shown at (3.8):

$$P \cdot \left(1 + \frac{re + DM}{100} \cdot B\right) = C + 100\left(\frac{re_2 + QM}{re_2 + DM}\right). \quad (3.8)$$

A gross redemption yield for an FRN can only be calculated if one assumes unchanged market reference rates during the remaining life of the bond, so that future coupon rates may be predicted. Under this restrictive assumption we may set an FRN's redemption yield as (3.9) below:

$$P = \sum_{n=1}^{N} C_i \cdot \nu^{B+ti} + M \cdot \nu^{B+tn} \quad (3.9)$$

where

n	is the number of coupon payments to redemption
t_i	is the time in periods from the next to the ith coupon payment
t_n	is the time in interest periods to redemption date
ν	is the discount factor, that is, $\nu = 1/(1 + y/h)$
y	is the required redemption yield compounded m times per year.

Selected bibliography and references

Brown, P.J., *Bond Markets: Structures and Yield Calculations*, Glenlake Publishing Company, 1998

Kish, R.J., Livingston, M., 'The determinants of the call feature on corporate bonds', *Journal of Banking and Finance*, 16, 1992, pp. 687–703

Levy, H., *Introduction to Investments*, South-Western, 1999

Livingston, M., *Money and Capital Markets*, 2nd edition, New York Institute of Finance, 1993

Narayan, M.P., Lim, S.P., 'The call provision on corporate zero-coupon bonds', *Journal of Financial and Quantitative Analysis*, 24, March 1989, pp. 91–103

4 Hybrid Securities

In this chapter we describe in generic format some of the more exotic or structured notes that have been introduced into the fixed income market. The motivations behind the development and use of these products are varied, but include the desire for increased yield without additional credit risk, as well as the need to alter, transform or transfer risk exposure and risk-return profiles. Certain structured notes were also developed as hedging instruments. The instruments themselves have been issued by banks, corporate institutions and sovereign authorities. By using certain types of notes, investors can gain access to different markets, sometimes synthetically, that were previously not available to them. For instance by purchasing a structured note an investor can take on board a position that reflects her views on a particular exchange rate and anticipated changes in yield curve but in a different market. The investment instrument can be tailored to suit the investor's particular risk profile.

We describe a number of structured notes that are currently available to investors today, although often investors will seek particular features that suit their needs, and so there are invariably detail variations in each note. We stress that this is only the tip of the iceberg, and many different types of notes are available; indeed, if any particular investor or issuer requirement has not been made available, it is a relatively straightforward process whereby an investment bank can structure a note that meets one or both specific requirements.

4.1.1 *Indexed amortising note*

Description

Another type of hybrid note is the Indexed Amortising Note or IAN. They were introduced in the US domestic market in the early 1990s at the demand of investors in asset-backed notes known as collateralised mortgage obligations or CMOs. IANs are fixed-coupon unsecured notes issued with a nominal value that is not fixed. That is, the nominal amount may reduce in value ahead of the legal maturity according to the levels recorded by a specified reference index such as six-month Libor. If the reference remains static or its level decreases, the IAN value will amortise in nominal value. The legal maturity of IANs is short- to medium-term, with the five-year maturity being common. The notes have been issued by banks and corporates, although a large volume has been issued by US government agencies. The yield payable on IANs is typically at a premium above that of similar credit quality conventional debt. The amortisation schedule on an IAN is linked to the movement of the specified reference index, which is easily understood. This is considered an advantage to certain mortgage-backed notes, which amortise in accordance with less clearly defined patterns such as a *prepayment schedule.*

An issuer of IANS will arrange a hedge that makes the funding obtained more attractive, for example a straight Libor-type exposure. This is most commonly arranged through a swap arrangement that mirrors the note structure. A diagrammatic representation is shown in Figure 4.1, with a swap hedge arrangement shown in Figure 4.2. In fact it is more

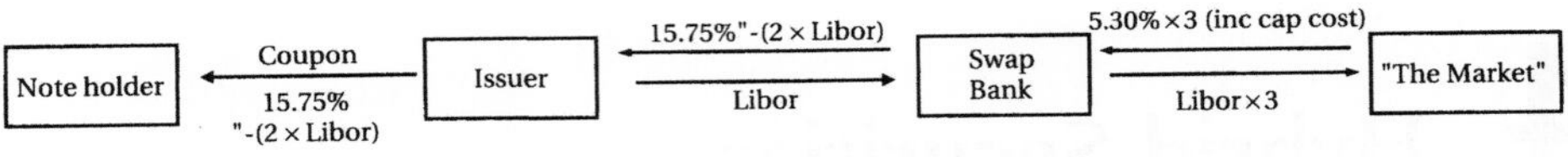

Figure 4.1: IAN structure.

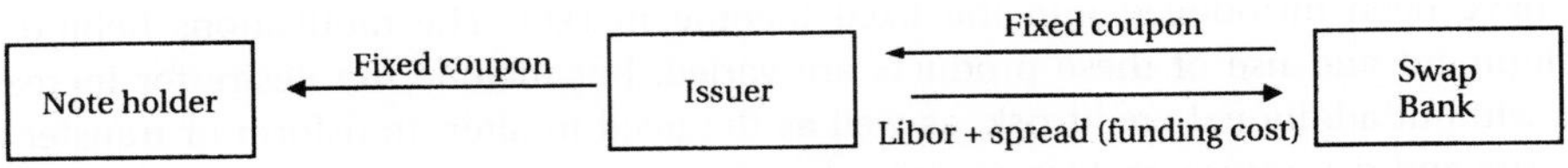

Figure 4.2: IAN hedge arrangement.

common for the swap arrangement to involve a series of options on swaps. The coupon available on an IAN might be attractive to investors when the volatility on *swaptions* is high and there is a steep positively sloping yield curve; under such an environment the option-element of an IAN would confer greatest value.

The terms of an hypothetical IAN issue are given at Table 4.1.

Under the terms of issue of the note summarised in Table 4.1, the coupon payable is the current two-year government benchmark plus a fixed spread of 1%. The note has a legal maturity of six years, however it will mature in three years if the six-month Libor rate is at a level of 6.00% or below two years from the date of issue. If the rate is above 6.00%, the maturity of the note will be extended. The 'lock-out' of three years means that the note has a minimum life of three years, irrespective of what happens to Libor rates. Amortisation takes place if on subsequent rate-fixing dates after the lock-out period the Libor rate rises. The maximum maturity of the note is six years. If at any time there is less than 20% of the nominal value in issue, the note is cancelled in full.

Issuer	Mortgage agency	
Nominal value	\$250,000,000	
Legal maturity	6 years	
Coupon	2-year Treasury plus 100 bps	
Interest basis	Monthly	
"Lock-out period"	Three years	
Reference index	6-month Libor	
6 m Libor fixing on issue	5.15%	
Minimum level of note	20%	
Average life sensitivity		
Libor rate	Amortisation rate	Average life (years)
5.15%	100%	3
6.00%	100%	3
7.00%	21%	4.1
8.00%	7%	5.6
9.00%	0.00%	6

Table 4.1: Hypothetical IAN issue.

Advantages to investors

The IAN structure offers advantages to investors under certain conditions. If the credit quality is acceptable, the notes offer a high yield over a relatively low term to maturity. The amortisation structure is easier to understand than that on mortgage-backed securities, which contain prepayment schedules that are based on assumptions that may not apply. This means that investors will know with certainty how the amortisation of the note will proceed, given the level of the reference index at any given time. The 'lock-out' period of a note is usually set at a period that offers investor comfort, such as three years; during this time no amortisation can take place.

As with the other instruments described here, IANs can be tailored to meet individual investor requirements. The legal maturity and lock-out period are features that are most frequently subject to variation, with the yield premium decreasing as the lock-out period becomes closer to the formal maturity. The reference index can be a government benchmark or interbank rate such as the swap rate. However the most common reference is the Libor rate.

4.1.2 *Synthetic convertible note*

Description

Synthetic convertible notes are fixed-coupon securities whose total return is linked to an external source such as the level of an equity index, or the price of a specific security. The fixed-coupon element is typically at a low level, and the investor has greater exposure to the performance of the external index. A common arrangement has the note redeeming at par, but redeemable at a greater amount if the performance of the reference index exceeds a stated minimum. However the investor has the safety net of redemption at par. Another typical structure is a zero-coupon note, issued at par and redeemable at par, but redeemable at a higher level if a specified equity index performs above a pre-specified level.

Table 4.2 lists the terms of an hypothetical synthetic convertible note issue that is linked to the FTSE-100 equity index. This note will pay par on maturity, but if the level of the FTSE-100 has increased by more than 10% from the level on note issue, the note will be redeemed at par plus this amount. Note however that this is an investment suitable only for someone who is very bullish on the prospects for the FTSE-100. If this index does not rise by the minimum level, the investor will have received a coupon of 0.5%, which is roughly five percentage points below the level for two-year sterling at this time.

Investor benefits

Similarly to a convertible bond, a synthetic convertible note provides investors with a fixed coupon together with additional market upside potential if the level of the reference index performs above a certain level. Unlike the convertible however, the payoff is in the form of cash.

The reference can be virtually any publicly quoted source, and notes have been issued whose payout is linked to the exchange rate of two currencies, the days on which Libor falls within a specified range, the performance of a selected basket of stocks (say 'technology stocks'), and so on.

Nominal value	£50,000,000
Term to maturity	Two years
Issue date	17-Jun-99
Maturity date	17-Jun-01
Issue price	£100
Coupon	0.50%
Interest basis	Semi-annual
Redemption proceeds	Min [100, Formula level]
Formula level	100 + [100 × (R(I) − (1.1 × R(II))/R(II)]
Index	FTSE-100
R(I)	Index level on maturity
R(II)	Index level on issue
Hedge terms	
Issuer pays	Libor
Swap bank pays	Redemption proceeds in accordance with formula

Table 4.2: Terms of a synthetic convertible note issue.

4.1.3 *Interest differential notes*

Interest differential notes or IDNs are hybrid securities which are aimed at investors who wish to put on a position that reflects their view on the interest-rate differential between rates of two different currencies. Notes in the US market are usually denominated in US dollars, whereas Euromarket notes have been issued in a wide range of global currencies.

There are a number of variations of IDNs. Notes may pay a variable coupon and a fixed redemption amount, or a fixed coupon and a redemption amount that is determined by the level or performance of an external reference index. IDNs have also been issued with payoff profiles that are linked to the differentials in interest rates of two specified currencies, or between one currency across different maturities.

Example of IDN

Here we discuss a five-year note that is linked to the differential between US dollar Libor and euro-libor.

The return on this note is a function of the spread between the US dollar Libor rate and euro-libor. An increase in the spread results in a higher coupon payable on the note, while a narrowing of the spread results in a lower coupon payable. Such a structure will appeal to an investor who has a particular view on the USD and EUR yield curves. For instance assume that the US dollar curve is inverted and the euro curve is positively-sloping. A position in an IDN (structured as above) on these two currencies allows an investor to avoid outright yield curve plays in each currency, and instead put on a trade that reflects a view on the relative level of interest rates in each currency. An IDN in this environment would allow an investor to earn a high yield while taking a view that is different to the market consensus.

When analysing an IDN, an investor must regard the note to be the equivalent to a fixed-coupon bond together with a double indexation of an interest-rate differential. The effect of this double indexation on the differential is to create two long positions in a five-year USD fixed-rate note and two short positions in a EUR fixed-rate note. The short position in the EUR note means that the EUR exchange-rate risk is removed and the investor has an exposure only to the EUR interest-rate risk, which is the desired position.

The issuer of the note hedges the note with a swap structure as with other hybrid securities. The arrangement involves both USD and EUR interest-rate swaps. The swap bank takes the opposite position in the swaps.

Table 4.3 also illustrates the return profiles possible under different interest-rate scenarios. One possibility shows that the IDN provides 95 basis point yield premium over the five-year government benchmark yield, however this assumes rather unrealistically that the interest differential between the USD and EUR interest rates remains constant through to the final coupon setting date. More significantly though we see that the yield premium available on the note increases as the spread differential between the two rates increases. In a spread tightening environment, the note offers a premium over the government yield as long as the tightening does not exceed 100 basis points each year.

Benefits to investors

IDN-type instruments allow investors to put on positions that reflect their view on foreign interest rate direction and/or levels, but without having to expose themselves to currency (exchange-rate) risk at the same time. The notes may also be structured in a way that allows investors to take a view on any maturity point of the yield curve. For instance the coupon may be set in accordance with the differential between the 10-year government benchmark yields of two specified countries. As another approach, investors can arrange combinations of different maturities in the same currency, which is a straight yield curve or relative value trade in a domestic or foreign currency.

Term to maturity	Five years	
Coupon	[(2 × USD Libor) −(2 × EUR Libor) − .50%]	
Current USD Libor		6.15%
Current EUR Libor		3.05%
Rate differential		2.65%
First coupon fix		5.70%
Current five-year benchmark		4.75%
Yield spread over benchmark		0.95%

Change in Libor spread (bps p.a.)	Libor spread at rate reset	Spread over benchmark
75	4.78%	2.34%
50	3.90%	1.88%
25	3.15%	1.21%
0	2.65%	0.95%
−25	1.97%	0.56%
−50	1.32%	0.34%
−75	0.89%	0.12%
−100	0.32%	−0.28%

Table 4.3: IDN example.

The risk run by a note holder is that the interest-rate differential moves in the opposite direction to that sought, which reduces the coupon payable and may even result in a lower yield than that available on the benchmark bond.

Selected bibliography and references

Fabozzi, F., (editor) *Handbook of Fixed Income Securities*, 6th edition, McGraw-Hill 2000

Part II
Corporate Debt Markets

The market for corporate debt is large and diverse. In fact it is in the corporate markets that the most exciting innovations and the most exotic products are observed, as government markets are fairly plain vanilla in nature. In part II we review the most important instruments that form part of this market. There is also a chapter dealing with credit analysis.

The bonds described here are not exclusively corporate instruments; many sovereign governments for example issue Eurobonds. Not surprisingly the quality of paper issued ranges from triple-A risk-free, such as World Bank bonds, to high-yield and un-rated bonds. Bonds that feature embedded options, such as callable bonds and convertibles, are now traded under a much more rigorous analytical regime than previously; most banks will use a binomial valuation model to price these bonds. This serves to illustrate that the corporate debt markets continuously benefit from the latest developments in financial engineering, and it is here that one will observe the latest structures and innovations.

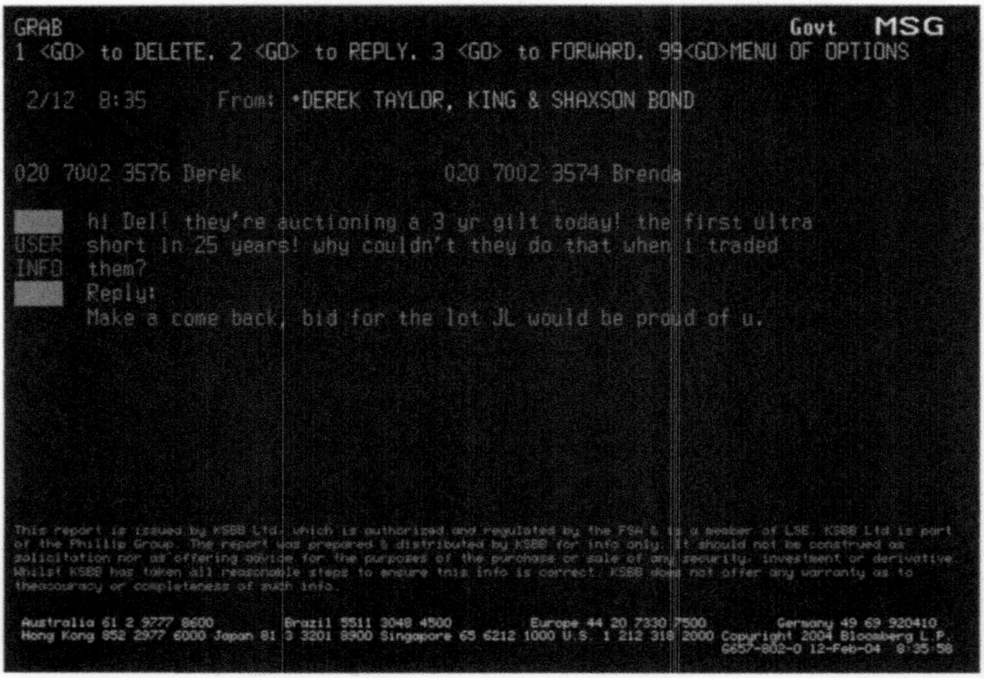
GRAB
Govt MSG
1 <GO> to DELETE. 2 <GO> to REPLY. 3 <GO> to FORWARD. 99<GO>MENU OF OPTIONS
2/12 8:35 From: *DEREK TAYLOR, KING & SHAXSON BOND
020 7002 3576 Derek
020 7002 3574 Brenda
USER
INFO
hi Del! they're auctioning a 3 yr gilt today! the first ultra short in 25 years! why couldn't they do that when i traded them?
Reply:
Make a come back, bid for the lot JL would be proud of u.
This report is issued by KSBB Ltd, which is authorized and regulated by the FSA & is a member of LSE. KSBB Ltd is part of the Phillip Group. The report was prepared & distributed by KSBB for info only. It should not be construed as solicitation nor as offering advice for the purposes of the purchase or sale of any security, investment or derivative. Whilst KSBB has taken all reasonable steps to ensure this info is correct, KSBB does not offer any warranty as to theaccuracy or completeness of such info.
Australia 61 2 9777 8600 Brazil 5511 3048 4500 Europe 44 20 7330 7500 Germany 49 69 920410
Hong Kong 852 2977 6000 Japan 81 3 3201 8900 Singapore 65 6212 1000 U.S. 1 212 318 2000 Copyright 2004 Bloomberg L.P.
G657-802-0 12-Feb-04 8:35:58

5 Corporate Debt Markets

In this and the next 11 chapters we review the corporate bond markets. The corporate markets cover a wide range of instruments and issuer currencies. There is a great variety of structures and products traded in the corporate markets, many of which easily could be the subject of separate books in their own right. All instruments serve the same primary purpose however, of serving as an instrument of corporate finance. The exotic structures that exist have usually been introduced in order to attract new investors, or retain existing investors, in what is an extremely competitive market.

Generally the term 'corporate markets' is used to cover bonds issued by non-government borrowers. The bonds issued by regional governments and certain public sector bodies, such as national power and telecommunications utilities, are usually included as 'government' debt, as they almost always are covered by an explicit or implicit government guarantee. All other categories of borrower are therefore deemed to be 'corporate' borrowers. The combined market is a large one. Table 5.1 shows non-government international bond issuance from 1996, split by currency. The majority of bonds are denominated in US dollars, euros, and Japanese yen.

The euro, introduced in twelve countries of the European Union in January 1999, has already become a popular currency for corporate bond issuers. This is indicated in Figure 5.1 which shows that the volume of issues in the euro currency was already over twice that in the first eight months of the year compared to issue volumes for the twelve currencies separately during the whole of 1998. Corporate bond issues in sterling are detailed in Figure 5.2, split into maturity bands of short-, medium- and long-dated bond issues.

5.1 Introduction

Corporate bonds are tradeable debt instruments issued by non-government borrowers. The majority of corporate bonds are plain vanilla instruments, paying a fixed coupon and with a fixed term to maturity. Corporate debt covers a wide range of instruments traded in the primary and secondary markets. Corporate issuers will use the debt capital markets to raise finance for short-, medium- and long-term requirements and projects. Corporate borrowers

	US$	Sterling	Euro	Other	Total
2000	261	51	153	108	573
2001	334	63	148	86	631
2002	342	78	209	65	693
2003*	249	52	260	38	599

* January-June 2003
Volumes are $ billion

Table 5.1: Non-government international bond issuance. Source: CapitalData Bondware; Bank of England.

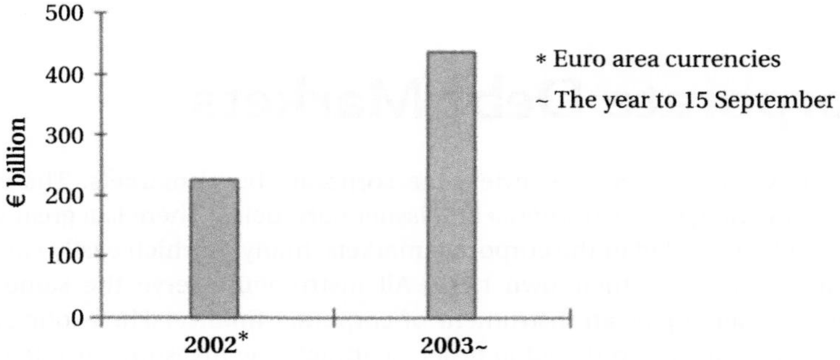

Figure 5.1: International bonds issued in euro. Source: *The Economist.*

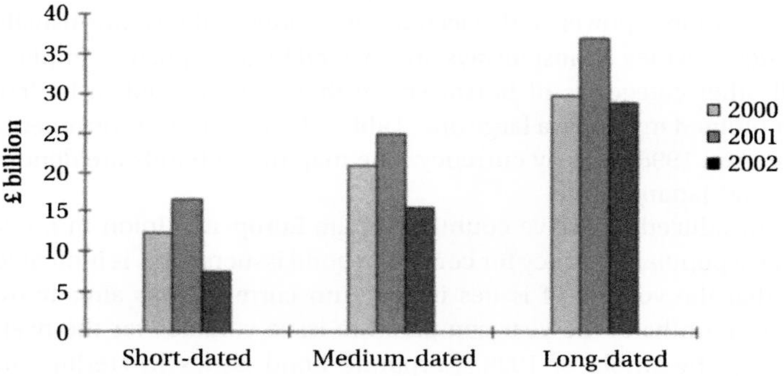

Figure 5.2: Sterling non-government bond issuance. Source: BoE.

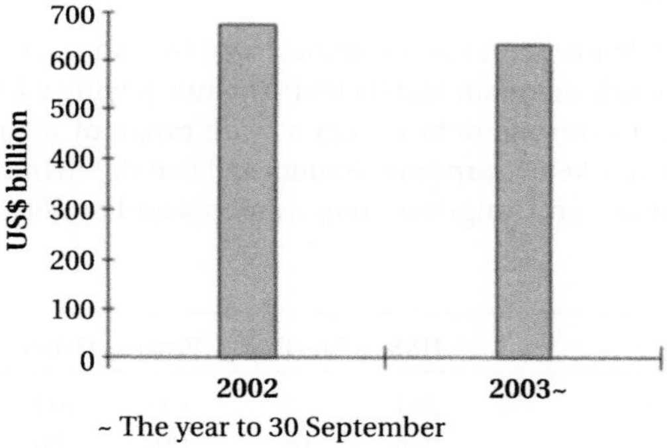

Figure 5.3: US dollar corporate bond issuance. Source: BoE.

will raise both *secured* and *unsecured debt*, with the former type of borrowing secured on assets of the company. The ease with which a corporation can raise unsecured finance in the public market is a function of its *credit rating*. Often corporate bonds are classified by the type of issuer, for example banks and financial services companies, utility companies and so on. Issuer classification is then broken down further, for example utility companies will be subdivided into electricity companies, water companies and gas distribution companies.

Under the terms of any corporate bond issue, the borrower is obliged to pay the periodic interest on the loan, represented by the coupon rate, as well as repay the principal on maturity of the debt. If the borrower fails to pay interest on the loan as it is due, or to repay the principal on maturity, this is known as *default* and the borrower will be in breach of the terms of the issue. This is a serious event. In the event of default[1] bondholders are entitled to enforce payment via the legal process and the courts. As providers of debt finance, bondholders rank higher than preferred and ordinary shareholders in the event of a winding-up of the company. Depending on the level of the *security* associated with the particular bond issue, bondholders may rank ahead of other creditors. The issue of the *credit risk* of a specific issuer is the key concern for corporate bond investors.

The yield on corporate bonds is set by the market and reflects the credit quality of the issuer of the paper, as well as the other considerations relevant to price setting such as level of liquidity, yield on similar bonds, supply and demand and general market conditions. Yields are always at a *spread* above the similar maturity government bond. A well-received corporate bond will trade at a relatively low spread over the government yield curve. Although the common perception is that bonds are held by investors for their income, and are less price volatile than equities, this is an over-generalisation. Certain bonds are highly volatile, while others are held for their anticipated price appreciation.

Certain corporate issues are aimed at only the professional (institutional) market and have minimum denominations of $10,000 or £10,000. Generally however they are issued in denominations of $1,000 (or £1,000, €1,000, etc). In the US domestic market the par value for corporate bonds is sometimes taken to be $1,000 instead of the more conventional $100. A market order to purchase '100 bonds' (or simply '100') would therefore mean $100,000 nominal of the bond. In other markets though the standard convention is followed of using 100 as the par value of the bond.

5.1.1 *Basic provisions*

The majority of corporate bonds are term bonds, that is, they will have a fixed term to maturity, at which point they must be redeemed by the borrower. Only companies of the highest quality can issue bonds of maturity much greater than 10 years at anything less than prohibitive cost; however it is common to see long-dated bonds of up to 30 years maturity or longer issued by high credit-quality companies. Let us look at some other relevant features.

- **Bond security.** A corporate that is seeking lower cost debt, or that does not have a sufficiently high credit rating, may issue secured debt. As security the issuer will pledge either fixed assets such as land and buildings, or personal property. The security offered may be *fixed*, in which case a specific asset is tied to the loan, or *floating*, meaning that the general assets of the company are offered as security for the loan, but not any specific asset. A *mortgage debenture* gives bondholders a charge over the pledged assets, called a *lien* (a lien is a legal right to sell mortgaged property to satisfy unpaid obligations

[1] The term *technical default* is used to refer to non-payment or delay of a coupon as it becomes due, when the issuer is still otherwise financially solvent.

to creditors). Where companies do not own fixed assets or other real property they often offer as collateral securities of other companies that they hold. A *debenture* bond is secured not by a specific pledge of property but bondholders have a claim over company assets in general, often ahead of other creditors.

- **Provisions for paying off bonds.** In some cases a corporate issue will have a call provision that gives the issuer the option to buy back all or part of the issue before maturity. The issuer will find a call option useful as it means that debt can be refinanced when market interest rates drop below the rate currently being paid, without having to wait until the bond's maturity. At the same time such a provision is disadvantageous to the bondholder, who will require a higher yield as compensation. Call provisions can take various forms. There may be a requirement for the issuer to redeem a pre-determined amount of the issue at regular intervals. Such a provision is known as a *sinking fund* requirement. This type of provision for repayment of corporate debt may be designed to retire all of a bond issue by the maturity date, or it may be arranged to pay off only a part of the total by the end of the term. If only a part is paid off, the remaining balance is known as a *balloon maturity*. The purpose of a sinking fund is to reduce the credit risk attached to the bond. Investors will derive comfort from the fact that provisions have been made regarding the final redemption of the bond, and will be more willing to buy the bond. Clearly this may be necessary for borrowers of lower credit quality.

In most cases the issuer will satisfy any sinking fund requirement by either making a cash payment of the face amount of the bonds to be redeemed to the bond trustee, who will call the bonds for repayment by drawing serial numbers randomly, or by delivering to the trustee bonds with a total face value equal to the amount that must be retired from bonds purchased in the open market. The sinking fund call price, as with callable bonds generally, is the par value of the bonds, although in a few cases there may be a set percentage of par that is redeemable.

These are only a sample of the features that can be attached to corporate bonds. We will consider them and certain others in the remainder of this chapter and in the following chapters.

5.2 Determinants of the development of a corporate market

Corporate bond markets generally develop after a functioning market in government securities has been established. A study by the International Monetary Fund[2] has found that six general areas of the debt markets, concerned with the infrastructure and regulation of the markets, are generally required to be in place before corporate markets can develop. Some of these six areas are described below.

- **Money markets.** The IMF study found that an already established and liquid money market will facilitate the development of a corporate market. This is essentially because in order to develop a yield curve against which corporate debt can be priced, the short-end of the yield curve must be established first, as short-date rates form the

[2] Schinasi and Todd Smith, IMF Working Paper 98/173, 1998. The full reference is stated in the bibliography.

cornerstone for longer-dated benchmark interest rates (Schinasi states that the short-end 'anchors' the rest of the yield curve). A liquid market in short-term instruments serves as a benchmark for corporate bonds that offer different levels of liquidity, credit quality and terms to maturity. A well-established money market, particularly a repo market, also enables market participants to finance both long and short positions in other bond instruments.

- **Regulatory infrastructure.** A common observation is that regulatory policies have an influence in either encouraging or inhibiting the development of a corporate market. Generally the essential prerequisite is that *supervision* provision should be well established in order to provide comfort to investors that the market is well policed. However regulation should not be unnecessarily cumbersome or bureaucratic as this will drive business elsewhere. Overly strict financial regulations often result in the growth of 'offshore' markets, witness the development of the Eurobond market in London and the growth of Singapore and Hong Kong as financial trading centres for the products of several Asian countries. Capital controls in the United States are said to have been the prime factor behind the development of the 'Eurodollar' market, the offshore market in US dollars.[3] This is a topical issue, for instance towards the end of 1999 the European Union, as part of an effort to harmonise tax policies across its member countries, was debating the introduction of a withholding tax for cross-border investments. The UK government was resisting the implementation of such a tax, on the grounds that this would drive the Eurobond market away from London, with a consequent loss in trading income and employment opportunities. Excessive regulation and taxation policies are considered to be partly behind the slow growth of the money markets in countries such as France, Germany, Italy and Japan; for example the *commercial paper* market in these countries has grown only slowly.[4] Taxation policies also impact the development of markets, and may serve to force debt issuance offshore. It is common for developed markets to allow gross payment of coupon to overseas investors, while corporate accounting policy often enables companies to offset the interest payable on debt against their income tax liability.
- **Investor base.** Another ingredient that is believed to be important in the development of corporate debt markets is a professional and diversified investor base. In advanced economies it is institutional investors such as life companies and pension funds that are the largest investing firms. At the shorter end of the yield curve, banks and corporates are important investors. In the US, money market mutual funds are also heavily invested in short-dated instruments. An institutional investor base will lead to a demand for corporate debt, which will facilitate the market's development.

Other areas cited by the IMF study (1998) include the concentration of market power amongst financial firms and the culture of corporate finance in the domestic market.

---

3 The term 'Eurodollar' originally referred to a deposit of US dollars outside the United States, originally in Europe. A Eurodollar deposit can of course be in any country outside of the US, not just in Europe.

4 See Alworth and Borio (1993).

5.3 The primary market

The issue of corporate debt in the capital markets requires a primary market mechanism. The first requirement is a collection of merchant banks or investment banks that possess the necessary expertise. Investment banks provide advisory services on corporate finance as well as *underwriting* services, which is a guarantee to place an entire bond issue into the market in return for a fee.[5] As part of the underwriting process the investment bank will either guarantee a minimum price for the bonds, or aim to place the paper at the best price available. The IMF study (1998) notes that investment banking expertise is something that is acquired over time. This is one reason why the major underwriting institutions in emerging economies are often branch offices of the major integrated global investment banks.

Small size bond issues may be underwritten by a single bank. It is common however for larger issues, or issues that are aimed at a cross-border investor base, to be underwritten by a *syndicate* of investment banks. This is a group of banks that collectively underwrite a bond issue, with each syndicate member being responsible for placing a proportion of the issue. The bank that originally won the *mandate* to place the paper invites other banks to join the syndicate. This bank is known as the *lead underwriter, lead manager* or *book-runner*. An issue is brought to the market simultaneously by all syndicate members, usually via the *fixed price re-offer* mechanism. This is designed to guard against some syndicate members in an offering selling stock at a discount in the grey market, to attract investors, which would force the lead manager to buy the bonds back if it wished to support the price. Under the fixed price re-offer method, price undercutting is not possible as all banks are obliged not to sell their bonds below the initial offer price that has been set for the issue. The fixed price usually is in place up to the first settlement date, after which the bond is free to trade in the secondary market.

A corporate debt issue is priced over the same currency government bond yield curve. A liquid benchmark yield curve therefore is required to facilitate pricing. The extent of a corporate bond's yield spread over the government yield curve is a function of the market's view of the credit risk of the issuer (for which formal credit ratings are usually used) and the perception of the liquidity of the issue. The pricing of corporate bonds is sometimes expressed as a spread over the equivalent maturity government bond, rather than as an explicit stated yield, or sometimes as a spread over another market reference index such as Libor. If there is no government bond of the same maturity as the corporate bond, the issuing bank will price the bond over an interpolated yield, obtained from the yields of two government bonds with maturities lying either side of the corporate issue. If there is no government bond that has a maturity beyond the corporate issue, the practice in developed economies is to take a spread over the longest dated government issue. In developing markets however, the bond would probably not be issued.

Formal credit ratings are important in the corporate markets. Investors usually use both a domestic rating agency in conjunction with an established international agency such as Moody's or Standard & Poor's. As formal ratings are viewed as important by investors, it is

---

[5] If the bank cannot sell an entire issue to its customers or other institutions in the market, it will take the remaining stock onto its own books. The fee payable by the borrower is compensation to the bank for taking on this underwriting risk.

in the interest of issuing companies to seek a rating from an established agency, especially if it is seeking to issue foreign currency debt and/or place its debt across national boundaries.

5.4 The secondary market

Corporate bonds virtually everywhere are traded on an over-the-counter (OTC) basis, that is, directly between counterparties over the telephone. Bonds are usually listed on an exchange though, as many institutional investors have limitations on the extent to which they may hold non-listed instruments. Eurobonds for example are usually listed on the London Stock Exchange or Luxembourg Stock Exchange, while those issued by Asian borrowers are frequently also listed on the Hong Kong or Singapore exchanges. In the United States there are more corporate bond issues listed on the New York Stock Exchange (NYSE) than there are equities, and the dollar value of daily bond trading is at least as high as that in equities. On the NYSE a low volume of trading in bonds does take place on the exchange itself, but this dwarfed by the volume of trading in the OTC market.

The level of liquidity varies greatly for corporate bonds, ranging from completely liquid (for example, a World Bank global bond issue) to completely illiquid, which is common when investors have bought the entire issue of a bond and held it to maturity. The number of market makers in a particular issue will also determine its liquidity. In return for providing liquidity, market makers also retain a major market privilege because they have exclusive access to inter-dealer broker price screens.

Another factor that is important to secondary market liquidity is the clearance and settlement system. In Japan for example, the settlement system until very recently was a decentralised, paper-based system, which acted as a barrier to market liquidity. A computerised, de-materialised 'book-entry' system for settling corporate bonds, as represented by Euroclear and Clearstream, contributes to liquidity because it assists market participants to trade without being exposed to delivery or payment risk.

Total issues	**1985**	**1990**	**1991**	**1992**	**1993**	**1994**	**1995**	**1996**	**1997**	**1998**
	165.7	299.9	389.8	471.1	646.6	498	573.2	n.a.	n.a.	n.a.
By type of offering:										
Public, domestic	119.6	189.3	286.9	379.1	486.9	365.2	408.8	386.3	397.2	374.1
Private placement, domestic	46.2	87	74.9	65.9	116.2	76.1	87.5	n.a.	n.a.	78.4
Foreign sales and other issues *	–	23.6	28.0	27.1	43.5	56.7	76.9	74.8	79.2	n.a.
By industry:										
Manufacturing	52.1	53.1	86.6	82.1	88.0	43.4	61.1	42.0	58.5	55.4
Commercial and miscellaneous	15.1	40.0	36.7	43.1	60.4	40.7	50.7	34.1	41.3	38.0
Transportation	5.7	12.7	13.6	9.8	10.8	6.9	8.4	5.1	6.9	5.5
Public utility	13.0	17.5	23.9	49.1	56.3	13.3	13.8	8.2	9.7	8.9
Communication	10.5	6.7	9.4	15.4	32.0	13.3	23.0	13.3	18.5	15.3
Real estate and financial	69.3	169.3	219.6	272.9	394.1	380.4	416.3	358.5	386.4	378.1

* Includes foreign sales only.

Note: Includes all debt security issues with a maturity greater than one year.

Table 5.2: Bond market financing by US Firms (in US$ billion).
Source: Federal Reserve Bulletin.

	Households	Foreign	Banks	Insurance	Private pensions	Public pensions	Mutual funds	Brokers dealers	Others
1985	9.4	14.3	11.7	35.6	11.3	12.2	2.9	2.6	0
1992	12.6	12.8	11.3	38.5	8.8	9.9	4.5	1.7	0
1993	16.2	12.5	10.7	37.1	8.8	6.9	5.7	2.2	0
1994	14.5	12.3	10.4	36.9	9.2	7.2	6.9	2.5	0
1995	14.6	11.8	9.6	35.5	9.1	6.8	8.7	3.2	0.7
1996	13.7	12.7	9	36.1	9.5	6.6	8.2	2.6	1.5
1997	15.1	13.3	8	35.2	9.7	5.8	8.3	2.8	1.8
1998	14.4	13.7	7.7	35.2	9.8	6	8.6	2.7	1.9

Table 5.3: Holders of US Corporate and Yankee bonds (in per cent of total). Source: Flow of Funds, Board of Governors of the Federal Reserve Board; IMF.

5.5 Fundamentals of corporate bonds

The market generally classifies corporate bonds by credit rating and by sector of issuer. In the US for example issuers are classified as public utilities, transport companies, industrial companies, banking and financial institutions, and international (or *Yankee*) borrowers. Within these broad categories issuers are broken down further, for example transportation companies are segmented into airlines, railway companies and road transport companies. In other respects corporate bonds have similar characteristics to those described in Chapter 1, although it is often in the corporate market that exotic or engineered instruments are encountered, compared to the generally plain vanilla government market.

5.5.1 *Term to maturity*

In the corporate markets, bond issues usually have a stated term to maturity, although the term is often not fixed because of the addition of call or put features. The convention is for most corporate issues to be medium- or long-dated, and rarely to have a term greater than 20 years. In the US market prior to the Second World War it was once common for companies to issue bonds with maturities of 100 years or more, but this is now quite rare. Only the highest rated companies find it possible to issue bonds with terms to maturity greater than 30 years; during the 1990s such companies included Coca-Cola, Disney and British Gas.

Investors prefer to hold bonds with relatively short maturities because of the greater price volatility experienced in the markets since the 1970s, when high inflation and high interest rates were common. A shorter-dated bond has lower interest rate risk and price volatility compared to a longer-dated bond. There is thus a conflict between investors, whose wish is to hold bonds of shorter maturities, and borrowers, who would like to fix their borrowing for as long a period as possible. Although certain institutional investors such as pension fund managers have an interest in holding 30-year bonds, it would be difficult for all but the largest, best-rated companies, to issue debt with a maturity greater than this.

5.5.2 *Bond interest payment*

Corporate bonds pay a fixed or floating-rate coupon. Floating-rate bonds were reviewed in Chapter 4. Zero-coupon bonds are also popular in the corporate market, indeed corporate zero-coupon bonds differ from zero-coupon bonds in government markets in that they are actually issued by the borrower, rather than simply being the result of a market-maker stripping a conventional coupon bond.

The fixed interest rate payable by a conventional bond is called the bond *coupon*, and we used this term when describing bonds in Chapter 1. The term originates from the time when bonds were *bearer* instruments, and were issued with coupons attached to them. The bondholder would tear off each coupon and post it to the issuer as each interest payment became due. These days bonds are *registered* instruments, and the investor receives the interest payment automatically from the issuer's registrar or paying agent. Therefore it is technically incorrect to refer to a bond's 'coupon' but the convention persists from earlier market infrastructure. Many bond issues including Eurobonds and US Treasuries are held in 'de-materialised' form, which means only one 'global' certificate is issued, which is held with the clearing or custody agent, and investors receive a computer print-out detailing their bond holding.

Zero-coupon bonds are issued in their own right in the corporate markets, but are otherwise similar to zero-coupon bonds in government markets. Note that the term 'strip' for a zero-coupon bond is usually used only in the context of a government bond strip. In the US market zero-coupon bonds or 'zeros' were first issued in 1981 and initially offered tax advantages for investors, who avoided the income tax charge associated with coupon bonds.[6] However the tax authorities in the US implemented legislation that treated the capital gain on zeros as income, thus wiping out the tax advantage. The tax treatment for zeros is similar in most jurisdictions. Zeros are still popular with investors however because they carry no reinvestment risk. The lack of reinvestment risk is appreciated more by investors in a declining interest rate environment, whereas in a rising interest rate environment investors may prefer to have coupons to reinvest. Zeros are also preferred during a period of relatively high interest rates, as the compounding effect is greater.

As a zero-coupon bond is issued at a discount to its face value, and then repaid at par, there is a significant liability for the borrower on maturity. For a long-dated bond this liability can be very large. This may be a concern for bondholders, so it is usually only highly-rated borrowers that are able to place zero-coupon bonds. Lower-rated borrowers in the US domestic market have issued *deferred-interest bonds*, also known as *zero/coupon bonds*. With a deferred-interest bond the investor receives no interest payments for a set period after issue, say the first five years of the bond's life. At the end of the deferred interest period, the accumulated interest is paid out. The rate payable is usually considerably higher than the market level. This feature makes the bond attractive for lower-rated companies or start-up companies who might be expected to suffer from cash-flow problems in their early years. The thinking behind deferred-interest bonds is that, after the no coupon period, the issuer will be in a financially stable state and able to pay off the accumulated interest, and indeed redeem the bond and refinance at a lower rate of interest.

In the case of default, bankruptcy laws in the US for example, allow the bondholder to claim back the value of the purchase price plus 'accrued' interest up to the time the issuer

---

6 The first offer of zero-coupon bonds was by J.C. Penney Co, Inc in the domestic US market in 1981.

when into liquidation. This value is essentially the value of the bond at the time. The face value of the bond of course, cannot be claimed.

5.6 Bond security

International bonds and bonds sold in the Euro markets are unsecured. It is sometimes said that the best type of security is a company in sound financial shape that is able to service its debt out of its general cash flow, or a company with a high credit rating. While this is undoubtedly true, a secured bond is sometimes preferred by investors. In domestic markets, corporate bonds are often issued with a form of security attached in order to make them more palatable to investors. The type of security that is offered varies and can be either *fixed* or *floating*, that is a specific or general charge on the assets of the borrowing company. The type of security sometimes defines the market that the bond trades in, for example a mortgage-backed bond or a debenture. We consider the main types of security below.

5.6.1 *Mortgage bonds*

A bond that is secured with a *lien* over some or all of the issuer's mortgaged properties is known as a *mortgage bond*. A lien is the legal right to sell mortgaged property in the event that the borrower is unable to meet obligations arising from its bond issue. The coupon payable is lower than would otherwise be payable if the bond was issued without a first charge on the issuer's properties. In the US market such an unsecured bond is called a *debenture*, although confusingly a debenture in the UK domestic market is a bond that *is* secured, although on a floating rather than fixed asset.

An example of a bond with collateral in the form of a charge over property is the Annington Finance No. 4 plc issue (AF4), which dates from December 1997. This is a sterling bond and is described in Example 5.1 below.

Example 5.1: Annington Finance No. 4 plc

- Annington Finance is a public limited company incorporated in England, whose share capital is owned by Annington Homes Limited, a subsidiary of Annington Holdings plc. The holding company was established in 1996 to purchase housing stock from the United Kingdom's Ministry of Defence (MoD), who had previously run the housing for the benefit of members of the country's armed forces and their families. This housing was known as the Married Quarters Estate (MQE). Annington Holdings plc purchased the housing stock from the MoD and then leased it back to it.

  As part of the purchase proceeds, Annington Holdings plc issued bonds secured on the assets themselves. The bonds consisted of:

  £1.24 billion Class A Zero-coupon notes due December 2022
  £1 billion Class B Zero-coupon notes due January 2023
  £900 million Secured floating-rate notes due January 2023

  The floating-rate notes pay interest at Libor plus 40 basis points up to 2008, after which the interest steps up to Libor plus 100 basis points. The issuer has an option to redeem the floating-rate notes after 2008.

The collateral for the issue consists of a first fixed security on the housing stock of the MQE, which is made up of 760 sites throughout the UK and approximately 55,000 housing units. The MQE was leased back to the MoD who pay rental fees on it. The cash flows for the bond issue are financed by these rental proceeds, as well as the proceeds from the occasional disposal of individual residential properties. On the basis of this security the bonds were rated 'A2' by Moody's and 'A' by Fitch IBCA. Duff & Phelps rated the class A notes as 'AAA' and the other notes as 'A'. The class A notes rank ahead of the class B notes. On maturity the issuer is required to repay the interest and principal outstanding on all the notes.

Mortgage bonds may be issued as part of a *series*. This often happens when companies wish to finance their operations continuously through the issue of long-dated debt. This means that as one bond issue matures, another series is issued under the same mortgage.

There are restrictions on the amount of debt that may be issued with a charge over the same property. Generally the terms of a mortgage bond issue state that property purchased by the borrower after the issue of the bonds is still covered by the lien attached to those bonds. This is known as an *after-acquired clause*. Additional borrowing secured by the properties is usually set as a percentage of the value of the after-acquired assets.

5.6.2 *Other collateral*

Debt is often issued by firms that do not possess fixed assets such as property or factories. These companies may offer security for bonds they issue in the form of other collateral that they own, such as government bonds and bonds and equity of other companies. In the US market bonds that have been secured with collateral of this form are known as *collateral trust bonds*. Assuming the bonds are issued at par, the nominal value of an issue is always lower than the market value of the collateral pledged, to provide an element of safety for investors. Under the terms of the issue the borrower delivers the collateral that has been pledged into the safe custody of the bond's trustee or paying agent, which will hold them for the term of the bond's life. In the event of default, bondholders are entitled to ownership of the collateral; if part of this is equity, the voting rights of the equity are transferred to the bondholders at the same time.

Terms of issue of a collateral trust bond include certain provisions to protect investors. The main one is that the value of the collateral must remain at a specified level above the nominal value of the bonds, and if there is decline in value of the collateral the issuer must provide additional collateral to make up the shortfall. This is similar to a margin call in a repo transaction.

5.6.3 *Debentures*

In the US market a debenture bond is one that is not secured by a pledge on a specific fixed asset or property. Bondholders have only a claim on the assets of the issuer in the event of default in line with general creditors. In the UK market a *debenture* is a secured bond, one that is secured on the general assets of the issuing company rather than a specified fixed asset.

US market debentures generally are of two types, those that are issued by highly-rated borrowers who do not need necessarily to provide security for investors, and those issued by borrowers who have already issued bonds secured on their assets, such as mortgage bonds. This second type of debenture pays a higher coupon than both the other debentures as well as the secured bonds of its issuer. A company that has debenture bonds outstanding but no secured bonds may provide a *negative pledge clause*, which states that the debenture issue will rank equally with any secured bonds that may be issued subsequently. This protects existing bondholders. Other terms under which the bonds are issued include a limitation on the amount of dividends that the company can pay, or the proportion of current earnings that can be used to pay a dividend. With share dividends themselves becoming increasingly unfashionable in the US, these restrictions are seen less in the domestic bond market.

5.6.4 *Subordinated bonds*

Debt issued by companies that ranks behind both secured debt and debentures is known as *subordinated* debt. A subordinated bond therefore has the highest credit risk of any domestic bond issue, because it is not backed with security of any kind. As well as ranking behind secured bonds and debentures, subordinated bonds may also in some cases rank after other creditors such as trade creditors. For this reason subordinated bonds pay the among the highest yields in a domestic market. They are often issued with other features that are designed to make them more attractive. Such features may include an option to convert the bond into the ordinary shares of the issuing company at a specified date or dates. A bond with such a feature is then a *convertible*. Another common feature is a *step-up* feature, which states that the bond will pay a higher coupon after a set period of time, say ten years if it is not redeemed at that point. The higher coupon is often set at a punitive rate, say 100 basis points higher than the initial coupon, which acts as an incentive to the issuer to redeem the bond after the initial period. Step-up subordinated bonds are common in the sterling market, in both fixed-date and perpetual form, and have been issued by smaller borrowers such as independent merchant banks.[7]

The US market has also been tapped by borrowers issuing subordinated bonds that are convertible into the ordinary shares of another company. These are known as *exchangeable bonds*.

5.7 Redemption provisions

Highly-rated corporate borrowers often are able to issue bonds without indicating specifically how they will be redeemed (by implication, maturity proceeds will be financed out of the company's general cash flows or by the issue of another bond). This luxury is not always available to borrowers with low ratings. To make their debt issue more palatable to investors, they may make specific provisions for paying off a bond issue on its maturity date. We consider the most common provisions in this section.

---

7 For example in 1994 perpetual step-up sterling notes were issued by banks such as NM Rothschild, Barings and Robert Fleming.

5.7.1 *Sinking funds*

The term *sinking fund* originally referred to a ring-fenced sum of cash that was put aside to form the proceeds used in the repayment of a fixed-term bond. Although the operation of sinking funds has since changed, the term is still used. Essentially a sinking fund facility is where a set proportion of a bond issue is redeemed every year, say 5% of the nominal value, until the final year when the remaining outstanding amount is repaid. This outstanding amount is known as a *balloon maturity*. Although it is still possible to encounter the original type of sinking fund, the majority of them are those that pay off a small part of an issue each year during its life. Sinking funds that are set up for and apply to a specific issue are known as *specific* sinking funds. There are also sinking funds that are set up by issuers and apply to their entire range of bonds. These are known as *blanket* or *aggregate* sinking funds.

In most cases the issuer will pass the correct cash proceeds to the bond's trustee, who will use a lottery method to recall bonds representing the proportion of the total nominal value outstanding that is being repaid. The trustee usually publishes the serial numbers of bonds that are being recalled in a newspaper such as *The Wall Street Journal* or the *Financial Times*. Another method by which bonds are repaid is that the issuer will purchase the required nominal value of the bonds in the open market; these are then delivered to the trustee, who cancels them. There are two types of sinking funds, those that pay off the same amount of the issue each year, say 5% of the outstanding nominal value, or those that pay a progressively greater amount each year, say 5% in the first year and then 1% more each year until maturity, when the entire amount is redeemed. It is common to find utility and energy companies in the US that have bond sinking funds that incorporate this variable provision. A *doubling option* in a sinking fund entitles the issuer to repay double the amount that was originally specified as going to be repaid, while a provision that allows the issuer to repay an amount larger than the specified value is known as an *accelerated provision.*

The price at which bonds are redeemed by a sinking fund is usually par. If a bond has been issued above par, the sinking fund may retire the bonds at the issue price and gradually decrease this each year until it reaches par. Sinking funds reduce the credit risk applying to a bond issue, because they indicate to investors that provision has been made to repay the debt. However there is a risk associated with holding them, in that at the time bonds are paid off they may be trading above par due to a decline in market interest rates. In this case investors will suffer a loss if it is their holding that is redeemed.

5.7.2 *Redemption and asset sales*

Bonds that are secured through a charge on fixed assets such as property or plant often have certain clauses in their offer documents that state that the issuer cannot dispose of the assets without making provision for redemption of the bonds, as this would weaken the collateral backing for the bond. These clauses are known as *release-of-property* and *substitution-of-property* clauses. Under these clauses, if property or plant is disposed, the issuer must use the proceeds (or part of the proceeds) to redeem bonds that are secured by the disposed assets. The price at which the bonds are retired under this provision is usually par, although a special redemption price other than par may be specified in the repayment clause.

5.7.3 *Call and refund provisions*

A large number of corporate bonds, especially in the US market, have a call provision on dates ahead of the stated maturity date. Borrowers prefer to have this provision attached to their bonds as it enables them to refinance debt at cheaper levels when market interest rates have fallen significantly below the level they were at at the time of the bond issue. A call provision is a negative feature for investors, as bonds are only paid off if their price has risen above par. Although a call feature indicates an issuer's interest in paying off the bond, because they are not attractive for investors callable bonds pay a higher yield than non-callable bonds of the same credit quality and maturity.

In general callable bonds are not callable for the first five or 10 years of their life, a feature that grants an element of protection for investors. Thereafter a bond is usually callable on set dates up to the final maturity date. In the US market another restriction is the *refunding redemption.* This prohibits repayment of bonds within a set period after issue with funds obtained at a lower interest rate or through issue of bonds that rank with or ahead of the bond being redeemed. A bond with refunding protection during the first five or 10 years of its life is not as attractive to a borrower as a bond with absolute call protection. Bonds that are called are usually called at par, although it is common also for bonds to have a call schedule that states that they are redeemable at specified prices above par during the call period.

There are also bonds that are callable in part rather than in whole. In this case the issuer or trustee will select the bonds to be repaid on a random basis, with the serial numbers of the bonds being called published in major news publications.

5.8 Corporate bond risks

The market risks associated with holding corporate bonds are identical to those reviewed in Chapter 1. Corporate bonds however hold additional risk for investors, unlike the developed market government bonds that were (implicitly) the subject of the earlier chapters. In this section we introduce the additional risks to investors of holding corporate debt.

5.8.1 *Credit risk*

Unlike a (developed economy) government bond, holding a corporate bond exposes investors to *credit risk,* also known as *default risk.* This is the risk that the issuing company will default on its bond's coupon payments or principal repayment, resulting in a loss to the bondholders. Default may occur due to general financial difficulties, which may turn out to be short-term in nature, or a prelude to bankruptcy and liquidation. In the most extreme case it may be many years, if ever, before investors receive some of their money back.

The price of a corporate bond reflects the market's view of the credit risk associated with holding it. If the credit risk is perceived to be low, the *spread* of the issuer's bonds over the equivalent-maturity government bond will be low, while if the credit risk is deemed to be high, the yield spread will be correspondingly higher. This yield spread is sometimes referred to as the *credit spread* or *quality spread.* A 10-year bond issued by a

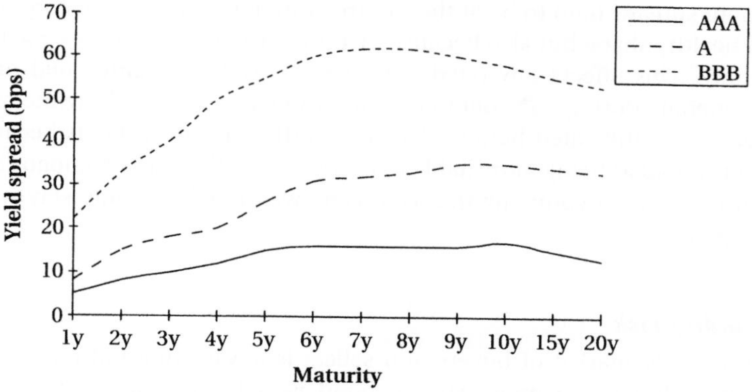

Figure 5.4: Credit structure of interest rates.

highly rated corporate borrower will have a lower spread than a 10-year bond issued by a borrower with a lower credit rating. The higher yield on the bond issued by the lower-rated borrower is the compensation required by investors for holding the paper. Bond issuers are rated for their credit risk by both investment houses' internal credit analysts and by formal rating agencies such as Standard & Poor's, Moody's, and Fitch.

Figure 5.4 illustrates an hypothetical 'credit structure of interest rates'. The credit structure is dynamic and will fluctuate with changes in market conditions and the general health of the economy.

Credit spreads over government yields and between corporate borrowers of different credit quality fluctuate with market conditions and in line with the business cycle. Spreads are highest when an economy is in a recession and corporate health is relatively weak. A significant downward market correction also tends to widen credit spreads as investors embark on a 'flight to quality' that depresses government bond yields. At the height of an

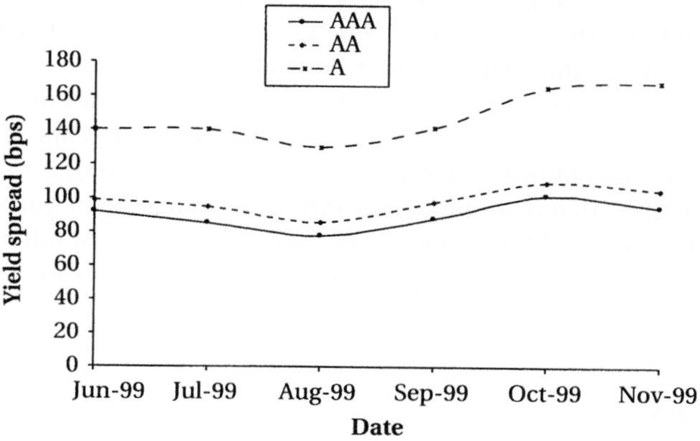

Figure 5.5: Sterling bonds 10-year yield spreads over gilts. Source: Halifax plc.

economic boom spreads tend to be at their narrowest, not only because corporate balance sheets are in healthy shape but also because investors become less risk averse in times of a strong economy. This affects low-rated borrowers as well as highly-rated ones, so that spreads fall generally during an economic boom. In Figure 5.4 note how the credit spread for the hypothetical BBB-rated bonds falls as maturity increases; this is because analysts view the credit spread as being more liable to improve over time, as a company is upgraded, while a bond issued by a company that is already well-rated can only stay where it is or suffer a downgrade.

5.8.2 *Liquidity risk*

A bond with a ready market of buyers and sellers is always more attractive to investors than one that is difficult to trade. Such a bond is called a *liquid* bond. Liquidity is a function of the ease with which market participants may buy or sell a particular bond, the number of market makers that are prepared to quote prices for the bond, and the spread between the buying and selling price (the bid-offer spread). Illiquid bonds will have wide spreads and perhaps a lack of market makers willing to quote a bid price for them. Although some government bonds can sometimes be illiquid, liquidity risk, which is the risk that a bond held by an investor becomes illiquid, is primarily a corporate bond market risk. The yield on a bond that is, or about to become, illiquid, will be marked up by the market in compensation for the added risk of holding it. The best gauge of an issue's liquidity is the size of its bid-offer spread. Government bonds frequently have a spread of 0.03 per cent or less, which is considered very liquid. Corporate spreads are wider but a spread of 0.10 to 0.25, up to 0.50 of one per cent is considered liquid. A bid-offer spread wider than this is considered illiquid, while a spread of say 1% or more is virtually non-tradeable. Some bonds are not quoted with a bid price or an offer price, indicating they are completely illiquid.

5.8.3 *Call risk*

In the previous section we stated that many domestic bond issues in the US market have call or refunding features attached to them. Such callable bonds have an added risk associated with holding them, known as *call risk*. This is the risk that the bond will be called at a time and price that is disadvantageous to bondholders or exposes them to loss. For example consider a 10-year bond with a call provision that states that the bond may be called at any time after the first five years, at par. For the last five years of the bond's life, if market interest rates fall below the bond's coupon rate, the price of the bond will not rise above par by as much as that of a similar maturity (and similar credit quality) bond that has no call feature. The price/yield relationship of a bond callable at par differs from a conventional bond, as the price will be less responsive to downward moves in yield once the price is at par.

5.8.4 *Event risk*

Event risk is peculiar to corporate bonds. This is the risk that, as a result of an unexpected corporate event, the credit risk of a bond increases greatly, so that the yield of the bond rises

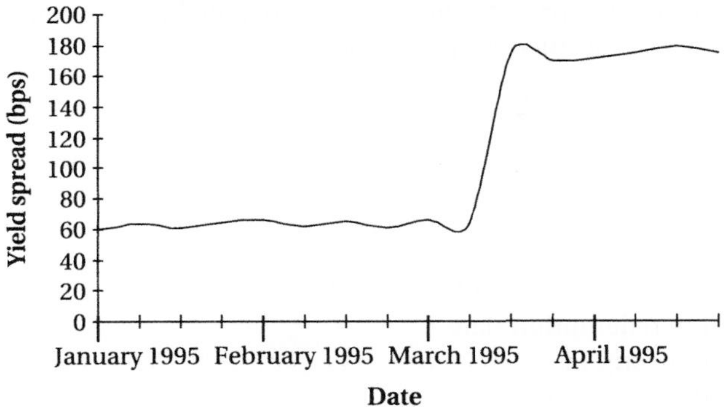

Figure 5.6: Impact of Barings Bank crisis on yield spread of bonds issued by similar companies. Source: ABN Amro Hoare Govett Sterling Bonds Limited.

very quickly to much higher levels. The events can be external to the company, such as a natural disaster or regulatory change, or internal such as a merger or acquisition. A natural disaster may be an earthquake or flood, while regulatory change might be a change in the accounting or tax treatment of certain types of corporate debt. Event risk can affect companies across an industry. An example of this was the fall of Barings Bank in 1995. The owners of Barings subordinated perpetual bonds suffered a loss as a result of the bankruptcy of the company, however holders of bonds issued by similar companies also suffered losses as the market marked the yields on these bonds up as well. Figure 5.6 shows the change in average yield spread for bonds issued by N.M. Rothschild and Robert Fleming at the time of the Barings crash.

A takeover is another example of an event that may result in loss for bondholders. For example if, as a result of a merger or takeover the debt of the amalgamated company is downgraded, bondholders will suffer a loss in capital value. To protect against event risk, bonds may have provisions in them that require an acquiring company to repurchase them, under specified conditions. Such provisions are known as *poison puts*. Other features that may be included in the terms of corporate bonds are *maintenance of net worth* and *offer to redeem* clauses. The former provision states that if an issue falls below a certain level of net worth, the borrower must redeem the bond at par. The latter clause is similar except that it does not apply to an entire issue, but only to those bonds whose holders wish to redeem.

5.8.5 *Spens clause*

In corporate markets a *Spens clause* is sometimes included in a bond's issue terms. This relates to the redemption proceeds of the bond. Under the terms of the clause, if there is a change in control of the issuing company, the company is required to redeem the notes within 45 days of the change of ownership. If the bonds are not redeemed in this time, bondholders may give notice to the issuer that the bond must be retired. The redemption amount is determined in accordance with (5.1) below, which essentially states that the yield at which the bond is redeemed is a spread over the benchmark government bond against which the corporate bond is priced. This spread is negotiable between the issuer and the bondholders, unless it is specified in the Spens clause itself.

$$P_{red} = \sum_{t=N_{red}}^{t=N_{mat}} \frac{(C+M)}{(1+ry)((t-N_{red})/B)} \tag{5.1}$$

where

P_{red}	is the redemption proceeds
N_{mat}	is the maturity date of the bond
N_{red}	is the redemption date
C	is the coupon
M	is the principal repayment
ry	is $(1 + \frac{rm}{2})^2 - 1$
rm	is the yield to maturity of the benchmark bond over which the bond is priced
t	is each coupon date and the number of days between N_{red} and N_{mat}
$t - N_{red}$	is the number of days between t and N_{red}
B	is the day-count base (360 or 265).

5.9 High-yield corporate bonds

High-yield bonds were developed in the US corporate bond market, and have not as yet emerged as a significant investment outside the dollar market, except perhaps in the UK. The bonds were previously known as *junk bonds*, and this term is still used occasionally. They refer to bond issues with very low credit ratings, typically below BBB (S&P rating). Bonds in this category may not necessarily have started life as high-yield debt; they may have been rated as investment grade when originally issued and then suffered successive rating downgrades until rated as non-investment grade. The majority of high-yield bonds however were rated as below investment grade at the time of issue. Some of the bond structures are quite sophisticated examples of financial engineering, as when they have been issued as part of a 'leveraged buy-out' finance package or as part of a re-capitalisation that results in higher levels of debt. For example a high-yield bond structure may include deferred coupons, with no coupon payments for a number of years after issue. This recognises the fact that the debt burden of the issuer may result in severe cash flow problems in the early years, so that coupons are deferred. Where there is a deferred coupon structure, the bond may include a *step-up* feature, so that after a period of time the coupon rate is increased, to compensate for the low (or zero) coupon rate at the start of the bond's life.

5.10 Corporate bond offering circular

The following is an example of a typical bond issue offering circular, relating to a plain vanilla US dollar bond issued by an hypothetical company in the Euro markets. The bond has been underwritten by an hypothetical syndicate of banks, with two hypothetical banks involved as joint lead-managers, Jones Brothers International (Europe) and John Paul George Corporation. The content of the circular is fairly representative of a bond issue in the international markets, and there will be differences where for example, the bond structure is not plain vanilla. These will only be detail differences however; the following can be taken to be a standard and fairly representative document.

OFFERING CIRCULAR

JACKFRUIT CORPORATION

(INCORPORATED IN SURREY, ENGLAND)

U.S. $500,000,000

6¾% Senior Notes due 7 June 2009

Issued pursuant to its

EURO MEDIUM-TERM NOTE PROGRAM

The U.S. $500,000,000 67/8 % Senior Notes due on 7 June 2009 (the 'Notes') of Jackfruit Corporation (the 'Issuer') will be issued pursuant to the Issuer's Euro Medium-Term Note Program (the 'Program'). Interest on the Notes will be payable annually on 7 June of each year, commencing on 7 June 1999, and at maturity. The Notes will not be redeemable prior to maturity except in certain circumstances affecting taxation, as more fully described in the Information Memorandum referred to below under the heading 'Terms and Conditions of the Notes.'

Applications have been made for listing of and permission to deal in the Notes on The Stock Exchange of Singapore Limited and The Stock Exchange of Hong Kong Limited, which are expected to be effective on or about 23 June 1998 and 24 June 1998, respectively. Application will be made to The London Stock Exchange Limited (the 'London Stock Exchange') for the Notes to be issued under the Issuer's Program, which will be amended in order to, among other things, increase the maximum principal amount of medium-term notes outstanding at any one time. An Information Memorandum and Information Memorandum Addendum, each expected to be dated 26 June 1998, together with the Issuer's Annual Report on for the year ended 31 December 1997 and its Quarterly Report for the quarter ended 31 March 1998, will comprise the listing particulars expected to be approved by the London Stock Exchange (the 'London Listing Particulars'). Draft copies of such documents expected to comprise the London Listing Particulars may be inspected during normal business hours on any weekday (excluding Saturdays) at the principal place of business of the Issuer and at the offices of the Fiscal Agent in London. It is expected that the Notes will be admitted to the Official List of the London Stock Exchange, subject to the satisfaction of certain conditions, with effect on or about 2 July 1998.

The Notes will initially be represented by a temporary global Note without coupons which will be deposited with a common depositary acting on behalf of Cedel Bank and Euroclear on or about 20 June 1998 and will be exchangeable for definitive Notes in bearer form with coupons not earlier than 30 July 1998, upon certification of non-U.S. beneficial ownership.

This Offering Circular (including the Pricing Supplement relating to the Notes set forth herein) is supplemental to, and should be read in conjunction with, the Information Memorandum and Information Memorandum Addendum, each dated 19 June 1997, as may be amended or superseded from time to time (collectively, the 'Information Memorandum'), which are annexed hereto. Terms defined in the Information Memorandum shall have the same meaning when used in this Offering Circular. References herein to 'Dollars,' '$' and 'U.S.$' are to the lawful currency of the United States of America.

JONES BROTHERS INTL (EUROPE)	**JOHN PAUL GEORGE CORPORATION**
NATIONAL CREDIT BANK	SANBIN INTERNATIONAL
AKERS MARKETS	HENRY MARSHALL SECURITIES LIMITED
STEGAS SECURITIES LIMITED	CAPE LIMITED
THE ABC BANK plc	CLAXTON CAPITAL MARKETS (EUROPE)
LIMITED	

The date of this document is 18 June 1998.

TERMS OF THE NOTES

The Terms and Conditions of the Notes will include the information set forth in the Information Memorandum under the heading 'Terms and Conditions of the Notes,' as supplemented and modified by the Pricing Supplement set forth below.

Pricing Supplement Dated 18 June, 1998

Jackfruit Corporation
U.S. $500,000,000
67/8% Senior Notes due 7 June 2009 (the 'Notes')
Issued pursuant to its
Euro Medium-Term Note Program

Terms used herein shall be deemed to be defined as such for the purposes of the Conditions; items in the form of pricing supplement included in the Information Memorandum that are not applicable to the Notes are omitted. The terms for the issue of the Notes are as follows:

TYPE OF NOTE

Form of Notes to be initially issued:	Temporary global Note in bearer form. Temporary Globe Note is exchangeable for a Permanent Global Note on 30 days'notice
Ranking	The Notes are Senior Notes and will constitute direct unconditional and unsecured obligations of the Issuer and will rank pari passu in right of payment with all outstanding unsecured senior debt of the Issuer
Fixed Rate/Floating Rate/Zero Coupon/ Original Issue Discount/Indexed Redemption Amount/Indexed Interest/Dual Currency/Partly Paid/ Installment/Extendible/Renewable/ combination/other:	Fixed Rate
Convertible automatically or at the option of the Issuer and/or Noteholders into Note(s) of another Interest Basis:	No

DESCRIPTION OF THE NOTES

Provisions for exchange of Notes:	Interests in the temporary global Note in bearer form are exchangeable for definitive Notes in bearer form on or after the Exchange Date following certification as to the non-U.S. beneficial ownership thereof.
Talons for future Coupons to be attached to definitive Notes in bearer form:	No
Series Number:	10
Nominal Amount (Face Amount) of Notes to be issued:	U.S. $500,000,000
Specified Currency:	United States Dollars
Specified Denomination (s):	U.S. $1,000, U.S. $10,000 and U.S. $100,00
Issue Price:	99.264%
Issue Date:	20 June 1998
Proceeds to Issuer:	U.S. $488,254,800

PROVISIONS RELATING TO INTEREST PAYABLE

Interest Basis:	Fixed Rate
Fixed Rate of Interest:	$6\frac{3}{4}$%
Fixed Interest Dates:	7 June of each year, beginning 7 June 1999

PROVISIONS REGARDING REDEMPTION/MATURITY

Maturity Date:	7 June 2009
Redemption at Issuer's option:	No, except in certain circumstances affecting taxation, as set forth in Condition 10(b)
Redemption at Noteholder's option:	No
Final Redemption Amount for each Note:	100%

GENERAL PROVISIONS APPLICABLE TO THIS ISSUE OF NOTES

Additional sales restrictions:

In addition to the sales restrictions set forth in the Information Memorandum under the heading 'Subscription and Sale,' the following restrictions apply:

United Kingdom: With regard to the United Kingdom, references to Article 11 (3) of the Financial Services Act 1986 (Investment Advertisements) (Exemptions) Order 1995 in the Information

Memorandum shall be deemed to refer to Article 11 (3) of the Financial Services Act 1986 (Investment Advertisements) (Exemptions) Order 1996 (as amended).

Hong Kong: Each Manager has represented and agreed that it has not offered or sold and will not offer or sell in Hong Kong by means of any document, any Notes other than to persons whose ordinary business it is to buy or sell shares or debentures (whether as principal or agent) or in circumstances which do not constitute an offer to the public within the meaning of the Companies Ordinance of Hong Kong.

Each Manager has represented and agreed that until such time as the listing of the Notes on The Stock Exchange of Hong Kong Limited has been formally approved or unless it is a person permitted to do so under the securities laws of Hong Kong, it has not issued or had in its possession for the purpose of issue, and will not issue or have in its possession for the purpose of issue, in Hong Kong, any advertisement, invitation or document relating to the Notes, other than with respect to Notes intended to be disposed of to persons outside Hong Kong or to be disposed of in Hong Kong only to persons whose business involves the acquisition, disposal or holding of securities, whether as principal or agent.

Singapore: No prospectus in connection with the offer of the Notes will be registered with the Registrar of Companies in Singapore and the Notes will be offered in Singapore pursuant to an exemption invoked under Section 106C of the Companies Act, Chapter 50 of Singapore (the 'Singapore Companies Act'). Accordingly each Manager has represented and agreed that documents or material prepared in connection with the offer of the Notes may not be, and have not been, circulated, and the Notes may not be, and have not been, offered or

	sold, directly or indirectly to the public or any member of the public in Singapore other than (i) to an institutional investor or other person specified in Section 106C of the Singapore Companies Act, (ii) to a sophisticated investor, and in accordance with the conditions, specified in Section 106D of the Singapore Companies Act or (iii) otherwise pursuant to, and in accordance with the conditions of, any other applicable provision of the Singapore Companies Act.
Method of distribution:	Syndicated Lead Managers: Jones Brothers International (Europe) John Paul George Corporation Co-Lead Managers: National Credit Bank Sanbin International Akers Securities Henry Marshall Securities Limited Stegas Securities The ABC Bank plc Claxton Capital Markets (Europe) Limited
Commissions:	0.275% Management and Underwriting 1.35% Selling
Stabilizing Dealer/Manager:	In connection with the issue of the Notes, Jones Brothers International (Europe) may over-allot or effect transactions which stabilize or maintain the market price of the Notes at a level which might not otherwise prevail. Such stabilizing, if commenced, may be discontinued at any time. Such stabilizing shall be in compliance with all relevant laws and regulations.
Notes to be listed: Stock Exchange(s):	Yes The London Stock Exchange Limited The Stock Exchange of Singapore Limited The Stock Exchange of Hong Kong Limited With regard to the London Stock Exchange listing of this issue of Notes, see 'Other terms or special conditions' below.
Common Code for Euroclear and Cedel Bank and ISIN:	Common Code: 001234554321 ISIN: XS001234554321

Selected bibliography

Alworth, J.S., Borio, C.E.V., 'Commercial Paper Markets: A Survey', BIS Economic Papers No. 37, Bank for International Settlements, 1993
Bank of England, *Quarterly Bulletin*, August 1999
Economist, 'Much indebted to EU', 18 September 1999
Fabozzi, F.J., *Bond Markets, Analysis and Strategies*, 2nd edition, Prentice Hall, 1993
Schinasi, G.J., Todd Smith, R., 'Fixed Income Markets in the United States, Europe, and Japan: Some Lessons for Emerging Markets', a Working Paper of the International Monetary Fund, No. 98/173, December 1998
Wilson, R.S., Fabozzi, F.J., *Corporate Bonds; Structures and Analysis*, FJF Associates, 1996

6 Callable Bonds

In Chapter 1 we reviewed the yield to maturity calculation, the main measure of bond return used in the fixed income markets. For conventional bonds the yield calculation is relatively straightforward because the issue's redemption date is known and fixed. This means that the future cash flows that make up the total cash flows of the bond are known with certainty. As such the cash flows that are required to calculate the yield to maturity are easily ascertained. Callable, put-able and sinking fund bonds, generally termed bonds with *embedded options*, are not as straightforward to analyse. This is because some aspect of their cash flows, such as the timing or the value of their future payments, are not certain. The term *embedded* is used because the option element cannot be separated from the bond itself. Since callable bonds have more than one possible redemption date, the collection of future cash flows contributing to their overall return is not clearly defined. If we wish to calculate the yield to maturity for such bonds, we must assume a particular redemption date and calculate the yield to this date. The market convention is to assume the first possible maturity date as the one to be used for yield calculation if the bond is priced above par, and the last possible date if the bond is priced below par. The term *yield-to-worst* is sometimes used to refer to a redemption yield calculation made under this assumption; this is the Bloomberg term. If the actual redemption date of a bond is different to the assumed redemption date, the measurement of return will be meaningless and irrelevant.

The market therefore prefers to use other measures of bond return for callable bonds. The most common method of return calculation is something known as *option-adjusted spread analysis* or OAS analysis; a very good account of OAS analysis is contained in Windas (1994). In this chapter we present one of the main methods by which callable bonds are priced. Although the discussion centres on callable bonds, the principles apply to all bonds with embedded option elements in their structure.

6.1 Understanding embedded option elements in a bond

Consider an hypothetical sterling corporate bond issued by ABC plc with a 6% coupon on 1 December 1999 and maturing on 1 December 2019. The bond is callable after five years, under the schedule shown at Table 6.1. We see that the bond is first callable at a price of 103.00, after which the call price falls progressively until December 2014, after which the bond is callable at par.

Although our example is hypothetical, this form of call provision is quite common in the corporate debt market. The basic case can be stated quite easily; in our example the ABC plc bond pays a fixed semi-annual coupon of 6%. If the market level of interest rates rises after the bonds are issued, ABC plc effectively gain because it is paying below-market financing costs on its debt. If rates decline however, investors gain from a rise in the capital value of their investment, but in this instance their upside is capped by the call provisions attached to the bond.

The difference between the value of a callable bond and that of an (otherwise identical) non-callable bond of similar credit quality is the value attached to the option element of the

Date	Call Price	Date	Call Price
01-Dec-2004	103.00	01-Dec-2009	101.75
01-Dec-2005	102.85	01-Dec-2010	101.25
01-Dec-2006	102.65	01-Dec-2011	100.85
01-Dec-2007	102.50	01-Dec-2012	100.45
01-Dec-2008	102.00	01-Dec-2013	100.25
		01-Dec-2014	100.00

Table 6.1: Call schedule for 'ABC plc' 6% bond due December 2019.

callable bond. This is an important relationship and one that we will consider, but first a word on the basics of option instruments.

6.1.1 *Basic features of options*

An option is a contract between two parties. The buyer of an option has the right, but not the obligation, to buy or sell an underlying asset at a specified price during a specified period or at a specified time (usually the expiry date of the option contract). The price of an option is known as the *premium*, which is paid by the buyer to the seller or *writer* of the option. An option that grants the holder the right to buy the underlying asset is known as a *call* option; one that grants the right to sell the underlying asset is a *put* option. The option writer is short the contract; the buyer is long. If the owner of the option elects to *exercise* her option and enter into the underlying trade, the option writer is obliged to execute under the terms of the option contract. The price at which an option specifies that the underlying asset may be bought or sold is known as the exercise or *strike* price. The expiry date of an option is the last day on which it may be exercised. Options that can be exercised anytime from the time they are struck up to and including the expiry date are called *American* options. Those that can be exercised only on the expiry date are known as *European* options.

The profit/loss profiles for option buyers and sellers are quite different. The buyer of an option has her loss limited to the price of that option, while her profit can in theory be unlimited. The seller of an option has her profit limited to the option price, while her loss can in theory be unlimited, or at least potentially very substantial.

The value or price of an option is comprised of two elements, its *intrinsic value* and its *time value.* The intrinsic value of an option is the value to the holder of an option if it were exercised immediately. That is, it is the difference between the strike price and the current price of the underlying asset. The holder of an option will only exercise it if there is underlying intrinsic value. For this reason, the intrinsic value is never less than zero. To illustrate, if a call option on a bond has a strike price of £100 and the underlying bond is currently trading at £103, the option has an intrinsic value of £3. An option with intrinsic value greater than zero is said to be *in-the-money.* An option where the strike price is equal to the price of the underlying is said to be *at-the-money* while one whose strike price is above (call) or below (put) the underlying is said to be *out-of-the-money.*

The time value of an option is the difference between the intrinsic value of an option and its total value. An option with zero intrinsic value has value comprised solely of time value. That is,

$$\text{Time value of an option} = \text{Option price} - \text{Intrinsic value}$$

The time value reflects the potential for an option to move into the money during its life, or move to a higher level of being in-the-money, before expiry. Time value diminishes steadily for an option up to its expiry date, when it will be zero. The price of an option on expiry is comprised solely of intrinsic value.

Later in this chapter we will illustrate how the price of a bond with an embedded option is calculated by assessing the value of the 'underlying' bond and the value of its associated option. The basic issues behind the price of the associated option are considered here.[1] The main factors influencing the price of an option on an interest-rate instrument such as a bond are:

- the strike price of the option;
- the current price of the underlying bond, and its coupon rate;
- the time to expiry;
- the short-term risk-free rate of interest during the life of the option;
- the expected volatility of interest rates during the life of the option.

The effect of each of these factors will differ for call and put options and American and European options. There are a number of option pricing models used in the market, the most well-known of which is probably the Black–Scholes model. Market participants often use their own variations of models or in-house developed varieties. The fundamental principle behind the Black–Scholes model is that a synthetic option can be created and valued by taking a position in the underlying asset and borrowing or lending funds in the market at the risk-free rate of interest. Although it is the basis for certain subsequent option models and is still used widely in the market, it is not necessarily appropriate for certain interest-rate instruments. For instance Fabozzi (1997) points out the unsuitability of the Black–Scholes model for certain bond options, based on its underlying assumptions. As a result a number of other methods have been developed for callable bonds analysis.

6.1.2 *The call provision*

A bond with early redemption provisions essentially is a portfolio containing an underlying conventional bond, with the coupon and maturity date of the actual bond, and a put or call option on this underlying issue. Analysis therefore is interest-rate dependent, it must consider the possibility of the option being exercised when valuing the bond. The value of a bond with an option feature is the sum of the values of the individual elements, that is the underlying bond and the option component. This is expressed at (6.1):

$$P_{bond} = P_{underlying} + P_{option}. \tag{6.1}$$

Expression (6.1) above states simply that the value of the actual bond is composed of the value of the underlying conventional bond together with the value of the embedded option(s). The relationship would hold for a true conventional bond, as the option component value would be zero. For a put-able bond, an embedded put option is an attractive feature for investors as the put feature contributes to its value by acting as a floor on the

---

1 For a technical review of option pricing, see Chapters 43–46 in the author's book *The Bond and Money Markets* (Butterworth-Heinemann 2001).

bond's price. Thus the greater the value of the put, the greater the value of the actual bond. We can express this by re-writing (6.1) as (6.2):

$$P_{bond} = P_{underlying} + P_{put}. \qquad (6.2)$$

The expression at (6.2) above states that the value of a put-able bond is equal to the sum of the values of the underlying conventional bond and the embedded put option. If any of the components of the total price were to increase in value, then so would the value of the put-able bond itself.

A callable bond is viewed as a conventional bond together with a short position in a call option, which acts as a cap on the actual bond's price. This 'short' position in a call option reduces the total value of the actual bond, so we present the bond price in the form (6.3):

$$P_{bond} = P_{underlying} - P_{call}. \qquad (6.3)$$

Equation (6.3) above states that the price of a callable bond is equal to the price of the underlying conventional bond less the price of the embedded call option. Therefore if the value of the call option were to increase, the value of the callable bond would decrease. That is, when a bondholder of such a bond sells a call option, they receive the option price; the difference between the price of the option-free bond and the callable bond at any time is the price of the embedded call option. The precise nature of the behaviour of the attached option element will depend on the terms of the callable bond issue. If the issuer of a callable bond is entitled to call the issue at any time after the first call date, the bondholder has effectively sold the issuer an American call option. However the call option price may vary with the date the option is exercised; this occurs when the call schedule for a bond has different call prices according to which date the bond is called. The underlying bond at the time the call is exercised is comprised of the remaining coupon payments that would have been received by the bondholder had the issue not been called. However for ease of explanation the market generally analyses a callable bond in terms of a long position in a conventional bond and a short position in a call option, as stated by (6.3) above. Note of course that the option is embedded; it does not trade in its own right. Nevertheless it is clear that embedded options are important elements not only in the behaviour of a bond but in its valuation as well.

6.2 The binomial tree of short-term interest rates

In an earlier chapter we illustrated how a coupon bond yield curve could be used to derive spot (zero-coupon) and implied forward rates. A forward rate is defined as the one-period interest rate for a term beginning at a forward date and maturing one period later. Forward rates form the basis upon which a *binomial* interest-rate tree is built. For an introduction to a binomial process, see Appendix 6.1.

An option model that used implied forward rates to generate a price for an option's underlying bond on a future date would implicitly assume that interest rates implied by the yield curve today for a date in the future would occur with certainty. Such an assumption would essentially repeat the errors associated with yield-to-worst analysis, which would be inaccurate because interest rates do not remain unchanged from a future today to a future pricing date. To avoid this inaccuracy, a binomial tree model assumes that interest rates do not remain fixed but fluctuate over time. This is done by treating implied forward rates, sometimes referred to as *short rates*,[2] as outcomes of a binomial process. In a binomial interest-rate process we construct a binomial tree of possible short rates for each future time period. In the binomial tree we model two interest rates as the possible outcomes of a previous time period, when the interest rate was known.

Example 6.1: An introduction to arbitrage-free pricing

- Consider an hypothetical situation. Assume that the short-term yield curve describes the following environment:

  Six-month rate: 5.00%
  One-year rate: 5.15%

Assume further that in six months' time the then six-month rate will be either 5.01% or 5.50%, and that the probability of either new rate is equal at 50% each. Our capital market is a semi-annual one, that is convention is for bonds to pay a semi-annual coupon, as in the US and UK domestic markets. We can illustrate this state in the following way:

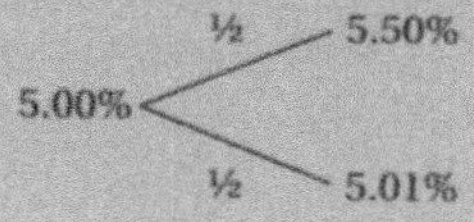

Figure 6.1

Figure 6.1 is a *binomial interest rate tree* or *lattice* for the six-month interest rate. The tree is called 'binomial' because there are precisely two possibilities for the future level of the interest rate. Using this lattice, we can calculate the tree for the prices of six-month and one-year zero-coupon bonds. The six-month zero-coupon bond price today is given by 100/(1 + (0.05/2)) or 97.56098. The price tree is given at Figure 6.2.

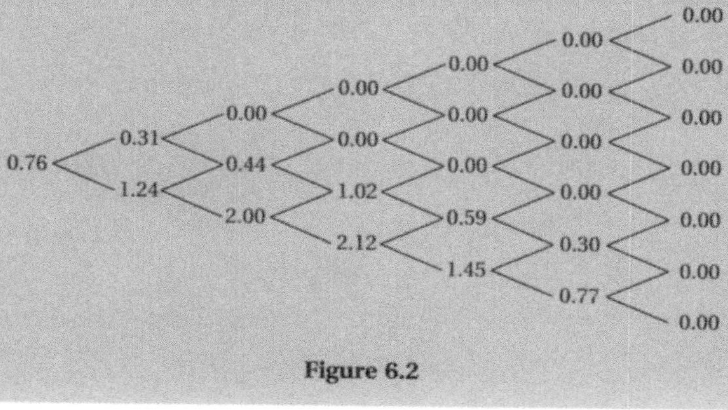

Figure 6.2

---

2 Although it is not strictly correct to refer to forward rates in this way.

Period 0 is today; period 1 is the point precisely six months from today. Given that we are dealing with a six-month zero-coupon bond, it is apparent that there is only one *state of the world* whatever the interest rate is in period 1; the maturity value of the bond, which is 100.

The binomial lattice for the one-year zero-coupon bond is given in Figure 6.3.

At period 0 the price of the one-year zero-coupon bond is $100/(1+(0.0515/2)^2)$ or 95.0423. The price of the bond at period 1, at which point it is now a six-month piece of paper, is dependent on the six-month rate at the time, shown in the diagram. At period 2 the bond matures and its price is 100. The model at Figure 6.3 demonstrates that the average or *expected* value of the price of the one-year bond at period 1 is $((0.5 \times 97.3236) + (0.5 \times 97.5562))$ or 97.4399. This is the expected price at period 1, therefore using this the price at period 0 is $97.4399/(1+(0.05/2))$ or 95.06332.

However, we know that the market price is 95.0423. This demonstrates a very important principle in financial economics, that markets do not price derivative instruments on the basis of their expected future value. At period 0 the one-year zero-coupon bond is a more risky investment compared to the shorter-dated bond; in the last six months of its life it will be worth either 97.32 or 97.55 depending on the direction of six-month rates. Investors' preference is for a bond that has a price of 97.4399 at period 1 with certainty. The price of such a bond at period 0 would be $97.4399/(1+(0.05/2))$ or 95.0633. In fact the actual price of the one-year bond at that date, 95.0423, indicates the *risk premium* that the market places on the bond.

We can now consider the pricing of an option. What value should be given to a six-month call option maturing in six months' time (period 1) written on 100 nominal of the six-month zero at a strike price of 97.40? The binomial tree for this option is given at Figure 6.4. This shows that at period 1 if the six-month rate is 5.50% the call option has no value, because the price of the bond is below the strike price. If on the other hand the six-month rate is at the lower level, the option has a value of 97.5562 – 94.40 or 0.1562.

How do we calculate the price of the option? Option pricing theory states that to do this one must construct a *replicating portfolio* and find the value of this portfolio. In our example we must set up a portfolio of six-month and one-year zero-coupon bonds today that will have no value at period 1 if the six-month rate rises to 5.50%, but will have a

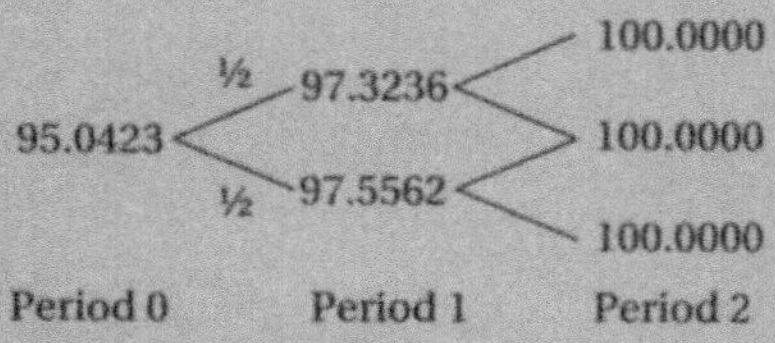

Figure 6.3

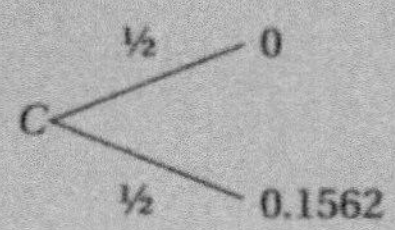

Figure 6.4

value of 0.1562 if the rate at that time is 5.01%. If we let the value of the six-month and one-year bonds in the replicating portfolio be $C1$ and $C2$ respectively at period 1, we may set the following equations:

$$C1 + 0.973236C2 = 0 \tag{6.4}$$

$$C1 + 0.975562C2 = 0.1562. \tag{6.5}$$

The value of the six-month zero-coupon bond in the replicating portfolio at period 1 is 100 as it matures. In the case of an interest-rate rise the value of the one-year bond (now a six-month bond) at period 1 is 97.3236. The total value of the portfolio is given by the first expression above, which states that this value must also be equal to the value of the option. The second expression gives the value of the replicating portfolio in the event that rates decrease, when the option value is 0.1562.

Solving the expressions above gives us $C1 = -65.3566$ and $C2 = 67.1539$. What does this mean? Basically to construct the replicating portfolio we purchase 67.15 of one-year zero-coupon bonds and sell short 65.36 of the six-month zero-coupon bond. However the original intention behind the replicating portfolio was because we wished to price the option: the portfolio and the option have equal values. The value of the portfolio is a known quantity, as it is equal to the price of the six-month bond at period 0 multiplied by $C1$ together with the price of the one-year bond multiplied by $C2$. This is given by

$$(0.9756 \times -65.3566) + (0.950423 \times 67.1539) = 0.0627.$$

That is, the price of the six-month call option is 0.06. This is the *arbitrage-free* price of the option; below this price a market participant could buy the option and simultaneously sell short the replicating portfolio and would be guaranteed a profit. If the option was quoted at a price above this, a trader could write the option and buy the portfolio. Note how the probability of the six-month rate increasing or decreasing was not part of the analysis. This reflects the arbitrage pricing logic. That is, the replicating portfolio must be equal in value to the option whatever direction interest rates move in. This means probabilities do not have an impact in the construction of the portfolio. This is not to say that probabilities do not have an impact on the option price, far from it. For example, if there is a very high probability that rates will increase (in our example), intuitively we can see that the value of an option to an investor will fall. However this is accounted for by the market in the value of the option or callable bond at any one time. If probabilities change, the market price will change to reflect this.

Let us now turn to the concept of *risk neutral* pricing. Notwithstanding what we have just noted about how the market does not price instruments using expected values, there exist risk-neutral probabilities for which the discounted expected value does give the actual price at period 0. If we let p be the risk-neutral probability of an interest rate increase and $(1-p)$ be the probability of a rate decrease, we may set p such that

$$\frac{97.3236p + 97.5562(1-p)}{1 + \frac{1}{2}0.05} = 95.0423.$$

That is, we can calculate a value for p such that the discounted expected value, using the probability p rather than the actual probability of 1/2 provides the true market price. The above expression solves to give $p = 0.5926$.

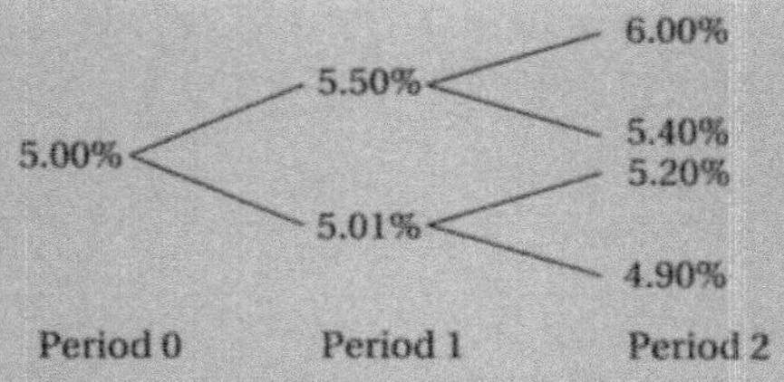

Figure 6.5

In our example from the option price tree in Figure 6.5, given the risk-neutral probability of 0.5926 we can calculate the option price to be

$$\frac{(0.5926 \times 0) + (0.4074 \times 0.1562)}{1 + \frac{1}{2}0.05} = 0.0621.$$

This is virtually identical to the 0.062 option price calculated above. Put very simply risk-neutral pricing works by first finding the probabilities that produce prices of the replicating or *underlying* security equal to the discounted expected value. An option on the security is valued by discounting this expected value under the risk-neutral probability.

We can now turn to binomial trees. In the description above we had a two-period tree, moving to period 2 we might have Figure 6.6.

This binomial tree is known as a *non-recombining tree*, because each node branches out to two further nodes. This might seem more logical, and such trees are used in practice in the market. However implementing it requires a considerable amount of computer processing power, and it is easy to see why. In period 1 there are two possible levels for the interest rate, and at period 2 there are four possible levels. After N interest periods there will be 2^N possible values for the interest rate. If we wished to calculate the current price a 10-year callable bond that paid semi-annual coupons, we would have over 1 million possible values for the last period set of nodes. For a 20-year bond we would have over 1 trillion possible values. (Note also that binomial models are not used with a six-month time step between nodes in practice, but have much smaller time steps, further increasing the number of nodes).

For this reason certain market practitioners prefer to use a *recombining* binomial tree, where the upward-downward state has the same value as the downward-upward state. This is shown below.

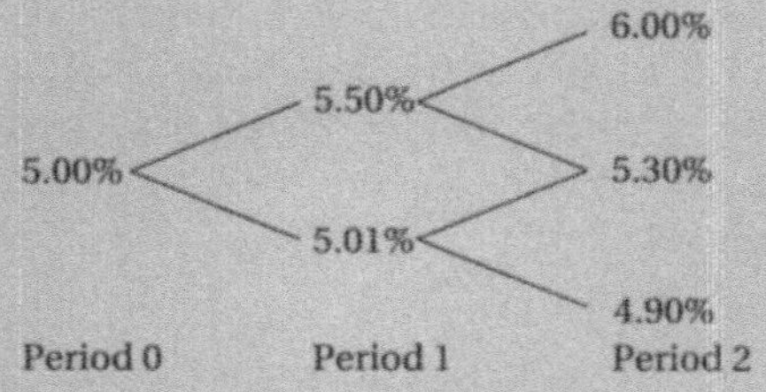

Figure 6.6

The number of nodes and possible values at the latest time step is much reduced in a recombining tree. For example the number of nodes used to price a 20-year bond that was being priced with one-week time steps would be $(52 \times 20) + 1$ or 1041. Implementation is therefore more straightforward with a recombining tree.

6.3 Pricing callable bonds

We can now consider a simple pricing method for callable bonds. We will assume a binomial term structure model. The background to this is given in the box above, *Introduction to arbitrage-free pricing.* It is well worth reading this box, especially if one is not familiar with binomial models or the principle of the arbitrage-free pricing of financial instruments. For a background on the binomial process itself see Appendix 6.1. Using the binomial model we can derive a *risk-neutral* binomial lattice, where each lattice carries an equal probability of upward or downward moves, for the evolution of the six-month interest rate. The time step in the lattice is six months. This model is then used to price an hypothetical semi-annual coupon bond with the following terms:

Coupon Maturity Call schedule:	**6% Three years**
Year 1	103.00
Year 1.5	102.00
Year 2	101.50
Year 2.5	101.00
Year 3	100.00

Table 6.2

The tree is shown at Figure 6.7.

In the first instance we construct the binomial tree that describes the price process followed by the bond itself, if we ignore its call feature. This is shown at Figure 6.8. Note that the maturity value of the bond on the redemption date is given as 100.00, that is, we perform the analysis on the basis of the bond's ex-coupon value. The final cash flow would of course be 103.00.

We construct the tree from the final date backwards. At each of the nodes at year 3, the price of the bond will be 100.00, the (ex-coupon) par value. At year 2.5 the price of the bond

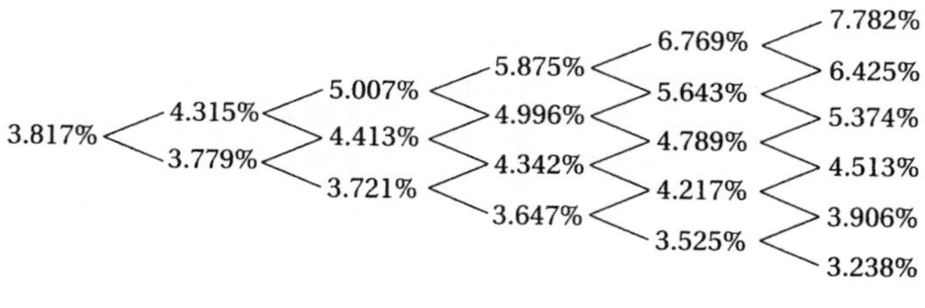

Figure 6.7

at the highest yield will be that at which the yield of the bond is 7.782%. At this point, the price of the bond after six months will be 103.00 in both the 'up' state and the 'down' state. Following risk-neutral pricing therefore the price of the bond at this node is

$$P_{bond} = \frac{0.5 \times 103 \ + \ 0.5 \times 103}{1 + (0.07782/2)} = 99.14237.$$

The same process is used to obtain the prices for every node at year 2.5. Once all these prices have been calculated, we repeat the process for the prices at each node in year 2. At the highest yield, 6.769%, the two possible future values are

$$99.14237 + 3.0 = 102.14237 \text{ and } 99.79411 + 3.0 = 102.79411.$$

Therefore the price of the bond in this state is given by

$$P_{bond} = \frac{0.5 \times 102.14237 \ + \ 0.5 \times 102.79411}{1 + (0.06769/2)} = 99.11374.$$

The same procedure is repeated until we have populated every node in the lattice. At each node the ex-coupon bond price is equal to the sum of the expected value and coupon, discounted at the appropriate six-month interest rate. The completed lattice is shown at Figure 6.8.

Once we have calculated the prices for the conventional element of the bond, we can calculate the value of the option element on the callable bond. This is shown in Figure 6.9. On the bond's maturity date the option is worthless, because it is an option to call at 100, which is the price the bond is redeemed at in any case. At all other node points a valuation analysis is called for.

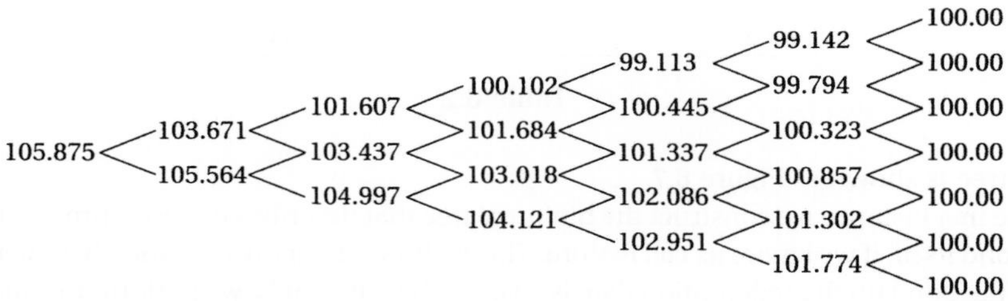

Figure 6.8

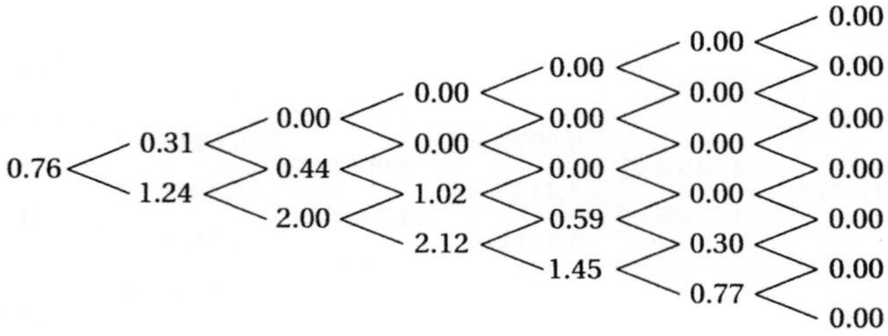

Figure 6.9

The holder of the option in the case of a callable bond is the issuing company. At any time during the life of the bond, the holder will either exercise the option on the call date or elect to hold it to the next date. The option holder must consider:

- the value of holding the option for an extra period, denoted by P_{Ct};
- the value of exercising the option straight away, denoted P_C.

If the value of the former exceeds that of the latter, the holder will elect to not exercise, and if the value at the exercise date is higher the holder will exercise immediately. At year 2.5 call date for example, there is no value in holding the option because it will be worthless at year 3. Therefore at any point where the option is in-the-money the holder will exercise.

We can express the general valuation as follows. The value of the option for immediate exercise is *Vt*; the value if one is holding on to the option for a further period is V_T. Additionally let *P* be the value of the bond at any particular node, *S* the call option price, and V_h and V_l the values of the option in the up-state and down-state respectively. The value of the option at any specified node is *V*. The six-month interest rate at any specified node point is *r*. We have

$$V_T = \frac{0.5V_h + 0.5V_l}{1 + \frac{1}{2}r} \qquad (6.6)$$

$$V_t = max(0, P - S)$$

while the expression for *V* is $V = max(V_T, V_t)$.

The rule is as demonstrated above, to work backwards in time and apply the expression at each node, which produces the option value binomial lattice tree.

The general rule with an option is they have more value 'alive than dead'. This means that sometimes it is optimal to run an in-the-money option rather than exercising straight away. The same is true for callable bonds. There are a number of factors that dictate whether an option should be exercised or not. The first is the asymmetric profile resulting when the price of the 'underlying' asset rises; option holders gain if the price rises, but will only lose the value of their initial investment if the price falls. Therefore it is optimal to run with the option position. There is also time value, which is lost if the option is exercised early. In the case of callable bonds, it is often the case that the call price decreases as the bond approaches maturity. This is an incentive to delay exercise until a lower exercise price is available. The issue that may influence the decision to exercise sooner is coupon payments, as interest is earned sooner.

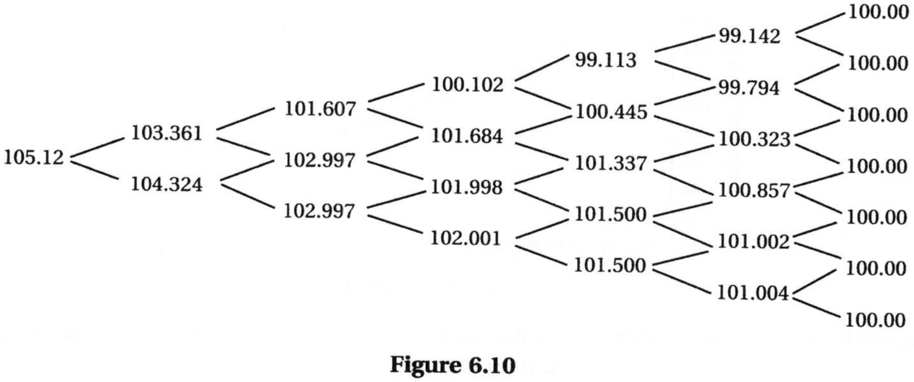

Figure 6.10

To return to our hypothetical example, we can now complete the price tree for the callable bond. Remember that the option in the case of a callable bond is held by the issuer, so the value of the option is subtracted from the price of the bond to obtain the actual value. We see from Figure 6.10 that the price of the callable bond today is 105.875 – 0.76 or 105.115. The price of the bond at each node in the lattice is also shown. By building a tree in this way, which can be programmed into a spreadsheet or as a front-end application, we are able to price a callable or putable bond.

6.4 Price and yield sensitivity

As we saw in Chapter 2, the price/yield relationship for a conventional vanilla bond is essentially convex in shape, while for a bond with an option feature attached this relationship changes as the price of the bond approaches par, at which the bond is said to exhibit *negative convexity*. This means that the rise in price will be lower than the fall in price for a large change in yield of a given number of basis points. We summarise the price/yield relationship for both conventional and option-feature bonds in Table 6.3.

The price/yield relationship for a callable bond exhibits negative convexity as interest rates fall. Option-adjusted spread analysis is used to highlight this relationship for changes in rates. This is done by effecting a parallel shift in the benchmark yield curve, holding the spread level constant and then calculating the theoretical price along the nodes of the binomial price tree. The average present value then becomes the projected price for the bond. General results for a hypothetical callable bond, compared to a conventional bond are shown at Figure 6.11. In our example once the market rate falls below the 10% level, the bond exhibits negative convexity.

Value of price change for		
Change in yield	Positive convexity	Negative convexity
Fall of 100 bp	X%	Lower than Y%
Rise of 100 bp	Lower than X%	Y%

Table 6.3

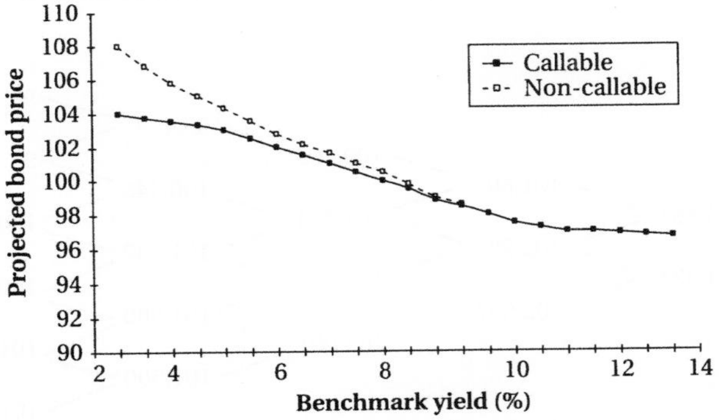

Figure 6.11: Projected prices for callable and conventional bonds with identical coupon and final maturity dates.

This is because it then becomes callable at that point, which acts as an effective cap on the price of the bond.

The market analyses bonds with embedded options in terms of a yield spread, with a 'cheap' bond trading at a higher yield spread and a 'dear' bond trading at a lower yield spread. The usual convention is to quote yield spreads as the difference between the redemption yield of the bond being analysed and the equivalent maturity government bond. This is not accurate because the redemption yield is in effect a meaningless number – there is not a single rate at which all the cash flows comprising either bond should be discounted but a set of spot or forward rates that are used for each successive interest period. The correct procedure for discounting therefore is to determine the yield spread over the spot or forward rate curve. With regard to the binomial tree what we require then, is the constant spread that, when added to all the short-rates on the binomial tree, makes the theoretical (model-derived) price equal to the observed market price. The constant spread that satisfies this requirement is known as the *option-adjusted spread* (OAS). The spread is referred to as an 'option-adjusted' spread because it reflects the option feature attached to the bond. The OAS will depend on the volatility level assumed in running the model. For any given bond price, the higher the volatility level specified, the lower will be the OAS for a callable bond, and the higher for a put-able bond. Since the OAS is calculated usually relative to a government spot or forward rate curve, it reflects the credit risk and any liquidity premium between the corporate bond and the government bond. Note that OAS analysis reflects the valuation model being used, and its accuracy is reflection of the accuracy of the model itself.

6.4.1 *Measuring bond yield spreads*

The binomial model evaluates the return of a bond by measuring the extent to which its return exceeds the returns determined by the risk-free short-rates in the tree. The difference between these returns is expressed as a spread and may be considered the *incremental return* of a bond at a specified price. Determining the spread involves the following steps:

1. the binomial tree is used to derive a theoretical price for the specified bond;
2. the theoretical price is compared with the bond's observed market price;
3. if the two prices differ, the rates in the binomial model are adjusted by a user-specified amount, which is the estimate of the spread;
4. using the adjusted rates a new theoretical price is derived and compared with the observed price;
5. the last two steps are repeated until the theoretical price matches the observed price.

The process can be carried out in a straightforward fashion using a software application.

6.5 Price volatility of bonds with embedded options

In Chapter 2 we reviewed traditional duration and modified duration measures for bond interest-rate risk. Modified duration is essentially a predictive measure, used to describe the expected percentage change in bond price for a 1% change in yield. The measure is a snapshot in time, based on the current yield of the bond and the structure of its expected cash flows. In analysing a bond with an embedded option, the bondholder must assume a fixed maturity date, based on the current price of the bond, and calculate modified duration based on this assumed redemption date. However under circumstances where it is not exactly certain what the final maturity is, modified duration may be calculated to the first call date and to the final maturity date. This would be of little use to bondholders in these circumstances, since it may be unclear which measure is appropriate. The problem is more acute for bonds that are continuously callable (or put-able) from the first call date up to maturity.

6.5.1 *Effective duration*

To recap from Chapter 2, the duration for any bond is calculated using (6.7) which assumes annualised yields.

$$D = \frac{\sum_{t=1}^{n} \frac{tC_t}{(1+rm)^t}}{P}. \tag{6.7}$$

Fabozzi (1997) describes how the measure can be approximated using (6.8):

$$D_{\text{approx}} = \frac{P_{-} - P_{+}}{2P_0(\Delta rm)} \tag{6.8}$$

where

P_0	is the initial price of the bond
P_{-}	is the estimated price of the bond if the yield falls by Δrm
P_{+}	is the estimated price of the bond if the yield rises by Δrm
Δrm	is the change in the yield of the bond.

The drawbacks of the traditional measure are overcome to a certain extent when OAS analysis is used to measure the *effective duration* of a bond. Whereas traditional duration seeks to predict a bond's price changes based on a given price and assumed redemption date, effective duration is solved from actual price changes resulting from specified shifts in interest rates. Applying the analysis to a bond with an embedded option means that the new prices resulting from yield changes reflect changes in the cash flow. Effective duration may be thought of as a duration measure which recognises that yield changes may change the future cash flow of the bond. For bonds with embedded options the difference between traditional duration and effective duration can be significant; for example for a callable bond the effective duration is sometimes half that its traditional duration measure. For mortgage-backed securities the difference is sometimes greater still.

To calculate effective duration using the binomial model and (6.8) we employ the following procedure:

- calculate the OAS spread for the bond;
- change the benchmark yield through a downward parallel shift;
- construct an adjusted binomial tree using the new yield curve;
- add the OAS adjustment to the short-rates at each of the node points in the tree;
- use the modified binomial tree constructed above to calculate the new value of the bond, which then becomes P_{+} for use in equation (6.8).

To determine the lower price resulting from a rise in yields we follow the same procedure but effect an upward parallel shift in the yield curve.

Effective duration for bonds that contain embedded options is often referred to as *option-adjusted spread duration*. There are two advantages associated with using this measure. These are that, by incorporating the binomial tree into the analysis, the interest-rate dependent nature of the cash flows is taken into account. This is done by holding the bond's OAS constant over the specified interest-rate shifts, in effect maintaining the credit spread demanded by the market at a constant level. This takes into account the behaviour of the embedded option as interest rates change. The second, and possibly more significant advantage is that OAS duration is calculated based on a parallel shift in the benchmark yield curve, which gives us an indication of the change in bond price with respect to changes in market interest rates rather than with respect to changes in its own yield.

The derivation of the expression for option-adjusted modified duration is given at Appendix 6.2.

6.5.2 *Effective convexity*

In the same way that we calculate an effective duration measure for bonds with embedded options, the standard measure of bond convexity may well be inappropriate for such bonds, for the same reason that the measure does not take into account impact of a change in market interest rates on a bond's future cash flows. The convexity measure for any bond may be approximated using (6.9), described in Fabozzi (1997).

$$CV = \frac{P_+ + P_- - 2P_0}{P_0(\Delta rm)^2}. \tag{6.9}$$

If prices input to (6.9) are those assuming that remaining cash flows for the bond do not change when market rates change, the convexity value is that for an option-free bond. To calculate a more meaningful value for bonds with embedded options, the prices used in the equation are derived by changing the cash flows when interest rates change, based on the results obtained from the binomial model. This measure is called *effective convexity* or *option-adjusted convexity*. The derivation of this measure is given at Appendix 6.3.

6.6 Sinking funds

In some markets corporate bond issuers set up *sinking fund* provisions. They are more widely used in the US corporate market. For example consider the following hypothetical bond issue:

Issuer	ABC plc
Issue date	01-Dec-99
Maturity date	01-Dec-19
Nominal	£100 million
Coupon	8%
Sinking fund provision	£5 million 1 December, 2009 to 2018

Table 6.4

In the example of the ABC plc 8% 2019 bond, a proportion of the principal is paid out over a period of time. This is the formal provision. In practice the actual payments made may differ from the formal requirements.

A sinking fund allows the bond issuer to redeem the nominal amount using one of two methods. The issuer may purchase the stipulated amount in the open market, and then deliver these bonds to the Trustee[3] for cancellation. Alternatively the issuer may call the required amount of the bonds at par. This is in effect a *partial call*, similar to a callable bond for which only a fraction of the issue may be called. Generally the actual bonds called are selected randomly by certificate serial numbers. Readers will have noticed however that the second method by which a portion of the issue is redeemed is actually a call option, which carries value for the issuer. Therefore the method by which the issuer chooses to fulfil its sinking fund requirement is a function of the level of interest rates. If interest rates have risen since the bond was issued, so that the price of the bond has fallen, the issuer will meet its sinking fund obligation by direct purchase in the open market. However if interest rates have fallen, the issuing company will call the specified amount of bonds at par. In the hypothetical example given at Table 6.4, in effect ABC plc has ten options embedded in the bond, each relating to £5 million nominal of the bonds. The options each have different maturities, so the first expires on 1 December 2009 and subsequent options maturing on 1 December each following year until 2018.[4] The decision to exercise the options as they fall due is made using the same binomial tree method that we discussed earlier.

Appendices

Appendix 6.1: An illustration of the binomial process

In general we observe that bonds that contain embedded options trade in the market with the option element possessing little or no *intrinsic* value. If a callable bond is not immediately exercisable, by definition the option has no intrinsic value. This will hold regardless of the difference between the option exercise price and the price of the underlying bond. Since the embedded options in most callable and put-able bonds have no intrinsic value, the value that is attached to them is composed entirely of *time* value. It is important to measure this time value when analysing option-embedded bonds. There are several valuation methodologies that are used in the market to facilitate this. Whatever the model that is used, the objective is to derive a price distribution of the underlying security at a future date. This enables the analyst to measure the future intrinsic value and then calculate its present value today, which enables her to determine if the option will be exercised at that future date.

The binomial model is a commonly encountered valuation model. This is best illustrated using the example of tossing a coin, where the probabilities of the two expected outcomes from tossing a coin are precisely equal. To illustrate the principles involved, assume a coin-toss process whereby an outcome of 'heads' results in a payout of £20, while an outcome of 'tails' results in a payout of £0. There is an equal probability of achieving

[3] Bond issuers appoint a Trustee that is responsible for looking after the interests of bondholders during the life of the issue. In some cases the Trustee is appointed by the underwriting investment bank or the Issuer's solicitors. Specialised arms of commercial and investment banks carry out the Trustee function, for example JPMorgan Chase Bank, Deutsche Bank, Bank of New York, Citibank and others.

[4] The 'options' are European options, in that they can only be exercised on the expiry date.

heads or tails for every coin toss. On a single toss of the coin the only possible outcome is a payout of £20 or £0. Over a large number of coin tosses we would expect the outcome to be heads 50% of the time and tails 50% of the time. In general the expected payoff of one toss is calculated by weighting the payoff associated with each possible outcome by the probability that the outcome will occur. This is expressed as (6.10):

$$E(w) = \sum_{i=1}^{n}(w_i \times p(i)) \tag{6.10}$$

where

$E(w)$	is the expected payoff from one coin toss
w_i	is the payout received from an outcome i
$p(i)$	is the probability that an outcome i will occur
n	is the number of possible different outcomes
i	is 1, 2, 3, ... m.

In our case of a £20 gain from achieving a 'heads' the expected payoff from one toss of a coin would therefore be calculated as follows:

$$= (w_1 \times p(1)) + (w_2 \times p(2)) = ((20) \times (50\%)) + ((0) \times (50\%))$$
$$= £10.$$

Note that the expected outcome is £10, despite the fact that the only outcome from a single toss of the coin is £20 or £0. The way to interpret the result is that the payoff from a large number of tosses is an average of £10 per toss. In other words the payoff from n coin tosses is n multiplied by the expected payoff from one coin toss. This is expressed formally as (6.11):

$$E(nw) = nE(w). \tag{6.11}$$

From (6.11) we would calculate that the expected payoff from 10 coin tosses would be £100.

As our hypothetical process has an expected payoff of £10 per coin toss, it is described as having value. To quantify the extent of this value, consider the following situation, where we are given the following choice:

- paying today for 10 tosses of the coin, to take place one year from today;
- buying today a *risk-free* one-year Treasury bill with a nominal value of £100, at a price of £95.18.

The payoff from 10 tosses of the coin is not certain. Although the highest probability outcome is a payoff of £100, it is of course possible to receive considerably more or less than this. This is because there is a probability that the outcome is more or less than five 'heads'. The outcome in the second case is certain: the Treasury bill will pay out £100 on maturity. The difference between these two choices is that the coin toss outcome has an element of risk, whereas there is no risk associated with the T-bill.

The gain achieved from purchasing the T-bill is the difference between the redemption amount and the current price, which is £4.82. This gain is risk-free, in that if we pay £95.18 today we will receive £100 in one year's time, a gain of £4.82. This gain is 5.064%, or an approximate bond-equivalent return of 5.00% This is referred to as the *risk-free rate of return*. Given that this is the risk-free rate of return available to anyone in the market, it is also the minimum return we would accept from investing in the coin-toss, which means that the maximum we would pay for that investment is £95.18. A rational investor would not pay more than this because at that price a risk-free return is available in the shape of the T-bill. Therefore £95.18 represents the maximum present value of the expected outcome of 10 coin tosses, as determined by the 5% risk-free rate. A feature of the market is that the present value of an expected future payoff is determined by the risk-free rate of return during the intervening period.

The coin toss illustration is an example of a *binomial* process. In a binomial process each action has only two possible outcomes. A *trinomial* process would have precisely three possible outcomes.

The binomial distribution

If any process meets the following conditions:

- there is a specified discrete number of trials;
- there are only two possible outcomes from each trial (for example, heads, tails; or defective, not defective);
- the probability of the outcomes in each trial does not change;
- the trials are independent, that is, the outcome of the previous trial has no bearing on the outcome of the current trial;

then it said to be a binomial distribution. Under these conditions we may use the binomial formula to calculate directly the probabilities of any process. The formula is given at (6.12):

$$p(r) = {}^{n}C_{r}p(r)q^{(n-r)} \tag{6.12}$$

where

${}^{n}C_{r}$	is the term for determining the number of different ways an event can occur
p	is the probability of the outcome from the trial under investigation
q	is $(1 - p)$, the probability of the specified outcome from the trial not occurring
n	is the number of trials
r	is the specified number of outcomes.

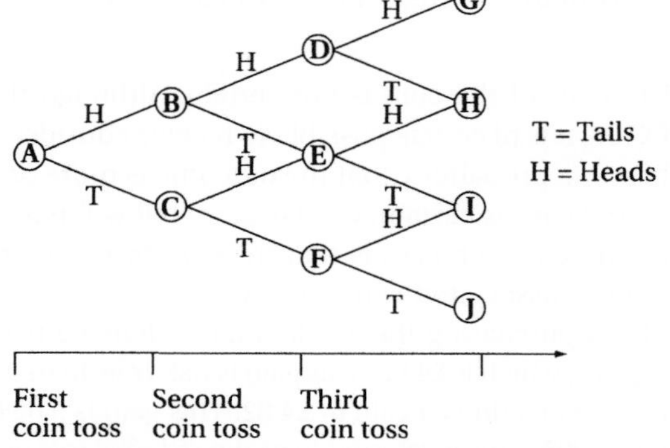

Figure 6.12: Binomial tree of outcome of tossing a coin three times.

The term ^nC_r is calculated as follows:

$$^nC_r = \frac{n!}{r!(n-r)!}$$

where ! is a factorial.

It is not always necessary to make the calculation of the probability directly as binomial tables exist; however the tables typically show only the probabilities for certain combinations of n and p. Binomial tables are contained in standard statistics textbooks and are not reproduced here.

The binomial tree diagram illustrates the properties of a binomial process. These properties form the basis for the model used to evaluate options embedded in bonds. It is usually referred to as the *binomial tree of interest rates* and is demonstrated in the chapter.

Appendix 6.2: Deriving the modified duration expression for a bond with an embedded option

Consider a callable bond, the price of which may be expressed as (6.13):

$$P_{cbond} = P_{underlying} - P_{call}. \tag{6.13}$$

Differentiating (6.13) with respect to the bond yield rm we obtain (6.14):

$$\frac{\mathrm{d}P_{cbond}}{\mathrm{d}rm} = \frac{\mathrm{d}P_{underlying}}{\mathrm{d}rm} - \frac{\mathrm{d}P_{call}}{\mathrm{d}rm}. \tag{6.14}$$

Dividing both sides of (6.14) by the price of the callable bond results in (6.15):

$$\frac{\mathrm{d}P_{cbond}}{\mathrm{d}rm}\frac{1}{P_{cbond}} = \frac{\mathrm{d}P_{underlying}}{\mathrm{d}rm}\frac{1}{P_{cbond}} - \frac{\mathrm{d}P_{call}}{\mathrm{d}rm}\frac{1}{P_{cbond}}. \tag{6.15}$$

We then multiply the numerator and denominator of the right-hand side of (6.15) by the price of the underlying bond, shown as (6.16):

$$\frac{\mathrm{d}P_{cbond}}{\mathrm{d}rm}\frac{1}{P_{cbond}} = \frac{\mathrm{d}P_{underlying}}{\mathrm{d}rm}\frac{1}{P_{underlying}}\frac{P_{underlying}}{P_{cbond}} - \frac{\mathrm{d}P_{call}}{\mathrm{d}rm}\frac{1}{P_{underlying}}\frac{P_{underlying}}{P_{cbond}}. \tag{6.16}$$

The components of (6.16) measure duration and modified duration of the underlying and callable bond, as shown by (6.17) and (6.18):

$$\frac{\mathrm{d}P_{cbond}}{\mathrm{d}rm}\frac{1}{P_{cbond}} = -MD_{cbond} \tag{6.17}$$

$$\frac{\mathrm{d}P_{underlying}}{\mathrm{d}rm}\frac{1}{P_{underlying}} = D_{underlying}. \tag{6.18}$$

This relationship is demonstrated in Chapter 7 of the author's book *The Bond and Money Markets*. We omit the negative sign in (6.17) as it does not have any impact on how the option-adjusted duration is derived.

Therefore we may state that:

$$MD_{cbond} = D_{underlying}\frac{P_{underlying}}{P_{cbond}} - \frac{\mathrm{d}P_{call}}{\mathrm{d}rm}\frac{1}{P_{underlying}}\frac{P_{underlying}}{P_{cbond}}. \tag{6.19}$$

The change in the value of the embedded call for a change in yield is expressed by (6.20):

$$\frac{dP_{call}}{drm}. \tag{6.20}$$

Any change in the value of the embedded call is dependent on the change in the price of the underlying bond for a specified yield change. This may be expressed as (6.21):

$$\begin{aligned} P_{call} &= fn(P_{underlying}) \\ P_{underlying} &= g(rm). \end{aligned} \tag{6.21}$$

By applying calculus equation (6.20) may be expressed as (6.22):

$$\frac{dP_{call}}{drm} = \frac{dP_{call}}{dP_{underlying}} \frac{dP_{underlying}}{drm}. \tag{6.22}$$

The change in the value of the embedded call resulting from a change in price of the underlying is contained in the first term of the right-hand side of (6.22). This is the definition of the *Delta* of an option. Therefore we may state the following:

$$\frac{dP_{call}}{drm} = \text{Delta} \times \frac{dP_{underlying}}{drm}. \tag{6.23}$$

Equation (6.23) may be used to obtain the expression for the call-adjusted duration of a callable bond; by substituting it into (6.19) and rearranging it we obtain (6.24), which is the duration of a callable bond, adjusted for the call feature.

$$MD_{cbond} = D_{underlying} \times \frac{P_{underlying}}{P_{cbond}} \times (1 - \text{Delta}). \tag{6.24}$$

Appendix 6.3: Option-adjusted convexity measure

This derivation is undertaken again for a callable bond, broken down as shown by (6.13). The convexity measure is the second derivative of the price/yield function, obtained by multiplying the second derivative by the reciprocal of the price of the bond at that point. Equation (6.14) above is the first derivative of the price of a callable bond. Applying calculus allows us to express (6.14) as (6.25):

$$\frac{dP_{cbond}}{drm} = \frac{dP_{underlying}}{drm} - \frac{dP_{call}}{dP_{underlying}} \frac{dP_{underlying}}{drm}. \tag{6.25}$$

The second derivative of this expression is (6.26):

$$\frac{d^2P_{cbond}}{drm^2} = \frac{d^2P_{underlying}}{drm^2} - \left(\frac{d^2P_{call}}{dP^2_{underlying}} \left(\frac{dP_{underlying}}{drm} \right)^2 + \frac{dP_{call}}{dP_{underlying}} \frac{d^2P_{underlying}}{drm^2} \right). \tag{6.26}$$

The right-hand side of (6.26) contains the terms for establishing the value of the first and second derivatives. The first term on the right-hand side is the second derivative of the price of the underlying bond with respect to change in yield. Multiplying this term by the price of the underlying bond results in (6.27):

$$\frac{d^2P_{underlying}}{drm^2} \times \frac{P_{underlying}}{P_{underlying}}. \tag{6.27}$$

The expression at (6.27) is in fact simply the convexity of the underlying bond multiplied by its price, which we can express as (6.28):

$$CV_{underlying} \times P_{underlying}. \tag{6.28}$$

Consider next the term below:

$$\frac{d^2 P_{underlying}}{dP^2_{underlying}} \left(\frac{dP_{underlying}}{drm}\right)^2.$$

The first term is the expression for the rate of change of the delta of the call option component with respect to the change in the price of the underlying. This is in fact the definition of the *gamma* of an option, so that we may write:

$$\text{Gamma} \times \left(\frac{dP_{underlying}}{drm}\right)^2, \text{ which may also be expressed as:}$$

$$\text{Gamma} \times \left(\frac{dP_{underlying}}{drm}\right)^2 \times \frac{P^2_{underlying}}{P^2_{underlying}}. \text{ This is equivalent to (6.29):}$$

$$\text{Gamma} \times (D_{underlying})^2 \times P^2_{underlying}. \tag{6.29}$$

We may also set the second derivative of the price of the underlying bond in the following terms:

$$Delta \times CV_{underlying} \times P_{underlying}. \tag{6.30}$$

Substituting (6.28), (6.29) and (6.30) into (6.25) results in (6.31):

$$\frac{d^2 P_{cbond}}{drm^2} = CV_{underlying} \times P_{underlying} - \Big(\text{Gamma} \times (D_{underlying})^2 \times P^2_{underlying} + \text{Delta} \times CV_{underlying} \times P_{underlying}\Big). \tag{6.31}$$

If we multiply the right-hand side of (6.30) by the reciprocal of the price of the callable bond, and then rearrange the terms for the convexity, we obtain the expression for the option-adjusted convexity of a callable bond, shown as (6.32):

$$CV_{cbond} = \frac{P_{underlying}}{P_{cbond}} \Big(CV_{underlying} \times (1 - \text{Delta}) - P_{underlying}. \times \text{Gamma} \times (D_{underlying})^2\Big). \tag{6.32}$$

Selected bibliography

Bodie, Z., Taggart, R., 'Future Investment Opportunities and the Value of the Call Provision on a Bond', *Journal of Finance* 33, 1978, pp. 1187–2000

Fabozzi, F.J., *Fixed Income Mathematics: Analytical and Statistical Techniques*, 3rd edition, McGraw-Hill, 1997, Chapter 16

Kalotay, A., Williams, G.O., Fabozzi, F.J., 'A model for the Valuation of Bonds and Embedded Options', *Financial Analysts Journal*, May–June 1993, pp. 35–46

Kish, R., Livingstone, M., 'The Determinants of the Call Feature on Corporate Bonds', *Journal of Banking and Finance* 16, 1992, pp. 687–703

Mitchell, K., 'The Call, Sinking Fund, and Term-to-Maturity Features of Corporate Bonds: An Empirical Investigation', *Journal of Financial and Quantitative Analysis* 26, June 1991, pp. 201–222

Narayanan, M.P., Lim, S.P., 'On the Call Provision on Corporate Zero-Coupon Bonds', *Journal of Financial and Quantitative Analysis* 24, March 1989, pp. 91–103

Tuckman, B., *Fixed Income Securities,* Wiley, 1996, Chapter 17

Van Horne, J.C., *Financial Management and Policy,* Prentice Hall, 1986

Windas, T., *An Introduction to Option-Adjusted Spread Analysis,* Bloomberg Publications, 1994

7 Convertible Bonds I

A *convertible* bond is a corporate security that gives the bondholder the right, without imposing an obligation, to convert the bond into another security under specified conditions, usually the ordinary shares of the issuing company. The decision to convert is solely at the discretion of the bondholder.[1] Once converted into ordinary shares, the shares cannot be exchanged back into bonds. As a result of their structure and option feature, in the market convertibles display the characteristics of both debt and equity instruments; as such they are often referred to as *hybrid* instruments. In addition to convertible bonds, there are also *convertible preferred stock*, which are essentially preference shares that are convertible into ordinary shares, again under terms specified at the time of issue. Convertibles are an important element of corporate finance and have benefited from the development of complex valuation models as applied in the option markets. Due to their hybrid nature, convertibles have presented some issues in their analysis and valuation in the past, but modern techniques have essentially resolved this and issue volumes have been steadily increasing during the 1990s, with volumes usually highest during rising stock markets. The sustained bull-run in global equities markets during the second half of the 1990s, led by Wall Street but also observed in other markets, has also witnessed growth in convertibles volumes. This reflects the fact that issuing a right to share in future equity price growth is most attractive during times of rising markets, and this allows corporates to issue convertibles on favourable terms.

In this chapter we review the basic characteristics of convertible securities, and the advantages and disadvantages of the bonds for both issuers and investors. The following chapter reviews the valuation and analysis of convertible bonds.

7.1 Basic description

Convertible bonds are typically fixed coupon securities that are issued with an option to be converted, at the bondholder's discretion, into the equity of the issuing company under specified terms and conditions. They are usually subordinated securities, and may only be issued by companies with a strong enough credit rating to tap the markets. The view of the market on the performance of the issuing company's shares is also a key factor, because investors are buying into the right to subscribe for the shares at a later date and, if exercised, at a premium on the open market price. For this reason the price of a convertible bond at any time will reflect changes in the price of the underlying ordinary shares; it also reflects changes in interest rates. Convertibles are typically medium- to long-dated instruments, and are usually issued with maturities of 10 to 20 years. The coupon on a convertible is

1 Although generally a corporate financing instrument, convertibles have also been issued by governments, where the bond is usually convertible into another debt instrument. Certain corporate issues are also convertible into the ordinary shares of another company, these are known as *exchangeable* bonds.

Convertible bond issues in 2002 by currency	$billion
US dollars	106
Euros	66
Sterling	18
Other currencies	7

Table 7.1: Convertible bond issuance in 2002.
Source: Strata Consulting.

always below the level payable on the same issuer's non-convertible bond of the same maturity. The bonds are usually convertible into ordinary shares of the issuing company under a set ration and a specified price.

In addition to the basic fixed coupon convertible there is a range of other instruments available to corporate borrowers. These include the *zero-coupon convertible,* which trades similarly to a zero-coupon vanilla bond and is issued at a deep discount. There is usually a low possibility of conversion with these bonds. A similar instrument to this is the *discount convertible.*

Some convertibles are also callable by the issuer, under pre-specified conditions. These are known as *convertible calls* and remove one of the advantages of the straight convertible – that conversion is at the discretion of the bondholder – because by calling a bond the issuer is able to force conversion, on potentially unfavourable terms. Put-able convertible bonds are the opposite of this and allow bondholders to redeem the bond as well as effect conversion at their discretion. The *premium put convertible* may be converted on only one date during its life, compared to the *rolling put convertible* which may be converted on a series of dates during its life; it is generally issued with a lower coupon than a conventional convertible. The addition of a put feature in a convertible is regarded as an extra inducement for investors, as they offer downside price protection. The *exchangeable* security is a bond that is issued by one company, but is convertible into the shares of another company, usually one in which the issuer holds a substantial interest. The *bond with warrant* is a convertible bond that is issued with an attached warrant, which may be detached and traded separately in the secondary market. Bonds with warrants are issued at a lower coupon than those issued as traditional convertibles. *Step-up convertible* bonds and preference shares are a more recent innovation. These pay a fixed coupon for a specified first part of their life, say the first five years, and then pay a higher coupon until they mature or are converted.

Convertible bonds have a long history in the capital markets, having been issued by utility companies in the United States in the 19th century. In 1997 the global convertibles market was estimated at over $360 billion. The US is the largest issuer of convertibles, and historically the biggest issuers were utility and transport companies. Unlike domestic and international securities, the market is essentially an exchange-traded one, with bonds listed on an exchange such as the New York Stock Exchange or the London Stock Exchange. This provides an added advantage in that the instruments may be more liquid than OTC market domestic bonds, and are also more transparent. However liquidity is also a function of the number of market makers in the stock and the amount of an issue available for trading, so that some convertibles will be more illiquid than conventional bonds.

7.1.1 *Terms and conditions*

Consider a standard convertible bond issued by our hypothetical borrower ABC plc. In the example ABC plc has issued a bond that gives the right, but not the obligation, to the bondholder to convert into the underlying shares of ABC plc at a specified price during the next ten years (see Table 7.2 below).

Issuer	ABC plc
Coupon	10%
Maturity	December 2009
Issue size	£50,000,000
Face value	£1,000
Number of bonds	50,000
Issue price	£100
Current price	£103.50
Conversion price	£8.50
Dividend yield	3.50%

Table 7.2: ABC plc 10% Convertible 2009.

For our hypothetical issue the conversion right or *option* may or may not be taken up at any time during the life of the bond, known as an *American* option, as opposed to a *European* option convertible which may only be converted on the maturity date of the bond. The majority of convertibles are American-style.

The ratio of exchange between the convertible bond and the ordinary shares can be stated either in terms of a *conversion price* or a *conversion ratio*. Bonds are always issued at a premium, which is the amount by which the conversion price, also known as the *exercise* or *strike* price, lies above the current share price.

The ABC plc bond has a face value of £1000, and a conversion price of £8.50, which means that each bond is convertible into 117.64 ordinary shares. To obtain this figure we have simply divided the face value of the bond by the conversion price to obtain the conversion ratio, which is £1000/£8.50 = 117.64 shares. This is also known as the *conversion ratio* and is given by (7.1):

$$\text{Conversion ratio} = \text{Bond denomination/Conversion price} \tag{7.1}$$

The terms and conditions under which a convertible is issued, and the terms under which it may be converted into the issuer's ordinary shares, are listed in the offer particulars or *prospectus*. The legal obligations of issuers and the rights of bondholders are stated in the *indenture* of the bond.

The conversion privilege can be stated in terms of either the conversion price or the conversion ratio. Conversion terms for a convertible do not necessarily remain constant over time. In certain cases convertible issues will provide for increases or *step ups* in the conversion price at periodic intervals. A £1000 denomination face value bond may be issued with a conversion price of say, £8.50 a share for the first three years, £10 a share for the next three years and £12 for the next five years, and so on. Under this arrangement the bond will convert to fewer ordinary shares over time which, given that the share price is expected to rise during this period, is a logical arrangement. The conversion price is also adjusted for any corporate actions that occur after the convertibles have been issued, such as rights issues or stock dividends. For example, if there was a 2 for 1 rights issue, the conversion price would be halved. This provision protects the convertible bondholders and is known as an *anti-dilution* clause.

The *parity* or *intrinsic value* of a convertible refers to the value of the underlying equity, expressed as a percentage of the nominal value of the bond. Parity is given by (7.2):

$$\begin{aligned}\text{Parity} &= \text{Share price/Conversion price } \textit{or}\\ &\quad\ \text{Share price/Conversion ratio.}\end{aligned} \tag{7.2}$$

The bond itself may be analysed – in the first instance – as a conventional fixed income security, so using its coupon and maturity date we may calculate a current yield (running yield) and yield to maturity. The *yield advantage* is the difference between the current yield and the *dividend yield* of the underlying share, given by (7.3):

$$\text{Yield advantage} = \text{Current yield} - \text{Dividend yield.} \tag{7.3}$$

In this case the current yield of the bond is 9.66%, which results in a yield advantage of 6.16%. Equity investors also use another measure, the *break-even* value which is given by (7.4):

$$\text{Break-even} = (\text{Bond price} - \text{Parity})/\text{Yield advantage.} \tag{7.4}$$

7.1.2 *Investor analysis*

The analytical requirements of the market investor are slightly different to those of the market maker or trader. In this section we consider the former. When evaluating convertible securities the investor must consider the expected performance of the underlying shares, the future prospects of the company itself and the relative attraction of the bond as a pure fixed income instrument in the event that the conversion feature proves to be worthless. In addition the assessment of the bond will take into account the credit quality of the issuer, the yield give-up suffered as a result of purchasing the convertible over a conventional bond, the conversion premium ratio, and the fixed income advantage gained over a purchase of the underlying shares in the first place.

We have already referred to the conversion ratio, which defines the number of shares of common stock that is received when the bond is converted. The conversion price is the actual price paid for the shares when conversion occurs.

$$\text{Conversion price} = \frac{\text{Par value of bond}}{\text{Conversion ratio}}. \tag{7.5}$$

The *conversion premium* is the percentage by which the conversion price exceeds the current share price. Using our previous illustration for ABC plc, the convertible has a conversion ratio of 117.64 (that is, 117.64 shares are received in return for the bond with a par value of £1000) and therefore a conversion price of £8.50. If the current price of the share is £6.70, then we have:

$$\begin{aligned}\text{Percentage conversion premium} &= \frac{\text{Conversion price} - \text{Share price}}{\text{Share price}}\\ &= \frac{£8.50 - £6.70}{£6.70}\\ &= 26.87\%\end{aligned}$$

The *conversion value* of the bond shows the current value of the shares received in exchange for the bond. It is given by:

$$\text{Conversion value} = \text{Share price} \times \text{Conversion ratio}. \quad (7.6)$$

As the current share price is £6.70, then the current conversion value would be:

$$\text{Conversion value} = £6.70 \times £117.64 = £788.19.$$

Assume that the bond is trading at 103.50 (per 100), then the *percentage conversion price premium*, or the percentage by which the current bond price exceeds the current conversion value is given by (7.7) below.

$$\text{Percentage conversion price premium} = \frac{\text{Price of bond} - \text{Conversion value}}{\text{Conversion value}} \quad (7.7)$$

In our example the premium value is $\dfrac{1035 - 788.19}{788.19} = 31.32\%$

The premium value in a convertible may be illustrated as shown in Figure 7.1. Investors are concerned with the point at which the ratio of the parity of the bond to the investment value moves far above the bond floor. At this point the security trades more like equity than debt. The opposite to this is when the equity price falls to low levels, to the point at which it will need to appreciate by a very large amount before the conversion option has any value; at this point the convertible trades like a pure fixed income instrument. Investors sometimes view a convertible bond price in terms of where it is standing in terms of the premium line in Figure 7.1, and assess its chances of moving into the 'hybrid' part of the chart. This analysis has no value however.

The value of a convertible bond may be broken down and viewed as the sum of the value of two instruments, the straight bond of the issuer and a call option on the issuer's equity. Considering Figure 7.1, the value of the convertible bond minus the conversion feature is represented by the line AB. It is sometimes referred to as the *straight line* value and is the conventional redemption yield measure. As we noted above the value of a convertible if it is converted straight away is the conversion value. Therefore the minimum value of a convertible bond is the higher of its straight line value and conversion value.

As a convertible is viewed as a conventional bond with a warrant attached, its fair price is a combination of the price of a vanilla bond and the price of a call option, not withstanding

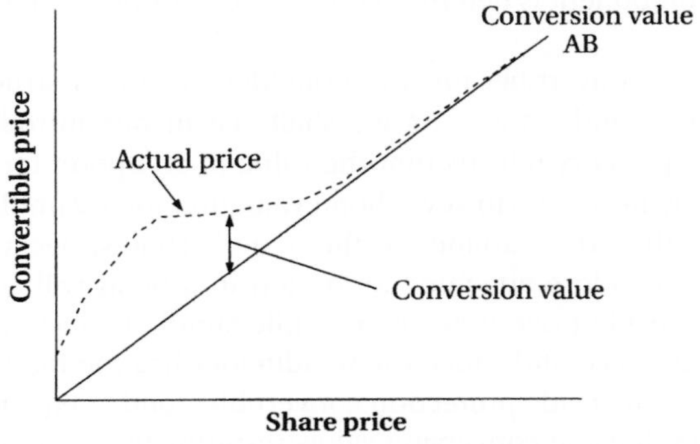

Figure 7.1: Convertible bond and conversion premium.

the dilution effect of the new shares that are issued and the coupon payments that are saved as a result of conversion.

The proportionate increase in the number of shares outstanding if all the bonds were to be converted, referred to as p, is given by (7.9):

$$p = \frac{\text{Number of convertible bonds} \times \text{Conversion ratio}}{\text{Number of shares outstanding before conversion}} \tag{7.8}$$

The fair value of a convertible is given by (7.9):

$$\text{Price of convertible} = \text{Price of vanilla bond} + \frac{P_C}{1+p} \times \textit{Conversion ratio}. \tag{7.9}$$

where P_C is the value of an American call option with an exercise price equal to the conversion price and an expiry date equal to the maturity of the bond. The price of the vanilla bond is calculated in exactly the same way as a standard bond in the same risk class.

Equation (7.9) will give us the fair price of a convertible if the bond is not callable. However some convertibles are callable at the issuer's option prior to the final maturity date. The issuer can therefore effect conversion when the share price has risen to the point where the value of the shares received on conversion equals the call price of the bond. As the firm has an incentive to call the bond when this occurs, the call price puts an effective ceiling on the price of the convertible given by (7.9).

We can calculate a realistic call date for a callable convertible by using the expression at (7.10):

$$\text{Call price} = \text{Current share price} \times (1+g)t \times \text{Conversion ratio} \tag{7.10}$$

where g is the expected growth rate in the share price and t is the time in years. Let us then assume that the call price of the hypothetical ABC plc bond is £100 (that is, par per face value of £1000), the conversion ratio is 117.64 and the current share price is £6.70 and is growing at 8.25 per cent per year. Given that the right-hand side of expression (7.10) is the conversion value of the convertible in t years' time, we can calculate at what point the conversion value will equal the call price.

If we look again at (7.9) and using our assumed terms and values, we can see that the price of the convertible depends on the price of a vanilla bond with identical years to maturity (and a terminal value of £100) and a call option with the same years to expiry. The value of the option component is determined using equity option models and is considered in Chapter 8.

The attraction of a convertible for a bondholder lies in its structure being one of a combined vanilla bond and option. As we shall see in our introductory discussion of options, option pricing theory tells us that the value of an option increases with the price variance of the underlying asset. However bond valuation theory implies that the value of a bond decreases with the price variance of the issuer's shares, because the probability of default is increased. Therefore attaching an option to a bond will act as a kind of hedge against excessive downside price movement, while simultaneously preserving the upside potential if the firm is successful, since the bondholder has the right to convert to equity. Due to this element of downside protection convertible bonds frequently sell at a premium over both their bond value and conversion value, resulting in the premium over conversion value that we referred to earlier. The conversion feature also leads to convertibles generally trading at a premium over bond value as well; the higher the market price of the ordinary share relative to the conversion price, the greater the resulting premium.

Example 7.1

- Consider the following Euro convertible bond currently trading at 104.80.

Denomination:	£1000
Coupon:	4.50%
Maturity:	15 years
Conversion price:	£25 per share

The issuer's shares are currently trading at £19.50

1. Number of shares into which the bond is convertible:

   Conversion ratio = £1000/25 = 40.

2. Parity or conversion value:

   $$\frac{\text{Current share price}}{\text{Conversion price}} \times 100 = 78\%.$$

3. Effective conversion price:

   $$\frac{\text{Price of convertible}}{\text{Conversion ratio}} = 2.62 \text{ (that is, £26.30 per £1000).}$$

4. Conversion premium:

   $$\frac{((3.) - \text{Current share price})}{\text{Current share price}} \times 100 = 34.36\%.$$

5. Conversion premium – alternative formula:

   Convertible price/Parity = 34.36%.

6. What do the following represent in terms of intrinsic value and time value?

Parity: parity value reflects the equity value of the bond
Premium: the ratio of the bond price divided by parity value; this includes a measure of time value

7.2 Advantages of issuing and holding convertibles

7.2.1 *Borrowers' advantages*

The main advantage to a borrowing company in issuing convertible bonds is that the cost of the loan will be lower than a straight issue of debt. This is because, as a result of providing an equity option feature with the instrument, the coupon payable is lower than would be the case with a conventional bond. The bondholder accepts a lower coupon as the price for being able to share in the success of the company during the life of the bond, without having the direct exposure to the equity market that a holding in the ordinary shares would entail. The yield spread below which a convertible may be sold varies over time and with the quality of the issuer. Credit rating agencies generally rate convertible issues one grade below the straight debt of the issuer, although this would appear to reflect the price volatility of convertibles more than credit concerns. The second advantage to an issuer is that, under certain circumstances, it may be able to sell ordinary shares at a more favourable price via conversion than through a direct issue in the market. This may occur when, for example, the price of shares in a direct offer is lower because the shares represent investment in a project that is not expected to show returns until a period into the future. The company can issue callable convertibles with an exercise price above the direct market price, and then call the bond at a later date, forcing conversion at the higher price.

A disadvantage of issuing convertibles is where the company experiences a significant rise in its share price; in this case the interest cost may turn out to have been prohibitive and the company would have gained if it had issued shares directly. This however is only known in hindsight. The same occurs if there is a substantial drop in the share price after convertibles have been issued; here there is no incentive for bondholders to convert and the company is left with debt on its balance sheet until maturity, when it might have expected to have converted this to equity capital.

7.2.2 *Investors' advantages*

The advantages to an investor in holding convertible bonds centres on the ability to participate in the fortunes of the company without having to have a direct equity holding. The bondholder has a fixed coupon income stream, together with the advantages of senior debt (so it ranks above equity but below secured debt). If the underlying share price rises, the value of the convertible will rise as well, reflecting the increase in value of the embedded option, and if the conversion premium disappears the investor is able to realise an instant gain. This is the upside advantage. There is also downside advantage, because if the price of the underlying share falls, the convertible price will fall only to the point at which it represents fair value for an equivalent conventional fixed interest security. Although the coupon available with a convertible is lower than that available on a conventional vanilla bond, it will be higher than the dividend yield available from holding the share directly. If there is a rise in interest rates, there is further downside protection available in the time value of the embedded option, which may also add a floor to the price. Therefore in theory convertibles offer the downside protection of a debt instrument as well as the upside potential of an equity instrument.

The disadvantages to an investor in holding convertibles mirror the effects of the advantages: the main one is that the investor must accept a lower yield compared to bonds of identical maturity and credit quality. If a convertible is also callable, then this is an additional disadvantage for the investor, as the issuer may force conversion of the bond at its choosing, under potentially unfavourable conditions for the investor. The other disadvantages of holding convertibles are only apparent in hindsight: if the issuer's share price does not appreciate, the investor will have accepted a below-market coupon level for the life of the bond, and possibly a drop in the price of the bond below its issue price.

There a range of investor classes that may be interested in holding convertibles at one time or another. These include equity fund managers who are currently bearish of the market: purchasing convertibles allows them an element of downside market protection, whilst still enabling them to gain from upside movements. Equity managers who wish to enhance the income from their portfolios may also be interested in convertibles. For bond fund managers, convertibles provide an opportunity to obtain a limited exposure to the growth potential and upside potential associated with an option on equities.

Selected bibliography and references

Calamos, J., *Convertible Securities*, McGraw-Hill, 1998

Connolly, K., *Pricing Convertible Bonds*, Wiley, 1998

Fabozzi, F., *Bond Markets, Analysis and Strategies*, Prentice Hall, 1991

Kitter, G., *Investment Mathematics for Finance and Treasury Professionals*, Chapter 6, John Wiley and Son, 1999

8 Convertible Bonds II

In the previous chapter we reviewed convertible bond instruments and the features that differentiated them from conventional fixed interest bonds. In this chapter we consider the pricing and valuation of these securities.

8.1 Traditional valuation methodology

Let us consider another hypothetical security issued by ABC plc, a 20-year convertible bond with a coupon of 8%. 'One' bond has a nominal amount of £100 and may be converted into 10 ordinary shares of ABC plc. In November 1999 the bond is trading at £102 and the underlying shares at £2.50. In 1999 the company paid a dividend of £0.08 per share, a dividend yield of 3.20%.

If an investor buys just £100 nominal of the convertible, the premium paid over a direct purchase of the ordinary shares is equal to (100 × 102%) − (2.50 × 10) or £77 per bond. The compensation for this premium is the cash flow differential between the convertible and the underlying shares, which is calculated as (£100 × 8%) − (25 × 3.20%) or £7.20. The number 25 above is the parity value for the convertible obtained by multiplying the current share price by the conversion ratio. The annual cash flow differential measure implies that the investor receives £7.20 per annum more income from holding the convertible than would be received in the form of dividends from a holding of 10 ordinary shares in the company. This gives us a *payback period* measure of £77/7.20 or 10.694 years. Using the above analysis we may derive the formula at (8.1) below as an expression for the payback period for a convertible bond.

$$\text{Payback} = \frac{\dfrac{premium}{1+premium}}{rc - \dfrac{rd}{1+premium}} \tag{8.1}$$

where *rc* is the running yield on the convertible bond and *rd* is the dividend yield on the underlying ordinary shares. Note that (8.1) assumes a fixed coupon stream and therefore can only be used for bonds that pay a constant coupon. Bonds that have variable coupon payments, such as step-up convertibles, as well as bonds with no cash flow such as zero-coupon convertibles, cannot be analysed using (8.1). If we input the same parameters to (8.1) we will obtain the same value for the payback period of 10.694 years.

The concept of payback analysis for convertible securities is similar to payback or *breakeven* analysis in corporate finance: the length of time after which the initial outlay in a capital project is recouped as a result of investment returns from the project. However much corporate finance analysis now uses net present value and the concept of the internal rate of return for project appraisal. The assumptions behind payback period are also restrictive; if we consider (8.1) we see that for the measure to be meaningful it requires a constant dividend yield and a flat yield curve. It also does not discount cash flows and ignores cash flows beyond the payback period. Although it is possible to introduce certain variations into the analysis, for example a (constant) dividend growth rate and discounting of cash flows, the measurement does not take into account the option element of the convertible and the downside price floor available to investors. The value of a convertible must consider not only its premium over the underlying share price but also the fact that investors have the right, but not the obligation, to convert their holding and conversion is at their discretion. The decision to exercise is closely related to the future level of the issuer's share price, and therefore cannot be predicted. As well as holding a call option on the issuer's ordinary shares, bondholders are also holding in effect a put option, because if the share price falls and makes conversion uneconomic, they will elect to hold the bond to maturity and receive the redemption payment instead. Any fair valuation of a convertible should therefore ideally consider both option features of the bond.

The remainder of this chapter reviews a convertible valuation model that incorporates the likelihood of the option feature being exercised during the life of the bond.

8.2 Fair value of a convertible bond

The current analytical approach to convertible bond valuation is to consider the instrument as a conventional vanilla bond and an embedded option(s). That is, the value of a convertible is the sum of its bond value and the value of the embedded option. The bond element is valued using the standard redemption yield method. The option element is valued using a binomial option pricing model, which we review in this section.

8.2.1 *The binomial model*

The first option pricing model was developed by Fischer Black and Myron Scholes and was described in the *Journal of Political Economy* in 1973. Another approach, later termed the *binomial model* was described by Cox, Ross and Rubinstein (1979). Convertible bond analysis, like callable and put-able bonds analysis, frequently uses the binomial model.

The fair price of a convertible bond is the one that provides no opportunity for arbitrage profit, that is, it precludes a trading strategy of running simultaneous but opposite positions in the convertible and the underlying equity in order to realise a profit. There is no need to take a view on the price expectations of the equity to arrive at such a fair price. In this section we consider an application of the binomial model to value a convertible security. Under the conditions of an option pricing model such as Black–Scholes or the binomial model, we assume no dividend payments, no transaction costs and a risk-free interest rate with no bid-offer spreads.

In similar fashion to the description in Chapter 6, application of the binomial model requires the binomial tree detailing the price outcomes from the start period. In the case of a convertible bond this will refer to the prices for the underlying asset, which is the ordinary share of the issuing company. This is shown in Figure 8.1 below.

If we accept that the price of the equity follows such a path, we assume that it follows a *multiplicative binomial process*. This is a geometric process which accelerates as the share price increases and decelerates as the share price falls. This assumption is key to the working of the model and has been the subject of some debate. Although it is not completely accurate, by assuming that market returns follow this pattern we are able to model a series of share price returns that in turn enable us to calculate the fair value of an instrument containing an embedded option.

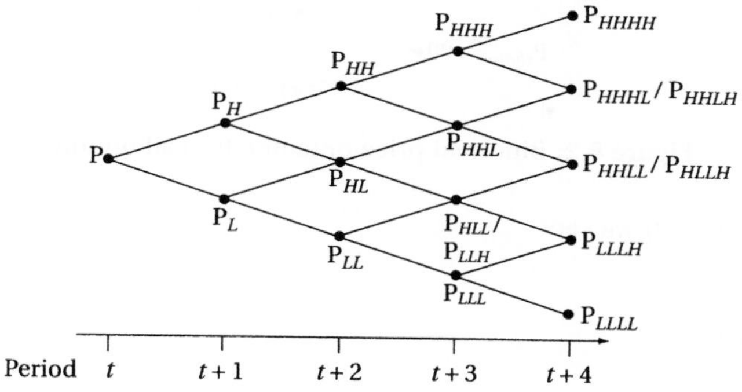

Figure 8.1: Underlying equity price binomial tree.

In Figure 8.1 the current price of the underlying share is given as P, in period 1 at time t. In the next period, time $t+1$, the share price can assume a price of P_H or P_L, with P_H higher than P and P_L lower than P. If the price is P_H in period 2, the price in period 3 can be P_{HH} or P_{HL}, and so on. The tree may be drawn for as many periods as required.

The value of a convertible bond is a function of a number of variables; for the purposes of this analysis we set the different parameters required as shown below.

P_{conv}	is the price of the convertible bond
P_{share}	is the price of the underlying equity
C	is the bond coupon
r	is the risk-free interest rate
N	is the time to maturity
d	is the risk of default
σ	is the annualised share price volatility
c	is the call option feature
p	is the put option feature
rd	is the dividend yield on the underlying share

In the first instance we wish to calculate the value of a call option on the underlying shares of a convertible bond. For Figure 8.1 if we state that the probability of a price increase is 50%, this leaves the probability of a price decrease as $1-p$ or 50%. If we were to construct a portfolio of δ shares, funded by M pounds sterling, which mirrored the final payoff of the call option, we can state that the call option must be equal to the value of the portfolio, to remove any arbitrage possibilities. To solve for this we set the following constraints:

$$\delta P_H + rM = P_H - X \tag{8.2}$$

$$\delta P_L + rM = 0 \tag{8.3}$$

where X is the strike price of the option. If we say that the exercise price is 100 then it will be higher than P_L and lower than P_H. This is illustrated by Figure 8.2.

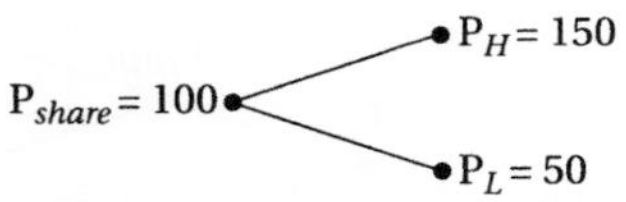

Figure 8.2: Binomial price outcome for call option.

From equation (8.3) we set:

$$rM = -\delta P_L \tag{8.4}$$

$$M = \frac{-(\delta P_L)}{r}. \tag{8.5}$$

Substituting (8.5) into (8.2) gives us:

$$\delta P_H - \delta P_L = P_H - X$$

$$\Rightarrow \delta = \frac{P_H - X}{P(H - L)}. \tag{8.6}$$

The number of shares that would be held in the portfolio is δ, which is known as the *delta* or *hedge ratio*.

We use the relationships above to solve for the value of the borrowing component M, by substituting (8.6) into (8.3), giving us:

$\frac{P_H - X}{P(H - L)} \cdot P_L + rM = 0$, and rearranging for M we obtain:

$$M = \frac{-L(P_H - X)}{r(H - L)}. \tag{8.7}$$

Given the relationships above then we may set the fair value of a call option as (8.8):

$$c = \delta P + r. \tag{8.8}$$

Following Black–Scholes, an estimate of the extent of the increase and decrease in prices from period 1 is given by:

$$H = e^{r+\sigma} \tag{8.9}$$

$$L = e^{r-\sigma} \tag{8.10}$$

where r is the risk-free interest rate and σ is the volatility of the share price at each time period.

We are now in a position to apply this analysis to a convertible security. Table 8.1 sets the terms and parameters for an hypothetical convertible bond and underlying share price.

Using the parameters above we may calculate the value of the underlying equity, which is priced at 100 in period 1. The volatility is assumed constant at 10%, and the maturity of the bond is five years or 1825 days. The price is calculated over ten periods, with each period equal to a half-year or 180 days. The risk-free interest rate is 4%, however this must be continuously compounded, which is calculated as follows:

$$r = ln(1.04) = 0.039220$$

and over one time period or 180 days this is 0.02017 or 2.017%. This is therefore the risk-free interest rate. The volatility level of 10% is an annualised figure, following market convention.

Equity price	100
Conversion price	100
Coupon	5% s/a
Time to maturity	5 years
Volatility	10%
r	4%
'H'	1.095138
'L'	0.950716

Table 8.1

This may be broken down per time period as well, and this is calculated by multiplying the annual figure by the square root of the time period required. This is shown below:

$$\sigma \times \sqrt{t/N} = 0.10 \times \sqrt{0.5} = 0.07071.$$

This allows the calculation of H and L which are given below:

$$H = e^{0.012518 + 0.1424} = 1.095138$$

$$L = e^{0.012518 - 0.1424} = 0.950716.$$

Using these parameters the price tree for the underlying equity, from time periods t to $t+10$ under the assumptions given is shown at Table 8.2, with $t+10$ representing the last period five years from now.

The valuation now proceeds to the conventional bond element of the convertible. The bond has a coupon of 5.0% payable semi-annually and a maturity of five years. We assume a 'credit spread' of 200 basis points above the risk-free interest rate, so a discount rate of 6.00% is used as the market rate required to value the bond. This credit spread is a subjective measure based on the perceived credit risk of the bond issuer. On maturity the bond must be priced at par or 100, while the final coupon is worth 2.50. Therefore the value of the bond on maturity in the final period (at $t+10$) must be 102.50. This is shown at Table 8.3. The value of the bond at earlier nodes along the binomial tree is then calculated using straightforward discounting,

Period	**0**	**1**	**2**	**3**	**4**	**5**	**6**	**7**	**8**	**9**	**10**
0	100.00	114.89	124.51	144.08	179.06	205.12	235.69	269.07	294.45	341.25	398.74
1		89.02	100.05	115.94	125.86	155.86	174.60	189.98	245.49	276.48	315.68
2			79.32	88.05	101.04	118.59	136.98	154.87	181.46	207.63	237.87
3				70.14	81.13	90.89	103.74	120.46	138.37	168.74	192.58
4					57.43	67.63	79.03	90.65	103.58	128.41	142.35
5						49.06	56.90	69.05	84.14	94.18	106.41
6							40.14	50.05	61.29	74.85	83.34
7								35.89	45.20	55.04	67.32
8									31.24	42.03	51.26
9										27.67	33.49
10											22.07

Table 8.2: Underlying share price tree.

Period	0	1	2	3	4	5	6	7	8	9	10
0	98.23	98.60	98.98	99.38	99.79	100.21	100.64	101.08	101.54	102.01	102.50
1		98.60	98.98	99.38	99.79	100.21	100.64	101.08	101.54	102.01	102.50
2			98.98	99.38	99.79	100.21	100.64	101.08	101.54	102.01	102.50
3				99.38	99.79	100.21	100.64	101.08	101.54	102.01	102.50
4					99.79	100.21	100.64	101.08	101.54	102.01	102.50
5						100.21	100.64	101.08	101.54	102.01	102.50
6							100.64	101.08	101.54	102.01	102.50
7								101.08	101.54	102.01	102.50
8									101.54	102.01	102.50
9										102.01	102.50
10											102.50

Table 8.3: Conventional bond price tree.

using the 6% discount rate. For example at $t+9$ the valuation is obtained by taking the maturity value of 102.5 and discounting at the credit-adjusted interest rate, as shown below:

$$P = (102.5/1.03) + 2.5 = 102.01.$$

This process is continued all the way to time t.

We may take the analysis further for a conventional convertible bond plus embedded option. Table 8.4 shows the price tree for the conventional bond where the share price and conversion price is equal to 100 in the current time period. If we assume the share price in period $t+9$ is 94.18, then in period $t+10$ the share can assume only one of two possible values, 106.41 or 83.34 (see Table 8.2). In these cases the value of the call option c_H and c_L will be equal to the higher of the bond's conversion value or its redemption value, which is 106.41 if there is a rise in the price of the underlying or 102.50 if there is a fall in the price of the underlying. These are the range of possible final values for the bond, however we require the current (present) value, which must be discounted at the appropriate rate. To determine the correct rate to use, consider the corresponding price of the conventional bond when the share price is 27.67 at period $t+9$. The price of the bond is calculated on the

Period	0	1	2	3	4	5	6	7	8	9	10
0	113.91	120.21	134.70	158.87	188.08	207.34	237.69	270.61	295.12	341.25	398.74
1		106.32	108.73	126.95	135.73	159.09	178.05	190.65	246.67	276.48	315.68
2			104.50	107.12	118.40	125.40	142.28	155.87	182.43	207.63	237.87
3				102.47	105.39	112.58	118.79	122.86	138.98	168.74	192.58
4					101.05	103.41	106.08	108.43	112.79	128.41	142.35
5						100.21	102.76	103.36	103.08	106.07	106.41
6							100.64	101.98	101.75	102.01	102.50
7								101.08	101.54	102.01	102.50
8									101.54	102.01	102.50
9										102.01	102.50
10											102.50

Table 8.4: Convertible bond price tree.

basis that on maturity the bond will be redeemed irrespective of what happens to the share price. Therefore the appropriate interest rate to use when discounting a conventional bond is the credit-adjusted rate, as this is a corporate bond carrying credit risk. However this does not apply at a different share price; consider the corresponding conventional bond price when the underlying share price is 341.25, in the same time period. The hedge ratio at this point on the binomial price tree is calculated using:

$$\delta = \frac{(c_H - c_L)}{P(H - L)} = 1.$$

The position of a bondholder at this point is essentially long of the underlying stock and also receiving a coupon. A position equivalent to a risk-free bond may be put on synthetically by holding the convertible bond and selling short one unit of the underlying equity. In the event of default the position is hedged, therefore in this case the correct discount rate to use is the risk-free interest rate. The correct rate to use is dependent on the price of the underlying share and how this affects the behaviour of the convertible, and will be either the risk-free rate or a credit-adjusted rate. The adjusted rate can be obtained using (8.11) and indeed all the convertible prices at period $t + 9$ are obtained using (8.11). The process is then carried out 'backwards' to complete the entire price tree. At period t with the share price at 100 then the fair value of the convertible is seen to be 113.91.

$$r_{adjusted} = \delta \cdot r + (1 - \delta) \cdot credit\ adjustment. \tag{8.11}$$

8.2.2 *Analysis for call and put features*

Convertible bonds are sometimes issued with call and/or put provisions embedded within them. Such features may be analysed using the same binomial tree as was used for valuing the straight convertible bond. Using the same hypothetical bond considered in the previous section, assume now that the bond additionally is callable at set dates, as specified below.

Call provision	
Year 2	115
Year 3	110
Year 4	105
Year 5	100

As specified above, the bond is not callable for the first two years after issue, after which it is callable at specified prices on each anniversary of issue until maturity. The call feature is academic after year 4 because the bond is redeemable at par on the maturity date in any case. As part of the analysis we assume that the issuer will act in its interests, and will call the bond if there is material advantage to be gained from so doing. This then enables us to introduce the call feature into the binomial tree.

The issuer will effect *forced conversion* at nodes on the binomial tree (that occur on bond issue anniversary dates from year 2) where the share price or parity value is greater than the exercise price. It is worthwhile for the issuer to call the bond in such cases because the option is worth more 'alive' than 'dead'. We may consider forced conversion using the price tree at Table 8.5.

The callable bond price at $t + 8$ of 294.45 corresponds with the underlying share price at this time period. The holding period return of the convertible at this point may be calculated from the corresponding value at this point for the straight convertible bond, which is 295.12.

Period	0	1	2	3	4	5	6	7	8	9	10
0	109.34	118.69	130.46	158.87	187.98	206.34	236.89	268.56	294.45	341.25	398.74
1		102.35	110.60	125.95	134.63	158.67	177.27	190.07	245.49	276.48	315.68
2			102.80	105.68	117.64	123.85	141.08	155.28	181.46	207.63	237.87
3				100.76	105.56	108.55	115.75	121.05	138.37	168.74	192.58
4					102.57	101.21	103.45	105.43	103.58	128.41	142.35
5						100.21	100.91	102.06	103.08	106.07	106.41
6							100.64	101.98	101.75	102.01	102.50
7								101.08	101.54	102.01	102.50
8									101.54	102.01	102.50
9										102.01	102.50
10											102.50

Table 8.5: Convertible bond with call feature, binomial price tree.

It is worthwhile for the issuer to call the bond at this point (at a call price of 105) because this value is higher than the value of the bond if it is converted. Therefore we assume the issuer will call the bond at 105 and pay the accrued interest to date. Note that this is academic however because the bondholder will elect to convert and receive the higher of the parity value or 294.45, albeit at the cost of accrued interest.

If the underlying share price is lower than the conversion price, for example at 31.24 in period $t+8$, the holding value of the convertible is of course the straight bond price of 101.54. There is no value to the company of calling the bond at this point.

Essentially if the holding value of the bond plus accrued interest is higher than the call price, then the fair value of the bond will be equal to the higher of the call price plus accrued or parity value; otherwise the bond value will be equal to the higher of the holding value or the call price. In our illustration the straight convertible bond had a value today of 113.91. The addition of a call feature has reduced the price of the bond (that is, increased the yield, as we would expect) to 109.34, so the call provision is worth 4.57.

8.2.3 *Model parameters*

The binomial model reviewed in the previous two sections will calculate the fair value for a convertible where certain parameters have been specified. It is immediately apparent that altering any of the inputs to the model will have an impact on the price calculation. In this section we consider the effect of changing one of these parameters.

Share price

The price of the underlying share is a key parameter of the model. A change in the value of the underlying share will result in a change in the value of the convertible; specifically a rise in the underlying will result in a rise in the price of the convertible, and a fall in the price of the underlying will result in a fall in the price of the convertible. The *delta* of an option instrument measures the extent of this change. Figure 8.3 depicts a graph drawn from the values in Table 8.2. It shows that when the share price is at low levels relative to the conversion price, the sensitivity of the convertible to movements in the share price is low. However when the share price is high, this sensitivity or *delta* approaches unity, so that a unit move in the price of the share is matched by a unit move in the price of the bond. In the former case the option is

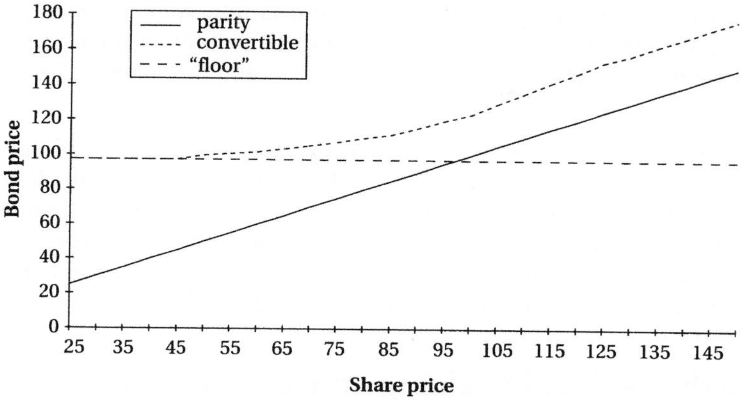

Figure 8.3: Convertible bond price sensitivity.

said to be 'out-of-the-money', while in the latter case the option is 'in-the-money'. Where the delta approaches unity the option is said to be 'deeply in-the-money'.

The measure of the change in the price of the convertible with respect to a change in the price of the underlying equity is given by the delta of the convertible, that is

$$\delta = \frac{\text{change in convertible price}}{\text{change in underlying price}}. \tag{8.12}$$

As we will note again in the introductory chapter on options the delta is defined as the first derivative of the price of an instrument with respect to the price of the underlying asset. Here we are concerned with the delta being the measure of the change in the price of the convertible bond with respect to change in the price of the underlying share. The value of delta in our illustration is given by the gradient of the convertible price line as shown in Figure 8.3. When the option feature of the convertible is deeply in-the-money, the convertible behaves more or less in the same way as the underlying share itself, but one that pays a coupon rather than a dividend.

The second derivative of the price change function, *gamma*, is the measure of the rate of change of delta with respect to the rate of change of the underlying share price, and is given by (8.13):

$$\gamma = \frac{\Delta\delta}{\Delta P_{share}}. \tag{8.13}$$

At low price levels for the underlying share, gamma is very low. This reflects the fact that at this price the delta is close to zero and the convertible behaves more like a conventional bullet bond, so that for small changes in the share price the delta will be unchanged. This pattern is repeated at high share price levels, where the delta is unity and gamma is close to zero: when a convertible is deep in-the-money and the delta is one, small increases in the share price will not affect the delta.

Volatility

A change in the volatility of the underlying share price will affect the price of the convertible, given that under the binomial model its value has been calculated based on a volatility level for the share. The measure of sensitivity of the convertible price to a change in the volatility of the underlying share is given by *vega*. Put simply, an increase in the volatility of the underlying has the effect that there is a greater probability of nodes on the binomial price tree being reached. This has a the effect of increasing the value of the convertible.

Interest rate

A change in the risk-free interest rate will have an impact on the price of the convertible. The measure of sensitivity of a convertible bond's price to changes in the level of interest rates is given by *rho*. The key factor is that the price of deeply out-of-the-money convertibles is sensitive to changes in interest rates, because at this point the convertible behaves similarly to a conventional straight bond. Deep in-the-money convertibles behave more like the underlying equity and are hardly affected by changes in interest rates.

8.3 Further issues in valuing convertible bonds

8.3.1 *Dilution*

Up to now the discussion has focused on treating the convertibility feature of the convertible bond much as a call option on the underlying stock. There are practical reasons why a convertible is not precisely identical to a call option however. In the first instance when a convertible bond is converted into the underlying shares, this results in the issue of new shares. This does not happen in the exercise of an equity call option, for which already existing shares are delivered. The effect on existing shareholders of a further issue of ordinary shares is termed *dilution*. In practice the effect of dilution is not often accounted for in the pricing of a convertible, although it is relevant.

The basic effect is given as (8.14) below, which we illustrate for an equity warrant. The exercise of a warrant results in the issue of new shares, upon which it may be shown that:

$$P_{warrant} = max\ ((P_{share} - E)/(1 + \lambda), 0) \tag{8.14}$$

where E is the exercise price and λ is the dilution factor resulting from the exercise of the warrant. This means that the holder of the warrant will receive the maximum of the diluted difference between the share price and exercise price, and zero. However the share price will reflect the effect of the approaching exercise date, that is it will incorporate the impact of the anticipated dilution. Logically this should have an impact on the price of the warrant or convertible, but is a function of how much in the-the-money the convertible is. In a binomial model the probabilities can be adjusted to one and zero for the final price path, if the convertible is deeply in- or out-of-the-money. With certain probabilities entered, the analyst may work backwards along the tree to arrive at the probability of conversion at each node. The effect of dilution could then be ignored for deeply out-of-the-money convertibles.

A new issue of convertible bonds can be expected to have an effect on the volatility of the share price and its likely path along a binomial tree. As the bond approaches maturity a commonly observed phenomenon is of it being 'pulled to the money'. The share price is effectively capped as a significant rise would result in share selling as the hedge ratio approached 100%, with selling by market makers who are long the convertible.

8.3.2 *Volatility level*

The pricing model reviewed in the previous section assumed a constant volatility level for the price returns of the underlying equity. This is clearly unrealistic over periods of time, although it is accepted by the market for short periods; this is because changes in volatility levels appear to occur quite slowly. Such changes also appear to be largely random rather than systematic, that is volatility appears to be *stochastic*. There is a considerable literature on incorporating changing volatility levels into pricing models, although it is common for banks to use the static model described in this chapter. This is because the binomial model appears to perform well in practice. Instruments such as convertible bonds have relatively long maturities, and are less sensitive to jumps in short-term volatility levels. That is, the impact of a change in volatility is viewed as not material when pricing long-dated instruments.

There are a number of issues that it is worthwhile to consider however. One of the most important is the concept of *mean reversion*. This is the term for a commonly observed behaviour pattern of volatility levels, whereby volatility levels return to a mean level after a period of corrections or market crashes. For example after the 1987 stock market crash or 'Black Monday' in the sterling market in 1992, individual volatility levels achieved very high figures (certain stock volatilities exceeded 100%), but it was only a matter of time before they reverted to a mean level. The same has been observed for commodity prices, for example the crude oil price in the aftermath of the Gulf crisis of 1990/91.

The *implied volatility* levels of longer-dated instruments such as convertible bonds reflect the fact that the market anticipates mean reversion. Observation of market behaviour also confirms that the volatility levels of individual shares tend to move in the same direction. This is logical, in the same way that share prices themselves reflect an element of specific company issues and an element that is attributed to the market in general. Another observation from the market is that share prices tend to be inversely related to changes in volatility levels. This is common for both individual shares as well as for market indices. The common explanation for this behaviour is that when share prices fall (rise), the debt/equity ratio rises (falls), which implies a higher (lower) risk level for equities. This indicates *skewed* distribution of returns. So far we have not discussed the distribution of stock price returns, which is generally assumed to follow a *normal* distribution, which is an assumption of the Black–Scholes and binomial models.[1] The market also accepts that this is not completely accurate, and that the distribution of returns tends to have fatter tails than a conventional normal distribution, a phenomenon known as *leptokurtosis*.[2] The existence of fatter tails will have an impact on pricing models, as deeply in or out-of-the-money options will tend to be mispriced.

These issues are reviewed in Part V of the author's book *The Bond and Money Markets*.

8.4 Convertible bond default risk

Virtually all convertible bonds are issued by corporates and therefore expose their holders to an element of *default* risk.[3] This is defined as the risk of a corporate failing to meet its contractual obligations regarding the payment of coupon or redemption proceeds.

---

1 Strictly speaking for the Black–Scholes model the assumption is that market returns follow a *geometric Brownian motion*.

2 This is discussed in Chapter 37 of the author's book *The Bond and Money Markets*.

3 Certain developed country governments have issued convertible bonds, including the United Kingdom, but these are convertible into another debt issue.

Although shareholders are at risk of the issuing company going bankrupt, strictly speaking this is not default risk because shares do not promise to pay a fixed interest cash flow for a set period of time in the future. The presence of default risk introduces further issues in the valuation of convertible bonds, which are considered in this section.

8.4.1 *Credit ratings*

The most commonly quoted ratings are those issued by Standard & Poor's and Moody's. Within domestic markets there are other local agencies that may be more influential or more frequently used. Rating agencies assign a formal credit rating to the individual issue of a corporate, although it is common for the market to refer to say, a 'double A-rated company'. The ratings fall into two main categories, *investment grade* and *speculative grade.* There is also a third category, companies in default. The role of the formal rating agencies is reviewed in Chapter 16; the main areas that they assess include the debt/equity ratio, the asset base, volatility of earnings per share, and the level of subordination of debt. The agencies analyse published accounting data as well as qualitative data such as the credibility and strength of senior management, and publish forecasts on company performance.

The credit rating of a company is a major determinant of the yield that will be payable by that company's bonds. This is because, in an increasingly integrated and global capital market, *name recognition* (the traditional major determinant) plays a decreasing role. The yield spread of a corporate bond over the risk-free bond yield is known as the *default premium.* In practice the default premium is composed of two elements, the compensation element specific to the company and the element related to market risk. This is because, in an environment where the default of one company was completely unrelated to the default of other companies, the return from a portfolio of corporate bonds would equal that of the risk-free bond, as the gains from bonds of companies that did not default compensated for the loss from those that did default. The additional part of the default premium, the *risk premium* is the compensation for risk exposure that cannot be diversified away in a portfolio, known as *systematic* or *non-diversifiable* risk. Observation of the market tells us that in certain circumstances the default patterns of companies are related, for example in a recession there are more corporate defaults, and this fact is reflected in the risk premium.

8.4.2 *The credit spread*

Earlier in this chapter we reviewed a binomial pricing model for convertible bonds. One of the parameters of the model is the credit-risk adjusted discount rate. The appropriate rate to use for this parameter is not always clear cut, as it is a subjective matter as to what credit spread to apply to the risk-free rate. The analysis is less problematic if there is an equivalent-maturity conventional bond from the same issuer in existence. The yield spread between such a bond and the convertible bond can be said, simplistically, to reflect the market's appetite for the convertible over the straight bond. If this is not available, it may be appropriate to consider the conventional bond issued by a company that is in the same

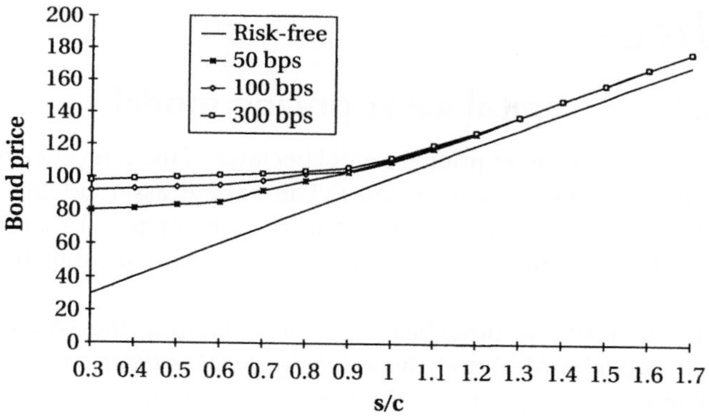

Figure 8.4: Price sensitivity of credit spread.

industry as the issuer, and has a similar capital structure. For deeply out-of-the money convertibles, the yield may be taken to be the equivalent of a conventional bond, and therefore it is possible to view the theoretical spread directly.

The sensitivity of the theoretical yield spread of a convertible bond to moves in the underlying equity price varies with credit rating. This is to be expected, since, in addition to their yields, lower-rated bonds have higher price volatility levels. This sensitivity is at its highest during times of extreme volatility in the equity market and during times of recession, during which yield spreads widen most significantly. It is possible to plot this sensitivity, shown as Figure 8.4.

The graph at Figure 8.4 shows the theoretical price profile of the hypothetical 1.50% coupon convertible bond introduced earlier, with different credit spreads selected. The risk-free interest rate is 1.50%, and the constant volatility level is 20% as before. The price profile is then plotted for credit-adjusted spreads of 50 basis points, 100 basis points and 300 basis points. When a convertible is deeply in-the-money, default risk is less significant, and at a delta value approaching unity, the risk-free rate becomes the relevant rate at which to value the bond; at this point, a change in the credit spread has little or no impact on the price of the convertible. The opposite is true when the convertible is deeply out-of-the-money and/ or when the delta approaches zero.

Appendices

Appendix 8.1: Capital asset pricing model

We briefly discuss the capital asset pricing model because of the relevance of the underlying equity value in the valuation of convertibles. The capital asset pricing model (CAPM), attributable to Sharpe (1964), is a cornerstone of modern financial theory and originates from analysis of the cost of capital. The cost of capital of a company may be broken down as shown by Figure 8.5.

The three most common approaches used for estimating the cost of equity are the *dividend valuation model*, CAPM and the *arbitrage pricing theory*. CAPM is in a class of market models known as *risk premium* models which rely on the assumption that every individual holding a risk-carrying security will demand a return in excess of the return they would receive from holding a risk-free security. This excess is the investor's compensation for her risk exposure. The risk premium in CAPM is measured by *beta*, it is known as *systematic*, *market* or *non-diversifiable* risk. This risk is caused by macroeconomic factors such as inflation or political events, which affect the returns of all companies. If a company is affected by these macroeconomic factors in the same way as the market (usually measured by a stock index), it will have a beta of 1, and will be expected to have returns equal to the market. Similarly if a company's systematic risk is greater than the market, then its capital will be priced such that it is expected to have returns greater than the market. Essentially therefore beta is a measure of volatility, with a company's relative volatility being measured by comparing its returns to the market's returns. For example if a share has a beta of 2.0, then on average for every 10% that the market index has returned above the risk-free rate, the share is expected to have returned 20%. Conversely for every 10% the market has under-performed the risk-free rate, the share is expected to have returned 20% below. Beta is calculated for a share by measuring its variance relative to the variance of a market index such as the FTSE All Share or the S&P 500. The most common method of estimating beta is with standard regression techniques based on historical share price movements over say, a five-year period.

To obtain the CAPM estimate of the cost of equity for a company, two other pieces of data are required, the risk-free interest rate and the equity risk premium. The risk-free rate represents the most secure return that can be achieved in the market. It is theoretically defined as an investment that has no variance and no covariance with the market; a perfect proxy for the risk-free rate therefore would be a security with a beta equal to zero, and no

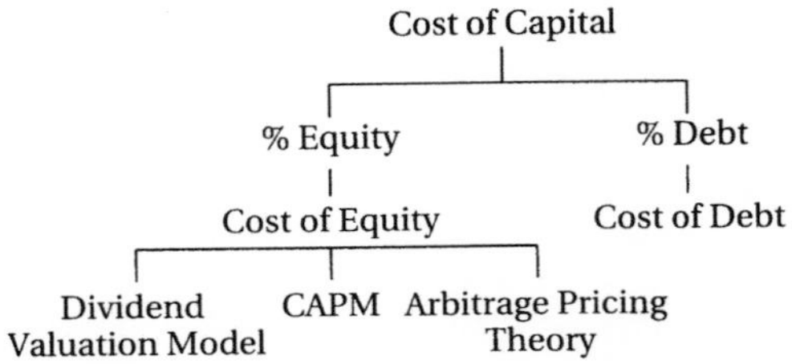

Figure 8.5: Components of the cost of capital.

volatility. Such an instrument does not, to all intents and purposes, exist. Instead the market uses the next-best proxy available, which in a developed economy is the government issued Treasury bill, a short-dated debt instrument guaranteed by the government.

The equity risk premium represents the excess return above the risk-free rate that investors demand for holding risk-carrying securities. The risk premium in the CAPM is the premium above the risk-free rate on a portfolio assumed to have a beta of 1.0. The premium itself may be estimated in a number of ways. A common approach is to use historical prices, on the basis that past prices are a satisfactory guide to the future[4] and use these returns over time to calculate an arithmetic or geometric average. Research has shown that the market risk premium for the US and UK has varied between 5.5% and 11% historically (Mills 1994), depending on the time period chosen and the method used.

Once the beta has been determined, the cost of equity for a corporate is given by CAPM as (8.15):

$$k_e = r_f + (\beta \times r_e) \tag{8.15}$$

where

k_e	is the cost of equity
r_f	is the risk-free interest rate
r_e	is the equity risk premium
β	is the share beta.

The primary assumption behind CAPM is that all the market-related risk of a share can be captured in a single indicator, the beta. This would appear to be refuted by evidence that fund managers sometimes demand a higher return from one portfolio than another when both apparently are equally at risk, having betas of 1.0. The difference in portfolio returns cannot be due to differences in specific risk, because diversification nearly eliminates such risk in large, well-balanced portfolios. If the systematic risk of the two portfolios were truly identical, then they would be priced to yield identical returns. Nevertheless the CAPM is often used by analysts to calculate cost of equity and hence cost of capital.

If we consider the returns on an individual share and the market as positively sloping lines on a graph plotting return, beta is usually given by (8.16):

$$r_s = \alpha_{sl} + \beta_{sl} r_l + \varepsilon_{sl} \tag{8.16}$$

where

r_s	is the return on security s
r_l	is the return on the market (usually measured for a given index)
α_{sl}	is the intercept between s and I, often termed the 'alpha'
β_{sl}	is the slope measurement or beta
ε	is a random error term.

4 Not that any self-respecting independent financial advisor would say this!

Selected bibliography

Bhattacharya, M., Zhu, Y., 'Valuation and Analysis of Convertible Securities', in Fabaozzi, F., *The Fixed Income Handbook*, 5th edition, McGraw-Hill, pp. 791–817

Bierman, H., 'The cost of warrants', *Journal of Financial and Quantitative Analysis*, June 1973, pp. 499–503

Black, F., Scholes, M., 'The pricing of options and corporate liabilities', *Journal of Political Economy* 81, 1973, pp. 637–659

Brennan, M., Schwartz, E., 'Analysing convertible bonds', *Journal of Financial and Quantitative Analysis* 15, November 1980, pp. 907–929

Calamos, J.P., *Investing in Convertible Securities*, Longman, 1988

Cooper, I., *The relationship between two methods of valuing convertible bonds*, London Business School, 1988

Cowan, A.R., Nandkumar N., Singh, A.K., 'Calls and out of the money convertible bonds', *Financial Management* 22, 1993, pp. 105–116

Cox, J., Ross, S., Rubinstein, M., 'Option pricing: a simplified approach', *Journal of Financial Economics* 7(3), September 1979, pp. 229–263

Dunn, K., Eades, K., 'Voluntary conversion of convertible securities and the option call strategy', *Journal of Financial Economics* 23, 1989, pp. 273–301

Gemmill, G., *Options Pricing*, McGraw-Hill International, 1993

Ho, T.S.Y., Lee, S., 'Term structure movements and pricing interest rate contingent claims', *Journal of Finance*, December 1986, pp. 1–22

Ingersoll, J., Jr., 'An examination of convertible call policies on convertible securities', *Journal of Finance* 32, May 1977, pp. 463–478

Kim Yong-Cheol, Stultz, R., 'Is there a global market for convertible bonds?', *Journal of Business* 65, 1992, pp. 75–92

King, R., 'The effect of convertible bond equity values on dilution and leverage', *The Accounting Review* 59, 1984, pp. 419–431

Liebowitz, M., 'Understanding convertible securities', *Financial Analysts Journal* 30, 1974, pp. 57–67

Lewis, C., 'Convertible debt: valuation and conversion in complex capital structures', *Journal of Banking and Finance* 15, 1991, pp. 665–682

McGuire, S., *Convertibles*, Woodhead-Faulkner, 1990

Mills. R., *Strategic Value Analysis*, Mars Business Associates, 1994

Sharpe, W., 'Capital Asset Prices: A Theory of Market Equilibrium Under Conditions of Risk', *Journal of Finance*, September 1964

Walter, J., Que, A., 'The valuation of convertible bonds', *Journal of Finance* 28, 1973, pp. 713–732

9 The Eurobond Market

Virtually nowhere has the increasing integration and globalisation of the world's capital markets been more evident than in the Eurobond market. It is an important source of funds for many banks and corporates, not to mention central governments. The Eurobond market has benefited from much of the advances in financial engineering, and has undergone some innovative changes in the debt capital markets. It continues to develop new structures, in response to the varying demands and requirements of specific groups of investors. The range of innovations has customised the market to a certain extent and often the market is the only opening for certain types of government and corporate finance. Investors also often look to the Eurobond market due to constraints in their domestic market, and Euro securities have been designed to reproduce the features of instruments that certain investors may be prohibited from investing in their domestic arena. Other instruments are designed for investors in order to provide tax advantages. The traditional image of the Eurobond investor, the so-called 'Belgian dentist', has changed and the investor base is both varied and geographically dispersed.

The key feature of Eurobonds is the way they are issued, internationally across borders and by an international underwriting syndicate. The method of issuing Eurobonds reflects the cross-border nature of the transaction, and unlike government markets where the auction is the primary issue method, Eurobonds are typically issued under a 'fixed price re-offer' method or a 'bought deal'. There is also a regulatory distinction as no one central authority is responsible for regulating the market and overseeing its structure.

This chapter reviews the Eurobond market in terms of the structure of the market, the nature of the instruments themselves, the market players, the issuing process and technical aspects such as taxation and swap arrangements. A subsequent chapter reviews the secondary market.[1]

9.1 Eurobonds

A Eurobond is a debt capital market instrument issued in a 'Eurocurrency' through a syndicate of issuing banks and securities houses, and distributed internationally when issued, that is sold in more than one country of issue and subsequently traded by market participants in several international financial centres. The Eurobond market is divided into sectors depending on the currency in which the issue is denominated. For example US dollar Eurobonds are often referred to as *Eurodollar* bonds, similar sterling issues are called *Eurosterling* bonds. The prefix 'Euro' was first used to refer to deposits of US dollars in continental Europe in the 1960s. The Euro-deposit now refers to any deposit of a currency outside the country of issue of that currency, and is not limited to Europe. For historical reasons and also due to the importance of the US economy and investor base, the major

---

1 Note that Eurobonds are also known as international securities. All Eurobonds settle or 'clear' in the Euroclear and Clearstream settlement systems.

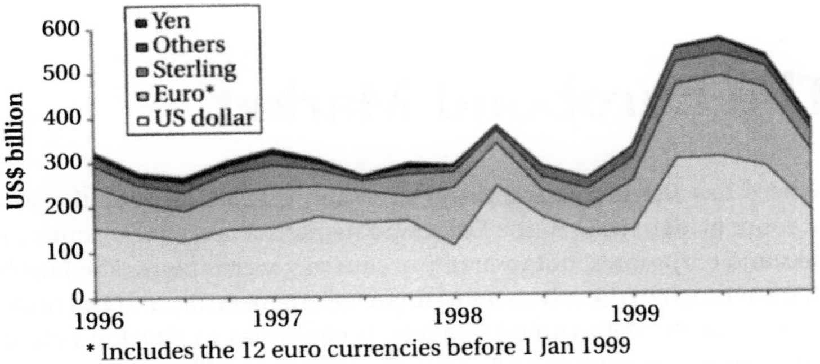

Figure 9.1: Non-government international bond issuance, 1996–1999. Source: BoE.

currency in which Eurobonds are denominated has always been US dollars. The volume of non-sovereign Eurobond issues from 1996 to 1999 is shown at Figure 9.1.

The first ever Eurobond is generally considered to be the issue of $15 million nominal of ten-year 5 ½% bonds by Autostrada, the Italian state highway authority, in July 1963.[2] The bonds were denominated in US dollars and paid an annual coupon in July each year. This coincides with the imposition in the United States of the Interest Equalisation Tax, a withholding tax on domestic corporate bonds, which is often quoted as being a prime reason behind the establishment of overseas deposits of US dollars.

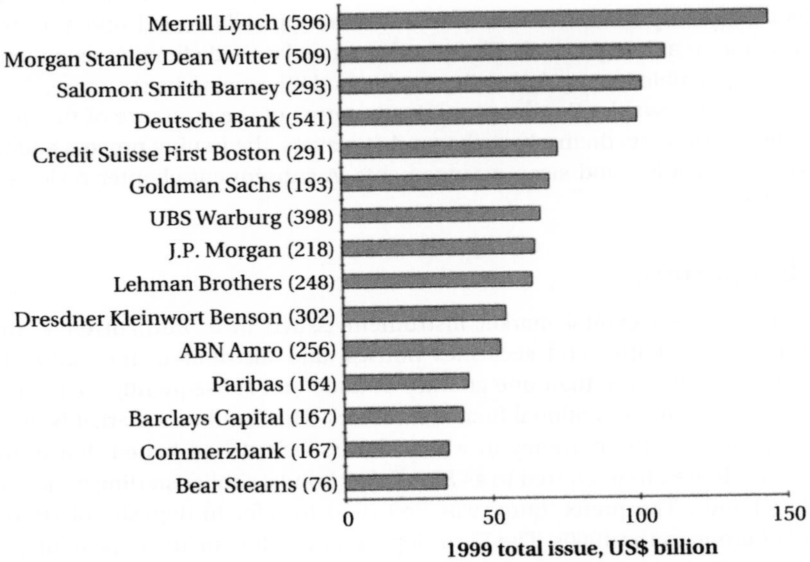

Figure 9.2: International Bond Issues in 1999, with leading book-runners (the number in brackets is the number of issues). Source: *The Economist.*

2 Decovny (1998) states that the first Eurobond issue was in 1957, but its identity is not apparent.

9.2 Foreign bonds

At this stage it is important to identify 'foreign bonds' and distinguish them from Eurobonds. Foreign bonds are debt capital market instruments that are issued by foreign borrowers in the domestic bond market of another country. As such they trade in a similar fashion to the bond instruments of the domestic market in which they are issued. They are usually underwritten by a single bank or a syndicate of domestic banks, and are denominated in the currency of the market in which they are issued. For those familiar with the sterling markets the best example of a foreign bond is a *Bulldog* bond, which is a sterling bond issued in the UK by a non-UK domiciled borrower. Other examples are *Yankee* bonds in the United States, *Samurai* bonds in Japan, *Rembrandt* bonds in the Netherlands, *Matador* bonds in Spain, and so on. Hence a US company issuing a bond in the UK, denominated in sterling and underwritten by a domestic bank would be issuing a Bulldog bond, which would trade as a gilt, except with an element of credit risk attached. In today's integrated global markets however, the distinction is becoming more and more fine. Many foreign bonds pay gross coupons and are issued by a syndicate of international banks, so the difference between them and Eurobond may be completely eroded in the near future.

The most important domestic market for foreign bond issues has been the US dollar market, followed by euros, Swiss francs and Japanese yen. There are also important markets in Canadian and Australian dollars, and minor markets in currencies such as Hong Kong dollars, Kuwaiti dinars and Saudi Arabian riyals.

9.3 Eurobond instruments

There is a wide range of instruments issued in the Eurobond market, designed to meet the needs of borrowers and investors. We review the main types in this section.

9.3.1 *Conventional bonds*

The most common type of instrument issued in the Euro markets is the conventional vanilla bond, with fixed coupon and maturity date. Coupon frequency is on annual basis. The typical face value of such Eurobonds is \$1000, e1000, £1000 or so on. The bond is unsecured, and therefore depends on the credit quality of its issuer in order to attract investors. Eurobonds have a typical maturity of five to ten years, although many high quality corporates have issued bonds with maturities of thirty years or even longer. The largest Eurobond market is in US dollars, followed by issues in Euros, Japanese yen, sterling and a range of other currencies such as Australian, New Zealand and Canadian dollars, South African rand and so on. Issuers will denominate bonds in a currency that is attractive to particular investors at the time, and it is common for bonds to be issued in more 'exotic' currencies, such as East European, Latin American and Asian currencies.

Eurobonds are not regulated by the country in whose currency the bonds are issued. They are typically registered on a national stock exchange, usually London or Luxembourg. Listing of the bonds enables certain institutional investors, who are prohibited from holding assets that are not listed on an exchange, to purchase them. The volume of trading on a registered stock exchange is negligible however; virtually all trading is on an over-the-counter (OTC) basis directly between market participants.

Interest payments on Eurobonds are paid gross and are free of any withholding or other taxes. This is one of the main features of Eurobonds, as is the fact that they are 'bearer'

Issuer	Rating	Coupon	Maturity	Volume e mn	Launch spread (benchmark) bps
Pearson	Baa1/BBB+	4.625%	July 2004	400	82
Lafarge	A3/A	4.375%	July 2004	500	52
Mannesmann	A2/A	4.875%	September 2004	2500	75
Enron	Baa2/BBB+	4.375%	April 2005	400	90
Swissair	–	4.375%	June 2006	400	78
Renault	Baa2/BBB+	5.125%	July 2006	500	88
Continental Rubber	–	5.25%	July 2006	500	100
Yorkshire Water	A2/A+	5.25%	July 2006	500	75
British Steel	A3/A–	5.375%	August 2006	400	105
International Paper	A3/BBB+	5.375%	August 2006	250	105
Hammerson	Baa1/A	5%	July 2007	300	92
Mannesmann	A2/A	4.75%	May 2009	3000	70

Table 9.1: Selected euro-denominated Eurobond issues in 1999. Source: Bloomberg.

bonds, that is there is no central register. Historically this meant that the bond certificates were bearer certificates with coupons attached; these days bonds are still designated 'bearer' instruments but are held in a central depository to facilitate electronic settlement.

9.3.2 *Floating rate notes*

An early innovation in the Eurobond market was the floating rate note (FRN). They are usually short- to medium-dated issues, with interest quoted as a spread to a reference rate. The reference rate is usually the London interbank offered rate (Libor), or the Singapore interbank offered rate for issues in Asia (Sibor). The euro interbank rate (Euribor) is also now commonly quoted. The spread over the reference rate is a function of the credit quality of the issuer, and can range from 10 to 150 basis points over the reference rate or even higher. Bonds typically pay a semi-annual coupon, although quarterly coupon bonds are also issued. The first FRN issue was by ENEL, an Italian utility company, in 1970. The majority of issuers are financial institutions such as banks and securities houses.

There are also perpetual, or undated, FRNs, the first issue of which was by National Westminster Bank plc in 1984. They are essentially similar to regular FRNs except that they have no maturity date and are therefore 'perpetual'. Most perpetual FRNs are issued by banks, for whom they are attractive because they are a means of raising capital similar to equity but with the tax advantages associated with debt. They also match the payment characteristics of the banks' assets. Traditionally the yield on perpetuals is higher than both conventional bonds and fixed-term FRNs.

9.3.3 *Zero-coupon bonds*

An innovation in the market from the late 1980s was the zero-coupon bond, or *pure discount* bond, which makes no interest payments. Like zero-coupon bonds initially in government markets, the main attraction of these bonds for investors was that, as no interest was payable, the return could be declared entirely as capital gain, thus allowing the bondholder to avoid income tax. Most jurisdictions including the US and UK have adjusted their tax legislation so that the return on zero-coupon bonds now counts as income and not capital gain.

9.3.4 *Convertible bonds*[3]

Another instrument that is common in the Eurobond market is the convertible bond. A Eurobond is convertible if it may be exchanged at some point for another instrument, usually the ordinary shares (equity) of the issuing company. The decision to elect to convert is at the discretion of the bondholder. Convertibles are analysed as a structure comprised of a conventional bond and an embedded option.

The most common conversion feature is an *equity convertible*, which is a conventional bond that is convertible into the equity of the issuer. The conversion feature allows the bondholder to convert the Eurobond, on maturity or at specified times during the bond's life, into a specified number of shares of the issuing company at a set price. In some cases the bond is convertible into the shares of the company that is guaranteeing the bond. The issuing company must release new shares in the event of conversion. The price at which the bond is convertible into shares, known as the exercise price, is usually set at a premium above the market price of the ordinary shares in the market on the day the bond is issued. Investors will exercise their conversion rights only if the market price has risen sufficiently that a gain will be realised by converting. The incorporation of a conversion feature in a bond is designed to make the bond more attractive to investors, as it allows them to gain from a rise in the issuing company's share price. The conversion feature also acts as a floor for the bond price. The advantages of convertibles for borrowers include the following:

- as the bond incorporates an added attraction in the form of the conversion feature, the coupon payable on the bond is lower than it otherwise would be; this enables the borrower to save on interest costs;
- issuing convertibles is one method by which companies can broaden the geographical base of their equity holders;
- companies are usually able to raise a higher amount at one issue if the bond is convertible, compared to a conventional bond.

Against these factors must be weighed certain disadvantages associated with convertibles, which include the following:

- the investor's insurance against the volatility of share price movements, an attraction of the convertible, is gained at the cost of a lower coupon than would be obtained from a conventional bond;
- convertibles are often issued by companies that would have greater difficulty placing conventional paper. Convertibles are usually subordinated and are often viewed more as equity rather than debt. The credit and interest-rate risk associated with them is consequently higher than for conventional bonds.

---

3 Convertible bonds are reviewed in Chapters 7–8.

There have been variations on the straight convertible bond in the Eurobond market. This includes the *convertible preference share*. This is a combination of a perpetual debt instrument cash flow with an option to convert into ordinary shares. Sometimes these issues are convertible not into shares of the issuer, but rather into the equity of a company in which the issuer has a significant shareholding.

Another variation is the *equity note*, which is a bond that is redeemed in shares and not in cash. The equity note is not a true convertible, since the conversion feature is not an option for the bondholder but a condition of the bond issue, and is guaranteed to take place. A more accurate description of an equity note would be an 'interest bearing equity future' note.

Eurobonds have also been issued with a feature that allows conversion into other assets such as crude oil or gold, or into other bonds with different payment characteristics. These are known as *asset convertibles*. Examples of such bonds include FRNs that are convertible under specified circumstances into fixed-rate bonds. One version of this was the *drop-lock* bond, which was first introduced in the early 1980s during a period of high interest rates. Drop-lock bonds are initially issued as FRNs but convert to a fixed-rate bond at the point that the reference rate falls to a pre-set level. The bond then pays this fixed rate for the remainder of its life. During the 1990s as interest rate volatility fell to relatively lower levels, drop-locks fell out of favour and it is now rare to see them issued.

Currency convertibles are bonds that are issued in one currency and are redeemed in another currency or currencies. Often this is at the discretion of the bondholder; other currency convertibles pay their coupon in a different currency to the one they are denominated in. In certain respects currency convertibles possess similar characteristics to a conventional bond issued in conjunction with a forward contract. The conversion rate is specified at the time of issue, and may be either a fixed-rate option or a floating-rate option. With a fixed-rate option the exchange rate between the currencies is fixed for the entire maturity of the bond at the time it is issued; with a floating-rate option the exchange rate is not fixed and is the rate prevailing in the market at the time the conversion is exercised. Initially most currency convertibles offered a fixed-rate option, so that the foreign exchange risk resided entirely with the issuer. Floating-rate options were introduced in the 1970s when exchange rates began to experience greater volatility.

9.3.5 *Eurowarrants*

The Eurobond warrant or *Eurowarrant* is essentially a call option attached to a conventional bond. The call option is convertible into either ordinary shares or other bonds of the issuing company, or rarely, another company. A typical Eurobond warrant will be comprised of a conventional bond, issued in denominations of $1,000 or $10,000, paying a fixed coupon. The attached warrant will entitle the bondholder to purchase shares (or bonds) at a specified price at set dates, or a set time period, up until maturity of the warrant, whereupon the warrant expires worthless. Warrants are often detached from their host bond and traded separately.

The exercise price of a warrant is fixed at a premium over the market price of the equity at issue. This premium is separate to the premium associated with a warrant in the secondary market, which is the total premium cost connected with buying the warrant and immediately exercising it into the equity, and not the cost associated with a purchase of the equity in the open market.

There are several advantages that Eurobond warrants hold for investors. They are composed of two assets that are usually traded separately in the secondary market; indeed warrants are often attached to bonds as a 'sweetener' for investors. Investors have an interest in the performance of the shares of the issuer without having a direct exposure to them. Should the intrinsic value of the warrant fall to zero, there is still time value associated with the warrant up until the maturity of the bond. Warrants typically possess high *gearing*, which is defined as the ratio of the cost of the warrant to the cost of the shares that the warrant holder is entitled to purchase. Borrowers may also gain from attaching warrants to their bond issues. The advantages include being able to pay a lower coupon than might otherwise have been the case. The exercise of a warrant results in the issuer receiving cash for the shares that are purchased (albeit at a below-market rate), compared with a convertible bond where the issuer receives only bonds that are subsequently cancelled. This is a feature of the warrant's gearing, as the value of the warrant is always less than the price at which the company guarantees to issue new equity to the warrant holder. The disadvantage at the time the warrant is exercised is that the company is receiving a below-market price for its shares at a time when they are trading at a historically high level; however there is a form of compensation for this since the company would have issued the bonds at a lower coupon rate than would have been the case had the warrants not been attached.

9.4 The issuing process: market participants

When a company raises a bond issue its main concerns will be the success of the issue, and the interest rate that must be paid for the funds borrowed. An issue is handled by an international syndicate of banks. A company wishing to make a bond issue will invite a number of investment banks and securities houses to bid for the role of lead manager. The bidding banks will indicate the price at which they believe they can get the issue away to investors, and the size of their fees. The company's choice of lead manager will be based on the bids, but also the reputation and standing of the bank in the market. The lead manager when appointed, will assemble a syndicate of other banks to help with the issue. This syndicate will often be made up of banks from several different countries. The lead manager has essentially agreed to underwrite the issue, which means that he guarantees to take the paper off the issuer's hands (in return for a fee). If there is an insufficient level of investor demand for the bonds the lead manager will be left holding ('wearing') the issue, which in addition to being costly will not help its name in the market. When we referred to an issuer assessing the reputation of potential lead managers, this included the company's view on the 'placing power' of the bank, its perceived ability to get the entire issue away. The borrowing company would prefer the issue to be over-subscribed, which is when demand outstrips supply.

In many cases the primary issue involves a *fixed price re-offer* scheme. The lead manager will form the syndicate which will agree on a fixed issue price, a fixed commission and the distribution amongst themselves of the quantity of bonds they agreed to take as part of the syndicate. The banks then re-offer the bonds that they have been allotted to the market, at the agreed price. This technique gives the lead manager greater control over a Eurobond issue. It sets the price at which other underwriters in the syndicate can initially sell the bonds to investors. The fixed price re-offer mechanism is designed to prevent underwriters from selling the bonds back to the lead manager at a discount to the original issue price, that is 'dumping' the bonds.

Before the bond issue is made, but after its basic details have been announced, it is traded for a time in the *grey market*. This is a term used to describe trading in the bonds before they officially come to the market, mainly market makers selling the bond short to other market players or investors. Activity in the grey market serves as useful market intelligence to the lead manager, who can gauge the level of demand that exists in the market for the issue. A final decision on the offer price is often delayed until dealing in the grey market indicates the best price at which the issue can be got away.

Let us now consider the primary market participants in greater detail.

9.4.1 *The borrowing parties*

The range of borrowers in the Euromarkets is very diverse. From virtually the inception of the market, borrowers representing corporates, sovereign and local governments, nationalised corporations, supranational institutions, and financial institutions have raised finance in the international markets. The majority of borrowing has been by governments, regional governments and public agencies of developed countries, although the Eurobond market is increasingly a source of finance for developing country governments and corporates.

Governments and institutions access the Euromarkets for a number of reasons. Under certain circumstances it is more advantageous for a borrower to raise funds outside its domestic market, due to the effects of tax or regulatory rules. The international markets are very competitive in terms of using intermediaries, and a borrower may well be able to raise cheaper funds in the international markets. Other reasons why borrowers access Eurobond markets include:

- a desire to diversify sources of long-term funding. A bond issue is often placed with a wide range of institutional and private investors, rather than the more restricted investor base that may prevail in a domestic market. This gives the borrower access to a wider range of lenders, and for corporate borrowers this also enhances the international profile of the company;
- for both corporates and emerging country governments, the prestige associated with an issue of bonds in the international market;
- the flexibility of a Eurobond issue compared to a domestic bond issue or bank loan, illustrated by the different types of Eurobond instruments available.

Against this are balanced the potential downsides of a Eurobond issue, which include the following:

- for all but the largest and most creditworthy of borrowers, the rigid nature of the issue procedure becomes significant during times of interest and exchange rate volatility, reducing the funds available for borrowers;
- issuing debt in currencies other than those in which a company holds matching assets, or in which there are no prospects of earnings, exposes the issuer to foreign exchange risk.

Generally though the Euromarket remains an efficient and attractive market in which a company can raise finance for a wide range of maturities.

The nature of the Eurobond market is such that the ability of governments and corporates to access it varies greatly. Access to the market for a first-time borrower has historically been difficult, and has been a function of global debt market conditions. There is a general set of criteria, first presented by van Agtmael (1983) that must be fulfilled initially, which for corporates include the following:

- the company should ideally be domiciled in a country that is familiar to Eurobond issuers, usually as a result of previous offerings by the country's government or a government agency. This suggests that it is difficult for a corporate to access the market ahead of a first issue by the country's government;
- the borrowing company must benefit from a level of name recognition or, failing this, a sufficient quality credit rating;
- the company ideally must have a track record of success, and needs to have published financial statements over a sufficient period of time, audited by a recognised and respected firm, and the company's management must make sufficient financial data available at the time of the issue;
- the company's requirement for medium-term or long-term finance, represented by the bond issue, must be seen to fit into a formal strategic plan.

Generally Eurobond issuers are investment-grade rated, and only a small number, less than 5%[4], are not rated at all.

9.4.2 *The underwriting lead manager*

Issuers of debt in the Eurobond market select an investment bank to manage the bond issue for them. This bank is known as the underwriter because in return for a fee, it takes on the risk of placing the bond amongst investors. If the bond cannot be placed in total, the underwriting bank will take on the paper itself. The issuer will pick an investment bank with whom it already has an existing relationship, or it may invite a number of banks to bid for the mandate. In the event of a competitive bid, the bank will be selected on the basis of the prospective coupon that can be offered, the fees and other expenses that it will charge, the willingness of the bank to support the issue in the secondary market, the track record of the bank in placing similar issues and the reach of the bank's client base. Often it is a combination of a bank's existing relationship with the issuer and its reputation in the market for placing paper that will determine whether or not it wins the mandate for the issue.

After the mandate has been granted, and the investment bank is satisfied that the issuer meets its own requirements on counterparty and reputational risk, both parties will prepare a detailed financing proposal for the bond issue. This will cover topics such as the specific type of financing, the size and timing of the issue, approximate pricing, fees and so on. The responsibilities of the lead manager include the following:

- analysing the prospects of the bond issue being accepted by the market; this is a function of both the credit quality of the issuer and the market's capacity to absorb the issue;
- forming the *syndicate* of banks to share responsibility for placing the issue. These banks are co-lead managers and syndicate banks;

---

4 Source: IMF.

- assisting the borrower with the prospectus, which details the bond issue and also holds financial and other information on the issuing company;
- assuming responsibility for the legal issues involved in the transaction, for which the bank's in-house legal team and/or external legal counsel will be employed;
- preparing the documentation associated with the issue;
- taking responsibility for the handling of the fiduciary services associated with the issue, which is usually handled by a specialised agent bank;
- if deemed necessary, establishing a pool of funds that can be used to stabilise the price of the issue in the *grey market*, used to buy (or sell) bonds if required.

These duties are usually undertaken jointly with other members of the syndicate. For first-time borrowers the prospectus is a very important document, as it is the main communication medium used to advertise the borrower to investors. In a corporate issue, the prospectus may include the analysis of the company by the underwriters, financial indicators and balance sheet data, a detailed description of the issue specifications, the members of the underwriting syndicate, and details of placement strategies. In a sovereign issue, the prospectus may cover a general description of the economy of the country, including key economic indicators such as balance of payments figures and export and import levels, the state of the national accounts and budget, a description of the political situation (with an eye on the stability of the country), current economic activity, and a statement of the current external and public debt position of the country.

9.4.3 *The co-lead manager*

The function of the co-lead manager in Eurobond issues developed as a consequence of the distribution of placing ability across geographic markets. For example, as the Eurobond market developed, underwriters who were mainly US or UK banks did not have significant client bases in say, the continental European market, and so banking houses that had a customer base there would be invited to take on some of the issue. For a long time the ability to place $500 000 nominal of a new Eurobond issue was taken as the benchmark against a potential co-lead manager.

The decision by a lead manager to invite other banks to participate will depend on the type and size of the issue. Global issues such as those by the World Bank, which have nominal sizes of $1 billion or more, have a fairly large syndicate. The lead manager will assess whether it can place all the paper or, in order to achieve geographic spread (which may have been stipulated by the issuer) it needs to form a syndicate. It is common for small issues to be placed entirely by a single lead manager.

9.4.4 *Investors*

The structure of the Eurobond market, compared to domestic markets, lends a certain degree of anonymity, if such is desired, to end-investors. This is relevant essentially in the case of private investors. The institutional holders of investors are identical to those in the domestic bond markets, and include institutional investors such as insurance companies, pension funds, investment trusts, commercial banks, and corporations. Other investors include central banks and government agencies; for example the Kuwait Investment Office and the Saudi Arabian Monetary Agency both have large Eurobond holdings. In the United

Kingdom, banks and securities houses are keen holders of FRN Eurobonds, usually issued by other financial institutions.

9.5 Fees, expenses and pricing

9.5.1 *Fees*

The fee structure for placing and underwriting a Eurobond issue are relatively identical for most issues. The general rule is that fees increase with maturity and decreasing credit quality of the issuer, and decrease with nominal size. Fees are not paid directly but are obtained by adjusting the final price paid to the issuer, that is, taken out of the sale proceeds of the issue. The allocation of fees within a syndicate can be slightly more complex, and in the form of an *underwriting allowance*. This is usually paid out by the lead manager.

Typical fees will vary according to the type of issue and issuer, and also whether the bond itself is plain vanilla or more exotic. Fees range from 0.25% to 0.75% of the nominal of an issue. Higher fees may be charged for small issues

9.5.2 *Expenses*

The expenses associated with the launch of a Eurobond issue vary greatly. Table 9.2 illustrates the costs associated with a typical Eurobond transaction. Not every bond issue will incur every expense, however these elements are common.

The expense items in Table 9.2 do not include the issuer's own expenses with regard to financial accounting and marketing. The reimbursement for underwriters is intended to cover such items as legal expenses, travel, delivery of bonds and other business expenses.

In general Eurobonds are listed on either the London or Luxembourg stock exchanges. Certain issues in the Asian markets are listed on the Singapore exchange. To enable listing to take place an issuer will need to employ a listing agent, although this is usually arranged by the lead manager. The function of the listing agent is to (i) provide a professional opinion on the prospectus, (ii) prepare the documentation for submission to the stock exchange and (iii) make a formal application and conduct negotiations on behalf of the issuer.

9.5.3 *Pricing*

One of the primary tasks of the lead manager is the pricing of the new issue. The lead manager faces an inherent conflict of interest between its need to maximise its returns from the syndication process and its obligation to secure the best possible deal for the issuer, its client. An inflated issue price invariably causes the yield spread on the bond to rise as soon as the bond trades in the secondary market. This would result in a negative impression being associated with the issuer, which would affect its next offering. On the other hand, too low a price can permanently damage a lead manager's relationship with the client.

Printing (prospectus, certificates, etc)	Clearing and bond issuance
Legal counsel (issuer and investment bank)	Paying agent
Stock exchange listing fee	Trustee
Promotion	Custodian
Underwriters expenses	Common depositary

Table 9.2: Expense elements, Eurobond issue.

For Eurobonds that are conventional vanilla fixed income instruments, pricing does not present too many problems in theory. The determinants of the price of a new issue are the same as those for a domestic bond offering, and include the credit quality of the borrower, the maturity of the issue, the total nominal value, the presence of any option feature, and the prevailing level and volatility of market interest rates. Eurobonds are perhaps more heavily influenced by the target market's ability to absorb the issue, and this is gauged by the lead manager in its preliminary offering discussions with investors. The credit rating of a borrower is often similar to that granted to it for borrowings in its domestic market, although in many cases a corporate will have a different rating for its foreign currency debt compared to its domestic currency debt.

In the grey market the lead manager will attempt to gauge the yield spread over the reference pricing bond at which investors will be happy to bid for the paper. The reference bond is the benchmark for the maturity that is equivalent to the maturity of the Eurobond. It is commonly observed that Eurobonds have the same maturity date as the benchmark bond that is used to price the issue. As lead managers often hedge their issue using the benchmark bond, an identical maturity date helps to reduce basis risk.

9.6 Issuing the bond

The three key dates in a new issue of Eurobonds are the announcement date, the offering day and the closing day. Prior to the announcement date the borrower and the lead manager (and co-lead managers if applicable) will have had preliminary discussions to confirm the issue specifications, such as its total nominal size, the target coupon and the offer price. These details are provisional and may well be different at the time of the closing date. At these preliminary meetings the lead manager will appoint a fiscal agent or trustee, and a principal paying agent. The lead manager will appoint other members of the syndicate group, and the legal documentation and prospectus will be prepared.

On the announcement date the new issue is formally announced, usually via a press release. The announcement includes the maturity of the issuer and a coupon rate or range in which the coupon is expected to fall. A telex is also sent by the lead manager to each prospective underwriter, which is a formal invitation to participate in the syndicate. These banks will also receive the preliminary offering circular, a timetable of relevant dates for the issue, and documentation that discloses the legal obligations that they are expected to follow should they decide to participate in the issue. The decision to join is mainly, but not wholly, a function of the bank's clients interest in the issue, which the bank needs to sound out.

The *pricing day* signals the end of the subscription period, the point at which the final terms and conditions of the issue are agreed between the borrower and the syndicate group. If there has been a significant change in market conditions, the specifications of the bond issue will change. Otherwise any required final adjustment of the price is usually undertaken by a change in the price of the bond relative to par. The ability of the lead manager to assess market conditions accurately at this time is vital to the successful pricing of the issue.

Once the final specifications have been determined, members of the syndicate have roughly 24 hours to accept or reject the negotiated terms; the bonds are then formally offered on the *offering day*, the day after the pricing day, when the issuer and the managing group sign the subscription or underwriting agreement containing the final specifications of the issue. The underwriting syndicate then enters into a legal commitment to purchase the bonds from the issuer at the price announced on the pricing day. A final offering circular is produced, and the lead manager informs the syndicate of the amount of their allotments. The lead manager may wish to either over-allocate or under-allocate the number of available bonds, depending on its view on future levels and direction of interest rates. There then begins the *stabilisation period*, when the bonds begin to trade in the secondary period, where Eurobonds trade in an over-the-counter market. About 14 days after the offering day, the *closing day* occurs. This is when syndicate members pay for bonds they have purchased, usually by depositing funds into a bank account opened and run by the lead manager on behalf of the issuer. The bond itself is usually represented by a *global note*, held in Euroclear or Clearstream, initially issued in temporary form. The temporary note is later changed to a *permanent* global note. Tranches of an issue targeted at US investors may be held in the Depository Trust Corporation as a registered note.

9.6.1 *The grey market*

The subscription period of a new Eurobond issue is characterised by uncertainty about potential changes in market conditions. After the announcement of the issue, but before the bonds have been formally issued, the bonds trade in the *grey market*. The grey market is where bonds are bought and sold for settlement on the first settlement date after the offering day. Grey market trading enables the lead manager to gauge the extent of investor appetite for the issue, and make any adjustment to coupon if required. A grey market that functions efficiently will at any time, reflect the market's view on where the bond should trade, and what yield the bond should be offered. It enables investors to trade in the primary market possessing information as to the likely price of the issue in the secondary market.

Another principal task of the lead manager is to stabilise the price of the bond issue for a short period after the bond has started trading in the secondary market. This is known as the stabilisation period, and the process is undertaken by the lead manager in concert with some or all of the syndicate members. A previously established pool of funds may be used for this purpose. The price at which stabilisation occurs is known as the *syndicate bid*.

9.6.2 *Alternative issue procedures*

In addition to the traditional issue procedure where a lead manager and syndicate offer bonds to investors based on a price set, on pricing day, based on a yield over the benchmark bond, there are a number of other issue procedures that are used. One of these methods include the *bought deal*, where a lead manager or a managing group approaches the issuer with a firm bid, specifying issue price, amount, coupon and yield. Only a few hours are allowed for the borrower to accept or reject the terms. If the bid is accepted, the lead manager purchases the entire bond issue from the borrower. The lead manager then has the option of selling part of the issue to other banks for distribution to investors, or doing so itself. In a volatile market the lead manager will probably parcel some of the issue to other banks for placement. However it is at this time that the risk of banks dumping bonds on the secondary market is highest; in this respect lead managers will usually pre-place the bonds with institutional investors before the bid is made. The bought deal is focused primarily on institutional rather than private investors. As the syndicate process is not used, the bought deal requires a lead manager with sufficient capital and placement power to enable the entire issue to be placed.

In a *pre-priced offering* the lead manager's bid is contingent on its ability to form a selling group for the issue. Any alterations in the bid required for the formation of the group must be approved by the borrower. The period allocated for the formation of the group is usually 2–4 days, and after the group has been formed the process is identical to that for the bought deal.

Yet another approach is the *auction issue,* under which the issuer will announce the maturity and coupon of a prospective issue and invite interested investors to submit bids. The bids are submitted by banks, securities houses and brokers and include both price and amount. The advantages of the auction process are that it avoids the management fees and costs associated with a syndicate issue. However the issuer does not have the use of a lead manager's marketing and placement expertise, which means it is a method that can only be employed by very high quality, well-known borrowers.

9.7 Covenants

Eurobonds are unsecured and as such the yield demanded by the market for any particular bond will depend on the credit rating of the issuer. Until the early 1980s Eurobonds were generally issued without covenants, due to the high quality of most issuers. Nowadays it is common for covenants to be given with Eurobond issues. Three covenants in particular are frequently demanded by investors:

- a negative pledge;
- a disposal of assets covenant;
- a gearing ratio covenant.

Negative pledge

A negative pledge is one that restricts the borrowings of the group which ranks in priority ahead of the debt represented by the Eurobond. In the case of an unsecured Eurobond issue this covenant restricts new secured borrowings by the issuer, as well as new unsecured borrowings by any of the issuer's subsidiaries, since these would rank ahead of the unsecured borrowings by the parent company in the event of the whole group going into receivership.

Disposal of assets covenant

This sets a limit on the amount of assets that can be disposed of by the borrower during the *tenor* (term to maturity) of the debt. The limit on disposals could be typically, a cumulative total of 30 per cent of the gross assets of the company. This covenant is intended to prevent a break-up of the company without reference to the Eurobond investors.

Gearing ratio covenant

This places a restriction on the total borrowings of the company during the tenor of the bond. The restriction is set as a maximum percentage say, 150–175 per cent of the company's or group's net worth (share capital and reserves).

9.8 Trust services

A Eurobond issue requires an agent bank to service it during its life. The range of activities required are detailed below.

9.8.1 *Depositary*

The depositary for a Eurobond issue is responsible for the safekeeping of securities. In the Euromarkets well over 90% of investors are institutions, and so as a result issues are made in dematerialised form, and are represented by a global note. Trading and settlement is in computerised book-entry form via the two main international clearing systems, Euroclear and Clearstream. Both these institutions have appointed a group of banks to act on their behalf as depositaries for book-entry securities; this is known as *common depositaries*, because the appointment is common to both Euroclear and Clearstream. Both clearing firms have appointed separately a network of banks to act as specialised depositaries, which handle securities that have been issued in printed note or *definitive* form.

As at February 2000 there were 21 banks that acted as common depositaries on behalf of Euroclear and Clearstream, although the majority of the trading volume was handled by just three banks, Citibank NA, Chase Manhattan and Deutsche Bankers Trust. The common depositary is responsible for:

- representing Euroclear and Clearstream, and facilitating delivery-versus-payment of the primary market issue by collecting funds from the investors, taking possession of the temporary global note (which allows securities to be released to investors), and making a single payment of funds to the issuer;
- holding the temporary global note in safe custody, until it is exchanged for definitive notes or a permanent global note;
- making adjustments to the nominal value of the global note that occur after the exercise of any options or after conversions, in line with instructions from Euroclear or Clearstream and the fiscal agent;
- surrendering the cancelled temporary global note to the fiscal agent after the exchange into definitive certificates or a permanent global note, or on maturity of the permanent global note.

A specialised depositary will hold definitive notes representing aggregate investor positions held in a particular issue; on coupon and maturity dates it presents the coupons or bond to the paying agent and passes the proceeds on to the clearing system.

9.8.2 *Paying agent*

Debt issuance in the Euromarkets requires a fiscal or principal paying agent, or in the case of a programme of issuance (for example a Euro-MTN programme) an issuing and paying agent. The responsibility of the paying agent is to provide administrative support to the issuer throughout the lifetime of the issue. The duties of a paying agent include:

- issuing securities upon demand in the case of a debt programme;
- authenticating definitive notes;

- collecting funds from the issuer and paying these out to investors as coupon and redemption payments;
- in the case of global notes, acting on behalf of the issuer to supervise payments of interest and principal to investors via the clearing systems, and in the case of definitive notes, paying out interest and coupon on presentation by the investor of the relevant coupon or bond to the paying agent;
- transferring funds to sub-paying agents, where these have been appointed. A security that has been listed in Luxembourg must have a local sub-paying agent appointed for it;
- maintaining an account of the cash flows paid out on the bond;
- arranging the cancellation and subsequent payment of coupons, matured bonds and global notes, and sending destroyed certificates to the issuer.

A paying agent will act solely on behalf of the issuer, unlike a Trustee who has an obligation to look after the interests of investors. For larger bond issues there may be a number of paying agents appointed, of which the *principal paying agent* is the coordinator. A number of *sub-paying agents* may be appointed to ensure that bondholders in different country locations may receive their coupon and redemption payments without delay. The term *fiscal agent* is used to describe a paying agent for a bond issue for which no trustee has been appointed.

9.8.3 *Registrar*

The role of the registrar is essentially administrative and it is responsible for keeping accurate records of bond ownership for registered securities. As most Eurobonds are issued in bearer form, there is not a great deal of work for registrars in the Euromarket, and the number of holders of registered notes is normally quite low.

The responsibilities of the registrar include:

- maintaining a register of all bondholders, and records of all transfers of ownership;
- coordinating the registration, transfer or exchange of bonds;
- issuing and authenticating new bonds should any transfer or exchange take place;
- maintaining a record of the outstanding principal value of the bond;
- undertaking administrative functions relating to any special transfers.

9.8.4 *Trustee*

An issuer may appoint a trustee to represent the interests of investors. In the event of default, the trustee is required to discharge its duties on behalf of bondholders. In certain markets a trustee is required by law, for instance in the United States a trustee has been a legal requirement since 1939. In other markets an issuer may appoint a trustee in order to make the bond issue more attractive to investors, as it means that there is an independent body to help look after their interests. This is particularly important for a secured issue, where the trustee sometimes holds collateral for the benefit of investors. Assets that are held by the trustee can be protected from the creditors of the issuer in the event of bankruptcy. A trustee has a variety of powers and discretion, which are stated formally in the issue trust deed, and these include its duties in relation to the monitoring of covenants, and duties to bondholders.

9.8.5 *Custodian*

A custodian provides safekeeping services for securities belonging to a client. The client may be an institutional investor such as a pension fund, that requires a portfolio of securities in many locations to be kept in secure custody on their behalf. As well as holding securities, the custodian usually manages corporate actions such as dividend payments.

9.9 Form of the bond

Eurobonds are issued in temporary global form or permanent global form. If issued in temporary form, the note is subsequently changed into either permanent global form or *definitive* form, which may be either a bearer note or registered.

9.9.1 *Temporary global form*

On issue the majority of Eurobonds are in the form of a single document known as a temporary global bond. This document represents the entire issue, executed by an officer of the issuer and certified by the fiscal agent or principal paying agent. After a period of time the temporary global bond, as its name suggests, is exchanged for either a permanent global bond or bonds in definitive form, which are separate certificates representing each bond holding.

The main reason bonds are issued in temporary form is because of time constraints between the launch of issue, when the offer is announced to the market, and closing, when the bonds are actually issued. This period differs according to the type of issue and instrument, for example for a plain vanilla issue it can be as little as two weeks whereas for more exotic issues (such as a securitisation) it can be a matter of months. The borrower will be keen to have the periods as short as possible, as the financing is usually required quickly. As this results in there being insufficient time to complete the security printing and authentication of the certificates, which represent the final definitive form, a temporary bond is issued to enable the offering to be closed and be placed in a clearing system, while the final certificates are produced. Bonds are also issued in temporary form to comply with certain domestic selling regulations and restrictions, for example a US regulation that definitive bonds cannot be delivered for a 40-day period after issue. This is known as the *lock-up* period.

9.9.2 *Permanent global bond*

Like the temporary bond the permanent global bond is a word-processed document and not a security printed certificate, issued on the closing date. It represents the entire issue and is compiled by the underwriter's legal representatives. In most cases it is actually held for safe-keeping on behalf of Euroclear and Clearstream by the trust or clearing arm of a bank, known as the *common depositary*. Borrowers often prefer to issue notes in permanent global form because this carries lower costs compared to definitive notes, which are security printed.

9.9.3 *Definitive form*

Under any circumstances where it is required that investors have legal ownership of the debt obligation represented by a bond issue they have purchased, a borrower is obliged to issue the bond in definitive form. The situations under which this becomes necessary are listed on the permanent global bond document, and include the following:

- where an investor requires a definitive bond to prove legal entitlement to the bond(s) he has purchased, in the case of any legal proceedings undertaken concerning the bond issue;
- in the event of default, or if investors believe default to have occurred;
- where for any reason the bonds can no longer be cleared through a clearing system, in which case they must be physically delivered in the form of certificates.

Bonds issued in definitive form may be either *bearer* or *registered* securities. A bearer security has similar characteristics to cash money, in that the certificates are documents of value and the holder is considered to be the beneficiary and legal owner of the bond. The bond certificate is security printed and the nature of the debt obligation is detailed on the certificate. Transfer of a bearer security is by physical delivery. Some of the features of traditional bearer securities include:

- *coupons*, attached to the side of the certificate, and which represent each interest payment for the life of the bond. The holder is required to detach each coupon as it becomes due and send it to the issuer's paying agent;[5]
- a *promise to pay*, much like a bank note, which confirms that the issuer will pay the bearer the face value of the bond on the specified maturity date;
- in some cases, a *talon*; this is the right for the bond holder to claim a further set of coupons once the existing set has been used (this only applies to bonds that have more than 27 interest payments during their lifetime, as IPMA rules prohibit the attachment of more than 27 coupons to a bond on issue).

The administrative burdens associated with bearer securities is the main reason why the procedures associated with them are carried out via the clearing systems and paying agents, rather than individually by each investor.

9.9.4 *Registered bonds*

Bonds issued in registered form are transferred by an entry on a *register* held by the issuer or its agent; the promise to pay is made to those names that appear on the register. Most Eurobonds are issued in bearer form for ease in clearing. Issues that are placed wholly or partly in the United States do however include an option allowing investors to take the bonds in registered form. This is done as most issues in the US are sold under *private placement*, in order to be exempt from SEC selling restrictions, and private placement in that country requires that the bonds are in registered form. In such cases the issuer will appoint a New York *registrar* for the issuer, usually the trust arm of a bank.

---

5 This is the origin of the term 'coupon' to refer to the periodic interest payments of a bond. There is a marvellous line in the film *Mission Impossible* when the character played by Tom Cruise, discussing terms in the back of a car with the character played by Vanessa Redgrave, demands payment in the form of US Treasury securities 'with coupons attached.' This is wonderfully out-of-date, but no less good fun for it!

9.9.5 *Fiscal agent*

A Eurobond issuer will appoint either a fiscal agent or a Trustee; both perform similar roles but under differing legal arrangements. The fiscal agent is appointed by and is the representative of the issuer, so unlike a Trustee it does not represent the bondholders. The main responsibilities of the fiscal agent are to pay the principal and interest payments, and it performs a number of administrative roles as well, such as the publication of financial information and notices to investors.

9.9.6 *Listing agent*

Issuers must appoint a listing agent if they wish to list the bond on the London or Luxembourg stock exchanges, as this is a requirement of the rules of the exchange. The listing agent communicates with the exchange on behalf of the issuer, and lodges the required documentation with it. In the UK the listing agent must be authorised under financial regulatory legislation (at the time of writing, the Financial Services Act 1986, although this in the process of being updated with new legislation covering the new Financial Services Authority regulatory body) and is usually the lead manager for the issue, although it is also common for a fiduciary service provider to be appointed to this role.

9.10 Clearing systems

The development of the international bond market has taken place alongside the introduction of specialised clearing systems, which are responsible (among other things) for the settlement and safekeeping of Eurobonds. The two main clearing systems are Euroclear and Clearstream.[6]

Euroclear was created by the Morgan Guaranty Trust Company of New York in 1968. Ultimately ownership passed to a consortium of banks and it is now run by Euroclear Clearance Systems plc, and operated by a co-operative company in Brussels.

The original Cedel was created in 1970 in Luxembourg and is owned by a consortium of around 100 banks, no one of which may hold more than 5% of the company. The two clearing systems do not restrict their operations to the settlement and custody of Eurobonds.

Both clearing systems exist to avoid the physical handling of bearer instruments, both on issue and in the secondary market. This means that on issue the actual bond certificates, which may be in *definitive bearer* or *global* form are passed on to a 'trust' bank, known as the *depositary* for safekeeping. The clearing system will track holdings via a book entry. To participate in the clearing system set up, an investor must have two accounts with it, which may be its own accounts or accounts held by their bank who will act as a nominee on their behalf; these are a *securities clearance* account, to which a security is credited, and a *cash* account, through which cash is received or paid out.

The clearing system will allocate a unique identification code, known as the International Securities Identification Number (ISIN) to each Eurobond issue, and a 'Common Code' is derived from the ISIN. The Common Code is essentially the identification used for each bond issue whenever an instruction is sent to the clearing agent to deal in it. The ISIN will be in addition to any number issued by a domestic clearing agent, for example the Stock

6 Clearstream was previously known as Cedel Bank.

Exchange number (SEDOL) for London listed securities. Both clearing systems have specific roles in both the primary and secondary markets. In the primary market they accept a new issue of Eurobonds, and on *closing* the required number of bonds are credited to the securities clearance account of the banks that are part of the issue syndicate. Securities are then transferred (electronic book entry) to securities accounts of investors.

The clearance systems keep a record on the coupon payment and redemption dates for each bond, and 'present' the bonds for payment on each appropriate date. Investors therefore do not need to present any coupons or certificates themselves, which is why the system is now paperless.

9.11 Market associations

9.11.1 *International Securities Market Association*

The International Securities Market Association (ISMA) is a self-regulatory body based in Zurich whose membership (from over 60 countries) consists of firms dealing in the international securities markets. It was originally known as the Association of International Bond Dealers. The body provides a regulatory framework for the international markets and has established uniform practices that govern nearly all transactions in Eurobonds between members. ISMA has also:

- introduced a standard method of calculating yields for Eurobonds;
- contributed towards the harmonisation of procedures for settling market transactions, and co-operation between the two main settlement institutions, Euroclear and Cedel;
- introduced TRAX, a computerised system for matching and reporting transactions in the market.

Dealers in the international markets must cooperate with national governments and ensure that market practice is consistent with national laws. ISMA provides a point of contact between the markets and government bodies. The ISMA centre at the University of Reading in England has also established itself as a leading research body, concentrating on the financial and securities markets, as well as offering Masters degrees in a range of capital markets subjects.

9.11.2 *International Primary Market Association*

The International Primary Market Association (IPMA) is a trade association of the leading underwriters in the primary international capital markets. It is also a self-regulatory association that has issued practical guidelines it expects members to follow. Its specific interest is with new issues, the co-operation between underwriters in a syndicate and standardised documentation. Members of IPMA are required to belong to ISMA. The IPMA recommendations are applicable to new issues and relate to matters such as:

- early disclosure of the terms of an issue;
- underwriting commitments;
- allotments of securities with investors;
- payment of commissions;
- delivery of bond/share certificates;
- fixed price offerings and re-offer schemes.

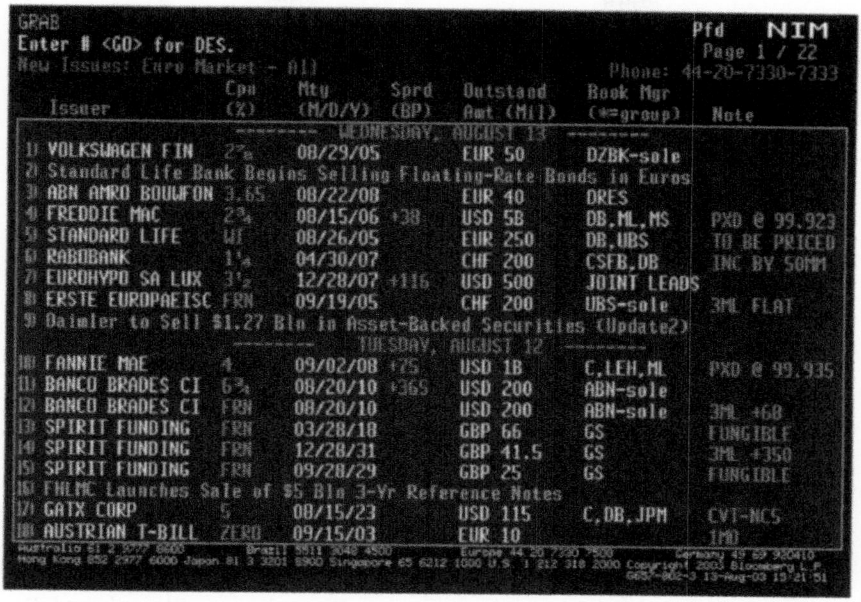

Figure 9.3: Eurobond new issues monitor on Bloomberg. © Bloomberg L.P. Used with permission.

The IPMA has also issued statements of best practice concerned with topics on a range of issuance procedures, for example in 1985 it published guidelines on the process of stabilisation. These guidelines emphasised the importance of correct pricing by lead managers.

9.12 Bloomberg screens

Eurobonds can be analysed using all the Bloomberg screens available for bonds generally. Figure 9.3 shows screen NIM on the Bloomberg which is the new issues monitor. It shows all new and recent issues in the market, in this case as at 13 August 2003. Issues that were placed on preceding days are also shown. We see that on the day in question seven bonds were placed in the market; another two were announced or were beginning to be placed by their underwriters.

Figure 9.4 shows a screen that can be obtained from the FMC menu page on Bloomberg, which stands for 'Fair Market Curve'. Using this page a user can select the yield curve for a number of market sectors; our example shows AAA, A and BBB-rated euro-denominated Eurobond curves as at 13 August 2003. The curves are labelled 'composite' because they take Eurobonds of the required rating from a number of different sectors, such as telecoms, utilities, industrials companies and so on.

9.13 Secondary market

Here we present the basic features of secondary market trading. Most Eurobonds are tradeable. Although in theory transfer is by physical delivery because the bonds are bearer instruments, the great majority of bonds will settle by the Euroclear or Clearstream

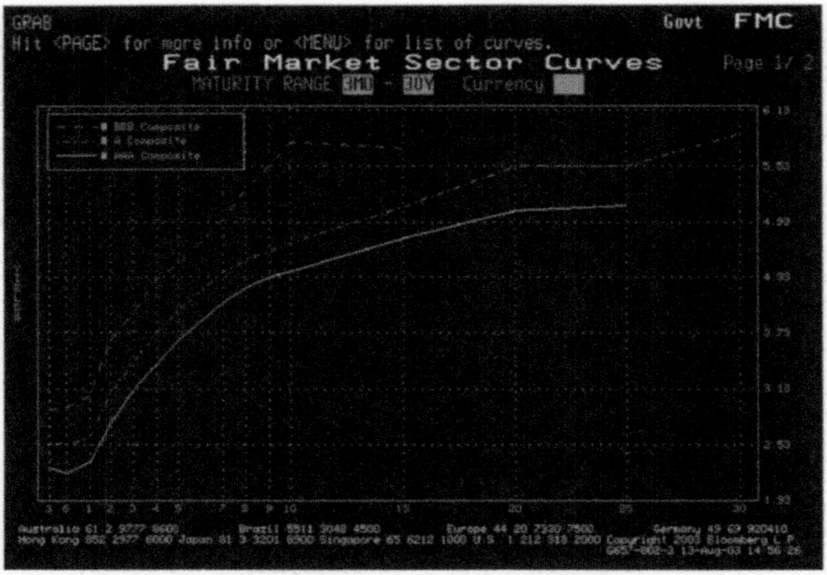

Figure 9.4: Composite fair market curves on Bloomberg © Bloomberg L.P. Used with permission.

International ('Clearstream') settlement systems.[7] Liquidity in the market varies over time and for individual issues will be a function of:

- size of issue;
- level of investor demand for the paper;
- commitment of market makers to support the issue.

A large number of Eurobonds are illiquid and market makers will quote a bid price only. No offer price is made because the market maker (unless he actually owns some of the issue) will be unable to find bonds to deliver to the buyer if it is illiquid. Many Eurobonds issued in the second tier currencies, such as Greek drachma, will have been issued and then immediately asset swapped, and hence there will be no paper available to trade (many large issuers will issue Eurobonds in a currency other than that which they require, in order to meet a specific customer demand for paper in that currency; after issue the proceeds are swapped into the desired currency. In the meantime the bonds will be held to maturity by the investors and usually not traded in the secondary market).

High-quality Eurobond issues will trade almost as government paper. For example issues by the World Bank or the European Investment Bank (EIB) trade at very low spreads above the same currency government bonds and are highly liquid. For example at times EIB sterling Eurobonds have traded at only 7–9 basis points above the same maturity gilt.

---

[7] In 1999 Cedel Bank and Deutsche Terminbourse merged their operations, and the resulting entity was named Clearstream International or simply Clearstream. Cedel Bank had originally been known as Cedel.

9.14 Settlement

Settlement of Eurobond transactions takes place within 28 days for primary market issues and T + 3 days for secondary market trades. Virtually all trades settle within the two main clearing systems, Euroclear and Clearstream. Euroclear was established in Brussels in 1968 by an international group of banks, the original entity known as Cedel was established in Luxembourg in 1970. Both clearing systems will settle in T + 3 days, however the facility exists to settle trades in T + 1 if both parties to a trade wish it.

In the Euroclear system bonds are placed in the custody of the clearing system, through a Europe-wide network of depository banks. The transfer of bonds on settlement is undertaken by means of a computer book-entry. This was the basic concept behind the introduction of Euroclear, the substitution of book entries for the physical movement of bonds. The actual physical securities to which a trading party has title are not identified in the majority of transactions made through Euroclear. The clearing system is made possible because the terms and conditions of any Eurobond issue are objectively specified, so that all bonds of a particular issue are standardised, and so fungible for one another. There is no requirement to assign a specific bond serial number to an individual holder, which occurs with registered bonds. Clearstream operates on much the same basis. Participants in either system must be institutions with their own account (they may have an agent settle for them). Settlement takes place through the simultaneous exchange of bonds for cash on the books of the system. An 'electronic bridge' connecting the two systems allows transfer of securities from one to the other.

9.15 Legal and tax issues

Investor and borrowers in the Eurobond market may at any one time fall under the auspicies of a number of countries laws and regulations. These relate to the withholding tax on the bond coupons, income tax, disclosure and prospectus requirements and restrictions on sales to certain classes of investor. The most important legal considerations for professional participants relate to (i) the possibility that the bonds are eventually distributed to residents in the United States, which is prohibited, and (ii) London, as the principal financial centre where the sale and trading of bonds takes place. The first consideration means that the market is subject to legislation in the US that dates from 1933[8] and Federal income tax regulations. The second consideration means that the market comes under certain aspects of English law. With regard to taxation, the key features of Eurobonds are that:

- the bonds are 'bearer' rather than registered securities;
- interest and principal payments are not subject to withholding tax at source in the country where the issuer is resident for tax purposes.

The fact that payments of interest and principal on Eurobonds are not subject to any form of withholding tax at source in the country where the borrower is deemed to be resident for tax purposes is the primary feature of Eurobonds for investors, generally cited to be of key importance in making the market attractive for investors across a range of

[8] The US Securities Act of 1933.

countries. Non-resident investors in Eurobonds are usually subject to the withholding tax requirements of the resident country of the bond issuer when that party repays interest or principal on bonds held by these non-residents. The tax advantages to an investor from the absence of withholding tax (combined with the fact that the bonds are issued in bearer form) are significant. A large proportion of Eurobonds are held by private investors, and much of this is made anonymously by means of external discretionary accounts, such as those run by Swiss banks. This is a source of some frustration to tax authorities in certain countries. The absence of withholding tax also confers a certain benefit to issuers of Eurobonds. Where a bond issue was subject to withholding tax, an issuer would need to make the terms of the issue more attractive, that is a higher coupon, in order to make the bond as attractive as the Eurobond issuer. This will carry higher associated costs for the issuer.

9.16 The secondary market

The market in trading Eurobonds is conducted on an over-the-counter basis. In 1998 a number of automated electronic trading systems were also introduced. The pre-eminence of London as the main trading centre for the Eurobond market is well-established, although Brussels, Frankfurt, Zurich and Singapore are also important trading centres. The advantages of London as a trading centre are generally regarded as being:

- a low level of regulatory interference in the functioning of the market;
- the presence of well-established infrastructure and institutions, as well as experienced human resources;
- the use of the English language as the market's main language of communication.

There are over 40 different market makers registered with ISMA, and although in theory they are all required to make two-way prices in their chosen markets, the level of commitment is very varied. The bid-offer spread can be as low as 0.10 for very liquid issues such as World Bank and EIB bonds, to no offer price quoted for illiquid issues. In between there are a range of spread sizes. The normal market size also varies, from £100,000 nominal to £500,000.

The valuation of Eurobonds is usually done on the basis of a yield spread over the relevant government bond yield curve. This yield spread is a function of the credit quality of the bond, its liquidity in the market and the level of supply and demand. The bonds also move in line with general moves in interest rates, so that if there is a change in the gilt yield curve, a sterling Eurobond will change in yield, irrespective of whether the bond's issuer was perceived as being a weaker or a stronger credit. A market maker wishing to hedge a position in Eurobonds will usually use either the benchmark government against which the bond is priced or, if a non-cash option is preferred, will use bond futures contracts to hedge the position. These topics are all covered in chapters elsewhere.

9.17 Eurobonds and swap transactions

Readers who are unfamiliar with swap instruments may wish to consult a standard derivatives text first. The issue of new Eurobonds and the use of 'asset swaps' in conjunction with issues is a vital part of the market, with investment banks keeping a close observation of the asset swap curve to spot any opportunities that may arise that makes a new issue of paper more attractive. New issues of Eurobonds are often launched to facilitate a swap which has been arranged in advance.

The existence of the currency swap and asset swap market is one of the key reasons for the growth and popularity of the Eurobond market. A borrower can issue bonds in virtually any liquid and convertible currency, according to where there is demand and what the yield curve looks like, and swap the proceeds into the currency that it requires. The cost of borrowing is usually significantly lower than if the borrower had issued bonds in the required currency. Swap driven issues are very common in the Eurobond market, and the key motivator is that borrowing costs will be cheaper. If this cheap borrowing opportunity is not available, it is unlikely that the bond will be issued, because entering into a swap exposes the issuer to additional credit risk. Swap financing will require a borrower to obtain debt initially that has undesirable currency and/or coupon characteristics. If the counterparty to a swap defaults, the borrower will be left with a risk exposure on the original debt. However swap financing remains attractive because of the opportunity to obtain cheaper borrowing costs, despite the additional exposure to credit risk entailed in the transaction.

The market in swaps is governed by the International Swap Dealers Association (ISDA). In the market the majority of transactions are plain vanilla in nature, and involve one of the following:

- cross-currency fixed-rate swaps, usually referred to as *currency swaps*;
- interest-rate swaps;
- cross-currency hybrid swaps;
- basis swaps.

Currency swaps are very common in the market. Under the plain vanilla version, two counterparties issue fixed-rate debt denominated in different currencies. They then exchange the interest (and sometimes) the principal repayments on their respective debt obligations. Under the conventional pattern the amounts exchanged remain fixed at maturity. We will not cover the mechanics of a currency swap here as this is reviewed in any number of derivatives texts; likewise interest-rate swaps and the concepts of comparative advantage and the fixed- versus floating-rate legs of an interest-rate swap. Swap agreements do not always involve the exchange of debt repayment streams. In certain cases one of the revenue streams exchanged in a swap can represent the income interest stream on an asset, or conventional security such as a corporate bond. Eurobond issues are frequently brought to the market primarily for the purpose of such 'asset swapping'. For the investment bank, swapping asset base interest payments is one means by which bond issues can be re-packaged.

Other instruments used include *basis swaps*, which involve the exchange of two floating-rate payments streams, each of which is based on a short-term interest rate. The most common of these instruments have the following reference rates:

- Libor versus the US commercial paper rate;
- Libor versus the Prime rate.

Basis swaps are not the primary motivators of Eurobond issues, but are often included in more complex swap agreements which may involve Eurobond borrowing.

Selected bibliography

Andersen, T., 'How the grey market became respectable', *Euromoney,* May 1982

Crawford, A., 'Stabilization brings the jitters', *Euromoney,* April 1987, p. 277

Decovny, S., *Swap,* FT Prentice Hall, 1998, p. 68

Kerr, I., *A History of the Eurobond Market,* Euromoney Publications, 1984

Van Agtmael, A., 'Issuance of Eurobonds: Syndication and Underwriting Techniques and Costs', in George, A., Giddy, I. (eds.), *International Financial Handbook,* Section 5.2, Wiley, 1983

10 Warrants

10.1 Introduction

A warrant entitles its holder to purchase a specified asset at a set price at a specified date or dates. The terms defining a warrant usually remain unchanged during its entire life, and the asset may be bonds, equities, an index, commodities or other instruments. Hence a warrant is an option issued by a firm to purchase a given number of shares in that firm (*equity warrant*) or more of the firm's bonds (*bond warrant*), at a given exercise price at any time before the warrant expires. If the warrant is exercised, the firm issues new shares (or bonds) at the exercise price and so raises additional finance. Warrants generally have longer maturities than conventional options (five years or longer, although there is usually a liquid market in very long-dated over-the-counter equity options), and some warrants are perpetual.

Warrants are usually attached to bonds (*host bond*) to start with, in most cases such warrants are detachable and can be traded separately. Equity warrants do not carry any shareholders rights until they are exercised, for example they pay no dividends and have no voting rights. Bond warrants can either be exercised into the same class of bonds as the host bond or into a different class of bond. In valuing a warrant it is important to recognise that exercising the warrant (unlike exercising an ordinary call option) will increase the number of shares outstanding. This will have the effect of diluting earnings per share and hence reducing the share price. Hence although equity warrants are often valued in the same way as an American call option, the pricing must also take into account this dilution effect. Warrants are often used in conjunction with a new bond issue, to act as a 'sweetener', and are common instruments in the Japanese bond and equity markets. If the issuing company performs well, the investor can eventually exercise the warrant to purchase the company's equity at the exercise price fixed at the time the warrant was issued. During this time, in the same way as for a convertible bondholder, the investor has the security of holding the company's fixed interest debt, which acts as a type of security in the event that the company's share price declines.

In the UK some companies use warrants to obtain a steady flow of new investment. For example, every year from 1988 the London-listed company BTR has issued bonus warrants free to its shareholders, with the exercise price set just out-of-the-money. From the investor's viewpoint warrants may be used as a means of having an exposure to a company's shares but with a relatively low capital outlay at the start. They also allows the investor already holding shares to sell them while still maintaining an equity stake. This is known as *cash extraction* and is a straightforward strategy. The investor sells the shares, uses some of the proceeds to buy warrants representing the same number of shares, and invests the remaining cash in interest-bearing instruments. The price of warrants, just like convertibles, does not move one-for-one with the underlying equity unless they are deep in-the-money however, so a rise in the share price will not be matched by the same rise in the warrant price. In the short term therefore an investor following a cash extraction strategy may miss out on share price performance, in addition to any dividend payments.

Example 10.1: Tate & Lyle warrants

- Tate & Lyle plc issued 5 3/4% 10-year bonds in March 1991, with 37,200 share warrants attached. The bond was issued with a face value of £5,000. Each share warrant entitles the holder to subscribe for 866 ordinary shares up to March 2001. The exercise price was £3,968.90 per warrant, or 458.3p per share until 20 March 1993, rising in annual increments to £5,143.75 per warrant (594p per share) from 20 March 2000. Alternatively a warrant may be exercised by surrendering one bond for the same number of shares, rather than making a cash payment.

10.2 Analysis

As with ordinary options the value of a warrant has two components, an intrinsic value (which in the warrant market is known as *formula value*) and a time value (*premium* over formula value). Although the term *premium* is used in the options market to refer to the price paid for an option, in the warrant market the conventional term *price* is used. The *warrant premium* is usually used to refer to the amount by which the warrant price plus the exercise price exceeds the current underlying share price.

The formula value is determined by equation (10.1):

$$\begin{aligned}\text{Formula value} &= (\text{Share price} - \text{Exercise price})\\ &\quad \times \text{Number new shares issued on exercise.}\end{aligned} \tag{10.1}$$

If the exercise price exceeds the share price, the formula value is zero and the warrant is said to be 'out-of-the-money'. If the share price exceeds the exercise price the warrant is in-the-money and the formula value is positive. The time value is always positive up until expiry of the warrant. As with options the time value declines as the expiry date approaches and on the expiry date itself the time value is zero.

The fair price of a warrant is given by (10.2):

$$\text{Warrant value} = \frac{P_c}{1+p} \times \text{number of new shares issued if warrant is exercised} \tag{10.2}$$

where p is the proportionate increase in the number of shares outstanding if all the warrants were exercised, and P_c is the value of an American call option with the same exercise price and expiry date as the warrant.

If a company issues new shares in a rights issue at a price below the market price or issues convertible bonds or new warrants, the value of any existing warrants already in issue will be affected. It is usual therefore for companies to issue warrants with a provision that allows for the exercise price to be reduced in the event of any corporate action that adversely affects the current warrant price.

A warrant is attractive to investors because if the firm is successful and its share price rises accordingly, the warrant can be exercised and the holder can receive higher-value shares at the lower exercise price. Virtually all warrants are issued by corporations and are equity warrants. In the late 1980s the Bank of England introduced *gilt warrants* which could be exercised into gilts; however none are in existence at present. However it is of course possible to trade in OTC call options on gilts with a number of banks in the City of London.

Covered warrants are issued by a securities house or investment bank rather than the company itself. The aim of the securities house is to create an active and liquid market in the warrants, and to earn profit from making a market in them. When covered warrants are exercised there is no recourse to the company, and the company does not issue new shares. There is thus no dilution effect. The securities house must settle the warrant holder's application to subscribe for shares, either by providing shares already in issue or by the payment of sufficient cash to allow the warrant holder to buy shares in the market.

10.3 Bond warrants

Very occasionally bonds are issued with debt warrants attached. For example an issue of bonds with a coupon of 5% could be made with warrants that give the holder the right to subscribe at a future date for more 5% bonds at a fixed price. The warrants would be attractive to investors who expect interest rates to fall in the future; a fall in rates could result in the warrants being exercised or sold on at a profit, as the lower rates would now make them more valuable.

Say that a bond warrant entitles its holder to purchase bonds with a face value of M at a price of E. The bonds issued on exercise of the warrants may be either a further tranche of an existing issue or a new issue. The exercise cost of purchasing the underlying bond via the warrant is given by (10.3):

$$Cost = \left(P_w + \frac{E \times M}{100}\right) \times \frac{100}{M} \qquad (10.3)$$

where

P_w is the price of the warrant
E is the exercise price
M is the par value of the underlying bonds which may be purchased per warrant.

When a bond warrant is exercised, the cost to the purchaser includes the accrued interest up to the exercise date.

If the warrant entitles the holder to the right to purchase a bond which is already in existence, a premium or discount resulting from purchasing the bond via the warrant, as opposed to directly in the market, may be calculated using (10.4):

$$\text{Premium }\% = \left(\frac{\text{Exercise cost}}{P_{bond}} - 1\right) \times 100 \qquad (10.4)$$

where P_{bond} is the clean price of the underlying bond.

Example 10.2: ABC plc bond warrant

- ABC plc warrant with the right to subscribe for 8% 2005 bonds. Each warrant gives the holder the right to subscribe for £1,000 nominal amount of the company's 8% bond due 2005, at the exercise price of 100 per cent of the nominal amount plus accrued interest from the previous coupon date (payable 7 June and 7 December each year). The warrants are exercisable up to and including 7 June 2001.

If the price of the warrant is £24, the exercise cost of purchasing the £1,000 nominal amount of the 8% bonds is:

$$(24 + (100 \times 1000)/100) \times 100/1000$$

which is 102.4% in addition to any accrued interest.

If the bonds are trading in the market at 98.00, as the exercise cost of the bonds via the warrant is 102.4%, the premium is (102.4/98) – 1 which is 4.490%.

10.4 Comparison of warrants and convertibles

Warrants and convertibles are both hybrid instruments, both are issued by companies in the international markets. They are essentially similar in many respects, including:

- **valuation:** the theoretical value for a warrant is often calculated using the Black–Scholes or a similar model. In practice however investors are willing to pay only a fraction of the theoretical price of a warrant compared to convertibles, which trade near to or at fair value. Investors often pay more for the conversion premium on an issue of convertibles than they will pay for warrants in an issue of bonds with warrants attached. It is often the case therefore that companies are able to raise more capital by issuing convertibles rather than by issuing bonds with warrants attached;
- **investor base:** although warrants can have a long term to maturity, often they are held by short-term investors who buy them in the expectation of re-selling them at a profit when the company's share price rises by a sufficient amount. Until the exercise date approaches, many investors do not intend to hold the warrants in order to subscribe for shares in the future. The opposite is usually true for convertible bonds, whose investors are more likely to hold convertibles until conversion or redemption;
- **call flexibility:** bonds with warrants attached are often non-callable. The company cannot therefore force warrant holders into an immediate decision whether or not to subscribe for shares. A call option is only rarely a feature of a warrant bond;
- **maturity:** the maturity of a bond with warrants attached is predictable (unless a call feature is also included), as the bond portion remains outstanding until maturity. In contrast a convertible could remain outstanding for a proportionately much shorter time of its life, and be converted into equity. It is more common for convertibles to have call and/or put features attached. If a company required certainty of redemption dates for its financial planning, warrant bonds would be preferable to convertibles for this reason.

Generally however warrants are issued as a 'sweetener' attached to a main issue, whereas convertibles are important corporate finance instruments in their own right. In certain markets though, for example in Japan, warrants are an important financing instrument.

Selected bibliography and references

Bird, A., 'Evaluating warrants', *The Investment Analyst*, December 1971

Chen, A.H.Y., 'A model of warrant pricing in a dynamic market', *Journal of Finance* 25, December 1970, pp. 1041–1060

Connolly, K.B., Phillips, G.A., *Japanese Warrant Markets*, Macmillan, 1992

Crouhy, M., Galai, D., *Warrant valuation and equity volatility*, HEC, 1988

Emmanuel, D., 'Warrant valuation and exercise strategy', *Journal of Financial Economics* 12, August 1983, pp. 211–236

Galai, D., Schneller, M., 'Pricing warrants and the value of the firm', *Journal of Finance* 33, December 1978, pp. 1333–1342

Giguere, G., 'Warrants: a mathematical model of evaluation', *Analysts Journal* 14, November 1958

Green, R., 'Investment incentives, debt and warrants', *Journal of Financial Economics* 13, 1984, pp. 115–136

Lauterbach, B., Schultz, P., 'Pricing warrants: an empirical study of the Black–Scholes model and its alternatives', *Journal of Finance* 45(4), 1990, pp. 1181–1209

Noreen, E., Wolfson, M., 'Equilibrium warrant pricing models and accounting for executive stock options', *Journal of Accounting Research* 19, Autumn 1981, pp. 384–398

Schulz, G., Trautman, S., 'Valuation of warrants: theory and empirical tests for warrants written on German stocks', unpublished paper, University of Stuttgart, 1990

Schwartz, E., 'The valuation of warrants: implementing a new approach', *Journal of Financial Economics* 4, January 1977, pp. 79–93

Shelton, J., 'The relation of the pricing of a warrant to the price of its associated common stock', *Financial Analysts Journal* 23, 1967, pp. 88–99

Spatt, C., Sterbenz, F., 'Warrant exercise, dividends and re-investment policy', *Journal of Finance* 43, 1988, pp. 493–506

11 Medium-Term Notes

Medium-term notes (MTNs) are corporate bonds that have evolved into an important source of corporate funding. They are not exclusively corporate instruments however and have been issued by sovereigns, supranationals and federal and local authorities. The first MTN was issued by the General Motors corporation in 1972, and was sold directly to investors rather than via an agent bank. During the 1970s the MTN market was largely illiquid, and in 1981 the volume of outstanding issues was less than $1 billion. In that year Merrill Lynch issued an MTN for Ford Motor Credit and also undertook to make a secondary market in the paper. Since then the MTN market has grown into a major corporate finance instrument, traded both domestically and internationally, and at the end of 1998 the outstanding volume of MTN issues around the world was approaching $1 trillion (see Table 11.1).

A medium-term note is essentially a plain vanilla debt security with a fixed coupon and maturity date. The term 'medium-term' is something of a misnomer, as the bonds range in maturity from nine months to 30 years or more; however the first MTNs generally had maturities of five years or less. They were originally designed to bridge the gap between *commercial paper* and long-dated bonds. An MTN is an unsecured debt, therefore the majority of MTNs are investment grade quality. In terms of the way they trade in the market, MTNs are virtually identical to conventional corporate bonds, and the main difference between an MTN and a corporate bond is the manner in which it is issued in the primary market. The unique characteristic of MTNs is that they are offered to investors continually over a period of time by an agent of the issuer, as part of an MTN *programme*. MTNs are usually offered in the market by investment banks acting as agents, and sold on a 'best efforts' basis. The issuing bank does not act as an underwriter of the bonds, unlike with a conventional bond issue, and therefore the borrowing company is not guaranteed to place all its paper. As MTNs are usually offered as part of a continuous programme, they are issued

Market	Nominal outstanding ($ bln)
United States	
Domestic corporate issues	275
Federal agency	174
Other	46
Sub-total	495
International markets	
Euro-MTNs	475
Domestic markets	26
Sub-total	501
Total	996

Table 11.1: Size of the global MTN market, year-ending 2001.
Source: Strata Consulting.

in smaller amounts than conventional bonds, which are generally sold in larger amounts at one time. Notes can be issued either as *bearer* securities or *registered* securities. A Euromarket in MTNs developed in the mid-1980s. Euro MTNs (EMTNs) trade in a similar fashion to Eurobonds; they are debt securities issued for distribution across markets internationally.

The majority of MTNs are conventional bonds with fixed coupon rate and single maturity date. There is a wide range of structures available however, and MTNs have been issued with floating-rate coupons, call and put features, amortising nominal amounts, multi-currency structures or as part of more exotic structures such as asset swaps. Certain MTN issues are underwritten by investment banks as well, making them indistinguishable from conventional corporate bonds.

11.1 Introduction

The first MTN issue was made by General Motors Acceptance Corporation (GMAC) in the United States in 1972. At that time the instrument was seen as a longer-dated version of commercial paper, which for regulatory reasons in the US may not have a longer maturity than nine months or 270 days. GMAC and (shortly after) other motor car manufacturers were interested in sources of finance that matched the maturity of their car loans to consumers, which were cheaper to issue than conventional bond offerings. For this reason the first MTNs were issued to investors directly, thus avoiding underwriting fees. However this resulted in a lack of liquidity in the secondary market. A requirement of the Securities and Exchange Commission (SEC) that regulatory approval be obtained for any change to a registered public offering also resulted in higher transaction costs for borrowers, some of whom issued MTNs via private placement. In the 1980s the market began to grow in volume after investment banks issued MTNs as agent and acted as market makers in the secondary market.[1]

A new regulation instituted by the SEC, Rule 415, also assisted market development as it allowed for *shelf registration* of an MTN programme. Under regulations in the United States, any corporate debt issued with a maturity of more than 270 days must be registered with the SEC. In 1982 the SEC adopted Rule 415 which permitted shelf registration of new corporate debt issues. A continuous MTN programme can be registered in this way. The issuer must file with the SEC details on (i) historical and current financial information and (ii) the type and amount of securities it plans to issue under the programme. This is known as 'filing a shelf'. The adoption of Rule 415 made the administration of continuously offered notes relatively straightforward for the issuer. Under shelf registration, bonds may be sold for up to two years after the registration date without requiring another registration statement every time there is a new offer. Borrowers are able to issue paper at short notice in response to favourable market conditions, such as a drop in market interest rates or investor demand for their paper, without having to register each new offering, as long as it is within the two year period. For issues outside a shelf registration there is a delay between the filing with the SEC and the actual date of public offering, which may be up to five days and potentially prevent the borrower from taking advantage of market conditions.

The adoption of financial engineering techniques has also contributed to the growth of the market. Companies are able to publish a single prospectus that encompasses the entire

---

[1] Initially the banks would only quote prices for their own issues.

MTN programme, and within the programme issue bonds with a variety of structures and in different currencies, to suit specific conditions and requirements. Individual issues within a single programme may have a range of coupons, maturity dates and other structures. For example, MTNs have been issued as zero-coupon bonds, floating-rate bonds, with step-up or step-down coupons, denominated in a foreign currency or indexed to an exchange-rate or commodity; they are frequently issued in conjunction with a swap structure. Floating-rate MTNs pay coupons linked to a reference rate such as LIBOR, but have been linked to the commercial paper rate, the T-bill rate, Federal funds rate and the *prime* rate. Floating-rate MTNs often pay monthly or quarterly coupons, compared to conventional FRNs which usually pay a semi-annual coupon. The larger borrowers issue debt as part of global MTN programmes, which enable them to place debt in their domestic market and internationally in the Euro market, in any liquid currency they wish. The MTN market is flexible and individual programmes may be adapted to suit the requirements of borrowers and investors alike; some of the most innovative structures have been observed in the MTN market before their introduction in the conventional corporate bond market.[2]

11.2 The primary market

MTN issues are arranged within a programme. A continuous MTN programme is established with a specified issue limit, and sizes can vary from $100 million to $5,000 million or more. Within the programme MTNs can be issued at any time, daily if required. The programme is similar to a revolving loan facility; as maturing notes are redeemed, new notes can be issued. The issuer usually specifies the maturity of each note issue within a programme, but cannot exceed the total limit of the programme.

Example 11.1: ABC plc

- ABC plc establishes a five-year $200 million MTN programme and immediately issues the following notes:
  $50 million of notes with a one-year maturity
  $70 million of notes with a five-year maturity

ABC plc can still issue a further $80 million of notes; however in one year's time when $50 million of notes mature, it will be able to issue a further $50 million if required. The total amount in issue at any one time never rises above $200 million.

The first step for the borrower is to arrange shelf registration with the SEC. This ensures the widest possible market for the programme; there are also no re-sale or transfer restrictions on the bonds themselves. The shelf registration identifies the investment bank or banks that will be acting as agents for the programme and who will distribute the paper to the market. A domestic programme may have only one agent bank, although two to four banks are typical. Global and Euro-MTN programmes usually have more agent banks. Once

2 In July 1993 Walt Disney issued an MTN with a 100-year maturity as part of its rolling global Euro-MTN programme. This is equal to the longest-dated maturity conventional debt instrument issued in recent years.

registration is complete the borrower issues a prospectus supplement detailing the terms and conditions of the programme. Often a draft prospectus is issued first, and only issued in final once the issuing bank has gauged market reaction. A draft prospectus is known as a *red herring*. Within a programme a borrower may also issue conventional corporate bonds, underwritten by an investment bank, but there is none of the flexibility available compared to an MTN issue, which can be arranged at very short notice, so conventional bond offerings within a programme are rare.

The agent banks sometimes publicise the maturities and yield spreads that are to be offered as part of the programme; a typical example for an hypothetical programme in the sterling market is given at Table 11.2.

The exact date of a particular maturity issue is not always known at the time the programme is announced, so yields are often given as a spread over the equivalent maturity government bond. If the borrower has a particular interest to tap the market at specific points of the yield curve, the spread offered at that point is increased in order to attract investors. Once the required funds have been raised, offer spreads are usually reduced. If the full amount stated in the registration details is raised, US domestic market borrowers need to file a new registration with the SEC. The size of individual issues within a programme varies with the funding strategy of the borrower. Certain companies have a preference to raise large amounts at once, say $100 to $200 million, and raise funds using fewer issues. This also maintains a 'scarcity value' for their paper compared to borrowers who tap the market more frequently. Other companies adopt the opposite approach, with small size issues of between $5 to $10 million spread over more dates.

Domestic market MTNs are primarily offered on an agency basis, although issues within a programme are sometimes sold using other methods. Agent banks sometimes acquire the paper for their own book, trading it later in the secondary market. Specific issues may be underwritten by an agent bank, or sold directly to investors by the corporate treasury arm of the borrowing company.

The main issuers of MTNs in the US market are:

- general finance companies, including automobile finance companies, business credit institutions and securities houses;
- banks, both domestic and foreign;
- governments and government agencies;

Maturity	Yield spread (bps)	Benchmark bond	Current yield
9 months	20	13% 2000	5.80
12–24 months	25	7% 2001	6.25
2–3 years	35	7% 2002	6.37
3–4 years	45	6.5% 2003	6.38
4–5 years	50	6.75% 2004	6.34
5–6 years	55	8.5% 2005	6.36
9–11 years	50	5.75% 2009	5.77
15–20 years	30	8% 2021	5.02

Table 11.2: MTN programme offer, October 1999.

- supranational bodies such as the World Bank;
- domestic industrial and commercial companies, primarily motor car and other industrial manufacturing companies, telecommunications companies and other utilities;
- savings and loan institutions.

During the 1980s the MTN market was dominated by financial institutions, accounting for over 90% of issue volume. This share was reduced to approximately 70% by 1992 (Crabbe 1992), the remainder of the issues being accounted for by other categories of borrower.

There is a large investor demand in the US for high-quality corporate paper, much more so than in Europe where the majority of bonds are issued by financial companies. This demand is particularly great at the short- to medium-term maturity end. As the market has a large number of issuers, investors are able to select issues that meet precisely their requirements for maturity and credit rating. The main investors are:

- investment companies;
- insurance companies;
- banks;
- savings and loan institutions;
- corporate treasury departments;
- state institutions.

It can be seen that the investor base is very similar to the issuer base!

All the main US investment banks make markets in MTNs, including Merrill Lynch, Goldman Sachs, Morgan Stanley, CSFB and Salomon Smith Barney. In the UK active market makers in MTNs include RBS Financial Markets and Barclays Capital.

11.3 MTNs and corporate bonds

A company wishing to raise a quantity of medium-term or long-term capital over a period of time has the choice of issuing MTNs or long-dated bonds. An MTN programme is a series of issues over time, matching the issuer's funding requirement, and therefore should be preferred over a bond by companies that do not need all the funding at once, nor for the full duration of the programme. Corporate bonds are preferred where funds are required immediately. They are also a better choice for issuers that expect interest rates to rise in the near future and wish to lock in a fixed borrowing rate for all the funds required. The decision on whether to raise finance using MTNs or corporate bonds will be taken after consideration of the interest cost and flexibility offered by each instrument. That MTNs offer financing advantages over conventional bonds under certain circumstances is reflected in the growth and current size of the market; however the same borrowers are evident in both markets, which implies that both instruments possess advantages over the other under specific conditions.

The main difference between MTNs and corporate bonds is the process by which they are sold and distributed. There are other differentiating features however. MTNs are almost invariably sold at par on issue, whereas conventional bonds are usually offered at a slight discount to par. The proceeds on the day of issue are settled on the same day for MTNs (making them similar to money market instruments in this respect), while the settlement for new issue traditional bonds is the following day, or T + 3 for international issues. In the US market, corporate bonds pay semi-annual coupon on either the 1st or the 15th of the month; the latter is identical to Treasury securities. MTNs however have coupon dates payable on a fixed cycle basis, irrespective of their issue or maturity date. This payment convention means that MTNs have a long or short first coupon, and a short final coupon, whereas conventional bonds would always have a regular final coupon. MTNs pay interest on a 30/360 day-count basis, similar to Eurobonds and US domestic corporate bonds.

Example 11.2

- An MTN programme pays semi-annual interest on 1 June and 1 December each year and on maturity of the individual note. An issue within the programme of £10 million 6.75% bonds with a two-year maturity on 1 July would pay a short first coupon of £281,250 on the first coupon date in December, regular coupons of £337,500 on the next three coupon dates and a short final coupon of £56,250 on the maturity date.

11.3.1 *Issue size and liquidity*

The size of an issue has the most significant impact on the relative cost of an MTN issue versus a straight bond. For large issues, which are regarded as nominal amounts of over $400 million borrowed over a medium or long term, the all-in cost of a straight bond issue is generally lower than the all-in cost of an MTN programme. This reflects the economies of scale that may be achieved when issuing such an amount on one date, as well as the greater secondary market liquidity of larger-sized issues. For this reason borrowers who have a heavy funding requirement for a specific period in time will usually prefer to raise the funds with a straight bond issue. The liquidity premium associated with large volume issues is not known with certainty, but is estimated at around 5 to 10 basis points (Kitter 1999); for large amounts this saving would be substantial. However this premium is indicative of the improved liquidity in the MTN market.

Another factor that borrowers consider is the cost saving associated with the distribution process for MTNs. To fully place a large bond issue, perhaps because the whole issue has not been taken up by customers, the bond may need to be offered at a higher yield, which raises the coupon for the borrower. If an individual bond within an MTN programme is not fully placed,[3] borrowers have the option of raising the remaining sum by offering another bond at a different maturity, or as part of a different structure to another group of investors. Since all the funding from an MTN issue need not be priced at the coupon

[3] For example the lead manager may have client orders for $460 million of a $500 million issue; in order to attract customer interest for the remaining paper, the coupon may need to be raised by 10–25 basis points.

required by the marginal buyers, and may be raised at slightly different times, the financing costs for MTNs are often below those of a straight bond issue.[4]

11.3.2 *MTN issue options*

The flexibility afforded by an MTN programme is often behind the corporate treasurer's decision to employ them as funding instruments, irrespective of the interest cost advantage of straight bonds. A major flexibility of MTNs is their term to maturity. It is common for MTNs to be issued with non-standard terms to maturity, such as 15 months, 3.5 years and so on. This contrasts with straight bonds which are usually issued with maturities of 2, 5, 7, 10 and 30 years in the US market and often just 5 or 10 years in the Euro market. This makes MTNs the preferred instrument when exact maturity terms are required, for example when a borrower wishes to precisely match assets with liabilities. The cost of a bond underwriting makes small issues prohibitively expensive, and it is rare to see a bond offered with total nominal value outstanding of less than $100–150 million. If a corporate has a requirement for a smaller amount, it is more practical to issue an MTN. Some individual issues within MTN programmes have been for as little as $5 million; again, this flexibility allows companies to meet their funding requirements more precisely.

A continuous programme of MTN issues has the potential benefit of a lower average interest cost, compared to a single straight bond issue. For example, over a six-month period, five MTN issues of $20 million each may have a lower average interest cost than a single issue of $100 million in the same period. This may compensate for the lower interest cost of straight bonds, mentioned earlier, and is more likely during periods of relatively high interest rate volatility.

Once a programme has secured shelf registration, the process of issuing an MTN can be very quick, often less than half a day. This enables agent banks to issue debt on behalf of a borrower in response to specific investor requirements, or to changes in the yield or swap curves. In fact a substantial amount of MTN issues originate as a result of *reverse enquiry*. This is when investors have a requirement for debt products of a certain maturity and credit quality. For example a bond fund manager may be interested in 10-year paper with an A-rating, paying at least 50 basis points above the government yield. This is detailed to their investment bank, who is also an MTN agent bank, and if the requirements suit the borrower, there will be an issue of bonds from within the borrower's MTN programme. Bonds issued in response to reverse enquiry are often the most exotic instruments in the MTN market, due to investor requirements. This includes some of the example bonds described later in this chapter. This flexibility again makes MTNs an attractive option for borrowers.

Finally a significant volume of MTNs are placed privately with investors, directly or via an agent bank. An advantage of this distribution method is that it avoids publicity, as the transaction details may be known only to the investor and borrower (and agent). Companies may wish to avoid raising funds in the bond market, and the publicity associated with this, during times of market correction or volatility, or if they are in a state of financial distress. This makes the MTN market particularly attractive during recessions and market

---

4 Another consideration is the commission to the agent bank, generally around 0.125% to 0.75% of the nominal value. Underwriting fees in a conventional bond offering range from 0.25% to 1.50%, and may be higher for international issues.

downturns. The private placement market is also used by overseas borrowers that seek to place paper in the US market, as SEC approval is only required for a public offering. However generally the financing costs are lower in the public market than the private placement market, with its lower liquidity, so the majority of domestic borrowers use the public offering method.

11.4 Issue mechanism

11.4.1 *The issue process*

Issuers of MTNs usually specify an Issuing and Paying Agent (IPA) responsible for providing investors with the ability to present interest coupons and notes in various locations around the world. The IPA function required for medium term note programmes is usually viewed as a processing and administration function, and is therefore normally of most interest to the settlements and processing areas of an issuing organisation.

Once an agent has been selected as the IPA for a new programme, and draft legal documentation is available, it will allocate the transaction to a documentation department. This department will review the documentation from a legal perspective, and often calls in external legal firms to assist in the review. However the primary functions that the IPA performs is to receive an issuer's instructions, arrange for the issuance of the security to the relevant dealer via the international clearing systems, and then to service the security throughout its term. Generally Euro-MTN transactions are represented by a single security, known as the *global note*. When an issuer and underwriting bank agree a new transaction, both parties will advise the IPA of the transaction details, such as the currency, amount, issue date, interest basis, maturity, issue price and so on. Although the dealer is not obligated to advise the IPA of the trade details, market practices are such that this has now become the norm. The IPA issues the security after receiving the instructions of the issuer together with an authorised pricing supplement, which is the term sheet listing the issue details.

Once trade details have been received, the IPA will contact Euroclear and Clearstream and advise them of the trade information. The clearing systems will then advise the IPA of the unique security codes, known as International Securities Identification Number (ISIN) and the Common Code, which are used to identify the security during its term. The IPA will then input the trade and settlement information into a 'new issuance account', while the dealer will input its instructions into the relevant clearing system. The IPA's instruction will be a securities delivery versus payment instruction, while the dealer's will be a securities receipt versus payment instruction. Processing the transaction on this basis means that all parties are protected and that the securities will never be issued unless the correct issue proceeds are paid. On the actual issuance date, the IPA will receive the cash proceeds from the dealer and will make onward payment to the issuer; it also creates the global note that represents the issue and delivers this to the *common depositary* for Euroclear and Clearstream. The common depositary is usually called the *custodian*.

11.4.2 *Servicing the issue*

The IPA is responsible for servicing the MTN during its life. Approximately ten business days before an interest payment date, or before the maturity date of an issue, it will advise the issuer of the forthcoming interest payment and provide them with payment details for the repayment amount due. On the instalment due date, the IPA will pay the clearing system(s) the amount due to the investors holding via their computer systems, and will also credit the proceeds to the relevant investor's account. Investors holding securities outside of a clearing system have to physically present their EMTNs (and Eurobonds as well) for payment at one of the designated paying agents for the issue.

The activities described above summarise the core function that is performed by an IPA; in addition throughout the life of a programme the IPA also performs numerous other activities on behalf of the issuer. Such activities include:

- being responsible for the safekeeping of the master global notes;
- the submission of any reports required by regulatory entities, such as the Bank of England, Japanese Ministry of Finance and the Bundesbank;
- acting as the calculation agent service for cash flows paid by floating rate, indexed linked, and dual-currency note issues;
- arranging for the listing of the note issues at a relevant stock exchange;
- arranging for the publication of notices in the financial press;
- maintaining comprehensive details of all transactions on its computer systems; and
- responding to external enquiries, such as requests made by auditors.

The process followed by IPAs is very similar to that used in the Eurobond market (see Chapter 9).

11.5 The secondary market

A liquid secondary market in MTNs was first established in the US market by Merrill Lynch which undertook to quote bid prices to any investor wishing to sell MTNs before maturity, provided that the investor had originally bought the notes through them. In other words Merrill Lynch was guaranteeing a secondary market to borrowers that issued notes through it. This undertaking was repeated by other banks, resulting in a market that is now both large and liquid. That said, MTNs are not actively traded and market makers do not quote real-time prices on dealing screens. The relatively low volume of secondary market trading stems from a disinclination of investors to sell notes they have bought, rather than a lack of market liquidity.

There is a wide range of maturities available for MTNs in the secondary market. The maturity of individual issues reflects the funding requirements of their issuers; for example bonds issued by motor car finance companies usually match the duration of loans to their customers, so they tend to have three-year to five-year maturities. Bonds issued by industrial and manufacturing companies have longer maturities. The maturity profile of MTNs in the US market is shown at Figure 11.1.

The yield on MTNs is a function of the credit quality of the issuer, as well as the liquidity of the paper in the secondary market and market maker's support. In the US domestic market MTNs are quoted on a yield basis, often as a spread over the equivalent maturity Treasury security. The highest yield spread is observed on the lowest rated bonds. Spreads vary according to market conditions and the business cycle (for example, they are at their widest during times of recession and after a market correction), as illustrated by Figure 11.2.

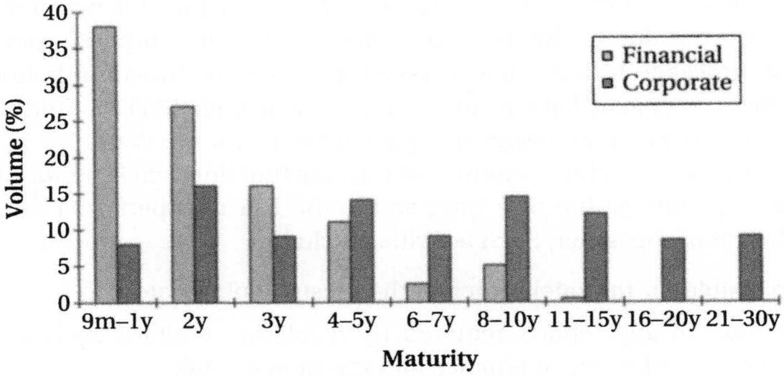

Figure 11.1: Maturity profile of US MTN market, 2002. Source: JPMorgan.

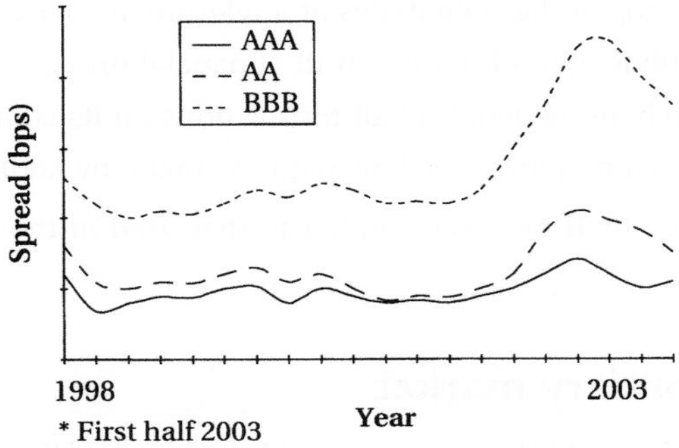

Figure 11.2: Credit structure of yield spreads, 10-year sterling MTNs, 1998–2003. Source: Greenwich NatWest.

The MTN market is a major instrument of corporate finance in the US market, and is growing in importance in the Euro market. An indication of its significance is given by its growing share of total investment-grade debt issuance. For instance in the US debt market, MTNs accounted for 47% of total investment grade debt issued in 1995, where total debt comprised MTNs and straight bond issues. This is an increase from around 12% in the early 1980s (Roland 1999).

11.5.1 *Credit rating*

MTNs are unsecured debt. A would-be issuer of MTNs will usually seek a credit rating for its issue from one or more of the main rating agencies such as Moody's or Standard & Poor's. The rating is given by the agency for a specific amount of possible new debt; should the issuer decided to increase the total amount of MTNs in issue it will need to seek a review of its credit rating. As MTNs are unsecured paper only the higher rated issuers, with an 'investment grade' rating for their debt, are usually able to embark on a revolving facility. Although there are 'junk' rated MTNs, there is no liquid market in them, and they account for less than 1% of outstanding volume.

Companies issuing MTNs generally have high ratings within the 'investment grade' category. During 1995, $65 billion of the $99 billion of MTNs issued in the US domestic market represented debt with a rating of 'A' or higher, while at the end of that year approximately 98% of the outstanding debt in the US market was rated at investment grade level.

Example 11.3: Reverse FRN with swap

- A subsidiary of a global integrated banking house that engages in investment activity requires US dollar funding. A proportion of its funds are raised as part of a $5 billion Euro-MTN programme. Due to demand for sterling assets they issue a five-year pounds sterling reverse floating rate medium-term note as part of the MTN programme, with the following details.

Issue size	£15 million
Issue date	20 January 1998
Maturity	21 January 2003
Rate payable	9% from 20/1/98 to 20/7/98
	19% – (2 × LIBOR6mo) thereafter to maturity
Price at issue	99.92
Proceeds	£14,988,000

As the issuer requires US dollar funding, it swaps the proceeds into dollars in the market in a cross-currency swap, and pays US dollar three-month Libor for this funding. On termination the original currencies are swapped back and the note redeemed.

11.6 The Euro-MTN market

The development of a market in offshore or internationally-traded MTNs was originally due to US companies seeking sources of finance overseas. The Euro-MTN market has since expanded dramatically and it is now an important source of corporate funding for US, European, Japanese and Asian domiciled companies. Euro-MTNs trade essentially as Eurobonds, that is they are international bonds that can be bought and sold across international boundaries. There is also a domestic market in MTNs in the UK, France, Germany and several other European countries, as well as Japan.[5] The main trading centre is in London, where most of the major underwriters and market making banks trade out of. The growth of the Euro market has been even more rapid than the US one, rising from approximately $10 billion in 1990 to just under $500 billion in 1998 (Roland 1999). The flexibility of an MTN programme, which was behind much of the growth in the US domestic market, is the key reason behind the expansion of the Euro market.

5 Note that there is a cross-over in terminology, and the terms 'international' and 'Euro' are frequently interchanged. A bond issued in a domestic market in Europe is not a Eurobond, equally there are domestic MTN programmes in several European countries. In this chapter the term 'Euro-MTN' is used to refer to MTNs that trade across international boundaries, and can be in any currency.

Euro-MTNs are essentially identical to MTNs in the US domestic market, with the key exception that they are not subject to national regulations or national registration requirements. The issuer base in the Euro market is much more concentrated among financial institutions and banks, and there is a lower appetite for lower-grade credit quality paper. In 1998 over 65% of Euro-MTNs were rated at AAA or AA, compared to just 13% of domestic US MTNs (Roland 1999). Another slight difference is in the maturity structure; most Euro-MTNs have maturities of 5 to 10 years, and it is rare to encounter maturities of 30 years. However there is a diverse range of structured Euro-MTNs in the market, according to Roland (1999) structured transactions account for up to 60% of Euro-MTN issues, compared to under half of that in the US market. As one might expect, currency swap structures such as those described in Example 11.3 are more common in the Euro market; note that the bonds in that example are part of the Euro-MTN programme of a major integrated banking house.

11.7 Structured MTNs

The application of financial engineering techniques has resulted in the introduction of exotic MTN structures. As a result both borrowers and investors have had their requirements met precisely through the use of tailor-made bond structures. Put simply, in a structured MTN, the borrowing company issues an MTN, which may or may not be a plain vanilla instrument itself, that is part of a swap agreement that changes the nature of the interest payments that the borrower makes. The first structured notes involved the issue of a conventional MTN in conjunction with an interest-rate swap. If the MTN was a fixed-coupon bond, the issuer would enter into an interest-rate swap whereby it received fixed interest and paid floating-rate interest; the end result would be that the issuer now had a floating-rate interest rate liability and not a fixed-rate one. The relevant swap terms are identical to the MTN ones, that is the fixed-rate payments are on the same date as the MTN coupon dates, and on the same interest basis. The borrower might do this because such an arrangement saves it interest payments not available through the issue of a straight floating-rate MTN. For borrowers, the primary motivation for entering into structured note arrangements is because a reduction in interest costs can be achieved. The interest savings must be sufficient to offset the increased transaction costs of structured deals, because these frequently require additional tax, accounting and legal advice, which may be supplied by the agent bank or by a separate advisory firm.

The flexibility of the MTN market has resulted in many structured transactions being created as a result of a reverse enquiry. An investor who has an interest in acquiring an instrument with specific terms, such as a link to an exotic exchange rate, equity index or commodity, may not be able to meet their requirements in the conventional market. If, via an agent bank, a borrower is able to issue an instrument that meets the specific needs of the enquiry, the investor will be able to purchase an instrument that fulfils its requirements precisely. The establishment of the inverse-floater MTN market in the US in the early 1990s was in response to investor needs; the issuers of inverse floaters usually hedged their interest-rate risk exposure in the swap market.

The other drivers of structured deals are the investment banks themselves, who may present an idea for a particular deal to their investor clients. Often this occurs when the structured finance team at the bank has spotted an area of the market where value may be obtained for the client, or a price anomaly may be exploited. According to Crabbe (1993), structured deals in the US market accounted for between 20% to 30% of MTN issue volume in the first six months of 1993, from a figure of under 5% ten years previously. The growth of structured deals is further evidence of the flexibility of the MTN market, although of course many of the structures have also been observed in the conventional bond market. In the remainder of this section we present examples of structured MTNs that have been issued as part of a global US dollar Euro-MTN programme by an investment banking group. They illustrate the wide range of features available to investors; in fact it is probably accurate to say that the range of arrangements available is limited only by market participants' imagination.

In Example 11.4 we present a description of some of the structured MTN deals that have taken place during 1998 and 1999. The issuer and counterparty banks are all large investment banking groups.

Example 11.4: Medium-Term Notes issued as part of a global $5 billion Euro-MTN programme

- The issuer is an integrated banking house, a subsidiary of which is an investment vehicle in the United States. As such the subsidiary's funding requirement is exclusively in US dollars, however it issues paper wherever there is customer demand. Foreign currency issues are swapped into dollars, on which the issuer pays floating-rate interest. The subsidiary has a AAA-rating.

Japanese yen MTN

Issue size	JPY500 million
Maturity	5 years
Rate payable	0.1%
Issue price	100 per cent
Proceeds	JPY500 million

This bond was swapped into US dollars, the equivalent amount of which was $3.56 million. During the life of the bond the issuer pays floating-rate interest on the US dollars, while the yen interest payments are made by the swap bank; on maturity the exact start proceeds are swapped back, enabling the issuer to redeem the bond. The structure is illustrated at Figure 11.3.

Swiss franc step-up notes

Issue date	25/3/1997	
Maturity	25/3/2002	
Issue size	CHF 15 million	
Issue price	100 per cent	
Coupon	2.40% to 25/3/1999	Callable 25/3/1999
	2.80% to 25/3/2000	25/3/2000
	3.80% to 25/3/2001	25/3/2001
	4.80% to 25/3/2002	

This bond was issued in conjunction with a currency swap, that is the CHF15 million was swapped into $10.304 million, on which the issuer pays floating-rate interest. These amounts were to be swapped back on termination, although the bond was in fact called at the first call date and the swap cancelled. The structure is illustrated at Figure 11.4.

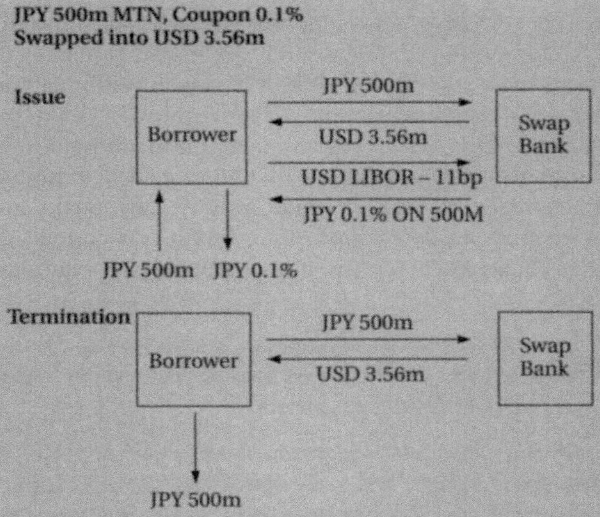

Figure 11.3: Structured MTN issue.

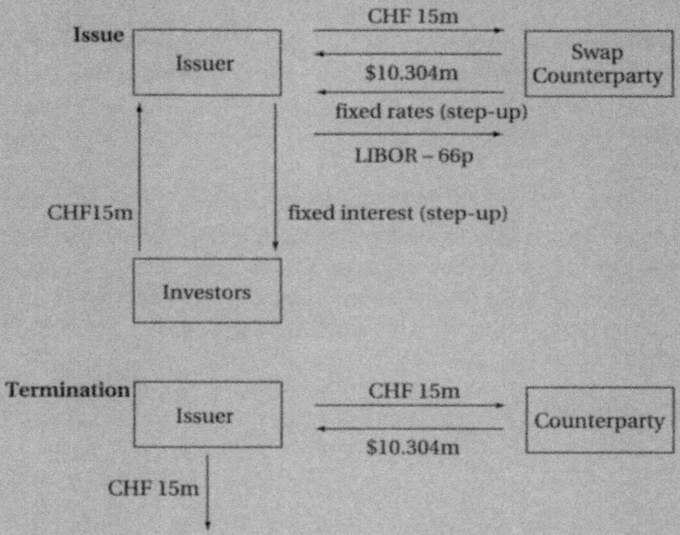

Figure 11.4: Structured MTN issue.

€6.15 million zero-coupon equity basket notes due January 2004

Issue date	22/1/1999
Maturity	22/1/2004
Issue price	100 per cent
Interest basis	Zero coupon

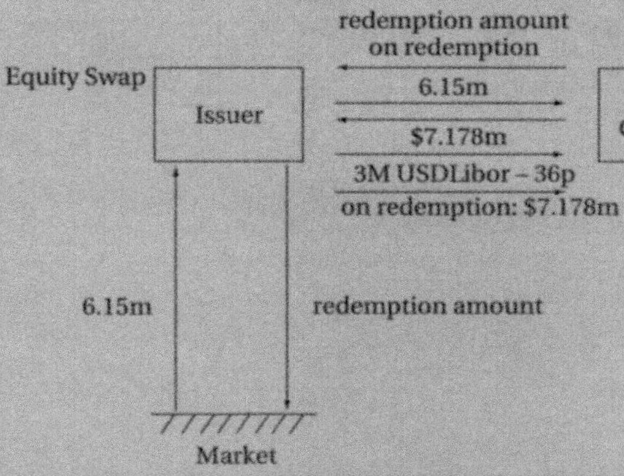

Issuer pays 3m $ LIBOR –3bp during life of swap on notional of $7.178m.

Figure 11.5: Structured MTN equity swap issue.

Final redemption amount:
The greater of
(i) 100%, or
(ii) 100% + (50% × (X_m – 2704/2704)),
subject to a maximum of 133%, where X_m is the level of the FTSE Eurotop 100 stock index.

The proceeds are swapped into dollars, an equivalent amount of $7.178 million, on which the issuer pays floating-rate interest of three-month LIBOR minus 3 basis points, during the life of the bond. This is illustrated in Figure 11.5.

Belgian franc 'DEM LIBOR Accrual' note

Issue date	13/7/1998
Maturity	17/7/1999
Issue size	BEF300 million
Coupon	(3-month BEF-LIBOR + 0.90)% × (Accrual factor), where the coupon rate will accrue for each day on which the DEM-LIBOR rate is within a range of 3.42%–4.03%

The terms of this issue included an unusual feature, a collar within which interest can accrue. The collar was the Deutschmark LIBOR rate; if the rate moved outside this stated range, no interest was payable on the note. In return for this the investor received a relatively high interest-rate from what was in effect a triple-A risk. The structure is illustrated as Figure 11.6.

USD Brazil credit-linked notes

Issue date	11/3/1998
Maturity	11/9/2000
Issue size	$30 million

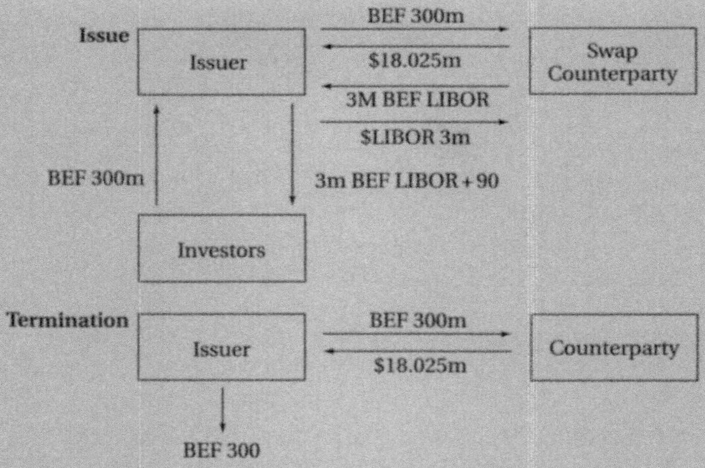

Figure 11.6: Structured MTN issue.

Issue price	100 per cent
Interest basis	Six-month USD-LIBOR + 430 basis points, not payable if a 'Brazilian Credit Event' has occurred

The redemption amount for this note is contingent on there being any relevant credit events occurring during the bond's life. A 'credit event' is defined in the MTN issue terms and conditions and is related to Brazilian corporate credit quality.

Japanese yen step-down notes due 2000

Issue date	4/1/1995
Maturity	29/3/2000
Issue size	JPY2.5 billion
Coupon	31% to 29/3/1995; thereafter 2.2% to redemption
Swap proceeds	$14 million

This is a straightforward MTN issue with yen proceeds swapped into dollars. Note however the very high initial coupon. The structure is illustrated in Figure 11.7.

ECU 12 million Korea Development Bank credit-linked zero-coupon notes due June 2000

Issue date	16/06/1998
Maturity	16/06/2000
Issue price	83.40%
Interest basis	Zero-coupon

The bonds are redeemable at par, or in the event of a 'credit event' (defined in the issue prospectus) prior to maturity are redeemable at a 'revised redemption amount', which is the greater of (a) zero and (b) a product of the Future Value percentage,

Recovery percentage and Accreted Notional, subject to a maximum of 100% (that is, redemption will be a maximum of ECU 12 million). The terms quoted here are defined in the issue prospectus.

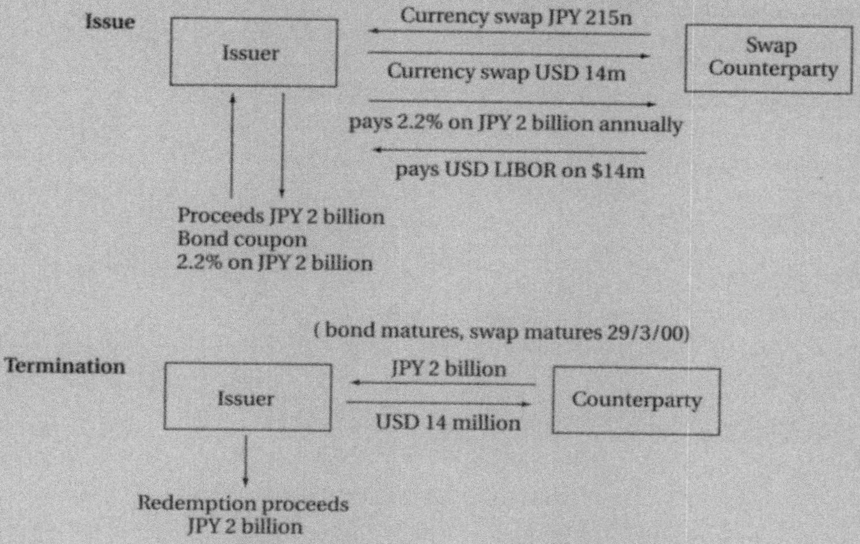

Figure 11.7: Structured MTN issue.

US dollar zero-coupon basket-linked notes due 2001

Issue	1/07/98
Maturity	1/07/2000
Issue price	100 per cent

Redemption amount:

The bond maturity value is $95\% + (82\% \times (X_m - 100/100))$, where X_m is the arithmetic mean of the values of a basket of global equities (the securities that constitute the equity basket are specified in the issue term sheet).

Selected bibliography and references

BPP Financial Publishing, *Corporate Debt Markets*, BPP Holdings plc, 1993

Crabbe, L., 'Anatomy of the Medium-Term Note Market', *Federal Reserve Bulletin*, August 1993, pp. 751–768

Crabbe, L., Corporate Medium-Term Notes', *The Continental Bank Journal of Applied Corporate Finance*, Winter 1992, pp. 90–102

Post, M., 'The Effect of SEC Amendments to Rule 2a-7 on the Commercial Paper Market', *Finance and Economics Discussion Series 1992* (Board of Governors of the Federal Reserve System, May 1992)

Fabozzi, F., *Bond Markets, Analysis and Strategies,* 2nd edition, Prentice Hall 1993, pp. 135–137

Roland, M., 'Sterling corporate debt and the MTN market', unpublished paper, Birkbeck, University of London, 2001

12 Commercial Paper

Strictly speaking *commercial paper* is a money market product, however CP is an important corporate finance instrument and it is worthwhile to review the subject.

Companies fund part of their medium- and long-term capital requirements in the debt capital markets, through the issue of bonds. Short-term capital and *working* capital is usually sourced directly from banks, in the form of bank loans. An alternative short-term funding instrument however is commercial paper (CP), which is available to corporates that have a sufficiently strong credit rating. Commercial paper is a short-term unsecured promissory note. The issuer of the note promises to pay its holder a specified amount on a specified maturity date. CP normally has a zero coupon and trades at a *discount* to its face value. The discount represents interest to the investor in the period to maturity. CP is typically issued in bearer form, although some issues are in registered form.

Outside of the United States CP markets were not introduced until the mid-1980s, and in 1986 the US market accounted for over 90% of outstanding commercial paper globally.[1] In the US however, the market was developed in the late nineteenth century, and as early as 1922 there were 2200 issuers of CP with $700 million outstanding. In 1998 there was just under $1 trillion outstanding, as shown in Table 12.1. CP was first issued in the United Kingdom in 1986, and subsequently in other European countries.

Originally the CP market was restricted to borrowers with high credit rating, and although lower-rated borrowers do now issue CP, sometimes by obtaining credit enhancements or setting up collateral arrangements, issuance in the market is still dominated by highly-rated companies. The majority of issues are very short-term, from 30 to 90 days in maturity; it is extremely rare to observe paper with a maturity of more than 270 days or nine months. This is because of regulatory requirements in the US,[2] which states that debt instruments with a maturity of less than 270 days need not be registered. Companies therefore issue CP with a maturity lower than nine months and so avoid the administration costs associated with registering issues with the SEC.

As with MTNs there are two major markets, the US dollar market with outstanding amount in 1998 just under $1 trillion as noted above, and the Eurocommercial paper market with outstanding value of $290 billion at the end of 1998.[3] Commercial paper markets are wholesale markets, and transactions are typically very large size. In the US over a third of all CP is purchased by money market unit trusts, known as mutual funds; other investors include pension fund managers, retail or commercial banks, local authorities and corporate treasurers.

Although there is a secondary market in CP, very little trading activity takes place since investors generally hold CP until maturity. This is to be expected because investors purchase CP that match their specific maturity requirement. When an investor does wish to sell

1 OECD (1989).
2 This is the Securities Act of 1933. Registration is with the Securities and Exchange Commission.
3 Source: BIS.

$bln	1985	1991	1992	1993	1994	1995	1996	1997	1998
Financial firms	213.9	414.7	395.5	398.1	399.3	430.7	486.6	590.8	765.8
Non-financial firms	87.2	147.9	133.4	147.6	155.7	164.6	188.3	184.6	200.9
All issuers	301.1	562.6	528.9	545.7	555	595.3	674.9	775.4	966.7

Table 12.1: The US Commercial Paper Market. Source: Federal Reserve Bulletin.

	US CP	Eurocommercial CP
Currency	US dollar	Any Euro currency
Maturity	1–270 days	2–365 days
Common maturity	30–50 days	30–90 days
Interest	Zero coupon, issued at discount	Usually zero-coupon, issued at discount
Quotation	On a discount rate basis	On a discount rate basis or yield basis
Settlement	T + 0	T + 2
Registration	Bearer form	Bearer form
Negotiable	Yes	Yes

Table 12.2: Comparison of US CP and Eurocommercial CP.

paper, it can be sold back to the dealer or, where the issuer has placed the paper directly in the market (and not via an investment bank), it can be sold back to the issuer.

12.1 Commercial paper programmes

The issuers of CP are often divided into two categories of company, banking and financial institutions and non-financial companies. The majority of CP issues are by financial companies, as noted in Table 12.1. Financial companies include not only banks but the financing arms of corporates such as General Motors, Ford Motor Credit and Chrysler Financial. Most of the issuers have strong credit ratings, but lower-rated borrowers have tapped the market, often after arranging credit support from a higher-rated company, such as a *letter of credit* from a bank, or by arranging collateral for the issue in the form of high-quality assets such as Treasury bonds. CP issued with credit support is known as *credit-supported commercial paper*, while paper backed with assets is known naturally enough, as *asset-backed commercial paper*. Paper that is backed by a bank letter of credit is termed *LOC paper*. Although banks charge a fee for issuing letters of credit, borrowers are often happy to arrange for this, since by so doing they are able to tap the CP market. The yield paid on an issue of CP will be lower than a commercial bank loan.

Although CP is a short-dated security, typically of three- to six-month maturity, it is issued within a longer term programme, usually for three to five years for euro paper; US CP programmes are often open-ended. For example a company might arrange a five-year CP programme with a limit of $100 million. Once the programme is established the company can issue CP up to this amount, say for maturities of 30 or 60 days. The programme is continuous and new CP can be issue at any time, daily if required. The total amount in issue cannot exceed the limit set for the programme. A CP programme can be used by a company to manage its short-term liquidity, that is its working capital requirements. New paper can be issued whenever a need for cash arises, and for an appropriate maturity.

Issuers often roll over their funding and use funds from a new issue of CP to redeem a maturing issue. There is a risk that an issuer might be unable to roll over the paper where there is a lack of investor interest in the new issue. To provide protection against this risk issuers often arrange a stand-by line of credit from a bank, normally for all of the CP programme, to draw against in the event that it cannot place a new issue.

There are two methods by which CP is issued, known as *direct-issued* or *direct paper* and *dealer-issued* or *dealer paper*. Direct paper is sold by the issuing firm directly to investors, and no agent bank or securities house is involved. It is common for financial companies to issue CP directly to their customers, often because they have continuous programmes and constantly roll-over their paper. It is therefore cost-effective for them to have their own sales arm and sell their CP direct. The treasury arms of certain non-financial companies also issue direct paper; this includes for example British Airways plc corporate treasury, which runs a continuous direct CP programme, used to provide short-term working capital for the company. Dealer paper is paper that is sold using a banking or securities house intermediary. In the US, dealer CP is effectively dominated by investment banks, as retail (commercial) banks were until recently forbidden from underwriting commercial paper. This restriction has since been removed and now both investment banks and commercial paper underwrite dealer paper.

Although CP is issued within a programme, like MTNs, there are of course key differences between the two types of paper, reflecting CP's status as a money market instrument. The CP market is issuer-driven, with daily offerings to the market. MTNs in contrast are more investor-driven; issuers will offer them when demand appears. In this respect MTNs issues are often 'opportunistic', taking advantage of favourable conditions in the market.

12.2 Commercial paper yields

Commercial paper is a discount instrument. There have been issues of coupon CP, but this is very unusual. Thus CP is sold at a discount to its maturity value, and the difference between this maturity value and the purchase price is the interest earned by the investor. The CP day-count base is 360 days in the US and euro markets, and 365 days in the UK. The paper is quoted on a discount yield basis, in the same manner as Treasury bills. The yield on CP follows that of other money market instruments and is a function of the short-dated yield curve. The yield on CP is higher than the T-Bill rate; this is due to the credit risk that the investor is exposed to when holding CP, for tax reasons (in certain jurisdictions interest earned on T-Bills is exempt from income tax) and because of the lower level of liquidity available in the CP market. CP also pays a higher yield than Certificates of Deposit (CD), due to the lower liquidity of the CP market.

Although CP is a discount instrument and trades as such in the US and UK, euro currency Eurocommercial paper trades on a yield basis, similar to a CD. The discount rate for an instrument is discussed in Chapter 2 of the author's book *The Bond and Money*

Markets. The expressions below are a reminder of the relationship between true yield and discount rate.

$$P = \frac{M}{1 + r \times \frac{\text{days}}{\text{year}}} \tag{12.1}$$

$$rd = \frac{r}{1 + r \times \frac{\text{days}}{\text{year}}} \tag{12.2}$$

$$r = \frac{rd}{1 - rd \times \frac{\text{days}}{\text{year}}} \tag{12.3}$$

where M is the face value of the instrument, rd is the discount rate and r the true yield.

Example 12.1

1. A 60-day CP note has a nominal value of \$100,000. It is issued at a discount of 7½ per cent per annum. The discount is calculated as:

$$Dis = \frac{\$100,000\ (0.075 \times 60)}{360}$$
$$= \$1,250.$$

The issue price for the CP is therefore \$100,000 – \$1,250, or \$98,750.
The money market yield on this note at the time of issue is:

$$\left(\frac{360 \times 0.075}{360 - (0.075 \times 60)}\right) \times 100\% = 7.59\%.$$

Another way to calculate this yield is to measure the capital gain (the discount) as a percentage of the CP's cost, and convert this from a 60-day yield to a one-year (360-day) yield, as shown below.

$$r = \frac{1,250}{98,750} \times \frac{360}{60} \times 100\%$$
$$= 7.59\%.$$

Note that these are US dollar CP and therefore have a 360-day base.

2. ABC plc wishes to issue CP with 90 days to maturity. The investment bank managing the issue advises that the discount rate should be 9.5 per cent. What should the issue price be, and what is the money market yield for investors?

$$Dis = \frac{100\ (0.095 \times 90)}{360}$$
$$= 2375.$$

The issue price will be 97.625.
The yield to investors will be:

$$\frac{2.375}{97.625} \times \frac{360}{90} \times 100\% = 9.73\%.$$

Asset-backed commercial paper

The rise in securitisation has led to the growth of short-term instruments backed by the cash flows from other assets, known as *asset-backed commercial paper* (ABCP). Securitisation is looked at in greater detail elsewhere in this book, here we discuss briefly the basic concept of ABCP.

Generally securitisation is used as a funding instrument by companies for three main reasons: it offers lower-cost funding compared with traditional bank loan or bond financing; it is a mechanism by which assets such as corporate loans or mortgages can be removed from the balance sheet, thus improving the lender's return on assets or return on equity ratios; and it increases a borrower's funding options. When entering into securitisation, an entity may issue term securities against assets into the public or private market, or it may issue commercial paper via a special vehicle known as a *conduit*. These conduits are usually sponsored by commercial banks.

Entities usually access the commercial paper market in order to secure permanent financing, rolling over individual issues as part of a longer-term *programme* and using interest-rate swaps to arrange a fixed rate if required. Conventional CP issues are typically supported by a line of credit from a commercial bank, and so this form of financing is in effect a form of bank funding.

Asset-backed conduits structures (AB-CP) are used for both funding and investment purposes. The first example is typified by a commercial bank that uses assets currently on its balance sheet (such as certain corporate or other loans, or corporate funding assets such as lease receivables) as collateral in a securitisation. This collateral is used as asset backing for the liabilities issued by the conduit in the form of CP. The second type of conduit is usually structured by investment banks that wish to invest in assets in an off-balance sheet capacity and fund these at the lower rates obtainable in the CP market. So, for example, the conduit may invest in long-dated assets such as investment-grade rated ABS, MBS and CDO notes, while funding these with short-dated CP. The conduit will be structured to receive the top short-term rating from the ratings agencies (A-1+, P-1, A-1). This enables it to issue CP at Libor-flat or Libor plus 1 or 2 basis points, which is a lower rate than the bank itself could have got if it had funded the assets directly from its own balance sheet.

The latest AB-CP structures make use of credit derivatives in their structure and are known as *synthetic* AB-CP vehicles. In a synthetic AB-CP conduit, the underlying assets are not held by the conduit itself; rather, the assets are referenced by a Total Return Swap (TRS) which pays out the CP interest on one side, while returning the economic performance of the assets ion the other side of the TRS. Alternatively, the conduit may hold an interest in the underlying asset by means of an option product issued at par, called a zero-strike call, instead of holding the assets themselves on its balance sheet.

Further details on synthetic AB-CP structures are given in Choudhry (2004).

Selected bibliography

Alworth, J., Borio, C., 'Commercial Paper Markets: A Survey', *BIS Economic Papers No.37*, 1993, Bank for International Settlements

Choudhry, M., *Fixed Income Markets: Instruments, Applications, Mathematics*, John Wiley & Sons, 2004

Corporate Finance, *A Guide to Commercial Paper in Europe 1991*, Euromoney Publications, September 1991

Corporate Finance, *Guide to International Commercial Paper*, Euromoney Publications, January 1993

OECD, *Competition in Banking*, OECD 1989

Stigum, M., *The Money Market*, Dow-Jones Irwin, 1990

13 Preference Shares and Preferred Stock

Preference shares, or *preferred stock* as they are known in the United States, are a class of shares that entitle the holder to preferences over those of the company's ordinary shares. The most usual preference concerns dividend rights, but other provisions may sometimes be included. They are non-equity shares, but are also described sometimes as equity. They are not debt instruments although they trade similarly to certain types of debt, and often the preference share market making desk is located within the bond division of a bank. Preference shares rank below debt instruments in the event of a wind-up of a company, but above ordinary shares. They have a long history; the market in preference shares was well established in both the United Kingdom and United States in the nineteenth century. The main types of preference share are fixed-dividend, adjustable-rate and auction market preference shares. These main variations will be reviewed later in the chapter.

Preference shares may be defined as shares which provide their holders with an entitlement to receive a dividend, but only up to a specific limit, which is usually a fixed amount every year. They may also give their holders a limited right to participate in any surplus in the event of a winding up, should there be a liquidation and sale of the company's assets. Preference shares may also be redeemable on fixed terms or on terms dictated by the issuing company. Despite their name however preference shares are similar to debt capital and this is why it is necessary to review their characteristics here. However preference shares are not debt, but are a form of ownership in a company, despite the fact that most forms of preference stocks do not grant their holders a voting right. The instruments might be fairly described as a peculiar cross between shares and bonds, and share some but not all characteristics of both. For example certain preference shares are unlike ordinary shares in that if a dividend is not paid in one year, it will *accumulate* and must be paid before ordinary share dividends. Unlike bonds however a failure to pay dividends is not a default, although there are several negative implications associated with such an action. They are similar to bonds in that they do not entitle holders a vote in the company (usually, as long as the dividend is paid), although voting rights are usually granted if a dividend is not paid. The preference share market making desk in a bank is usually situated in the fixed interest division, rather than in the equity division. This reflects that the valuation of preference shares fluctuates with the yield curve.

In this chapter we introduce the different types of preference shares, and how they differ from conventional fixed income securities. In the US and UK there is wide variety of preference shares in the market and we are only able to review them here; interested readers may wish to consult the references listed in the bibliography at the end of the chapter.

13.1 The size of the market

The majority of borrowers in the US domestic market are financial institutions. In the UK domestic market the instrument has been more popular with non-financial corporates, although banks have also been large-volume issuers. During the period 1983–1993 over $81 billion was raised in the US preferred market, of which around 62% was by financial companies.[1] Table 13.1 shows the level of issuance in the US market during this period.

Preference shares are purely a corporate financing instrument and credit ratings for individual share issues are as important as they are for corporate bonds. In the US domestic market, ratings are issued by four ratings firms, known as 'nationally recognised statistical rating organisations' or NRSROs, which are Standard & Poor's, Moody's, Duff and Phelps and Fitch Investors Service. The ratings issued by the NRSROs, although outwardly similar to the ratings for corporate bonds in some cases, need to be assessed differently however; this is because preferred stock should be analysed within the range of other preference shares, distinct from debt issues.

13.2 Description and definition of preference shares

13.2.1 *Introduction*

An annual preference dividend is payable, usually on a semi-annual basis, as a fixed percentage amount of the nominal value of the share. Unlike the interest payable on a conventional bond though, which is paid out of the pre-tax profits of the issuing company, preference share dividends are paid out of post-tax profits. The dividend on a preference share must be paid before any dividend can be paid to ordinary equity shareholders. The primary differentiating feature of preference shares compared to ordinary shares is the treatment of the dividend that is payable by them, which is at a fixed rate or variable rate. The dividend paid by a conventional preference share is at a fixed rate of the face value, or a fixed cash value per share. The dividend must be paid before any can be paid on ordinary shares; for

US preferred stock market	1983	1984	1985	1986	1987	1988	1989	1990	1991	1992	1993
Volumes ($ million)											
Fixed dividend	2,300	1,600	463	1,060	2,260	2,900	1,120	3,720	3,415	3,295	11,430
Variable dividend	2,800	4,375	3,180	5,480	6,290	5,325	5,980	2,480	1,370	6,740	3,990
Number of issues by industry sector											
Banks	19	32	26	54	73	62	49	21	14	28	31
Investment companies	–	–	–	–	–	–	20	7	12	25	24
Utility companies	49	42	21	13	32	42	16	11	16	23	54
Industrial/transportation companies	6	7	4	18	14	8	15	8	5	3	15

Table 13.1: US preferred stock market, 1983–1993. Source: IFC.

[1] Wilson (1997).

the majority of preference shares the dividend is in cash. During the bull market of the mid-1980s up to the crash of October 1987, some preference shares in the US market paid dividends in the form of more shares. These were known as *PIKs* preferred stock.

There are also preference shares that pay a variable rate dividend in the US market. Generally these pay a dividend that is adjusted or re-set quarterly at a fixed spread to the Treasury yield curve. The spread, known as the dividend reset spread, will lie above or at the level of one of three points on the yield curve, which are the three-month maturity point, the 10-year point and the 30-year point. Instead of using the redemption yield at these points, the adjusted dividend is based on the Treasury constant maturity (TCM) yield, which is calculated by the Federal Reserve. This means that the adjusted dividend is not a pure short- or long-term yield but a composite of the two. Variable rate preferred stock in the US is known as adjustable-rate preferred stocks or ARPS. They are singular instruments in that they are neither money market paper nor long-dated bonds. They possess some of the attributes of ordinary shares however, in that they do not exhibit the 'pull to par' effect of bonds with a fixed maturity. However they are related to the debt market yield curve and their value will fluctuate with this.

In the United Kingdom the coupon rate of preference dividend is shown net of tax, as the amount of dividend that shareholders will receive in cash. The gross pre-tax dividend is this net amount plus a *tax credit* for the amount of income tax deducted. If the tax credit is 25%, the gross dividend is multiplied by 100/75 of the net dividend.

13.2.2 *Rights in a liquidation*

In the event of a liquidation of the company, the order of entitlement to payment from the proceeds of selling off the company's assets is that preference shareholders rank behind trade creditors but ahead of ordinary shareholders. The amount receivable in a winding-up however is limited to the nominal value of the shares, and possibly also any unpaid dividend. Certain preference shares have issue terms that allow them to participate with the ordinary shares in the event of liquidation, which may seem to some to be a somewhat dubious advantage. For example, the preference share may entitle a holder to receive upon the company's liquidation, twice the amount per share distributed on each ordinary share. This is more common in the US market.

13.2.3 *Voting rights*

Preference shares do not, as a rule, entitle holders to a vote in the running of the company. This is perhaps the chief difference between preference shares and ordinary shares. The general understanding is that, because preference shareholders receive a regular and fixed dividend, they do not require voting rights. This is not always the case, and certain issues do entitle holders to a vote. For example the preferred stock of Southern California Edison, a US utility company, carries with it varying levels of voting rights. The cumulative preferred stockholders each have six votes per share, while the $100 cumulative preferred stock entitles its holders to two votes per share. The votes may be used cumulatively in the case of the election of company directors.

The general exception is when preference shares are in arrears after the non-payment of a dividend. In the US market if more than four dividends have not been paid, which in most cases would be over a two-year period, preference shares are allotted voting rights, sometimes just to be used in the election or re-election of directors. Where this provision is included in the terms of the share issue, they are known as *contingent voting stock*, because the right to vote is contingent on the preference shareholders not receiving the dividends to which they are entitled. When a dividend arrear(s) has been paid off, the voting rights will cease. Such provisions are common, sometimes because of regulatory requirements. The New York Stock Exchange for example, states that non-voting preferred stock must be contingent voting stock otherwise it cannot be listed on the exchange.

The other type of voting power that is often carried by preference shares relates to specific corporate actions that may affect the standing or value of the shares themselves. For instance preference shareholders may be entitled to vote on proposals to increase the authorised amount of any class of stock that would rank ahead of the preference shares, in terms of dividends or rights to assets in the event of a liquidation. The shareholders may also be entitled to give their approval on a merger or consolidation, the results of which might adversely affect the rights and preferences of the preference shares. Shares that have this privilege written into their terms is known as *vetoing stock*. However this veto power is usually available only if the preference shares are in dividend arrears, and will be removed if the arrears are paid off.

13.2.4 *Types of preference shares*

A 'straight' or conventional preference share has the following characteristics:

- interest is paid at a fixed annual rate, but only if profits are sufficiently high for the company to afford the dividend;
- when any due dividend is unpaid, the shareholders do not have the right to payment in arrears at a later date;
- the share is *perpetual*, that is it is irredeemable or 'permanent'.

In fact the majority of preference shares both in the US and the UK are not conventional, rather they incorporate one or more of the following features; they may be *cumulative*, *participating*, *redeemable* or *convertible*. Preference shares may have one or more, or all, of these features.

- **Cumulative preference shares** entitle their holder to a fixed rate of dividend, and if any dividend is not paid on the due date, the arrears remain payable and will accumulate. The preference shareholders must receive their arrears of dividend before any ordinary share dividend can be paid to equity shareholders. This provision is a significant restriction to the management of a company and would result in the ordinary shares being marked down; it is rare for such shares not to receive a dividend unless the company is in serious financial difficulty. Certain cumulative preference shares impose other restrictions in the event that a dividend is not paid. For example the issuer may not be able to redeem any stock that ranks below the preference shares. Shares that have a sinking fund attached to them may have their sinking payments suspended, with no funds being allowed to redeem preferred or ordinary shares.
- **Participating preference shares** have additional dividend rights. The holders of participating preference shares, in addition to receiving their fixed dividend, are also entitled to a share of the company's surplus profits. This extra *participating* dividend is usually set at a specified percentage of the dividend paid on the ordinary shares. In the US market

virtually all the preferred stock in the market is non-participating. Holders of such shares will not benefit from the company posting ever-increasing after-tax profits after every year, except indirectly in that the rating of their preference shares will receive a boost.

- **Redeemable preference shares** are shares that either will be redeemed at a specified future date, or could be redeemed at a specified future date at the option of the company or the preference shareholders. The shares are redeemed at par or at a premium to par value. In the US market preferred stock with no redemption provisions are rare, and are true perpetual securities. Most issues are callable during a time period after their initial issue, in whole or in part, at the option of the issuer and at pre-specified prices. The redemption value must include accrued dividend interest at the time of the call. The point at which the preferred stock is callable is often medium- to long-term after issue, and may not be for 10 or 20 years after the issue date. Callable issues are often protected from being called for a set period after the issue of debt or equity that ranks with or ahead of the preferred shares. This is to protect shareholders from capital loss arising from a new issue of stock, when the price would be expected to fall and the company could then cash in by redeeming the stock.
- **Convertible preference shares** entitle their holder to a right to convert the preference shares into ordinary shares of the company at a specified future date or between specified future dates, and at a specified rate of conversion. Convertible preference shares are usually redeemable; if they are not converted into equity they will eventually be redeemed. They are similar in many respects to convertible bonds, although the method of quoting prices differs according to which market they are traded in. In domestic markets the convention is to quote the shares in the same manner as ordinary shares; in international markets (Euromarkets) they are quoted in a similar way to bonds, that is as a percentage of nominal or par value.

Example 13.1

- A company with £10 million 6% cumulative preference shares of £1 nominal in issue was unable to pay the dividend on the last payment date, to both preference and ordinary shareholders. It would now like to resume dividend payments in the current year, beginning with an interim dividend. The company in fact is not able to pay an interim dividend to ordinary shareholders until the preference shareholders have been paid their dividend. This is £900,000, comprised of the arrears of the last dividend (6% of £10 million) and the interim dividend of half this amount (£300,000). If the preference shares had been non-cumulative, their holders would not be entitled to the arrears of the dividend and in the current year they would receive only the interim of dividend of £300,000.

Another instrument that is an example of the close similarities between convertible bonds and convertible preference shares are *convertible capital bonds*. These were first issued in the euroconvertibles market in 1989 by J. Sainsbury plc, a UK supermarket group. The bonds can be converted into redeemable convertible preference shares at the option of the company.

It is common for companies to have many classes of preference share in issue at any one time. The terms of each class will have been determined separately at the time of their respective issuance.

Example 13.2(i)

- The Rank Organisation plc, a UK leisure group, has an issue of 8 1/4% convertible redeemable preference shares of 20p each, convertible in any year from 1993–2003 into ordinary shares of 25p nominal value. The conversion rate is 10.6383 ordinary shares for every 100 of the preference shares. The company also has a call option and can redeem the shares at £1 per share at any time after 30 April 2003, and the shares will be redeemed in any event at £1 per share on 31 July 2007. The shares are listed on the London Stock Exchange are priced in the same way as ordinary shares, that is in pence per share.

Example 13.2 (ii)

- Tate & Lyle plc has convertible cumulative preference shares in issue. They are convertible in any year up to 2008 into ordinary shares at a conversion ratio of 11.299 ordinary shares for every 25 of the preference shares. The preference shares have a nominal value of 12.5p each and are redeemable at £1 per share on the maturity date of 28 February 2013, but at the issuer's option at any time from 1 September 2008.

Example 13.2 (iii)

- Thorn EMI (another UK leisure group) issued redeemable convertible preference shares in the Euromarket in 1989. The shares are convertible into the company's ordinary shares and had a maturity of ten years. Although the bonds were described as preference shares they had most of the characteristics of convertible bonds, and in fact were referred to as 'bonds' by most market analysts. The price of the shares was quoted as an amount per cent, for example 129 per 100 nominal. The bonds offered a put option that entitled holders to redeem them at 130.22% on 2 February 1994 and 180.64% on 2 February 1999, when they matured. The bonds were also callable.

13.2.5 *Sinking funds*

A *sinking fund* provision in a preference share issue will operate in a similar fashion to a sinking fund with a bond. It will provide for the periodic redemption of a proportion of the issue, most commonly on an annual basis. For example, the sinking fund may pay off 5% of the original number of shares each year. Preference shares that are callable and also have sinking finds may set different dates when the two features are applicable, so that the sinking fund may come into operation after the stock ceases to be callable. Sinking fund payments may be made in shares of stock purchased in the open market or by the call of the required number of shares at the sinking fund call price, which is normally par or another stated value. As with the payment of dividends, the failure to make a sinking fund payment is not considered a default, unlike with a bond, and the company could not be placed in bankruptcy.

Certain preferred issues have *purchase funds*. These are essentially optional on the part of the issuer because it will have to use its best efforts to retire a portion of the shares at periodic intervals if they can be purchased in the open market, or otherwise through a tender, at below the redemption price. If the shares are trading above the purchase price, the purchase fund cannot operate. A purchase fund can act as a floor for the price of the shares, at a time of high dividend yields, but would not operate in a low yield environment.

13.3 Cost of preference share capital

The gross yield that investors expect from preference shares and bonds of the same issuing company was historically the same, although liquidity considerations meant that the yield on preference shares would be slightly higher. The yield on preference shares in the UK market is now considerably higher than in the bond market, as a result of tax changes introduced by the Labour government in 1997.[2] This has resulted in there being no real advantage to a UK company in raising capital in the preference share market, which may well become illiquid in the near future. For the purposes of analysis, let us consider an historical example that illustrates the considerations involved, which would apply in other markets.

Example 13.3

- In March 1993 General Accident plc, a UK insurance group that subsequently merged with another insurer (Commercial Union) and is now known as CGU plc,[3] issued 110 million 7.875% cumulative irredeemable preference shares of £1 each at an issue price of 100.749p per share. The tax credit on UK dividends at that time was 25%, or 25/75 of the net cash dividend. The rate of interest payable on long-dated corporate bonds was then approximately 10.50%. What is the cost of the capital?

The dividend of 7.875% is net of tax (at that time). The gross dividend is treated as an advance payment of corporation tax by the company, and the annual profit that the company needs to cover the dividend payments is £8,662,500, obtained by multiplying the nominal value of the shares and multiplying this by the coupon. If the company pays corporation tax at a rate of say 33%, a bond issue paying a gross yield of 10.50% would have an after-tax cost of approximately 7%, obtained by multiplying the coupon rate of 10.50% by (100–33)%. The higher cost of the preference shares therefore might be attributable to the premium required for holding them because they are irredeemable.

Companies that are regarded as higher risk will pay a higher yield on their preference shares compared to their bonds. The yield on preference shares is usually shown as a current yield or, in the case of redeemable shares, a redemption yield. Preference shares that have an embedded option feature may be analysed using a yield-to-call or yield-to-put. The yield calculation uses an actual/360 or 30/360 basis in the US market and an actual/365 basis in the UK market. It is important to remember that the yield calculation is in effect a net yield, so that the value must be 'grossed up' if returns are being compared to those of bond instruments. This is because the convention is to quote gross yields for bonds.

---

2 The legislation did not take effect until the following year.
3 It subsequently purchased Norwich Union plc and is now CGNU plc.

13.4 The preference share market

In the UK domestic market preference shares are traded in the same way as ordinary shares that is, they are listed on an exchange. Trading is on the exchange via its dealing system. Domestic issues of preference shares can be relatively small size, and they are often issued as part of a company financial re-structuring or through a private placement to a small group of investors. In 1996 the Bank of Ireland issued conventional preference shares to raise part of the financing required in its take-over of the Bristol & West building society. The preference shares were also used to pay some of the membership of the building society, who were entitled to a share of the society's reserves in return for giving up ownership of it. In the US under half of all publicly issued preference shares are listed on the NYSE or the American Stock Exchange, with the remainder trading in the OTC market. The normal unit of trading is 100 shares but this is not universal and some issues trade in lots of 10 shares. It is possible to deal in odd-lots of shares. Listing an issue may lead to a lower dividend yield for an issuer if it improves its marketability. This is more significant if the issue itself is a relatively large size one. Dealing via an exchange system also makes an issue more transparent in the market.

In international markets companies usually issue redeemable convertible preference shares, which are regarded as part of the Euroconvertibles market, together with convertible bonds and equity warrant bonds.

13.5 Auction market preferred stock (Amps)

Auction market preferred stock (Amps) is a particular type of preference share. Its main distinguishing feature is that the dividend payable on the shares is determined by auction at regular intervals. The Amps market was developed in the US and the instrument has been issued by a number of foreign borrowers in the domestic US market.

Amps are placed through an investment bank or securities house that acts as lead manager for the issue. They are sold to investors through the auction process. They cannot be offered for sale to the general public, nor may they be traded on a stock exchange. A panel of investors is invited to participate in the auction, and they submit bids for the dividend rate that they will accept in return for purchasing a quantity of the stock. The stock is sold at a fixed price to the investors bidding at the lowest dividend level.

Example 13.4

- A US company is issuing Amps and a group of investment institutions is invited to bid for the stock. The size of the issue is $100 million. Bids are received for $60 million at a dividend yield of 6%, $90 million at a yield of 6 1/4% and $150 million at a yield of 6 1/2%. The shares will be sold to the investors bidding the lowest dividend yield, which is paid on the entire issue. Given the ratio of the bidding amount, the yield payable in our simple example is 6 1/4%. The investors who bid 6% will receive the full quantity of stock they bid for, on a yield of 6 1/4%, while the remaining $40 million will be allotted to investors bidding at this level on a pro-rata basis. The stock is issued at par.

Auctions occur at regular intervals, sometimes as frequently as every four weeks. Investors wishing to buy Amps at an auction may submit a bid to receive a dividend yield of their choice; at subsequent auctions existing holders may sell part or all of their holding to bidders. After the primary issue existing holders can opt to hold their stock, bid for more of the shares or sell to another bidder. When all orders have been submitted an 'auction agent' is responsible for deciding the allocation.

The number of Amps for which bid orders have been received is compared with the volume of Amps available. If the volume of orders exceeds the quantity of stock available the dividend rate is set at the lowest rate at which all the Amps will be taken up, and holders will subsequently receive this dividend level. At this point Amps must be sold by existing holders who bid at a higher rate to successful new purchasers who bid at a lower rate. At each auction there is a maximum rate of dividend that will be paid on the stock. This level is a function of the credit rating of the stock at the time of the auction and is determined by a pre-set formula. If the credit rating is downgraded, the maximum rate payable will be raised, and this new rate of dividend is used as a default rate. The dividend rate payable until the next auction, which must not be held for a minimum of 28 days, is the default rate. There may be an insufficient number of bidders in an auction for the quantity of Amps that are available below the maximum (default) rate. When this happens, existing holders who wish to sell will be unable to do so.

Example 13.5

- ABC Inc, a US company, has an issue of $500 million of Amps. In an auction bids are submitted for $300 million of stock at yields ranging from 6 1/2% to 7% and there are hold orders for $150 million. The maximum rate is 7%. Therefore there are insufficient bids for the stock. Bidders for $300 million will be able to buy the stock, and existing holders of $150 million of stock will retain their holding. Holders of a further $50 million who wished to sell their stock will be unable to do so. They must hold their paper until at least the next auction. The dividend rate payable to the next auction is the default rate of 7%.

Dividends on Amps are paid at pre-determined fixed intervals and sometimes match the auction cycle. For example British Aerospace (now known as BAE Holdings) Amps pay a dividend every 49 days. Although they are known as 'preferred stock' Amps are similar in many respects to bonds. The dividend on Amps is usually around 100 basis points above the yield on straight short-term fixed debt, but the advantages are that there are no covenants of any kind attached to Amps issues and they are redeemable only at the issuer's option. The cost of Amps to the issuer will increase however if its credit rating is downgraded. The default rate of dividend that applies if an auction is unsuccessful could be raised at the next auction.

Issues of Amps vary in size, although in the mid-1990s UK company issues in the US domestic market ranged in size from $100 million to $700 million.

Amps are only redeemable at the option of the issuer and in theory therefore are perpetual. They are issued without any form of covenant and a failure to pay a dividend on an Amps does not constitute a default (as is the case for all preference shares). Holders of

Amps are not able to demand redemption in the event of non-payment of a dividend. The inability of shareholders to demand redemption was used at one point to argue that Amps should be regarded as equity finance. This was not accepted by the UK authorities. Amps may not be 'perpetual' finance, as a company, having issued Amps could find that its credit rating was downgraded. The dividend that would be payable would then rise at subsequent auctions, and if the downgrade were sufficiently great, the cost of paying dividends on the Amps might then become so high as to cause the issuer to redeem them. In the UK in the early 1990s rising dividend costs on Amps made redemption an attractive option. For example BET plc announced a £200 million rights issue in July 1992 in order to finance a redemption of most of its outstanding Amps. The cost of the dividend payment on the Amps had risen from a level just below the US commercial paper rate in 1991 to a premium of over 21% above CP rates in mid-1992. The extract below from the *Financial Times* for 15 July 1992 suggested that domestic US investors were not sufficiently familiar with the name to believe it was worthwhile holding the paper without substantial rise in the dividend yield to compensate for whatever trouble they thought the company was getting into.

> 'The history of suspicion and misunderstanding of these instruments in the UK may seem odd to a US observer. But the market for Amps consists wholly of US investors who are interested primarily in big, familiar, triple-A US corporations like Coca-Cola and Exxon, rather than unknown foreign minnows.'
>
> (FT, 15 July 1992)

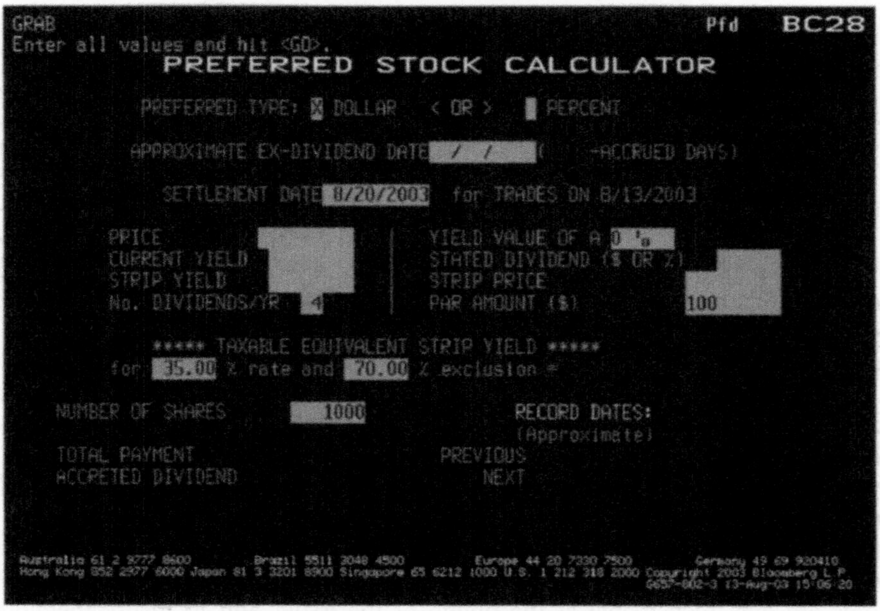

Figure 13.1: Preferred stock analysis screen on Bloomberg. © Bloomberg L.P. Used with permission.

During this period other UK companies also redeemed their Amps issues. For example Rank Organisation plc redeemed its $200 million Amps issue in April 1991 after its credit rating was downgraded from A- to BBB- by Standard & Poors.

13.6 Bloomberg screens

Preference shares can be analysed on Bloomberg using the same screens that are used for both fixed income and equities, depending on their particular terms and conditions. The specific preference share calculator is screen BC28, the preferred stock calculator. This is shown at Figure 13.1.

Selected bibliography

Brealey, R., Myers, S., *Principles of Corporate Finance,* McGraw-Hill, 1996

Finnerty, J.D., 'Financial Engineering in Corporate Finance: An Overview', *Financial Management 17,* Winter 1988, pp. 14–31

Ross, S., Westerfield, R., Jaffe, J., *Corporate Finance,* Irwin/McGraw-Hill, 1998

Wilson, R., 'Nonconvertible Preferred Stock', in Fabozzi, F., *The Handbook of Fixed Income Securities,* 5th edition, McGraw-Hill, 1997, Chapter 14, pp. 263–286

14 The US Municipal Bond Market

Municipal bonds in the United States are securities issued by state and local governments as well as institutions created by them. Until recently the municipal bond market was viewed as being akin to the US Treasury market, ranking only slightly behind Treasuries in terms of credit quality. Although in theory this is an accurate view, investors nowadays view municipal securities as more similar to corporate bonds, with significantly higher credit risk than Treasury bonds. This is considered to be the case irrespective of whether individual bonds are rated at investment-grade or not. Since municipal bonds trade at yields that are closer to corporate bonds than Treasury bonds, they are reviewed here in the section on corporate debt markets.[1] The principal difference between municipal bonds and Treasury bonds, aside from the credit considerations, is that municipal bonds are tax-exempt, that is interest is exempt from federal income taxation. The bonds may not necessarily be exempt from state or local income taxes, however as Treasuries are liable to federal taxes, municipal bonds are known as tax-exempt securities. However although there are both tax-exempt and taxable municipal bonds, the sector is sometimes referred to as the tax-exempt market. More than 50,000 entities have issued municipal bonds in the United States. They are issued for a variety of reasons, along the entire length of the yield curve. Short-dated paper is often issued to cover local authority cash flows, ahead of the receipt of taxation proceeds. Long-dated paper is issued for capital and other projects, for example to assist in the financing of say, schools, hospitals, and communication and infrastructure facilities such as airports.

The exemption from federal taxation makes municipal bonds particularly attractive to individual retail investors, approximately 75% of all outstanding paper is held by individuals. The remaining bonds are held by banks, mutual funds and property companies.[2] Banks are attracted to municipal bonds for various reasons; they include the tax advantage but also for liquidity purposes,[3] for which municipal bonds are often preferred to Treasury bonds. Municipal bonds are eligible to be used as collateral when commercial banks borrow funds from the Federal Reserve. Additionally banks may serve as underwriters of municipal bond issues and will frequently emerge from such activity holding an inventory of the paper. Property companies are attracted to municipal bonds because of the tax advantages

1 The municipal bond markets were also affected by several high profile instances of local authorities getting into financial difficulty, which resulted in the widening of spreads on bonds issued by them. These included the financial crisis in the City of New York in 1975, as well as the default of Orange County, California twenty years later. In addition to this, federal bankruptcy law effective from 1979 makes it more straightforward for municipal bond issuers to seek protection from bondholders by filing for bankruptcy.

2 Feldstein/Fabozzi 1997.

3 By liquidity we mean funding liquidity and not trading liquidity. The US term is that banks are required to be 'collateralised', that is deposits must be backed with short-dated high quality assets. Generally banking liquidity books invest in T-Bills, clearing banks Certificates of Deposit, short-dated government bonds and local authority bonds.

and also because their profits follow a highly cyclical pattern; municipal bonds are purchased during times of high profit, to lower their income tax liability.

14.1 Description of municipal bonds

The municipal bond in the United States is essentially a plain vanilla bond market. The majority of municipal securities are conventional fixed interest bonds; there are also a considerable number of floating-rate securities. Floating-rate municipal bonds will pay a spread over a specified reference interest rate. The reference rate may be a Treasury rate, the prime rate, or a municipal index such as the Municipal Bond Buyer index or the Merrill Lynch Index. The municipal market has also seen the issue of inverse floating-rate bonds, whose coupon is adjusted in the opposite direction to the move in the reference rate. Municipal zero-coupon bonds are known as *original-issue discount bonds* or OIDs. These bonds are similar to government zero-coupon securities, but the return to the investor is exempt from federal tax. There is also an almost unique type of zero-coupon municipal bond known as a *municipal multiplier* or *compound interest bond*. This bond is issued at par and pays interest. However the interest payments themselves are not distributed to the bondholder until the maturity date; in the meantime the issuer reinvests the undistributed coupon payments at the redemption yield level at which the bond was issued. Essentially this guarantees the investor a fixed interest rate on her coupons for the life of the bond, so in effect the redemption yield becomes a true redemption yield, unlike that quoted for a conventional bond. The maturity value of such bonds is calculated using standard present value techniques, as illustrated in Example 14.1.

Example 14.1

- A 6.00% 20-year municipal multiplier bond is issued at par. What is the value of the bond on maturity?

The bond is sold at 100 so that the redemption yield is 6.00%. The market has a semi-annual coupon convention, so the maturity value is given by the future value of the stream of coupon payments. This is:

$$100 \times (1.03)^{40} = \$326.21.$$

- If the issuing authority wishes to place 20-year bonds at a yield of 6.00% with a maturity value of 100, at what price must they be sold? This is a standard present-value calculation and is given by:

$$100 \times \frac{1}{(1.03)^{40}} = \$30.65568.$$

The maturity date on municipal bonds may be a conventional fixed date, or a dual date. Fixed term bonds have maturity terms of up to 40 years from the date of issue, although there may be a sinking fund that kicks in after the first say, ten years. It is also common for municipal bonds to mature over a number of years, which is known as a serial maturity. Such securities are known as *serial bonds*. Municipal bonds with serial maturities may have as many as 10 or more maturity dates. A serial maturity structure requires a proportion of the outstanding debt to be redeemed each year.

Municipal bonds may be broken down into two basic types, known as *general obligation bonds* and *revenue bonds*. The two types are not mutually exclusive and it is possible to encounter bonds that exhibit features of both types. They are reviewed next.

14.1.1 *General obligation bonds*

Municipal bonds that are issued by entities such as states, cities, towns and local districts are known as general obligation bonds. The unlimited tax-raising powers of the issuing body serves as the security for the issue of the bonds. This source of revenue is to all intents guaranteed, although amounts will fluctuate with the general health of the economy; however this fixity of income renders municipal bonds a lower credit risk than corporate bonds, at least in theory. A large borrower such as a state or large city will have a wide range of tax-raising sources, including income tax, corporation tax, value-added tax and property tax. Some general obligation bonds are issued without an unlimited tax-raising backing, and instead are secured with a tax base that is limited, such as a form of rates or property tax. The smaller entities such as local districts often issue bonds that are secured by this more limited tax-raising power. It is worth noting the term *double-barrelled security*, which refers to a general obligation bond that is backed with two income sources; these are the general tax-raising ability and other specific charges or fees, which are an additional source of funds for the issuing authority.

14.1.2 *Revenue bonds*

Revenue bonds are issued to finance a specific project or undertaking such as a bridge or road. The bonds are backed with the income that will be received from the running of the completed project itself. The terms of the issue must stipulate that revenues generated from the running of the particular project will be used to pay the interest costs associated with the bond issue. The redemption proceeds may well be financed through another issue of bonds. Revenues from the operation of the enterprise may be ring-fenced in a *revenue fund*, as a further protection for bondholders. Revenue bonds that have been issued include *airport revenue bonds, college and university bonds, hospital revenue bonds, public power revenue bonds, seaport revenue bonds, student loan revenue bonds, toll road revenue bonds* and *water revenue bonds*. The purpose and security of these bonds is evident from their names, except perhaps for the hospital revenue bond. These are issued to finance the construction of a hospital, and the security backing is the government and other funding that is provided to certain types of patient in US hospitals, which include the Medicare and Medicaid programmes as well as private insurance payments from insurance companies.

Note that if the facility or enterprise that is the purpose of a revenue bond is destroyed, say as a result of an act of nature or for any reason, the bond itself must be called by the issuer. This call provision is known as a *catastrophic call*.

14.2 The municipal bond market

The market in municipal securities is large and liquid. Paper is issued by a number of borrowers on a weekly basis. The issue process is similar to that for corporate bonds, and paper may be placed through a public offering to investors, via an investment bank or securities house, or via a private placement. A public offering will be underwritten by a bank or syndicate of banks. Regulation for the issue of a public offer differs slightly from state to state; for example some states have a requirement that all general obligation bonds be placed via a competitive auction.

Bonds are traded in the OTC market. Liquidity is variable and ranges from as liquid as Treasuries for the larger issues to a lower level for smaller issues, which may be supported only by smaller brokers and regional banks. There are a large number of issues that are quite illiquid however, usually due either to their small size or because there is an absence of paper to trade. The staggering of maturity dates also means that individual issues experience relatively thin trading. This consequently results in a wide bid-offer spread, which further discourages liquidity. Details of issue prices and offer sizes are detailed in a publication produced by Standard & Poor's known as *The Blue List.* An interesting feature of the municipal secondary market is that bonds are quoted on a yield basis, as opposed to a price basis.[4] Generally a redemption yield or yield-to-call is used, and the 'price' of a municipal bond is known as a *basis price.* The general formula for the price of a municipal bond is given at Appendix 14.1.

As municipal bonds are exempt from tax, their redemption yield is lower than equivalent-maturity Treasury bonds. The level at which this yield differs from Treasury yields is a function of the rate of income tax; for example the lowering of the marginal rate of tax as a result of the 1986 Tax Act made the tax-exempt nature of municipal bonds less attractive to investors, thus raising their yield. If the return on municipal bonds is compared to other bonds, the yield measure of one security must be adjusted to make the two values comparable. The common approach is to convert the municipal yield to an *equivalent taxable yield,* which is given by (14.1):

$$\text{Equivalent taxable yield} = \frac{\text{Tax} - \text{exempt yield}}{(1 - \text{tax rate})}. \tag{14.1}$$

To illustrate, if the marginal tax rate is 30% and a municipal bond is trading at a yield of 7.00%, the equivalent taxable yield is:

$$\text{Equivalent taxable yield} = \frac{0.07}{(1 - 0.30)} \text{ or } 10.00\%.$$

The equivalent taxable yield is not completely suitable for discounted issue municipal bonds or zero-coupon bonds. This is because, for these types of bonds, only the coupon interest is exempt from federal income tax. The redemption yield on these securities therefore is calculated assuming a tax level payable on the capital gain achieved by the bondholder, and this is used in the numerator of (14.1). The maturity value of the bond is not used to calculate the yield, rather the net proceeds after payment of capital gains tax is used as the redemption amount. Capital gains tax is payable at the investor's marginal rate of income tax.

The yields payable by municipal bonds are a function of the credit quality of the issuer, supply and demand, and differences between the local and general capital markets. The spread over equivalent-maturity Treasury bonds will reflect general economic conditions, so for example during a recession or market downturn spreads

---

4 First apparent to the author during a visit to the trading floor at Fidelity Capital Markets in Boston in 1996! Municipal bonds also trade on a 30/360 basis, unlike Treasury securities.

will widen, while they will narrow in a healthy economic climate. This is perhaps the best indication that municipal bonds trade in a similar fashion to corporate bonds. A peculiar phenomenon is that the yield on bonds issued by certain states will trade at lower levels than bonds of other states of similar credit rating. This is partly explained by tax treatment of certain state bonds compared to paper issued by other states; for example one state may exempt local holders of its own bonds from state and local income taxes, but not the bonds of other states. A state with a high level of local income tax will thus find that there is a higher demand for its paper compared to the paper of other issuers. The local income taxes of states are not uniform, for example the rates in New York are higher than those in Florida.

By far the greatest proportion of municipal bonds are held by retail investors. A bondholder is exposed to credit risk because municipal bonds reflect, like corporate bonds, the credit risk of the issuer. Investors are exposed to an additional risk, which is termed *tax risk*. This is the risk that the level of federal income tax is lowered, which will lower the value of the municipal bond. As is apparent from (14.1) the value of a municipal bond increases (that is, its yield decreases) as the tax rate is increased. A fall in the level of the tax rate will reduce the value of a municipal bond.

14.3 Municipal bonds credit ratings

After a number of high profile incidents when the issuers of municipal bonds found themselves in financial difficulty, thus affecting holders of their debt, the credit ratings assigned to municipal bonds assumed ever greater importance, and today formal ratings are used by investors to assess the credit risk associated with holding municipal debt. The process is essentially similar to the credit analysis of corporate bonds. Securities issued by municipal borrowers are no longer viewed as being risk-free securities, indeed far from it. For example bonds issued by the Washington Public Power Supply System were assigned the highest possible rating – Aaa and AAA – by Moody's and Standard & Poor's in the early 1980s. In 1990 around 25% of the entire issue was in default.[5] There have been other instances of default since 1975, all of which occurred amongst issuers whose paper had been granted investment-grade ratings. Although institutional investors often employ their own in-house credit analysts, the market pays close attention to the ratings assigned by the formal credit rating agencies, the three most quoted of which are Standard & Poor's, Moody's and FitchIBCA. The ratings used by these agencies for long-dated bonds are similar to the ones they employ for corporate bonds generally (see Chapter 16). The ratings for short-dated instruments including tax-exempt commercial paper, are shown in Tables 14.1 and 14.2.

Due to the nature of security backing for municipal bonds, undertaking credit analysis on them, although following a similar process to that for corporate bonds requires a different approach. The similarities include collating data on the issuer's debt structure, to determine the overall level of the debt burden. Additional analysis is carried out on the political leadership of the borrowing entity, including its capacity and reputation for

5 Feldstein/Fabozzi 1997.

Rating		Definition
Moody's	S&P	
MIG 1	SP-1	Best quality; very strong capacity to pay principal and interest. S&P ratings are given a '+' to indicate very strong safety characteristics
MIG 2	SP-2	High quality
MIG 3		Favourable quality.
MIG 4	SP-3	Adequate quality; S&P rating defined as 'speculative' capacity to pay principal and interest
'MIG' denotes Moody's Investment Grade		

Table 14.1: Municipal Note Credit Ratings. Source: Moody's, S&P.

Rating		Definition
Moody's	S&P	
Prime 1	(P-A-1 + 1)	Superior capacity for repayment; highest degree of safety
Prime 2	A-1	Strong capacity for repayment
Prime 3	A-2	Acceptable capacity for repayment
	A-3	Satisfactory degree of safety

Table 14.2: Tax-Exempt Commercial Paper Ratings. Source: Moody's, S&P.

maintaining budgetary discipline. Generally the credit rating agencies will look for a balanced budget over the last five years or so. Credit analysts will also consider the specific taxes and revenues that are available to the borrower, and the scope of its tax-raising power. There is a final issue to consider which is more qualitative in nature, regarding the general social and economic conditions in the state or local area as a whole. This includes the level of unemployment, incomes, population and the expected impact of these issues on the economic health of the area.

14.4 Bond insurance

Certain issuers of municipal bonds set up insurance cover for their bonds, as cover in the event of default. Under a bond insurance policy, an insurer agrees to service the debt on a bond when it is not paid by the issuer. Municipal bond insurance agreements are means by which, in return for the payment of a premium, the credit risk exposure of a bond holding may be reduced for investors. In the event of default, the principal will be paid to the investor by the insurance company. The insurance contract may be set up on purchase of the bond, and have a duration up to the maturity date. In 1995 approximately 25% of all new municipal bond issues were insured.[6]

6 Feldstein/Fabozzi 1997.

Bonds whose issuers have a low standing in the market benefit most from bond insurance. A borrower will be able to increase the marketability of its bond issue if it obtains bond insurance. In order for the insurance contract to be viable however, the saving in interest costs to the issuer must exceed the premium payable to the insurer for arranging the insurance contract. Therefore it is only low-rated borrowers that have an incentive to arrange bond insurance. It has been observed that although insured municipal bonds trade at yield levels that are lower than they would otherwise be without the insurance, they generally exhibit yields that are higher than highly-rated bonds such as deep-discounted bonds. There are specialised firms that operate in bond insurance, the best known of which are the Financial Guaranty Insurance Company (FGIC), the Financial Security Assurance, Inc (FSA), the Municipal Bond Investors Assurance Corporation (MBIA Corp.) and Connie Lee Insurance Company.

14.5 Taxation issues

The key tax consideration for investors in municipal bonds is the rate of federal income tax. This is not the sole interest for investors however, and state and local taxes and the tax treatment of interest expenses are also significant.

We noted early in this chapter that there are differences in the tax treatment of municipal bonds, and this treatment differs from state to state. An individual state may impose income tax on coupon income, capital gains tax on any capital gain and also a personal property tax. Most states do indeed charge income tax, and while certain states may exempt coupon income earned on any municipal bond, other states exempt only the bonds that they themselves issued. In certain states coupon income on all municipal bonds is liable to income tax. The treatment of capital gains is similarly not uniform, but in most cases where coupon income is exempted from income tax, any capital gain is still taxable. The term 'personal property tax' as levied in certain states is in effect another income tax.

Institutional investors often borrow funds to purchase assets that they wish to invest in. This is also common amongst bond traders and dealers, and the gain to the investor is the extra yield they receive on their assets compared to the interest cost on their borrowed funds. In the course of ordinary business, the interest payable on borrowed funds that are used to buy securities is tax deductible. This does not apply if the funds are used to purchase tax-exempt securities, a result of a specific ruling by the US Internal Revenue Service (IRS). The same rule applies to banks that invest in municipal bonds, unless the bonds are *bank qualified issues*. A bank qualified issue is defined as one that is a tax-exempt issue but not one issued for private activities, and is designated by the issuer as so qualified. There are also limitations on the amount of paper that may be issued.

14.6 Exotic municipal bonds

There are a range of municipal bonds with special characteristics, which are known as *hybrid bonds*. There have also been issues linked to derivative products. A common special feature bond is a *refunded* bond. This is a bond that originally was issued as a conventional general obligation or revenue security, but is now secured by an *escrow fund,* which holds direct federal government obligations. A municipal borrower may wish to retire an issue using an escrow fund for a number of reasons. The main one is where an original revenue bond was issued with a range of restrictive covenants, which the borrower now wishes to remove. Setting up an escrow fund enables the issuer to remove these covenants without breaching any legal considerations.

The municipal market was one of the first to introduce structures that combined a floating-rate note with an *inverse floating-rate note.* This combination is created from an original issue fixed-rate bond, with the total issue size being split into the FRN and the inverse floater. The rate on the FRN moves in line with a reference interest rate index, while the rate on the inverse floater moves in an opposite direction to the reference index. The net interest payment from the two newly created bonds must equal the fixed coupon rate that was paid by the original bond, which is known as the *collateral.* In order to achieve this, a cap is usually set on the FRN, while the inverse floater note will have a floor, usually zero, to prevent its interest rate moving to a negative value.

Investment banks have introduced proprietary derivative products in the municipal market. For example the inverse floating rate notes developed by Merrill Lynch are known as RITES, from Residual Interest Tax Exempt Securities, while those issued by Lehman Brothers are known as RIBS (Residual Interest Bonds).

14.7 Municipal money market instruments

Short-dated instruments in the municipal market are known as notes. There are also tax-exempt commercial paper, and variable-rate obligations which are similar to floating-rate notes. Notes in the municipal market are given special names, for example there are *revenue anticipation notes* (RANs), *tax anticipation notes* (TANs), *grant anticipation notes* (GANs) and *bond anticipation notes* (BANs). They are similar to discount instruments in the money markets, and are often issued as short-term borrowings to be redeemed after receipt of tax or other proceeds. Essentially the notes are issued to provide working capital, because the receipt of cash flows from taxation and other local government sources is irregular. The typical maturity of a note is three months, while the longest maturity is 12 months. In most cases tax-exempt notes are issued with credit backing in the form of a bank letter of credit, a bond insurance policy or a lending line at a bank.

Municipal borrowers issue commercial paper, which is similar to corporate CP and may have a maturity ranging from 1 to 270 days. It is known as tax-exempt commercial paper.

Another money market instrument is the *variable-rate demand obligation* (VRDO). This is a floating-rate security that has a long-dated maturity but has a coupon that is re-set at the very short-dated interest rate, either the overnight rate or the seven-day rate. The securities are issued with a put feature that entitles the bondholder to put the issue back to the borrower at any time, upon giving seven days' notice. The bonds may be out to the issuer at par.

Appendices

Appendix 14.1: The price of a municipal bond

The price of a municipal bond may be expressed as a function of the term structure, assuming that there is no default risk associated with the bond. For a discounted bond, expressed in terms of an annuity A and a zero-coupon bond of equivalent maturity of n years with a discount factor for that term of Dfn, the price is given by (14.2):

$$P_M = \frac{CA + 100(1-t)Df_n}{1 - tDf_n}. \tag{14.2}$$

For bonds redeemable at par the price is given by (14.3):

$$P_M = CA + 100Df_n. \tag{14.3}$$

Although they are exempt from income tax, discounted bonds are liable to capital gains tax on maturity, at the income tax level of t. There is no tax liability for conventional coupon bonds.

Selected bibliography and references

Fabozzi, F., Feldtsein, S., Pollack, I. (eds.), *The Municipal Bond Handbook: Volume I*, Dow-Jones Irwin, 1983

Fabozzi, F., Feldtsein, S., Pollack, I. (eds.), *The Municipal Bond Handbook: Volume II*, Dow-Jones Irwin, 1983

Feldstein, S., Fabozzi, F., 'Municipal Bonds', in Fabozzi, F., *The Handbook of Fixed Income Securities*, 5th edition, McGraw-Hill, 1997

Fortune, P., 'The Municipal Bond Market, Parts I and II', Federal Reserve Bank of Boston, *New England Economic Review*, September–October 1991, pp. 13–36 and May–June 1992, pp. 47–64

Heaton H., 'The Relative Yields on Taxable and Tax-Exempt Debt', *Journal of Money Credit and Banking* 18, 1986, pp. 482–494

Livingstone, M., 'The Pricing of Municipal Bonds', *Journal of Financial and Quantitative Analysis* 17, June 1982, pp. 179–193

Zipf, R., *How Municipal Bonds Work*, New York Institute of Finance, 1995

15 High-Yield Bonds

The high-yield corporate bond market developed in the United States during the 1980s, and was a symbol of market growth in that decade. The subsequent collapse of the 'junk bond' market in 1990 signalled a downturn in the market, but in recent years it has been re-developed into a liquid and relatively stable market, regarded as a viable source of capital for non-rated companies and companies that are rated below investment grade. It is now referred to as the *high-yield* bond market and an equivalent market has also developed in the United Kingdom and Europe. Economic performance through the second half of the 1990s, which has seen low inflation and steady growth in the US, and relatively low inflation and convergence of yields in Europe, as a result of introduction of the euro currency, has depressed bond yields to historically low levels across in developed countries. Investors who require higher yielding debt assets must look to 'emerging' markets or, increasingly, the high-yield market. In this chapter we provide a brief review of the US high-yield market, including the different types of securities that have been issued and the returns that were generated through the last decade.

15.1 Growth of the market

The US domestic high-yield market stood at approximately $200 billion nominal outstanding in 1990, and had grown to over $335 billion at the end of 1998.[1] The largest amount issued in one year was in 1993, when just under $70 billion was issued. Prior to 1990 around half of all issuance in the high-yield market was used to fund acquisitions and 'leveraged buy-outs' (LBOs), but by 1995 over half of new issues was used for the purposes of refinancing existing debt and as growth capital. The proportion used for LBOs had fallen to 4% in that year. The overall credit quality of the market improved steadily during the second half of the 1990s, which was explained by analysts as reflecting the performance and health of the US economy as a whole. Figure 15.1 shows the change of composition of the credit ratings in the market as a whole. The proportion of issuers rated at BB-grade had increased from 17% in 1987 to 48% in 1997.

Bonds have been issued by representatives of a number of industry sectors. The highest growth has been observed in the media, telecommunications and cable sectors, which represented over 15% of total debt outstanding in 1997. Outside the industrial sectors, high-yield bonds have been issued by energy, utility and finance companies, as well as by Canadian companies, whose bonds are officially designated as Yankee bonds.

---

1 The statistical data in this chapter is sourced from Bloomberg and Reuters, except where indicated.

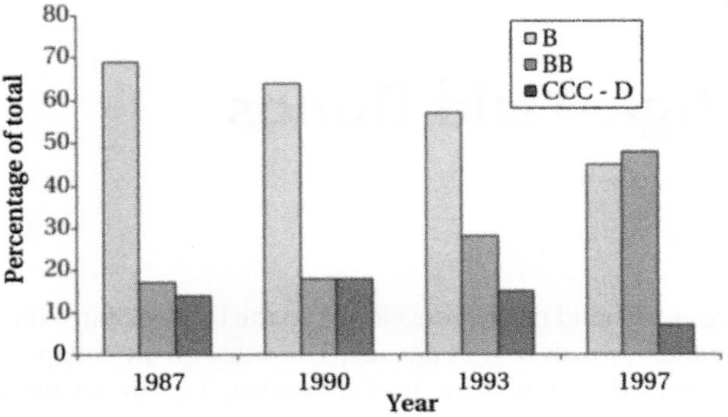

Figure 15.1: US high-yield bond market credit ratings, 1987–1997.
Source: Standard & Poor's.

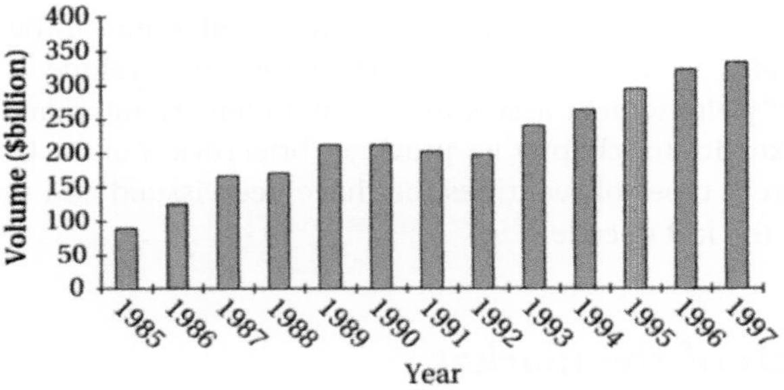

Figure 15.2: Growth of US high-yield bond market.
Source: Lehman Brothers.

15.2 High-yield securities

The high-yield market contains a range of securities, which have developed as investor interest in the market has grown. The majority of issues have been conventional plain vanilla issues however, although the market has also seen deferred-pay securities, which recognises that issuing companies will in all probability encounter cash-flow difficulties in their early years, as well as increasing-rate bonds. We present here a summary of the types of instruments traded in the market.

15.2.1 *Conventional securities*

The majority of bond issues are plain vanilla securities, with a fixed coupon; this type of security comprised over 90% of all domestic high-yield debt in 1997. The maturity of these bonds is between 7–12 years, although most bonds incorporate a call provision that is effective after the first three or five years. A call feature is important to issuers in the high-yield market, as it gives them an opportunity to refinance their debt at a lower interest rate when, as is hoped, their credit rating has improved.

15.2.2 *Split-coupon securities*

A *split-coupon* security is one that pays no coupon for the first few years of its life, and then transforms into a fixed-coupon bond for the remaining years of its life. They therefore begin life as zero-coupon bonds, typically for the first five years, although the no-interest period has been as low as two years and as high as seven years, before turning into conventional bonds. The bonds are issued at a discount, using the stated coupon as the discount rate. A split-coupon bond allows its issuer to build up its financial health before it has to service its debt. The most frequent issuers of split-coupon bonds have been operating in high-growth industry such as technology companies, or companies in the process of re-structuring their operations.

Another approach adopted by new companies has been to 'over-fund' their required proceeds, and use the overfunding to pay the interest charges on the debt for the first few years of the bond's life. This mirrors the effect achieved using a split-capital issue. For example a funding requirement of $60 million is met through the issue of $100 million of a 9% coupon bond; the extra capital raised is used to pay interest on the debt for the first four years.[2] An overfunded bond is designed to appeal to investors who have an appetite for high-yield debt but do not wish to purchase instruments that do not pay any interest.

15.2.3 *Payment-in-kind securities*

A *payment-in-kind* (PIK) bond is one that allows the issuer the option of paying coupon interest either in cash or similar securities. The option is usually set only for a short, limited period of time, say three or five years. If the issuer chooses to pay in the form of in-kind securities, the principal amount of the debt will increase, raising the liability of the issuer after the in-kind option falls away. When the in-kind option is in effect, PIK bonds trade differently to other high-yield bonds, because no interest is payable during this period. Hence the bonds trade without accrued interest, and the coupon payment is reflected in the accreted price of the security. This is similar to the method for quoting cumulative preference shares whose preferred dividend has not been paid in one year.

15.2.4 *Step-up coupon securities*

These types of bonds are common in conventional corporate markets, issued by companies who wish to make their paper more attractive to investors, or to a wider group of investors. A step-up bond is similar to the split-coupon bond, and is issued for similar reasons, except during the initial period a coupon is payable, rising to a higher coupon at a specified date. The higher coupon is set at the time of issue, and remains in force until the bond is redeemed. The initial period is usually for around five years, but can be for a shorter period.

15.2.5 *Exchangeable variable-rate notes*

Exchangeable variable-rate notes (EVRNs) are subordinated, medium-term instruments that pay a floating, quarterly coupon. The interest is actually fixed for a short term, known as the 'teaser' period, but after this initial period the rate changes to a floating one, linked to a reference rate such as the prime rate or the 90-day Treasury bill rate. In most cases the issuer has the option to exchange the notes for fixed-coupon notes with conventional

---

[2] There is 'spare' $4 million left over at the end of the four years, but this is invested at the time of the issue in the same way as the required $60 million.

features such as a fixed maturity date or call facility. The maximum maturity period of the bonds is usually five years.

15.2.6 *Bond and stock units*

Certain companies in high-growth and/or high-risk business sectors have issued combinations of bonds and equity. This is designed to appeal to investors who require an element of equity ownership in order to benefit from upside growth, to compensate them for the high risk incurred by debt holders. The resulting debt issue therefore has an element of equity attached, in the form of straight shares or warrants. Investors usually strip the equity or the warrants from the bonds on issue and may realise them immediately if they wish. Bonds issued with equity warrants are also known as *usable bonds.*

15.2.7 *Springing issues*

Start-up companies operating in a highly competitive, volatile environment sometimes issue securities that are specified to change one or more of their characteristics in response to a specific event occurring. For example the market has seen a springing warrant issue, which are exercisable only if another party attempted to acquire the issuer. Another version of a springing security was one that was originally issued as a subordinated bond, but was converted to senior debt once an old outstanding debenture had been discharged. The analysis of a springing security must take into account the probability that the security will change its terms and conditions and what impact such an event will have on the security's price.

15.2.8 *Extendible/reset securities*

An extendible or reset security allows the issuer to reset the coupon or extend the life of the bond on pre-specified dates. The general rule, stated on issue, is that the coupon must be reset to a level that results in it trading at a certain yield, and which is determined by a third-party bank (usually the issuing investment bank). The alternative is for the bond to be issued with a cap or floor, or both. The ability to reset the coupon can be a valuable asset if market rates have fallen since the time of issue, while it is also attractive to investors in a rising interest rate environment and as a form of protection against a decline in the issuer's credit quality. This will add to the overall debt burden of the issuer however, so may have negative effects.

Extendible bonds are issued with a final redemption date already stated. The issue may choose to have the bonds redeemed at one of a range of dates ahead of the final maturity date, and these dates are usually also associated with a *put* feature. If the issuer decides to extend the redemption date, a certain portion of the debt may have to be retired, or may be put back if investors so wish. This provision sometimes applies if the coupon is reset as well.

Only a small number of such issues were still trading in the US market in 1997.

15.2.9 *High-yield bank loans*

The development of a market in tradeable bank loans has served to break down many of the distinctions between high-yield loans and bonds. There has been a steady increase in secondary loan trading during the 1990s, indeed after the 'junk' bond market declines in 1990, high-yield bank loans comprised virtually all of the debt issued to non-investment grade companies in that year. Over $40 billion of high-yield bank loans were issued in 1997. Another type of bank loan that trades in the secondary market is the 'B loan', which is a long-dated loan that is serviced with interest payments only (that is, no repayment of principal) in the first few years after issue.

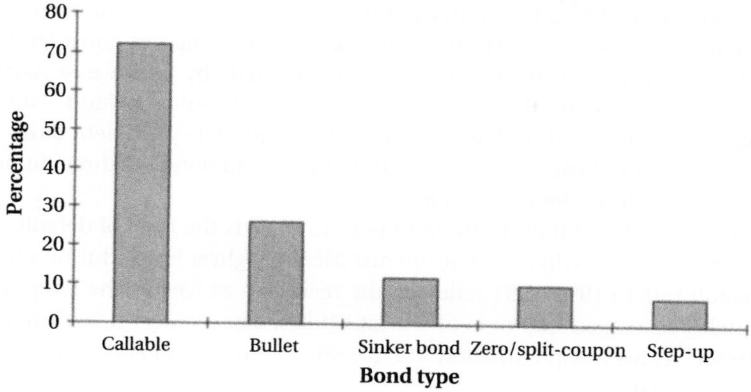

Figure 15.3: Types of high-yield securities, US domestic market, December 2001. Source: Lehman Brothers.

The main differences between high-yield bank loans and high-yield bonds are as follows:

- bank loans are typically floating-rate liabilities, while high-yield debt is almost invariably fixed-rate;
- bank loans are callable at any time;
- there is an element of security associated with most bank loans.

These differences ensure that the two markets remain distinct, if part of the overall 'high-yield' market.

Notwithstanding that the large majority of high-yield bonds are plain vanilla securities, there has been a proliferation of the types of instrument traded in the high-yield market. Bonds have been issued that offer investors a share in the firm's profits, as well as a fixed coupon. Other issues have been backed by commodities.

A common method of issue of high-yield debt in the US is via the SEC rule known as Rule 144A. Under this rule, securities sold initially through a private placement which are then offered for re-sale to institutional investors, are not subject to review by the SEC. The borrower must register the securities within a short period of time, usually one to three months after issuance. By placing debt under this rule, the issue may be got away fairly quickly and at minimal cost. The type of bond issued is not relevant: any of the securities described here may be issued pursuant to Rule 144A.

15.3 High-yield bond performance

The performance of high-yield bonds in the US domestic market mirrors economic performance in the US overall. The yield spread of high-yield debt over investment grade corporate bonds is more of a function of the general outlook of the economy than of the health of the issuing companies themselves, although the latter is obviously important. Thus high-yield debt outperformed corporate bonds and other securities such as Treasury bonds and mortgage-backed securities in 1991 and 1992 as the US economy recovered from a recession, after having generated negative returns in 1990. During the period 1992–1995 the

US economy was marked by a favourable combination of steady economic growth and low inflation and spreads moved to historical lows, before widening out considerably after the 1997 and 1998 bond market downturns, brought on (first) by South-east Asian currency collapse and debt worries and then by the Russian bond technical default. This triggered a 'flight to quality' that affected both emerging market and high-yield debt alike.

Figure 15.4 illustrates how the yield spread on high-yield bonds of three different ratings compared during the late 1980s and 1990s.

Another key indicator of high-yield bond performance is the level of default. The level of defaults have not unexpectedly, been at the historically highest levels during times of recession. The default rate in 1990–1991 reflected the recession as well as the hangover from the large-scale highly-leveraged buy-outs of the late 1980s. The average default rate during the 1980s and 1990s has been approximately 3% to 3.5%. Figure 15.5 illustrates the actual default rates in the two decades.

Figure 15.6 shows the extent of high-yield bond spreads (over treasuries) for selected indices. Tables 15.1 and 15.2 are shown here to give a couple of issuer names and prices in the high-yield market.

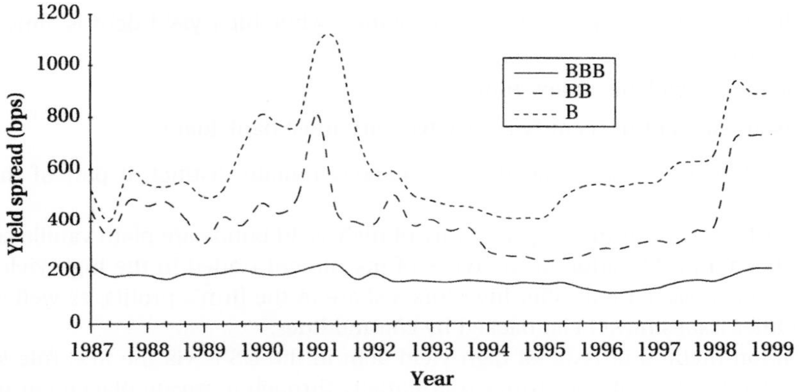

Figure 15.4: US high-yield bond spreads. Source: Standard & Poor's, Bloomberg.

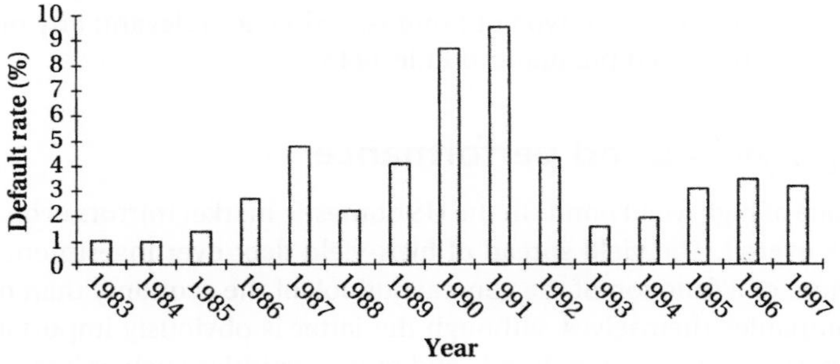

Figure 15.5: US high-yield market historical default rates, as percentage of outstanding debt. Source: Standard & Poor's, Lehman Brothers.

Issuer	Coupon (%)	Maturity	Nominal ($m)	Rating	Bid price	Spread (bp)
Adelphia Comms	Zero	Aug 2008	605	B1/BB–	42.000	464
Advanced Micro Devices	11.000	Aug 2003	400	B2/B	99.000	463
Advantica Rest Group	11.250	Jan 2008	550	B3/B	68.000	1,264
AK Stl	9.125	Dec 2006	546	Ba2/BB	98.250	279
Allied Waste North America	7.875	Jan 2009	875	Ba3/BB–	85.500	380
Amazon.Com	10.558	May 2008	530	Caa1/B	60.000	662
Budget Group	9.125	Apr 2006	400	B1/BB–	90.000	473
Caremark Rx	7.375	Oct 2006	450	B3/B	84.000	413
Chancellor Media Corp of LA	8.125	Dec 2007	500	B1/B	99.250	160
Charter Communication Holdings	8.625	Apr 2009	1,500	B2/B+	91.500	346
Crown Paper	11.000	Sep 2005	250	Caa1/CCC+	40.000	3,069
CSC Holdings	7.625	Jul 2018	500	Ba1/BB+	92.050	205
DR Horton	8.000	Feb 2009	385	Ba1/BB	87.000	364
Emmis Commun	8.125	Mar 2009	300	B2/B–	93.750	254
Exide	10.000	Apr 2005	300	B1/B+	95.250	449
Fairchild	10.750	Apr 2005	225	B3/B–	73.000	997
Flening Co	10.625	Dec 2001	300	B1/B+	100.000	397
Formica	10.875	Mar 2009	215	B3/B–	88.000	657
Fox Family Worldwide	10.250	Nov 2007	605	B1/B	64.000	640
Friendly Ice Cream	10.500	Dec 2007	200	B2/B	80.000	827
Gaylord Container	9.375	Jun 2007	200	Caa1/B–	90.500	464
Globalstar	11.375	Feb 2004	499	Caa1/B	59.000	2,283
HMH Pptys	7.875	Aug 2008	1,200	Ba2/BB	87.500	348
Intermedia Comms	11.250	Jul 2007	648	B2/B	78.750	403
Level 3 Comms	9.125	May 2008	1,999	B3/B	91.500	406
Lyondell Comms	10.875	May 2009	500	B2/B+	95.500	507
Mandalay Resort Group	9.250	Dec 2005	275	Ba2/BB+	99.000	275
Nextel Communications	9.963	Feb 2008	1,627	B1/B	70.000	432
Ocean Energy	8.875	Jul 2007	200	Ba3/BB–	98.750	244
Playtex Products	9.000	Dec 2003	360	B2/B	99.500	242
Pride International	9.375	May 2007	325	Ba3/BB	97.500	319
RBF Finance	11.000	Mar 2006	400	Ba3/BB–	105.750	301
REV Holdings	Zero	Mar 2001	770	Caa3/CCC+	23.000	19,344
Riverwood International	10.875	Apr 2008	400	Caa1/CCC+	95.000	520
Sterling Chemical	11.750	Aug 2006	275	Caa3/B	84.000	908
Tenet Healthcare	8.000	Jan 2005	900	Ba1/BB+	96.000	227
Time Warner Telecom	9.750	Jul 2008	400	B2/B	100.000	304
Trump Atlantic City Association	11.250	May 2006	1,200	B2/B–	70.000	1,316
WCI STL	10.000	Dec-04	300	B2/B+	99.500	337
Westpoint Stevens	7.875	Jun-05	525	Ba3/BB	88.000	417

Table 15.1: 'Focus 40' US high-yield bond index, February 2000.
Source: IFR, Thompson Financial Bank Watch.

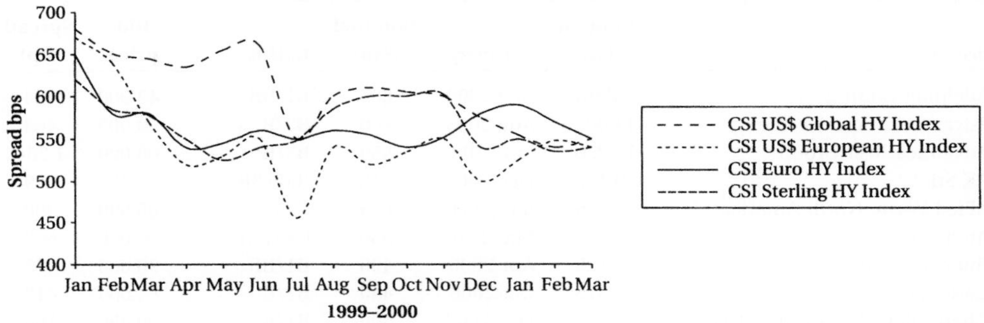

Figure 15.6: Average spreads in the European high-yield market, 1999–2000. Source: Chase Manhattan.

Issuer	Coupon (%)	Maturity	Currency	Nominal (mn)	Rating	Bid price	Spread (bp)
Atlantic Telecom	12.875	Feb 2010	EUR	200	B3/B–	113.00	510
Colt	7.625	Dec 2009	EUR	307	B1/B	96.00	290
Huntsman ICI	10.250	Jun 2009	EUR	200	B2/B+	105.00	375
IPC Magazines	9.625	Mar 2008	GBP	120	B3/B–	75.00	915
Jazztel	13.250	Dec 2009	EUR	400	Caa1/CCC+	105.00	680
Kappa	10.625	Jul 2009	EUR	370	B2/B	105.50	420
KPNQwest	7.125	Jun 2009	EUR	340	Ba1/BB	95.75	235
Luxfer	10.125	Mar 2009	GBP	160	B2/B	94.50	540
NTL	9.875	Nov 2009	EUR	350	B3/B–	100.50	435
NTL	9.500	Apr 2008	GBP	125	B3/B–	95.50	435
Telewest	9.875	Jan 2010	GBP	180	B1/B+	99.00	440
UPC	10.875	Aug 2009	EUR	300	B2/B–	98.00	570
UPC	13.375	Nov 2009	EUR	191	B2/B–	55.50	780
Versatel	11.875	Jul 2009	EUR	120	Caa1	107.00	510
William Hill	10.625	Apr 2008	GBP	150	B3/B–	101.00	440

Table 15.2: European high-yield bond pricing, February 2000. Source: IFR, Euroweek.

Selected bibliography and references

Barnhill, T. (ed.), *High-yield bonds: Market structure, valuation and portfolio strategies*, McGraw-Hill, 1999

Hickman, W., *Corporate Bond Quality and Investor Experience*, Princeton University Press and National Bureau of Economic Research, 1958

Howe, J.T., *Junk Bonds*, Probus Publishing, 1987

'Corporate Bond Defaults and Default Rates 1970–1992', *Moody's Special Report*, Moody's Investors Service, Inc., January 1993
Rubin, *Junk Bonds*, Prentice-Hall, 1990
Yago, G., *Junk Bonds: How high-yield securities restructured corporate America*, OUP, 1990

16 Corporate Bonds and Credit Analysis

The risks associated with holding a fixed interest debt instrument are closely connected with the ability of the issuer to maintain the regular coupon payments as well as redeem the debt on maturity. Essentially the *credit risk* is the main risk of holding a bond. Only the highest quality government debt, and a small number of supranational issues, may be considered to be entirely free of credit risk. Therefore at any time the yield on a bond reflects investors' views on the ability of the issuer to meet its liabilities as set out in the bond's terms and conditions. A delay in paying a cash liability as it becomes due is known as technical default and is a cause for extreme concern for investors; failure to pay will result in the matter being placed in the hands of the legal court as investors seek to recover their funds. To judge the ability of an issue to meet its obligations for a particular debt issue, for the entire life of the issue, requires judgemental analysis of the issuer's financial strength and business prospects. There are a number of factors that must be considered, and larger banks, fund managers and corporates carry out their own *credit analysis* of individual borrowers' bond issues. The market also makes a considerable use of formal *credit ratings* that are assigned to individual bond issues by a formal credit rating agency. In the international markets arguably the two most influential ratings agencies are Standard & Poor's Corporation (S&P) and Moody's Investors Service, Inc (Moody's), based in the US. Fitch Investors Service, Inc (Fitch) also has a high profile.[1]

The specific factors that are considered by a ratings agency, and the methodology used in conducting the analysis, differ slightly amongst the individual ratings agencies. Although in many cases the ratings assigned to a particular issue by different agencies are the same, they occasionally differ and in these instances investors usually seek to determine what aspect of an issuer is given more weight in an analysis by which individual agency. Note that a credit rating is not a recommendation to buy (or equally, sell) a particular bond, nor is it a comment on market expectations. Credit analysis does take into account general market and economic conditions; the overall purpose of credit analysis is to consider the financial health of the issuer and its ability to meet the obligations of the specific issue being rated. Credit ratings play a large part in the decision-making of investors, and also have a significant impact on the interest rates payable by borrowers.

---

1 Fitch subsequently merged with IBCA, another ratings agency, to become FitchIBCA and subsequently Fitch Investors Service, usually referred to simply as 'Fitch'.

In this chapter we review credit ratings and their function, and then go on to consider the main factors involved in corporate bond credit analysis.

16.1 Credit ratings

A credit rating is a formal opinion given by a rating agency, of the *credit risk* for investors in a particular issue of debt securities. Ratings are given to public issues of debt securities by any type of entity, including governments, banks and corporates. They are also given to short-term debt such as commercial paper as well as bonds and medium-term notes.

16.1.1 *Purpose of credit ratings*

Investors in securities accept the risk that the issuer will default on coupon payments or fail to repay the principal in full on the maturity date. Generally credit risk is greater for securities with a long maturity, as there is a longer period for the issuer potentially to default. For example if a company issues ten-year bonds, investors cannot be certain that the company will still exist in ten years' time. It may have failed and gone into liquidation some time before that. That said, there is also risk attached to short-dated debt securities, indeed there have been instances of default by issuers of commercial paper, which is a very short-term instrument.

The prospectus or offer document for an issue provides investors with some information about the issuer so that some credit analysis can be performed on the issuer before the bonds are placed. The information in the offer documents enables investors themselves to perform their own credit analysis by studying this information before deciding whether or not to invest. Credit assessments take up time however and also require the specialist skills of credit analysts. Large institutional investors do in fact employ such specialists to carry out credit analysis, however often it is too costly and time-consuming to assess every issuer in every debt market. Therefore investors commonly employ two other methods when making a decision on the credit risk of debt securities:

- name recognition;
- formal credit ratings.

Name recognition is when the investor relies on the good name and reputation of the issuer and accepts that the issuer is of such good financial standing, or sufficient financial standing, that a default on interest and principal payments is highly unlikely. An investor may feel this way about say, Microsoft or British Petroleum plc. However the experience of Barings in 1995 suggested to many investors that it may not be wise to rely on name recognition alone in today's marketplace. The tradition and reputation behind the Barings name allowed the bank to borrow at Libor and occasionally at sub-Libor interest rates in the money markets, which put it on a par with the highest-quality clearing banks in terms of credit rating. However name recognition needs to be augmented by other methods to reduce the risk against unforeseen events, as happened with Barings. Credit ratings are a formal assessment, for a given issue of debt securities, of the likelihood that the interest and principal will be paid in full and on schedule. They are increasingly used to make investment decisions about corporate or lesser-developed government debt.

16.1.2 *Formal credit ratings*

Credit ratings are provided by the specialist agencies. The major credit rating agencies are Standard & Poor's, Fitch and Moody's, based in the United States, and the UK-based IBCA. There are other agencies both in the US and other countries. On receipt of a formal request the credit rating agencies will carry out a rating exercise on a specific issue of debt capital. The request for a rating comes from the organisation planning the issue of bonds. Although ratings are provided for the benefit of investors, the issuer must bear the cost. However it is in the issuer's interest to request a rating as it raises the profile of the bonds, and investors may refuse to buy paper that is not accompanied with a recognised rating. Although the rating exercise involves a credit analysis of the issuer, the rating is applied to a specific debt issue. This means that in theory the credit rating is applied not to an organisation itself, but to specific debt securities that the organisation has issued or is planning to issue. In practice it is common for the market to refer to the creditworthiness of organisations themselves in terms of the rating of their debt. A highly-rated company such as Commerzbank is therefore referred to as a 'triple-A rated' company, although it is the bank's debt issues that are rated as triple-A.

The rating for an issue is kept constantly under review and if the credit quality of the issuer declines or improves, the rating will be changed accordingly. An agency may announce in advance that it is reviewing a particular credit rating, and may go further and state that the review is a precursor to a possible downgrade or upgrade. This announcement is referred to as putting the issue under *credit watch*. The outcome of a credit watch is in most cases likely to be a rating downgrade, however the review may re-affirm the current rating or possibly upgrade it. During the credit watch phase the agency will advise investors to use the current rating with caution. When an agency announces that an issue is under credit watch, the price of the bonds will fall in the market as investors look to sell out of their holdings. This upward movement in yield will be more pronounced if an actual downgrade results. For example in October 1992 the government of Canada was placed under credit watch and subsequently lost its AAA credit rating; as a result there was an immediate and sharp sell-off in Canadian government Eurobonds, before the rating agencies had announced the actual results of their credit review.

Credit ratings vary between agencies. Separate categories are used by each agency for short-term debt (with original maturity of 12 months or less) and long-term debt of over one year original maturity. It is also usual to distinguish between higher 'investment grade' ratings where the credit risk is low and lower quality 'speculative grade' ratings, where the credit risk is greater. High-yield bonds are speculative-grade bonds and are generally rated no higher than double-B, although some issuers have been upgraded to triple-B in recent years and a triple-B rating is still occasionally awarded to a high-yield bond. A summary of long-term ratings is shown at Table 16.1.

Ratings can be accessed on the Bloomberg system. A composite page is shown at Figure 16.1, the screen RATD.

16.2 Credit analysis

When ratings agencies were first set up the primary focus of credit analysis was on the default risk of the bond, or the probability that the investor would not receive the interest payments and the principal repayment as they fell due. Although this is still important, credit analysts

Duff & Phelps	FitchIBCA	Moody's	Standard & Poors	Summary Description
	Investment Grade – High credit quality			
AAA	AAA	Aaa	AAA	Gilt edged, prime, lowest risk, risk-free
AA+	AA+	Aa1	AA+	
AA	AA	Aa2	AA	High-grade, high credit quality
AA−	AA−	Aa3	AA−	
A+	A+	A1	A+	
A	A	A2	A	Upper-medium grade
A−	A−	A3	A−	
BBB+	BBB+	Baa1	BBB+	
BBB	BBB	Baa2	BBB	Lower-medium grade
BBB−	BBB−	Baa3	BBB−	
	Speculative – Lower credit quality			
BB+	BB+	Ba1	BB+	
BB	BB	Ba2	BB	Low grade; speculative
BB−	BB−	Ba3	BB−	
	B+	B1	B+	
B	B	B2	B	Highly speculative
	B−	B3	B−	
	Highly speculative, substantial risk or in default			
			CCC+	
CCC	CCC	Caa	CCC	Considerable risk, in poor standing
			CCC−	
	CC	Ca	CC	May already be in default, very speculative
	C	C	C	Extremely speculative
			CI	Income bonds – no interest being paid
	DDD			
DD	DD			Default
	D		D	

Table 16.1: Summary of credit rating agency bond ratings.[2] Source: Rating agencies.

these days also considers the overall economic conditions as well as the chance that an issuer will have its rating changed during the life of the bond. There are differences in approach depending on which industry or market sector the issuing company is part of.

In this section we review the main issues of concern to a credit analyst when rating bond issues. Analysts usually adopt a 'top-down' approach, or a 'big picture' approach, and concentrate on the macro-issues first before looking at the issuer specific points in detail. The process therefore involves reviewing the issuer's industry, before looking at its financial and balance sheet strength, and finally the legal provisions concerning the bond issue. There are also detail differences in analysis depending on which industry the issuer is in.

[2] Following subsequent mergers, Fitch Inc. incorporates Fitch, IBCA and Duff & Phelps.

Page N219n Govt **RATD**

LONG-TERM RATING SCALES COMPARISON

Page 1/2

MOODY'S	Aaa	Aa1	Aa2	Aa3	A1	A2	A3	Baa1	Baa2	Baa3
S&P	AAA	AA+	AA	AA-	A+	A	A-	BBB+	BBB	BBB-
COMP	AAA	AA1	AA2	AA3	A1	A2	A3	BBB1	BBB2	BBB3
TBW	AAA	AA+	AA	AA-	A+	A	A-	BBB+	BBB	BBB-
FITCH	AAA	AA+	AA	AA-	A+	A	A-	BBB+	BBB	BBB-
CBRS	AAA	AA+	AA	AA-	A+	A	A-	BBB+	BBB	BBB-
DOMINION	AAA	AAH	AA	AAL	AH	A	AL	BBBH	BBB	BBBL
R&I	AAA	AA+	AA	AA-	A+	A	A-	BBB+	BBB	BBB-
JCR	AAA	AA+	AA	AA-	A+	A	A-	BBB+	BBB	BBB-
MI	AAA		AA			A			BBB	

Page N219n Govt **RATD**

LONG-TERM RATING SCALES COMPARISON

Page 2/2

MOODY'S	Ba1	Ba2	Ba3	B1	B2	B3	Caa1	Caa2	Caa3	Ca	C	
S&P	BB+	BB	BB-	B+	B	B-	CCC+	CCC	CCC-	CC	C	D
COMP	BB1	BB2	BB3	B1	B2	B3	CCC1	CCC2	CCC3	CC2	C2	DDD2
TBW	BB+	BB	BB-	CCC+	CCC	CCC-	CC+	CC	CC-			D
FITCH	BB+	BB	BB-	B+	B	B-	CCC+	CCC	CCC-	CC	C	D
CBRS	BB+	BB	BB-	B+	B	B-					C	D
DOMINION	BBH	BB	BBL	BH	B	BL	CCCH	CCC	CCCL	CC	C	D
R&I	BB+	BB	BB-	B+	B	B-	CCC+	CCC	CCC-	CC+	CC	CC-
JCR	BB+	BB	BB-	B+	B	B-		CCC		CC	C	D
MI		BB			B			CCC		CC		DDD

Figure 16.1: Bloomberg screen RATD showing long-term ratings scales (© Bloomberg L.P., reproduced with permission).

16.2.1 *The issuer industry*

In the first instance the credit analysis process of a specific issue will review the issuer's industry. This is in order to place the subsequent company analysis in context. For example, a company that has recorded growth rates of 10% each year may appear to be a quality performer, but not if its industry has been experiencing average growth rates of 30%. Generally the industry analysis will review the following issues:

- **Economic cycle.** The business cycle of the industry and its correlation with the overall business cycle are key indicators. That is, how closely does the industry follow the rate of growth of its country's GNP? Certain industries such as the electricity and food retail sectors are more resistant to recession than others. Other sectors are closely tied to changes in population and birth patterns, such as residential homes, while the financial services industry is influenced by the overall health of the economy as well as by the level of interest rates. As well as the correlation with macro-factors, credit analysts review traditional financial indicators in context, for example the issuing company's *earnings per share* (EPS) against the growth rate of its industry.
- **Growth prospects.** This review is of the issuer industry's general prospects. A company operating within what is considered a high-growth industry is generally deemed to have better credit quality expectations than one operating in a low-growth environment. A scenario of anticipated growth in the industry has implications for the issuing company, for example the extent to which the company will be able cope with capacity demands and the financing of excess capacity. A fast-growth industry also attracts new entrants, which will lead to over-supply, intensified competition and reduced margins. A slow-growth industry has implications for diversification, so that a company deemed to have plans for diversifying when operating in stagnant markets will be marked up.
- **Competition.** A review of the intensity of competitive forces within an industry, and the extent of pricing and over- or under-capacity, is an essential ingredient of credit analysis. Competition is now regarded as a global phenomenon and well-rated companies are judged able to compete successfully on a global basis while concentrating on the highest-growth regions. Competition within a particular industry is related to that industry's structure and has implications for pricing flexibility. The type of market, for example, monopoly, oligopoly, and so on, also influences pricing policy and relative margins. Another issue arises if there is obvious over-capacity in an industry; this has been exemplified in the past in the airline industry and (in some countries) financial services, when over-capacity often leads to intense price competition and price wars. This is frequently damaging for the industry as a whole, as all companies suffer losses and financial deterioration in the attempt to maintain or grow market share.
- **Supply sources.** The availability of suppliers in an industry has influences for a company's financial well-being. Monopoly sources of supply are considered a restrictive element and have negative implications. A vertically-integrated company that is able to supply its own raw materials is less susceptible to economic conditions that might affect suppliers or leave it hostage to price rises. A company that is not self-sufficient in its factors of production but is nevertheless in a strong enough a position to pass on its costs is in a good position.

- **Research and development.** A broad assessment of the growth prospects of a company must also include a review of its research and development (R&D) position. In certain industries such as telecommunications, media and information technology, a heavy investment in R&D is essential simply in order to maintain market share. In a high-technology field it is common for products to obsolesce very quickly, therefore it is essential to maintain high R&D spend. In the short-term however a company with a low level of research expenditure may actually post above-average (relative to the industry) profits because it is operating at higher margins. This is not considered a healthy strategy for the long term though.

Evaluating the R&D input of a company is not necessarily a straightforward issue of comparing ratios however, as it is also important to assess correctly the direction of technology. That is, a successful company needs not only to invest a sufficient amount in R&D, it must also be correct in its assessment of the direction the industry is heading, technology-wise. A heavy investment in developing Betamax videos for example, would not have assisted a company in the early 1980s.

- **Level of regulation.** The degree of regulation in an industry, its direction and its effect on the profitability of a company are relevant in a credit analysis. A highly regulated industry such as power generation, production of medicines or (in certain countries) telecommunications can have a restrictive influence on company profits. On the other hand if the government has announced a policy of de-regulating an industry, this is considered a positive development for companies in that industry.
- **Labour relations.** An industry with a highly unionised labour force or generally tense labour relations is viewed unfavourably compared to one with stable labour relations. Credit analysts will consider historic patterns of say, strikes and production days lost to industrial action. The status of labour relations is also more influential in a highly labour-intensive industry than one that is more automated for example.
- **Political climate.** The investment industry adopts an increasingly global outlook and the emergence of sizeable tradeable debt markets in for example, 'emerging' countries means that ratings agencies frequently must analyse the general political and economic climate in which an industry is operating. Failure to foresee certain political developments can have far-reaching effects for investors, as recently occurred in Indonesia when that country experienced a change of government; foreign investors lost funds as several local banks went bankrupt.

16.2.2 *Financial analysis*

The traditional approach to credit analysis concentrated heavily on financial analysis. The more modern approach involves a review of the industry the company is operating in first, discussed above, before considering financial considerations. Generally the financial analysis of the issuer is conducted in three phases, namely:

- the ratio analysis for the bonds;
- analysing the company's return on capital;
- non-financial factors such as management expertise and extent of overseas operations.

Ratio analysis

There are a number of investor ratios that can be calculated. In themselves ratios do not present very much insight, although there are various norms that can be applied. Generally ratio analysis is compared to the levels prevalent in the industry, as well as historical values, in an effort to place the analysis in context and compare the company with those in its peer group. The ratios that can be considered are:

- pre-tax interest cover, the level of cover for interest charges in current pre-tax income;
- fixed interest charge level;
- *leverage*, which is commonly defined as the ratio of long-term debt as a percentage of the total capitalisation;
- level of leverage compared to industry average;
- nature of debt, whether fixed- or floating-rate, short- or long-term;
- cash flow, which is the ratio of cash flow as a percentage of total debt. Cash flow itself is usually defined as net income from continuing operations, plus depreciation and taxes, while debt is taken to be long-term debt;
- net assets, as a percentage of total debt. The liquidity of the assets – meaning the ease with which they can be turned into cash – is taken into account when assessing the net asset ratio.

The ratings agencies maintain benchmarks that are used to assign ratings, and these are monitored and if necessary modified to allow for changes in the economic climate. For example, Standard & Poor's guidelines for pre-tax interest cover, leverage level and cash flow in 1997 are shown in Table 16.2. A pre-tax cover of above 9.00 for example, is consistent with a double-A rating.

Other ratios that are considered include:

- intangibles, that is the portion of intangibles relative to the asset side of a balance sheet;
- unfunded pension liabilities; generally a fully-funded pension is not seen as necessary, however an unfunded liability that is over 10% of net assets would be viewed as a negative point;
- age and condition of plant;
- working capital.

Return on equity

There are range of performance measures used in the market that are connected with return on equity (generally the analysis concentrates on return on capital, or more recently return

Credit rating	Pre-tax interest cover	Leverage	Cash flow
AAA	17.99	13.2	97.5
AA	9.74	19.7	68.5
A	5.35	33.2	43.8
BBB	2.91	44.8	29.9

Table 16.2: S&P ratio benchmarks, 1997. Source: S&P.

on risk adjusted capital or RAROC). In analysing measures of return, analysts seek to determine trends in historical performance and comparisons with peer group companies. Different companies also emphasise different target returns in their objectives, usually an expression of their corporate philosophy, so it is common for companies in the same industry to have different return ratios. The range of ratios used by the credit ratings agencies is shown below. Note that 'EBIT' is 'earnings before interest and tax'.

$$\text{Return on net assets} = \frac{\text{Profit}}{\text{Net assets}} \times 100$$

$$\text{Return on sales} = \frac{\text{Profit}}{\text{Sales turnover}} \times 100$$

$$\text{Return on equity} = (\text{Return on net assets} \times \text{Gearing}) \times 100$$

$$\text{Pre-tax interest cover} = \frac{\text{Pre-tax income from continuing operations}}{\text{Gross interest}}$$

$$\text{EBIT interest cover} = \frac{\text{Pre-tax income from continuing operations} + \text{interest expense}}{\text{Gross interest}}$$

$$\text{Long-term debt as \% of capitalisation} = \frac{\text{Long-term debt}}{\text{Long-term debt} + \text{equity}} \times 100$$

$$\text{Funds flow as \% of debt} = \frac{\text{Funds from operations}}{\text{Total debt}} \times 100$$

$$\text{Free cash flow as \% of debt} = \frac{\text{Free cash flow}}{\text{Total debt}} \times 100$$

The agencies make available data that may be consulted by the public, for example Standard & Poor's has a facility known as 'CreditStats', which was introduced in 1989. It contains the main financial ratios for a large number of companies, organised by their industry sectors.

Non-financial factors

The non-financial element of a company credit analysis has assumed a more important role in recent years, especially with regard to companies in exotic or emerging markets. Credit analysts review the non-financial factors relevant to the specific company after they have completed the financial and ratio analysis. These include the strength and competence of senior management, and the degree of exposure to overseas markets. The depth of overseas exposure is not always apparent from documents such as the annual report, and analysts sometimes need to conduct further research to determine this. Companies with considerable overseas exposure, such as petroleum companies, also need to be reviewed with respect to the political situation in their operating locations. A bank such as Standard Chartered for example, has significant exposure to more exotic currencies in Asian, middle-eastern and African countries, and so is more at risk from additional market movements than a bank with almost exclusively domestic operations. The global, integrated nature of the bond markets also means that the foreign-exchange exposure of a company must be evaluated and assessed for risk.

The quality of management is a subjective, qualitative factor that can be reviewed in a number of ways. A personal familiarity with senior directors, acquired over a period of time, may help in the assessment. A broad breadth of experience, diversity of age, and strong internal competition for those aspiring to very senior roles, is considered positive. A company that had been founded by one individual, and in which there were no clear plans of 'succession', might be marked down.

16.3 Industry-specific analysis

Specific industries will be subject to review that is more relevant to the particular nature of the operations of the companies within them. In this section we briefly consider two separate industries, power generation, water and certain other public service companies (or utilities) and financial companies.

16.3.1 *Utility companies*

The industry for power generation, water supply and until recently telecommunications has a tradition of being highly regulated. Until the mid-1980s, utility companies were public sector companies, and the first privatisation of such a company was for British Telecom in 1984. In certain European countries utility companies are still nationalised companies, and their debt trades virtually as government debt. Credit analysis for utility companies therefore emphasises non-financial factors such as the depth of regulation and the direction in which regulation is heading, for example towards an easing or tightening. Even in a privatised industry for example, new government regulation maybe targeted only at the utility sector; for example, the Labour government in the UK imposed a 'windfall tax' on several privatised utility companies shortly after being elected in May 1997.

Another consideration concerns government direction on how the companies may operate, such as restrictions on where a power generation company may purchase coal from. In some countries such as Germany, coal must be bought from the country's own domestic coal industry only, which imposes costs on the generating company that it would escape if it were free to purchase coal from other, lower-cost producers.

The financial analysis of a utility company essentially follows the pattern we described earlier.

16.3.2 *Financial sector companies*

The financial sector encompasses a large and diverse group of companies. They conduct an intermediary function in that they are a conduit for funds between borrowers and lenders of capital. At its simplest, financial service companies such as banks may earn profit by taking the spread between funds lent and borrowed. They also play an important role in managing the risk exposure for industrial companies, utilising option structures. In analysing a financial sector company the credit analyst will consider the type of customer base served by the company, for example how much of a bank's lending is to the wholesale sector, how much is retail and so on. The financial strength and prospects of its customer base are important elements of a bank's credit rating.

Financial analysis of banks and securities houses is concerned (in addition to the factors discussed above) with the asset quality of the institution, for example the extent of diversification of a bank's lending book. Diversification can be across customer base as well as geographically. A loan book that is heavily concentrated in one sector is considered to be a negative factor in the overall credit assessment of the bank. A credit analyst will be concerned with the level of loans compared with levels in peer companies and the risk involved with this type of lending. For example the expected frequency of bad loans from direct unsecured retail customer loans is higher than for retail customer loans secured by a second mortgage on a property. The higher lending rate charged for the former is designed to compensate for this higher lending risk. There are a range of financial ratios that can be used to assess a bank's asset quality. These include:

- loss reserves/net charge-off level;
- net losses/average level of receivables;
- non-performing loans/average level of receivables.

However unlike the more 'concrete' financial ratios given earlier, there is a higher subjective element with these ratios as banks themselves will designate which loans are non-performing and those loans against which have been assigned charges. Nevertheless these ratios are useful indicators and may be used to identify trends across the sector as well. The loss reserves/net charge-off ratio is perhaps the most useful as it indicates the level of 'cushion' that a bank has; a falling ratio suggests that the bank may not be adding sufficient reserves to cover for future charge-offs. This trend, if continued, may then result in a future increase in the reserves and therefore a decrease in earnings levels as the expense of the reserves increases.

The leverage ratio is particularly important for financial sector companies as the industry and business itself are highly leveraged. Banks and securities companies are therefore permitted a significantly higher leverage level than other companies. For example in a diversified banking group with a high level of asset quality, a leverage ratio of 5:1 or even higher is considered satisfactory by ratings agencies.

Another important measure for financial companies is *liquidity*. Due to the nature of the industry and the capital structure of banks, liquidity or more accurately the lack of liquidity is the primary reason behind banking failures. A bank that is unable to raise funds sufficiently quickly to meet demand will most probably fail, and certainly so if external support is not provided. An inability to raise funds may arise due to internal factors, such as a deterioration in earnings or a very poorly performing loan book, connected perhaps with a downgrade in credit rating, or from external factors such as a major structural fault in the money markets. For credit analysis purposes the traditional liquidity measures are:

- cash;
- cash equivalents;
- level of receivables under one year/level of short-term liabilities.

A higher ratio indicates a greater safety cushion. A further consideration is the extent of lines of credit from other banks in the market.

Other measures of strength for financial companies are *asset coverage*, the bank's earnings record including *earnings per share* (profit attributable to shareholders/number of shares in issue) and finally, the size of the institution. There is an element of thought which states that a very large institution, measured by asset size, cannot go bankrupt. This type of thinking can lead to complacency however and did not prevent several large Japanese banks from getting into financial difficulty in the 1990s.[3]

16.4 The art of credit analysis

As bond markets become ever larger and integrated across a global market, the demand for paper is increasing and with it the demand for high quality credit research. There are now large numbers of companies for whom investors will have virtually no recognition at all, leading to a greater reliance on formal credit ratings. Also the rapid change in economic conditions and the effect of the business cycle frequently result in a company's credit outlook changing rapidly. Investors look to credit ratings as their main source of indicator of a borrower's health. The process by which a bond issue is rated is not purely quantitative however and analysts frequently apply their own qualitative criteria, to take account of changing environments and other, political and macro-economic factors.

Selected bibliography and references

Cohen, J., Zinbarg, E., Zeikel, A., *Investment Analysis and Portfolio Management,* Richard D Irwin, 1977
S&P, *Credit Week,* 8 November 1993, Standard & Poor's
S&P, *Credit Week,* 15 October 1999, Standard & Poor's
Mills, R., *Strategic Value Analysis,* Mars Business Associates, 1994
Wilson, R., Fabozzi., *Corporate Bonds: Structures and Analysis,* FJF Associates, 1996

3 In fact the Japanese government gave an implicit guarantee for the largest 20 'city' banks at one stage, shortly after the collapse of Yamaichi Securities in 1998.

Part III

Structured Financial Products

Structured products is the generic term used to refer to a wide variety of capital market instruments. They include bonds issued as part of a securitisation, such as asset-backed securities (ABS) and mortgage-backed securities (MBS), which are very well-established and were first introduced during the 1970s. A more recent product is the collateralised debt obligation (CDO), which is also well-established, the first such deal being introduced in 1988. Yet another well-established market is that in covered bonds (such as German Pfandbriefe) although this is a relatively new market in the United Kingdom. Structured products also include various classes of instruments that are also called *hybrid products,* combinations of two or more basic products such as vanilla bonds and interest-rate swaps, or vanilla bonds linked to external references or benchmarks. The literature on this subject is large and in-depth and need not concern us.

Structured credit products are products that combine securitisation technology with credit derivative instruments. As such they are also examples of *synthetic securitisation*: synthetic because they replicate the economic effects of securitisation without the actual 'true sale' event, which is the building block of traditional securitisation. The companion volume in the Fixed Income Markets Library, *An Introduction to Credit Derivatives,* discusses credit derivative instruments in detail. In this book we discuss the so-called synthetic structured products that are created from credit derivative instruments.

17 An Introduction to Securitisation[1]

In this chapter we introduce the basic concepts of securitisation and look at the motivation behind their use, as well as their economic impact. We illustrate the process with a brief hypothetical case study

17.1 The concept of securitisation

Securitisation is a well-established practice in the global debt capital markets. It refers to the sale of assets, which generate cashflows, from the institution that owns them, to another company that has been specifically set up for the purpose, and the issuing of notes by this second company. These notes are backed by the cashflows from the original assets. The technique was introduced initially as a means of funding for US mortgage banks. Subsequently, the technique was applied to other assets such as credit card payments and leasing receivables. It has also been employed as part of asset/liability management, as a means of managing balance sheet risk.

Securitisation allows institutions such as banks and corporates to convert assets that are not readily marketable – such as residential mortgages or car loans – into rated securities that are tradeable in the secondary market. The investors that buy these securities gain an exposure to these types of original assets that they would not otherwise have access to. The technique is well established and was first introduced by mortgage banks in the United States during the 1970s. The later synthetic securitisation market is much more recent, dating from 1997. The key difference between cash and synthetic securitisation is that in the former, as we have noted the assets in question are actually sold to a separate legal company known as a special purpose vehicle (SPV).[2] This does not occur in a synthetic transaction, as we shall see.

Sundaresan (1997) defines securitisation as,

> '....a framework in which some illiquid assets of a corporation or a financial institution are transformed into a package of securities backed by these assets, through careful packaging, credit enhancements, liquidity enhancements and structuring.' (page 359)

The process of securitisation creates *asset-backed bonds*. These are debt instruments that have been created from a package of loan assets on which interest is payable, usually on a floating basis. The asset-backed market was developed in the United States and is a large, diverse market containing a wide range of instruments. Techniques employed by investment banks today enable an entity to create a bond structure from any type of cash flow; assets that have been securitised include loans such as residential mortgages, car

---

1 This chapter was co-authored with Anuk Teasdale of YieldCurve.com.

2 An SPV is also referred to as a Special Purpose Entity (SPE) or a Special Purpose Company (SPC).

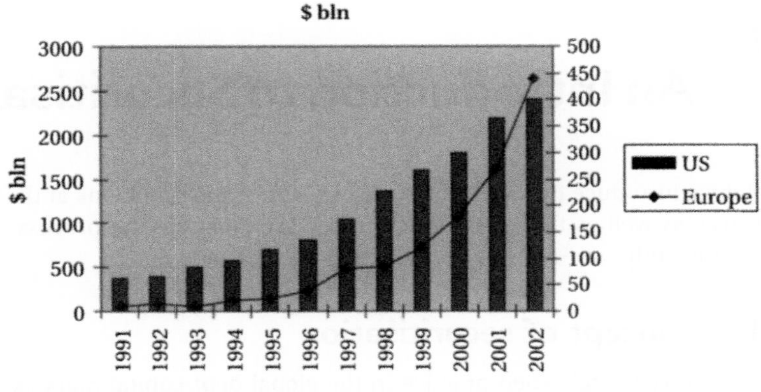

Figure 17.1: Asset-backed securities, notional amounts outstanding.
Source: BBA, ISMA, Federal Reserve.

loans, and credit card loans. The loans form assets on a bank or finance house balance sheet, which are packaged together and used as backing for an issue of bonds. The interest payments on the original loans form the cash flows used to service the new bond issue. Traditionally mortgage-backed bonds are grouped in their own right as mortgage-backed securities (MBS) while all other securitisation issues are known as asset-backed bonds or ABS.

Figure 17.1 shows the growth in securitisation markets during the 1990s.

17.2 Reasons for undertaking securitisation

The driving force behind securitisation has been the need for banks to realise value from the assets on their balance sheet. Typically these assets are residential mortgages, corporate loans, and retail loans such as credit card debt. Let us consider the factors that might lead a financial institution to securitise a part of its balance sheet. These might be for the following reasons:

- if revenues received from assets remain roughly unchanged but the size of assets has decreased, this will lead to an increase in the return on equity ratio;
- the level of capital required to support the balance sheet will be reduced, which again can lead to cost savings or allows the institution to allocate the capital to other, perhaps more profitable, business;
- to obtain cheaper funding: frequently the interest payable on ABS securities is considerably below the level payable on the underlying loans. This creates a cash surplus for the originating entity.

In other words the main reasons that a bank will securitise part of its balance sheet is for one or all of the following reasons:

- funding the assets it owns;
- balance sheet capital management;
- risk management and credit risk transfer.

We consider each of these in turn.

17.2.1 *Funding*

Banks can use securitisation to (i) support rapid asset growth, (ii) diversify their funding mix, and reduce cost of funding, and (iii) reduce maturity mis-matches. The market for asset-backed securities is large, with an estimated size of US$1,000 billion invested in ABS issues worldwide annually, of which US$150 billion is in the European market alone.[3] Access to this source of funding will enable a bank to grow its loan books at a faster pace than if they were reliant on traditional funding sources alone. For example in the United Kingdom a former building society-turned-bank, Northern Rock plc, has taken advantage of securitisation to back its growing share of the UK residential mortgage market. Securitising assets also allows a bank to diversify its funding mix. All banks will not wish to be reliant on only a single or a few sources of funding, as this can be high-risk in times of market difficulty. Banks aim to optimise their funding between a mix of retail, interbank and wholesale sources. Securitisation has a key role to play in this mix. It also enables a bank to reduce its funding costs. This is because the securitisation process de-links the credit rating of the originating institution from the credit rating of the issued notes. Typically most of the notes issued by SPVs will be higher-rated than the bonds issued directly by the originating bank itself. While the liquidity of the secondary market in ABS is frequently lower than that of the corporate bond market, and this adds to the yield payable by an ABS, it is frequently the case that the cost to the originating institution of issuing debt is still lower in the ABS market because of the latter's higher rating. Finally, there is the issue of maturity mis-matches. The business of bank asset-liability management (ALM) is inherently one of maturity mis-match, since a bank often funds long-term assets such as residential mortgages, with short-asset liabilities such as bank account deposits or interbank funding. This can be removed via securitisation, as the originating bank receives funding from the sale of the assets, and the economic maturity of the issued notes frequently matches that of the assets.

17.2.2 *Balance sheet capital management*

Banks use securitisation to improve balance sheet capital management. This provides (i) regulatory capital relief (ii) economic capital relief and (iii) diversified sources of capital. As stipulated in the Bank for International Settlements (BIS) capital rules,[4] also known as the Basel rules, banks must maintain a minimum capital level for their assets, in relation to the risk of these assets. Under Basel I, for every $100 of risk-weighted assets a bank must hold at least $8 of capital; however the designation of each assets risk-weighting is restrictive. For example with the exception of mortgages, customer loans are 100% risk-weighted regardless of the underlying rating of the borrower or the quality of the security held. The anomalies that this raises, which need not concern us here, is being addressed by the Basel II rules which become effective from 2007. However the Basel I rules, which have been in place since 1988 (and effective from 1992), are another driver of securitisation. As an SPV is not a bank, it is not subject to Basel rules and needs only such capital that is economically required by the nature of the assets they contain. This is not a set amount, but is

---

3 Source: CSFB, *Credit Risk Transfer*, 2 May 2003.

4 For further information on this see Choudhry (2001).

significantly below the 8% level required by banks in all cases. Although an originating bank does not obtain 100% regulatory capital relief when it sells assets off its balance sheet to an SPV, because it will have retained a 'first-loss' piece out of the issued notes, its regulatory capital charge will be significantly reduced after the securitisation.[5]

To the extent that securitisation provides regulatory capital relief, it can be thought of as an alternative to capital raising, compared with the traditional sources of Tier 1 capital (equity), preferred shares, and perpetual loan notes with step-up coupon features. By reducing the amount of capital that has to be used to support the asset pool, a bank can also improve its return-on-equity (ROE) value. This will be received favourably by shareholders.

17.2.3 *Risk management*

Once assets have been securitised, the credit risk exposure on these assets for the originating bank is reduced considerably and, if the bank does not retain a first-loss capital piece (the most junior of the issued notes), it is removed entirely. This is because assets have been sold to the SPV. Securitisation can also be used to remove non-performing assets from banks' balance sheets. This has the dual advantage of removing credit risk and removing a potentially negative sentiment from the balance sheet, as well as freeing up regulatory capital as before. Further, there is a potential upside from securitising such assets: if any of them start performing again, or there is a recovery value obtained from defaulted assets, the originator will receive any surplus profit made by the SPV.

17.3 Benefits of securitisation to investors

Investor interest in the ABS market has been considerable from the market's inception. This is because investors perceive asset-backed securities as possessing a number of benefits. Investors can:

- diversify sectors of interest;
- access different (and sometimes superior) risk-reward profiles;
- access sectors that are otherwise not open to them.

A key benefit of securitisation notes is the ability to tailor risk-return profiles. For example, if there is a lack of assets of any specific credit rating, these can be created via securitisation. Securitised notes frequently offer better risk-reward performance than corporate bonds of the same rating and maturity. While this might seem peculiar (why should one AA-rated bond perform better in terms of credit performance than another just because it is asset-backed?), this often occurs because the originator holds the first-loss piece in the structure.

A holding in an ABS also diversifies the risk exposure. For example, rather than invest $100 million in an AA-rated corporate bond and be exposed to 'event risk' associated with the issuer, investors can gain exposure to for instance, 100 pooled assets. These pooled assets will clearly have lower concentration risk.

---

5 We discuss first-loss in the chapter on synthetic CDOs.

17.4 The process of securitisation

We look now at the process of securitisation, the nature of the SPV structure and issues such as credit enhancements and the cashflow waterfall.

17.4.1 *Securitisation process*

The securitisation process involves a number of participants. In the first instance is the *originator*, the firm whose assets are being securitised. The most common process involves an *issuer* acquiring the assets from the originator. The issuer is usually a company that has been specially set up for the purpose of the securitisation, which is the SPV and is usually domiciled offshore. The creation of an SPV ensures that the underlying asset pool is held separate from the other assets of the originator. This is done so that in the event that the originator is declared bankrupt or insolvent, the assets that have been transferred to the SPV will not be affected. This is known as being bankruptcy-remote. Conversely, if the underlying assets begin to deteriorate in quality and are subject to a ratings downgrade, investors have no recourse to the originator.

By holding the assets within an SPV framework, defined in formal legal terms, the financial status and credit rating of the originator becomes almost irrelevant to the bondholders. The process of securitisation often involves *credit enhancements*, in which a third-party guarantee of credit quality is obtained, so that notes issued under the securitisation are often rated at investment grade and up to AAA-grade.

The process of structuring a securitisation deal ensures that the liability side of the SPV – the issued notes – carries lower cost than the asset side of the SPV. This enables the originator to secure lower cost funding that it would not otherwise be able to obtain in the unsecured market. This is a tremendous benefit for institutions with lower credit ratings. Figure 17.2 illustrates the process of securitisation in simple fashion.

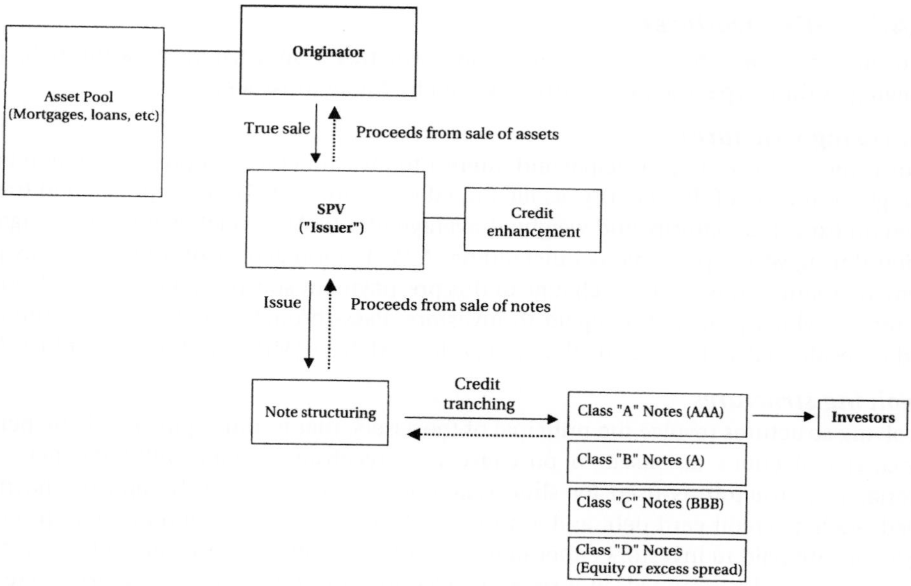

Figure 17.2: Securitisation process.

Mechanics of securitisation

Securitisation involves a 'true sale' of the underlying assets from the balance sheet of the originator. This is why a separate legal entity, the SPV, is created to act as the issuer of the notes. The assets being securitised are sold onto the balance sheet of the SPV and are, therefore, ring-fenced from those of the originating institution. The process involves:

- undertaking 'due diligence' on the quality and future prospects of the assets;
- setting up the SPV and then effecting the transfer of assets to it;
- underwriting of loans for credit quality and servicing;
- determining the structure of the notes, including how many tranches are to be issued, in accordance to originator and investor requirements;
- the notes being rated by one or more credit rating agencies;
- placing of notes in the capital markets.

The sale of assets to the SPV needs to be undertaken so that it is recognised as a true legal transfer. The originator will need to hire legal counsel to advise it in such matters. The credit rating process will consider the character and quality of the assets, and also whether any enhancements have been made to the assets that will raise their credit quality. This can include *overcollateralisation*, which is when the principal value of notes issued is lower than the principal value of assets, and a liquidity facility provided by a bank.

A key consideration for the originator is the choice of the underwriting bank, which structures the deal and places the notes. The originator will award the mandate for its deal to an investment bank on the basis of fee levels, marketing ability and track record with assets being securitised.

17.4.2 *SPV structures*

There are essentially two main securitisation structures, amortising (pass-through) and revolving. A third type, the master trust, is used by frequent issuers.

Amortising structures

Amortising structures pay principal and interest to investors on a coupon-by-coupon basis throughout the life of the security, as illustrated in Figure 17.3. They are priced and traded based on expected maturity and weighted-average lifer (WAL), which is the time-weighted period during which principal is outstanding. A WAL approach incorporates various pre-payment assumptions, and any change in this pre-payment speed will increase or decrease the rate at which principal is repaid to investors. Pass-through structures are commonly used in residential and commercial mortgage-backed deals (MBS), and consumer loan ABS.

Revolving structures

Revolving structures revolve the principal of the assets; that is, during the revolving period, principal collections are used to purchase new receivables which fulfil the necessary criteria. The structure is used for short-dated assets with a relatively high pre-payment speed, such as credit card debt and auto-loans. During the amortisation period, principal payments are paid to investors either in a series of equal instalments (*controlled amortisation*) or principal is 'trapped' in a separate account until the expected maturity date and then paid in a single lump sum to investors (*soft bullet*).

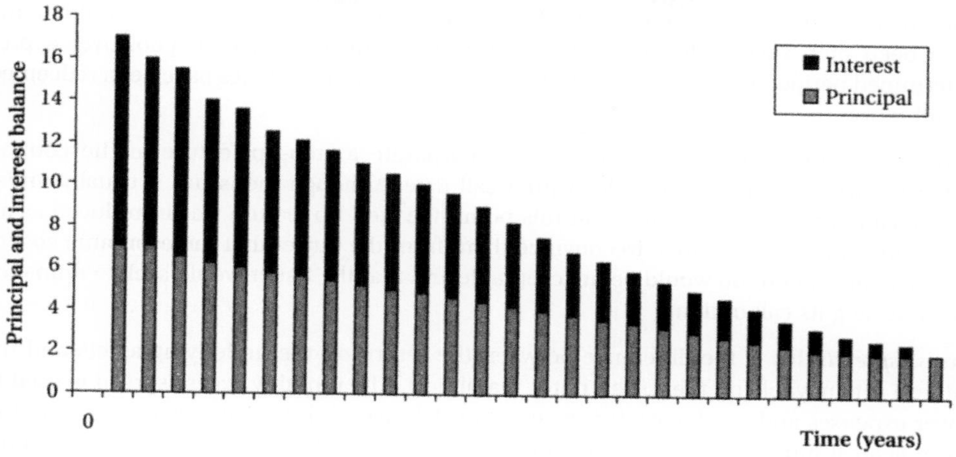

Figure 17.3: Amortising structure.

Master trust

Frequent issuers under US and UK law use *master trust* structures, which allow multiple securitisations to be issued from the same SPV. Under such schemes, the originator transfers assets to the master trust SPV. Notes are then issued out of the asset pool based on investor demand. Master trusts have been used by MBS and credit card ABS originators.

Securitisation note tranching

As illustrated in Figure 17.2, in a securitisation the issued notes are structured to reflect specified risk areas of the asset pool, and thus are rated differently. The senior tranche is usually rated AAA. The lower-rated notes usually have an element of *over-collateralisation* and are thus capable of absorbing losses. The most junior note is the lowest-rated or non-rated. It is often referred to as the *first-loss piece,* because it is impacted by losses in the underlying asset pool first. The first-loss piece is sometimes called the *equity piece* or equity note (even though it is a bond) and is usually held by the originator.

17.4.3 *Credit enhancement*

Credit enhancement refers to the group of measures that can be instituted as part of the securitisation process for ABS and MBS issues so that the credit rating of the issued notes meets investor requirements. The lower the quality of the assets being securitised, the greater the need for credit enhancement. This is usually by either of the following methods:

Over-collateralisation: where the nominal value of the assets in the pool are in excess of the nominal value of issued securities.

Pool insurance: an insurance policy provided by a composite insurance company to cover the risk of principal loss in the collateral pool. The claims paying rating of the insurance company is important in determining the overall rating of the issue.

Senior/junior note classes: credit enhancement is provided by subordinating a class of notes ('class B' notes) to the senior class notes ('class A' notes). The class B note's right to its proportional share of cash flows is subordinated to the rights of the senior noteholders.

Class B notes do not receive payments of principal until certain rating agency requirements have been met, specifically satisfactory performance of the collateral pool over a pre-determined period, or in many cases until all of the senior note classes have been redeemed in full.

Margin step-up: a number of ABS issues incorporate a step-up feature in the coupon structure, which typically coincides with a call date. Although the issuer is usually under no obligation to redeem the notes at this point, the step-up feature was introduced as an added incentive for investors, to convince them from the outset that the economic cost of paying a higher coupon would be unacceptable and that the issuer would seek to refinance by exercising its call option.

Excess spread: this is the difference between the return on the underlying assets and the interest rate payable on the issued notes (liabilities). The monthly excess spread is used to cover expenses and any losses. If any surplus is left over, it is held in a reserve account to cover against future losses or (if not required for that), as a benefit to the originator. In the meantime the reserve account is a credit enhancement for investors.

All securitisation structures incorporate a *cash waterfall* process, whereby all the cash that is generated by the asset pool is paid in order of payment priority. Only when senior obligations have been met can more junior obligations be paid. An independent third-party agent is usually employed to run 'tests' on the vehicle to confirm that there is sufficient cash available to pay all obligations. If a test is failed, then the vehicle will start to pay off the notes, starting from the senior notes. The waterfall process is illustrated in Figure 17.4.

17.4.4 *Impact on balance sheet*

Figure 17.5 illustrates by an hypothetical example the effect on the liability side of an originating bank's balance sheet from a securitisation transaction. Following the process, selected assets have been removed from the balance sheet, although the originating bank will usually have retained the first-loss piece. With regard to the regulatory capital impact, this first-loss amount is deducted from the bank's total capital position. For example, assume a bank has $100 million of risk-weighted assets and a target Basel ratio of 12%,[6] and securitises all $100 million of these assets. It retains the first-loss tranche which forms 1.5% of the total issue. The remaining 98.5% will be sold on to the market. The bank will still have to set aside 1.5% of capital as a buffer against future losses, but it has been able to free itself of the remaining 10.5% of capital.

17.5 Illustrating the process of securitisation

To illustrate the process of securitisation, we consider an hypothetical airline ticket receivables transaction, being originated by the fictitious ABC Airways plc and arranged by the equally fictitious XYZ Securities Limited. We show the kind of issues that will be considered by the investment bank that is structuring the deal.

---

6 The minimum is 8% but many banks prefer to set aside an amount well in excess of this minimum required level.

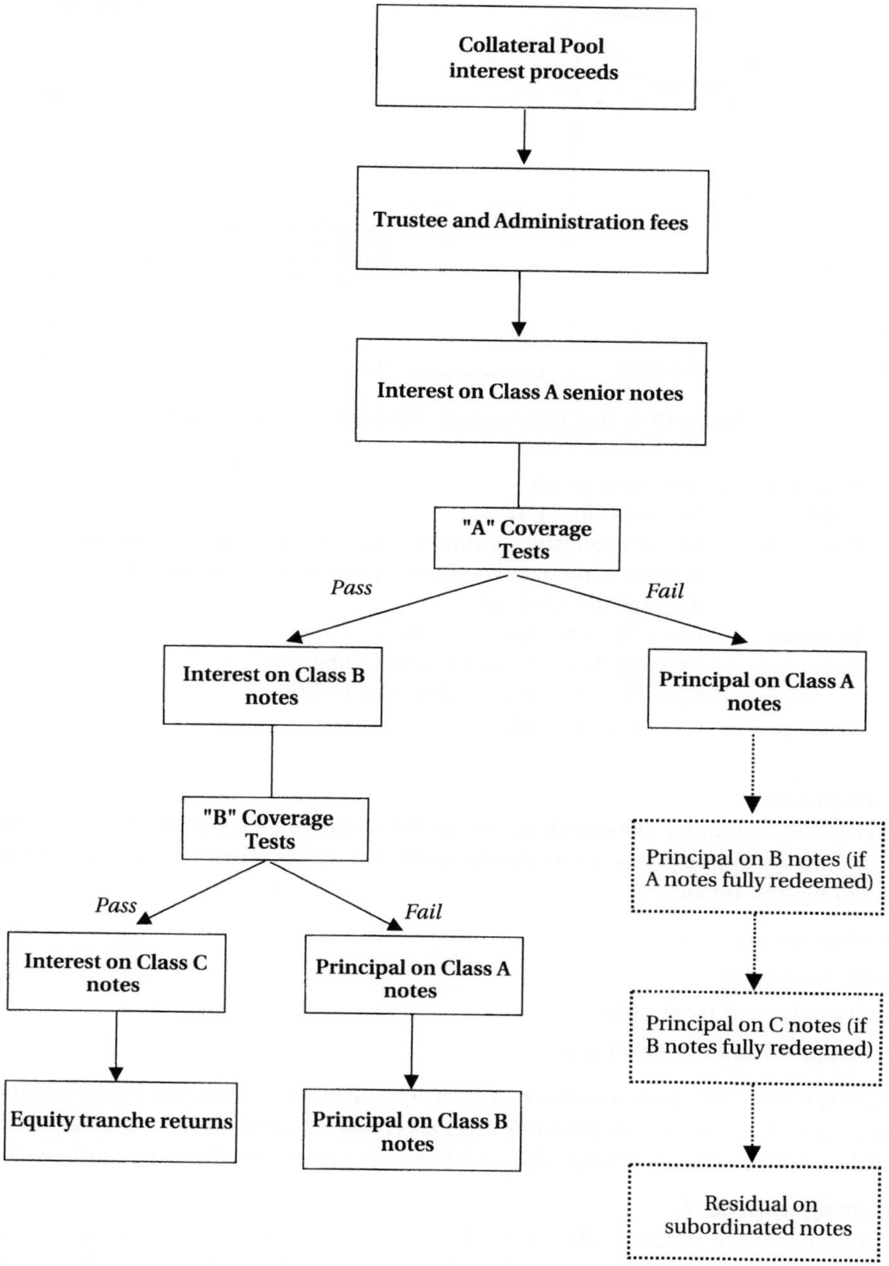

Figure 17.4: Cashflow waterfall (priority of payments).

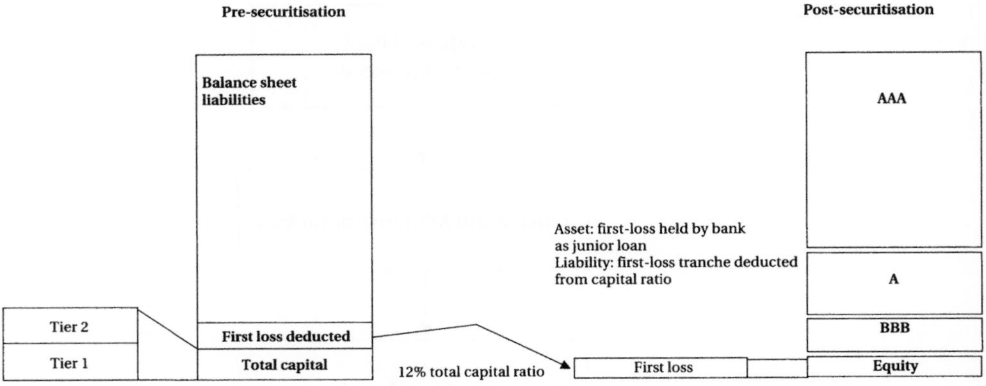

Figure 17.5: Regulatory capital impact of securitisation.

Originator	ABC Airways plc
Issuer	'Airways No 1 Ltd'
Transaction	Ticket receivables airline future flow securitisation bonds
	€200 m three-tranche floating rate notes, legal maturity 2010
	Average life 4.1 years
Tranches	Class 'A' note (AA), Libor plus [ ] bps
	Class 'B' note (A), Libor plus [ ] bps
	Class 'E' note (BBB), Libor plus [ ] bps
Arranger	XYZ Securities plc

Due diligence

XYZ Securities will undertake due diligence on the assets to be securitised. For this case, it will examine the airline performance figures over the last five years, as well as model future projected figures, including:

- total passenger sales
- total ticket sales
- total credit card receivables
- geographical split of ticket sales.

It is the future flow of receivables, in this case credit card purchases of airline tickets, that is being securitised. This is a higher-risk asset class than say, residential mortgages, because the airline industry has a tradition of greater volatility of earnings than say, mortgage banks.

Marketing approach

The present and all future credit card ticket receivables generated by the airline will be transferred to an SPV. The investment bank's syndication desk will seek to place the notes with institutional investors across Europe. The notes are first given an indicative pricing ahead of the issue, to gauge investor sentiment. Given the nature of the asset class, during November 2002 the notes would be marketed at around three-month Libor plus 70–80 basis points (AA note), 120–130 basis points (A note) and 260–270 basis points (BBB note).

The notes are 'benchmarked' against recent issues with similar asset classes, as well as the spread level in the unsecured market of comparable issuer names.

Deal structure

The deal structure is shown at Figure 17.6.

The process leading to issue of notes is as follows:

- ABC Airways plc sells its future flow ticket receivables to an offshore SPV set up for this deal, incorporated as Airways No 1 Ltd;
- the SPV issues notes in order to fund its purchase of the receivables;
- the SPV pledges its right to the receivables to a fiduciary agent, the Security Trustee, for the benefit of the bondholders;
- the Trustee accumulates funds as they are received by the SPV;
- the bondholders receive interest and principal payments, in the order of priority of the notes, on a quarterly basis.

In the event of default, the Trustee will act on behalf of the bondholders to safeguard their interests.

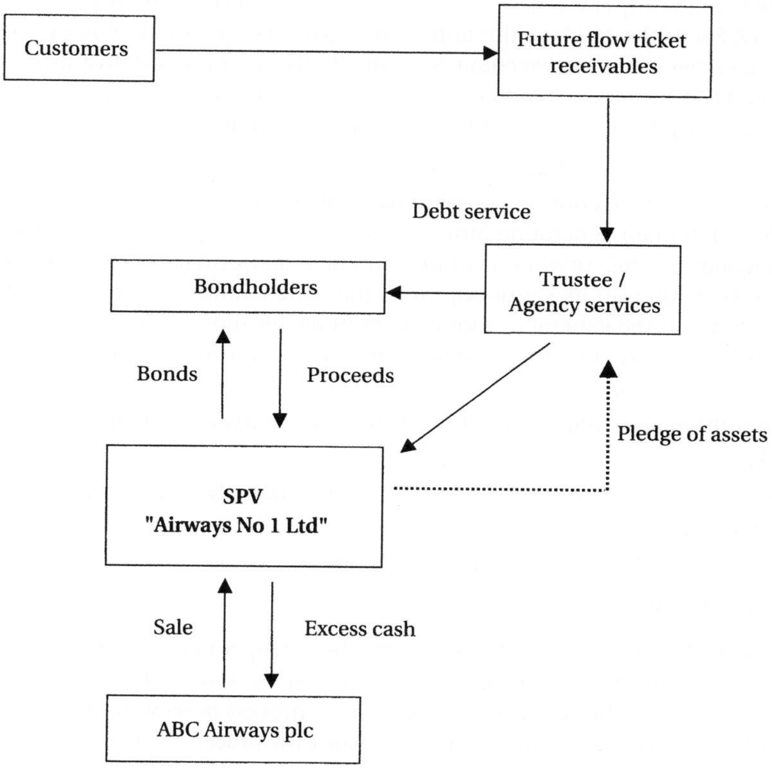

Figure 17.6: Airways No1 Limited deal structure.

Financial guarantors

The investment bank will consider if an insurance company, known as a monoline insurer, should be approached to 'wrap' the deal by providing a guarantee of backing for the SPV in the event of default. This insurance is provided in return for a fee.

Financial modelling

XYZ Securities will construct a cashflow model to estimate the size of the issued notes. The model will consider historical sales values, any seasonal factors in sales, credit card cash flows, and so on. Certain assumptions will be made when constructing the model, for example growth projections, inflation levels, tax levels, and so on. The model will consider a number of different scenarios, and also calculate the minimum asset coverage levels required to service the issued debt. A key indicator in the model will be the debt service coverage ratio (DSCR). The more conservative the DSCR, the more comfort there will be for investors in the notes. For a residential mortgage deal, this ratio might be approximately 2.5–3.0; however for an airline ticket receivables deal, the DSCR would be unlikely to be lower than 4.0. The model will therefore calculate the amount of notes that can be issued against the assets, whilst maintaining the minimum DSCR.

Credit rating

It is common for securitisation deals to be rated by one or more of the formal credit ratings agencies such as Moody's, Fitch or Standard & Poor's. A formal credit rating will make it easier for XYZ Securities to place the notes with investors. The methodology employed by the ratings agencies takes into account both qualitative and quantitative factors, and will differ according to the asset class being securitised. The main issues in a deal such as our hypothetical Airway No 1 deal would be expected to include:

- corporate credit quality: these are risks associated with the originator, and are factors that affect its ability to continue operations, meet its financial obligations, and provide a stable foundation for generating future receivables. This might be analysed according to the following: (i) ABC Airways' historical financial performance, including its liquidity and debt structure; (ii) its status within its domicile country, for example whether it is state-owned; (iii) the general economic conditions for industry and for airlines and (iv) the historical record and current state of the airline, for instance its safety record and age of its aeroplanes;
- the competition and industry trends: ABC Airways' market share, the competition on its network;
- regulatory issues, such as need for ABC Airways to comply with forthcoming legislation that would impact its cash flows;
- legal structure of the SPV and transfer of assets;
- cash flow analysis.

Based on the findings of the ratings agency, the arranger may re-design some aspect of the deal structure so that the issued notes are rated at the required level.

This is a selection of the key issues involved in the process of securitisation. Depending on investor sentiment, market conditions and legal issues, the process from inception to closure of the deal may take anything from three to 12 months or more. After the notes have been issued, the arranging bank will no longer have anything to do with the issue; however the bonds themselves require a number of agency services for their remaining life until they mature or are paid off. These agency services include paying agent, cash manager and custodian.

17.6 Sample transactions

Case study 1
Fosse Securities No 1 plc

This was the first securitisation undertaken by Alliance & Leicester plc, a former UK building society which converted into a commercial bank in 1997. The underlying portfolio was approximately 6,700 loans secured by first mortgages on property in the UK. The transaction was a £250 million securitisation via the SPV, named Fosse Securities No 1 plc. The underwriter was Morgan Stanley Dean Witter, which placed the notes in November 2000. The transaction structure was:

- a senior class 'A' note with AAA/Aaa rating by Standard & Poor's and Moody's, which represented £235 million of the issue, with a legal maturity of November 2032;
- a class 'B' note rated Aa/Aa3 of nominal £5 million;
- a class 'C' note rated BBB/Baa2 of nominal £10 million.

The ratings agencies cited the strengths of the issue as:[7] the loans were *prime* quality; there was a high level of *seasoning* in the underlying asset pool, with average age of 35 months; the average level of the loan-to-value ratio (LTV) was considered low, at 73.5%; and there were low average loan-to-income multiples amongst underlying borrowers.

Case study 2
SRM Investment No 1 Limited

Sveriges Bostadsfinansieringsaktiebolag (SBAB) is the Swedish state-owned national housing finance corporation. Its second ever securitisation issue was the EUR 1 billion SRM Investment No 1 Limited, issued in October 2000. The underlying asset backing was Swedish residential mortgage loans, with properties being mainly detached and semi-detached single-family properties. The issue was structured and underwritten by Nomura International.

The underlying motives behind the deal were that it allowed SBAB to:

- reduce capital allocation, thereby releasing capital for further lending;
- remove part of its mortgage loan-book off the balance sheet;
- obtain a more diversified source for its funding.

The transaction was structured into the following notes:

- senior class 'A1' floating-rate note rated AAA/Aaa by S&P and Moody's, issue size EUR755 million, with a legal maturity date in 2057;
- senior class 'A2' fixed coupon note, rated AAA/Aaa and denominated in Japanese yen, incorporating a step-up facility, legal maturity 2057; issue size JPY 20 billion;

7 Source: ISR, November 2000.

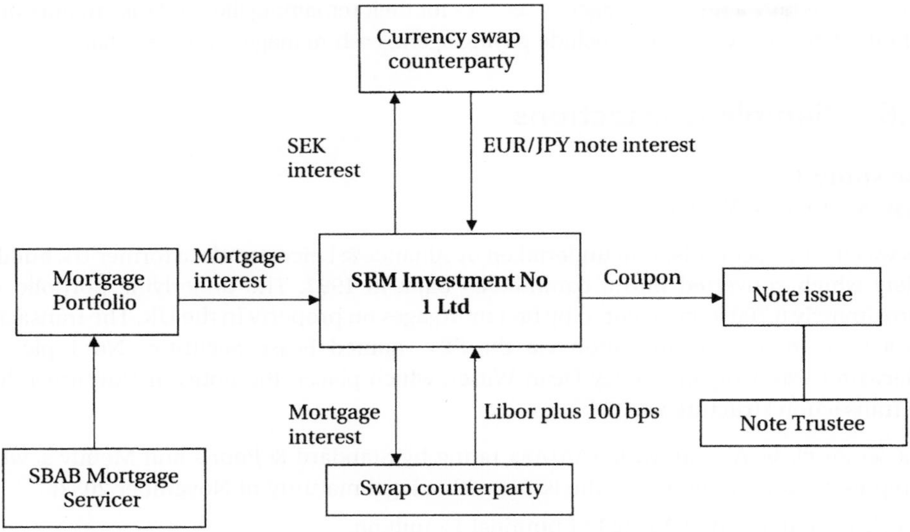

Figure 17.7: SRM Investment No 1 Limited.

- class 'M' floating-rate note rated A/A2, due 2057; issue size EUR 20 million;
- class 'B' floating-rate note, rated BBB/Baa2, issue size EUR 10 million.

The yen tranche reflects the targeting of a Japanese domestic investor base. On issue the class A1 notes paid 26 basis points over euribor. The structure is illustrated in Figure 17.7.

References and bibliography

Bhattacharya, A., Fabozzi, F., (eds.), *Asset-Backed Securities*, FJF Associates, 1996

Choudhry, M., *The Bond and Money Markets: Strategy, Trading, Analysis*, Butterworth-Heinemann 2001

Hayre, L., (editor), *The Salomon Smith Barney Guide to Mortgage-Backed and Asset-Backed Securities*, John Wiley and Sons 2001

Martellini, L., P., Priaulet, S., Priaulet, *Fixed Income Securities*, John Wiley and Sons 2003

Morris, D., *Asset Securitisation: Principles and Practices*, Executive Enterprise 1990

Sundaresan, S., *Fixed Income Markets and Their Derivatives*, South-Western Publishing 1997, chapter 9

18 Mortgage-Backed Securities I

In Chapter 3 we introduced *asset-backed bonds*, debt instruments created from a package of loan assets on which interest is payable, usually on a floating basis. The asset-backed market was developed in the United States and is a large, diverse market containing a wide variety of instruments. The characteristics of asset-backed securities (ABS) present additional features in their analysis, which are investigated in this and the next two chapters. Financial engineering techniques employed by investment banks today enable an entity to create a bond structure from any type of cash flow; the typical forms are high volume loans such as residential mortgages, car loans, and credit card loans. The loans form assets on a bank or finance house balance sheet, which are packaged together and used as backing for an issue of bonds. The interest payments on the original loans form the cash flows used to service the new bond issue.

In this chapter we consider *mortgage-backed securities*, the largest of the asset-backed bond markets. The remaining chapters deal with the other asset-backed instruments available.[1]

18.1 Mortgage-backed securities

A mortgage is a loan made for the purpose of purchasing property, which in turn is used as the security for the loan itself. It is defined as a debt instrument giving conditional ownership of an asset, and secured by the asset that is being financed. The borrower provides the lender a mortgage in exchange for the right to use the property during the term of the mortgage, and agrees to make regular payments of both principal and interest. The mortgage lien is the security for the lender, and is removed when the debt is paid off. A mortgage may involve residential property or commercial property and is a long-term debt, normally 25 to 30 years; however it can be drawn up for shorter periods if required by the borrower. If the borrower or *mortgagor* defaults on the interest payments, the lender or *mortgagee* has the right to take over the property and recover the debt from the proceeds of selling the property. Mortgages can be either fixed-rate or floating-rate interest. Although in the US mortgages are generally amortising loans, known as *repayment* mortgages in the UK, there are also *interest only* mortgages where the borrower only pays the interest on the loan; on maturity the original loan amount is paid off by the proceeds of a maturing investment contract taken out at the same time as the mortgage. These are known as *endowment* mortgages and are popular in the UK market, although their popularity has been waning in recent years.

---

1 Many texts place mortgage-backed securities in a separate category, distinct from asset-backed bonds (for example, see the highly recommended Fabozzi, F., *Handbook of Structured Finance Products*, 1998). Market practitioners also tend to make this distinction. Generally, the market is viewed as being composed of mortgage-backed securities and asset-backed securities (which encompass all other asset types).

A lending institution may have many hundreds of thousands of individual residential and commercial mortgages on its book. If the total loan book is pooled together and used as collateral for the issue of a bond, the resulting instrument is a *mortgage-backed security*. This process is known as *securitisation*, which is the pooling of loan assets in order to use them as collateral for a bond issue. Sometimes a *special purpose vehicle* (SPV) is set up specifically to serve as the entity representing the pooled assets. This is done for administrative reasons and also sometimes to enhance the credit rating that may be assigned to the bonds. In the UK some SPVs have a triple-A credit rating, although the majority of SPVs are below this rating, while retaining investment grade status. In the US market certain mortgage-backed securities are backed, either implicitly or explicitly, by the government, in which case they trade essentially as risk-free instruments and are not rated by the credit agencies. In the US a government agency, the Government National Mortgage Association (GNMA, known as 'Ginnie Mae') and two government-sponsored agencies, the Federal Home Loan Corporation and the Federal National Mortgage Association ('Freddie Mac' and 'Fannie Mae' respectively), purchase mortgages for the purpose of pooling them and holding them in their portfolios; they may then be securitised. Bonds that are not issued by government agencies are rated in the same way as other corporate bonds. On the other hand non-government agencies sometimes obtain mortgage insurance for their issue, in order to boost its credit quality. When this happens the credit rating of the mortgage insurer becomes an important factor in the credit standing of the bond issue.

18.1.1 *Growth of the market*

The mortgage-backed market in the US is the largest in the world and witnessed phenomenal growth in the early 1990s. One estimate put the size of the total market at around $1.8 trillion at the end of 1995, with around $400 billion issued in that year alone.[2] The same study suggested the following advantages of mortgage-backed bonds:

- although many mortgage bonds represent comparatively high quality assets and are collateralised instruments, the yields on them are usually higher then corporate bonds of the same credit quality. This is because of the complexity of the instruments and the uncertain nature of the mortgage cash flows. In the mid-1990s mortgage-backed bonds traded at yields of around 100–200 basis points above Treasury bonds;
- the wide range of products offers investors a choice of maturities, cash flows and security to suit individual requirements;
- agency mortgage-backed bonds are implicitly backed by the government and therefore represent a better credit risk than triple-A rated corporate bonds; the credit ratings for non-agency bonds is often triple-A or double-A rated;
- the size of the market means that it is very liquid, with agency mortgage-backed bonds having the same liquidity as Treasury bonds;
- the monthly coupon frequency of mortgage-backed bonds makes them an attractive instrument for investors who require frequent income payments; this feature is not available for most other bond market instruments.

---

2 Hayre, L., Mohebbi, C., Zimmermann, T., 'Mortgage Pass-Through Securities', in Fabozzi, F.,(ed.) *The Handbook of Fixed Income Securities*, 5th edition, McGraw-Hill, 1997.

	1986	1987	1988	1989	1990	1991	1992	1993	1994	1995	1996
GNMA	45	100	89	48	49	52	64	76	120	108	65
FHLMC	44	100.5	82	52	65	55	98	170	130	105	55
FNMA	25	65	55	52	75	80	115	175	240	130	120
Private	4.4	8	9	11	13	20	40	90	95	45	31

Table 18.1: Issue of mortgage pass-through securities 1986–1996.
Source: Federal Reserve Board Bulletin.

In the UK the asset-backed market has also witnessed rapid growth, and many issues are triple-A rated because issuers create a *special purpose vehicle* that is responsible for the issue. Various forms of credit insurance are also used. Unlike the US market, most bonds are floating-rate instruments, reflecting the variable-rate nature of the majority of mortgages in the UK.

The growth in selected markets in the US is shown in Table 18.1 (approximate nominal value in $ billion).

18.1.2 *Mortgages*

In the US market, the terms of a conventional mortgage, known as a *level-payment fixed-rate mortgage*, will state the interest rate payable on the loan, the term of the loan and the frequency of payment. Most mortgages specify monthly payment of interest. These are in fact the characteristics of a level-payment mortgage, which has a fixed interest rate and fixed term to maturity. This means that the monthly interest payments are fixed, hence the term 'level-pay'.

The singular feature of a mortgage is that, even if it charges interest at a fixed rate, its cash flows are not known with absolute certainty. This is because the borrower can elect to repay any or all of the principal before the final maturity date. This is a characteristic of all mortgages, and although some lending institutions impose a penalty on borrowers who retire the loan early, this is a risk for the lender, known as *prepayment risk*. The uncertainty of the cash flow patterns is similar to that of a callable bond, and as we shall see later this feature means that we may value mortgage-backed bonds using a pricing model similar to that employed for callable bonds.

The monthly interest payment on a conventional fixed-rate mortgage is given by (18.3), which is derived from the conventional present value analysis used for an annuity. Essentially the primary relationship is:

$$M_{m0} = I\left(\frac{1 - (1/(1+r)^n)}{r}\right) \tag{18.1}$$

from which we can derive:

$$I = \frac{M_{m0}}{\frac{1-(1/(1+r)^n)}{r}} \tag{18.2}$$

This is simplified to:

$$I = M_{m0}\frac{r(1+r)^n}{(1+r)^n - 1} \tag{18.3}$$

where

M_{m0}	is the original mortgage balance (the cash amount of loan)
I	is the monthly cash mortgage payment
r	is the simple monthly interest rate, given by (annual interest rate/12)
n	is the term of the mortgage in months.

The monthly repayment includes both the interest servicing and a repayment of part of the principal. In Example 18.1 after the 264th interest payment, the balance will be zero and the mortgage will have been paid off. Since a portion of the original balance is paid off every month, the interest payment reduces by a small amount each month, that is, the proportion of the monthly payment dedicated to repaying the principal steadily increases. The remaining mortgage balance for any particular month during the term of the mortgage may be calculated using (18.4):

$$M_{mt} = M_{m0}\frac{r(1+r)^n - (1+r)^t}{(1+r)^n - 1} \tag{18.4}$$

where M_{mt} is the mortgage cash balance after t months and n remains the original maturity of the mortgage in months.

The level of interest payment and principal re-payment in any one month during the mortgage term can be calculated using the equations below. If we wish to calculate the value of the principal repayment in a particular month during the mortgage term, we may use (18.5):

$$p_t = M_{m0}\frac{r(1+r)^{t-1}}{(1+r)^n - 1} \tag{18.5}$$

where p_t is the scheduled principal repayment amount for month t, while the level of interest payment in any month is given by (18.6):

$$i_t = M_{m0}\frac{r\left((1+r)^n - (1+r)^{t-1}\right)}{(1+r)^n - 1} \tag{18.6}$$

where i_t is the interest payment only in month t.

Example 18.1: Mortgage contract calculations

A mortgage borrower enters into a conventional mortgage contract, in which he borrows £72,200 for 22 years at a rate of 7.99%. What is the monthly mortgage payment?

This gives us n equal to 264 and r equal to (0.0799/12) or 0.0066583. Inserting the above terms into (18.3) we have:

$$I = 72,200\left(\frac{0.0066583(1.0066583)^{264}}{(1.0066583)^{264} - 1}\right)$$

or I equal to £581.60

The mortgage balance after ten years is given below, where t is 120:

$$M_{m120} = 72,200\left(\frac{(1.0066583)^{264} - (1.0066583)^{120}}{(1.0066583)^{264} - 1}\right)$$

or a remaining balance of £53,756.93.

In the same month the scheduled principal repayment amount is:

$$p_{120} = 72,200\frac{0.0066583(1.0066583)^{120-1}}{(1.0066583)^{264} - 1}$$

or £222.19.

The interest only payable in month 120 is shown below:

$$i_{120} = 72,200\frac{0.0066583\left((1.0066583)^{264} - (1.0066583)^{120-1}\right)}{(1.0066583)^{264} - 1}$$

and is equal to £359.41. The combined mortgage payment is £581.60, as calculated before.

Some mortgage contracts incorporate a *servicing fee*. This is payable to the mortgage provider to cover the administrative costs associated with collecting interest payments, sending regular statements and other information to borrowers, chasing overdue payments, maintaining the records and processing systems and other activities. Mortgage providers also incur costs when re-possessing properties after mortgagors have fallen into default. Mortgages may be serviced by the original lender or another third-party institution that has acquired the right to service it, in return for collecting the fee. When a servicing charge is payable by a borrower, the monthly mortgage payment is comprised of the interest costs, the principal repayment and the servicing fee. The fee incorporated into the monthly payment is usually stated as a percentage, say 0.25%. This is added to the mortgage rate.

Another type of mortgage in the US market is the *adjustable-rate mortgage* or ARM, which is a loan in which the interest rate payable is set in line with an external reference rate. The re-sets are at periodic intervals depending on the terms of the loan, and can be on a monthly, six-monthly or annual basis, or even longer. The interest rate is usually fixed at a spread over the reference rate. The reference rate that is used can be a market-determined rate such as the prime rate, or a calculated rate based on the funding costs for US savings and loan institutions or *thrifts*. The cost of funds for thrifts is calculated using the monthly average funding cost on the thrifts' activities, and there are 'thrift indexes' that are used to indicate to the cost of funding. The two most common indices are the Eleventh Federal Home Loan Bank Board District Cost of Funds Index (COFI) and the National Cost of Funds Index. Generally borrowers prefer to fix the rate they pay on their loans to reduce uncertainty, and this makes fixed-rate mortgages more popular than variable rate mortgages. A common incentive used to entice borrowers away from fixed-rate mortgages is to offer a below-market interest rate on an ARM mortgage, usually for an introductory period. This comfort period may be from two to five years or even longer.

Mortgages in the UK are predominantly *variable rate mortgages*, in which the interest rate is moves in line with the clearing bank base rate. It is rare to observe fixed-rate mortgages in the UK market, although short-term fixed-rate mortgages are more common (the rate reverts to a variable basis at the termination of the fixed-rate period).

A *balloon mortgage* entitles a borrower to long-term funding, but under its terms, at a specified future date the interest rate payable is re-negotiated. This effectively transforms a long-dated loan in to a short-term borrowing. The balloon payment is the original amount of the loan, minus the amount that is amortised. In a balloon mortgage therefore the actual maturity of the bonds is below that of the stated maturity.

A *graduated payment mortgage* (GPM) is aimed at lower-earning borrowers, as the mortgage payments for a fixed initial period, say the first five years, are set at lower the level applicable for a level-paying mortgage with an identical interest rate. The later mortgage payments are higher as a result. Hence a GPM mortgage will have a fixed term and a mortgage rate, but the offer letter will also contain details on the number of years over which the monthly mortgage payments will increase and the point at which level payments will take over. There will also be information on the annual increase in the mortgage payments. As the initial payments in a GPM are below the market rate, there will be little or no repayment of principal at this time. This means that the outstanding balance may actually increase during the early stages, a process known as *negative amortisation*. The higher payments in the remainder of the mortgage term are designed to pay off the entire balance in maturity. The opposite to the GPM is the *growing equity mortgage* or GEM. This mortgage charges fixed-rate interest but the payments increase over time; this means that a greater proportion of the principal is paid off over time, so that the mortgage itself is repaid in a shorter time than the level-pay mortgage.

In the UK market it is more common to encounter hybrid mortgages, which charge a combination of fixed-rate and variable-rate interest. For example the rate may be fixed for the first five years, after which it will vary with changes in the lender's base rate. Such a mortgage is known as *fixed/adjustable hybrid mortgage*.

18.1.3 *Mortgage risk*

Although mortgage contracts are typically long-term loan contracts, running usually for 20 to 30 years or even longer, there is no limitation on the amount of the principal that may be repaid at any one time. In the US market there is no penalty for repaying the mortgage ahead of its term, known as a mortgage prepayment. In the UK some lenders impose a penalty if a mortgage is prepaid early, although this is more common for contracts that have been offered at special terms, such as a discounted loan rate for the start of the mortgage's life. The penalty is often set as extra interest, for example six months' worth of mortgage payments at the time when the contract is paid off. As a borrower is free to prepay a mortgage at a time of their choosing, the lender is not certain of the cash flows that will be paid after the contract is taken out. This is known as *prepayment risk*.

A borrower may pay off the principal ahead of the final termination date for a number of reasons. The most common reason is when the property on which the mortgage is secured is subsequently sold by the borrower; this results in the entire mortgage being paid off at once. The average life of a mortgage in the UK market is eight years, and mortgages are most frequently prepaid because the property has been sold.[3] Other actions that result

3 Source: Halifax plc.

in the prepayment of a mortgage are when a property is repossessed after the borrower has fallen into default, if there is a change in interest rates making it attractive to refinance the mortgage (usually with another lender), or if the property is destroyed due to accident or natural disaster.

An investor acquiring a pool of mortgages from a lender will be concerned at the level of prepayment risk, which is usually measured by projecting the level of expected future payments using a financial model. Although it would not be possible to evaluate meaningfully the potential of an individual mortgage to be paid off early, it is tenable to conduct such analysis for a large number of loans pooled together. A similar activity is performed by actuaries when they assess the future liability of an insurance provider who has written personal pension contracts. Essentially the level of prepayment risk for a pool of loans is lower than that of an individual mortgage. Prepayment risk has the same type of impact on a mortgage pool's performance and valuation as a call feature does on a callable bond. This is understandable because a mortgage is essentially a callable contract, with the 'call' at the option of the borrower of funds.

The other significant risk of a mortgage book is the risk that the borrower will fall into arrears, or be unable to repay the loan on maturity (in the UK). This is known as *default risk*. Lenders take steps to minimise the level of default risk by assessing the credit quality of each borrower, as well as the quality of the property itself. A study has also found that the higher the deposit paid by the borrower, the lower the level of default.[4] Therefore lenders prefer to advance funds against a borrower's *equity* that is deemed sufficient to protect against falls in the value of the property. In the UK the typical deposit required is 25%, although certain lenders will advance funds against smaller deposits such as 10% or 5%.

18.1.4 *Securities*

Mortgage-backed securities are bonds created from a pool of mortgages. They are formed from mortgages that are for residential or commercial property or a mixture of both. Bonds created from commercial mortgages are known as *commercial mortgage-backed securities*. There are a range of different securities in the market, known in the US as *mortgage pass-through securities*. There also exist two related securities known as *collateralised mortgage securities* and *stripped mortgage-backed securities*. Bonds that are created from mortgage pools that have been purchased by government agencies are known as *agency mortgage-backed securities*, and are regarded as risk-free in the same way as Treasury securities.

A mortgage-backed bond is created by an entity out of its mortgage book or a book that it has purchased from the original lender (there is very often no connection between a mortgage-backed security and the firm that made the original loans). The mortgage book will have a total nominal value comprised of the total value of all the individual loans. The loans will generate cash flows, consisting of the interest and principal payments, and any prepayments. The regular cash flows are received on the same day each month, so the pool resembles a bond instrument. Therefore bonds may be issued against the mortgage pool. Example 18.2 is a simple illustration of a type of mortgage-backed bond known as a *mortgage pass-through security* in the US market.

---

[4] Brown, S., *et al.*, *Analysis of Mortgage Servicing Portfolios*, Financial Strategies Group, Prudential-Bache Capital Funding, 1990.

Example 18.2: Mortgage pass-through security

An investor purchases a book consisting of 5000 individual mortgages, with a total repayable value of $500,000,000. The loans are used as collateral against the issue of a new bond, and the cash flows payable on the bond are the cash flows that are received from the mortgages. The issuer sells 1000 bonds, with a face value of $500,000. Each bond is therefore entitled to 1/1000 or 0.02% of the cash flows received from the mortgages.

The prepayment risk associated with the original mortgages is unchanged, but any investor can now purchase a bond with a much lower value than the mortgage pool but with the same level of prepayment risk, which is lower than the risk of an individual loan. This would have been possible if an investor was buying all 100 mortgages, but by buying a bond that represents the pool of mortgages, a smaller cash value is needed to achieve the same performance. The bonds will also be more liquid than the loans, and the investor will be able to realise her investment ahead of the maturity date if she wishes. For these reasons the bonds will trade at higher prices than would an individual loan. A mortgage pass-through security therefore is a way for mortgage lenders to realise additional value from their loan book, and if it is sold to another investor (who issues the bonds), the loans will be taken off the original lender's balance sheet, thus freeing up lending lines for other activities.

A *collateralised mortgage obligation* (CMO) differs from a pass-through security in that the cash flows from the mortgage pool are distributed on a prioritised basis, based on the class of security held by the investor. In Example 18.2 this might mean that three different securities are formed, with a total nominal value of $100 million each entitled to a pro-rata amount of the interest payments but with different priorities for the repayment of principal. For instance, $60 million of the issue might consist of a bond known as 'class A' which may be entitled to receipt of all the principal repayment cash flows, after which the next class of bonds is entitled to all the repayment cash flow; this bond would be 'class B' bonds, of which say, $25 million was created, and so on. If 300 class A bonds are created, they would have a nominal value of $200,000 and each would receive 0.33% of the total cash flows received by the class A bonds. Note that all classes of bonds receive an equal share of the interest payments; it is the principal repayment cash flows received that differ. What is the main effect of this security structure? The most significant factor is that, in our illustration, the class A bonds will be repaid earlier than any other class of bond that is formed from the securitisation. It therefore has the shortest maturity. The last class of bonds will have the longest maturity. There is still a level of uncertainty associated with the maturity of each bond, but this is less than the uncertainty associated with a pass-through security.

Let us consider another type of mortgage bond, the *stripped mortgage-backed security*. As its name suggests, this is created by separating the interest and principal payments into individual distinct cash flows. This allows an issuer to create two very interesting securities, the IO-bond and the PO-bond. In a stripped mortgage-backed bond the interest and principal are divided into two classes, and two bonds are issued that are each entitled to receive one class of cash flow only. The bond class that receives the interest payment cash flows is known as an *interest-only* or IO class, while the bond receiving the principal repayments is known as a *principal only* or PO class. The PO bond is similar to a zero-coupon bond in that it is issued at a discount to par value. The return achieved by a PO-bond holder is a function of the rapidity at which prepayments are made; if prepayments are received in a relatively short time the investor will realise a higher return. This would be akin to the buyer of a zero-coupon bond receiving the maturity payment ahead of the redemption date, and the highest possible return that a PO-bond holder could receive would occur if all the mortgages were prepaid the instant after the PO bond was bought! A low return will be achieved if all the mortgages are held until maturity, so that there are no prepayments. Stripped mortgage-backed bonds present potentially less advantage to an issuer compared to a pass-through security or a CMO, however they are liquid instruments and are often traded to hedge a conventional mortgage bond book.

The price of a PO-bond fluctuates as mortgage interest rates change. As we noted earlier in the US market the majority of mortgages are fixed-rate loans, so that if mortgage rates fall below the coupon rate on the bond, the holder will expect the volume of prepayments to increase as individuals refinance loans in order to gain from lower borrowing rates. This will result in a faster stream of payments to the PO-bond holder as cash flows are received earlier than expected. The price of the PO rises to reflect this, and also because cash flows in the mortgage will now be discounted at a lower rate. The opposite happens when mortgage rates rise and the rate of prepayment is expected to fall, which causes a PO bond to fall in price. An IO bond is essentially a stream of cash flows and has no par value. The cash flows represent interest on the mortgage principal outstanding, therefore a higher rate of prepayment leads to a fall in the IO price. This is because the cash flows cease once the principal is redeemed. The risk for the IO-bond holder is that prepayments occur so quickly that interest payments cease before the investor has recovered the amount originally paid for the IO-bond. The price of an IO is also a function of mortgage rates in the market, but exhibits more peculiar responses. If rates fall below the bond coupon, again the rate of prepayment is expected to increase. This would cause the cash flows for the IO to decline, as mortgages were paid off more quickly. This would cause the price of the IO to fall as well, even though the cash flows themselves would be discounted at a lower interest rate. If mortgage rates rise, the outlook for future cash flows will improve as the prepayment rate falls, however there is also a higher discounting rate for the cash flows themselves, so the price of an IO may move in either direction. Thus IO bonds exhibit a curious characteristic for a bond instrument, in that their price moves in the same direction as market rates. Both versions of the stripped mortgage bond are interesting instruments, and they have high volatilities during times of market rate changes. Note that PO and IO bonds could be created from the hypothetical mortgage pool described above; therefore the combined modified duration of both instruments must equal the modified duration of the original pass-through security.

The securities described so far are essentially plain vanilla mortgage-backed bonds. Currently, there are more complicated instruments trading in the market.

18.2 Cash flow patterns

We stated that the exact term of a mortgage-backed bond cannot be stated with accuracy at the time of issue, because of the uncertain frequency of mortgage prepayments. This uncertainty means that it is not possible to analyse the bonds using the conventional methods used for fixed coupon bonds. The most common approach used by the market is to assume a fixed prepayment rate at the time of issue and use this to project the cash flows, and hence the life span, of the bond. The choice of prepayment selected therefore is significant, although it is recognised also that prepayment rates are not stable and will fluctuate with changes in mortgage rates and the economic cycle. In this section we consider some of the approaches used in evaluating the prepayment pattern of a mortgage-backed bond.

18.2.1 *Prepayment analysis*

Some market analysts assume a fixed life for a mortgage pass-through bond based on the average life of a mortgage. Traditionally a '12-year prepaid life' has been used to evaluate the securities, as market data suggested that the average mortgage has been paid off after the twelfth year. This is not generally favoured because it does not take into account the effect of mortgage rates and other factors. A more common approach is to use a *constant prepayment rate* (CPR). This measure is based on the expected number of mortgages in a pool that will be prepaid in a selected period, and is an annualised figure. The measure for the monthly level of prepayment is known as the *constant monthly repayment*, and measures the expected amount of the outstanding balance, minus the scheduled principal, that will be prepaid in each month. Another name for the constant monthly repayment is the *single monthly mortality rate* or SMM. In Fabozzi (1997) the SMM is given by (18.7) and is an expected value for the percentage of the remaining mortgage balance that will be prepaid in that month.

$$SMM = 1 - (1 - CPR)^{1/12}. \tag{18.7}$$

Example 18.3: Constant prepayment rate

The constant prepayment rate for a pool of mortgages is 2% each month. The outstanding principal balance at the start of the month is £72,200, while the scheduled principal payment is £223. This means that 2% of £71,977, or £1,439 will be prepaid in that month. To approximate the amount of principal prepayment, the constant monthly prepayment is multiplied by the outstanding balance.

In the US market the convention is to use the prepayment standard developed by the Public Securities Association (PSA), which is the domestic bond market trade association.[5] The PSA benchmark, known as 100% PSA, assumes a steadily increasing constant prepayment rate each month until the 30th month, when a constant rate of 6% is assumed. The starting prepayment rate is 0.2%, increasing at 0.2% each month until the rate levels off at 6%.

For the 100% PSA benchmark we may set, if t is the number of months from the start of the mortgage, that if $t < 30$, the CPR $= 6\% \cdot t/30$ while if $t > 30$, then CPR is equal to 6%.

This benchmark can be altered if required to suit changing market conditions, so for example the 200% PSA has a starting prepayment rate and an increase that is double the 100% PSA model, so the initial rate is 0.4%, increasing by 0.4% each month until it reaches

[5] Since renamed the Bond Market Association.

12% in the 30th month, at which point the rate remains constant. The 50% PSA has a starting (and increases by a) rate of 0.1%, remaining constant after it reaches 3%.

The prepayment level of a mortgage pool will have an impact on its cash flows. As we saw in Example 18.1 if the amount of prepayment is nil, the cash flows will remain constant during the life of the mortgage. In a fixed-rate mortgage the proportion of principal and interest payment will change each month as more and more of the mortgage amortises. That is, as the principal amount falls each month, the amount of interest decreases. If we assume that a pass-through security has been issued today, so that its coupon reflects the current market level, the payment pattern will resemble the bar chart shown at Figure 18.1 below.

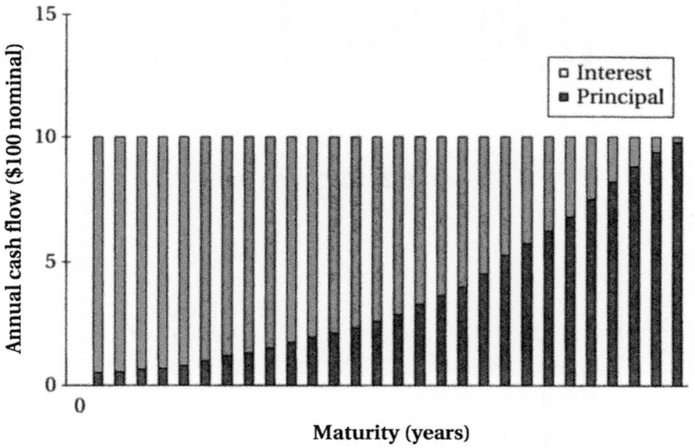

Figure 18.1: Mortgage pass-through security with 0% constant prepayment rate.

When there is an element of prepayment in a mortgage pool, for example as in the 100% PSA or 200% PSA model, the amount of principal payment will increase during the early years of the mortgages and then becomes more steady, before declining for the remainder of the term; this is because the principal balance has declined to such an extent that the scheduled principal payments become less significant. The two examples are shown at Figures 18.2 and 18.3 below.

The prepayment volatility of a mortgage-backed bond will vary according to the interest rate of the underlying mortgages. It has been observed that where the mortgages have interest rates of between 100 and 300 basis points above current mortgage rates, the prepayment volatility is the highest. At the bottom of the range, any fall in interest rates often leads to a sudden increase in refinancing of mortgages, while at the top of the range, an increase in rates will lead to a decrease in the prepayment rate.

The actual cash flow of a mortgage pass-through of course is dependent on the cash flow patterns of the mortgages in the pool. The relationships described in Example 18.1 can be used to derive further expressions to construct a cash flow schedule for a pass-through security, using a constant or adjustable assumed prepayment rate. Fabozzi (1997) describes the projected monthly mortgage payment for a level-paying fixed rate mortgage in any month as

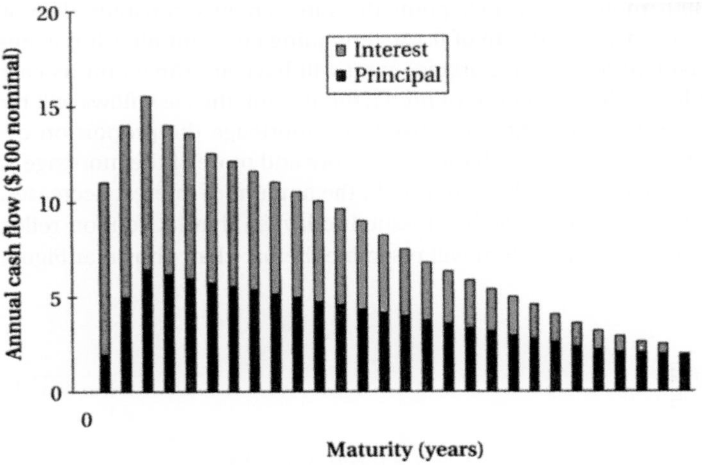

Figure 18.2: 100% PSA model.

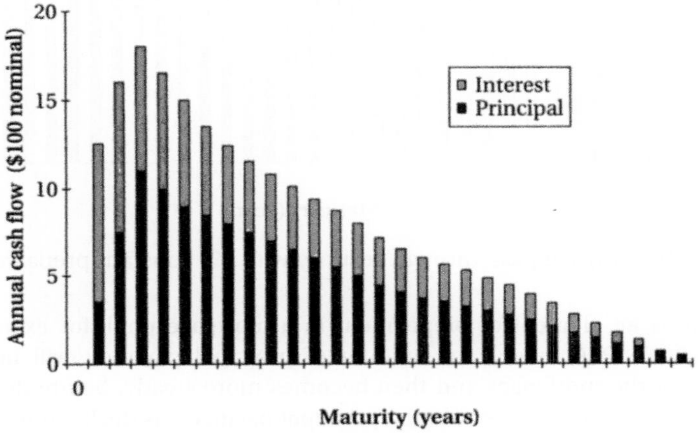

Figure 18.3: 200% PSA model.

$$\bar{I}_t = \overline{M}_{mt-1} \frac{r(1+r)^{n-t+1}}{(1+r)^{n-t+1} - 1} \tag{18.8}$$

where

$\bar{I}_t$ is the projected monthly mortgage payment for month t

$\overline{M}_{mt-1}$ is the projected mortgage balance at the end of month t assuming that prepayments have occurred in the past.

To calculate the interest proportion of the projected monthly mortgage payment we use (18.9) where i_t is the projected monthly interest payment for month t.

$$\bar{i}_t = M_{mt-1} \cdot i. \tag{18.9}$$

Expression (18.9) states that the projected monthly interest payment can be obtained by multiplying the mortgage balance at the end of the previous month by the monthly interest rate. In the same way the expression for calculating the projected monthly scheduled principal payment for any month is given by (18.10), where $\overline{p}_t$ is the projected scheduled principal payment for the month t.

$$\overline{p}_t = \overline{I}_t - \overline{i}_t. \tag{18.10}$$

The projected monthly principal prepayment, which is an expected rate only and not a model forecast, is given by (18.11):

$$\overline{pp}_t = SMM_t(\overline{M}_{mt-1} - \overline{p}_t) \tag{18.11}$$

where $\overline{pp}_t$ is the projected monthly principal prepayment for month t.

The above relationships enable us to calculate values for:

- the projected monthly interest payment;
- the projected monthly scheduled principal payment;
- and the projected monthly principal prepayment.

These values may be used to calculate the total cash flow in any month that a holder of a mortgage-backed bond receives which is given by (18.12) below, where *cft* is the cash flow receipt in month t.

$$cf_t = \overline{i}_t + \overline{p}_t + \overline{pp}_t. \tag{18.12}$$

The practice of using a prepayment rate is a market convention that enables analysts to evaluate mortgage-backed bonds. The original PSA prepayment rates were arbitrarily selected, based on the observation that prepayment rates tended to stabilise after the first 30 months of the life of a mortgage. A linear increase in the prepayment rate is also assumed. However this is a market convention only, adopted by the market as a standard benchmark. The levels do not reflect seasonal variations in prepayment patterns, or the different behaviour patterns of different types of mortgages.

The PSA benchmarks can be (and are) applied to default assumptions to produce a default benchmark. This is used for non-agency mortgage-backed bonds only, as agency securities are guaranteed by the one of the three government or government-sponsored agencies. Accordingly the PSA *standard default assumption* (SDA) benchmark is used to assess the potential default rate for a mortgage pool. For example the standard benchmark, 100SDA assumes that the default rate in the first month is 0.02% and increases in a linear fashion by 0.02% each month until the 30th month, at which point the default rate remains at 0.60%. In month 60 the default rate begins to fall from 0.60% to 0.03% and continues to fall linearly until month 120. From that point the default rate remains constant at 0.03%. The other benchmarks have similar patterns.

18.2.2 *Prepayment models*

The PSA standard benchmark reviewed in the previous section uses an assumption of prepayment rates and can be used to calculate the prepayment proceeds of a mortgage. It is not, strictly speaking, a prepayment *model* because it cannot be used to estimate actual prepayments. A prepayment model on the other hand does attempt to predict the prepayment cash flows of a mortgage pool, by modelling the statistical relationships between the various factors that have an impact on the level of prepayment. These factors are the current mortgage rate, the characteristics of the mortgages in the pool, seasonal factors and the general business cycle. Let us consider them in turn.

The prevailing mortgage interest rate is probably the most important factor in the level of prepayment. The level of the current mortgage rate and its spread above or below the original contract rate will influence the decision to refinance a mortgage; if the rate is materially below the original rate, the borrower will prepay the mortgage. As the mortgage rate at any time reflects the general bank base rate, the level of market interest rates has the greatest effect on mortgage prepayment levels. The current mortgage rate also has an effect on housing prices, since if mortgages are seen as 'cheap' the general perception will be that now is the right time to purchase: this affects housing market turnover. The pattern followed by mortgage rates since the original loan also has an impact, a phenomenon known as *refinancing burnout.*

Observation of the mortgage market has suggested that housing market and mortgage activity follows a strong seasonal pattern. The strongest period of activity is during the spring and summer, while the market is at its quietest in the winter. The various factors may be used to derive an expression that can be used to calculate expected prepayment levels. For example a US investment bank uses the following model to calculate expected prepayments:[6]

$$\text{Monthly prepayment rate} = (\textit{Refinancing incentive}) \times (\textit{Season multiplier}) \times (\textit{Month multiplier}) \times (\textit{Burnout}).$$

18.3 Evaluation and analysis of mortgage-backed bonds

18.3.1 *Term to maturity*

The term to maturity cannot be given for certain for a mortgage pass-through security, since the cash flows and prepayment patterns cannot be predicted. To evaluate such a bond therefore it is necessary to estimate the term for the bond, and use this measure for any analysis. The maturity measure for any bond is important, as without it it is not possible to assess over what period of time a return is being generated; also, it will not be possible to compare the asset to any other bond. The term to maturity of a bond also gives an indication of its sensitivity to changes in market interest rates. If comparisons with other securities such as government bonds are made, we cannot use the stated maturity of the mortgage-backed bond because prepayments will reduce this figure. The convention in the market is to use other estimated values, which are *average life* and the more traditional duration measure.

The *average life* of a mortgage-pass through security is the weighted-average time to return of a unit of principal payment, made up of projected scheduled principal payments and principal prepayments. It is also known as the *weighted-average life*. It is given by (18.13):

$$\text{Average life} = \frac{1}{12}\sum_{t=1}^{n}\frac{t(\text{Principal received at } t)}{\text{Total principal received}} \tag{18.13}$$

where n is the number of months remaining. The time from the term measured by the average life to the final scheduled principal payment is the bond's *tail.*

6 Fabozzi (1997).

To calculate duration (or Macaulay's duration) for a bond we require the weighted present values of all its cash flows. To apply this for a mortgage-backed bond therefore it is necessary to project the bond's cash flows, using an assumed prepayment rate. The projected cash flows, together with the bond price and the periodic interest rate may then be used to arrive at a duration value. The periodic interest rate is derived from the yield. This calculation for a mortgage-backed bond produces a periodic duration figure, which must be divided by 12 to arrive at a duration value in years (or by 4 in the case of a quarterly-paying bond).

Example 18.4: Macaulay duration

- A 25-year mortgage security with a mortgage rate of 8.49% and monthly coupon is quoted at a price of \$98.50, a bond-equivalent yield of 9.127%. To calculate the Macaulay duration we require the present value of the expected cash flows using the interest rate that will make this present value, assuming a constant prepayment rate, equate the price of 98.50. Using the expression below,

$$rm = 2((1 + r)^n - 1)$$

where rm is 9.127% and $n = 5$, this is shown to be 9.018%.

For the bond above this present value is 6,120.79. Therefore the mortgage security Macaulay duration is given by:

$$D_m = \frac{6,120.79}{98.50} = 6214.$$

Therefore the bond-equivalent Macaulay duration in years is given by $D = \frac{6214}{12} = 5.178$.

18.3.2 *Calculating yield and price: static cash flow model*

There are a number of ways that the yield on a mortgage-backed bond can be calculated. One of the most common methods employs the *static cash flow model*. This assumes a single prepayment rate to estimate the cash flows for the bond, and does not take into account how changes in market conditions might impact the prepayment pattern.

The conventional yield measure for a bond is the discount rate at which the sum of the present values of all the bond's expected cash flows will be equal to the price of the bond. The convention is usually to compute the yield from the *clean* price, that is excluding any accrued interest. This yield measure is known as the bond's *redemption yield* or *yield-to-maturity*. However for mortgage-backed bonds it is known as a *cash flow yield* or *mortgage yield*. The cash flow for a mortgage-backed bond is not known with certainty, due to the effect of prepayments, and so must be derived using an assumed prepayment rate. Once the projected cash flows have been calculated, it is possible to calculate the cash flow yield. The formula is given by (18.14):

$$P = \sum_{n=1}^{N} \frac{C(t)}{(1 + ri/1200)^{t-1}}. \tag{18.14}$$

Note however that a yield so computed will be for a bond with monthly coupon payments,[7] so it is necessary to convert the yield to an annualised equivalent before any comparisons are made with conventional bond yields. In the US and UK markets, the bond-equivalent yield is calculated for mortgage-backed bonds and measured against the relevant government bond yield, which (in both cases) is a semi-annual yield. Although it is reasonably accurate to simply double the yield of a semi-annual coupon bond to arrive at the annualised equivalent,[8] to obtain the bond equivalent yield for a monthly paying mortgage-backed bond we use (18.15):

$$rm = 2((1 + ri_M)^6 - 1) \tag{18.15}$$

where rm is the bond equivalent yield and ri_M is the interest rate that will equate the present value of the projected monthly cash flows for the mortgage-backed bond to its current price. The equivalent semi-annual yield is given by (18.16):

$$rm_{s/a} = (1 + ri_M)^6 - 1. \tag{18.16}$$

The cash flow yield calculated for a mortgage-backed bond in this way is essentially the redemption yield, using an assumption to derive the cash flows. As such the measure suffers from the same drawbacks as it does when used to measure the return of a plain vanilla bond, which are that the calculation assumes a uniform reinvestment rate for all the bond's cash flows and that the bond will be held to maturity. The same weakness will apply to the cash flow yield measure for a mortgage-backed bond. In fact the potential inaccuracy of the redemption yield measure is even greater with a mortgage-backed bond because the frequency of interest payments is higher, which makes the reinvestment risk greater. The final yield that is returned by a mortgage-backed bond will depend on the performance of the mortgages in the pool, specifically the prepayment pattern.

Given the nature of a mortgage-backed bond's cash flows, the exact yield cannot be calculated, however it is common for market practitioners to use the cash flow yield measure and compare this to the redemption yield of the equivalent government bond. The usual convention is to quote the spread over the government bond as the main measure of value. When measuring the spread, the mortgage-backed bond is compared to the government security that has a similar duration, or a term to maturity similar to its average life.

It is possible to calculate the price of a mortgage-backed bond once its yield is known (or vice-versa). As with a plain vanilla bond, the price is the sum of the present values of all the projected cash flows. It is necessary to convert the bond-equivalent yield to a monthly yield, which is then used to calculate the present value of each cash flow. The cash flows of IO and PO bonds are dependent on the cash flows of the underlying pass-through security, which is itself dependent on the cash flows of the underlying mortgage pool. Again, to calculate the price of an IO or PO bond, a prepayment rate must be assumed. This enables us to determine the projected level of the monthly cash flows of the IO and the principal payments

---

[7] The majority of mortgage-backed bonds pay interest on a monthly basis, since individual mortgages usually do as well; certain mortgage-backed bonds pay on a quarterly basis.

[8] See Chapter 1 for the formulae used to convert yields from one convention basis to another.

of the PO. The price of an IO is the present value of the projected interest payments, while the price of the PO is the present value of the projected principal payments, comprising the scheduled principal payments and the projected principal prepayments.

18.3.3 *Bond price and option-adjusted spread*

The concept of option-adjusted spread (OAS) and its use in the analysis and valuation of bonds with embedded options was first considered in Chapter 6, when OAS was discussed in the context of callable bonds. The behaviour of mortgage securities often resembles that of callable bonds, because effectively there is a call feature attached to them, in the shape of the prepayment option of the underlying mortgage holders. This option feature is the principal reason why it is necessary to use average life as the term to maturity for a mortgage security. It is frequently the case that the optionality of a mortgage-backed bond, and the volatility of its yield, have a negative impact on the bond holders. This is for two reasons: the actual yield realised during the holding period has a high probability of being lower than the anticipated yield, which was calculated on the basis of an assumed prepayment level, and mortgages are frequently prepaid at the time when the bondholder will suffer the most; that is, prepayments occur most often when rates have fallen, leaving the bondholder to reinvest repaid principal at a lower market interest rate.

These features combined represent the biggest risk to an investor of holding a mortgage security, and market analysts attempt to measure and quantify this risk. This is usually done using a form of OAS analysis. Under this approach the value of the mortgagor's prepayment option is calculated in terms of a basis point penalty that must be subtracted from the expected yield spread on the bond. This basis point value is calculated using a binomial model or a simulation model to generate a range of future interest rate paths, only some of which will cause a mortgagor to prepay her mortgage. The interest rate paths that would result in a prepayment are evaluated for their impact on the mortgage bond's expected yield spread over a government bond.[9] As OAS analysis takes account of the option feature of a mortgage-backed bond, it will be less affected by a yield change than the bond's yield spread. Assuming a flat yield curve environment, the relationship between the OAS and the yield spread is given by:

$$\text{OAS} = \text{Yield spread} - \text{Cost of option feature.}$$

This relationship can be observed occasionally when yield spreads on current coupon mortgages widen during upward moves in the market. As interest rates fall, the cost of the option feature on a current coupon mortgage will rise, as the possibility of prepayment increases. Put another way, the option feature begins to approach being in-the-money. To adjust for the increased value of the option traders will price in higher spreads on the bond, which will result in the OAS remaining more or less unchanged.

---

9 The yield spread from OAS analysis is based on the discounted value of the expected cash flow using the government bond-derived forward rate. The yield spread of the cash flow yield to the government bond is based on yields-to-maturity. For this reason, the two spreads are not strictly comparable. The OAS spread is added to the entire yield curve, whereas a yield spread is a spread over a single point on the government bond yield curve.

18.3.4 *Effective duration and convexity*

The modified duration of a bond measures its price sensitivity to a change in yield; the calculation is effectively a snapshot of one point in time. It also assumes that there is no change in expected cash flows as a result of the change in market interest rates. Therefore it is an inappropriate interest rate risk for a mortgage-backed bond, whose cash flows would be expected to change after a change in rates, due to the prepayment effect. Hence mortgage-backed bonds react differently to interest rate changes compared to conventional bonds, because when rates fall, the level of prepayments is expected to rise (and vice-versa). Therefore when interest rates fall, the duration of the bond may also fall, which is opposite to the behaviour of a conventional bond. This feature is known as *negative convexity* and is similar to the effect displayed by a callable bond. The prices of both these types of security react to interest rate changes differently compared to the price of conventional bonds.

For this reason the more accurate measure of interest rate sensitivity to use is *effective duration* described by Fabozzi (1997). Effective duration is the approximate duration of a bond as given by (18.17):

$$D_{app} = \frac{P_- - P_+}{2P_0(\Delta rm)} \tag{18.17}$$

where

P_0	is the initial price of the bond
P_-	is the estimated price of the bond if the yield decreases by Δrm
P_+	is the estimated price of the bond if the yield increases by Δrm
Δrm	is the change in the yield of the bond.

The approximate duration is the effective duration of a bond when the two values P_- and P_+ are obtained from a valuation model that incorporates the effect of a change in the expected cash flows (from prepayment effects) when there is a change in interest rates. The values are obtained from a pricing model such as the static cash flow model, binomial model or simulation model. The calculation of effective duration uses higher and lower prices that are dependent on the prepayment rate that is assumed. Generally analysts will assume a higher prepayment rate when the interest rate is at the lower level of the two.

Figure 18.4 illustrates the difference between modified duration and effective duration for a range of agency mortgage pass-through securities, where the effective duration for each bond is calculated using a 20 basis point change in rates. This indicates that the modified duration measure effectively overestimates the price sensitivity of lower coupon bonds. This factor is significant when hedging a mortgage-backed bond position, because using the modified duration figure to calculate the nominal value of the hedging instrument will not prove effective for anything other than very small changes in yield.

The formula to calculate approximate convexity (or *effective convexity*) is given below as (18.18); again if the values used in the formula allow for the cash flow to change, the convexity value may be taken to be the effective convexity. The effective convexity value of a mortgage pass-through security is invariably negative.

$$CV_{app} = \frac{P_+ + P_- - 2P_0}{P_0(\Delta rm)^2}. \tag{18.18}$$

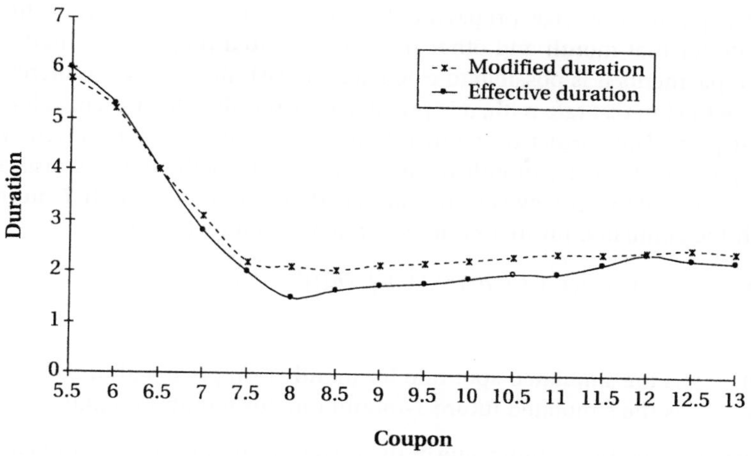

Figure 18.4: Modified duration and effective duration for agency mortgage-backed bonds.

18.3.5 *Simulation modelling*

The earlier section alluded to the main shortcomings of the static cash flow model when used for valuation and analysis, and usually to determine the spread between the cash flow yield of the mortgage-backed bond and the redemption yield of the equivalent government bond. In short the main weaknesses of this model are that:

- neither yield measure takes sufficient account of the real government bond term structure (the spot yield curve);
- the cash flow yield ignores the cash flow effects of a change in yields.

To overcome these drawbacks certain analysts use simulation methodology to value mortgage-backed bonds. Put simply this involves generating a set of cash flows based on simulated future mortgage refinancing rates, which themselves imply simulated prepayment rates. The simulation model used is usually a Monte Carlo simulation. Although running a simulation in order to generate future prices is straightforward enough to describe, it is in fact a complex procedure, and one that requires a considerable amount of computing power. In this section we describe only the concept behind the simulation model.

To run a simulation to generate future interest-rates and hence future prices, a model requires the current government bond zero-coupon yield curve, and an assumption of interest rate volatility. The current zero-coupon curve, also known as the spot curve or the term structure of interest rates, is the starting point of the simulation, while the interest rate volatilities are used to generate a range of values for future interest rates. The average of this range of future spot rates for any maturity is equal to the current spot rate for that maturity. The simulation is run by generating scenarios of future interest rate paths. For each future month, a monthly interest rate and a mortgage rate are generated; this mortgage rate is in effect the refinancing rate for that month. The monthly mortgage rates are used to discount the projected cash flows in the scenario, and as a refinancing rate it is used to calculate the cash flow, as it represents the opportunity cost the mortgage borrower is facing at that point. Mortgage prepayments are determined by inputting the projected mortgage rate for that month and other parameters into a prepayment model. Using the projected prepayments it is possible to calculate the cash flow along an interest-rate path. Once we have the interest rate path, it is possible to determine the present value of the cash flow on that path. The correct discount rate to use to calculate the present value is the simulated spot rate for each month on the interest-rate path (there is also a spread to consider). The relationship between the simulated spot rate for month T on interest-rate path n, with the simulated future one-month rate is given by (18.19):

$$s_T(n) = ((1 + f_1(n))(1 + f_2((n)) \cdots (1 + f_T(n)))^{1/T} - 1 \tag{18.19}$$

where

$sT\ (n)$ is the simulated spot rate for month T on price path n
$f_1\ (n)$ is the simulated future 1-month rate for month I on path n.

Hence we may set the present value of the cash flow for month T on interest-rate path n discounted at the simulated spot rate for month T, together with an amount of spread as given by (18.20):

$$PV(C_T(n)) = \frac{C_T(n)}{(1 + s_T(n) + K)^{1/T}} \tag{18.20}$$

where

$PV(C_T(n))$ is the present value of the cash flow for month T on path n
$C_T\ (n)$ is the cash flow for month T on path n
K is the spread.

The present value of path n is then the sum of all the present values of the cash flows for each month along path n, shown as (18.21):

$$PV(\text{path}(n)) = \sum_{t=1}^{T} PV(C_T(n)). \tag{18.21}$$

We are now in a position to calculate a market fair value or theoretical value for the bond. If a particular interest-rate path n is actually realised, the present value of that path, determined using (18.21) is the theoretical price of the mortgage-backed bond for that path. Therefore the theoretical price of the bond is the average of all the theoretical values for all the interest rate paths, shown as (18.22). This theoretical value is then compared to the actual observed price to determine if the bond is trading cheap or dear in the market.

$$P_{theo} = \frac{PV(\text{path}(1)) + PV(\text{path}(2)) + \cdots + PV(\text{path}(N))}{N} \tag{18.22}$$

where N is the number of interest-rate paths.

18.3.6 *Total return*

To assess the value of a mortgage-backed bond over a given investment horizon it is necessary to measure the return generated during the holding period from the bond's cash flows. This is done using what is known as the *total return* framework. The cash flows from a mortgage-backed bond are comprised of (1) the projected cash flows of the bond (which are the projected interest payments and principal repayments and prepayments), (2) the interest earned on the reinvestment of all the payments, and (3) the projected price of the bond at the end of the holding period. The first sum can be estimated using an assumed prepayment rate during the period the bond is held, while the second cash flow requires an assumed reinvestment rate. To obtain (3) the bondholder must assume first, what the bond equivalent yield of the mortgage bond will be at the end of the holding period, and second what prepayment rate the market will assume at this point. The second rate is a function of the projected yield at the time. The total return during the time the bond is held, on a monthly basis, is then given by (18.23),

$$\left(\frac{\text{Total future cash flow amount}}{P_m}\right)^{1/n} - 1 \qquad (18.23)$$

which can be converted to an annualised bond-equivalent yield using (18.15) or (18.16).

Note that the return calculated using (18.23) is based on a range of assumptions, which render it almost academic. The best approach to use is to calculate a yield for a range of different assumptions, which then give some idea of the likely yield that may be generated over the holding period, in the form of a range of yields (that is, an upper and lower limit).

Example 18.5: Mortgage-backed bond issue

- **Bradford & Bingley Building Society £1 billion three-tranche MBS due 2031**

Bradford & Bingley is a UK building society that plans to list on the London Stock Exchange (and convert to a bank) during 2000/2001. In August 2000 it issued a mortgage-backed security that was underwritten by UBS Warburg, via Aire Valley Finance (No. 2), a special purpose vehicle.

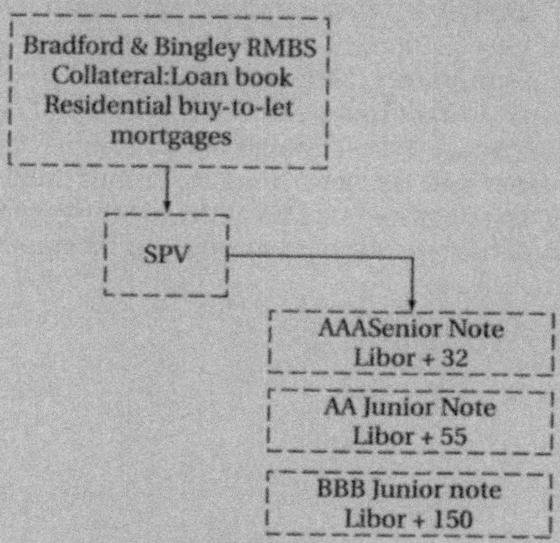

Figure 18.5

Loan portfolio

The underlying collateral consists of approximately 14,000 residential mortgages with an average loan balance of £74,000. Around two-thirds of the mortgages are on properties located in London and the south-east of England. An interesting feature of the mortgages is that they are *buy-to-let* loans; the issuer had previously undertaken a securitisation of its owner-occupier mortgage portfolio. These buy-to-let mortgages allow overpayment of the principal without penalty, consequently early prepayment is more likely with this type of collateral.

Bond structure

The issue is callable, with the structure composed of the following notes:

- £892.5 million senior note with AAA-rating, offered at a yield of three-month Libor plus 32 bps;
- £57.5 million junior note with AA-rating, offered at three-month Libor plus 55 bps;
- £50 million junior note with BBB-rating, offered at Libor plus 150 bps.

Although the issue has a legal maturity to 2031, it is callable and the senior note has a feature that raises its coupon to Libor plus 80 bps if it is not called after September 2008. This makes it likely that the bond will be called at that time.

Investor profile

The issue was placed with around 50 institutional investors, with other UK banks and large building societies and European banks being the largest buyers of the senior notes; fund managers were purchasers of the junior notes.

Selected bibliography and references

Fabozzi, F., Ramsey, C., Ramirez, F., *Collateralized Mortgage Obligations: Structures and Analysis*, FJF Associates 1994, Chapter 3

Fabozzi, F., *Fixed Income Mathematics*, McGraw-Hill, 1997

Fabozzi, F. (ed.), *Handbook of Structured Financial Products*, FJF Associates, 1998

Hayre, L., Mohebbi, C., 'Mortgage Pass-Through Securities', in Fabozzi, F. (ed.), *Advances and Innovations in the Bond and Mortgage Markets*, Probus Publishing, 1989, pp. 259–304

Pinkus, S., Chandoha, M., 'The Relative Price Volatility of Mortgage Securities', in Fabozzi, F. (ed), *Mortgage-Backed Securities: New Strategies, Applications and Research*, Probus Publishing, 1987

19 Mortgage-Backed Bonds II

The previous chapter introduced mortgage-backed securities and discussed the salient features of the main type of this bond, the mortgage pass-through security. Part of the discussion reviewed the use, in general terms, of a simulation model to value a mortgage security, given that the cash flow pattern of such a bond cannot be determined with certainty. This subject is investigated further in this chapter, where we review a valuation methodology based on the binomial model. However, the mathematical derivations are not included. The second part of the chapter considers the position and risk implications associated with running a portfolio of mortgage securities, and the issues concerned in tracking an index.

19.1 Basic concepts

Mortgage-backed bonds present some slight difficulty in their valuation, due to the uncertain nature of their cash flow stream, as well as the option feature that is attached to them. This option feature is the freedom of the underlying mortgage borrowers to repay their loan, known as *prepayment*, before the full term of the mortgage has run, at their option. This prepayment ability is in effect a call option on the underlying mortgage. Although an investor has no way of ascertaining when this option will be exercised, it is possible to come to an informed idea of when the most likely time of exercise will occur, based on an assessment of the current mortgage rate, the path interest rates have taken to now, the market's views on the likely direction of future interest rates, and the general economic climate at the time (and forecast). The market standard approach to pricing a mortgage security is to use the assessment of the above factors, in conjunction with another process we shall look at shortly, to arrive at a set of all the possible future interest rate paths that the bond may take, and the cash flows that will arise at each price path. The valuation must consider all the expected cash flows (both interest and principal payments) in addition to the level of prepayment and the possibility that this level might increase in the near future. The most common method used to generate the interest rate (hence price) paths and hence the valuations is to run a simulation on the likely path of future interest rates, to the point when the last scheduled principal payment for the underlying mortgages is due.

Overall the valuation process follows the three phases noted below:

- generate an 'arbitrage-free' interest rate scenario, derived from the current government spot yield curve or 'term structure of interest rates';
- generate expected cash flows for the mortgage security for each interest rate path or scenario that was calculated in the previous step; this requires a model that can

generate, usually using a constant prepayment rate, the prepayment pattern of mortgage borrowers, in conjunction with the general business climate around at the time;

- calculate the present value of the cash flows at each price path, using the model generated interest rates as the discount rates, and sum these to arrive at a net present value, which is the price of the bond, or to determine the option-adjusted spread premium over the government bond yield curve.

The projected cash flows generated in the last step up, which are arrived at under certain assumptions, can also be used to calculate the total return generated from a holding of the bond during a specified period. This is known as the *holding period return*.

19.2 Pricing and modelling techniques

19.2.1 *Valuation*

The fair value of a conventional fixed income bond is given as the present value of all its expected cash flows, discounted at the current market interest rate. The discount rate that is normally used is the government or *risk-free* rate. This has been formally modelled in several instances, for example the Cox–Ingersoll–Ross model amongst others.[1] The general approach is to use a path-dependent model, where a binomial or Monte Carlo simulation is used to generate the range of possible interest rates; the financial instrument is broken down into its cash flows which are valued using the discount rates at each point; the average of all of the present values is used to determine the theoretical value for the instrument.

The first step in pricing a security therefore requires a model of the term structure of interest rates. One approach is to use a binomial model[2]. The binomial lattice is reproduced here as Figure 19.1.

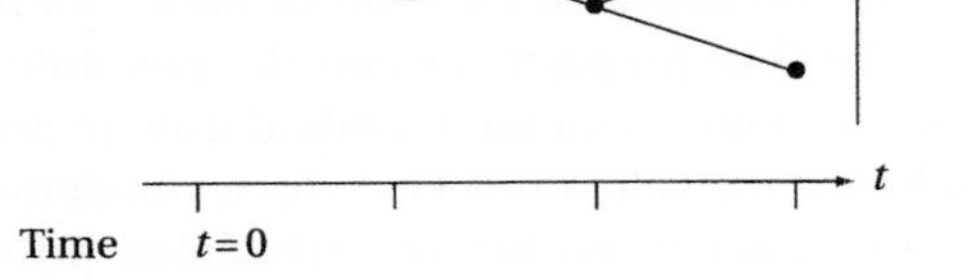

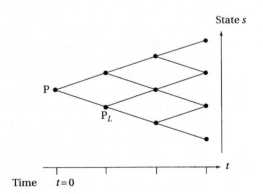

Figure 19.1: A binomial tree of path-dependent interest rates.

1 See Cox, J.C., Jr., Ingersoll, J.E., Ross, S.A., 'A Theory of the Term Structure of Interest Rates', *Econometrica*, March 1985, pp. 385–407.

2 See Black, F., Derman, E., Toy, W., 'A One-Factor Model of Interest Rates and its Application to Treasury Bond Options', *Financial Analysts Journal*, Jan–Feb 1990, pp. 33–39.

In a binomial tree there are discrete time periods, at each point of which the future possible short-term interest rate may move to only two possible points, either up or down. Using the tree it is possible to set all possible short-term rates using the base rate r at time t_0 and interest rate volatility levels σ and then modelling the possible future rate at time points 1, 2, 3, and so on to time T using the volatility level at each of these points. The discrete time points may be set at any interval, for example daily, monthly or six-monthly. The short-term interest rate at any state s of the binomial tree at any point t is then given by (19.1):

$$r_t^s = r_t^s(\sigma_t^s). \tag{19.1}$$

The base rate and volatility levels are set using historic market data. For a model such as Black–Derman–Toy,[3] the parameters required are the term structure of interest rates and the term structure of interest rate volatilities.

Say that S_0 is the set of different interest rate scenarios that evolve from the initial zero state of the binomial tree. If we let r_t^s denote the short-term discount rate at time t that is associated with scenario $s \in S_0$ and set C_{jt}^s as the cash flow paid by security j at time t, it can be shown that the fair price for the security is given by (19.2):

$$P_{j0} = \frac{1}{|S_0|}\sum_{s=1}^{|S_0|}\sum_{t=1}^{T}\frac{C_{jt}^s}{\prod_{i=1}^{t}(1+r_t^s)}. \tag{19.2}$$

Equation (19.2) is the basic price equation that has been used to develop more advanced pricing tools that we consider later in this section, principally with respect to the price of security at a future time period τ. The complexity of the equation is apparent given that we are calculating the price outcome that emanates from the number of paths in the binomial model. From the point of origin of the lattice the number of paths in the tree is 2^T, a very large number over even a short period of time. For plain vanilla bonds the process is essentially straightforward, requiring the calculation of discounted cash flows at the vertices of the binomial tree, of which there are $T^2/2$. For bonds with embedded option features attached, including mortgage-backed bonds, because the cash flows from the bond are path-dependent, it is necessary to consider the outcome of interest rates that result from the binomial tree paths. For mortgage securities the ultimate cash flows depend not only on the current level of interest rates, but also the path that interest rates followed from the issue of the bond until the valuation date. This is because prepayment rates for mortgage bonds are affected by the path followed by interest rates subsequent to the start dates of the underlying mortgages. The prepayment rate for a mortgage-backed bond, and the cash flows, are therefore path dependent.

19.2.2 *Using the option-adjusted spread*

Strictly speaking the equation at (19.2) is not applicable to corporate bonds because they are not priced using the risk-free discount rates derived from the government bond coupon yield curve. Corporate bond yields reflect their credit risk and liquidity, and for bonds such as mortgage securities, the option element represented by the prepayment risk. Therefore the valuation of mortgage-backed bonds, as with callable bonds must

[3] *Ibid.*

account for the *option-adjusted spread* included in the instrument's yield.[4] The OAS analysis estimates the adjustment factor required for the government risk-free rates that will equate the current observed market price for the bond with the theoretical fair value calculated from the expected present value of the bond's cash flows. Any difference between the observed market price and the theoretical price of a bond reflects the additional risks that the bond exposes its holders to, which are not contained in a government bond. It may also reflect uncertainties in the market about where the bond should be priced.

The OAS for a given instrument, given here as ρ_j is estimated based on the current market price P_{j0}. It is given by the non-linear equation at (19.3):

$$P_{j0} = \frac{1}{|S_0|}\sum_{s=1}^{|S_0|}\sum_{t=1}^{T}\frac{C_{jt}^s}{\prod_{i=1}^{t}(1+\rho_j r_t^s)}. \tag{19.3}$$

Expression (19.3) cannot be solved analytically, at least not initially. This is because it sets the price of security j as a function of the option-adjusted spread ρ. However this spread premium is calculated using the market price of the security. It is not possible to price a risky bond unless we are able to quantify the risks associated with it. Therefore for non-vanilla bonds such as mortgage securities, a value for the option-adjusted spread premium is input to equation (19.3) from values observed in the market for already-existing securities that have similar characteristics to the bond we wish to price. This OAS premium is then used in (19.3) to calculate the price of a new bond, or current bonds with similar characteristics. Any difference in spread premium between bonds that are deemed to be similar is also an indication of securities that are mis-priced.

After we have obtained the current price of the bond it is possible to use the interest-rate model to calculate the bond price at some future time period which is dependent on the state of the vertices of the binomial lattice. If we assume a set of interest rate scenarios S_s originating from the state s at time period τ, the option-adjusted price of the bond $P_{j\tau}^S$ is given by (19.4) below, which is equation (19.3) modified to calculate the price at time period τ.

$$P_{j\tau}^s = \frac{1}{|S_0|}\sum_{s=1}^{|S_0|}\sum_{t=1}^{T}\frac{C_{jt}^s}{\prod_{i=\tau}^{t}(1+\rho_j r_i^s)}. \tag{19.4}$$

Note that the price of the bond is dependent not only on the state s at the final vertex of the lattice, but also on the path of interest rates during the period $t=0$ to $t=\tau$ that pass through this state. The cash flows payable by a mortgage-backed bond after time τ will reflect the economic conditions experienced prior to this point. For instance if the bond has experienced a relatively low level of prepayment, a subsequent change in mortgage rates will have a higher impact on the generated cash flows. The economic situation up to point τ is therefore used when estimating the cash flows C_{jt}^s for the time period after τ.

4 See for example Babbel, D., Zenios, S., 'Pitfalls in the Analysis of Option-Adjusted Spreads' *Financial Analysts Journal*, Jul–Aug 1992, pp. 65–69.

Therefore to price the bond at the future point τ we sample interest-rate paths from $t=0$ that pass through state s at time $t=\tau$. If we denote the group of such paths as $S_{0,s}$ and set $P_{j\tau}$, $s \in S_{0,s}$ as the price of the bond at state s after applying (19.4), then the expected price of the bond at s is given by (19.5):

$$P^{s}_{j\tau} = \frac{1}{|S_{0,s}|} \sum_{s \in S_{0,s}} P^{s}_{j\tau}. \tag{19.5}$$

19.2.3 *Assumptions of OAS analysis*

The application of the path-dependent pricing model to mortgage-backed securities assumes a number of conditions, without which the price calculation will not have any value. The most important assumption is that prepayment rates and market interest rates are related. If the relationship between market rates and prepayment rates over time is not correlated, the price of a mortgage security calculated using OAS analysis will be inaccurate. A change in the level of prepayment rates will alter the price calculated using the OAS model. Another important assumption is that market interest rates follow what is known as a Gaussian diffusion process. The majority of interest rate models assume that market rates follow a random log-normal process and are *mean reverting*, that is the path drift centres on the mean of the rates over the time period. The log-normal distribution assumption implies that rates will centre on the implied forward rates. In a positively sloping yield curve environment, the implied forward rates indicate that short-term rates will be moving higher. This may or may not reflect the market's view of short-term rates. Using implied forward rates however forces long-dated instruments to have yields that are higher than short-dated instruments if they are to be fairly priced, and is a constituent of option pricing theory.

All interest rate models including the binomial model are sensitive to the volatility level that is assumed for interest rates. A higher volatility level will result in a greater dispersion of simulated interest-rate paths, which will increase the price of the option element of a bond. Mortgage-backed bonds have an implied call option feature, given the prepayment of the underlying mortgages, therefore a higher volatility will increase the value of the option element. This will decrease the amount of the option-adjusted spread.

Interest rate models simulate a set of randomly generated interest-rate paths, which carry an element of uncertainty as to their accuracy. The more interest-rate paths that are generated in a model, the less uncertain the simulated outcomes are deemed to be. The price calculated by an interest-rate model is therefore assumed to carry less uncertainty with the more price paths that it simulates.

19.3 Interest rate risk

The most common interest rate measure applied to vanilla bonds is duration, and the related sensitivity measure modified duration. As conventionally defined they cannot be calculated for mortgage-backed bonds, because the cash flows and the maturity date for such instruments cannot be stated with certainty. Although the average life of a mortgage security is often used as a crude measure of interest rate sensitivity, with longer term bonds deemed to carry greater interest rate risk, it is not accurate enough for most applications.

Using the OAS methodology however it is possible to calculate meaningful values for both duration and convexity. In the first instance we can shift the simulated interest-rate paths either upwards or downwards by a small amount, while keeping the OAS constant, and measure the difference between the two prices. Essentially the average percentage price change can be used to calculate a bond's OAS *effective duration*, and then measuring the *effective convexity* by observing the rate of change of the effective duration. As they are based on OAS prices the effective duration measure includes the effect of the prepayment option and also may be used for hedging purposes.

More formally we may use the OAS model to estimate the sensitivity of the model-generated prices to changes in market rates. To allow for the complex dependency of the cash flows of a mortgage-backed bond to changes in the market term structure we may use a model such as a Monte Carlo simulation. Assuming that interest rates follow a *stochastic* process, we generate a range of interest rate paths based on the current term structure, and calculate the OAS premium ρ_j implied by the current market price P_{j0} given by (19.3). We then shift the term structure by some specified amount, say -10 basis points, and then regenerate the stochastic process of interest rates. The interest rate paths (r_t^{-s}) from the initial stochastic process are sampled and used to calculate the OAS price, with assumed cash flows from the bond input to the price equation (19.6):

$$P_j^- = \frac{1}{|S_0|}\sum_{s=1}^{|S_0|}\sum_{t=1}^{T}\frac{C_{jt}^s}{\prod_{i=1}^{t}(1+\rho_j r_i^{-s})}. \tag{19.6}$$

We then shift the term structure by $+10$ basis points and recalibrate the stochastic process of interest rates. The price under the new term structure is then calculated in the same way as before. If we denote the first price calculated as P_j^- and the second price as P_j^+ then the *option-adjusted duration* of the bond is given by (19.7):

$$D_{jOAS} = \frac{P_j^+ - P_j^-}{100}. \tag{19.7}$$

The option-adjusted convexity is given by (19.8):

$$CV_{jOAS} = \frac{P_j^+ - 2P_{j0} + P_j^-}{50^2}. \tag{19.8}$$

The OAS-adjusted duration measure is often used to judge the level of prepayment risk of a mortgage security. Prepayment risk may be defined as a measure of the exposure to unforeseen changes in the market's assumed long-term prepayment rates, above those expected to occur with movements in interest rates. Such a change can take place for a number of reasons, including changes in mortgage finance that alters prepayment forecasts or changes in the attitude of mortgagors about prepayment. For obvious reasons a change in prepayment rates can have a significant impact on the performance of a portfolio that is composed of mortgage securities. The OAS-adjusted duration measure for a mortgage security is sometimes called *prepayment duration*, its percentage price change assuming constant OAS resulting from a specified change in projected prepayment rates. Figure 19.2 shows the prepayment duration of selected mortgage-backed bonds as calculated on Bloomberg. Note that a bond such as a current-coupon pass-through security has a relatively low sensitivity to prepayment rates, whereas bonds such as interest-only (IO) or principal only (PO) bonds have a much higher prepayment sensitivity. We can also see that an IO or a high-coupon

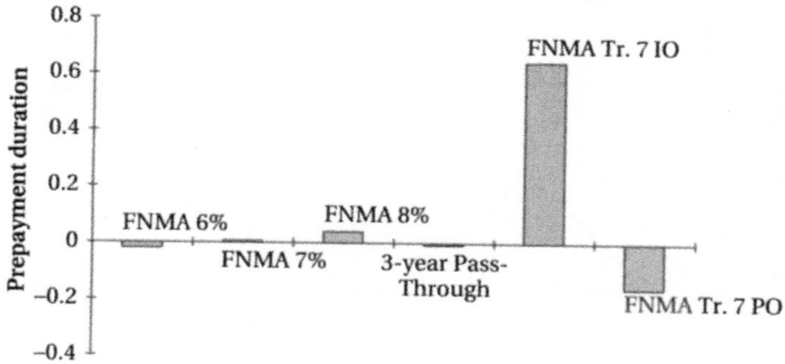

Figure 19.2: Prepayment duration of selected mortgage-backed bonds, May 1998. Source: Bloomberg.

pass-through has a positive prepayment sensitivity, indicating that its price will fall if prepayment rates increase, whereas the opposite is true for a PO or discount mortgage, which have a negative prepayment sensitivity. This characteristic was described in the previous chapter, when we observed that PO bond prices will rise following an increase in prepayment rates.

Under certain conditions, under small changes in market rate the binomial lattice model produces errors and sometimes the wrong sign for the convexity value. For the specific situations where this occurs a simulation pricing model will produce more accurate results. A good exposition of this problem is contained in the paper by Douglas Howard (1997), listed in the selected bibliography section.

19.4 Portfolio performance

There are additional considerations in measuring the return of a portfolio of mortgage-backed securities. The market uses the valuation methods described earlier to generate scenarios of returns achieved during a specified holding period. The scenarios are usually generated using a simulation model such as Monte Carlo simulation.

The rate of return of a bond j during a holding period τ is determined by the price of the security at the end of the holding period, together with the accrued value of the cash flows that have been generated by the bond. For a mortgage-backed bond it is necessary to estimate the value of the principal, interest, and prepayments made during the holding period, and then calculate the price of the unpaid balance of the bond at the end of the holding period. This requires the simulation of different scenarios of the term structure, and the prepayment activity that is projected under each different scenario. For any given interest rate scenario s the rate of return of security j during τ is given by (19.9):

$$R^s_{j\tau} = \frac{F^s_{j\tau} + PV^s_{j\tau}}{PP_{j0}} \tag{19.9}$$

where

$P^s_{j\tau}$ is the accrued value of the cash flows generated by the security, reinvested at the short-term interest rate generated for scenario s

P_{j0} is the current market price of the bond.

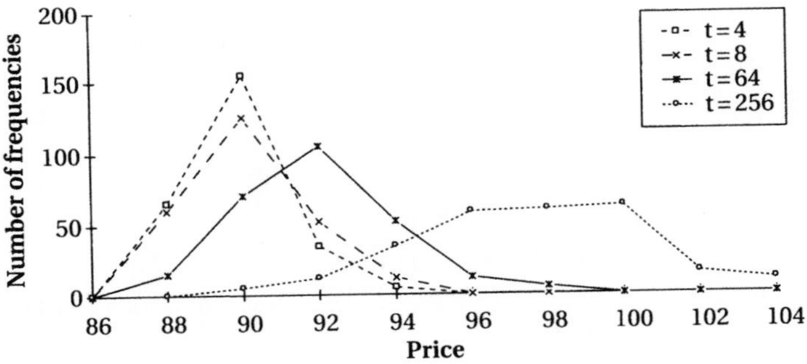

Figure 19.3: Distribution of the computed prices of a mortgage-backed bond at different discrete time points, using Monte Carlo simulation.

PV^s_{jT} is the value of the unpaid balance of the bond at the end of the holding period, conditional under scenario s. This is given by:

$$PV^s_{jT} = M^s jT \times P^s_{jT}$$

where M^s_{jT} is the unpaid balance of the mortgage security and P^s_{jT} is the price per unit nominal value of the bond. Both values are calculated at the end of the holding period and are conditional on scenario s.

Figure 19.3 shows the computed price for the FNMA 7% under different holding period horizons. For shorter time period horizons the price distribution is very sensitive to the number of simulations, which reflects the value of the embedded prepayment option. Under longer holding periods, and as the period approaches the bond's average life maturity, the prepayment option declines in value and the computed prices are more symmetric. As the bond approaches maturity the average price of the bond approaches par, which is similar to the 'pull to par' effect on a conventional plain vanilla bond.

Selected bibliography and references

Boyce, W., Koenigsberg, M., *Effective Duration of Callable Bonds: The Salomon Brothers Term Structure-Based Option Pricing Model*, Salomon Brothers Inc., April 1987

Douglas Howard, C., *Numerical Pitfalls of Lattice-Based Duration and Convexity Calculations*, working paper, Department of Applied Mathematics and Physics, Polytechnic University, 1997

Herskovitz, M.D., 'Option-Adjusted Spread Analysis for Mortgage-Backed Securities', in Fabozzi, F. (ed.), *The Handbook of Fixed-Income Options*, Probus Publishing, 1989, Chapter 21

Waldman, M., Modzelewski, S., 'A Framework for Evaluating Treasury-Based Adjustable Rate Mortgages', in Fabozzi, F. (ed.), *The Handbook of Mortgage-Backed Securities*, Probus Publishing, 1985

20 Asset-Backed Securities

The market in asset-backed securities contains instruments that have widely varying payment terms and conditions, and different collateral bases. The subject matter is a large one and so in this chapter we present only a summary of the main instruments. Interested readers may wish to consult the texts listed under the selected bibliography. Here we review the characteristics of the main asset-backed instruments, which were introduced in the US market but are also now issued in other markets including those in the United Kingdom and Europe. The instruments we will consider are:

- collateralised mortgage obligations, (in the US market) both agency and non-agency;
- commercial mortgage-backed securities;
- auto-loan-backed securities;
- credit card-backed securities.

We also present some further issues connected with the analysis of these securities.

20.1 Collateralised mortgage securities

Mortgage-backed bonds were introduced in Chapter 18. In this section we review some of the newer structures of these instruments. A large number of the instruments in the US market are collateralised mortgage obligations (CMOs), the majority of which are issued by government-sponsored agencies and so offer virtual Treasury bond credit quality but at significantly higher yields. This makes the paper attractive to a range of institutional investors, as does the opportunity to tailor the characteristics of a particular issue to suit the needs of a specific investor. The CMO market in the US experienced rapid growth during the 1990s, with a high of $324 billion issued in 1993; this figure had fallen to just under $100 billion during 1998.[1] The growth of the market has brought a range of new structures, for example bondholders who wished to have a lower exposure to prepayment risk have invested in *planned amortisation classes* (PACs) and *targeted amortisation classes* (TACs). The uncertain term to maturity of mortgage-backed bonds has resulted in the creation of bonds that were guaranteed not to extend beyond a stated date, which are known as *very accurately defined maturity* (VDAM) bonds. In the United Kingdom and certain overseas markets mortgage-backed bonds pay a floating-rate coupon, and the interest from foreign investors in the US domestic market led to the creation of bonds with coupons linked to the LIBOR rate. Other types of instruments in the market include interest-only (IO) and principal-only (PO) bonds, also sometimes called Strips, and inverse floating-rate bonds, which are usually created from an existing fixed-rate bond issue. Figure 20.1 illustrates the relative size of the different instruments in the US market at the beginning of 1999.

---

1 The source for statistical data in this section is *Inside Mortgage Securities*, Chase Manhattan, February 1999 and *Asset-Backed Alert* (www.ABAlert.com). Used with permission.

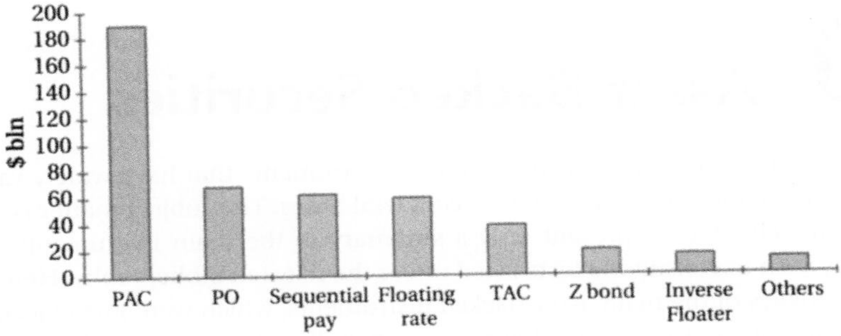

Figure 20.1: US market agency CMOs in issue 1999. Source: Chase Manhattan.

The primary features of US-market CMOs are summarised as follows:

- **Credit quality.** CMOs issued by US government agencies have the same guarantee as agency pass-through securities, so may be considered risk-free. These bonds therefore do not require any form of credit insurance or credit enhancement. Whole-loan CMOs do not carry any form of government guarantee, and are rated by credit rating agencies. Most bonds carry a triple-A rating, either because of the quality of the mortgage pool or issuing vehicle or because a form of credit enhancement has been used.
- **Interest frequency.** CMOs typically pay interest on a monthly basis, which is calculated on the current outstanding nominal value of the issue.
- **Cash flow profile.** The cash flow profile of CMOs is based on an assumed prepayment rate. This rate is based on the current market expectation of future prepayment levels and expected market interest rates, and is known as the *pricing speed*.
- **Maturity.** Most CMOs are long-dated instruments, and originally virtually all issues were created from underlying mortgage collateral with a 30-year stated maturity. During the 1990s issues were created from shorter-dated collateral, including 5–7 year and 15–20 year mortgages.
- **Market convention.** CMOs trade on a yield, as opposed to a price, basis and are usuall quoted as a spread over the yield of the nearest maturity Treasury security. The yields are calculated on the basis of an assumed prepayment rate. Agency CMOs are settled or a T + 3 basis via an electronic book-entry system known as 'Fedwire', the clearing system run by the Federal Reserve. Whole-loan CMOs also settle on a T + 3 basis, anc are cleared using either physical delivery or by electronic transfer. New issue CMOs settle from one to three months after the initial offer date.

Originally mortgage-backed bonds were created from individual underlying mortgages Agency CMOs are created from mortgages that have already been pooled and securitised usually in the form of a pass-through security (see Chapter 18). Issuers of *whole loan* CMO do not therefore need to create a pass-through security from a pool of individual mortgages but structure based on cash flows from the entire pool. In the same way as for agency pass through securities, the underlying mortgages in a whole-loan pool are generally of the sam risk type, maturity and interest rate. The other difference between whole-loan CMOs an agency pass-throughs is that the latter are comprised of mortgages of up to a state maximum size, while larger loans are contained in CMOs. There are essentially two CMO structures, those issues that re-direct the underlying pool interest payments and issues re-directing both interest and principal. The main CMO instrument types pay out both interest and principal and are described below.

Whole-loan CMO structures also differ from other mortgage-backed securities in terms of what is known as *compensating interest.* Virtually all mortgage securities pay principal and interest on a monthly basis, on a fixed coupon date. The underlying mortgages however may be paid off on any day of the month. Agency mortgage securities guarantee their bondholders an interest payment for the complete month, even if the underlying mortgage has been paid off ahead of the coupon date (and so has not attracted any interest). Whole-loan CMOs do not offer this guarantee, and so any *payment interest shortfall* will be lost, meaning that a bondholder would receive less than one month's worth interest on the coupon date. Some issuers, but not all, will pay a compensating interest payment to bondholders to make up this shortfall

20.1.1 *Planned amortisation class*

The first issue of *planned amortisation classes* (PACs) was in 1986, after a period of sustained falls in the market interest rates led to a demand for less interest-rate volatile mortgage-backed structures. PAC structures are designed to reduce prepayment risk and also the volatility of the weighted average life measure, which is related to the prepayment rate. The securities have a principal payment schedule that is maintained irrespective of any change in prepayment rates. The process is similar to a corporate bond sinking fund schedule, and is based on the minimum amount of principal cash flow that is produced by the underlying mortgage pool at two different prepayment rates, known as *PAC bands.* The PAC bands are set as a low and high PSA standard, for example 50%PSA and 250%PSA. This has the effect of constraining the amount of principal repayment, so that in the early years of the issue the minimum of principal received is at the level of the lower of the two bands, while later in the bond's life the payment schedule is constrained by the upper PAC band. The total principal cash flow under the PAC schedule will determine the value of PACs in a structure.

A PAC schedule follows an arrangement whereby cash flow uncertainty of principal payment is directed to another class of security known as *companions,* or *support classes.* When prepayment rates are high, companion issues support the main PACs by absorbing any principal prepayments that are in excess of the PAC schedule. When the prepayment rate has fallen, the companion amortisation rates are delayed if the level of principal prepayment is not sufficient to reach the minimum level stipulated by the PAC bands. Essentially then the structure of PACs results in the companion issues carrying the prepayment uncertainty, since when prepayment rates are high the average life of the companions will be reduced as they are paid off, and when prepayment rates are low the companions will see their measure of average life increase as they remain outstanding for a longer period.

The principal cash flows of PACs and companions can be divided sequentially, similar to a sequential-pay structure, which are reviewed in the next section. PACs have a lower price volatility than other mortgage securities, the level of which is relatively stable when the prepayment rates are within the PAC bands. When prepayment rates move outside the bands, the volatility increases by a lower amount than they otherwise would, because the prepayment risk is transferred to the companions. For this reason, PAC issues trade at lower spreads to the Treasury yield curve than other issues of similar average life. The companion bonds are always priced at a higher spread than the PACs, reflecting their higher prepayment risk.

PAC bonds that have a lower prepayment risk than standard PACs are known as *Type II* and *Type III PACs*. A Type II PAC is created from an existing PAC/companion structure, and has a narrower band than the original PAC. This reduces the prepayment risk. If prepayment rates remain within the bands, Type II PACs trade as PACs. If prepayment rates move outside the narrower band, the extra cash flow is redirected to the companion. Type II PACs are second in priority to the PACs and so carry a higher yield. If prepayment rates remain high over a period of time such that all the companions are redeemed, the Type II PACs take over the function of companion, so that they then carry higher prepayment risk. A further PAC with yet narrower bands, created from the same structure, is known as a *Type III PAC*.

The upper and lower bands in a PAC may 'drift' during the life of the CMO, irrespective of the level that actual prepayment rates are at. This drift arises because of the interaction between actual cash prepayments and the bands, and changes in collateral balance and the ratio between the PAC and companion nominal values. The impact of this drift differs according to where the prepayment rate is. The three possible scenarios are:

- **prepayment level lies within the current bands:** in this case the PAC will receive principal in line with the payment schedule, while any prepayments above the schedule amount will be re-directed to the companion issue. The effect of this if it continues is that both the lower and upper bands will drift upwards; this is because any prepayment that occurs is within the bands. This causes the upper band to rise, the rationale being that as prepayments have been below it, they have been received at a slower rate than expected, leaving more companion issues to receive future prepayments. The lower band rises as well, the reasoning being that prepayments have been received faster than expected (as they have been above the minimum level) so that a lower amount of collateral is available to generate future principal payments. It has been observed that upper bands tend to rise at a higher rate than the lower rate, so that prepayment levels lying within the bands causes them to widen over time;
- **prepayment level lies above the upper band:** where prepayment rates are above the upper band, the PAC will receive principal in line with the payment schedule until it is paid off. If the prepayment rates stays above the upper band, the two bands will begin to narrow, because the number of companions available to receive faster prepayments will fall. The two bands will converge completely once all the companion bonds have been redeemed, and the PAC will trade as a conventional sequential pay security after that until it is paid off;
- **prepayment level lies below the lower band:** if prepayment rates lie below the lower PAC band, the upper band will drift upwards as more companion bonds are available to receive a greater level of prepayments in the future; the lower band may also rise by a small amount. This situation is relatively rare however as PAC have the highest priority of all classes in a CMO structure until the payment schedule is back on track.

The band drift process occurs over a long time period and is sometimes not noticeable. Significant changes to the band levels only take place if the prepayment rate is outside the band for a long period. Prepayment rates that move outside the bands over a short time period do not have any effect on the bands.

20.1.2 *Sequential-pay classes*

One of the requirements that CMOs were designed to meet was the demand for mortgage-backed bonds with a wider range of maturities. Most CMO structures re-direct principal payments *sequentially* to individual classes of bonds within the structure, in accordance with the stated maturity of each bond. That is, principal payments are first used to pay off the class of bond with the shortest stated maturity, until it is completely redeemed, before being re-allocated to the next maturity band class of bond. This occurs until all the bonds in the structure are retired.

Sequential pay CMOs are attractive to a wide range of investors, particularly those with shorter-term investment horizons, as they are able to purchase only the class of CMO whose maturity terms meets their requirements. In addition investors with more traditional longer-dated investment horizons are protected from prepayment risk in the early years of the issue, because principal payments are used to pay off the shorter-dated bonds in the structure.

20.1.3 *Targeted amortisation class*

These bonds were created to cater for investors who require an element of prepayment protection but at a higher yield than would be available with a PAC. Targeted amortisation class bonds (TAC) offer a prepayment principal in line with a schedule, providing that the level of prepayment is within the stated range. If the level of principal prepayment moves outside of the range, the extra principal amounts are used to pay off TAC companion bonds, just as with PACs. The main difference between TACs and PACs is that TACs have extra prepayment risk if the level of prepayments falls below the amount required to maintain the payment schedule; this results in the average life of the TAC being extended. Essentially a TAC is a PAC but with a lower 'PAC band' setting. The preference to hold TACs over PACs is a function of the prevailing interest rate environment; if current rates are low and/or are expected to fall, there is a risk that increasing prepayments will reduce the average life of the bond. In this scenario, investors may be willing to do without the protection against an increase in the average life (deeming it unlikely to be required), and take the extra yield over PACs as a result. This makes TACs attractive compared to PACs under certain conditions, and because one element of the 'PAC band' is removed, TACs trade at a higher yield.

20.1.4 *Z-class bonds*

This type of bond is unique to the domestic US market, and has a very interesting structure. The Z-class bond (or *Z-bond*) is created from a CMO structure and has re-allocation of both principal and interest payments. It is essentially a coupon-bearing bond that ranks below all other classes in the CMO's structure, and pays no cash flows for part of its life. When the CMO is issued, the Z-bond has a nominal value of relatively small size, and at the start of its life it pays out cash flows on a monthly basis as determined by its coupons. However at any time that the Z-bond itself is receiving no principal payments, these cash flows are used to retire some of the principal of the other classes in the structure. This results in the nominal value of the bond being increased each month that the coupon payments are not received, so that the principal amount is higher at the end of the bond's life than at the start. This process is known as *accretion*. At the point when all classes of bond ahead of the Z-bond are retired, the Z-bond itself starts to pay out principal and interest cash flows.

The following example of a Z-bond cash flow structure is one described in Chapter 28 of *The Handbook of Fixed Income Securities*, edited by Frank Fabozzi (1997). The table is reproduced with the kind permission of McGraw-Hill.

Example 20.1: Sample Z-bond cash flows

- This is an example of a Z-bond created from a 7½% 30-year mortgage pass-through bond. The nominal value of the bond on issue is $118,000, but the initial coupon payments of $737.50 (the bond pays a monthly coupon) are used as principal prepayments for other bonds in the CMO structure. These cash flows therefore accrete to the nominal value of the Z-bond. The accretion amounts increase as the principal amount increases. In month 133 though, the last sequential-pay bond in the structure is paid off, leaving the Z-class as the only note left in the structure. At this point the bond has a principal value of $270,203. From the next month the bond receives all the interest and principal payments and prepayments that are paid out by the underlying mortgage collateral.

In the conventional sequential pay structure, the existence of a Z-bond will increase the principal prepayments in the CMO structure. The other classes in the structure receive some of their principal prepayments from the Z-bond, which lowers their average life volatility. Creating a Z-bond in a CMO structure reduces therefore the average life volatility

Sequential Pay Z-Bond Structure
CMO created from 7.50% 30-year Mortgage Pass-Through Security
Cash flows $

Month	Starting balance	Coupon accretion	Coupon cash flow	Amortisation	Ending balance	Total cash flows
1	118,000.00	737.50	0.00	0.00	118,737.50	0.00
2	118,737.50	742.11	0.00	0.00	119,479.61	0.00
3	119,479.61	746.75	0.00	0.00	120,226.36	0.00
:	:	:	:	:	:	0.00
:	:	:	:	:	:	0.00
131	265,245.57	1,657.78	0.00	0.00	266,903.35	0.00
132	266,903.35	1,668.15	0.00	0.00	268,571.50	0.00
133	268,571.50	1,678.57	0.00	47.44	270,202.63	47.44
134	270,202.63	0.00	1,688.77	3131.55	267,071.08	4,820.31
135	267,071.08	0.00	1,669.19	3,099.51	263,971.57	4,768.70

Table 20.1: Example of Z-Bond cash flows in CMO structure.
Source: Ames, C., 'Collateralized Mortgage Obligation', in Fabozzi, F., *The Handbook of Fixed Income Securities*, 5th edition, McGraw-Hill, 1997. Reproduced with permission.

of all the classes in the structure. Z-bonds are an alternative to investors who might otherwise purchase Treasury zero-coupon bonds, with a similar feature of no reinvestment risk. They also offer the added attraction of higher yields compared to those available on Treasury strips with a similar average life.

20.1.5 *Interest-only and principal-only class*

Stripped coupon mortgage securities were introduced in Chapter 18. They are created when the coupon cash flows payable by a pool of mortgages are split into interest-only (IO) and principal-only (PO) payments. The cash flows will be a function of the prepayment rate, since this determines the nominal value of the collateral pool. IO issues, also known as IO strips, gain whenever the prepayment rate falls, as interest payments are reduced as the principal amount falls. If there is a rise in the prepayment rate, PO bonds benefit because they are discount securities and a higher prepayment rate result in the redemption proceeds being received early. Early strip issues were created with an unequal amount of coupon and principal, resulting in a synthetic coupon rate that was different to the coupon on the underlying bond. These instruments were known as *synthetic coupon pass-throughs*. Nowadays it is more typical for all the interest to be allocated to one class, the IO issue, and all the principal to be allocated to the PO class. The most common CMO structures have a portion of their principal stripped into IO and PO bonds, but in some structures the entire issue is made up of IO and PO bonds. The amount of principal used to create stripped securities will reflect investor demand. In certain cases IO issues created from a class of CMO known as *real estate mortgage investment conduits* (REMICs) have quite esoteric terms. For example the IO classes might be issued with an amount of principal attached known as the nominal balance. The cash flows for bonds with this structure are paid through a process of amortising and prepaying the nominal balance. The balance itself is a small amount, resulting in a very high coupon, so that the IO has a multi-digit coupon and very high price (such as 1183% and 3626–12).[2]

Strips created from whole-loan CMOs trade differently from those issued out of agency CMOs. Agency CMOs pay a fixed coupon, whereas whole-loan CMOs pay a coupon based on a weighted average of all the individual mortgage coupons. During the life of the whole-loan issue this coupon value will alter as prepayments change the amount of principal. To preserve the coupon payments of all issues within a structure therefore, a portion of the principal and interest cash flows are stripped from the underlying mortgages, leaving collateral that has a more stable average life. This is another reason that IOs and POs may be created.

IO issue prices exhibit the singular tendency of moving in the same direction as interest rates under certain situations. This reflects the behaviour of mortgages and prepayment rates: when interest rates fall below the mortgage coupon rate, prepayment rates will increase. This causes the cash flow for an IO strip to fall, as the level of the underlying principal declines, which causes the price of the IO to fall as well. This is despite the fact that the issue's cash flows are now discounted at a lower rate. Figure 20.2 shows the price of a sensitivity of a 7% pass-through security compared to the prices of an IO and a PO that have been created from it. Note that the price of the pass-through is not particularly sensitive to a

2 Ames (1997).

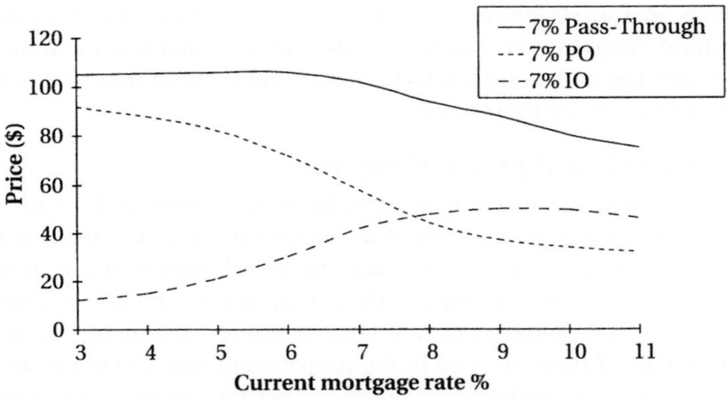

Figure 20.2: Price sensitivity of pass-through security, IO and PO to changes in mortgage rate. Price source and calculation: Bloomberg.

fall in the mortgage rate below the coupon rate of 7%. This illustrates the *negative convexity* property of pass-through securities. The price sensitivity of the two strip issues is very different. The PO experiences a dramatic fall in price as the mortgage rate rises above the coupon rate. The IO on the other hand experiences a rise in price in the same situation, while its price falls significantly if mortgage rates fall below the coupon rate.

Both PO and IO issues are extremely price volatile at times of moves in mortgage rates, and have much greater interest rate sensitivity than the pass-through securities from which they are created.

20.1.6 *Structuring a CMO*

The process of setting up a CMO structure can be quite involved, and is dependent on the level of customer demand for each of the different classes of instruments. Customer demand is a function of their individual requirements as well as the current market environment. Factors such as current mortgage rates and interest rate expectations also influence the demand for certain instruments. We can illustrate a CMO structure using a hypothetical example of an agency pass-through security. We have called this the 'Agency 7% issue'. The structuring bank then creates instruments to meet particular requirements. A series of sequential-pay CMOs are created first, which is typical but most frequent under expectations of stable interest and prepayment rates. The last of this series of issues is a Z-bond, aimed at investors who believe that interest rates will rise, and hence that prepayment rates will fall. Part of the cash flows from the Z-bond issue are used to provide principal payments to support a VADM issue. These are offered to investors who wish to purchase bonds that have the greatest protection against an extension in their average life. The structuring bank then creates an IO bond by stripping some of the interest cash flows. This may be done before or after the creation of any further issues. Assume that ½% of the coupon is stripped, leaving the original bond now with a coupon of 6½%. The different classes of instrument are shown in Figure 20.3.

In Figure 20.4 we show an alternative structure that might be set up in a different interest rate environment. If the market believes that interest rates and prepayment rates

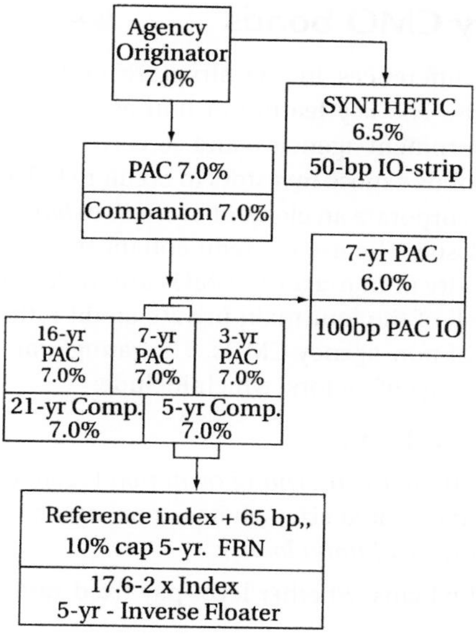

Figure 20.3: Hypothetical example of CMO structure.

will experience high volatility levels, the structuring bank may create instead a series of PACs (or TACs) and companion bonds. A share of the collateral is used to create the PACs and their companions, with a range of maturities (measured as average lives). In addition a floating-rate bond is created to meet demand from overseas investors, which is created from the five-year companion issue. The floating-rate bond is issued in conjunction with an inverse floater bond. The final element is an instrument created to meet the requirement of an investor who wishes to purchase a bond with lower coupon together with a strip. The 7-year PAC is used for this and split into the two new issues.

The examples illustrated at Figures 20.3 and 20.4 are an indication of how flexible CMO structures can be, and they are suitable for a wide range of investors with varying requirements.

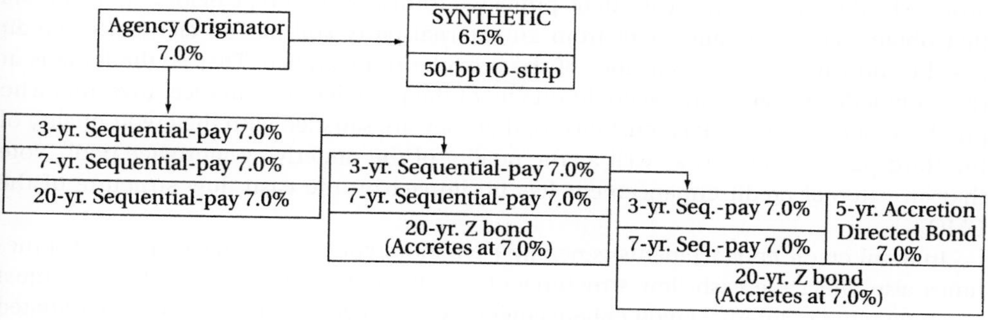

Figure 20.4: Alternative CMO structure.

20.2 Non-agency CMO bonds

There are no significant differences in the structure and terms of non-agency CMOs compared to agency CMOs. The key feature of non-agency CMOs however, is that they are not guaranteed by government agencies, and so carry an element of credit risk, in the same way that corporate bonds expose investors to credit risk. To attract investors therefore most non-agency CMOs incorporate an element of *credit enhancement* designed to improve the credit standing of the issue. The use of credit enhancement usually results in a triple-A rating, indeed a large majority of non-agency CMOs are triple-A rated, with very few falling below a double-A rating. All of the four main private credit rating agencies are involved in credit analysis and rating of non-agency CMOs. The rating granted to a particular issue of CMOs is dependent on a range of factors, which include:

- the term of the underlying loans;
- the size of the loans, whether *conforming* or *jumbo* (agency mortgages do not include mortgages above a certain stated size, whereas non-agency issues often are comprised of larger size loans known as *jumbo loans*);
- the interest basis for the loans, whether level-pay fixed-rate, variable or other type;
- the type of property;
- the geographical area within which the loans have been made;
- the purpose behind the loans, whether a first purchase or a refinancing.

In this section we discuss the credit enhancement facility that is used in non-agency CMOs.

20.2.1 *Credit enhancements*

CMOs are arranged with either an external or internal credit enhancement. An *external* credit enhancement is a guarantee made by a third-party to cover losses on the issue. Usually a set amount of the issue is guaranteed, such as 25%, rather than the entire issue. The guarantee can take the form of a letter of credit, bond insurance or *pool insurance*. A pool insurance policy would be written to insure against losses that arose as a result of default, usually for a cash amount of cover that would remain in place during the life of the pool. Certain policies are set up so that the cash coverage falls in value during the life of the bond. Pool insurance is provided by specialised agencies. Note that only defaults and foreclosures are included in the policy, which forces investors to arrange further cover if they wish to be protected from any other type of loss. A CMO issue that obtains credit enhancement from an external party still has an element of credit risk, but now linked to the fortunes of the provider of insurance. That is, the issue is at risk from a deterioration in the credit quality of the provider of insurance. Investors who purchase non-agency CMOs must ensure that they are satisfied with the credit quality of the third-party guarantor, as well as the quality of the underlying mortgage pool. Note that an external credit enhancement has no impact on the cash flow structure of the CMO.

Internal credit enhancements generally have more complex arrangements and sometimes also affect the cash flow structures of the instruments themselves. The two most common types of internal credit enhancement are *reserve funds* and a senior/subordinated structure.

- **Reserve funds.** There are two types of reserve funds. A *cash reserve fund* is a deposit of cash that has been built up from payments arising from the issue of the bonds. A portion of the profits made when the bonds were initially issued are placed in a separate fund. The fund in turn places this cash in short-term bank deposits. The cash reserve fund is used in the event of default to compensate investors who have suffered capital loss. It is often set up in conjunction with another credit enhancement product, such as a letter of credit. An *excess servicing spread account* is also a separate fund, generated from excess spread after all the payments of the mortgage have been made, that is the coupon, servicing fee and other expenses. For instance if an issue has a gross weighted average coupon of 7.50%, and the service fee is 0.10% and the net weighted average coupon is 7.25%, then the excess servicing amount is 0.15%. This amount is paid into the spread account, and will grow steadily during the bond's life. The funds in the account can be used to pay off any losses arising from the bond that affect investors.
- **Senior/subordinated structure.** This is the most common type of internal credit enhancement method encountered in the market. Essentially it involves a bond ranking below the CMO that absorbs all the losses arising from default, or other cause, leaving the main issue unaffected. The subordinated bond clearly has the higher risk attached to it, so it trades at a higher yield. Most senior/subordinated arrangements also incorporate a 'shifting interest structure'. This arranges for prepayments to be re-directed from the subordinated class to the senior class. Hence it alters the cash flow characteristics of the senior notes, irrespective of the presence of defaults or otherwise.

20.3 Commercial mortgage-backed securities

The mortgage-backed bond market includes a sector of securities that are backed by commercial, as opposed to residential, mortgages. These are known as *commercial mortgage-backed securities* (CMBS). They trade essentially as other mortgage securities but there are detail differences in their structure, which are summarised in this section.

20.3.1 *Issuing a CMBS*

As with a residential mortgage security, a CMBS is created from a pool or 'trust' of commercial mortgages, with the cash flows of the bond backed by the interest and principal payments of the underlying mortgages. A commercial mortgage is a loan made to finance or refinance the purchase of a commercial (business) property. There is a market in direct purchase of a commercial loan book in addition to the more structured CMBS transaction. An issue of CMBS is rated in the same was as a residential mortgage security and usually has a credit enhancement arrangement to raise its credit rating. The credit rating of a CMBS takes into account the size of the issue as well as the level of credit enhancement support.

Classes of bonds in a CMBS structure are usually arranged in a sequential-pay series, and bonds are retired in line with their rating in the structure; the highest-rated bonds are paid off first.

Commercial mortgages impose a penalty on borrowers if they are redeemed early, usually in the form of an interest charge on the final principal. There is not such a penalty in the US residential mortgage market, although early retirement fees are still a feature of residential loans in the UK. The early payment protection in a commercial loan can have

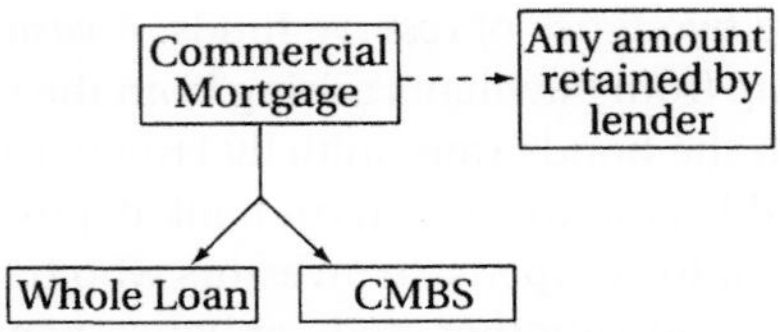

Figure 20.5: Commercial mortgage security issue.

other forms as well, such as a prepayment 'lockout', which is a contractual arrangement that prevents early retirement. This early prepayment protection is repeated in a CMBS structure, and may be in the form of call protection of the bonds themselves. There is already a form of protection in the ratings of individual issues in the structure, because the highest-rated bonds are paid off first. That is, the triple-A rated bonds will be retired ahead of the double-A rated bonds, and so on. The highest-rated bonds in a CMBS structure also have the highest protection from default of any of the underlying mortgages, which means that losses of principal arising from default will affect the lowest-rated bond first.

As well as the early retirement protection, commercial mortgages differ from residential loans in that many of them are *balloon* mortgages. A balloon loan is one on which only the interest is paid, or only a small amount of the principal is paid as well as the interest, so that all or a large part of the loan remains to be paid off on the maturity date. This makes CMBSs potentially similar to conventional vanilla bonds (which are also sometimes called 'bullet' bonds) and so attractive to investors who prefer less uncertainty on term to maturity of a bond.

20.3.2 *Types of CMBS structures*[3]

In the US market there are currently five types of CMBS structures. They are:

- liquidating trusts;
- multi-property single borrower;
- multi-property conduit;
- multi-property non-conduit;
- single property single-borrower.

We briefly describe the three most common structures here.

- **Liquidating trusts.** This sector of the market is relatively small by value and represents bonds issued against non-performing loans, hence the other name of *non-performing CMBS.* The market is structured in a slightly different way to regular commercial mortgage securities. The features include a *fast-pay structure,* which states that all cash flows from the mortgage pool be used to redeem the most senior bond first, and *over-collateralisation,* which is when the value of bonds created is significantly lower than the value of the underlying loans. This over-collateralisation results in bonds being paid off

[3] The structures described in this section borrow heavily from data contained in Dunlevy (1996), Chapter 30 in Fabozzi/Jacob (1996).

sooner. Due to the nature of the asset backing for liquidating CMBSs, bonds are usually issued with relatively short average lives, and will receive cash flows on only a portion of the loans. A target date for paying off is set and in the event that the target is not met, the bonds usually have a provision to raise the coupon rate. This acts as an incentive for the borrower to meet the retirement target.

- **Multi-property single borrower.** The single borrower/multi-property structure is an important and large-size part of the CMBS market. The special features of these bonds include *cross-collateralisation*, which is when properties that are used as collateral for individual loans are pledged against each loan. Another feature known as *cross-default* allows the lender to call each loan in the pool if any one of them defaults. Since cross-collateralisation and cross-default links all the properties together, sufficient cash flow is available to meet the collective debt on all of the loans. This influences the grade of credit rating that is received for the issue. A *property release provision* in the structure is set up to protect the investor against the lender removing or prepaying the stronger loans in the book. Another common protection against this risk is a clause in the structure terms that prevents the issuer from substituting one property for another.
- **Multi-borrower/conduit.** A *conduit* is a commercial lending entity that has been set up solely to generate collateral to be used in securitisation deals. The major investment banks have all established conduit arms. Conduits are responsible for originating collateral that meets requirements on loan type (whether amortising or balloon, and so on), loan term, geographic spread of the properties and the time that the loans were struck. Generally a conduit will want to have a diversified range of underlying loans, known as *pool diversification*, with a wide spread of location and size. A diversified pool reduces the default risk for the investor. After it has generated the collateral the conduit then structures the deal, on terms as similar to CMOs but with the additional features described in this section.

20.4 Auto-loan backed securities

20.4.1 *Description*

Bonds issued against car loan finance are known as *auto-loan-backed securities* (auto-ABS) in the US or simply as *car-loans* in the UK. The auto-loan-backed market in the US is one of the largest in the asset-backed market. It is also one of the oldest sectors, with the first deal being issued in May 1985.[4] Auto-loans are amortising private loans in the manner of residential mortgages, but are typically of much shorter duration than mortgages and carry no prepayment risk. This makes bonds that are issued against them attractive instruments for investors who are seeking more stable, shorter-dated paper of high credit quality but yielding more than Treasury bonds. As they are more straightforward, their analysis presents fewer problems than other asset-backed securities. Up to the middle of 1998 approximately $170 billion of auto-loan bonds had been issued in the US, and the sector is a liquid and fairly transparent one.

---

4 Statistics in this section are sourced from Zimmerman (1996) in Bhattacharya/Fabozzi (1996), Chapter 31 and *Asset-Backed News*, 2000 and 2001.

Car loans in the US are short-term amortising deals, ranging from three to six years in maturity. The average maturity is four years. Loans are made either direct at the dealership, in which case finance is supplied by an arm of the car manufacturer, or at a commercial (retail) bank. In the UK car loans are of two types, the amortising loan from a bank or a bullet loan usually taken from a finance house, known as leasing. Both types of loans are used as collateral in a car-loan bond issue. The US car loan market is dominated by the 'Big Three' car manufacturers General Motors, Ford Motor Corporation and Chrysler Corporation, who issued over 36% of all auto-ABS in 1998. The large commercial banks are also big issuers of auto-ABS bonds, and include Capital One, NationsBank and Chase Manhattan. Independent finance companies make up the third category of issuers, companies such as Western Financial and Union Acceptance Corporation. The independent houses are much more reliant on the auto-ABS market and can fund their book at lower rates directly as a result, since they create AAA securities out of securitised car loans that pay a lower yield than their individual credit standings would allow. To achieve a high credit rating most auto-ABS issues are structured with a form of credit enhancement. The most common form of enhancement is a senior/subordinated structure, similar to mortgage-backed bonds, although letters of credit and over-collateralisation are also used.

The underlying assets in an auto-ABS issue are bank or finance house car loans, which may be purchased or originated by a special purpose vehicle called a *special purpose corporation* (SPC). Interest payments from the original borrowers are passed to investors via the SPC. There are two main types of auto-ABS bonds, pass-through securities and *pay-through* securities. The majority of issues are pass-throughs.

The prepayment risk on auto-ABS bonds is low. Car loans have a very low response to changes in market interest rates, and loans are rarely repaid ahead of the maturity date. Auto-ABS bonds therefore do not exhibit the negative convexity of mortgage-backed bonds. There are non-interest-rate reasons why prepayment might occur however, such as customers 'trading up' to another car, or theft or destruction of the vehicle.

20.4.2 *Yield spreads*

The structure of auto-ABS bonds is relatively straightforward compared to other asset-backed securities, and possibly simpler than credit card-backed securities. They are amortising bonds (in the US) but because they have little prepayment risk they do not exhibit negative convexity. They are also shorter-dated securities compared to other ABS issues; most auto pass-throughs have average lives of 1.8 to 2.2 years, which is considerably lower than mortgage bonds. The yield spread over Treasury securities for auto-ABS issues is tighter than mortgage securities, but slightly over that for credit card securities. During 1996 they typically yielded around 10–25 basis points over credit card securities, and on average 30–40 basis points below manufactured housing mortgage securities. The market places a premium on auto-ABS bonds issued by the independent finance companies, which trade at around 5–10 basis points above issues made by the Big Three manufacturers and the commercial banks.

This is illustrated in Table 20.2. The Olympic 1996-A and Western Finance 1996-A were issued by independent finance houses, as was the UAC 1996-A. Note that each of these traded at a yield that was 6–8 basis points higher than the others, which were issued by commercial banks, although their relatively small issue will impact in their liquidity, for which there is a small yield premium.

Tranche Issues	Date	Amount ($m)	Average life (years)	Spread (bps)
Premier 1996–1	21-Mar-96	1,250	2.0	34
Olympic 1996-A	07-Mar-96	600	2.0	40
Western Finance	21-Mar-96	484	2.0	42
Pass-Throughs				
Chase 1996-A	14-Feb-96	1,474	1.6	41
Banc One 1996-A	15-Feb-96	537	1.6	42
Fifth Third 1996-A	19-Mar-96	408	1.7	43
UAC 1996-A	09-Feb-96	203	1.9	49

Table 20.2: Auto-ABS issues during 1996. Reprinted from Zimmerman, T., 'Auto-Loan-Backed Securities', in Fabozzi, F., *The Handbook of Fixed Income Securities*, 5th edition, McGraw-Hill, 1997. Used with permission.

Auto-ABS bonds have a wider range of payment windows than comparable securities and this makes their relative value more closely related to the shape of the yield curve. Securities such as credit card ABS bonds provide a higher return in an environment with a steeply positive short-date yield curve, due to their 'roll down' effect, so that in a steepening yield curve scenario auto-ABS bonds will be outperformed by credit card securities. This reflects that in a stable yield curve environment auto-ABS bonds will achieve a higher total return, compared to their spread, than credit card securities.

20.5 Credit card-backed securities

Another large sector in the asset-backed market is the credit card market. It experienced steady growth during the 1990s, with over $369 billion nominal outstanding in June 1998.[5] The rise in credit card securitisation reflects the increasing use of credit cards by consumers, such that it is now a significant national economic indicator. The public are now able to pay for a large number of goods and services using credit cards, and as a payment medium they are increasingly used for regular, 'day-to-day' purchases as well as larger size one-off transactions. The first example of a credit card securitisation was in 1987 in the US domestic market, as banks sought to move credit card assets off their balance sheets, thus freeing up lending lines, and diversify their funding sources. The first banks to securitise their credit card books were Capital One, MBNA and Advanta, among others. They were able to benefit from funding at triple-A rates, due to the credit enhancement used on the bond structures and consequently low charges on their capital. The largest issuers of credit card-backed bonds in the US market are shown at Table 20.3 below.

Credit card ABS bonds, along with auto-ABS issues, remain the most accessible instruments for investors who are interested in having an exposure in the asset-backed market. As they have maturities that are shorter than the average lives of mortgage-backed securities, as well as cash flow patterns that are more akin to conventional bonds, they are attractive investments to institutions such as banks and money market funds.

5 The source of the statistical data in this section is *Asset-Backed Alert*.

Securitising banks	$ billion
Citibank	41.5
MBNA America	22.3
Discover	13.6
First USA	12.1
First Chicago	11.9
Household	10.2
Capital One	7.1
Chase Manhattan	6.0
Advanta	5.1

Table 20.3: Largest issuers of credit card-backed bonds, US domestic market, June 1998. Source: Chase Manhattan.

In the US, and increasingly in the UK and Europe, the combination of credit card, auto-loan and mortgage-backed securities means that there are highly-rated asset-backed instruments, paying reasonable spreads over government securities, available along the entire yield curve.

20.5.1 *Issuing structures*

In the US market there are two different structures under which credit card debt is securitised. The *stand-alone trust* is a pool of credit card accounts that have been sold to a trust, and then used as collateral for a single security. As with CMOs there are usually several classes of bonds within a single issue. If a subsequent class of bonds is issued, the issuer must designate a new pool of *receivables* and sell these card accounts to a separate trust. This structure was used at the start of the market, but has been all but replaced by the *master trust*, which is a structure that allows the securitising bank to issue successive securities from the same trust, which are all backed by the same pool of credit card loan collateral. Under this arrangement the issuer retains greater flexibility for issuing securities, and without the cost associated with setting up a new trust each time a new issue is required.

Example 20.2: Credit Card ABS master trust structure

- An issuing bank transfers the cash flows represented by 100,000 credit card accounts, with a nominal value of $200 million, to a separate trust. It then issues different classes of securities, with different coupons, maturities and nominal values, all backed by the same collateral. At a later date if the issuer requires further funding it transfers the receivables from more card accounts to the same trust and issues more securities. The different tranches of receivables, transferred at two different times, are not differentiated from one another and are not segregated; that is, the combined receivables in the trust back all the bond issues made against the trust.

As a master trust will comprise receivables transferred to it over time, it will contain cash flows that have different payment terms and interest rates (or *annual payment rate* [APR], used in quoting credit card interest rates), reflecting the terms and conditions of cards issued at different times. For instance, a bank may issue cards under a special low interest rate as part of a special promotion designed to attract new customers. New cardholders will have accounts with different terms and cash flows to existing card holders. Investors in credit card ABS must be aware therefore that the composition of accounts in a master trust pool are liable to alter over time, sometimes significantly, as existing cardholder accounts are closed or fall dormant, and as new accounts are added, with or without different terms and conditions.

Issuers of credit card ABS in the US market are required to retain ownership, or a shared ownership, in the trust. This is so that the issuer can ensure that fluctuations in the balance of the receivables due to seasonal factors and factors such as returned goods and credit card fraud can be managed. It is also an incentive for the issuer to maintain the credit quality of the pool. The participation level is set at the minimum level of the receivables balance in the trust, which is 7% in the US market. This minimum level is set at 10% in the UK market and for sterling credit card ABS. If the level of its participation falls below the minimum required, the issuer must add further credit card accounts to the trust.

The issuing structure for credit card ABS is similar irrespective of the type of trust that is used. Generally there are three types of cash flow periods, which are *revolving, amortisation* (or otherwise *accumulation*) and *early amortisation*. Each period generates a different cash flow. This structure essentially replicates a conventional plain vanilla bond, with regular coupon payments and a single redemption amount on maturity, sometimes called the *bullet* payment. The main difference however is that credit card ABS pay monthly interest, instead of the traditional semi-annual interest basis. Credit card bonds also differ from other asset-backed securities because they do not have an amortising payment structure. Such an arrangement would not be appropriate for credit card bonds, since the average life of a receivable is shorter, ranging from between 5 months to 10 months. Under the amortising structure, which is used for mortgage-backed bonds and some auto-ABS bonds, payments of principal and interest are passed directly to investors each month. This would lead to an uncertain and volatile payment structure for credit card bonds. Therefore a revolving structure is used instead, with all cash flows being split into interest payments and principal payments. The monthly interest payment is used to cover the coupon on the bond, and cash flow that remains after this liability has been discharged, known as *excess spread*, is passed to the issuer or seller. The collection of principal differs according to the payment period, which is reviewed below.

- **Revolving period.** The revolving period in the structure is not fixed, and has ranged from 2 to 11 years. During the period bondholders receive only interest payments, when monthly payments of principal are used to purchase new receivables in accounts held in the trust; if there are no new receivables, the cash flows are used to purchase a share of the issuer's participation. If there are insufficient receivables available, this effects an early amortisation, as the issuer's participation would have fallen to below the minimum level. This is an incentive to the issuer to maintain a participation above the minimum.
- **Amortisation/accumulation.** This period starts after the revolving period has ceased. In amortisation or *controlled amortisation*, principal payments are no longer used for reinvestment in more receivables, but instead are used to pay off bondholders in a series

of amortisation payments. The size of these payments depends on how long the amortisation period runs for; the usual length is one year, so that investors receive 12 equal amortisation periods over the year. Excess principal payments received during this period are used to purchase new receivables, similar to the process followed in the revolving period. Accumulation is similar to controlled amortisation, but for investors the results of the process are akin to a conventional bond. The monthly principal payments are deposited in a trust account or *principal funding account* over the 12 month period, and then paid out to bondholders as one lump sum on the maturity date. During this time, interest payments are made each month on the balance of the total invested amount. Accumulation is therefore attractive to investors who wish the redemption payment to be a single bullet payment, and during the process they will not notice any change as the bond moves from the revolving period to the accumulation period.

- **Early amortisation.** An early amortisation is not a planned event, and is triggered if there is decline in asset quality, or the issuer is found to be in financial trouble. The bonds enter into an early amortisation so that investors start to receive their principal immediately, and not be subject to delays in repayment that might otherwise occur. The terms under which credit card ABS deals are issued specify a range of events that, if they occur, will cause the issue to enter early amortisation. These include failure to make required interest payments, failure to transfer receivables to the trust when required, and certain events of bankruptcy and default connected with the issuer. Other triggering events include if the excess spread falls to zero, and if the issuer's participation level falls below the minimum level. The occurrence of early amortisation is a rare event.

20.5.2 *Credit enhancement*

Bonds issued against credit card receivables are unsecured in that the receivables provide no collateral if cardholders default. Credit card bonds require therefore some form of credit enhancement if they are to receive investment-grade credit ratings, and the majority of them are highly rated once the enhancement has been set up. In this section we briefly describe the main types of credit enhancement that are arranged for credit card issues; many structures have two or more of these enhancements.

- **Excess spread.** The excess spread payment is the amount of cash flow over and above the amount required to discharge the bond's interest obligations. There is usually a significant excess spread due to the interest rate charged on credit cards being substantially higher than money market and bond market interest rates. For example, the average credit card APR in the UK market during 1998 was over 19%, and sometimes as high as 23%. This means that once the coupon on the bond has been issued and service and other charges paid, there is usually a substantial excess spread, often as high as 5%. The excess spread is used in one or more ways, including to pay the fees of credit enhancement institutions, being deposited in a trust reserve account or being released to the issuer.
- **Senior/subordinated notes.** Issues are often split into different classes of bonds, to suit investor taste. A common credit enhancement is the senior/subordinated structure, with bonds split into higher and lower rated issues. The subordinated notes absorb the losses in the structure ahead of the senior notes, if any other credit enhancement features have

not proved sufficient. On maturity or early amortisation the senior notes will be repaid ahead of the subordinated notes. The latter trade at a higher yield as a result.

- **Letter of credit.** As with other asset-backed markets, a bank letter of credit is a common form of credit enhancement used in the credit card market. This is a guarantee from a bank to provide payment in the event that the trust is unable to meet the commitments of the bond issue. The bank guarantee is up to an amount stipulated in the letter of credit. A fee is payable to the bank for providing the letter. This type of enhancement has proved less popular in recent years, after some issuers were themselves downgraded, leading to a downgrading of assets that they had provided letters of credit against.
- **Cash collateral account.** This is a segregated bank account for the benefit of the trust. It is set up and funded at the time of the issue, and funds in it may be used to cover occasions when there are insufficient payments received to cover required interest and principal payments. The funds in the account are borrowed from a third-party bank, and the terms of the issue usually provide for repayment of the cash collateral account only after all the bonds in the issue have been repaid. The excess spread may also be used to fund or top-up the account.
- **Collateral invested amount.** The collateral invested amount, also known as *collateral interest* or *enhancement invested amount* is a share of ownership in the trust and works in the same way as the cash collateral account. It is usually placed with a third-party bank, and is also funded by part of the excess spread.

20.5.3 *Credit analysis*

Credit card ABS are rated by the four major credit ratings agencies, in the same way as other asset-backed bonds. The variables in the credit card market mean that there are a larger number of scenarios that the agencies must consider. For example the quality of a pool of credit card receivables is a function of (among other issues):

- the type of credit cards in the pool, whether standard, low-rate, affinity cards, store cards, etc.;
- the credit scoring model used by the card issuer;
- the interest rates charged on the cards, whether fixed or floating, and the frequency with which rates are changed or re-set;
- amount of dormant cards in the pool;
- behaviour of cardholders in the pool;
- yield on the portfolio;
- monthly payment rate, which will fluctuate as the number of accounts changes, or as cardholders pay a smaller amount of their balance each month or pay off balances entirely;
- coupon on the bonds: a floating coupon on the bond is more at risk if it is backed with card receivables that are fixed rate, and vice-versa.

The credit rating a bond issue receives will also consider what possibility there exists that it will be forced into early amortisation. This is separate to the issue of credit enhancement, and unaffected by it. The rating of a credit card issue indicates the likelihood that the issue will be able to redeem in full all the bonds in the structure under any possible scenario. A triple-A rating indicates that investors should receive all their principal.

20.6 Static spread analysis of asset-backed bonds

It is apparent that the traditional gross redemption yield or yield-to-maturity method for measuring the return available from a particular instrument, and its relative value compared to the government yield curve, is not appropriate in the case of asset-backed bonds. In order to calculate a meaningful redemption yield measure, the cash flows for a particular instrument must be known with a degree of certainty. This is not the case for many asset-backed securities. The inaccuracy of the redemption yield measure also must take into account the fact that, even for conventional bonds, it ignores the reinvestment and dispersion of coupon payments, discounting them all at the same rate. This is, to all and intents and purposes, glossed over for conventional bonds because the calculation treats all bonds the same, creating in effect a level playing field.

Asset-backed bonds have subtle differences in cash flow profiles and prepayment rates, making it more difficult to analyse them all in the same way. The exception to this is most credit card-ABS issues, which have a single bullet payment on maturity and (usually, but not always) a fixed coupon payment every month. It would be in order to compare the yield on such a bond with a conventional corporate bond. Other asset-backed issues such as mortgage and car loan securities do not have such a stable cash flow, mainly due to the amortising nature of the underlying loans. The simplest way to analyse these securities is to price them as a spread to the yield of the government bond whose maturity is closest to the weighted average life of the bonds being analysed. This is still an approximate measure and can be inaccurate under certain circumstances, and the convention now is to use the *static spread* measure.

20.6.1 *Static spread analysis*

Static spread analysis assumes that a particular bond itself represents a portfolio of individual securities, so that each cash flow is viewed as a zero-coupon bond. Under the static spread method each of these individual cash flows is discounted using a rate made up of the relevant government zero-coupon rate plus a spread. The spot rate used is the one whose duration matches that of the specific cash flow.[6] The spread at which the sum of the discounted cash flows equalled their nominal price is known as the static spread, *zero-volatility spread*, or *Z-spread*.

This is illustrated with the following example, which uses three hypothetical securities. The first bond (Bond A) has a maturity of one year (12 months), while the remaining bonds B and C have average maturities of 12 months. Bond A has a single bullet redemption payment in exactly 12 months' time, exemplified by a conventional

6 In the US, UK and certain European markets there is a market in zero-coupon government bonds, known as strips. Therefore it is straightforward to find the appropriate spot rate to use in discounting the asset-backed bond cash flows, although banks frequently use an implied spot-rate curve because of liquidity effects of the observed zero-coupon curve. In the absence of an actual strip market, the implied spot rate calculated from the benchmark government bond yield curve is used.

corporate bond or certain credit card-backed bonds. Bond B repays its principal over a 12-month period beginning six months from now, similar to a credit card-backed bond that has a controlled amortisation process. Bond C has an amortising principal repayment pattern, so that the amount of repayment declines gradually starting in the next month and finishing 24 months from now. This bond resembles an auto-ABS bond and certain mortgage pass-through securities. The principal payment cash flows are shown as Figures 20.6 (i), (ii) and (iii). Assume that all bonds are trading at a yield to maturity of 6.33%. The one-year government bond is trading at a yield of 5.98%, therefore the yield spread on the three bonds is 35 basis points.[7] This spread is also called the *nominal spread*.

We know that the redemption yield calculation discounts each cash flow at the internal rate of return, here 6.33%, which has been based on the average maturity of 12 months for receipt of the principal. In a positively sloping short-term yield curve environment, cash flows received early on would be discounted at a rate that was above the actual rate for that term, while cash flows received later would be discounted at a rate that was below the actual

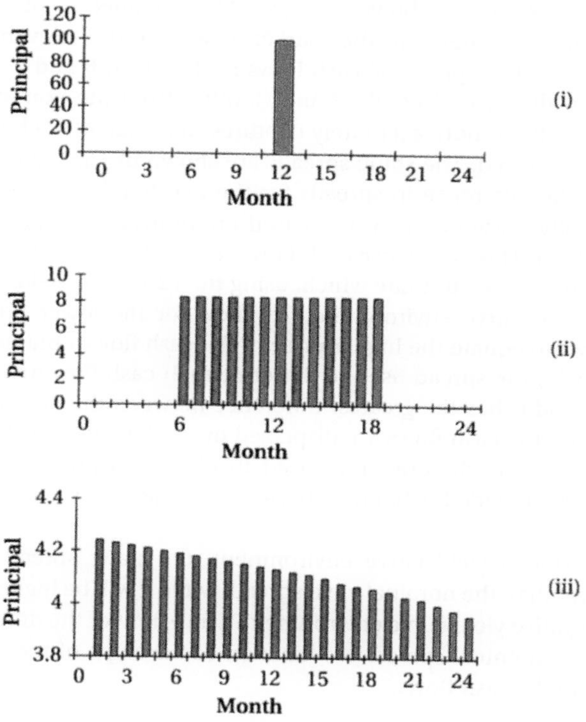

Figure 20.6: Cash flow profiles for bullet, controlled amortisation and amortised principal bonds (i), (ii), (iii).

7 The yields are based on market conditions for sterling asset-backed bonds in October 1999, against the gilt yield curve at that time.

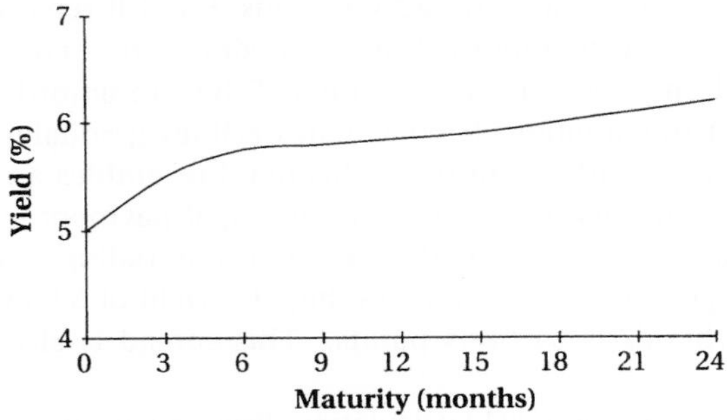

Figure 20.7: Short-term yield curve.

rate. This is an accepted drawback of the redemption yield method, and is accepted on the belief that the two effects will cancel each other out.

The static spread gives a more accurate picture yield. Assume that the short-term zero-coupon yield curve is as follows, shown in Figure 20.7, obtained by observing the yield of government discount instruments in the market. If we use the relevant yields from this curve to discount each of the principal cash flows for bonds A, B and C, the static spreads that are obtained, in the case of bonds B and C, differ from the nominal spread. This is because using this method more accurately captures the value of each cash flow over the period that they are received. The static spreads are shown in Table 20.4.

What is behind the difference in spreads for the two bonds with non-bullet principal repayment? Essentially these bonds, when based on an average maturity yield level plus spread, are over-valued. This is because cash flows received after the average maturity date are more sensitive to the discount rate which, using the 12-month yield, is below the actual rate in a positive yield curve environment. To allow for the lower present value of the individual cash flows to equate the higher price of the cash flows obtained using the single average maturity yield, the spread used to discount each cash flow must be lower. This is the static spread. Bond C has the greatest difference between the nominal spread and the static spread, because the cash flows are dispersed over a longer period, making each cash flow more sensitive to the discount rate used to obtain its present value. There is no difference in the two spreads for bond A, because the cash flow has been discounted at the correct rate.

In a positively sloped yield curve environment, the static spread on an amortising security will be lower than the nominal yield spread, while it will be higher than the nominal yield spread in a negative yield curve environment. The extent of the difference between the static spread and the nominal spread is a function of the slope of the yield curve and the dispersion of the bond's cash flows.

	Bond A	Bond B	Bond C
Nominal spread	35	35	35
Static spread	35	30	28

Table 20.4: Static and nominal spreads of hypothetical bonds A, B and C.

Example 20.3: Covered bonds

Covered bonds are similar in most economic aspects to residential MBS instruments but have detail differences in their structure and legal definition. The longest-established covered bond market is that in German Pfandbriefe; there are also covered bond markets in other European markets such as the Netherlands, Ireland, Spain and the United Kingdom.

The key difference between an RMBS and a mortgage-backed covered bond is that an SPV is not created and assets are not transferred to an SPV. Instead, a wholly-owned subsidiary is created within the originating bank or financial institution and assets are transferred to this legal entity. Hence, these assets are not taken off the originating entity's balance sheet, as they remain part of the Group assets.

As an example, consider the mortgage covered bond issued by Halifax plc (a former UK building society and part of the HBOS group). It is illustrated in Figure 20.8. This was created as follows:

- the arm of HBOS responsible for funding activity, HBOS Treasury, issued covered bonds to investors;
- funds raised by this issue were loaned to a new Group company, Halifax LLP, a wholly-owned subsidiary of HBOS group;
- the Group sold a pool of residential mortgages to Halifax LLP, at an overcollateralisation of 15%;
- Halifax LLP placed these assets under a security trust and guarantee which was given to investors.

Unlike a traditional securitisation, the liabilities on the issues notes were held by HBOS Treasury, not the new legal entity. It funded the liabilities out of its normal activities, not out of the cash flows represented by the mortgages transferred to Halifax LLP. Only in the event of default on the issued notes would investors have recourse to the assets held by Halifax LLP. This structure presented certain advantages over traditional RMBS issues as it was operated as a programme of rolling issues, and also appealed to a wider investor base.

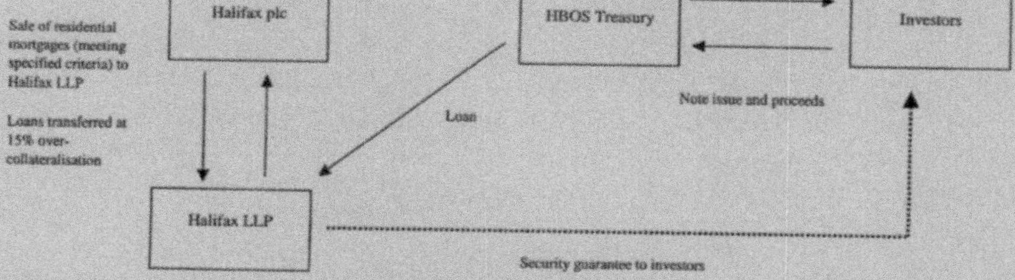

Figure 20.8: Halifax mortgage covered bond, July 2003 © HBOS. Reproduced with permission.

20.7 Conclusion

The asset-based markets represent a large and diverse group of securities which are suited to a varied group of investors. We have only touched upon them in these three chapters. Often they are the only way for institutional investors to pick up yield while retaining assets with high credit ratings. They are popular with issuers because they represent a cost-effective means of removing assets off the balance sheet, thus freeing up lending lines, and enabling them to have access to lower cost funding. Depending on the nature of the underlying asset backing, there are instruments available that cover the entire term of the yield curve. They are also available paying a fixed- or floating-rate coupon. Although the market was developed in the United States, there are also liquid markets in the United Kingdom and other European markets. In the UK it is common for mortgage-backed bonds to have a floating coupon, reflecting the interest basis of UK mortgages, although there have been structures paying fixed coupon rates.

Yield analysis of asset-backed securities must take into account their uncertain cash flows. We have demonstrated that the traditional redemption yield measure, calculated using the security's average life maturity, is inappropriate, because it does not allow for the dispersed nature of the bond's cash. A mortgage or auto-loan backed bond has a principal repayment structure that disperses the payments over a length of time, so the more accurate yield measure to use is static spread. As well as accounting for dispersion, this approach also overcomes the traditional drawback of yield-to-maturity as it discounts each cash flow at the correct rate for that cash flow's maturity.

Selected bibliography and references

Bear Stearns, *Asset-Backed Securities Special Report*, 5 December 1994

Bhattacharya, A., Fabozzi, F. (eds.), *Asset-Backed Securities*, FJF Associates, 1996

Fabozzi, F., Jacob, D., *The Handbook of Commercial Mortgage-Backed Securities*, FJF Associates, 1996

Fabozzi, F., Ramsey, C., Ramirez, F., *Collateralized Mortgage Obligations*, FJF Associates, 1994

Fabozzi, F., *Handbook of Structured Financial Products*, FJF Associates, 1998

Oppenheimer & Co., 'Qualitatively Assessing Prepayments of Current- and Discount-Coupon PassThroughs', *Mortgage Research*, Oppenheimer & Co., Inc., 20 October 1994

21 Collateralised Debt Obligations

Collateralised debt obligations (CDOs) are a form of securitised debt. The market in such bonds emerged in the US in the late 1980s, first as a form of repackaged high-yield bonds. The market experienced sharp growth in the second half of the 1990s, due to a combination of investor demand for higher yields allied to credit protection, and the varying requirements of originators, such as balance sheet management and lower-cost funding. The term 'CDO' is a generic one, used to cover what are known as *collateralised bond obligations* (CBOs) and *collateralised loan obligations* (CLOs). Put simply a CBO is an issue of rated securities backed or 'collateralised' by a pool of debt securities. A CLO on the other hand is an issue of paper that has been secured by a pool of bank loans. As the market has grown the distinction between the two types of structure has become blurred somewhat. Practitioners have taken to defining different issues in terms of the issuer's motivation, the type of asset backing and the type of market into which the paper is sold, for example the commercial paper market. Different structures are now more often categorised as being *balance sheet* transactions, usually a securitisation of assets in order to reduce regulatory capital requirements and provide the originator with an alternative source of funding, or *arbitrage* transactions, in which the originator sets up a managed investment vehicle in order to benefit from a funding gap that exists between assets and liabilities. Balance sheet transactions are issuer driven, whereas arbitrage transactions are typically investor driven.

Over $107 billion of CDOs was issued during 1999.[1] This included over $51 billion of CBOs backed by high-yield bonds and just under $45 billion of CLOs. During 1999 the combined CBO/CLO market was thought to account for approximately 18–20% of the total US asset-backed bond market.[2] In this chapter we provide an introduction to the most common CDO structures, as well as an overview of the analysis of these instruments. We also discuss the use of credit derivatives in the CDO market.

21.1 An overview of CDOs

21.1.1 *Introduction*

Collateralised debt obligation or CDO is the generic term for two distinct products, so-called balance sheet transactions and arbitrage transactions. The common thread between these structures is that they are both backed by some form of commercial or corporate debt or loan receivable. The primary differences between the two types are the type of collateral backing the newly-created securities in the CDO structure, and the

---

1 Source: *Risk*, 2000. This refers to CDO deals that had been rated by at least one of Moody's, S & P and Fitch rating agencies.

2 *Ibid.*

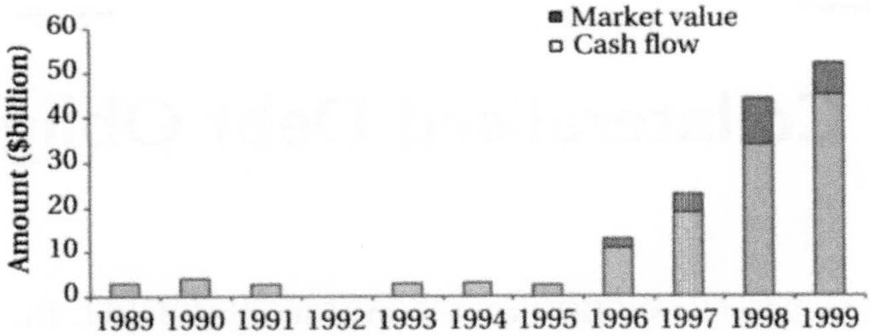

Figure 21.1: CDO issuance 1989–1999. Source: Moodys, Fitch, Bloomberg.

motivations behind the transaction. The growth of the market has been in response to two key requirements: the desire of investors for higher-yield investments in higher-risk markets, managed by portfolio managers skilled at extracting value out of poorly performing or distressed debt, and the need for banks to extract greater value out of assets on their balance sheet, almost invariably because they are generating a below-market rate of return. By securitising bond or loan portfolios, banks can lower their capital charge by removing them off their balance sheet and funding them at a lower rate. The market has its origins in investor-driven arbitrage transactions, with bank balance sheet transactions a natural progression after banks applied securitisation techniques to their own asset base. Figure 21.2 is a summary of the key differences between balance sheet arbitrage and CDOs.

Balance sheet CDOs are structured securities that are usually backed with bank-originated, investment grade commercial and corporate loans. Since this form of collateral is almost invariably loans, and very rarely bonds, these transactions are usually referred to as collateralised loan obligations or CLOs. Why would a bank wish to securitise part of its loan portfolio? In short, in order to improve its capital adequacy position. Securitising a bank's loans reduces the size of its balance sheet, thereby improving its capital ratio and lowering its capital charge. The first domestic balance sheet CLO in the US market was the NationsBank Commercial Loan Master Trust, series 1997–1 and 1997–2, issued in September 1997,

Collateralised Debt Obligations (CDOs)

Balance Sheet CDOs	**Arbitrage CDOs**
Collateral: High grade, bank-originated commercial and corporate loans ***Key motivations:*** Reducing balance sheet to improve capital ratios; obtain off-balance sheet treatment; obtain lower funding rates ***Typical issuers:*** Domestic and international banks Market liquidity: Generally lower than investor-driven trades	*Collateral:* High yield corporate bonds or corporate loans ***Key motivations:*** Arbitrage opportunity; increase assets under management; assets purchased in secondary market ***Typical issuers:*** Insurance companies; mutual funds; private equity funds

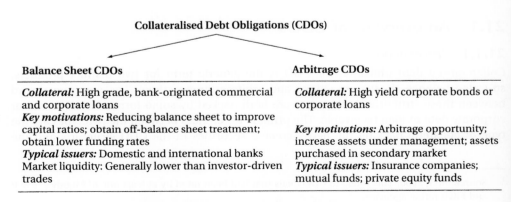

Figure 21.2: Collateralised debt obligations.

which employed what is known as a Master Trust structure to target investors who had previously purchased asset-backed securities.[3]

As balance sheet CLOs are originated mainly by commercial banks, the underlying collateral is usually part of their own commercial loan portfolios, and can be fixed term, revolving, secured and unsecured, syndicated and other loans. Although we note from Figure 21.6 that most CLOs have been issued by banks that are domiciled in the main developed economies, the geographical nature of the underlying collateral often have little connection with the home country of the originating bank. Most bank CLOs are floating-rate loans with average lives of five years or less. They are targeted mainly at bank sector Libor-based investors, and are structured with an amortising payoff schedule.

Arbitrage CDOs are backed with high-yield corporate bonds or loans. As the collateral can take either forms, arbitrage CDOs can be either CLOs or collateralised bond obligations (CBOs). Market practitioners often refer to all arbitrage deals as CDOs for simplicity, irrespective of the collateral backing them. The key motivation behind arbitrage CDOs is, unsurprisingly, the opportunity for arbitrage, or the difference between investment grade funding rates and high-yield investment rates. In an arbitrage CDO, the income generated by the high-yield assets should exceed the cost of funding, as long as no credit event or market event takes place.

Although CDOs are not a recent innovation, the market only experienced high growth rates from 1995 onwards, and certain investors are still prone to regard it as an 'emerging' asset class. However in terms of volume in the US market, CDOs are comparable to credit card and automobile loan asset-backed securities, as illustrated in Figure 21.3 below.

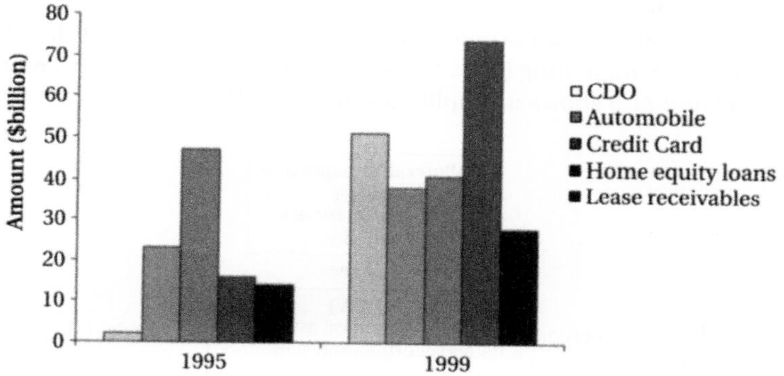

Figure 21.3: CDO supply versus other ABS products in US market, 1995 and 1999. Source: Bloomberg, Bank of America.

21.1.2 *Security structure*

Arbitrage and balance sheet CDOs generally have similar structures. In essence a special purpose vehicle (SPV) purchases loans or bonds directly from the originator or from the

[3] The Master Trust structure is a generic set up that allows originators to issue subsequent asset-backed deals under the same legal arrangement, thus enabling such issues to made quicker than they otherwise might be. Investors also welcome such a structure, as they indicate a commitment to liquidity by implying further issues into the market.

secondary market. SPVs have been set up in a number of ways, these include a *special purpose corporation*, a limited partnership or a limited liability corporation. An SPV will be bankruptcy-remote, that is unconnected to any other entities that support it or are involved with it. The parties involved in a transaction, apart from the investors, are usually a portfolio manager, a bond trustee appointed to look after the interests of the investors, a credit enhancer and a back-up servicer. Some structures involve a swap arrangement where this is required to alter cash flows or set up a hedge, so in such cases a swap counterparty is also involved. A basic structure is shown in Figure 21.4, which is applicable to both CBOs and CLOs.

Invariably the SPV will issue a number of classes of debt, with credit enhancements included in the structure such that different tranches of security can be issued, each with differing levels of credit quality. Other forms of protection may also be included, including a cash reserve.

A further development has been the issue of *synthetic* CDOs. Synthetic CLO structures use credit derivatives that allow the originating bank to transfer the risk of the loan portfolio to the market. In a synthetic structure there is no actual transfer of the underlying reference assets; instead the economic effect of a traditional CDO is synthesised by passing to the end investor(s) an identical economic risk associated with the underlying assets, the same that would have been transferred had the SPV actually purchased the assets. This effect is achieved by the provision by a counterparty of a *credit default swap*, or by the issue of *credit-linked notes* by the originating bank, or by a combination of these approaches. In a credit-linked CLO the loan portfolio remains on the sponsoring bank's balance sheet, and investors in the securities are exposed to the credit risk of the bank itself, in addition to the market risk of the collateralised portfolio. Therefore, the credit rating of the CLO can be no higher than that of the originating bank. We will look at these structures in more detail later in Chapter 22. Figure 21.5 shows a simplified synthetic CDO structure.

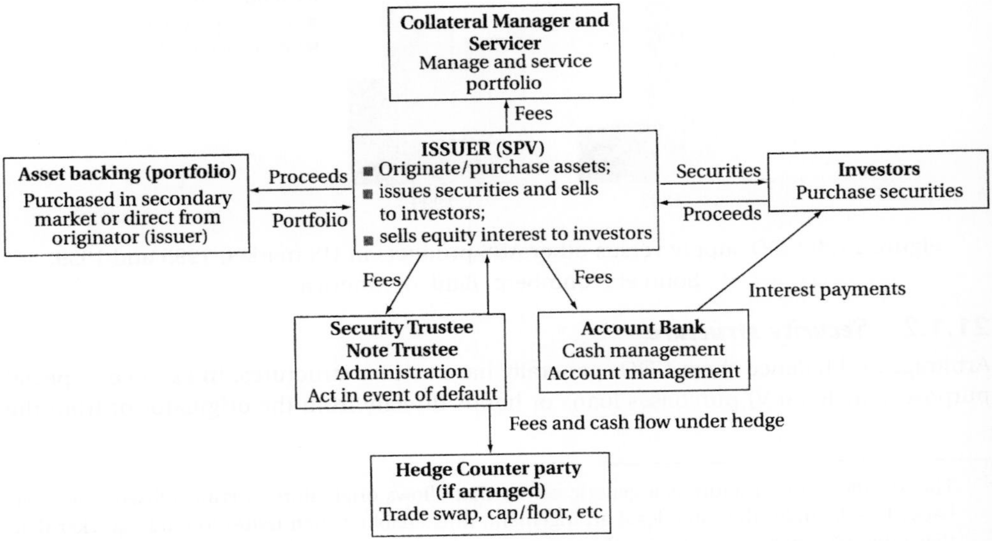

Figure 21.4: Basic CDO structure.

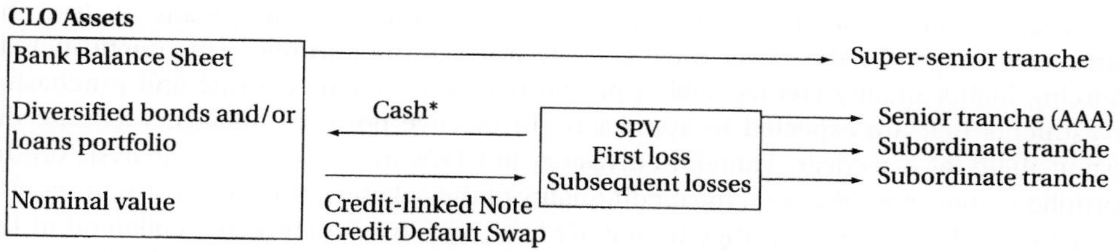

*Cash raised by the SPV goes to the originating bank in "linked" transactions or is invested in Treasury securities in "delinked" transactions.

Figure 21.5: Synthetic CDO structure.

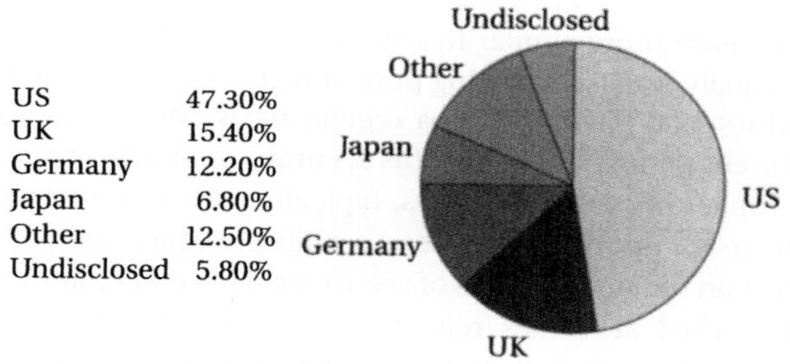

Figure 21.6: Outstanding bank CLOs by country of originating bank in 1999. Source: Fitch, Bank of America.

21.1.3 *Comparisons with other asset-backed securities*

The CDO asset class has similarities in its fundamental structure with other securities in the ABS market. Like other asset-backed securities, a CDO is a debt obligation issued by a special purpose vehicle, secured by a form of receivable. In this case though, the collateral concerned is high yield loans or bonds, rather than say, mortgage or credit card receivables. Again similar to other ABS, CDO securities typically consist of different credit tranches within a single structure, and the credit ratings range from AAA to B or unrated. The rating of each CDO class is determined by the amount credit enhancement in the structure, the ongoing performance of the collateral, and the priority of interest in the cash flows generated by the pool of assets. The credit enhancement in a structure is among items scrutinised by investors, who will determine the cash flow *waterfalls* for the interest and principal, the prepayment conditions, and the methods of allocation for default and recovery. Note that the term 'waterfall' is used in the context of asset-backed securitisations that are structured with more than one tranche, to refer to the allocation of principal and interest to each tranche in a series. If there is excess cash and this can be shared with other series, the cash flows are allocated back through the waterfall, running over the successive tranches in the order of priority determined at issue.

A significant difference between CDOs and other ABS is the relationship to the servicer. In a traditional ABS the servicing function is usually performed by the same entity that sources and underwrites the original loans. These roles are different in a CDO transaction;

for instance there is no servicer that can collect on non-performing loans. Instead the portfolio manager for the issuer must actively manage the portfolio. This might include sourcing higher quality credits, selling positions before they deteriorate and purchasing investments that are expected to appreciate. In essence portfolio managers assume the responsibility of a servicer. Therefore investors in CDOs must focus their analysis on the portfolio manager as well as on the credit quality of the collateral pool. CDO structures also differ from other ABS in that they frequently hold non-investment grade collateral in the pool, which is not a common occurrence in traditional ABS structures. Finally CDO transactions are (or rather, have been to date) private and not public securities.

21.1.4 *CDO asset types*

The arbitrage CDO market can be broken down into two main asset types, *cash flow* and *market value* CDOs. Balance sheet CDOs are all cash flow CDOs.

Cash flow CDOs share more similarities to traditional ABS than market value transactions. Collateral is usually a self-amortising pool of high-yield bonds and loans, expected to make principal and interest payments on a regular basis. Most cash flow CDO structures allow for a reinvestment period, and while this is common in other types of ABS, the period length tends to be longer in cash flow CDOs, typically with a minimum of four years. The cash flow structure relies upon the collateral's ability to generate sufficient cash to pay principal and interest on the rated classes of securities. This is similar to an automobile ABS, in which the auto-backed securities rely upon the cash flows from the fixed pool of automobile loans to make principal and interest payments on the liabilities. Trading of the CDO collateral is usually limited, for instance in the event of a change in credit situation, and so the value of the portfolio is based on the par amount of the collateral securities.

Market value CDOs, which were first introduced in 1995, resemble hedge funds more than traditional ABS. The main difference between a cash flow CDO and a market value CDO is that the portfolio manager has the ability to freely trade the collateral. This means investors focus on expected appreciation in the portfolio, and the portfolio itself may be quite different in say, three months' time compared to its composition today. This leads to the analogy with the hedge fund. Investors in market value CDOs are as concerned with the management and credit skills of the portfolio manager as they are with the credit quality of the collateral pool. Market value CDOs rely upon the portfolio manager's ability to generate total returns and liquidate the collateral in timely fashion, if necessary, in order to meet the cash flow obligations (principal and interest) of the CDO structure.

Different portfolio objectives result in distinct investment characteristics. Cash flow CDO assets consist mainly of rated, high-yield debt or loans that are *current* in their principal and interest payments, that is they are not in default. In a market value CDO the asset composition is more diversified. The collateral pool might consist of say, a 75:25 percentage split between assets to support liability payments and investments to produce increased equity returns. In this case, the first 75% of assets of a market value CDO assets will resemble those of a conventional cash flow CDO, with say 25% invested in high-yield bonds and 50% in high-yield loans. These assets should be sufficient to support payments on 100% of the liabilities. The remaining 25% of the portfolio might be invested in 'special situations' such as distressed debt, foreign bank loans, hybrid capital instruments and other investments. The higher yielding investments are required to produce the higher yields that are marketed to equity investors in market value CDOs.

We have described in general terms the asset side of a CDO. The liability side of a CDO structure is similar to other ABS structures, and encompasses several investment grade and non-investment grade classes with an accompanying equity tranche that serves as the first loss position. In say, a mortgage-backed transaction the equity class is not usually offered but instead held by the issuer. Typically in the US market rated CDO liabilities have a 10–12 year legal final maturity. The four main rating agencies[4] all actively rate cash flow CDOs, although commonly transactions carry ratings from only one or two of the agencies.

Liabilities for market value CDOs differ in some ways from cash flow CDOs. In most cases senior bank facilities provide more than half of the capital structure, with a 6–7 year final maturity. When a market value transaction is issued, cash generated by the issuance is usually not fully invested at the start. There is a *ramp-up* period to allow the portfolio manager time to make investment decisions and effect collateral purchases. Ramp-up periods result in a risk that cash flows on the portfolio's assets will not be sufficient to cover liability obligations at the start. Rating agencies consider this ramp-up risk when evaluating the transaction's credit enhancement. Ramp-up periods are in fact common to both cash flow and market value CDOs, but the period is longer with the latter transactions, resulting in more significant risk.

We noted that although CDOs were created at almost the same time as the first ABS issues, with the first structure appearing in 1988, it was only in the latter half of the 1990s that the product evolved sufficiently and in enough volume to be regarded as a distinct investment instrument. The US market has witnessed the most innovative structures, but interesting developments have also taken place in the UK and Germany. Figure 21.7 summarises the evolution in the CDO product in the US market from its first appearance to present arrangements. In particular collateral types backing the securities have grown considerably, with increasing sophistication in structure and cash flow mechanics. In 1999 CDOs covered a wide spectrum of credit risk and investment returns, from a diverse pool of high-yielding assets. Investors analyse CDOs as investment instruments in their own right and also with regard to the relative value offered by them vis-à-vis other ABS products.

Early CDO balance sheet	
Assets	*Liabilities*
US domestic high yield bonds	Fixed-rate private securities Equity
Present-day CDO balance sheet	
Assets	*Liabilities*
US domestic high yield bonds	AAA to BBB fixed rate securities
US domestic high yield loans	AAA to BBB floating rate securities
Emerging market debt	
Special situation/distressed debt	BB Mezzanine securities Contingent interest securities
Foreign bank loan	Credit-linked notes Equity

Figure 21.7: CDO product evolution.

4 That is, Standard & Poor's, Moody's, Fitch IBCA and Duff & Phelps. [Since this was written, the last two have merged to become Fitch IBCA, Duff & Phelps].

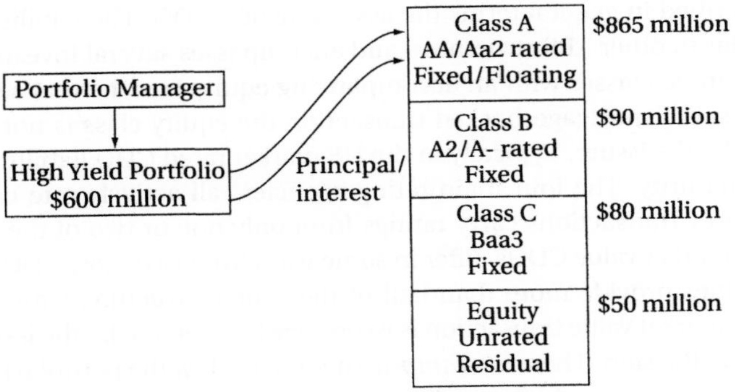

Figure 21.8: Hypothetical cash flow CBO structure.

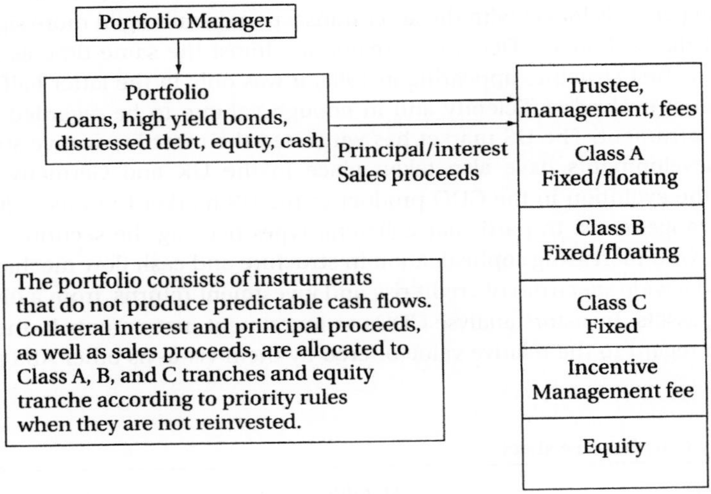

Figure 21.9: Hypothetical market value CBO structure.

21.2 Relative value analysis

Investors have a number of motivations when considering the CDO market both in their domestic market and abroad. These include:

- the opportunity to gain exposure to a high-yield market on a diversified basis, without committing significant resources;
- the ability to choose from a number of portfolio managers that manage the CDO;
- CDOs acting as an initial entry point into the high yield market;
- with respect to lower-rated (BBB and below) tranches, achieving leveraged returns while gaining benefit from a diversified portfolio;

- the appeal of a wide investor base, with ratings ranging from AAA to B and maturities from four years to as long as 20 years;
- wide variety of collateral.

CDOs offer investors a variety of risk/return profiles, as well as market volatilities, and their appeal has widened as broader macroeconomic developments in the global capital markets have resulted in lower yields on more traditional investments.

Investors analysing CDO instruments will focus on particular aspects of the market. For instance those with a low appetite for risk will concentrate in the higher rated classes of cash flow transactions. Investors that are satisfied with greater volatility of earnings but still wish to hold AA- or AAA-rated instruments may consider market value deals. The 'arbitrage' that exists in the transaction may be a result of:

- industry diversification;
- differences between investment grade and high-yield spreads;
- the difference between implied default rates in the high yield market and expected default rates;
- the liquidity premium embedded in high yield investments;
- the LIBOR rate versus the Treasury spread.

The CDO asset class cannot be compared in a straightforward fashion to other ABS classes, which makes relative value analysis difficult. Although a CDO is a structured finance product, it does not have sufficient common characteristics with other such products. The structure and cash flow of a CDO are perhaps most similar to a commercial mortgage-backed security; the collateral backing the two types share comparable characteristics. Commercial mortgage pools and high yield bonds and loans both have fewer obligors and larger balances than other ABS collateral, and each credit is rated. On the other hand CDOs often pay floating-rate interest and are private securities,[5] whereas commercial MBS (in the US market) pay fixed rate and are often public securities.

Historically during 1998 and 1999 CDO spreads offered greater opportunity for spread tightening than traditional ABS, as CDO yields were observed to take a longer time to recover from the bond bear market that existed in the second half of 1998. This is illustrated in Figure 21.10, with a comparison to commercial mortgage-backed securities. Although these had returned to pre-bear market levels, CDO spreads remained at the higher levels, that is they required a longer recovery period. From this picture at the start of the second quarter in 1999, CDO spreads had potentially a significant scope for tightening before reaching historical low spreads. This was in fact confirmed in the second half of the

---

[5] In the US market, they are also filed under Rule 144A, as opposed to public securities which must be registered with the Securities and Exchange Commission. Rule 144A securities may only be sold to investors classified as professional investors under specified criteria. Rule 144A provides an exemption from the registration requirements of the Securities Act (1933) for resale of privately placed securities to qualified institutional buyers. Such buyers are deemed to be established and experienced institutions, and so the SEC does not regulate or approve disclosure requirements.

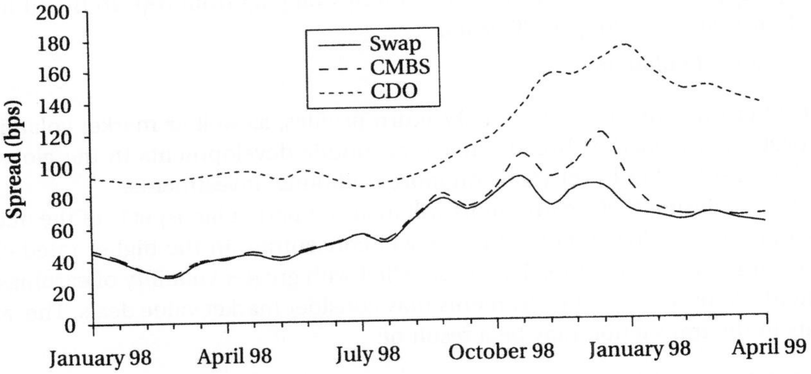

Figure 21.10: Historical spreads January 1998–March 1999. Source: Bloomberg, Bank of America.

year, when spreads came in to lower levels. In assessing relative value therefore an investor will assess the difference in spreads between CDOs and other ABS asset classes.

We have presented only an overview here; interested readers may wish to consult the references at the end of this chapter, principally Fabozzi (1998; Chapter 18) and the study by ING Barings.

21.3 Credit derivatives

Credit derivatives include a range of instruments designed to transfer credit risk without requiring the sale or purchase of bonds or loans. They originated in the eary 1990s in the US market, among banks that wished to manage the credit risk in their loan portfolios while preserving customer relationships. Here we consider their use in the CDO market.

Credit derivatives allow banks to provide the following enhanced services to their clients:

- tailored exposure to credit risk;
- the ability to take short positions in credits of underlying securities without having to take a position in the security itself;
- providing investors with access to the bank loan market, generally on a leveraged basis;
- the ability to extract and hedge specific sections of credit risk, for example defaulted par, defaulted coupon and credit rating migration.

The use of credit derivatives has added to the liquidity in the CDO market, by providing a more accurate asset-liability in CBO/CLO structures, increasing diversification in CBO collateral portfolios and repackaging illiquid CBO bonds to tailor risk to specific investor preferences.

The main credit derivative instruments are credit default swaps, total return swaps and credit-linked notes.

21.3.1 *Application of credit derivatives*

Synthetic CDOs originated for balance sheet purposes are intended to reduce regulatory capital requirements. Examples include *Glacier* in September 1997 and *Bistro* in December 1997, issued by (the then) Swiss Bank Corporation and JP Morgan respectively. These are believed to be the first structures that included credit derivatives. As we noted earlier, in a synthetic CDO a financial institution sets up an SPV to finance asset purchases. However as it is a synthetic structure, total return swaps (TRS) are used to pass through underlying security returns to a credit-linked note. These notes are in turn placed in an SPV that sells a range of liabilities. The use of TRSs in such structures allows for the maintenance of client confidentiality as well as a reduction in credit exposure. Compared to traditional structures, synthetic CDOs require a higher return, a downside for issuers, and this is achieved via the leverage offered by TRSs.

Another application of credit derivatives is in subordinated debt and default protection. The subordinated or mezzanine debt in a cash flow CBO is debt protected by an equity layer and an excess spread. One method by which liquidity of the mezzanine debt can be increased is to extract the mezzanine cash flows and place them inside a credit derivative. These repackaged cash flows can in turn be sold as an investment grade security to investors.

Here we illustrate the application of credit derivatives in CDO deals with the following hypothetical examples.

Example 21.1

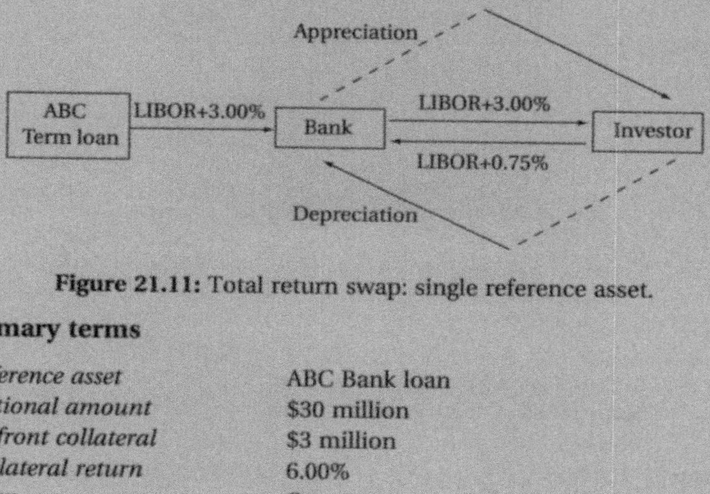

Figure 21.11: Total return swap: single reference asset.

1(i) Summary terms

Reference asset	ABC Bank loan
Notional amount	$30 million
Upfront collateral	$3 million
Collateral return	6.00%
Term	One year
Initial price	100
Investor (buyer) pays	LIBOR + 0.75% plus price depreciation
Investor receives	Interest + fees + price appreciation

1(ii) Remarks

This structure preserves the capital structure for the originating bank and requires minimal administration. However it allows the bank access to off-balance sheet financing.

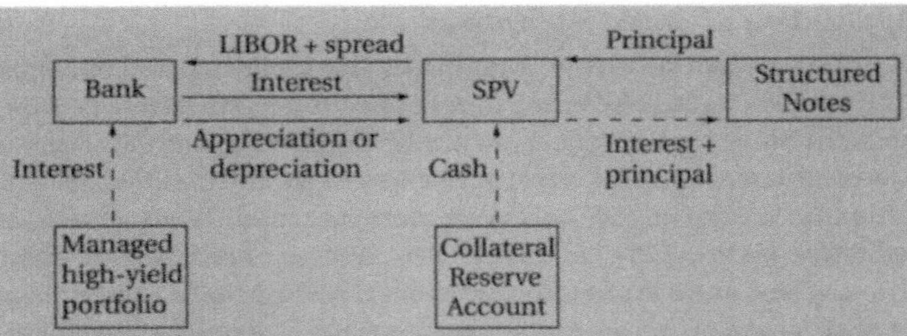

Figure 21.12: Synthetic CBO using total return swaps: TRS financing.

2(i) Summary terms

Reference asset	High yield loan portfolio
Notional amount	$500 million
Collateral return	LIBOR + 3%
Term	12 years
Initial price	100
Investor (buyer) pays	Price of note
Investor receives	Interest + par

2(ii) Remarks

This structure enables investors to have access to the bank loan market, and provides protection against market downside. It generates high return for investors with lower transaction costs, and for originators is an efficient use of capital.

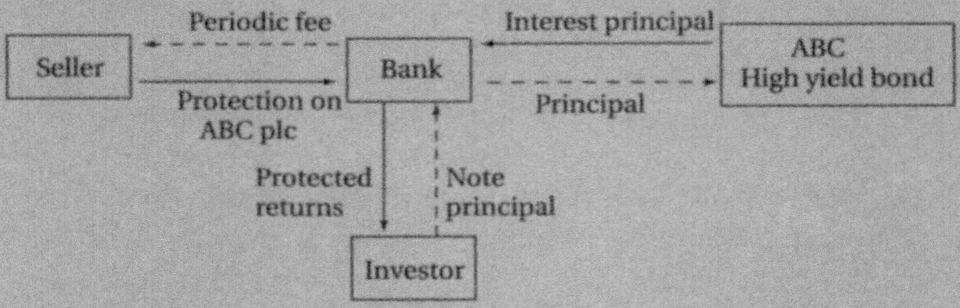

Figure 21.13: Credit-linked note: single reference asset.

3(i) Summary terms

Reference asset	High yield bond
Notional amount	$50 million
Collateral return	9.00%
Term	Two years
Initial price	100
Investor (buyer) pays	Price of note
Investor receives	Interest + par

3(ii) Remarks

A simple structure with minimal administration. Another form of off-balance sheet financing.

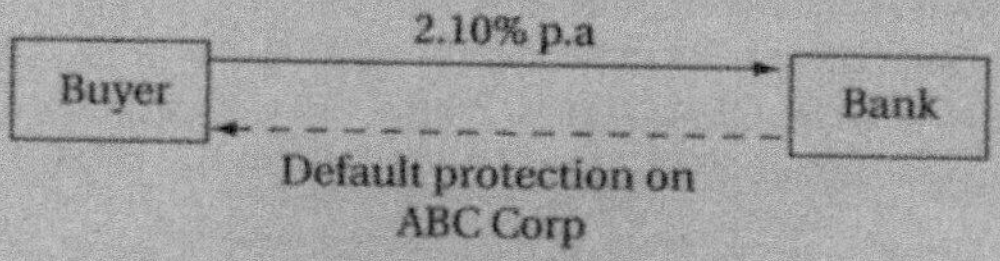

Figure 21.14: Credit default swap: purchase swap.

4(i) Summary terms

Reference asset	ABC Corporation bond (8.5% December 2005)
Notional amount	\$10 million
Term	Five years
Buyer pays	2.10% per annum
Buyer receives	Notional amount × (100% – market price) if credit event occurs

4(ii) Remarks

This is a simple credit default protection for the holder of the corporate bond, with the asset remaining on the balance sheet

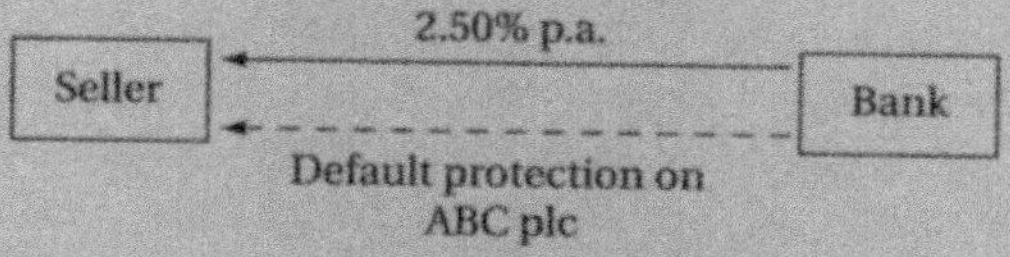

Figure 21.15: Credit default swap: sell swap.

5(i) Summary terms

Reference asset	ABC plc senior secured revolving loan (due 2005)
Notional amount	\$30 million
Term	Two years
Investor receives	2.50% per annum
Investor pays	Notional amount × (100% – market price) if credit event occurs

5(ii) Remarks

This is an unfounded investment that is off-balance sheet. It requires minimal administration and can be flexible in terms of maturity.

Selected bibliography

Braddock, J., *Derivatives demystified: using structured finance products*, John Wiley and Sons, 1997
Fabozzi, F., *Handbook of Structured Financial Products*, FJF Associates, 1998
ING Barings, *International Asset Securitisation*, 1999
Mattoo, M., *Structured Derivatives*, Pitman, 1996
Norton Rose, *Collateralised Debt Obligations*, 2000
Peng, S., Dattatreya, R., *The Structured Note Market*, Pitman, 1994

22 Synthetic Collateralised Debt Obligations

The Collateralised Debt Obligation (CDO) was a natural advancement of securitisation technology, first introduced in 1988. A CDO is essentially a structured finance product in which a distinct legal entity known as a special purpose vehicle issues bonds or notes against an investment in cashflows of an underlying pool of assets. These assets can be bonds, commercial bank loans or a mixture of both bonds and loans. Originally CDOs were developed as repackaging structures for high-yield bonds and illiquid instruments such as certain convertible bonds, but they have developed into sophisticated investment management vehicles in their own right. Through the 1990s CDOs were the fastest growing asset class in the asset-backed securities market, due to a number of features that made them attractive to issuers and investors alike. A subsequent development was the *synthetic* CDO, a structure that uses credit derivatives in its construction, and which is the subject of this chapter.

22.1 Introduction

22.1.1 *Cash flow CDO structures*

Generally cashflow CDOs were introduced in chapter 21 and are categorised as either balance sheet or arbitrage deals. Arbitrage CDOs are further categorised as cashflow or market-value deals. A later development, the *synthetic* CDO, now accounts for a growing number of transactions. We show a 'family tree' of CDOs in Figure 22.1.

The total issuance of all cashflow deals in 2000 and 2001 is shown in Figure 22.2.

Cash flow CDO

These are similar to other asset-backed securitisations involving an SPV. Bonds or loans are pooled together and the cash flows from these assets used to back the liabilities of the notes issued by the SPV into the market. As the underlying assets are sold to the SPV, they are removed from the originator's balance sheet; hence the credit risk associated with these assets is transferred to the holders of the issued notes. The originator also obtains funding by issuing the notes. The generic structure is illustrated at Figure 22.3.

Banks and other financial institutions are the primary originators of *balance sheet CDOs*. These are deals securitising banking assets such as commercial loans of investment grade or sub-investment grade rating. The main motivations for entering into this arrangement are:

- to obtain regulatory relief;
- to increase return on capital via the removal of lower yielding assets from the balance sheet;
- to secure alternative and/or cheaper sources of funding.

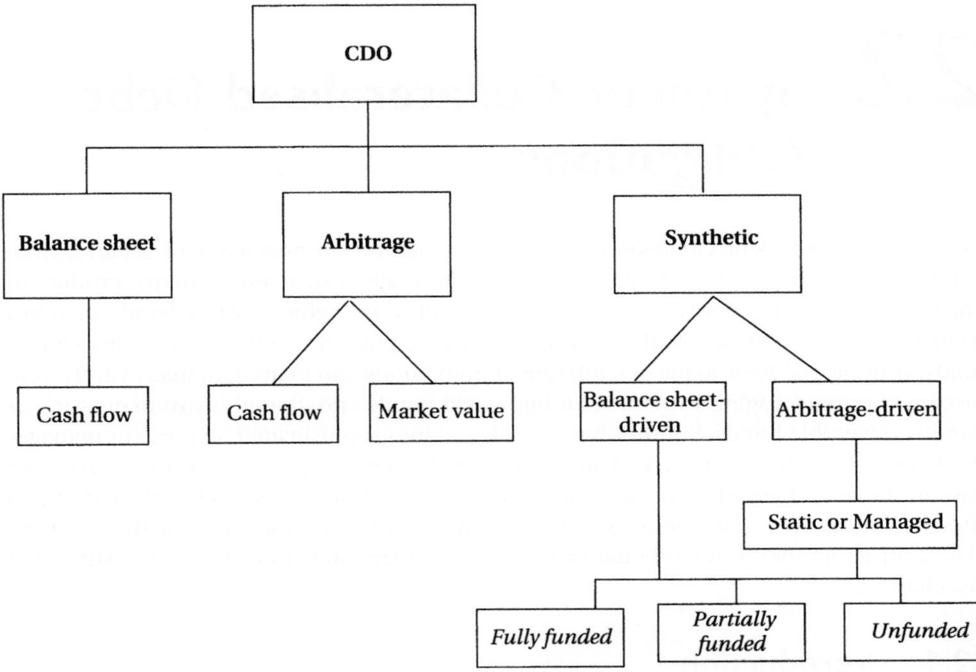

Figure 22.1: The CDO family.

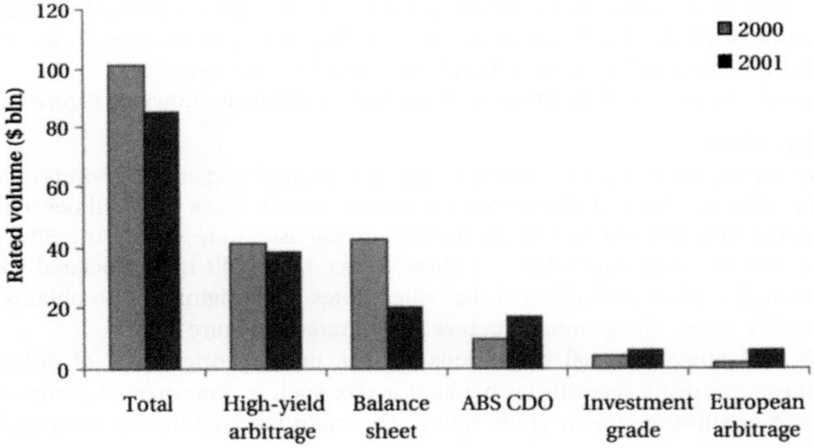

Figure 22.2: Global issuance of cashflow CDOs in 2000 and 2001.(Source: Risk, May 2002)

Investors are often attracted to balance sheet CDOs because they are perceived as offering a higher return than say, credit card ABS at a similar level of risk exposure. They also represent a diversification away from traditional structured finance investments. The asset

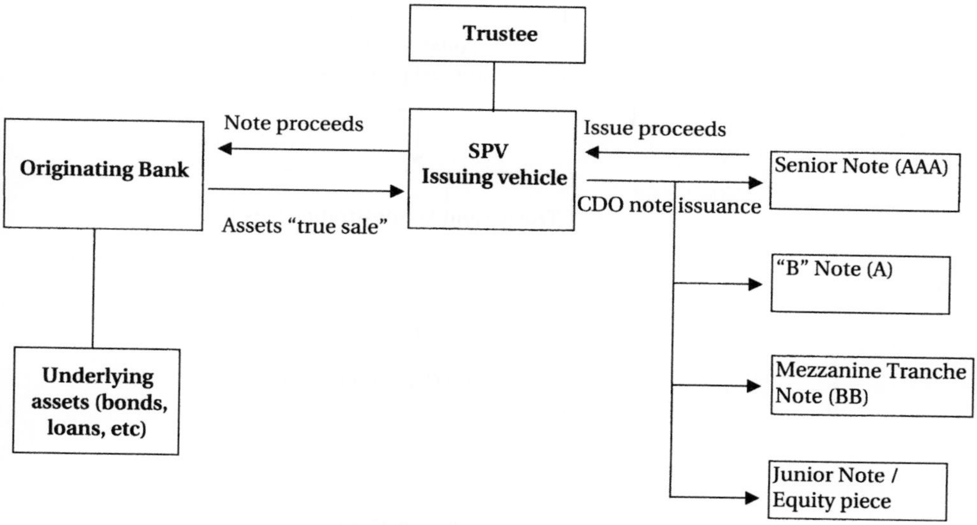

Figure 22.3: Generic cashflow CDO.

pool in a balance sheet CDO is static, that is it is not traded or actively managed by a portfolio manager; for this reason the structure is similar to more traditional ABS or repackaging vehicles. The typical note tranching is:

- senior note, AAA-rated, and 90%–95% of the issue;
- subordinated note, A-rated, 3%–5%;
- mezzanine note, BBB-rated, 1%–3%;
- equity note, non-rated, 1%–2%.

The cash flows of the underlying assets are used to fund the liabilities of the overlying notes. As the notes carry different ratings, there is a *priority of payment* that must be followed, which is the cashflow waterfall. The most senior payment must be paid in full before the next payment can be met, all the way until the most junior liability is discharged. If there are insufficient funds available, the most senior notes must be paid off before the junior liabilities can be addressed.

The waterfall process for interest payments is shown at Figure 22.4. Before paying the next priority of the waterfall, the vehicle must pass a number of compliance tests on the level of its underlying cash flows. These include interest coverage and principal (par) coverage tests.

During the life of the CDO transaction, a portfolio administrator will produce a periodic report detailing the quality of the collateral pool. This report is known as an investor or *Trustee* report and also shows the results of the compliance tests that are required to affirm that the notes of the CDO have maintained their credit rating.

Arbitrage CDOs are classified into either cash flow CDOs or market value CDOs. An arbitrage CDO will be designated as one of these two types depending on the way the

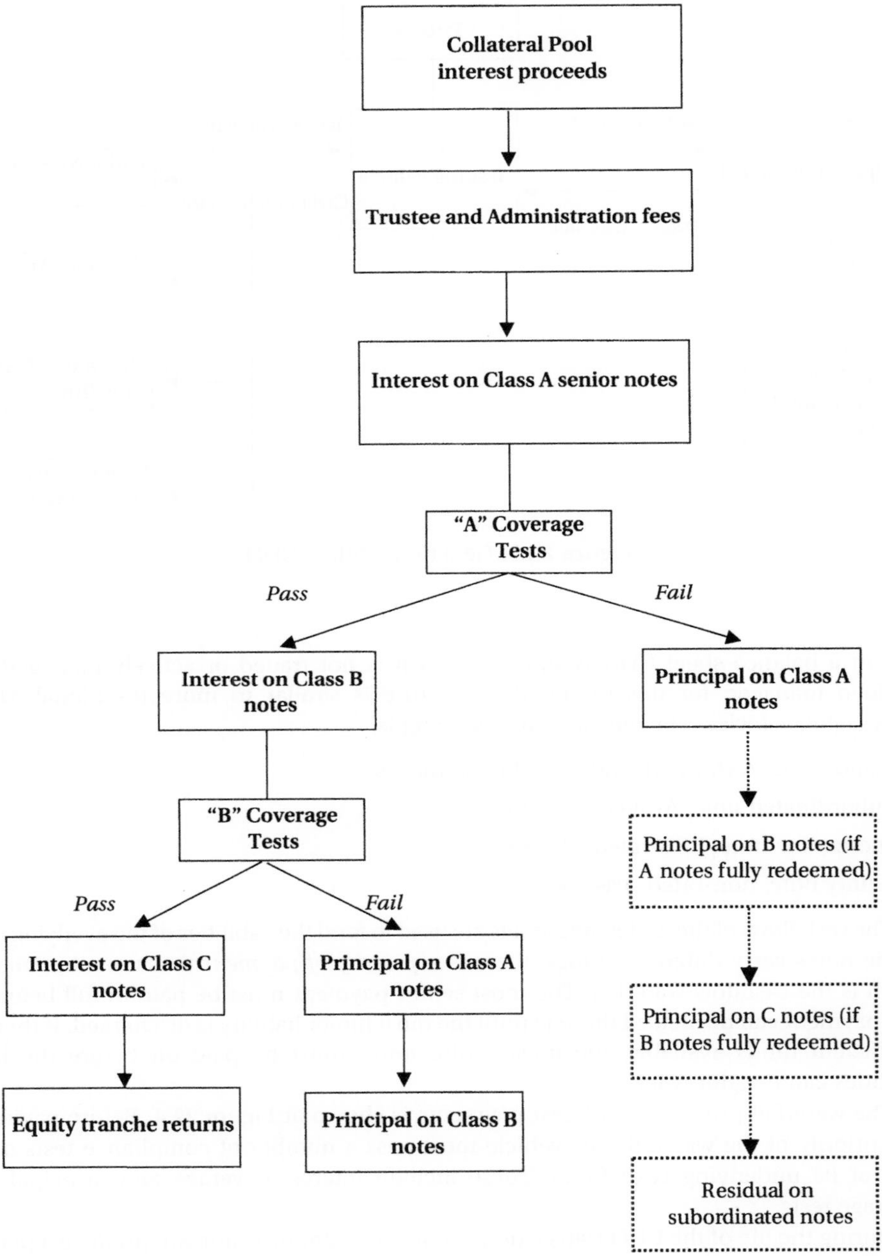

Figure 22.4: Interest cash flow waterfall for cash flow CDO.

underlying asset pool is structured to provide value (cash proceeds) in the vehicle. The distinction is that:

- a cash flow CDO will have a collateral pool that is usually static, and which generates sufficient interest to cover fees, expenses and overlying liabilities, and sufficient principal to repay notes on maturity; whereas
- in a market value CDO the collateral pool is usually actively traded, and marked-to-market on a daily basis. The daily mark for all the assets indicates the total value of the collateral pool and this value must always be sufficient to cover the principal and interest liabilities.

A cash flow arbitrage CDO has certain similarities with a balance sheet CDO, and if it is a static pool CDO it is also conceptually similar to an ABS deal.[1] The priority of payments is similar, starting from expenses, Trustee and servicing fees, senior noteholders, and so on down to the most junior noteholder. Underlying assets on cash flow arbitrage deals are commonly lower-rated bonds, commercial bank loans, high-yield debt and emerging market sovereign bonds. The basic structure is designed to split the aggregate credit risk of the collateral pool into various tranches, which are the overlying notes, each of which has a different credit exposure from the other. As a result each note figures a different risk/reward profile, and so will attract itself to different classes of investor.

The different risk profiles of the issued notes results because they are subordinated, that is, the notes are structured in descending order of seniority. In addition the structure makes use of *credit enhancements* to varying degrees, which include:

- over-collateralisation: the overlying notes are lower in value compared to the underlying pool; for example, $250 million nominal of assets are used as backing for $170 million nominal of issued bonds;
- cash reserve accounts: a reserve is maintained in a cash account and used to cover initial losses; the funds may be sourced from part of the proceeds;
- excess spread: cash inflows from assets that exceed the interest service requirements of liabilities;
- insurance wraps: insurance cover against losses suffered by the asset pool, for which an insurance premium is paid for as long as the cover is needed.

The quality of the collateral pool is monitored regularly and reported on by the portfolio administrator, who produces the investor report. This report details the results of various *compliance tests*, which are undertaken at individual asset level as well as aggregate level. Compliance tests include:

- weighted average spread and weighted average rating: the average interest spread and average credit rating of the assets, which must remain at a specified minimum;
- concentration: there will be a set maximum share of the assets that may be sourced from particular emerging markets, industrial sectors, and so on;

---

1 Except that in a typical ABS deal such as a consumer or trade receivables deal, or a residential MBS deal, there are a large number of individual underlying assets, whereas with a CBO or CLO there may be as few as 20 underlying loans or bonds.

- diversity score: this is a statistical value that is calculated via a formula set by the rating agency analysing the transaction. It measures the level of diversity of the assets, in other words how different they are – and hence how uncorrelated in their probability of default – from each other.

These tests are calculated on a regular basis and also each time the composition of the assets changes, for example because certain assets have been sold, new assets are purchased or because bonds have paid off ahead of their legal maturity date. If the test results fall below the required minimum, trading activity is restricted to only those trades that will improve the test results. Certain other compliance tests are viewed as more important, since if any of them are 'failed', the cash flows will be diverted from the normal waterfall and will be used to begin paying off the senior notes until the test results improve. These include:

- over-collateralisation: the over-collateralisation level vis-à-vis the issued notes must remain above a specified minimum, for instance it must be at 120% of the nominal value of the senior note;
- interest coverage: the level of interest receivables on assets must be sufficient to cover interest liabilities but also to bear default and other losses.

Compliance tests are specified as part of the process leading up to the issue of notes, in discussion between the originator and the rating agency.[2] The ratings analysis is comprehensive and focuses on the quality of the collateral, individual asset default probabilities, the structure of the deal and the track record and reputation of the originator.

Market value CDOs

The originators of market value CDOs are predominantly fund managers. With these transactions, the originator has rather more freedom to actively trade assets in and out of the collateral pool, and sometimes a wider range of assets to choose from when trading. Assets are marked-to-market by the portfolio administrator on a regular basis, possibly as frequently as daily. Investors are attracted by the perceived fund management credentials of the originator, and there is also the theoretical advantages that comes from the flexibility of being better able to manage losses when the market is experiencing a correction.

Market value deals frequently experience a *ramp-up* period when assets are built up in the collateral pool. This can take several months. There is also a liquidity or *revolver* facility, essentially a funding line distinct from the issue of notes, which is in place prior to the closing of the transaction and which is used to fund the acquisition of assets. The principal repayment of liabilities is funded when underlying assets are sold (traded out) of the pool, rather than when they mature.

22.1.2 *Synthetic CDOs*

The ongoing development of securitisation technology has resulted in more complex structures, illustrated perfectly by the synthetic CDO. These were introduced to meet differing needs of originators, where credit risk transfer is of more importance than funding

---

2 Deals may be rated by more than one rating agency.

considerations. Compared with conventional cashflow deals, which feature an actual transfer of ownership or *true sale* of the underlying assets to a separately incorporated legal entity, a synthetic securitisation structure is engineered so that the credit risk of the assets is transferred by the sponsor or originator of the transaction, from itself, to the investors by means of credit derivative instruments. The originator is therefore the credit protection buyer and investors are the credit protection sellers. This credit risk transfer may be undertaken either directly or via an SPV. Using this approach, underlying or *reference* assets are not necessarily moved off the originator's balance sheet, so it is adopted whenever the primary objective is to achieve risk transfer rather than balance sheet funding. The synthetic structure enables removal of credit exposure without asset transfer, so may be preferred for risk management and regulatory capital relief purposes. For banking institutions it also enables loan risk to be transferred without selling the loans themselves, thereby allowing customer relationships to remain unaffected.

The first synthetic deals were observed in the US market, while the first deals in Europe were observed in 1998. Market growth in Europe has been rapid; the total value of cash and synthetic deals in Europe in 2001 approached $120 billion, and a growing share of this total has been of synthetic deals. Figure 22.5 illustrates market volume, while Figure 22.6 shows the breakdown of arbitrage CDOs, whether cash flow, market value or synthetic deals, in 2000 and 2001. Figure 22.6 appears to suggest that synthetic deals were a very small part of the market, but the total reflects the funded element of each transaction, which grew to 9% of all arbitrage deals in 2001. However when the unfunded element of synthetic deals is included, we see that the synthetic deal share is substantially increased, shown at Figure 22.6(ii). Market share volumes reported by say, the rating agencies generally include the note element, however as a measure of actual risk transferred by a vehicle, it is logical to include the unfunded super-senior swap element as well. This suggests that in 2001 similar amounts of synthetic and cash business were transacted.

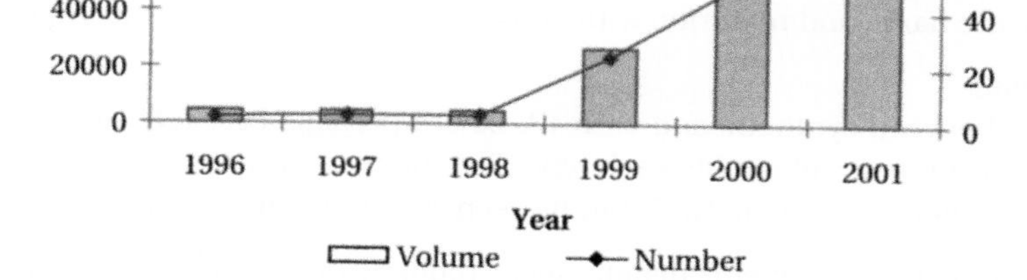

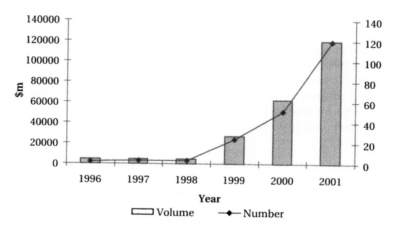

Figure 22.5: CDO market volume growth in Europe. Values for volume include rated debt and credit default swap tranches and unrated super-senior tranches for synthetic CDOs, and exclude equity tranches.(Source: Moodys)

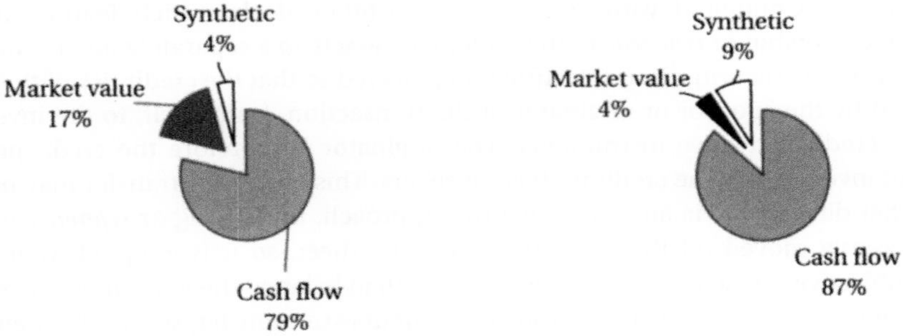

Figure 22.6: (i) Market share of arbitrage CDOs in 2000 and 2001 (Source: UBS Warburg, reproduced with permission).

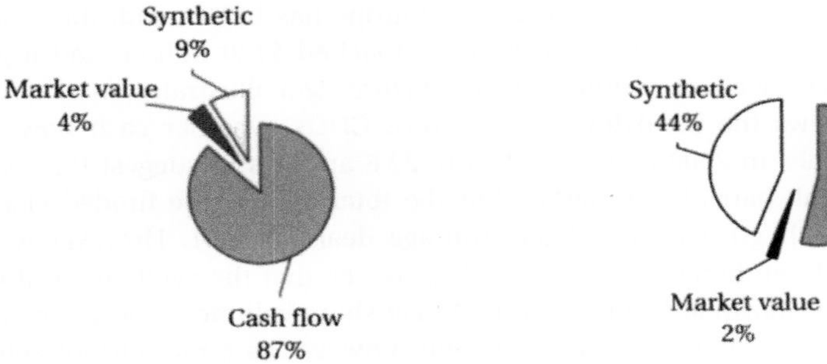

Figure 22.6: (ii) Market share of arbitrage CDOs in 2001, comparison when unfunded swap element of synthetic deals is included (Source: UBS Warburg, reproduced with permission).

The first European synthetic deals were balance sheet CLOs, with underlying reference assets being commercial loans on the originator's balance sheet. Originators were typically banking institutions. Arbitrage synthetic CDOs have also been introduced, typically by fund management institutions, and involve sourcing credit derivative contracts in the market and then selling these on to investors in the form of rated notes, at the arbitrage profit. Within the synthetic market, arbitrage deals were the most frequently issued during 2001, reflecting certain advantages they possess over cash CDOs. A key advantage has been that credit default swaps for single reference entities frequently trade at a lower spread than cash bonds of same name and maturity, with consequent lower costs for the originator.

Motivations

Differences between synthetic and cash CDOs are perhaps best reflected in the different cost-benefit economics of issuing each type. The motivations behind the issue of each type usually also differ. A synthetic CDO can be seen as being constructed out of the following:

- a short position in a credit default swap (bought protection), by which the sponsor transfers its portfolio credit risk to the issuer;
- a long position in a portfolio of bonds or loans, the cash flow from which enables the sponsor to pay liabilities of overlying notes.

The originators of the first synthetic deals were banks who wished to manage the credit risk exposure of their loan books, without having to resort to the administrative burden of true sale cash securitisation. They are a natural progression in the development of credit derivative structures, with single name credit default swaps being replaced by portfolio default swaps. Synthetic CDOs can be 'de-linked' from the sponsoring institution, so that investors do not have any credit exposure to the sponsor itself. The first deals were introduced (in 1998) at a time when widening credit spreads and the worsening of credit quality among originating firms meant that investors were sellers of cash CDOs which had retained a credit linkage to the sponsor. A synthetic arrangement also means that the credit risk of assets that are otherwise not suited to conventional securitisation may be transferred, while assets are retained on the balance sheet. Such assets include bank guarantees, letters of credit or cash loans that have some legal or other restriction on being securitised. For this reason synthetic deals are more appropriate for assets that are described under multiple legal jurisdictions.

The economic advantage of issuing a synthetic versus a cash CDO can be significant. Put simply, the net benefit to the originator is the gain in regulatory capital cost, minus the cost of paying for credit protection on the credit default swap side. In a partially funded structure, a sponsoring bank will obtain full capital relief when note proceeds are invested in 0% risk weighted collateral such as Treasuries or gilts. The super senior swap portion will carry a 20% risk weighting.[3] In fact a moment's thought should make clear to us that a synthetic deal would be cheaper: where credit default swaps are used, the sponsor pays a basis point fee, which for AAA security might be in the range 10–30 bps, depending on the stage of the credit cycle. In a cash structure where bonds are issued, the cost to the sponsor would be the benchmark yield plus the credit spread, which would be considerably higher compared to the default swap premium. This is illustrated in the example shown at Figure 22.7, where we assume certain spreads and premiums in comparing a partially funded synthetic deal with a cash deal. The assumptions are:

- that the super senior credit swap cost is 15 bps, and carries a 20% risk weight;
- the equity piece retains a 100% risk-weighting;
- the synthetic CDO invests note proceeds in sovereign collateral that pays sub-Libor.

Synthetic deals can be unfunded, partially funded or fully funded. An unfunded CDO would be comprised wholly of credit default swaps, while fully funded structures would be arranged so that the entire credit risk of the reference portfolio was transferred through the issue of credit-linked notes. We discuss these shortly.

Mechanics

A synthetic CDO is so-called because the transfer of credit risk is achieved 'synthetically' via a credit derivative, rather than by a 'true sale' to an SPV. Thus in a synthetic CDO the credit risk of the underlying loans or bonds is transferred to the SPV using credit default swaps and/or total return swaps (TRS). However the assets themselves are not legally transferred to the SPV, and they remain on the originator's balance sheet. Using a synthetic CDO, the

---

3 This is as long as the counterparty is an OECD bank, which is invariably the case.

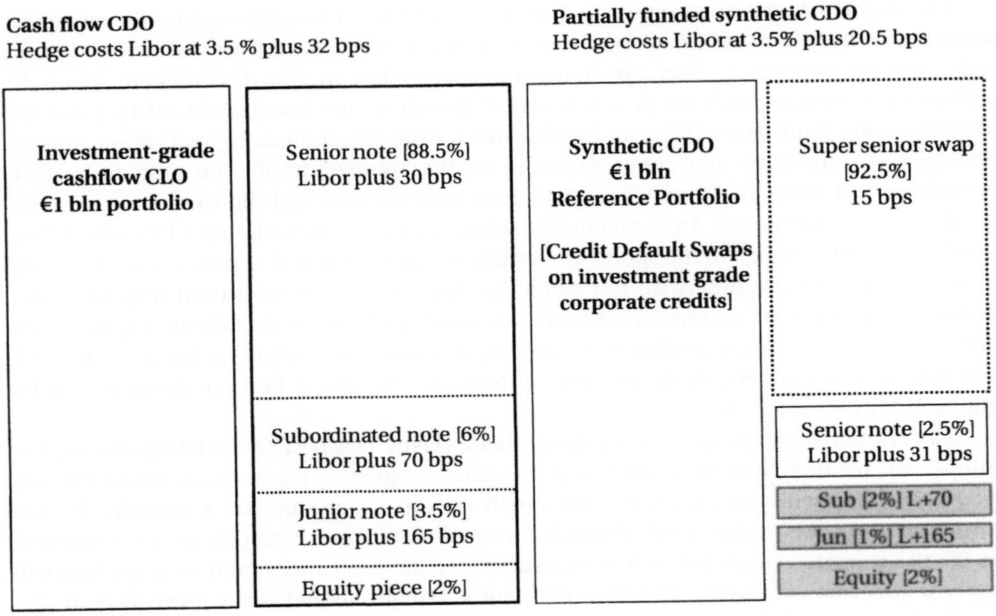

Regulatory capital relief
Cash CDO
Capital charge on assets reduces from 8% (100% RW) to 2% (equity piece only now 100% RW)
Regulatory capital relief is 6%
Synthetic CDO
Capital charge on assets reduces from 8% (100% RW) to 3.48% (equity piece plus super senior swap at 20% RW)
Regulatory capital relief is 4.52%

Figure 22.7: Comparing cashflow and synthetic deal economies.

originator can obtain regulatory capital relief[4] and manage the credit risk on its balance sheet, but will not be receiving any funding. In other words a synthetic CDO structure enables originators to separate credit risk exposure and asset funding requirements. The credit risk of the asset portfolio, now known as the reference portfolio, is transferred, directly or to an SPV, through credit derivatives. The most common credit contracts used are credit default swaps. A portion of the credit risk may be sold on as credit-linked notes. Typically a large majority of the credit risk is transferred via a 'super-senior' credit default swap,[5] which is dealt with a swap counterparty but usually sold to monoline insurance companies at a significantly lower spread over Libor compared with the senior AAA-rated tranche of cashflow CDOs. This is a key attraction of synthetic deals for originators. Most

[4] This is because reference assets that are protected by credit derivative contracts, and which remain on the balance sheet, will, under Basel rules, attract a lower regulatory capital charge.

[5] So called because the swap is ahead of the most senior of any funded (note) portion, which latter being 'senior' means the swap must be 'super-senior'.

deals are structured with mezzanine notes sold to a wider set of investors, the proceeds of which are invested in risk-free collateral such as Treasury bonds or Pfandbriefe securities. The most junior note, known as the 'first-loss' piece, may be retained by the originator. On occurrence of a credit event among the reference assets, the originating bank receives funds remaining from the collateral after they have been used to pay the principal on the issued notes, less the value of the junior note.

A generic synthetic CDO structure is shown at Figure 22.8. In this generic structure, the credit risk of the reference assets is transferred to the issuer SPV and ultimately the investors, by means of the credit default swap and an issue of credit-linked notes. In the default swap arrangement, the risk transfer is undertaken in return for the swap premium, which is then paid to investors by the issuer. The note issue is invested in risk-free collateral rather than passed on to the originator, in order to de-link the credit ratings of the notes from the rating of the originator. If the collateral pool was not established, a downgrade of the sponsor could result in a downgrade of the issued notes. Investors in the notes expose themselves to the credit risk of the reference assets, and if there are no credit events they will earn returns at least the equal of the collateral assets and the default swap premium. If the notes are credit-linked, they will also earn excess returns based on the performance of the reference portfolio. If there are credit events, the issuer will deliver the assets to the swap counterparty and will pay the nominal value of the assets to the originator out of the collateral pool. Credit default swaps are unfunded credit derivatives, while CLNs are funded credit derivatives where the protection seller (the investors) fund

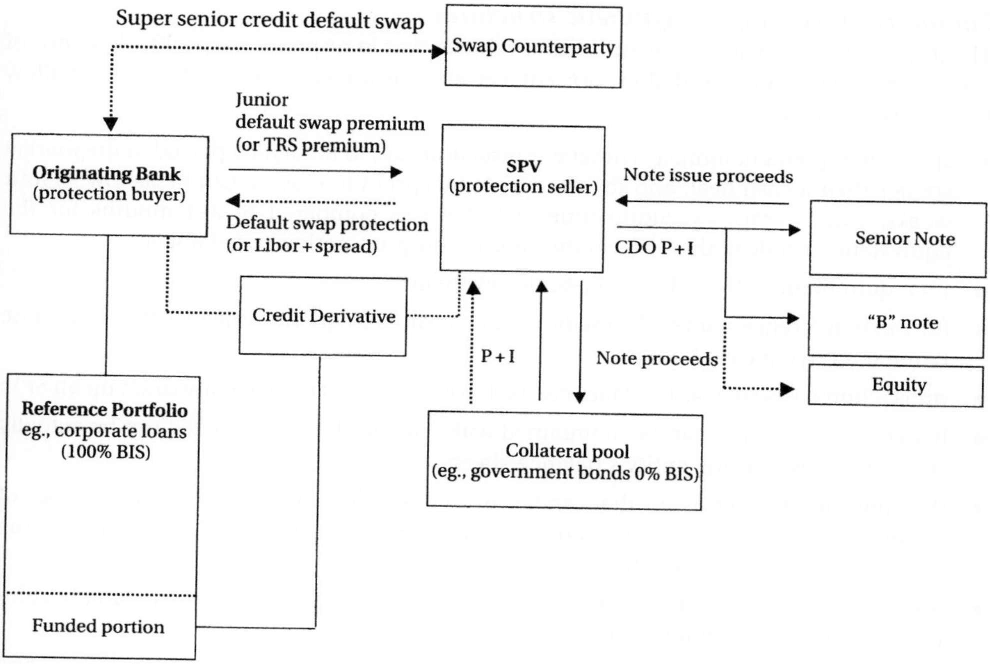

Figure 22.8: Synthetic CDO structure.

the value of the reference assets up-front, and will receive a reduced return on occurrence of a credit event.

Synthetic CDOs are popular in the European market due to less onerous legal documentation requirements. Across Europe the legal infrastructure is not uniform and in certain countries has not been sufficiently developed to enable true sale securitisation to be undertaken. In addition when the underlying asset pool is composed of bonds from different countries, a cash funded CDO may present too many administrative difficulties. A synthetic CDO removes such issues by using credit derivatives, and in theory can be brought to market more quickly than a cash flow arrangement (although in practice this is not always the case). It is also able to benefit from a shorter ramp-up period prior to closing.

Traditional cash CDOs suffer when only a portion of the portfolio is in place at time of closing, especially holders of the equity piece who may receive no cash inflow during the ramp-up. This cost may be reduced if a *warehouse* facility is set up prior to closing the transaction. A warehouse, which is provided by the portfolio administrator in return for a fee, enables the CDO issuer to begin purchasing bonds before closing. Using a warehouse arrangement, the issuer purchases target securities and hedges their interest-rate risk using futures, interest-rate swaps or by shorting government bonds. The credit risk on the bonds is not hedged of course, and equity holders bear losses if spreads widen due to credit deterioration (they will of course gain if spreads tighten). A shorter ramp-up period is a plus therefore, and although in a synthetic deal the manager will take some time while sourcing credit default swaps, this time is typically shorter than in a cashflow CDO.

Summary: advantages of synthetic structures

The introduction of synthetic securitisation vehicles was in response to specific demands of sponsoring institutions, and they present certain advantages over traditional cashflow structures. These include:

- speed of implementation: a synthetic transaction can, in theory, be placed in the market sooner than a cash deal, and the time from inception to closure can be as low as four weeks, with average execution time of 6–8 weeks compared to 3–4 months for the equivalent cash deal; this reflects the shorter ramp-up period noted above;
- no requirement to fund the super-senior element;
- for many reference names the credit default swap is frequently cheaper than the same name underlying cash bond;
- transaction costs such as legal fees can be lower as there is no necessity to set up an SPV;
- banking relationships can be maintained with clients whose loans need not be actually sold off the sponsoring entity's balance sheet;
- the range of reference assets that can be covered is wider, and includes undrawn lines of credit, bank guarantees and derivative instruments that would give rise to legal and true sale issues in a cash transaction;
- the use of credit derivatives introduces greater flexibility to provide tailor-made solutions for credit risk requirements;
- the cost of buying protection is usually lower as there is little or no funding element and the credit protection price is below the equivalent-rate note liability.

BISTRO: the first synthetic securitisation

Generally viewed as the first synthetic securitisation, BISTRO is a JPMorgan vehicle brought to market in December 1997. The transaction was designed to remove the credit risk on a portfolio of corporate credits held on JPMorgan's books, with no funding or balance sheet impact. The overall portfolio was $9.7 billion, with $700 million of notes being issued, in two tranches, by the BISTRO SPV. The proceeds of the note issue were invested in US Treasury securities, which in turn were used as collateral for the credit default swap entered into between JPMorgan and the vehicle. This is a five-year swap written on the whole portfolio, with JPMorgan as the protection buyer. BISTRO, the protection seller, pays for the coupons on the issued notes from funds received from the collateral pool and the premiums on the credit default swap. Payments on occurrence of credit events are paid out from the collateral pool.

Under this structure, JPMorgan has transferred the credit risk on $700 million of its portfolio to investors, and retained the risk on a first-loss piece and the residual piece. The first loss piece is not a note issue, but a $32 million reserve cash account held for the five-year life of the deal. First losses are funded out of this cash reserve which is held by JPMorgan. This is shown in the diagram below.

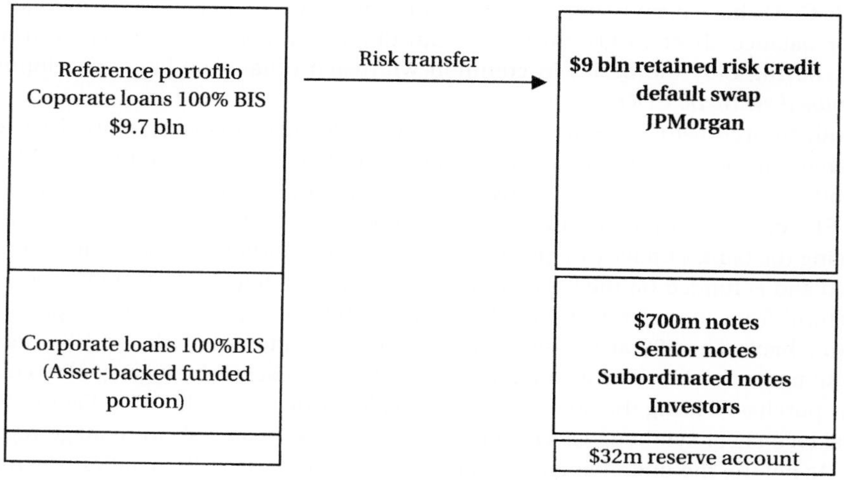

BISTRO structure

The asset pool is static for the life of the deal. The attraction of the deal for investors included a higher return on the notes compared to bonds of the same credit rating and a bullet-maturity structure, compared to the amortising arrangement of other ABS asset classes.

This does not mean that the cash transaction is now an endangered species. It retains certain advantages of its own over synthetic deals, which include:

- no requirement for an OECD bank (the 20% BIS risk-weighted entity) to act as the swap counterparty to meet capital relief requirements;
- lower capital relief available compared to the 20% risk weighting on the OECD bank counterparty
- larger potential investor base, as the number of counterparties is potentially greater (certain financial and investing institutions have limitations on the degree of usage of credit derivatives);
- lower degree of counterparty exposure for originating entity. In a synthetic deal the default of a swap counterparty would mean cessation of premium payments or more critically a credit event protection payment, and termination of the credit default swap.

Investment banking advisors will structure the arrangement for their sponsoring client that best meets the latter's requirements. Depending on the nature of these, this can be either a synthetic or cash deal.

22.1.3 *Variations in synthetic CDOs*

Synthetic CDOs have been issued in a variety of forms, labelled in generic form as arbitrage CDOs or balance sheet CDOs. Structures can differ to a considerable degree from one another, having only the basics in common with each other. The latest development is the *managed synthetic* CDO.

A synthetic arbitrage CDO is originated generally by collateral managers who wish to exploit the difference in yield between that obtained on the underlying assets and that payable on the CDO, both in note interest and servicing fees. The generic structure is as follows: a specially-created SPV enters into a total-return swap with the originating bank or financial institution, referencing the bank's underlying portfolio (the reference portfolio). The portfolio is actively managed and is funded on the balance sheet by the originating bank. The SPV receives the 'total return' from the reference portfolio, and in return it pays Libor plus a spread to the originating bank. The SPV also issues notes that are sold into the market to CDO investors, and these notes can be rated as high as AAA as they are backed by high-quality collateral, which is purchased using the note proceeds. A typical structure is shown at Figure 22.9.

A balance sheet synthetic CDO is employed by banks that wish to manage regulatory capital. As before, the underlying assets are bonds, loans and credit facilities originated by the issuing bank. In a balance sheet CDO the SPV enters into a credit default swap agreement with the originator, with the specific collateral pool designated as the reference portfolio. The SPV receives the premium payable on the default swap, and thereby provides credit protection on the reference portfolio. There are three types of CDO within this structure. A fully synthetic CDO is a completely *unfunded* structure which uses credit default swaps to transfer the entire credit risk of the reference assets to investors who are protection sellers. In a *partially funded* CDO, only the highest credit risk segment of the portfolio is transferred. The cash flow that would be needed to service the synthetic CDO overlying liability is received from the AAA-rated collateral that is purchased by the SPV with the proceeds of an overlying note issue. An originating bank obtains maximum regulatory capital relief by means of a partially funded structure, through a combination

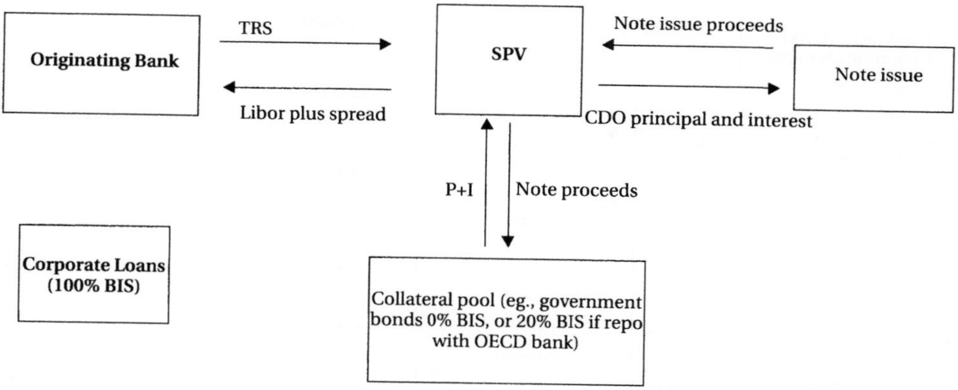

Figure 22.9: Synthetic arbitrage CDO structure.

of the synthetic CDO and what is known as a *super senior swap* arrangement with an OECD banking counterparty. A super senior swap provides additional protection to that part of the portfolio, the senior segment, that is already protected by the funded portion of the transaction. The sponsor may retain the super senior element or may sell it to a monoline insurance firm or credit default swap provider.

Some commentators have categorised synthetic deals using slightly different terms. For instance Boggiano, Waterson and Stein (2002) define the following types:

- balance sheet static synthetic CDO;
- managed static synthetic CDO;
- balance sheet variable synthetic CDO;
- managed variable synthetic CDO.

As described by Boggiano *et al*, the basic structure is as we described earlier for a partially funded synthetic CDO. In fact there is essentially little difference between the first two types of deal, in the latter an investment manager rather than the credit swap counterparty selects the portfolio. However the reference assets remain static for the life of the deal in both cases. For the last two deal types, the main difference would appear to be that an investment manager, rather than the originator bank, trades the portfolio of credit swaps under specified guidelines. In the author's belief this is not a structural difference and so for this article we will consider them both as managed CDOs, which are described later.

A generic partially funded synthetic transaction is shown at Figure 22.10. It shows an arrangement whereby the issuer enters into two credit default swaps; the first with an SPV that provides protection for losses up to a specified amount of the reference pool,[6] while the second swap is set up with the OECD bank or, occasionally, an insurance company.[7]

6 In practice, to date this portion has been between 5% and 15% of the reference pool.

7 An 'OECD' bank, thus guaranteeing a 20% risk weighting for capital ratio purposes, under Basel I rules.

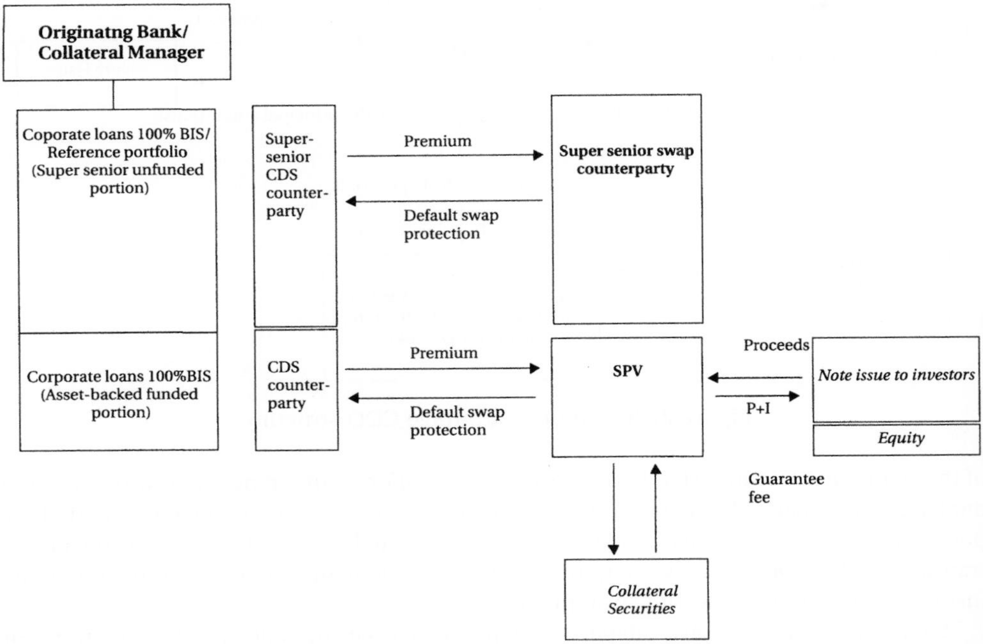

Figure 22.10: Partially funded synthetic CDO structure.

A *fully funded* CDO is a structure where the credit risk of the entire portfolio is transferred to the SPV via a credit default swap. In a fully funded (or just 'funded') synthetic CDO the issuer enters into the credit default swap with the SPV, which itself issues credit-linked notes (CLNs) to the entire value of the assets on which the risk has been transferred. The proceeds from the notes are invested in risk-free government or agency debt such as gilts, bunds or Pfandbriefe, or in senior unsecured bank debt. Should there be a default on one or more of the underlying assets, the required amount of the collateral is sold and the proceeds from the sale paid to the issuer to recompense for the losses. The premium paid on the credit default swap must be sufficiently high to ensure that it covers the difference in yield between that on the collateral and that on the notes issued by the SPV. The generic structure is illustrated at Figure 22.11.

Fully funded CDOs are relatively uncommon. One of the advantages of the partially funded arrangement is that the issuer will pay a lower premium compared to a fully funded synthetic CDO, because it is not required to pay the difference between the yield on the collateral and the coupon on the note issue (the unfunded part of the transaction). The downside is that the issuer will receive a reduction in risk weighting for capital purposes to 20% for the risk transferred via the super senior default swap.

The fully *unfunded* CDO uses only credit derivatives in its structure. The swaps are rated in a similar fashion to notes, and there is usually an 'equity' piece that is retained by the originator. The reference portfolio will again be commercial loans, usually 100% risk-weighted, or other assets. The credit rating of the swap tranches is based on the rating of the reference assets, as well as other factors such as the diversity of the assets and ratings performance correlation. The

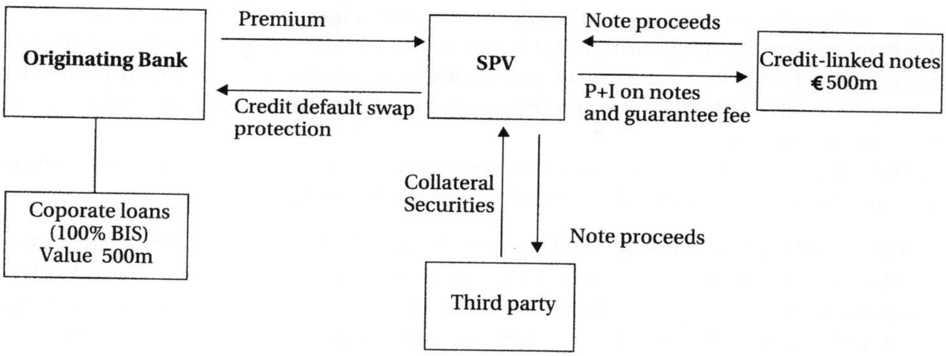

Figure 22.11: Fully funded synthetic balance sheet CDO structure.

typical structure is illustrated at Figure 22.12. As well as the equity tranche, there will be one or more junior tranches, one or more senior tranches and super-senior tranche. The senior tranches are sold on to AAA-rated banks as a portfolio credit default swap, while the junior tranche is usually sold to an OECD bank. The ratings of the tranches will typically be:

- super-senior: AAA
- senior: AA to AAA
- junior: BB to A
- equity: unrated.

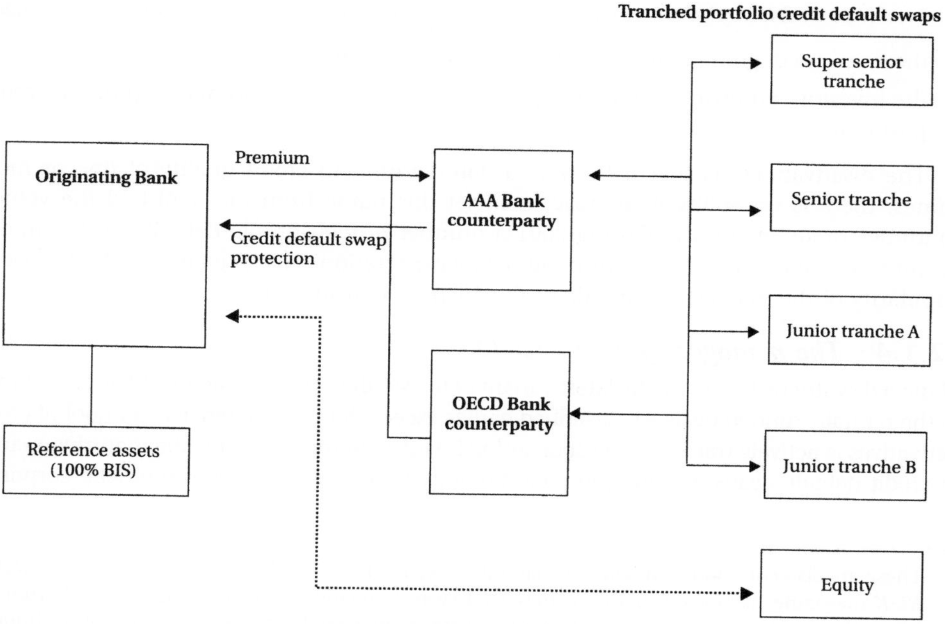

Figure 22.12: The fully synthetic or unfunded CDO.

The credit default swaps are not single-name swaps, but are written on a class of debt. The advantage for the originator is that it can name the reference asset class to investors without having to disclose the name of specific loans. Default swaps are usually cash-settled and not physically settled, so that the reference assets can be replaced with other assets if desired by the sponsor.

Within the European market static synthetic balance sheet CDOs are the most common structure. The reasons that banks originate them are two-fold:

- *capital relief*: banks can obtain regulatory capital relief by transferring lower-yield corporate credit risk such as corporate bank loans off their balance sheet. Under Basel I rules all corporate debt carries an identical 100% risk-weighting; therefore with banks having to assign 8% of capital for such loans, higher-rated (and hence lower-yielding) corporate assets will require the same amount of capital but will generate a lower return on that capital. A bank may wish to transfer such higher-rated, lower-yield assets from its balance sheet, and this can be achieved via a CDO transaction. The capital requirements for a synthetic CDO are lower than for corporate assets; for example the funded segment of the deal will be supported by high quality collateral such as government bonds, and arranged via a repo with an OECD bank would carry a 20% risk weighting. This is the same for the super senior element;
- *transfer of credit risk*: the cost of servicing a fully funded CDO, and the premium payable on the associated credit default swap, can be prohibitive. With a partially funded structure, the issue amount is typically a relatively small share of the asset portfolio. This lowers substantially the default swap premium. Also, as the CDO investors suffer the first loss element of the portfolio, the super senior default swap can be entered into at a considerably lower cost than that on a fully funded CDO.

Synthetic deals may be either static or managed. Static deals hold the following advantages:

- there are no ongoing management fees to be borne by the vehicle;
- the investor can review and grant approval to credits that are to make up the reference portfolio.

The disadvantage is that if there is a deterioration in credit quality of one or more names, there is no ability to remove or offset this name from the pool and the vehicle continues to suffer from it. During 2001 a number of high profile defaults in the market meant that static pool CDOs performed below expectation. This explains partly the rise in popularity of the managed synthetic deal, which we consider next.

22.1.4 *The managed synthetic CDO*

Managed synthetic CDOs are the latest variant of the synthetic CDO structure.[8] They are similar to the partially funded deals we described earlier except that the reference asset pool of credit derivatives is actively traded by the sponsoring investment manager. It is the maturing market in credit default swaps, resulting in good liquidity in a large number of synthetic corporate

---

8 These are also commonly known as collateralised synthetic obligations or CSOs within the market. *RISK* magazine has called them collateralised swap obligations, which handily also shortens to CSOs. Boggiano *et al* (2002) refer to these structures as managed variable synthetic CDOs, although the author has not come across this term in other literature.

credits, that has facilitated the introduction of the managed synthetic CDO. With this structure, originators can use credit derivatives to arbitrage cash and synthetic liabilities, as well as leverage off their expertise in credit trading to generate profit. The advantages for investors are the same as with earlier generations of CDOs, except that with active trading they are gaining a still-larger exposure to the abilities of the investment manager. The underlying asset pool is again, a portfolio of credit default swaps. However these are now dynamically managed and actively traded, under specified guidelines. Thus, there is greater flexibility afforded to the sponsor, and the vehicle will record trading gains or losses as a result of credit derivative trading. In most structures, the investment manager can only buy protection (short credit) in order to offset an existing sold protection default swap. For some deals, this restriction is removed and the investment manager can buy or sell credit derivatives to reflect its view.

Structure

The structure of the managed synthetic is similar to the partially funded synthetic CDO, with a separate legally incorporated SPV.[9] On the liability side there is an issue of notes, with note proceeds invested in collateral or *eligible investments* which is one or a combination of the following:

- a bank deposit account or guaranteed investment contract (*GIC*) which pays a pre-specified rate of interest;[10]
- risk-free bonds such as US Treasury securities, German Pfandbriefe or AAA-rated bonds such as credit-card ABS securities;
- a repo agreement with risk-free collateral;
- a liquidity facility with an AA-rated bank;
- a market-sensitive debt instrument, often enhanced with the repo or liquidity arrangement described above.

On the asset side the SPV enters into credit default swaps and/or total return swaps, selling protection to the sponsor. The investment manager (or 'collateral manager') can trade in and out of credit default swaps after the transaction has closed in the market.[11] The SPV enters into credit derivatives via a single basket credit default swap to one swap counterparty, written on a portfolio of reference assets, or via multiple single-name credit swaps with a number of swap counterparties. The latter arrangement is more common and is referred to as a *multiple dealer* CDO. A percentage of the reference portfolio will be identified at the start of work on the transaction, with the remainder of the entities being selected during the ramp-up period ahead of closing. The SPV enters into the other side of the credit default swaps by selling

---

9 We use the term SPV for *special purpose vehicle*. This is also referred to as a special purpose entity (SPE) or special purpose company (SPC).

10 A GIC has been defined either as an account that pays a fixed rate of interest for its term, or more usually an account that pays a fixed spread below Libor or euribor, usually three-month floating rolled over each interest period.

11 This term is shared with other securitisation structures: when notes have been priced, and placed in the market, and all legal documentation signed by all named participants, the transaction has *closed*. In effect this is the start of the transaction, and all being well the noteholders will receive interest payments during the life of the deal and principal repayment on maturity.

protection to one of the swap counterparties on specific reference entities. Thereafter the investment manager can trade out of this exposure in the following ways:

- buying credit protection from another swap counterparty on the same reference entity. This offsets the existing exposure, but there may be residual risk exposure unless premium dates are matched exactly or if there is a default in both the reference entity and the swap counterparty;
- unwinding or terminating the swap with the counterparty;
- buying credit protection on a reference asset that is outside the portfolio. This is uncommon as it will leave residual exposures and may affect premium spread gains.

The SPV actively manages the portfolio within specified guidelines, the decisions being made by the investment manager. Initially the manager's opportunity to trade may be extensive, but this will be curtailed if there are losses. The trading guidelines will extend to both individual credit default swaps and at the portfolio level. They may include:

- parameters under which the investment manager (in the guise of the SPV) may actively close out, hedge or substitute reference assets using credit derivatives;
- guidelines under which the investment manager can trade credit derivatives to maximise gains or minimise losses on reference assets that have improved or worsened in credit quality or outlook.

Credit default swaps may be cash settled or physically settled, with physical settlement being more common in a managed synthetic deal. In a multiple dealer CDO the legal documentation must be in place with all names on the counterparty dealer list, which may add to legal costs as standardisation may be difficult.

Investors who are interested in this structure are seeking to benefit from the following advantages compared to vanilla synthetic deals:

- active management of the reference portfolio and the trading expertise of the investment manager in the corporate credit market;
- a multiple dealer arrangement, so that the investment manager can obtain the most competitive prices for default swaps;
- under physical settlement, the investment manager (via the SPV) has the ability to obtain the highest recovery value for the reference asset.

A generic managed synthetic CDO is illustrated at Figure 22.13.

22.2 Risk and return on CDOs

22.2.1 *Risk-return analysis*

The return analysis for CDOs performed by potential investors is necessarily different to that undertaken for other securitised asset classes. For CDOs the three key factors to consider are:

- default probabilities and cumulative default rates;
- default correlations;
- recovery rates.

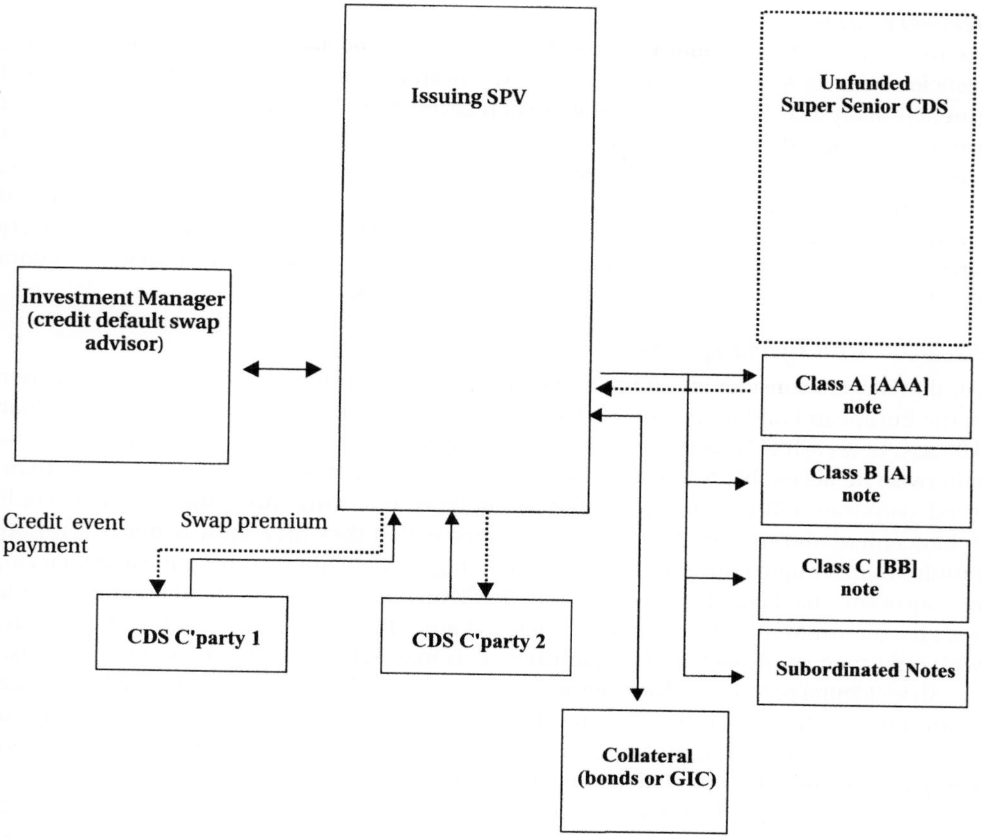

Figure 22.13: Generic managed synthetic CDO.

Analysts make assumptions about each of these with regard to individual reference assets, usually with recourse to historical data. We consider each factor in turn.

Default probability rates

The level of default probability rates will vary with each deal. Analysts such as the rating agencies will use a number of methods to estimate default probabilities, such as individual reference credit ratings and historical probability rates. Since there may be as much as 150 or more reference names in the CDO, a common approach is to use the average rating of the reference portfolio. Rating agencies such as Moody's provide data on the default rates for different ratings as an 'average' class, which can be used in the analysis.

Correlation

The correlation between assets in the reference portfolio of a CDO is an important factor in CDO returns analysis. A problem arises with what precise correlation value to use; these can be correlation between default probabilities, correlation between timing of default and correlation between spreads. The *diversity score* value of the CDO plays a part in this: it represents the number of uncorrelated bonds with identical par value and the same default probability.

Recovery rates
Recovery rates for individual obligors differ by issuer and industry classification. Rating agencies such as Moody's publish data on the average prices of all defaulted bonds, and generally analysts will construct a database of recovery rates by industry and credit rating for use in modelling the expected recovery rates of assets in the collateral pool. Note that for synthetic CDOs with credit default swaps as assets in the portfolio, this factor is not relevant.

Analysts undertake simulation modelling to generate scenarios of default and expected return. For instance they may model the number of defaults up to maturity, the recovery rates of these defaults and the timing of defaults. All these variables are viewed as random variables, so they are modelled using a stochastic process.

22.2.2 *CDO yield spreads*

Fund managers consider investing in CDO-type products as they represent a diversification in the European bond markets, with yields that are comparable to credit-card or auto-loan ABS assets. A cash CDO also gives investors exposure to sectors in the market that may not otherwise be accessible to most investors, for example credits such as small- or medium-sized corporate entities that rely on entirely bank financing. Also, the extent of credit enhancement and note tranching in a CDO means that they may show better risk/reward profiles than straight conventional debt, with a higher yield but incorporating asset backing and insurance backing. In cash and synthetic CDOs the issues notes are often bullet bonds, with fixed term to maturity, whereas other ABS and MBS product are amortising securities with only average (expected life) maturities. This may suit certain longer-dated investors.

An incidental perceived advantage of cash CDOs is that they are typically issued by financial institutions such as higher-rated banks. This usually provides comfort on the credit side but also on the underlying administration and servicing side with regard to underlying assets, compared to consumer receivables securitisations.

To illustrate yields, Figure 22.14 shows the spreads on a selected range of notes during January 2002 over the credit spectrum. Figure 22.15 shows a comparison of different asset classes in European structured products during February 2002. In Figure 22.16 we show the note spread at issue for a selected number of synthetic CDOs closed during 2001–2002. The regression of these and selected other AAA-rated note spreads against maturity shows an adjusted R^2 of 0.82, shown at Figure 22.17, which suggests that for a set of AAA-rated securities, the term to maturity is not the only consideration.[12] Other factors that may explain the difference in yields include perception of the asset manager, secondary market liquidity and the placing power of the arranger of the transaction.

22.3 Case studies

The latest manifestation of synthetic securitisation technology is the managed synthetic CDO or CSO. In Europe these have been originated by fund managers, with the first example being issued in 2000. Although they are, in effect, investment vehicles, the discipline required to manage what is termed a 'structured credit product' is not necessarily identical to those required

12 Calculated from 12 synthetic CDO senior (AAA-rated) notes issued in Europe during Jan–Jun 2002, yields obtained from Bloomberg.

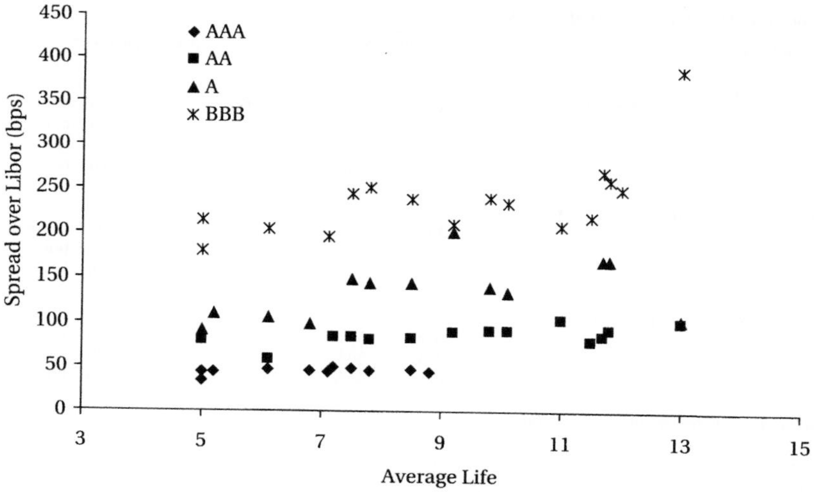

Figure 22.14: Rating spreads. (Source: JPMorgan)

for a corporate bond fund. Investment bank arrangers are apt to suggest that a track record in credit derivatives trading is an essential pre-requisite to being a successful CSO manager. There is an element of reputational risk at stake if a CDO suffers a downgrade; for example during 2001 Moody's downgraded elements of 83 separate CDO deals, across 174 tranches, as underlying pools of investment-grade and high-yield corporate bonds experienced default.[13] Thus managing a CDO presents a high-profile record of a fund manager's performance.

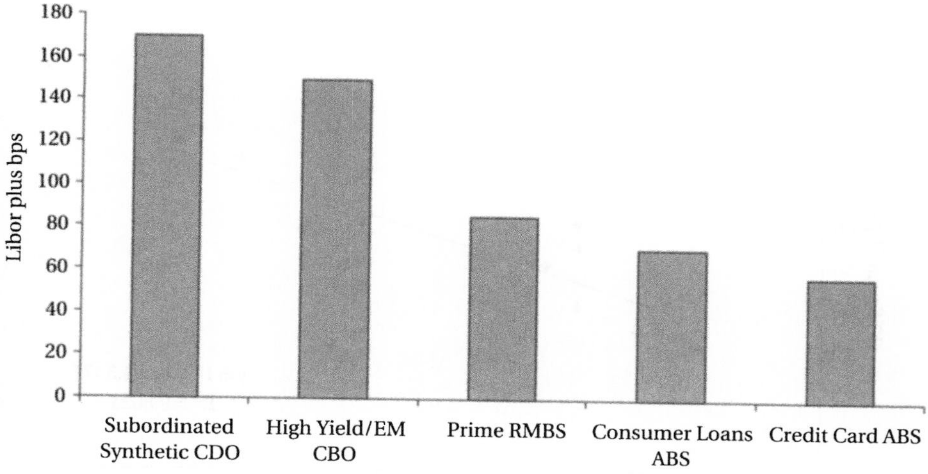

Figure 22.15: Comparing CDO yields to other securitisation asset classes. (Source: Bloomberg)

13 Source: CreditFlux, April 2002

Exhibit 15 SELECTED DEAL SPREADS AT ISSUE

Deal name plus close date	Moodys	S&P	Fitch	Spread bps	Index
Jazz CDO Mar-02					
Class A	Aaa	AAA		47	6m Libor
Class B	Aa2	AAA		75	6m Libor
Class C-1		A-		135	6m Libor
Class D		BBB		240	6m Libor
Robeco III CSO Dec-01					
Class A	Aaa			55	3m Libor/euribor
Class B	Aa2			85	3m Libor
Class C	Baa1			275	3m Libor
Marylebone Road CBO III Oct-01					
Class A-1	Aaa	AAA		45	3m Libor
Class A-2	Aa1	AAA		65	3m Libor
Class A-3	A2	AAA		160	3m Libor
Brooklands € referenced linked notes Jul-01					
Class A	Aaa		AAA	50	3m Libor
Class B	Aa3		AA-	80	3m Libor
Class C	Baa2		BBB	250	3m Libor
Class D-1	n/a		BBB-	500	3m Libor
North Street Ref. Linked Notes 2000-2 Oct-00					
Class A			AAA	70	6m Libor
Class B			AA	105	6m Libor
Class C			A	175	6m Libor

(Source: Bloomberg)

Figure 22.16: Selected synthetic deal spreads at issue.

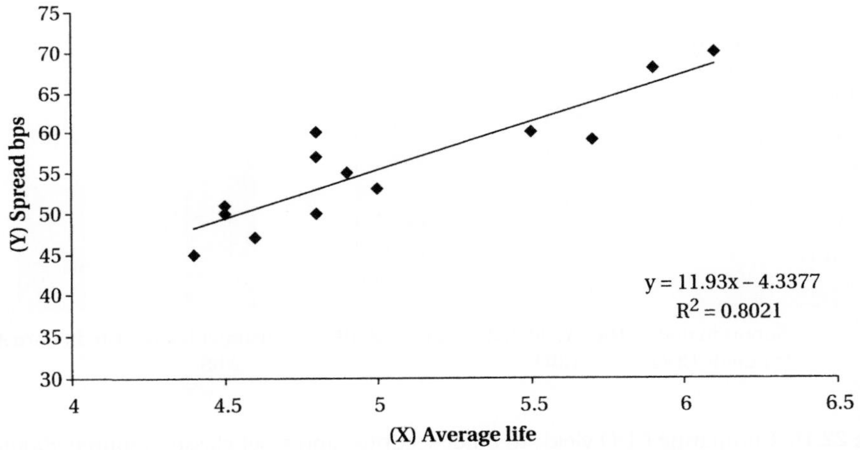

Figure 22.17: AAA spreads as at February 2002 (selected European CDO deals).

In Europe fund managers that have originated managed synthetic deals include Robeco, Cheyne Capital Management, BAREP Asset Management and Axa Investment Managers. In the second part of this chapter we look at three specific deals as case studies, issued in the European market during 2001 and 2002.

The deals discussed are innovative structures and a creative combination of securitisation technology and credit derivatives. They show how a portfolio manager can utilise vehicles of this kind to exploit its expertise in credit trading as well as provide attractive returns for investors. Managed synthetic CDOs also present fund managers with a vehicle to build on their credit derivatives experience. As the market in synthetic credit, in Europe at least, is frequently more liquid than the cash market for the same reference names, it is reasonable to expect more transactions of this type in the near future.

22.3.1 *Blue Chip Funding 2001–1 plc*

Blue Chip Funding is a managed synthetic CDO originated by Dolmen Securities, which closed in December 2001. The deal has a €1 billion reference portfolio, with the following terms:

Name	**Blue Chip Funding 2001–1 plc**
Manager	Dolmen Securities Limited
Arranger	Dolmen Securities Limited Dresdner Kleinwort Wasserstein
Closing date	17 December 2001
Portfolio	€1 billion of credit default swaps
Reference assets	80 investment-grade entities
Portfolio Administrator	Bank of New York

The structure is partially funded, with €80 million of notes issued, or 8% of the nominal value. The share of the unfunded piece is comparatively high. The proceeds from the notes issue are invested in AAA securities, which are held in custody by the third-party agency service provider, which must be rated at AA- or higher. The diversity of the structure is reflected in there being 80 different credits, with a weighted average rating of A-, with no individual asset having a rating below BBB-.

The structure is illustrated at Figure 22.18.

With this deal, the managers have the ability to trade the credit default swaps with a pre-specified panel of dealers. The default swap counterparties must have a short-term rating of A-1+ or better. Trading will result in trading gains or losses. This contrasts with a static synthetic deal, where investors have not been affected by trading gains or losses that arise from pool substitutions. The deal was rated by Standard & Poor's, which in its rating report described the management strategy as 'defensive trading' to avoid acute credit deteriorations. There are a number of guidelines that the manager must adhere to, such as:

- the manager may both sell credit protection and purchase credit protection; however the manager may only short credit (purchase credit protection) in order to close out or offset an existing previous sale of protection;
- there is a discretionary trading limit of 10% of portfolio value;

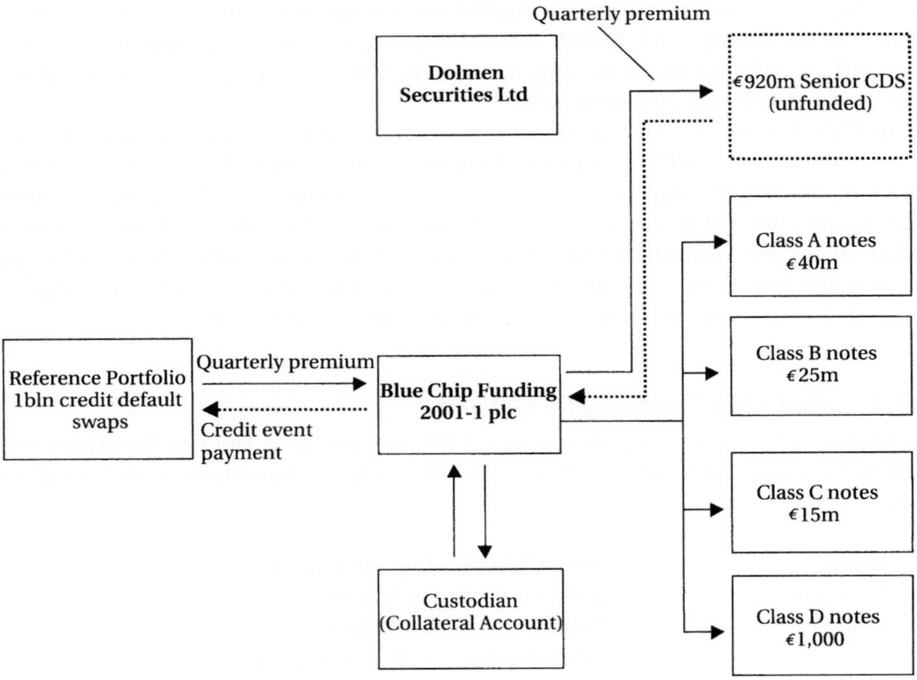

Figure 22.18: Blue Chip Funding managed synthetic CDO (Source: S&P).

- a minimum weighted average premium of 60 bps for swaps must be maintained;
- a minimum reinvestment test must be passed at all times: this states that if the value of the collateral account falls below €80 million, interest generated by the collateral securities must be diverted from the equity (Class C and D notes) to the senior notes until the interest cover is restored.

The issuer has sold protection on the reference assets. On occurrence of a credit event, the issuer will make credit protection payments to the swap counterparty (see Figure 22.18). If the vehicle experiences losses as a result of credit events or credit default swap trading, these are made up from the collateral account.

22.3.2 *Robeco CSO III B.V.*

The Robeco III CDO is described as the first stand-alone, multiple dealer managed synthetic CDO in Europe. It is a €1billion structure sponsored and managed by Robeco Asset Management in Rotterdam, Netherlands. The manager can trade in credit default swaps but, as with Blue Chip Funding, is limited to purchasing swaps only in order to offset an existing sold protection swap. The motivation behind structuring the trade was partly the liquidity and depth of the credit derivatives market for European corporate credits, deemed to be greater than the equivalent cash market bonds for the same names.[14]

[14] Source: *RISK*, March 2002

Name	**Robeco CSO III B.V.**
Manager	Robeco Institutional Asset Management B.V.
Arrangers	JPMorgan Chase Bank Robeco Alternative Investments
Closing date	15 December 2001
Maturity	September 2008
Portfolio	€1 billion of credit default swaps
Reference assets	80 investment-grade entities
Portfolio Administrator	JPMorgan Chase Bank Institutional Trust Services

The first managed synthetic deal in Europe, Robeco III-type structures have subsequently been adopted by other collateral managers. The principal innovation of the vehicle is the method by which the credit default swaps are managed, as part of a dynamically managed reference portfolio. The addition or offsetting of swaps at different spread levels creates trading gains or losses for the vehicle. The choice of reference credits on which swaps are written must, as expected with a CDO, follow a number of criteria set by the ratings agency, including diversity score, rating factor, weighted average spread, geographical and industry concentration, among others.

The reference portfolio is comprised of between 100 and 130 reference credits, of which at least 90% must be at investment grade rating. There is a minimum permitted weighted average credit rating of Baa2. On issue the average rating factor was at around 250–260. The structure is 70% unfunded, as shown at Figure 22.19. The remaining 30% is funded through the issue of credit-linked notes, and after payment of the initial fees and expenses of the Issuer, the proceeds of the note issue are invested in the following as collateral:

- €220 million invested in a unique ABS security, a credit card-backed bond issued by MBNA Bank and rated AAA, which has a scheduled maturity of September 2008;
- €80 million invested in a series of 'guaranteed investment contracts' (GIC) paying an average rate of Libor minus 10 basis points.

The structure is of interest to investors who wish to exploit the liquidity of the credit derivative market for European credits that are not well represented in the cash markets. Investors who wish to diversify across the market can also leverage the expertise of the CDO manager in the synthetic credit market.

Portfolio trading

Upon closure of the transaction, the issuer enters into credit default swaps with counterparties among a pre-selected list of seven swap dealers, building up over the ramp-up period to a maximum of €1 billion notional of swaps. At this point the portfolio of default swaps is dynamic, as the issuer may enter into additional default swaps, and unwind or offset existing swaps. The decisions on when and which swaps to trade is taken by the portfolio manager. The issuer sells credit protection through the network of established counterparties; it may buy protection but only to remove an existing reference entity exposure. The sale of a credit protection adds a new credit default swap to the portfolio, whereas buying a swap to offset an existing exposure adds a new swap but nets out the exposure. This trading leads to trading gains or losses. Trading gains are to the benefit of the vehicle and will increase the value of the collateral pool.

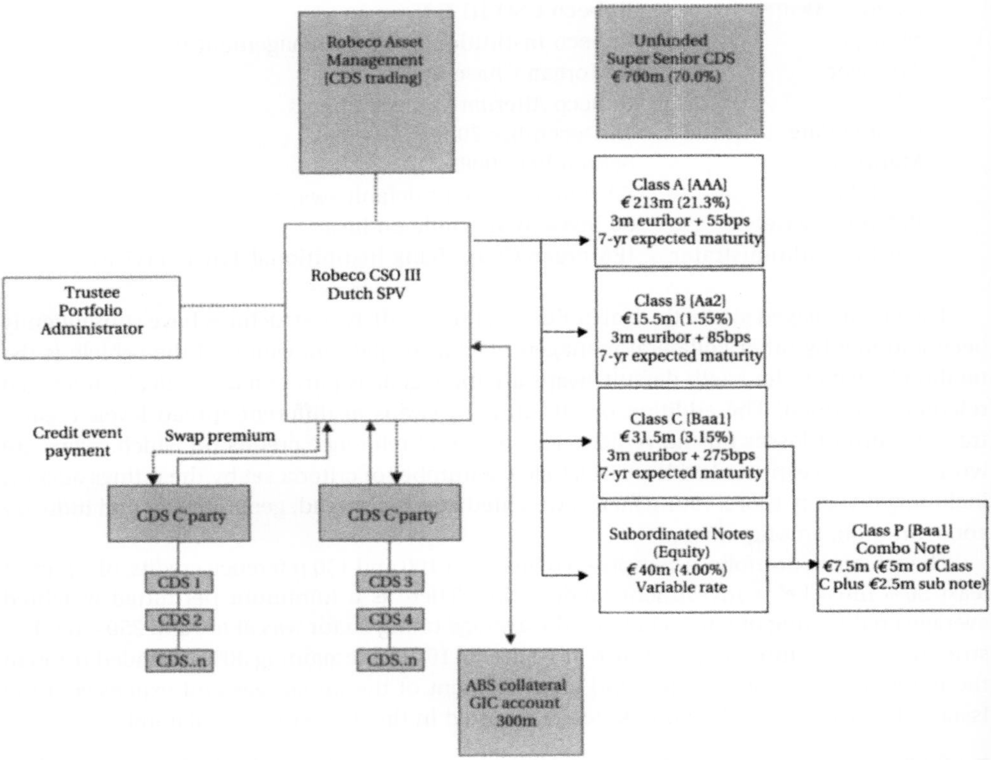

Figure 22.19: Robeco III structure and tranching.

Each credit default swap is a vanilla single-name contract, under which the counterparty pays the regular credit protection premium to the issuer. On occurrence of a credit event for the reference entity, the counterparty will calculate a net loss amount which is paid by the issuer to the counterparty. The loss amount is defined as the difference between the nominal value of the reference entity and its market value at time of the credit event. Payments required on occurrence of a credit event, and trading losses resulting from credit default swap activity, are both paid out of the collateral account.

The portfolio manager must follow certain trading guidelines when adding or removing default swaps. As set out by Moody's,[15] the manager may add reference credits to the portfolio only if the total credit default swap notional amount is below €1 billion, and if the outstanding loss amount is below € 25 million. For any single obligor name, the criteria are:

- a minimum rating of Ba3 or above;
- notional limits for single name of €5 m, €10 m or €12.5 m, depending on credit rating.

15 Robeco CSO III B.V., *Pre-sale report*, Moody's Investor Service, 7 December 2001.

Reference credits may be removed only if:

- there has been a fall in the reference credit default swap premium, so that trading it out creates a gain;
- the premium has increased by 25% (in other words, a kind of 'stop-loss');
- the reference entity has been subject to credit rating downgrade.

Returns analysis

The structure of the vehicle, with 30% level of funding, adds to the attraction of the transaction for investors. In effect the issuer represents a counterparty with 30% Tier 1 capital. This reduces the cost of capital of the vehicle and improves return for investors compared to a cash CDO. As reported by RISK,[16] a comparison with an equivalent cash vehicle resulted in returns of 20.1% compared to 11.9%, as shown in Figure 22.20. This reflected the significantly lower funding cost associated with the (lower) cost of the super-senior swap element, which was 70% of the structure.

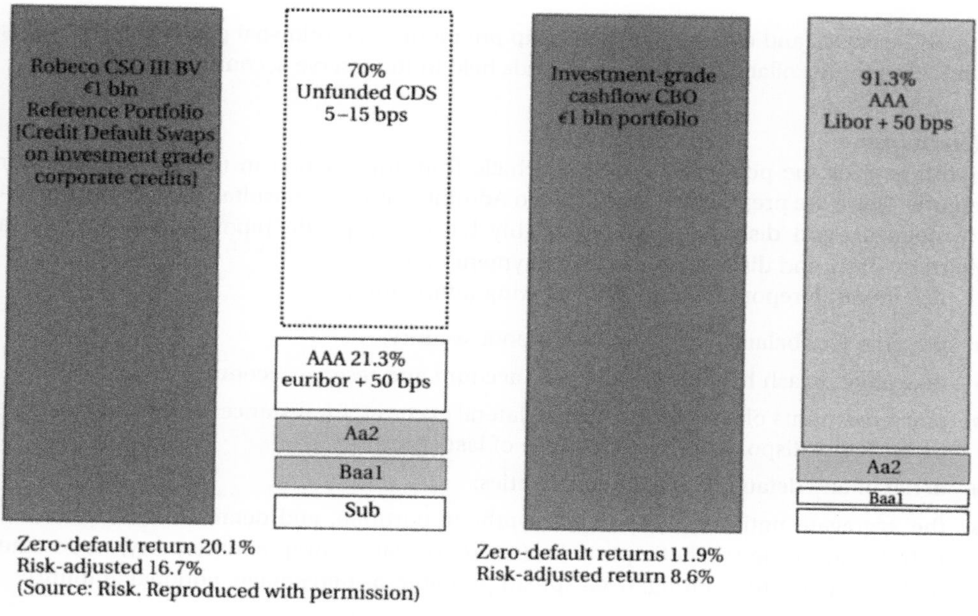

Figure 22.20: Robeco returns analysis.

Priority of payments

The priority of payments followed by the vehicle follows a familiar pattern for CDOs. On each payment date, payments will be made in accordance with the waterfall shown in Figure 22.21. These payments are funded by coupon from the collateral pool, including interest earned on

16 *RISK*, March 2002

Interest proceeds waterfall	Principal proceeds waterfall
Trustee fees, costs, expenses	Fees, costs, expenses
Management fee	Credit default swaps payment
Class A interest	Management fee
(If pass Class B interest trigger test), Class B interest	Unpaid Class A interest
(If pass Class C interest trigger), Class C interest	Class A principal
Interest to subordinated Class	Unpaid Class B interest
Loss amount reserve payment	Class B principal
(If Class B trigger event), interest to Class B and deferred interest	Unpaid Class C interest
(If Class C trigger event), interest to Class C	Class C principal
Subordinated Notes	Subordinated notes

(Source: Moody's)

Figure 22.21: Robeco waterfall schedule.

the GIC account, and the credit default swap premiums. The principal payments waterfall is funded from the collateral security and funds held in the reserve account.

Reporting

Investors track the performance of the vehicle from information in the periodic investor reports. These are prepared by the Portfolio Administrator, in consultation with the portfolio manager, and distributed on a monthly basis. A separate report is prepared on a quarterly basis and distributed on each payment date.

The monthly report includes the following information:

- the principal balance of the collateral pool security;
- the value of cash held in the collateral account and reserve accounts;
- any movements of securities in the collateral account, for instance securities or eligible investments disposed of since the date of last report;
- detail of any default in collateral securities;
- the aggregate notional value of the synthetic portfolio, and details of each reference entity held in the synthetic portfolio (reference name, swap counterparty, trade date, maturity date, credit rating, fixed spread premium as percentage, notional amount);
- the diversity score;
- compliance test results, including weighted average rating, weighted average spread and weighted average recovery;
- the outstanding loss amount.

It is a requirement of the ratings agencies that the portfolio report be produced, or at least verified, by an independent third-party to the deal. The investor report is sent to the issuer, swap counterparties, rating agency and noteholders.

Appendices

Appendix 22.1: An introduction to credit derivatives

Credit derivatives are a relatively recent innovation, having been introduced in significant volumes in the mid 1990s. They are financial instruments originally designed to protect banks and other institutions against losses arising from *credit events*. A succinct definition would be that they are instruments designed to lay off or take on credit risk. Since their inception, they have been used to trade credit for speculative purposes and as hedging instruments.

A payout under a credit derivative is triggered by a credit event. As banks may define default in different way, the terms under which a credit derivative is executed usually include a specification of what constitutes a credit event. Typically this can be:

- bankruptcy or insolvency of the reference asset obligor;
- a financial restructuring, for example occasioned under administration or as required under US bankruptcy protection;
- technical default, for example the non-payment of interest or coupon when it falls due;
- a change in credit spread payable by the obligor above a specified maximum level;
- a downgrade in credit rating below a specified minimum level.

A user of credit derivatives may be any institution that has an exposure to or desires an exposure to credit risk. This includes investment banks and commercial banks, insurance companies, corporates, fund managers, and hedge funds.

Credit default swaps

The most common credit derivative, and possibly the simplest, is the *credit default swap, default swap* or *credit swap*. This is a contract in which a periodic fixed fee or a one-off premium is paid to a *protection seller*, in return for which the seller will make a payment on the occurrence of a specified credit event. The fee is usually quoted as a basis point fee of the nominal value. The swap can refer to a single asset, known as the reference asset or underlying asset, or a basket of assets. The default payment can be paid in whatever way suits the protection buyer or both counterparties. For example it may be linked to the change in price of the reference asset or another specified asset, it may be fixed at a pre-determined recovery rate, or it may be in the form of actual delivery of the reference asset at a specified price. However it is structured, the credit default swap enables one party to transfer its credit exposure to another party, while retaining the asset on its balance sheet. Alternatively banks may use default swaps to trade sovereign and corporate credit spreads without trading the actual assets themselves; for example someone who has gone long a default swap (the protection buyer) will gain if the reference asset obligor suffers a rating downgrade or defaults, and can sell the default swap at a profit if he can find a buyer counterparty. This is because the cost of protection on the reference asset will have increased as a result of the credit event. The original buyer of the default swap need never have owned a bond issued by the reference asset obligor.

The maturity does not have to match the maturity of the reference asset and in most cases does not. On default the swap is terminated and default payment by the protection

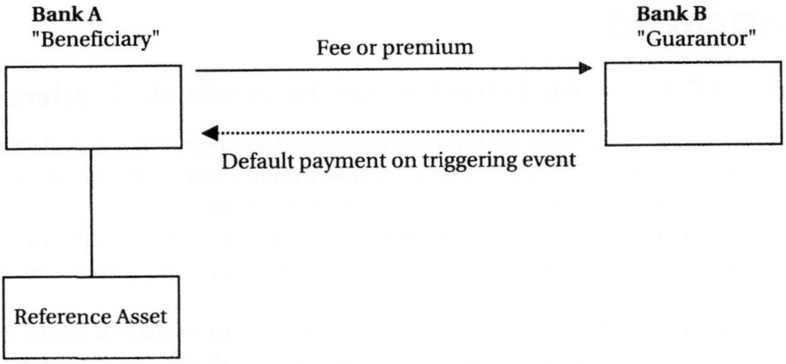

Figure 22.A1: Credit Default Swap.

seller or guarantor is calculated and handed over. The guarantor may have the asset delivered to him and pay the nominal value, or may cash settle the swap contract.

Total return swaps

Total return swaps (TRS)[17] are slightly different to credit default swaps. Anson (1999) makes the distinction that while default swaps are used to hedge credit risk exposure, a TRS is used to increase credit exposure. They are sometimes known as synthetic repos. A TRS is a bilateral contract in which the total return of an asset such as a bond or bank loan is exchanged in return for a funding cash flow, which is usually Libor plus a spread. The return of a bond is defined as the coupon income plus any appreciation in price per nominal. For taking on an exposure to an asset's total return, the purchaser of the swap (the receiver of the total return) pays the Libor floating rate plus spread.

If the total return payer owns the underlying asset (reference asset), it has in effect transferred its economic exposure to the total return receiver. In other words, by entering into the TRS the owner has effected a credit derivative transaction and transferred its credit risk. The net effect is that the owner of the asset has a neutral position that is earning it Libor plus a spread. The asset is not transferred off the owner's balance sheet, only its interest-rate and credit risk. This makes it similar to a repo, hence the name synthetic repo. The total return payer must continue to fund the underlying asset at its cost of funding capital.

On the other side of the swap, a TRS enables an investor to obtain an exposure to the economic benefits of an asset without having to own it. The investor is the total return receiver. On maturity of the swap the investor will pay the value of any decline in price of the asset to the TRS payer. If the asset has risen in price, the investor receives the difference in value between the higher current price and the original price at the time of the start of the trade. If the price of the asset has not changed, no final payment changes hands. In return for this exposure, the investor (TRS receiver) makes regular payments of Libor plus spread.

TRSs are attractive to investors who wish to gain a leveraged exposure to an asset such as a high-yield bond or bank loan without bearing the original cost, or who wish to diversify their portfolio credit exposure. The main difference compared to a credit default swap is

---

17 Also known as *total rate of return swaps* or TRORs.

that payments made to balance the change in value of the asset will take place irrespective of the occurrence of a credit event.

A TRS is illustrated at Figure 22.A2. The total return receiver is long of both interest and credit risk of the reference asset, while the total return payer *may* be long of the asset itself.

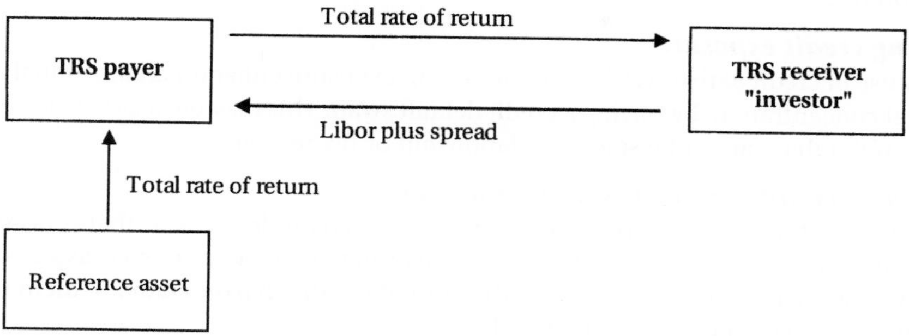

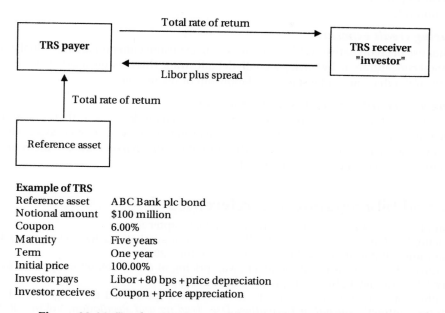

Example of TRS

Reference asset	ABC Bank plc bond
Notional amount	$100 million
Coupon	6.00%
Maturity	Five years
Term	One year
Initial price	100.00%
Investor pays	Libor + 80 bps + price depreciation
Investor receives	Coupon + price appreciation

Figure 22.A2: Total return swap, with terms for a generic example.

Credit-linked notes

Another type of credit derivative is the *credit-linked note* (CLN). These are considered in the next chapter.

Credit options

Credit options are another form of credit derivative. Like other options a credit option is a contract designed to meet specific hedging or speculative requirements of an entity, which may purchase or sell the option to meet its objectives. A credit call option gives the buyer the right without the obligation to purchase the underlying credit-sensitive asset, or a credit spread, at a specified price and specified time (or period of time). A credit put option gives the buyer the right without the obligation to sell the underlying credit-sensitive asset or credit spread. By purchasing credit options banks and other institutions can take a view on credit spread movements for the cost of the option premium only, without recourse to actual loans issued by an obligor. The writer of credit options seeks to earn fee income.

Use of credit derivatives

Banks use credit derivatives for a number of reasons. Some of these are summarised below.

Diversifying the credit portfolio

A bank may wish to take on credit exposure by providing credit protection on assets that it already owns, in return for a fee. This enhances income on their portfolio. They may sell credit derivatives to enable non-banking clients to gain credit exposures, if these clients do not wish to purchase the assets directly. In this respect the bank performs a credit intermediation role.

Reducing credit exposure

Another use of credit derivatives is to reduce credit exposure either for an individual asset or a sectoral concentration, by buying a credit default swap. This may be desirable for assets in their portfolio that cannot be sold for relationship or tax reasons.

Acting as a credit derivatives market maker

A bank may wish to set itself up as a market maker in credit derivatives, that is becoming a credit trader. In this case the trader may or may not hold the reference assets directly, depending on their appetite for risk and the liquidity of the market enabling them to offset derivative contracts as and when required.

Selected bibliography and references

Anson M., *Credit Derivatives,* FJF Associates 1999, Chapter 3

Boggiano, K., Waterson, and Stein, C., 'Four forms of synthetic CDOs', *Derivatives Week,* Euromoney Publications, Volume XI, No 23, 10 June 2002

Choudhry, M., 'Some issues in the asset-swap pricing of credit default swaps', *Derivatives Week,* Euromoney Publications, 2 December 2001

Choudhry, M., 'Trading credit spreads: the case for a specialised exchange-traded credit futures contract', *Journal of Derivatives Use, Trading and Regulation,* Volume 8, No 1, June 2002

Das, S., *Structured Products and Hybrid Securities,* John Wiley 2001, chapter 12

Fabozzi, F., Goodman, L., (editors), *Investing in Collateralised Debt Obligations,* FJF Associates 2001

Kasapi, A., *Mastering Credit Derivatives,* FT Prentice Hall 1999

23 Credit-Linked Notes

Credit-linked notes (CLNs) are a form of credit derivative. Credit derivative instruments enable participants in the financial market to trade in credit as an asset, as they isolate and transfer credit risk. They also enable the market to separate funding considerations from credit risk. A number of instruments come under the category of credit derivatives. In this chapter we consider a commonly encountered credit derivative instrument, the credit-linked note.

Irrespective of the particular instrument under consideration, all credit derivatives can be described under the following characteristics:

- the *reference entity*, which is the asset or name on which credit protection is being bought and sold;
- the credit event, or events, which indicate that the reference entity is experiencing, or about to experience, financial difficulty and which act as trigger events for payments under the credit derivative contract;
- the settlement mechanism for the credit derivative instrument, whether cash settled or physically settled;
- (under physical settlement), the deliverable obligation that the protection buyer delivers to the protection seller on the occurrence of a trigger event.

Credit derivatives are grouped into *funded* and *unfunded* variants. In an unfunded credit derivative, typified by a *credit default swap*, the protection seller does not make an upfront payment to the protection buyer. Credit default swaps have a number of applications and are used extensively for flow trading of single reference name credit risks or, in *portfolio swap* form, for trading a basket of reference credits.

In a funded credit derivative, typified by a credit-linked note, the investor in the note is the credit-protection seller and is making an upfront payment to the protection buyer when it buys the note. Thus, the protection buyer is the issuer of the note. If no credit event occurs during the life of the note, the redemption value of the note is paid to the investor on maturity. If a credit event does occur, then on maturity a value less than par will be paid out to the investor. This value will be reduced by the nominal value of the reference asset that the CLN is linked to. The exact process will differ according to whether *cash settlement* or *physical settlement* has been specified for the note. We will consider this later.

Credit default swaps and CLNs are used in structured products, in various combinations, and their flexibility has been behind the growth and wide application of the synthetic collateralised debt obligation and other credit hybrid products.

23.1 Description of CLNs

Credit-linked notes exist in a number of forms, but all of them contain a link between the return they pay and the credit-related performance of the underlying asset. A standard credit-linked note is a security, usually issued by an investment-graded entity, that has an interest payment and fixed maturity structure similar to a vanilla bond. The performance of the note however, including the maturity value, is linked to the performance of a specified underlying asset or assets as well as that of the issuing entity. Notes are usually issued at par. The notes are often used by borrowers to hedge against credit risk, and by investors to enhance the yield received on their holdings. Hence, the issuer of the note is the protection buyer and the buyer of the note is the protection seller.

Essentially, credit-linked notes are hybrid instruments that combine a pure credit-risk exposure with a vanilla bond. The credit-linked note pays regular coupons, however the credit derivative element is usually set to allow the issuer to decrease the principal amount, and/or the coupon interest, if a specified credit event occurs.

Figure 23.1 shows Bloomberg screen SND and their definition of the CLN.

To illustrate a CLN, consider a bank issuer of credit cards that wants to fund its credit card loan portfolio via an issue of debt. The bank is rated AA–. In order to reduce the credit risk of the loans, it issues a two-year CLN. The principal amount of the bond is 100 (par) as usual, and it pays a coupon of 7.50%, which is 110 basis points above the two-year benchmark. At the time of issue the equivalent spread for a vanilla bond issued by a bank of this rating would be of the order of 65 bps. With the CLN though, if the incidence of bad debt amongst credit card holders exceeds 10% then the terms state that note holders will only

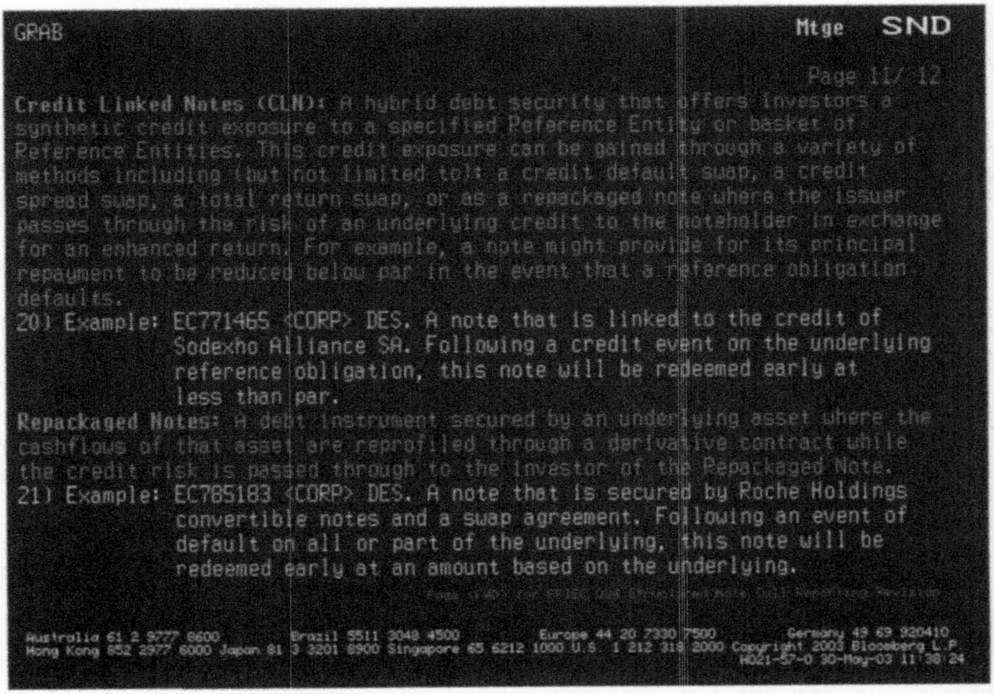
GRAB Mtge SND

Page 11/ 12

Credit Linked Notes (CLN): A hybrid debt security that offers investors a synthetic credit exposure to a specified Reference Entity or basket of Reference Entities. This credit exposure can be gained through a variety of methods including (but not limited to): a credit default swap, a credit spread swap, a total return swap, or as a repackaged note where the issuer passes through the risk of an underlying credit to the noteholder in exchange for an enhanced return. For example, a note might provide for its principal repayment to be reduced below par in the event that a reference obligation defaults.

20) Example: EC771465 <CORP> DES. A note that is linked to the credit of Sodexho Alliance SA. Following a credit event on the underlying reference obligation, this note will be redeemed early at less than par.

Repackaged Notes: A debt instrument secured by an underlying asset where the cashflows of that asset are reprofiled through a derivative contract while the credit risk is passed through to the investor of the Repackaged Note.

21) Example: EC785183 <CORP> DES. A note that is secured by Roche Holdings convertible notes and a swap agreement. Following an event of default on all or part of the underlying, this note will be redeemed early at an amount based on the underlying.

Australia 61 2 9777 8600 Brazil 5511 3048 4500 Europe 44 20 7330 7500 Germany 49 69 920410
Hong Kong 852 2977 6000 Japan 81 3 3201 8900 Singapore 65 6212 1000 U.S. 1 212 318 2000 Copyright 2003 Bloomberg L.P.
H021-57-0 30-May-03 11:38:24

Figure 23.1: Bloomberg screen SND: definition of credit-linked note (© Bloomberg L.P., reproduced with permission).

receive back 85 per 100 par. The credit card issuer has, in effect, purchased a credit option that lowers its liability in the event that it suffers from a specified credit event, which in this case is an above-expected incidence of bad debts. The cost of this credit option is paid in the form of a higher coupon payment on the CLN. The credit card bank has issued the CLN to reduce its credit exposure, in the form of this particular type of credit insurance. If the incidence of bad debts is low, the CLN is redeemed at par. However, if there is a high incidence of such debt, the bank will only have to repay a part of its loan liability.

Investors may wish to purchase the CLN because the coupon paid on it will be above what the credit card bank would pay on a vanilla bond it issued, and higher than other comparable investments in the market. In addition, such notes are usually priced below par on issue. Assuming the notes are eventually redeemed at par, investors will also have realised a substantial capital gain.

As with credit default swaps, credit-linked notes may be specified under cash settlement or physical settlement. Specifically:

- under cash settlement, if a credit event has occurred, on maturity the protection seller receives the difference between the value of the initial purchase proceeds and the value of the reference asset at the time of the credit event;
- under physical settlement, on occurrence of a credit event, the note is terminated. At maturity the protection buyer delivers the reference asset or an asset among a list of deliverable assets, and the protection seller receives the value of the original purchase proceeds minus the value of the asset that has been delivered.

Figure 23.2 illustrates a cash-settled credit-linked note.

CLNs may be issued directly by a financial or corporate entity or via a Special Purpose Vehicle (SPV). They have been issued with the form of credit-linking taking on one or more of a number of different guises. For instance, a CLN may have its return performance linked to the issuer's, or a specified reference entity's, credit rating, risk exposure, financial performance or circumstance of default. Figure 23.3 shows Bloomberg screen CLN and a list of the various types of CLN issue that have been made. Figure 23.4 shows a page accessed from Bloomberg screen 'CLN', which is a list of CLNs that have had their coupon affected by a change in the reference entity's credit rating.

The majority of CLNs are issued by issuers direct. An example of such a bond is shown in Figure 23.5. This shows Bloomberg screen DES for a CLN issued by British Telecom plc, the 8.125% note due in December 2010. The terms of this note state that the coupon will increase by 25 basis points for each one-notch rating downgrade below A-/A3 suffered by the issuer during the life of the note. The coupon will decrease by 25 basis points for each ratings upgrade, with a minimum coupon set at 8.125%. In other words, this note allows investors to take on a credit play on the fortunes of the issuer.

Figure 23.6 shows Bloomberg screen YA for this note, as at 29 May 2003. We see that a rating downgrade meant that the coupon on the note was now 8.375%.

CLNs have been issued with a number of different types of credit linking.

For instance, Figure 23.7 is the Bloomberg DES page for a USD-denominated CLN issued directly by Household Finance Corporation.[1] Like the British Telecom bond, this is

---

1 HFC was subsequently acquired by HSBC.

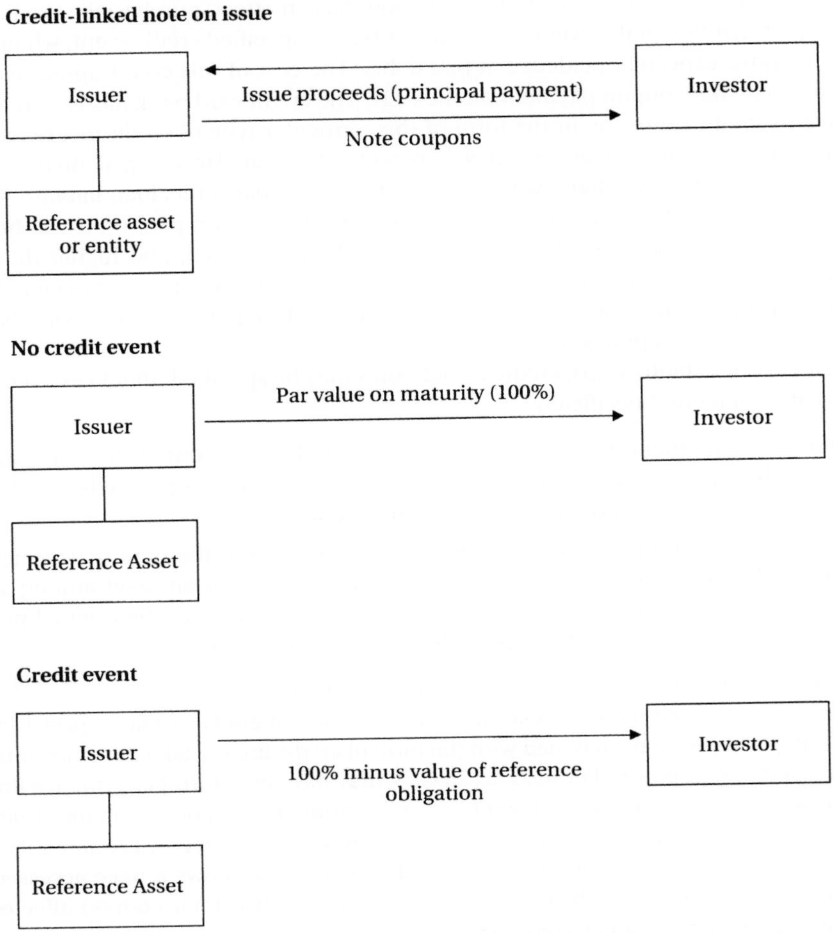

Figure 23.2: Credit-linked note cash settlement.

a CLN whose return is linked to the credit risk of the issuer, but in a different way. The coupon of the HFC bond was issued as floating USD-Libor, but in the event of the bond not being called from November 2001, the coupon would be the issuer's two-year 'credit spread' over a fixed rate of 5.9%. In fact the issuer called the bond with effect from the coupon change date. Figure 23.8 shows the Bloomberg screen YA for the bond and how its coupon remained as at first issue until the call date.

Another type of credit-linking is evidenced from the details shown in Figure 23.9. This is a JPY-denominated bond issued by Alpha-Sires, which is an MTN programme vehicle set up by Merrill Lynch. The note itself is linked to the credit quality of Ford Motor Credit. In the event of a default of the reference name, the note will be called immediately. Figure 23.10 shows the rate fixing for this note as at the last coupon date. The screen snapshot was taken on 6 June 2003.

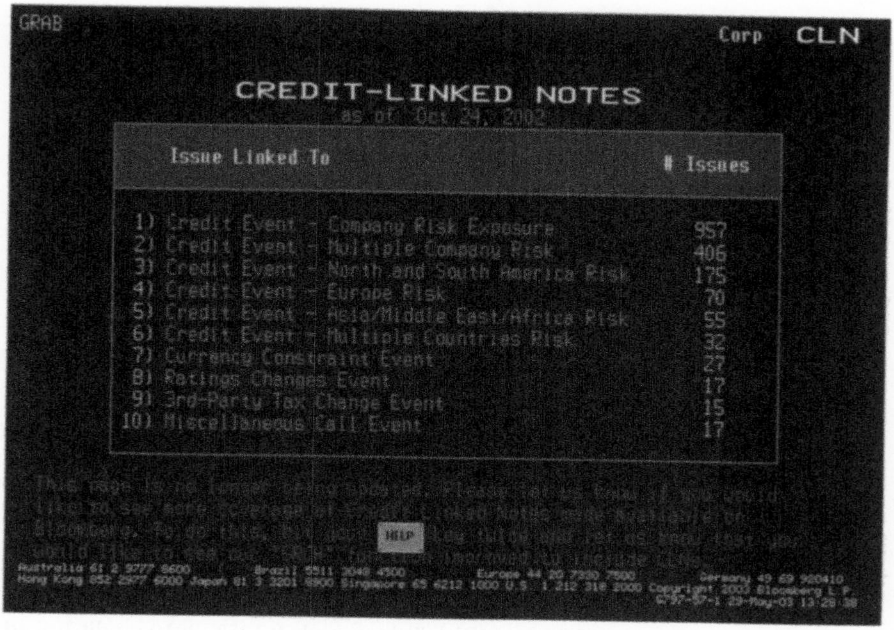

Figure 23.3: Bloomberg screen CLN (© Bloomberg L.P., reproduced with permission).

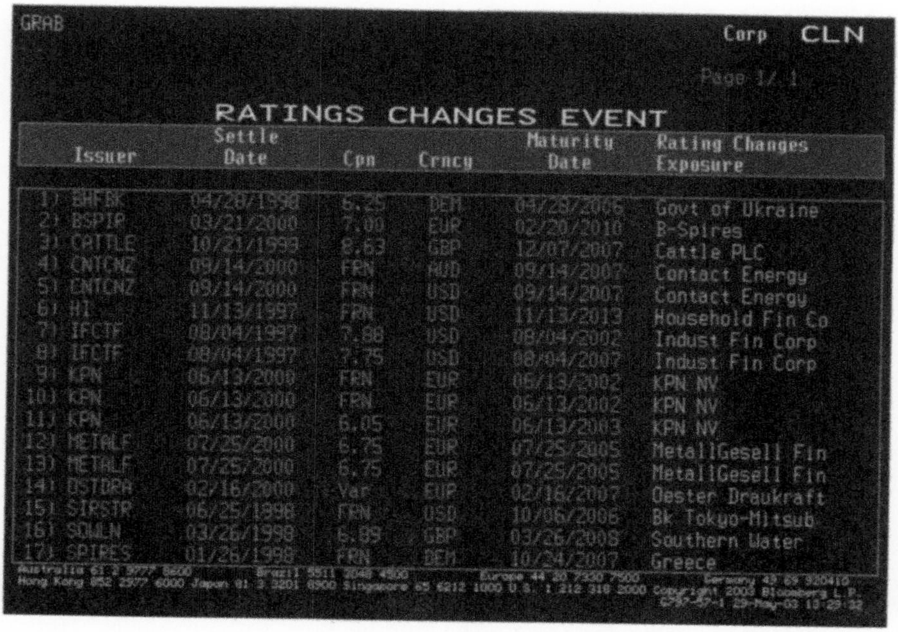

Issuer	Settle Date	Cpn	Crncy	Maturity Date	Rating Changes Exposure
1) BHFBK	04/28/1998	6.25	DEM	04/28/2006	Govt of Ukraine
2) BSPIR	03/21/2000	7.09	EUR	02/20/2010	B-Spires
3) CATTLE	10/21/1999	8.63	GBP	12/07/2007	Cattle PLC
4) CNTCNZ	09/14/2000	FRN	AUD	09/14/2007	Contact Energy
5) CNTCNZ	09/14/2000	FRN	USD	09/14/2007	Contact Energy
6) HI	11/13/1997	FRN	USD	11/13/2013	Household Fin Co
7) IFCTF	08/04/1997	7.88	USD	08/04/2002	Indust Fin Corp
8) IFCTF	08/04/1997	7.75	USD	08/04/2007	Indust Fin Corp
9) KPN	06/13/2000	FRN	EUR	06/13/2002	KPN NV
10) KPN	06/13/2000	FRN	EUR	06/13/2002	KPN NV
11) KPN	06/13/2000	6.05	EUR	06/13/2003	KPN NV
12) METALF	07/25/2000	6.75	EUR	07/25/2005	MetallGesell Fin
13) METALF	07/25/2000	6.75	EUR	07/25/2005	MetallGesell Fin
14) OSTDRA	02/16/2000	Var	EUR	02/16/2007	Oester Draukraft
15) SIRSTR	06/25/1998	FRN	USD	10/06/2006	Bk Tokyo-Mitsub
16) SOWLN	03/26/1998	6.89	GBP	03/26/2008	Southern Water
17) SPIRES	01/26/1999	FRN	DEM	10/24/2007	Greece

Figure 23.4: Bloomberg screen showing a sample of CLNs impacted by change in reference entity credit rating, October 2002 (© Bloomberg L.P., reproduced with permission).

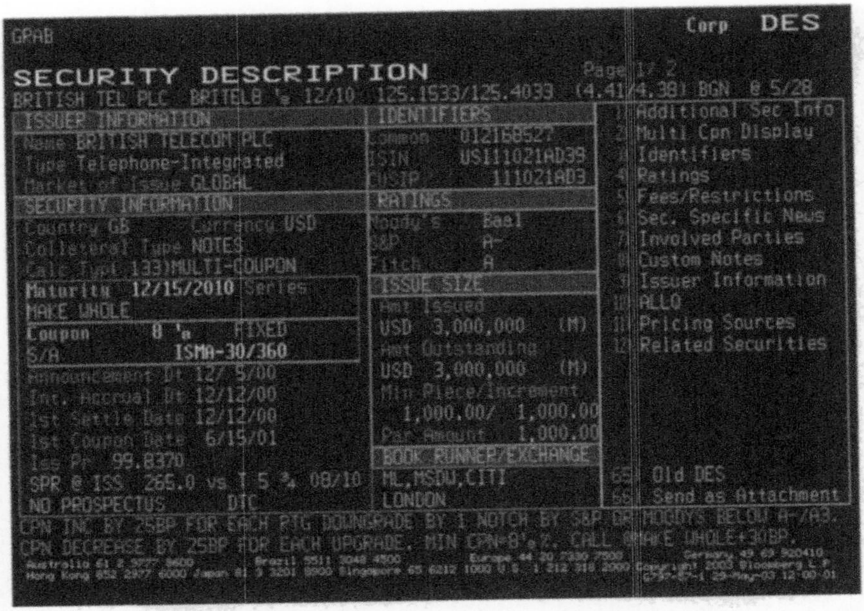

Figure 23.5: Bloomberg screen DES for British Telecom plc 8.125% 2010 credit-linked note issued on 5 December 2000 (© Bloomberg L.P., reproduced with permission).

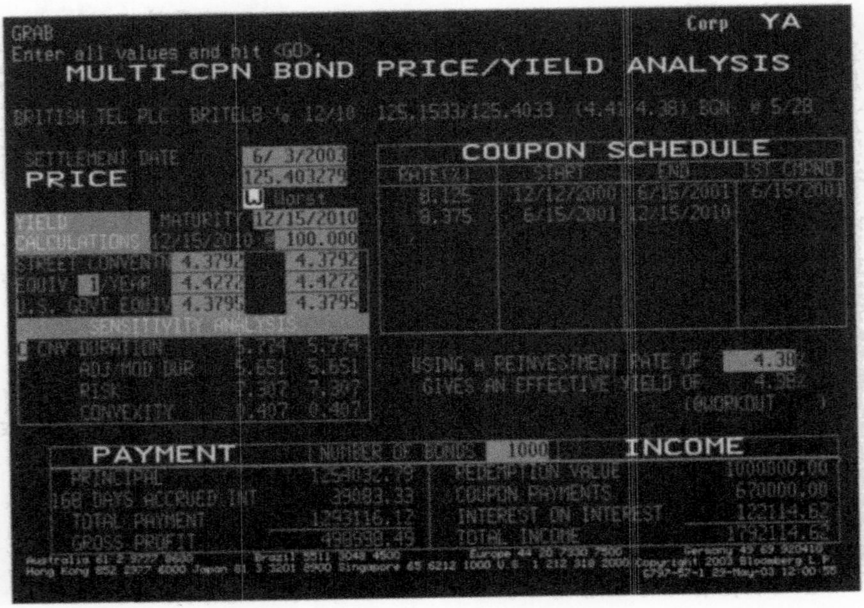

Figure 23.6: Bloomberg screen YA for British Telecom CLN, as at 29 May 2003 (© Bloomberg L.P., reproduced with permission).

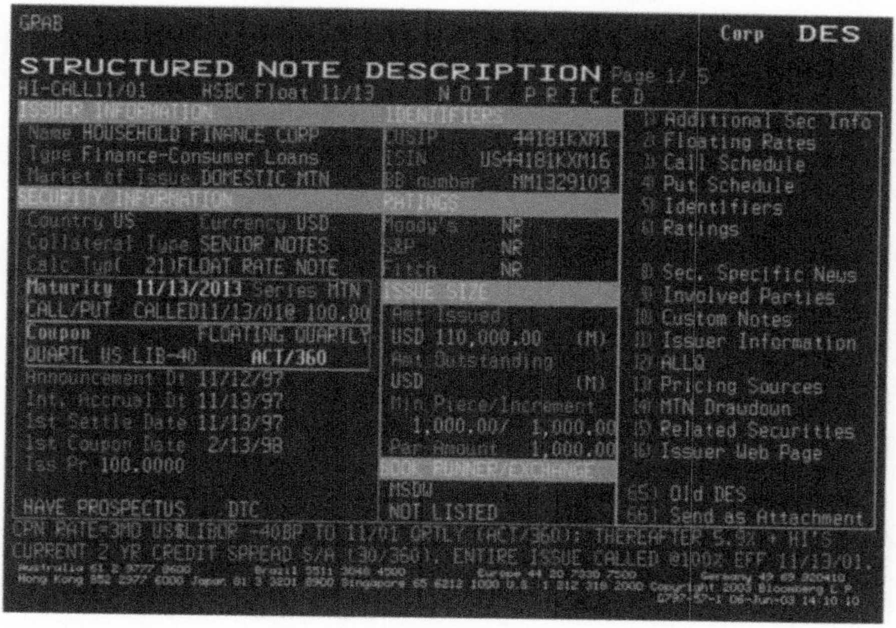

Figure 23.7: HFC bond, screen DES on Bloomberg (© Bloomberg L.P., reproduced with permission).

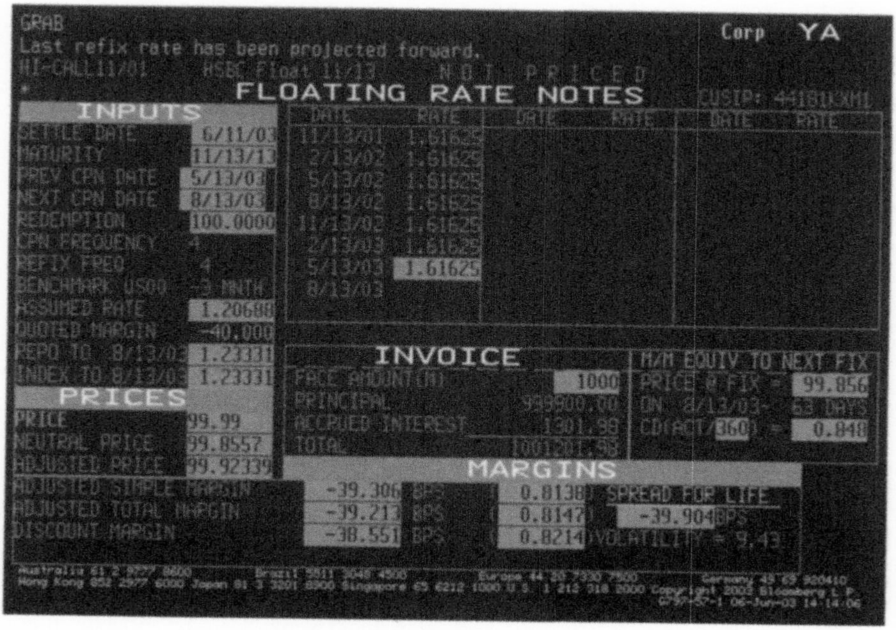

Figure 23.8: HFC bond YA screen (©Bloomberg L.P., reproduced with permission).

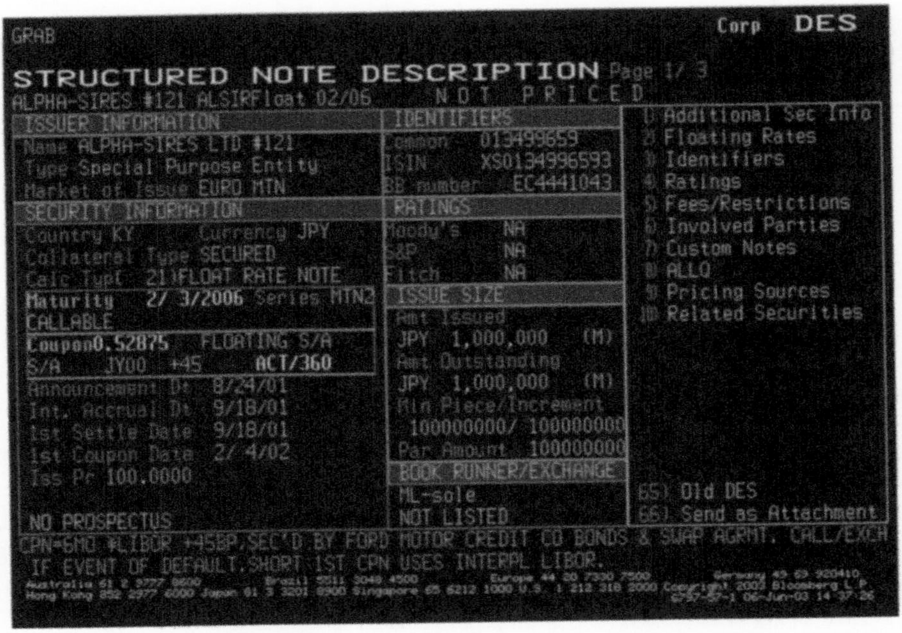

Figure 23.9: Ford CLN DES page (©Bloomberg L.P., reproduced with permission).

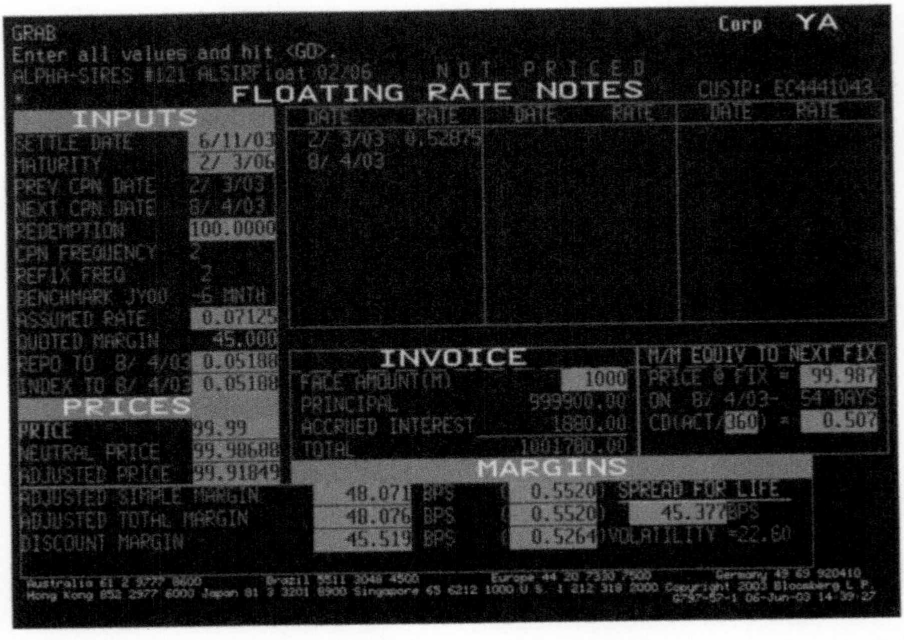

Figure 23.10: Ford CLN YA page (©Bloomberg L.P., reproduced with permission).

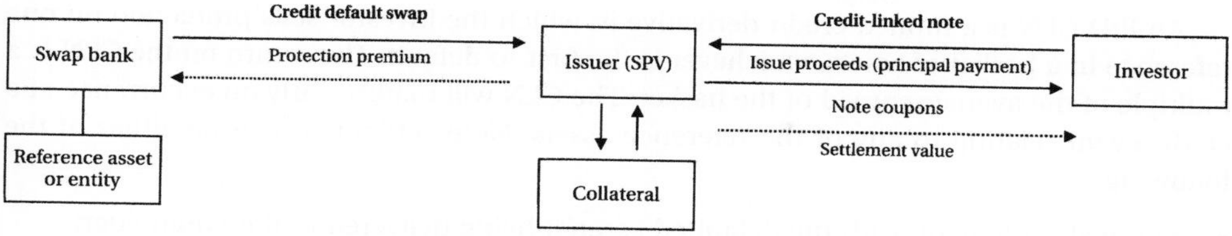

Figure 23.11: CLN and credit default swap structure on single reference name.

Structured products such as synthetic collateralised debt obligations (CDOs) may combine both CLNs and credit default swaps, to meet issuer and investor requirements. For instance, Figure 23.11 shows a credit structure designed to provide a higher return for an investor on comparable risk to the cash market. An issuing entity is set up in the form of a special purpose vehicle (SPV) which issues CLNs to the market. The structure is engineered so that the SPV has a neutral position on a reference asset. It has bought protection on a single reference name by issuing a funded credit derivative, the CLN, and simultaneously sold protection on this name by selling a credit default swap on this name. The proceeds of the CLN are invested in risk-free collateral such as T-bills or a Treasury bank account. The coupon on the CLN will be a spread over Libor. It is backed by the collateral account and the fee generated by the SPV in selling protection with the credit default swap. Investors in the CLN will have exposure to the reference asset or entity, and the repayment of the note is linked to the performance of the reference entity. If a credit event occurs, the maturity date of the CLN is brought forward and the note is settled as par minus the value of the reference asset or entity.

23.2 The first-to-default credit-linked note

A standard credit-linked note is issued in reference to one specific bond or loan. An investor purchasing such a note is writing credit protection on a specific reference credit. A CLN that is linked to more than one reference credit is known as a *basket credit-linked note.* A development of the CLN as a structured product is the First-to-Default CLN (FtD), which is a CLN that is linked to a basket of reference assets. The investor in the CLN is selling protection on the first credit to default.[2] Figure 23.12 shows this progression in the development of CLNs as structured products, with the *fully-funded synthetic* collateralised debt obligation (CDO) being the vehicle that uses CLNs tied to a large basket of reference assets.

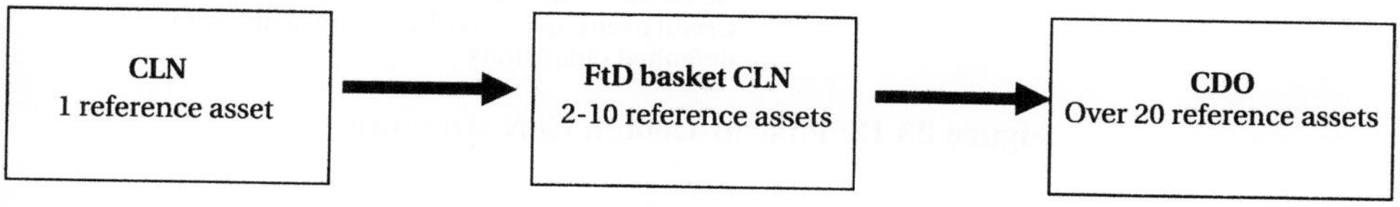

Figure 23.12: Progression of CLN development.

[2] 'Default' here meaning a credit event as defined in the ISDA definitions.

An FtD CLN is a funded credit derivative in which the investor sells protection on one reference in a basket of assets, whichever is the first to default. The return on the CLN is a multiple of the average spread of the basket. The CLN will mature early on occurrence of a credit event relating to any of the reference assets. Note settlement can be either of the following:

- physical settlement, with the defaulted asset(s) being delivered to the noteholder;
- cash settlement, in which the CLN issuer pays redemption proceeds to the noteholder calculated as (principal amount × reference asset recovery value).[3]

Figure 23.13 shows a generic FtD credit-linked note.

To illustrate, consider an FtD CLN issued at par with a term-to-maturity of five years and linked to a basket of five reference assets with a face value (issued nominal amount) of $10 million. An investor purchasing this note will pay $10 million to the issuer. If no credit event occurs during the life of the note, the investor will receive the face value of the note on maturity. If a credit event occurs on any of the assets in the basket, the note will redeem early and the issuer will deliver a deliverable obligation of the reference entity, or a portfolio of such obligations, for a $10 million nominal amount. An FtD CLN carries a similar amount of risk exposure on default to a standard CLN, namely the recovery rate of the defaulted credit. However, its risk exposure prior to default is theoretically lower than a standard CLN, as it can reduce default probability through diversification. The investor can obtain exposure to a basket of reference entities that differ by industrial sector and by credit rating.

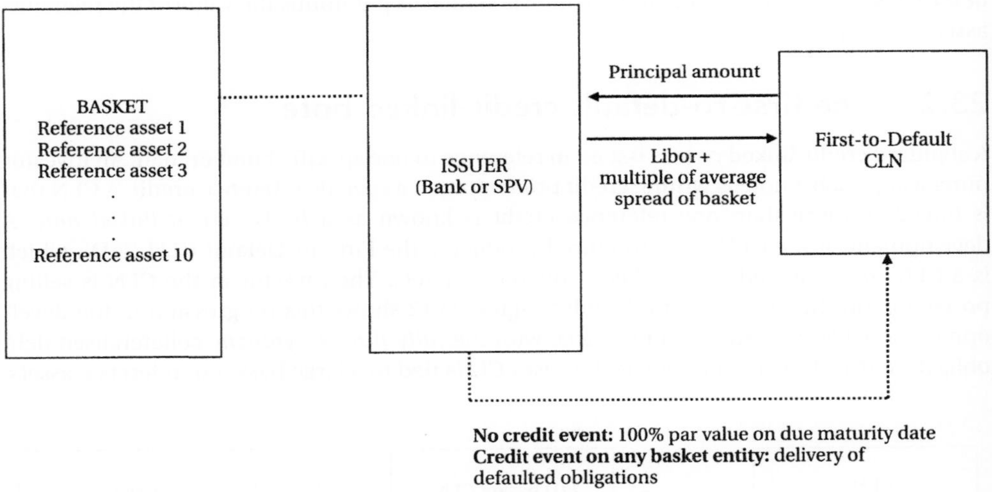

Figure 23.13: First-to-Default CLN structure.

3 In practice, it is not the 'recovery value' that is used but the market value of the reference asset at the time the credit event is verified. Recovery of a defaulted asset follows a legal process of administration and/or liquidation that can take some years, the final recovery value may not be known for certainty for some time.

	Automobiles	Banks	Electronics	Insurance	Media	Telecoms	Utilities
AAA							
Aa1							
Aa2				SunAlliance			
Aa3		RBoS					
A1							
A2							Powergen
A3	Ford					British Telecom	
Baa1			Philips		News Intl		
Baa2							
Baa3							

Figure 23.14: Diversified credit exposure to basket of reference assets: hypothetical reference asset mix.

The matrix in Figure 23.14 illustrates how an investor can select a credit mix in the basket that diversifies risk exposure across a wide range – we show an hypothetical mix of reference assets to which an issued FtD could be linked. The precise selection of names will reflect investors' own risk/return profile requirements.

The FtD CLN creates a synthetic credit entity that features a note return with enhanced spread. Investors receive a spread over Libor that is the average return of all the reference assets in the basket. This structure serves to diversify credit risk exposure while benefiting from a higher average return. If the pool of reference assets is sufficiently large, the structure becomes similar to a *single-tranche CDO*. This is considered in Choudhry (2004).

Bibliography

Choudhry, M., *Structured Credit Products: Credit Derivatives and Synthetic Securitisation*, John Wiley & Sons, 2004

Glossary

A

Accreting: An accreting principal is one which increases during the life of the deal. See **amortising, bullet**.

Accreting swap: Swap whose notional amount increases during the life of the swap (opposite of **amortising** swap).

Accrued benefit obligation: Present value of pension benefits that have been earned by an employee to date, whether vested in the employee or not. It can be an important measure when managing the asset/liability ration of pension funds.

Accrued interest: The proportion of interest or coupon earned on an investment from the previous coupon payment date until the value date

Accumulated value: The same as **future value**.

ACT/360: A day/year count convention taking the number of calendar days in a period and a 'year' of 360 days.

ACT/365: A day/year convention taking the number of calendar days in a period and a 'year' of 365 days. Under the ISDA definitions used for interest rate swap documentation, ACT/365 means the same as **ACT/ACT**.

ACT/ACT: A day/year count convention taking the number of calendar days in a period and a 'year' equal to the number of days in the current coupon period multiplied by the coupon frequency. For an interest rate sway, that part of the interest period falling in a leap year is divided by 366 and the remainder is divided by 365.

Add on factor: Simplified estimate of the potential future increase in the replacement cost, or market value, of a derivative transaction.

All-in price: See 'dirty price'.

All or nothing: Digital option. This option's **put** (call) pays out a pre-determined amount ('the all') if the index is below (above) the strike price at the option's expiration. The amount by which the **index** is below (above) the **strike** is irrelevant; the payout will be all or nothing.

American: An American option is one which may be exercised at any time during its life.

Amortising: An amortising principal is one which decreases during the life of a deal, or is repaid in stages during a loan. Amortising an amount over a period of time also means accruing for it pro rata over the period. See **accreting, bullet**.

Annuity: An investment providing a series of (generally equal) future cashflows.

Appreciation: An increase in the market value of a currency in terms of other currencies. See **depreciation, revaluation**.

Arbitrage: The process of buying securities in one country, currency or market, and selling identical securities in another to take advantage of price differences. When this is carried out simultaneously, it is in theory a risk-free transaction. There are many forms of arbitrage transactions. For instance in the cash market a bank might issue a money market instrument in one money centre and invest the same amount in another centre at a higher rate, such as an issue of three-month US dollar CDs in the United States at 5.5% and a purchase of three-month Eurodollar CDs at 5.6%. In the futures market arbitrage might involve buying three-month contracts and selling forward six-month contracts.

Arbitrageur: Someone who undertakes arbitrage trading.

Arch: (autoreggressive conditional heteroscedasticity) A discrete-time model for a random variable. It assumes that variance is stochastic and is a function of the variance of previous time steps and the level of the underlying.

Asian: An Asian option depends on the average value of the underlying over the option's life.

Ask: See **offer**.

Asset: Probable future economic benefit obtained or controlled as a result of past events or transactions. Generally classified as either current or long-term.

Asset & Liability Management (ALM): The practice of matching the term structure and cashflows of an organisation's asset and liability portfolios to maximise returns and minimise risk.

Asset allocation: Distribution of investment funds within an asset class or across a range of asset classes for the purpose of diversifying risk or adding value to a portfolio.

Asset securitisation: The process whereby loans, receivables and other illiquid assets in the balance sheet are packaged into interest-bearing securities that offer attractive investment opportunities.

Asset-backed security: A security which is collaterised by specific assets – such as mortgages – rather than by the intangible creditworthiness of the issuer.

Asset-risk benchmark: Benchmark against which the riskiness of a corporation's assets may be measured. In sophisticated corporate risk management strategies the dollar risk of the liability portfolio may be managed against an asset-risk benchmark.

Asset-sensitivity estimates: Estimates of the effect of risk factors on the value of assets.

Asset swap: An interest rate swap or currency swap used in conjunction with an underlying asset such as a bond investment. See **liability swap**.

At-the-money (ATM): An option is at-the-money if the current value of the underlying is the same as the strike price. See **in-the-money, out-of-the-money**.

Auction: A method of issue where institutions submit bids to the issuer on a price or yield basis. Auction rules vary considerably across markets

Average cap: Also known as an average rate cap, a cap on an average interest rate over a given period rather than on the rate prevailing at the end of the period. See also **average price (rate) option**.

Average price (rate) option: Option on a currency's average exchange rate or commodity's average spot price in which four variables have to be agreed between buyer and seller: the premium, the **strike** price, the source of the exchange rate or commodity price data and the sampling interval (each day, for example). At the end of the life of the option the **average spot exchange rate** is calculated and compared with the strike price. A cash payment is then made to the buyer of the option that is equal to the face amount of the option times the difference between the two rates (assuming the option is **in-the-money**; otherwise it expires worthless).

Average worst case exposure: The expression of an exposure in terms the average of the worst-case exposure over a given period.

B

Back-testing: The validation of a model by feeding it historical data and comparing the results with historical reality.

Backwardation: The situation when a forward or futures price for something is lower than the spot price (the same as forward discount in foreign exchange). See **contango**.

Balance sheet: Statement of the financial position of an enterprise at a specific point in time, giving assets, liabilities and stockholders' equity.

Band: The Exchange Rate Mechanism (ERM II) of the European Union links the currencies of Denmark and Greece in a system which limits the degree of fluctuation of each currency against the Euro within a band (of 15 percent for the drachma and 21/4 percent for the krone) either side of an agreed par value.

Banker's acceptance: See **Bill of Exchange**.

Barrier option: A barrier option is one which ceases to exist, or starts to exist, if the underlying reaches a certain barrier level. See **knock out/in**.

Base currency: Exchange rates are quoted in terms of the number of units of one currency (the variable or counter currency) which corresponds to one unit of the other currency (the base currency).

Basis: The underlying cash market price minus the futures price. In the case of a bond futures contract, the futures price must be multiplied by the conversion factor for the cash bond in question.

Basis points: In interest rate quotations, 0.01 percent.

Basis risk: A form of market risk that arises whenever one kind of risk exposure is hedged with an instrument that behaves in a similar, but not necessarily identical way. For instance a bank trading desk may use three-month interest rate futures to hedge its commercial paper or euronote programme. Although eurocurrency rates, to which futures prices respond, are well correlated with commercial paper rates they do not always move in lock step. If therefore commercial paper rates move by 10 basis points but futures prices dropped by only 7 basis points, the 3 bp gap would be the basis risk.

Basis swap: An interest rate swap where both legs are based on floating rate payments.

Basis trade: Buying the basis means selling a futures contract and buying the commodity or instrument underlying the futures contract. Selling the basis is the opposite.

Basket option: Option based on an underlying basket of bonds, currencies, equities or commodities.

Bearer bond: A bond for which physical possession of the certificate is proof of ownership. The issuer does not know the identity of the bondholder. Traditionally the bond carries detachable coupons, one for each interest payment date, which are posted to the issuer when payment is due. At maturity the bond is redeemed by sending in the certificate for repayment. These days bearer bonds are usually settled electronically, and while no register of ownership is kept by the issuer, coupon payments may be made electronically.

Bear spread: A spread position taken with the expectation of a fall in value in the underlying.

Benchmark: A bond whose terms set a standard for the market. The benchmark usually has the greatest liquidity, the highest turnover and is usually the most frequently quoted. It also usually trades expensive to the yield curve, due to higher demand for it amongst institutional investors.

Beta: The sensitivity of a stock relative to swings in the overall market. The market has a beta of one, so a stock or portfolio with a beta greater than one will rise or fall more than the overall market, whereas a beta of less than one means that the stock is less volatile.

Bid: The price at which a market maker will buy bonds. A tight bid-offer spread is indicative of a liquid and competitive market. The bid rate in a **repo** is the interest rate at which the dealer will borrow the **collateral** and lend the cash. See **offer**.

Bid figure: In a foreign exchange quotation, the exchange rate omitting the last two decimal places. For example, when EUR/USD is 1.1910/20, the bid figure is 1.19. See **points**.

Bid-offer: The two-way price at which a market will buy and sell stock.

Bilateral netting: The ability to offset amounts owed to a counterparty under one contract against amounts owed to the same counterparty under another contract – for example, where both transactions are governed by one master agreement. Also known as **'cherry-picking'**.

Bill: A *bill of exchange* is a payment order written by one person (the drawer) to another, directing the latter (drawee) to pay a certain amount of money at a future date to a third party. A bill of exchange is a bank draft when drawn on a bank. By accepting the draft, a bank agrees to pay the face value of the obligation if the drawer fails to pay, hence the term *bankers acceptance*. A *Treasury bill* is short-term government paper of up to one year's maturity, sold at a discount to principal value and redeemed at par.

Bill of exchange: A short-term, **zero-coupon** debt issued by a company to finance commercial trading. If it is guaranteed by a bank, it becomes a banker's acceptance.

Binomial tree: A mathematical model to value options, based on the assumption that the value of the underlying can move either up or down a given extent over a given short time. This process is repeated many times to give a large number of possible paths (the 'tree') which the value could follow during the option's life.

Black-Scholes: A widely used option pricing formula devised by Fischer Black and Myron Scholes.

Blended interest rate swap: Result of adding forward swap to an existing swap and blending the rates over the total life of the transaction.

Bloomberg: The trading, analytics and news service produced by Bloomberg LP; also used to refer to the terminal itself.

Bond basis: An interest rate is quoted on a bond basis if it is on an **ACT/365**, **ACT/ACT** or **30/360** basis. In the short term (for accrued interest, for example), these three are different. Over a whole (non-leap) year, however they all equate to 1. In general, the expression 'bond basis' does not distinguish between them and is calculated as ACT/365. See **money-market basis**.

Bond-equivalent yield: The yield which would be quoted on a US treasury bond which is trading at par and which has the same economic return and maturity as a given treasury bill.

Bootstrapping: Building up successive zero-coupon yields from a combination of coupon-bearing yields.

Bpv: Basis point value. The price movement due to a one basis point change in yield.

Bräss/Fangmeyer: A method for calculating the yield of a bond similar to the **Moosmüller** method, but in the case of bonds which pay coupons more frequently than annually, using a mixture of annual and less than annual **compounding**.

Break forward: A product equivalent to a straightforward option, but structured as a forward deal at an off-market rate which can be reversed at a penalty rate.

Broken date: A maturity date other than the standard ones (such as 1 week, 1, 2, 3, 6 and 12 months) normally quoted.

Broker-Dealers: Members of the London Stock Exchange who may intermediate between customers and market makers; may also act as principals, transacting business with customers from their own holdings of stock.

Bulldog: Sterling domestic bonds issued by non-UK domiciled borrowers. These bonds trade under a similar arrangement to Gilts and are settled via the Central Gilts Office (now CREST).

Bullet: A loan/deposit has a bullet maturity if the principal is all repaid at maturity. See **amortising**.

Bull spread: A spread position taken with the expectation of a rise in value in the **underlying**.

Business intelligence tools: Term used to describe the latest generation of access tools, which are expected to support both data extraction and subsequent analysis.

Buy/sell-back: Opposite of **sell/buy-back**.

C

Cable: The exchange rate for sterling against the US dollar.

CAD: The European Union's Capital Adequacy Directive.

Calendar spread: The simultaneous purchase/sale of a futures contract for one date and the sale/purchase of a similar futures contract for a different date. See **spread**.

Callable bond: A bond which provides the borrower with an option to redeem the issue before the original maturity date. In most cases certain terms are set before the issue, such as the date after which the bond is callable and the price at which the issuer may redeem the bond.

Call option: An option to purchase the commodity or instrument underlying the option. See put.

Call price: The price at which the issuer can call in a bond or preferred bond.

Cancellable swap: Swap in which the payer of the fixed rate has the option, usually exercisable on a specified date, to cancel the deal (see also **swaption**).

Cap: A series of borrower's **IRG**s, designed to protect a borrower against rising interest rates on each of a series of dates.

Capital market: Long term market (generally longer than one year) for financial instruments. See **money market**.

Capped option: Option where the holder's ability to profit from a change in value of the underlying is subject to a specified limit.

Caption: Option on a **cap**.

Cash: See **cash market**.

CBOT: The Chicago Board of Trade, one of the two futures exchanges in Chicago, USA and one of the largest in the world.

CD: See **certificate of deposit**

Cedel: Centrale de Livraison de Valeurs Mobilieres; a clearing system for Euro-currency and international bonds. Cedel is located in Luxembourg and is jointly owned by a number of European banks.

Ceiling: The same as **cap**.

Central Gilts Office: The office of the Bank of England which runs the computer-based settlement system for gilt-edged securities and certain other securities (mostly Bulldogs) for which the Bank acts as Registrar.

Central line theorem: The assertion that as sample size, *n*, increases, the distribution of the mean of a random sample taken from almost any population approaches a normal distribution.

Certificate of Deposit (CD): A money market instrument of up to one year's maturity (although CDs of up to five years have been issued) that pays a bullet interest payment on maturity. After issue, CDs can trade freely in the secondary market, the ease of which is a function of the credit quality of the issuer.

CGBCR: Central Government Net Cash Requirement.

CGBR: Central Government Borrowing Requirement.

CGO reference prices: Daily prices of gilt-edged and other securities held in CGO which are used by CGO in various processes, including revaluing stock loan transactions, calculating total consideration in a repo transaction, and DBV assembly.

Cheapest to deliver: (Or CTD). In a bond futures contract, the one underlying bond among all those that are deliverable, which is the most price-efficient for the seller to deliver.

Cherry-picking: See **bilateral netting**.

Classic repo: Repo is short for 'sale and repurchase agreement' – a simultaneous spot sale and forward purchase of a security, equivalent to borrowing money against a loan of collateral. A reverse repo is the opposite. The terminology is usually applied from the perspective of the repo dealer. For example, when a central bank does repos, it is lending cash (the repo dealer is borrowing cash from the central bank).

Clean deposit: The same as **time deposit**.

Clean price: The price of a bond excluding accrued coupon. The price quoted in the market for a bond is generally a clean price rather than a **dirty price**.

Close-out netting: The ability to net a portfolio of contracts with a given counterparty in the event of default. See also **bilateral netting**.

CMO: Central Moneymarkets Office which settles transactions in Treasury bills and other money markets instruments, and provides a depository.

CMTM: Current **mark-to-market** value. See **current exposure** and **replacement cost**.

Collar: The simultaneous sale of a **put (or call) option** and purchase of a call (or put) at different strikes – typically both **out-of-the-money**.

Collateral: Something of value, often of good creditworthiness such as a government bond, given temporarily to a counterparty to enhance a party's creditworthiness. In a **repo**, the collateral is actually sold temporarily by one party to the other rather than merely lodged with it.

Commercial paper: A short-term security issued by a company or bank, generally with a zero coupon.

Commodity swap: Swap where one of the cashflows is based on a fixed value for the underlying commodity and the other is based on a floating index value. The commodity is often oil or natural gas, although copper, gold, other metals and agricultural commodities are also commonly used. The end-users are consumers, who pay a fixed-rate, and producers.

Competitive bid: A bid for the stock at a price stated by a bidder in an auction. **Non-competitive bid** is a bid where no price is specified; such bids are allotted at the weighted average price of successful competitive bid prices.

Compound interest: When some interest on an investment is paid before maturity and the investor can reinvest it to earn interest on interest, the interest is said to be compounded. Compounding generally assumes that the reinvestment rate is the same as the original rate. See **simple interest**.

Compound option: Option on an option, the first giving the buyer the right, but not the obligation to buy the second on a specific date at a pre-determined price. There are two kinds. One, on currencies, is useful for companies tendering for overseas contracts in a foreign currency. The interest rate version comprises **captions** and **floortions**.

Consideration: The total price paid in a transaction, including taxes, commissions and (for bonds) accrued interest.

Contango: The situation when a forward or futures price for something is higher than the spot price (the same as forward premium in foreign exchange). See **backwardation**.

Contingent option: Option where the premium is higher than usual but is only payable if the value of the underlying reaches a specified level. Also known as a contingent premium option.

Continuous compounding: A mathematical, rather than practical, concept of compound interest where the period of compounding is infinitesimally small.

Contract date: The date on which a transaction is negotiated. See **value date**.

Contract for differences: A deal such as an **FRA** and some futures contracts, where the instrument or commodity effectively bought or sold cannot be delivered; instead, a cash gain or loss is taken by comparing the price dealt with the market price, or an index, at maturity.

Conventional gilts (includes double-dated): Gilts on which interest payments and principal repayments are fixed.

Conversion factor: In a bond futures contract, a factor to make each deliverable bond comparable with the contract's notional bond specification. Defined as the price of one unit of the deliverable bond required to make its yield equal the notional coupon. The price paid for a bond on delivery is the futures settlement price times the conversion factor.

Convertible currency: A currency that may be freely exchanged for other currencies.

Convexity: A measure of the curvature of a bond's price/yield curve (mathematically,/dirty price).

Correlation matrices: Statistical constructs used in the value-at-risk methodology to measure the degree of relatedness of various market forces.

Corridor: The same as **collar**.

Cost of carry: The net running cost of holding a position (which may be negative) – for example, the cost of borrowing cash to buy a bond less the coupon earned on the bond while holding it.

Cost volatility: Volatility relating to operational errors or the fines and losses a business unit may incur. Reflected in excess costs and penalty charges posted to the profit and losses. See also **revenue volatility**.

Counterparty risk weighting: See **risk weighting**.

Country risk: The risks, when business is conducted in a particular country, of adverse economic or political conditions arising in that country. More specifically, the credit risk of a financial transaction or instrument arising from such conditions.

Coupon: The interest payment(s) made by the issuer of security to the holders, based on the coupon rate and the face value.

Coupon swap: An interest rate swap in which one leg is fixed-rate and the other floating-rate. See **basis rate**.

Cover: To cover an exposure is to deal in such a way as to remove the risk – either reversing the position, or hedging it by dealing in an instrument with a similar but opposite risk profile. Also the amount by how much a bond auction is subscribed.

Covered call/put: The sale of a covered call option is when the option writer also owns the underlying. If the underlying rises in value so that the option is exercised, the writer is protected by his position in the underlying. Covered puts are defined analogously. See **naked**.

Covered interest arbitrage: Creating a loan/deposit in one currency by combining a loan/deposit in another with a forward foreign exchange swap.

CP: See **commercial paper**.

Credit (or default) risk: The risk that a loss will be incurred if a counter-party to a derivatives transaction does not fulfil its financial obligations in a timely manner.

Credit derivatives: Financial contracts that involve a potential exchange of payments in which at least one of the cashflows is linked to the performance of a specified underlying credit-sensitive asset or liability.

Credit-equivalent amount: As part of the calculation of the risk-weighted amount of capital the Bank for International Settlements (BIS) advises each bank to set aside against derivative credit risk, banks must compute a credit-equivalent amount for each derivative transaction. The amount is calculated by summing the **current replacement cost**, or market value, of the instrument and an **add-on factor**.

Credit risk (or default risk) exposure: The value of the contract exposed to default. If all transactions are marked to market each day, such positive market value is the amount of previously recorded profit that might have to be reversed and recorded as a loss in the event of counterparty default.

Credit spread: The interest rate spread between two debt issues of similar duration and maturity, reflecting the relative creditworthiness of the issuers.

Credit swaps: Agreement between two counterparties to exchange disparate cashflows, at least one of which must be tied to the performance of a credit-sensitive asset or to a portfolio or index of such assets. The other cashflow is usually tied to a **floating-rate index** (such as **Libor**) or a fixed rate or is linked to another credit-sensitive asset.

Credit value-at-risk (CVAR): See **value-at-risk (VAR)**.

CREST: The paperless share settlement system through which trades conducted on the London Stock Exchange can be settled. The system is operated by CRESTCo and was introduced in 1996.

CRND: Commissioners for the Reduction of the National Debt, formally responsible for investment of funds held within the public sector e.g., National Insurance Fund.

Cross: See **cross-rate**.

Cross-rate: Generally an exchange rate between two currencies, neither of which is the US dollar. In the American market, spot cross is the exchange rate for US dollars against Canadian dollars in its direct form.

CTD: See **cheapest to deliver**.

cum-dividend: literally 'with dividend', stock that is traded with interest or dividend accrued included in the price.

Cumulative default rate: See **probability of default**.

Currency option: The option to buy or sell a specified amount of a given currency at a specified rate at or during a specified time in the future.

Currency swap: An agreement to exchange a series of cashflows determined in one currency, possibly with reference to a particular fixed or floating interest payment schedule, for a series of cashflows based in a different currency. See **interest rate swap**.

Current assets: Assets which are expected to be used or converted to cash within one year or one operating cycle.

Current liabilities: Obligations which the firm is expected to settle within one year or one operating cycle.

Current yield: Bond coupon as a proportion of clean price per 100; does not take principal gain/loss or time value of money into account. See **yield to maturity**, **simple yield to maturity**.

Cylinder: The same as **collar**.

D

DAC-RAP: Delivery against collateral – receipt against payment. Same as **DVP**.

Daily range: The difference between the high and low points of a single trading day.

Day count: The convention used to calculate accrued interest on bonds and interest on cash. For UK gilts the convention changed to actual/actual from actual/365 on 1 November 1998. For cash the convention in sterling markets is actual/365.

DBV (delivery by value): A mechanism whereby a CGO member may borrow from or lend money to another CGO member against overnight gilt collateral. The CGO system automatically selects and delivers securities to a specified aggregate value on the basis of the previous night's CGO reference prices; equivalent securities are returned the following day. The DBV functionality allows the giver and taker of collateral to specify the classes of security to be included within the DBV. The options are: all classes of security held within CGO, including strips and bulldogs; coupon bearing gilts and bulldogs; coupon bearing gilts and strips; only coupon bearing gilts.

DEaR: Daily earnings at risk.

Debenture: In the US market, an unsecured domestic bond, backed by the general credit quality of the issuer. Debentures are issued under a trust deed or indenture. In the UK market, a bond that is secured against the general assets of the issuer.

Debt Management Office (DMO): An executive arm of the UK Treasury, responsible for cash management of the government's borrowing requirement. This includes responsibility for issuing government bonds (gilts), a function previously carried out by the Bank of England. The DMO began operations in April 1998.

Default correlation: The degree of covariance between the probabilities of default of a given set of counterparties. For example, in a set of counterparties with positive default correlation, a default by one counterparty suggests an increased probability of a default by another counterparty.

Default probability: See **probability of default**.

Default risk: See **credit risk**.

Default risk exposure: See **credit risk exposure**.

Default start options: Options purchased before their 'lives' actually commence. A corporation might, for example, decide to pay for a deferred start option to lock into what it perceives as current advantageous pricing for an option that it knows it will need in the future.

Deferred strike option: Option where the strike price is established at future date on the basis of the spot foreign exchange price prevailing at that future date.

Delegation costs: Incentive costs incurred by banks in delegating monitoring activities.

Deliverable bond: One of the bonds which is eligible to be delivered by the seller of a bond futures contract at the contract's maturity, according to the specifications of that particular contract.

Delivery: Transfer of gilts (in settlements) from seller to buyer.

Delivery versus payment (DVP): The simultaneous exchange of securities and cash. The assured payment mechanism of the CGO achieves the same protection.

Delta (Δ): The change in an option's value relative to a change in the underlying's value.

Depreciation: A decrease in the market value of a currency in terms of other currencies. See **appreciation, devaluation**.

Derivative: Strictly, any financial instrument whose value is derived from another, such as a forward foreign exchange rate, a futures contract, an option, an interest rate swap, etc. Forward deals to be settled in full are not always called derivatives, however.

Devaluation: An official one-off decrease in the value of a currency in terms of other currencies. See **revaluation, depreciation**.

Diffusion effect: The potential for increase over time of the credit exposure generated by a derivative: as time progresses, there is more likelihood of larger changes in the underlying market variables. Depending on the type and structure of the instrument this effect may be moderated by **amortisation effect**.

Digital option: Unlike simple European and American options, a digital option has fixed payouts and, rather like binary digital circuits, which are either on or off, pays out either this amount or nothing. Digital options can be added together to create assets that exactly mirror index price movements anticipated by investors. See **one touch all-or-nothing**.

Direct: An exchange rate quotation against the US dollar in which the dollar is the **variable currency** and the other currency is the **base currency**.

Dirty price: The price of a bond including accrued interest. Also known as the 'all-in' price.

Discount: The amount by which a currency is cheaper, in terms of another currency, for future delivery than for spot, is the forward discount (in general, a reflection of interest rate differentials between two currencies). If an exchange rate is 'at a discount'(without specifying to which of the two currencies this refers), this generally means that the **variable currency** is at a discount. See **premium**.

Discount house: In the UK money market, originally securities houses that dealt directly with the Bank of England in T-bills and bank bills, or discount instruments, hence the name. Most discount houses were taken over by banking groups and the term is not generally used, as the BoE now also deals directly with clearing banks and securities houses.

Discount rate: The method of market quotation for certain securities (US and UK treasury bills, for example), expressing the return on the security as a proportion of the face value of the security received at maturity – as opposed to a **yield** which expresses the yield as a proportion of the original investment.

Discount swap: Swap in which the fixed-rate payments are less than the internal rate of return on the swap, the difference being made up at maturity by a balloon payment.

Dividend discount model: Theoretical estimate of market value that computes the economic or the net present value of future cashflows due to an equity investor.

DMO: The UK Debt Management Office.

DMR: The Debt Management Report, published annually by HM Treasury.

Down-and-in option: Barrier option where the holder's ability to exercise is activated if the value of the underlying drops below a specified level. See also **up-and-in option**.

Down-and-out-option: Barrier option where the holder's ability to exercise expires if the value of the underlying drops below a specified level.

DRM: Debt and Reserves Management Team in HM Treasury.

Dual currency option: Option allowing the holder to buy either of two currencies.

Dual currency swap: Currency swap where both the interest rates are fixed rates.

Dual strike option: Interest rate option, usually a **cap** or a **floor**, with one floor or ceiling rate for part of the option's life and another for the rest.

Duration: A measure of the weighted average life of a bond or other series of cashflows, using the present values of the cashflows as the weights. See **modified duration**.

Duration gap: Measurement of the interest rate exposure of an institution.

Duration weighting: The process of using the modified duration value for bonds to calculate the exact nominal holdings in a spread position. This is necessary because £1 million nominal of a two-year bond is not equivalent to £1 million of say, a five-year bond. The modified duration value of the five-year bond will be higher, indicating that its 'basis point value' (bpv) will be greater, and that therefore £1 million worth of this bond represents greater sensitivity to a move in interest rates (risk). As another example consider a fund manager holding £10 million of five-year bonds. The fund manager wishes to switch into a holding of two-year bonds with the same overall risk position. The basis point values of the bonds are 0.041583 and 0.022898 respectively. The ratio of the bpvs are $0.041583/0.022898 = 1.816$. The fund manager therefore needs to switch into £10 m $\times$ 1.816 = £18.160 million of the two-year bond.

DVP: Delivery versus payment, in which the settlement mechanics of a sale or loan of securities against cash is such that the securities and cash are exchanged against each other simultaneously through the same clearing mechanism and neither can be transferred unless the other is.

E

Early exercise: The exercise or assignment of an option prior to expiration.

ECU: The European Currency Unit, a basket composed of European Union currencies, now defunct following introduction of euro currency.

Effective rate: An effective interest rate is the rate which, earned as simple interest over one year, gives the same return as interest paid more frequently than once per year and then compounded. See **nominal rate**.

Efficient frontier method: Technique used by fund managers to allocate assets.

Embedded option: Interest rate-sensitive option in debt instrument that affects its redemption. Such instruments include **mortgage-backed securities** and **callable bonds**.

End-end: A money market deal commencing on the last working day of a month and lasting for a whole number of months, maturing on the last working day of the correlation.

Epsilon (ε): The same as **vega**.

Equity: The residual interest in the net assets of an entity that remains after deducting the liabilities.

Equity options: Options on shares of an individual common stock.

Equity warrant: Warranty, usually attached to a bond, entitling the holder purchase share(s).

Equity-linked swap: Swap where one of the cashflows is based on an equity instrument or index, when it is known as an equity index swap.

Equivalent life: The weighted average life of the principal of a bond where there are partial **redemptions**, using the **present values** of the partial redemptions as the weights.

ERA: See **exchange rate agreement**.

Eta (η): The same as **vega**.

Euribor: The reference rate for the euro currency, set in Frankfurt.

Euro: The name for the domestic currency of the European Monetary Union. Not to be confused with **Eurocurrency**.

Euroclear: An international clearing system for Eurocurrency and international securities. Euroclear is based in Brussels and managed by Morgan Guaranty Trust Company.

Eurocurrency: A Eurocurrency is a currency owned by a non-resident of the country in which the currency is legal tender. Not to be confused with **Euro**.

Euro-issuance: The issue of gilts (or other securities) denominated in Euro.

Euromarket: The international market in which **Eurocurrencies** traded.

European: A European **option** is one that may be exercised only at **expiry**. See **American**.

Exchange controls: Regulations restricting the free convertibility of a currency into other currencies.

Exchange rate agreement: A **contract for differences** based on the movement in a **forward-forward** foreign exchange swap price. Does not take account of the effect of **spot** rate changes as an **FXA** does. See **SAFE**.

Exchange-traded: Futures contracts are traded on a futures exchange, as opposed to **forward** deals which are **OTC**. **Option** contracts are similarly exchange traded rather than **OTC**.

Ex-dividend (xd) date: A bond's record date for the payment of coupons. The coupon payment will be made to the person who is the registered holder of the stock on the xd date. For UK gilts this is seven working days before the coupon date.

Exercise: To exercise an **option** (by the **holder**) is to require the other party (the **writer**) to fulfil the underlying transaction. Exercise price is the same as **strike** price.

Expected (credit) loss: Estimate of the amount a derivatives counterparty is likely to lose as a result of default from a derivatives contract, with a given level of probability. The expected loss of any derivative position can be derived by combining the distributions of credit exposures, rate of recovery and probabilities of default.

Expected default rate: Estimate of the most likely rate of default of a counterparty expressed as a level of probability.

Expected rate of recovery: See **rate of recovery**.

Expiry: An option's expiry is the time after which it can no longer be **exercised**.

Exposure: Risk to market movements.

Exposure profile: The path of worst-case or expected exposures over time. Different instruments reveal quite differently shaped exposure profiles due to the interaction of the diffusion and amortisation effects.

Extinguishable option: Option in which the holder's right to exercise disappears if the value of the underlying passes a specified level. See also **barrier option**.

Extrapolation: The process of estimating a price or rate for a particular value date, from other known prices, when the value date required lies outside the period covered by the known prices. See **interpolation**.

F

Face value: The principal amount of a security generally repaid ('redeemed') all at maturity, but sometimes repaid in stages, on which the **coupon** amounts are calculated.

Fence: The same as **collar**.

Fixing: See **Libor fixing**.

Floating rate: An interest rate set with reference to an external index. Also an instrument paying a floating rate is one where the rate of interest is refixed in line with market conditions at regular intervals such as every three or six months. In the current market, an exchange rate determined by market forces with no government intervention.

Floating rate CD: CD on which the rate of interest payable is refixed in line with market conditions at regular intervals (usually six months).

Floating rate gilt: Gilt issued with an interest rate adjusted periodically in line with market interbank rates.

Floating rate note: Capital market instrument on which the rate of interest payable is refixed in line with market conditions at regular intervals (usually six months).

Floor: A series of lender's **IRGs**, designed to protect an investor against falling interest rates on each of a series of dates.

Floortion: Option on a **floor**.

Forward: In general, a deal for value later than the normal value date for that particular commodity or instrument. In the foreign exchange market, a forward price is the price quoted for the purchase or sale of one currency against another where the value date is at least one month after the **spot** date. See **short date**.

Forward band: Zero-cost collar that is, one in which the premium payable as a result of buying the **cap** is offset exactly by that obtained from selling the **floor**.

Forward break: See **break forward**.

Forward exchange agreement: A **contract for differences** designed to create exactly the same economic result as a foreign exchange cash **forward-forward** deal. See **ERA, SAFE**.

Forward/forward: Short-term exchange of currency deposits. (See also **forward/forward deposit**).

Forward rate agreement: Short-term interest rate **hedge**. Specifically, a contract between buyer and seller for an agreed interest rate on a notional deposit of a specified maturity on a predetermined future date. No principal is exchanged. At maturity the seller pays the buyer the difference if rates have risen above the agreed level, and vice versa.

Forward swap: Swap arranged at the current rate but entered into at some time in the future.

FRA: See **forward rate agreement**.

Framework document: Sets out the DMO's responsibilities, objectives and targets, its relationship with the rest of the Treasury and its accountability as an Executive Agency.

Fraption: Option on a forward rate agreement. Also known as an interest rate guarantee.

FRCD: See **floating rate CD**.

FRN: See **floating rate note**.

FSA: The Financial Services Authority, the body responsible for the regulation of investment business, and the supervision of banks and money market institutions in the UK. The FSA took over these duties from nine 'self-regulatory organisations' that had previously carried out this function, including the Securities and Futures Authority (SFA), which had been responsible for regulation of professional investment business in the City of London. The FSA commenced its duties in 1998.

FTSE-100: Index comprising 100 major UK shares listed on The International Stock Exchange in London. Futures and options on the index are traded at the London International Financial Futures and Options Exchange (**LIFFE**).

Funds: The **USD/CAD** exchange rate for value on the next business day (standard practice for **USD/CAD** in preference to **spot**).

Fungible: A financial instrument that is equivalent in value to another, and easily exchanged or substituted. The best example is cash money, as a £10 note has the same value and is directly exchangeable with another £10 note. A bearer bond also has this quality.

Future: A futures contract is a contract to buy or sell securities or other goods at a future date at a pre-determined price. Futures contracts are usually standardised and traded on an exchange.

Future exposure: See **potential exposure**.

Future value: The amount of money achieved in the future, including interest, by investing a given amount of money now. See **time value of money, present value**.

Futures contract: A deal to buy or sell some financial instrument or commodity for value on a future date. Unlike a **forward** deal, futures contracts are traded only on an exchange (rather than **OTC**), have standardised contract sizes and value dates, and are often only **contract for differences** rather than deliverable.

FXA: See **forward exchange agreement**.

G

G7: The 'Group of Seven' countries, the USA, Canada, UK, Germany, France, Italy and Japan.

Gamma (Γ): The change in an option's delta relative to a change in the underlying's value.

Gap ratio: Ratio of interest rate-sensitive assets to interest rate-sensitive liabilities; used to determine changes in the risk profile of an institution with changes in interest rate levels.

Gapping: Feature of commodity markets whereby there are large and very rapid price movements to new levels followed by relatively stable prices.

GDP: Gross domestic product, the value of total output produced within a country's borders.

GEMM: A gilt-edged market maker, a bank or securities house registered with the Bank of England as a market maker in gilts. A GEMM is required to meet certain obligations as part of its function as a registered market maker, including making two-way price quotes at all times in all gilts and taking part in gilt auctions. The Debt Management Office now make a distinction between conventional gilt GEMMs and index-linked GEMMs, known as 7IG GEMMs.

General collateral (GC): Securities, which are not 'special', used as collateral against cash borrowing. A repo buyer will accept GC at any time that a specific stock is not quoted as required in the transaction. In the gilts market GC includes DBVs.

GIC: Guaranteed investment contract.

Gilt: A UK Government sterling denominated, listed security issued by HM Treasury with initial maturity of over 365 days when issued. The term 'gilt' (or gilt-edged) is a reference to the primary characteristic of gilts as an investment: their security.

Gilt-edged market maker: See **GEMM**.

GNP: Gross national product, the total monetary value of a country's output, as produced by citizens of that country.

Gold warrant: Naked or attached warrant exercisable into gold at a predetermined price.

Gross redemption yield: The same as **yield to maturity**; 'gross' because it does not take tax effects into account.

GRY: See **gross redemption yield**.

H

Hedge ratio: The ratio of the size of the position it is necessary to take in a particular instrument as a hedge against another, to the size of the position being hedged.

Hedging: Protecting against the risks arising from potential market movements in exchange rates, interest rates or other variables. See **cover, arbitrage, speculation**.

Herstatt risk: See **settlement risk**.

High coupon swap: Off-market coupon swap where the coupon is higher than the market rate. The floating-rate payer pays a front-end fee as compensation. Opposite of low coupon swap.

Historic rate rollover: A **forward rate swap** in FX where the settlement exchange rate for the near date is based on a historic **off-market** rate rather than the current market rate. This is prohibited by many central banks.

Historic volatility: The actual **volatility** recorded in market prices over a particular period.

Historical simulation methodology: Method of calculating **value-at-risk (VAR)** using historical data to assess the likely effect of market moves on a portfolio.

Holder: The holder of an **option** is the party that has purchased it.

I

IDB: Inter-Dealer Broker, in this context a broker that provide facilities for dealing in bonds between market makers.

IG: Index-linked gilt whose coupons and final redemption payment are related to the movements in the Retail Price Index (RPI).

Immunisation: This is the process by which a bond portfolio is created that has an assured return for a specific time horizon irrespective of changes in interest rates. The mechanism underlying immunisation is a portfolio structure that balances the change in the value of a portfolio at the end of the investment horizon (time period) with the return gained from the reinvestment of cash flows from the portfolio. As such immunisation requires the portfolio manager to offset interest-rate risk and reinvestment risk.

Implied repo rate: The break-even interest rate at which it is possible to sell a bond **futures contract**, buy a **deliverable bond**, and **repo** the bond out. See **cash and carry**.

Implied volatility: The **volatility** used by a dealer to calculate an **option** price; conversely, the volatility implied by the price actually quoted.

Index option: An **option** whose **underlying** security is an index. Index options enable a trader to bet on the direction of the index.

Index swap: Sometimes the same as a **basis swap**. Otherwise a swap like an **interest rate swap** where payments on one or both of the legs are based on the value of an index – such as an equity index, for example.

Indexed notes: Contract whereby the issuer usually assumes the risk of unfavourable price movements in the instrument, commodity or index to which the contract is linked, in exchange for which the issuer can reduce the cost of borrowing (compared with traditional instruments without the risk exposure).

Indirect: An exchange rate quotation against the US dollar in which the dollar is the **base currency** and the other currency is the **variable currency**.

Initial margin: The excess either of cash over the value of securities, or of the value of securities over cash in a repo transaction at the time it is executed and subsequently, after margin calls.

Interbank: The market in unsecured lending and trading between banks of roughly similar credit quality.

Interest rate cap: See **cap**.

Interest rate floor: See **floor**.

Interest rate guarantee: An **option** on an **FRA**.

Interest rate option: Option to pay or receive a specified rate of interest on or from a predetermined future date.

Interest rate swap: An agreement to exchange a series of cashflows determined in one currency, based on fixed or **floating** interest payments on an agreed **notional** principal, for a series of cashflows based in the same currency but on a different interest rate. May be combined with a **currency swap**.

Intermarket spread: A spread involving futures contracts in one market spread against futures contracts in another market.

Internal rate of return: The yield necessary to discount a series of cashflows to an **NPV** of zero.

Interpolation: The process of estimating a price or rate for value on a particular date by comparing the prices actually quoted for value dates either side. See **extrapolation**.

Intervention: Purchases or sales of currencies in the market by central banks in an attempt to reduce exchange rate fluctuations or to maintain the value of a currency within a particular band, or at a particular level. Similarly, central bank operations in the money markets to maintain interest rates at a certain level.

In-the-money: A **call (put) option** is in-the-money if the underlying is currently more (less) valuable than the **strike** price. See **at-the-money**, **out-of-the-money**.

Intrinsic value: The amount by which an option is in-the-money.

IRG: See **interest rate guarantee**.

IRR: See **internal rate of return**.

IRS: See **interest rate swap**.

ISMA: The International Securities Market Association. This association drew up with the PSA (now renamed the Bond Market Association) the PSA/ISMA Global Master repurchase Agreement.

Issuer risk: Risk to an institution when it holds debt securities issued by another institution. (See also **credit risk**).

Iteration: The repetitive mathematical process of estimating the answer to a problem, by trying how well this estimate fits the data, adjusting the estimate appropriately and trying again, until the fit is acceptably close. Used, for example, in calculating a bond's **yield** from its price.

J

Junk bonds: The common term for high-yield bonds; higher risk, low rated debt.

K

Kappa (κ): An alternative term to refer to volatility; see **vega**.

Knock out/in: A knock out (in) **option** ceases to exist (starts to exist) if the underlying reaches a certain trigger level. See **barrier option**.

L

Lambda (λ): The same as **vega**.

Lender option: Floor on a single-period forward rate agreement.

Leptokurtosis: The non-normal distribution of asset-price returns. Refers to a probability distribution that has a fatter tail and a sharper hump than a normal distribution.

Level payment swap: Evens out those fixed-rate payments that would otherwise vary, for example, because of the amortisation of the principal.

Leverage: The ability to control large amounts of an underlying variable for a small initial investment.

Liability: Probable future sacrifice of economic benefit due to present obligations to transfer assets or provide services to other entities as a result of past events or transactions. Generally classed as either current or long-term.

Liability swap: An interest rate swap or currency swap used in conjunction with an underlying liability such as a borrowing. See **asset swap**.

LIBID: The London Interbank Bid Rate, the rate at which banks will pay for funds in the interbank market.

LIBOR: The London Interbank Offered Rate, the lending rate for all major currencies up to one-year set at 11am each day by the British Bankers Association.

Libor fixing: The Libor rate 'fixed' by the British Bankers Association (BBA) at 1100 hours each day, for maturities up to one year.

LIFFE: The London International Financial Futures and Options Exchange, the largest futures exchange in Europe.

Limean: The arithmetic average of Libor and Libid rates.

Limit up/down: **Futures** prices are generally not allowed to change by more than a specified total amount in a specified time, in order to control risk in very volatile conditions. The maximum movements permitted are referred to as limit up and limit down.

Liquidation: Any transaction that closes out or offsets a futures or options position.

Liquidity: A word describing the ease with which one can undertake transactions in a particular market or instrument. A market where there are always ready buyers and sellers willing to transact at competitive prices is regarded as liquid. In banking, the term is also used to describe the requirement that a portion of a banks assets be held in short-term risk free instruments, such as government bonds, T-Bills and high quality Certificates of Deposit.

Loan-equivalent amount: Description of derivative exposure which is used to compare the credit risk of derivatives with that of traditional bonds or bank loans.

Lognormal: A variable's **probability distribution** is lognormal if the logarithm of the variable has a normal distribution.

Lognormal distribution: The assumption that the log of today's interest rate, for example, minus the log of yesterday's rate is normally distributed.

Long: A long position is a surplus of purchases over sales of a given currency or asset, or a situation which naturally gives rise to an organisation benefiting from a strengthening of that currency or asset. To a money market dealer, however, a long position is a surplus of borrowings taken in over money lent out, (which gives rise to a benefit if that currency weakens rather than strengthens). See **short**.

Long-dated forward: Forward foreign exchange contract with a maturity of greater than one year. Some long-dated forwards have maturities as great as 10 years.

Long-term assets: Assets which are expected to provide benefits and services over a period longer than one year.

Long-term liabilities: Obligations to be repaid by the firm more than one year later.

Lookback option: Option that allows the purchaser, at the end of a given period of time, to choose as the rate for exercise any rate that has existed during the option's life.

Low coupon swap: Tax-driven swap, in which the fixed-rate payments are significantly lower than current market interest rates. The floating-rate payer is compensated by a front-end fee.

LSE: London Stock Exchange.

M

Macaulay duration: See **duration**.

Mapping: The process whereby a treasury's derivative positions are related to a set of risk 'buckets'.

Margin: Initial margin is **collateral**, placed by one party with a counterparty at the time of the deal, against the possibility that the market price will move against the first party, thereby leaving the counterparty with a credit risk. Variation margin is a payment or extra collateral transferred subsequently from one party to the other because the market price has moved. Variation margin payment is either in effect a settlement of profit/loss (for example, in the case of a **futures** contract) or the reduction of credit exposure (for example, in the case of a **repo**). In gilt **repos**, variation margin refers to the fluctuation band or threshold within which the existing collateral's value may vary before further cash or **collateral** needs to be transferred. In a loan, margin is the extra interest above a **benchmark** (e.g., a margin of 0.5 percent over **Libor**) required by a lender to compensate for the credit risk of that particular borrower.

Margin call: A request following marking-to-market of a repo transaction for the initial margin to be reinstated or, where no initial margin has been taken to restore the cash/securities ratio to parity.

Margin default rate: See **probability of default**.

Margin transfer: The payment of a **margin call**.

Market comparables: Technique for estimating the fair value of an instrument for which no price is quoted by comparing it with the quoted prices of similar instruments.

Market-maker: Market participant who is committed, explicitly or otherwise, to quoting two-way bid and offer prices at all times in a particular market.

Market risk: Risks related to changes in prices of tradable macroeconomics variables, such as exchange rate risks.

Mark-to-market: The act of revaluing securities to current market values. Such revaluations should include both coupon accrued on the securities outstanding and interest accrued on the cash.

Matched book: This refers to the matching by a repo trader of securities repoed in and out. It carries no implications that the trader's position is 'matched' in terms of exposure, for example to short-term interest rates.

Maturity date: Date on which stock is redeemed.

Mean: Average.

Minmax option: One of the strategies for reducing the cost of options by forgoing some of the potential for gain. The buyer of a currency option, for example, simultaneously sells an option on the same amount of currency but at a different strike price.

MLV: Maximum likely potential increase in value.

Modified duration: A measure of the proportional change in the price of a bond or other series of cashflows, relative to a change in yield. (Mathematically – / dirty price.) See **duration**.

Modified following: The convention that if a value date in the future falls on a non-business day, the value date will be moved to the next following business day, unless this moves the value date to the next month, in which case the value date is moved back to the last previous business day.

Momentum: The strength behind an upward or downward movement in price.

Money market: Short-term market (generally up to one year) for financial instruments. See **capital market**.

Money-market basis: An interest rate quoted on an ACT/360 basis is said to be on a money-market basis. See **bond basis**.

Monte Carlo simulation: Technique used to determine the likely value of a derivative or other contract by simulating the evolution of the underlying variables many times. The discounted **average** outcome of the simulation gives an approximation of the derivative's value. Monte Carlo simulation can be used to estimate the **value-at-risk (VAR)** of a portfolio. Here, it generates a simulation of many correlated market movements for the markets to which the portfolio is exposed, and the positions in the portfolio are revalued repeatedly in accordance with the simulated scenarios. This gives a probability distribution of portfolio gains and losses from which the **VAR** can be determined.

Moosmüller: A method for calculating the yield of a bond.

Mortgage-backed security (MBS): Security guaranteed by pool of mortgages. MBS markets include the US, UK, Japan and Denmark.

Moving average convergence/divergence: The crossing of two exponentially smoothed moving averages that oscillate above and below an equilibrium line. (MACD)

Multi-index option: Option which gives the holder the right to buy the asset that performs best out of a number of assets (usually two). The investor would typically buy a call allowing him or her to buy the **equity**.

N

Naked: A naked **option** position is one not protected by an off-setting position in the **underlying.** See **covered call/put**.

NAO: National Audit Office.

Negative divergence: When at least two indicators, indexes or averages show conflicting or contradictory trends.

Negotiable: A security which can be bought and sold in a **secondary market** is negotiable.

Net present value: The net present value of a series of cashflows is the sum of the present values of each cashflow (some or all of which may be negative).

NLF: National Loans Fund, the account which brings together all UK Government lending and borrowing.

Noise: Fluctuations in the market which can confuse or impede interpretation of market direction.

Nominal amount: Same as **face value** of a security.

Nominal rate: A rate of interest as quoted, rather than the **effective rate** to which it is equivalent.

Normal: A normal **probability distribution** is a particular distribution assumed to prevail in a wide variety of circumstances, including the financial markets. Mathematically, it corresponds to the probability density function.

Notional: In a bond futures contract, the bond bought or sold is a standardised non-existent notional bond, as opposed to the actual bonds which are **deliverable** at maturity. **Contracts for differences** also require a notional principal amount on which settlement can be calculated.

Novation: Replacement of a contract or, more usually, a series of contracts with one new-contract.

NPV: See **net present value**.

O

O/N: See **overnight**.

Odd date: See **broken date**.

Offer: The price at which a market maker will sell bonds. Also called 'ask'.

Off-market: A rate which is not the current market rate.

Off-market coupon swap: Tax-driven swap strategy, in which the fixed-rate payments differ significantly from current market rates. There are high and low coupon swaps.

One touch all-or-nothing: Digital option. The option's put pays out a predetermined amount (the 'all') if the index goes below (above) the strike price at any time during the option's life. How far below (above) the strike price the strike price the index moves is irrelevant; the payout will be the 'all' or nothing.

Open interest: The quantity of **futures** contracts (of a particular specification) which have not yet been closed out by reversing. Either all **long** positions or all **short** positions are counted but not both.

Opening leg: The first half of a repo transaction (see 'closing leg').

Operational Market Notice: Sets out the DMO's (previously the Bank's) operations and procedures in the gilt market.

Operational risk: Risk of loss occurring due to inadequate systems and control, human error, or management failure.

Opportunity cost: Value of an action that could have been taken if the current action had not been chosen.

Option: The right (but not the obligation) to buy or sell securities at a fixed price within a specified period.

Option forward: See **time option**.

Ornstein-Uhlenbeck equation: A standard equation that describes mean reversion. It can be used to characterise and measure commodity price behaviour.

OTC: Over the counter. Strictly speaking any transaction not conducted on a registered stock exchange. Trades conducted via the telephone between banks, and contracts such as FRAs and (non-exchange traded) options are said to be 'over-the-counter' instruments. OTC also refers to non-standard instruments or contracts traded between two parties; for example a client with a requirement for a specific risk to be hedged with a tailor-made instrument may enter into an OTC structured option trade with a bank that makes markets in such products.

Out-of-the-money: A **call (put) option** is out-of-the-money if the **underlying** is currently less (more) valuable than the strike price. See **at-the-money, in-the-money**.

Outright: An outright (or **forward** outright) is the sale or purchase of one foreign currency against another value on any date other than spot. See **spot, swap, forward, short date**.

Over the counter: An OTC transaction is one dealt privately between any two parties, with all details agreed between them, as opposed to one dealt on an exchange – for example, a **forward** deal as opposed to a **futures contract**.

Overborrowed: A position in which a dealer's liabilities (borrowings taken in) are of longer maturity than the assets (loans out).

Overlent: A position in which a dealer's assets (loans out) are of longer maturity than the liabilities (borrowings taken in).

Overnight: A deal from today until the next working day ('tomorrow').

P

Paper: Another term for a bond or debt issue.

Par: In foreign exchange, when the **outright** and **spot** exchange rates are equal, the **forward swap** is zero or par. When the price of a security is equal to the face value, usually expressed as 100, it is said to be trading at par. A par swap rate is the current market rate for a fixed **interest rate swap** against **Libor**.

Par yield curve: A curve plotting maturity against **yield** for bonds priced at par.

Parity: The official rate of exchange for one currency in terms of another which a government is obliged to maintain by means of intervention.

Participation forward: A product equivalent to a straightforward **option** plus a **forward** deal, but structured as a forward deal at an **off-market** rate plus the opportunity to benefit partially if the market rate improves.

Path-dependent: A path-dependent **option** is one which depends on what happens to the **underlying** throughout the option's life (such as the **American** or **barrier** option) rather than only at expiry (a **European** option).

Peak exposure: If the worst case or the expected credit risk exposures of an instrument is calculated over time, the resulting graph reveals a credit risk exposure profile. The highest exposure marked out by the profile is the peak exposure generated by the instrument.

Periodic resetting swap: Swap where the floating-rate payment is an average of floating rates that have prevailed since the last payment, rather than the interest rate prevailing at the end of the period. For example, the average of six one-month **Libor** rates rather than one six-month Libor rate.

Pips: See **points**.

Plain vanilla: See **vanilla**.

Points: The last two decimal places in an exchange rate. For example, when EUR/USD is 1.1910/1.1920, the points are 10/20. See **bid figure**.

Portfolio variance: The square of the **standard deviation** of a portfolio's return from the mean.

Positive cashflow collar: Collar other than a zero-cost collar.

Potential exposure: Estimate of the future replacement cost, or positive market value, of a derivative transaction. Potential exposure should be calculated using probability analysis based on broad confidence intervals (e.g., two standard deviations) over the remaining term of the transaction.

Preference shares: These are a form of corporate financing. They are normally fixed interest shares whose holders have the right to receive dividends ahead of ordinary shareholders. If a company were to go into liquidation, preference shareholders would rank above ordinary shareholders for the repayment of their investment in the company. Preference shares ('prefs') are normally traded within the fixed interest division of a bank or securities house.

Premium: The amount by which a currency is more expensive, in terms of another currency, for future delivery than for spot, is the forward premium (in general, a reflection of interest rate differentials between two currencies). If an exchange rate is 'at a premium' (without specifying to which of the two currencies this refers), this generally means that the **variable currency** is at a premium. See **discount**.

Present value: The amount of money which needs to be invested now to achieve a given amount in the future when interest is added. See **time value of money, future value**.

Pre-settlement risk: As distinct from credit risk arising from intra-day settlement risk, this term describes the risk of loss that might be suffered during the life of the contract if a counterparty to a trade defaulted and if, at the time default, the instrument had a positive economic value.

Price-earnings ratio: A ratio giving the price of a stock relative to the earnings per share.

Price factor: See **conversion factor**.

Primary market: The market for new debt, into which new bonds are issued. The primary market is made up of borrowers, investors and the investment banks which place new debt into the market, usually with their clients. Bonds that trade after they have been issued are said to be part of the secondary market.

Probability distribution: The mathematical description of how probable it is that the value of something is less than or equal to a particular level.

Probit procedures: Methods for analysing qualitative dependent methods where the dependent variable is binary, taking the values zero or one.

Put: A put option is an option to sell the commodity or instrument **underlying** the option. See **call**.

Q

Quanto: An option that has its final payoff linked to two or more underlying assets or reference rates.

Quanto swap: A **swap** where the payment's one or both legs are based on a measurement (such as the interest rate) in one currency but payable in another currency.

Quasi-coupon date: The regular date for which a **coupon** payment would be scheduled if there were one. Used for price/yield calculations for **zero-coupon** instruments.

R

Range forward: A **zero-cost collar** where the customer is obliged to deal with the same bank at spot if neither limit of the collar is breached at **expiry**.

Rate of recovery: Estimate of the percentage of the amount exposed to default – i.e., the credit risk exposure – that is likely to be recovered by an institution if a counterparty defaults.

Record date: A **coupon** or other payment due on a security is paid by the issuer to whoever is registered on the record date as being the owner. See **ex-dividend, cum-dividend**.

Redeem: A security is said to be redeemed when the principal is repaid.

Redemption yield: The rate of interest at which all future payments (coupons and redemption) on a bond are discounted so that their total equals the current price of the bond (inversely related to price).

Redenomination: A change in the currency unit in which the nominal value of a security is expressed (in context, from sterling to Euro).

Reduced-cost option: Generic term for options for which there is a reduced premium, either because the buyer undertakes to forgo a percentage of any gain, or because he or she offsets the cost by writing other options (e.g., minmax, range forward). See also zero-cost option.

Refer: The practice whereby a trader instructs a broker to put 'under reference' any prices or rates he has quoted to him, meaning that they are no longer 'firm' and the broker must refer to the trader before he can trade on the price initially quoted.

Register: Record of ownership of securities. For gilts, excluding bearer bonds, entry in an official register confers title.

Registered bond: A bond for which the issuer keeps a record (register) of its owners. Transfer of ownership must be notified and recorded in the register. Interest payments are posted (more usually electronically transferred) to the bondholder.

Registrar's Department: Department of the Bank of England which maintains the register of holdings of gilts.

Reinvestment rate: The rate at which interest paid during the life of an investment is reinvested to earn interest-on-interest, which in practice will generally not be the same as the original yield quoted on the investment.

Relative performance option: Option whose value varies in line with the relative value of two assets.

Replacement cost: The present value of the expected future net cashflows of a derivative instrument. Aside from various conventions dealing with the **bid/ask** spread, synonymous with the 'market value' or 'current exposure' of an instrument.

Repo: Usually refers in particular to **classic repo.** Also used as a term to include classic repos, **buy/sell-backs** and **securities lending**.

Repo rate: The return earned on a repo transaction expressed as an interest rate on the cash side of the transaction.

Repurchase agreement: See **repo**.

Return on assets: The net earnings of a company divided by its assets.

Return on equity: The net earning of a company divided by its equity.

Return on value-at-risk: An analysis conducted to determine the relative rates of return on different risks, allowing corporations to compare different risk capital allocations and capital structure decisions effectively. **(ROVAR)**

Revaluation: An official one-off increase in the value of a currency in terms of other currencies. See **devaluation.**

Reverse: See **reverse repo.**

Reverse repo: The opposite of a **repo**.

Rho (ρ)**:** The change in an option's value relative to a change in interest rates.

Risk reversal: Changing a long (or short) position in a call option to the same position in a put option by selling (or buying) forward, and vice versa.

Rollover: See **tom/next.** Also refers to a renewal of a loan.

Rump: A gilt issue so designated because it is illiquid, generally because there is a very small nominal amount left in existence.

Running yield: Same as **current yield**.

S

S/N: See **spot/next**.

S/W: See **spot-a-week**.

SAFE: See **synthetic agreement for forward exchange**.

Secondary market: The market in instruments after they have been issued. Bonds are bought and sold after their initial issue by the borrower, and the marketplace for this buying and selling is referred to as the secondary market. The new issues market is the *primary* market.

Securities and Exchange Commission: The central regulatory authority in the United States, responsible for policing the financial markets including the bond markets.

Securities Lending: When a specific security is lent against some form of collateral. Also known as stock lending.

Security: A financial asset sold initially for cash by a borrowing organisation (the 'issuer'). The security is often negotiable and usually has a maturity date when it is redeemed.

Sell/buy-back: Simultaneous spot sale and forward purchase of a security, with the forward price calculated to achieve an effect equivalent to a classic repo.

Settlement: The process of transferring stock from seller to buyer and arranging the corresponding movement of funds between the two parties.

Settlement bank: Bank which agrees to receive and make assured payments for gilts bought and sold by a CGO member.

Settlement date: Date on which transfer of gilts and payment occur, usually the next working date after the trade is conducted.

Settlement risk: The risk that occurs when there is a non-simultaneous exchange of value. Also known as 'delivery risk' and 'Herstatt risk'.

Sharpe ratio: A measure of the attractiveness of the return on an asset by comparing how much risk premium the investor can expect it to receive in return for the incremental risk (volatility) the investment carries. It is the ratio of the risk premium to the volatility of the asset.

Short: A short position is a surplus of sales over purchases of a given currency or asset, or a situation which naturally gives rise to an organisation benefiting from a weakening of that currency or asset. To a money market dealer, however, a short position is a surplus of money lent out over borrowings taken in (which give rise to a benefit if that currency strengthens rather than weakens). See **long**.

Short date: A deal for value on a date other than spot but less than one month after spot.

Simple interest: When interest on an investment is paid all at maturity or not reinvested to earn interest on interest, the interest is said to be simple. See **compound interest**.

Simple yield to maturity: Bond coupon plus principal gain/loss amortised over the time to maturity, as a proportion of the clean price per 100. Does not take time value of money into account. See **yield to maturity, current yield**.

SLA: Service Level Agreement, in this context between the DMO and service suppliers in the Bank and HM Treasury.

Special: A security which for any reason is sought after in the repo market, thereby enabling any holder of the security to earn incremental income (in excess of the *General Collateral* rate) through lending them via a repo transaction. The repo rate for a special will be below the GC rate, as this is the rate the borrower of the cash is paying in returning for supplying the special bond as collateral. An individual security can be in high demand for a variety of reasons, for instance if there is sudden heavy investor demand for it, or (if it is a benchmark issue) it is required as a hedge against a new issue of similar maturity paper.

Speculation: A deal undertaken because the dealer expects prices to move in his favour, as opposed to **hedging** or **arbitrage**.

Spot: A deal to be settled on the customary value date for that particular market. In the foreign exchange market, this is for value in two working days' time.

Spot/next: A transaction from **spot** until the next working day.

Spread: The difference between the bid and offer prices in a quotation. Also a strategy involving the purchase of an instrument and the simultaneous sale of a similar related instrument, such as the purchase of a **call option** at one **strike** and the sale of a call option at a different strike.

Square: A position in which sales exactly match purchases, or in which assets exactly match liabilities. See **long, short**.

Standard deviation (σ)**:** A measure of how much the values of something fluctuate around its mean value. Defined as the square root of the **variance**.

Step-down swap: Swap in which the fixed-rate payment decreases over the life of the swap.

Step-up swap: Swap in which the fixed-rate payment increases over the life of the swap.

Stock index future: Future on a stock index, allowing a hedge against, or bet on, a broad equity market movement.

Stock index option: Option on a stock index future.

Stock lending: See **securities lending**.

Stock option: Option on an individual stock.

Straddle: A position combining the purchase of both a call and put at the same strike for the same date. See **strangle**.

Strangle: A position combining the purchase of both a call and a put at different strikes for the same date. See **straddle**.

Street: The 'street' is a term for the market, originating as 'Wall Street'. A US term for market convention, so in the US market is the convention for quoting the price or yield for a particular instrument.

Stress testing: Analysis that gives the value of a portfolio under a range of **worst-case** scenarios.

Strike: The strike price or strike rate of an option is the price or rate at which the holder can insist on the underlying transaction being fulfilled.

Strip: A zero-coupon bond which is produced by separating a standard coupon-bearing bond into its constituent principal and interest components. To strip a bond is to separate its principal amount and its coupons and trade each individual cash flow as a separate instrument ('*s*eparately *t*raded and *r*egistered for *i*nterest and *p*rincipal'). Also, a strip of **futures** is a series of short-term futures contracts with consecutive delivery dates, which together create the effect of a longer term instrument (for example, four consecutive 3-month futures contracts as a **hedge** against a one-year swap). A strip of **FRAs** is similar.

Swap: A foreign exchange swap is the purchase of one currency against another for delivery on one date, with a simultaneous sale to reverse the transaction on another value date. See also **interest rate swap, currency swap**.

Swaption: An **option** on an **interest rate swap, currency swap**.

Switch: Exchanges of one gilt holding for another, sometimes entered into between the DMO and a GEMM as part of the DMO's secondary market operations.

Synthetic: A package of transactions which is economically equivalent to a different transaction (for example, the purchase of a **call option** and simultaneous sale of a **put** option at the same **strike** is a synthetic **forward** purchase.)

Synthetic agreement for forward exchange: A generic term for **ERAs** and **FXAs**.

T

T/N: See **tom/next**.

Tail: The exposure to interest rates over a forward-forward period arising from a mismatched position (such as a two-month borrowing against a three-month loan). A forward foreign exchange dealer's exposure to **spot** movements.

Tap: The issue of a gilt for exceptional market management reasons and not on a pre-announced schedule.

Term: The time between the beginning and end of a deal or investment.

Theta (Θ): The change in an option's value relative to a change in the time left to expiry.

Tick: The minimum change allowed in a futures price.

Time deposit: A non-**negotiable** deposit for a specific term.

Time option: A forward currency deal in which the value date is set to be within a period rather than on a particular day. The customer sets the exact date two working days before settlement.

Time value for money: The concept that a future cashflow can be valued as the amount of money which it is necessary to invest now in order to achieve that cashflow in the future. See **present value, future value**.

Today/tomorrow: See **overnight**.

Tom/next: A transaction from the next working day ('tomorrow') until the day after ('next day – i.e., **spot** in the foreign exchange market).

Total return swap: Swap agreement in which the total return of bank loans or credit-sensitive securities is exchanged for some other cashflow usually tied to **Libor**, or other loans, or credit-sensitive securities. It allows participants to effectively go **long** or **short** the credit risk of the **underlying** asset.

Traded option: Option that is listed on and cleared by an exchange, with standard terms and delivery months.

Tranche: One of a series of two or more issues with the same coupon rate and maturity date. The tranches become fungible at a future date, usually just after the first coupon date.

Transaction risk: Extent to which the value of transactions that have already been agreed is affected by market risk.

Transparent: A term used to refer to how clear asset prices are in a market. A transparent market is one in which a majority of market participants are aware of what level a particular bond or instrument is trading.

Treasury bill: A short-term security issued by a government, generally with a zero **coupon**.

Trigger option: See **barrier option**.

Tunnel: The same as **collar**.

Tunnel options: Set of collars, typically zero-cost, covering a series of maturities from the current date. They might, for example, be for dates 6, 12, 24 months ahead. The special feature of a tunnel is that strike price on both sets of options not just on the options bought is constant.

U

Uncovered option: When the writer of the option does not own the underlying security. Also known as a **naked option**.

Undated gilts: Gilts for which there is no final date by which the gilt must be redeemed.

Underlying: The underlying of a futures or option contract is the commodity or financial instrument on which the contract depends. Thus underlying for a bond option is the bond; the underlying for a short-term interest rate futures contract is typically a three-month deposit.

Underwriting: An arrangement by which a company is guaranteed that an issue of debt (bonds) will raise a given amount of cash. Underwriting is carried out by investment banks, who undertake to purchase any part of the debt issue not taken up by the public. A commission is charged for this service.

Unexpected default rate: The distribution of future default rates is often characterised in terms of an expected default rate (e.g., 0.05%) and a worst-case default rate (e.g., 1.05%). The difference between the worst-case default rate and the expected default rate is often termed the 'unexpected default' (i.e., 1% = 1.05 – 0.05%).

Unexpected loss: The distribution of credit losses associated with a derivative instrument is often characterised in terms of an **expected loss** or a **worst-case loss.** The unexpected loss associated with an instrument is the difference between these two measures.

Up-and-away option: See **up-and-out option**.

Up-and-in option: Type of barrier option which is activated if the value of the underlying goes above a predetermined level. See also **down-and-in option**.

Up-and-out option: Type of barrier option that is extinguished if the value of the underlying goes above a predetermined level. See also **down-and-out option**.

V

Value-at-risk (VAR): Formally, the probabilistic bound of market losses over a given period of time (known as the holding period) expressed in terms of a specified degree of certainity (known as the confidence interval). Put more simply, the VAR is the worst-case loss that would be expected over the holding period within the probability set out by the confidence interval. Larger losses are possible but with a low probability. For instance, a portfolio whose VAR is $20 million over a one-day holding period, with a 95% confidence interval, would have only a 5% chance of suffering an overnight loss greater than $20 million.

Value date: The date on which a deal is to be consummated. In some bond markets, the value date for coupon accruals can sometimes differ from the settlement date.

Vanilla: A vanilla transaction is a straightforward one.

VAR: See **value-at-risk**.

Variable currency: Exchange rates are quoted in terms of the number of units of one currency (the variable or counter currency) which corresponds to one unit of the other currency (the **base currency**).

Variance (σ^2): A measure of how much the value of something fluctuates around its mean value. Defined as the average of $(\text{value} - \text{mean})^2$. See **standard deviation**.

Variance-covariance methodology: Methodology for calculating the **value-at-risk** of a portfolio as a function of the **volatility** of each asset or liability position in the portfolio and the correlation between the positions.

Variation margin: The band agreed between the parties to a repo transaction at the outset within which the value of the collateral may fluctuate before triggering a right to call for cash or securities to reinstate the initial margin on the repo transaction.

Vega: The change in an option's value relative to a change in the **underlying's volatility**.

Volatility: The **standard deviation** of the continuously compounded return on the **under-**

lying. Volatility is generally annualised. See **historic volatility, implied volatility**.

W

Warrant: A security giving the holder a right to subscribe to a share or bond at a given price and from a certain date. If this right is not exercised before the maturity date, the warrant will expire worthless.

Warrant-driven swap: Swap with a warrant attached allowing the issuer of the fixed-rate bond to go on paying a floating rate in the event that he or she exercises another warrant allowing him or her to prolong the life of the bond.

When-issued trading: Trading a bond before the issue date; no interest is accrued during this period. Also known as the 'grey market'.

Worst-case (credit risk) exposure: Estimate of the highest positive market value a derivative contract or portfolio is likely to attain at a given moment or period in the future, with a given level of confidence.

Worst-case (credit risk) loss: Estimate of the largest amount a derivative counterparty is likely to lose, with a given level of probability, as a result of default from a derivatives contract or portfolio.

Worst-case default rate: The highest rates of default that are likely to occur at a given moment or period in the future, with a given level of confidence.

Write: To sell an option is to write it. The person selling an option is known as the **writer**.

Writer: The same as 'seller' of an **option**.

X

X: Used to denote the strike price of an option; sometimes this is denoted using the term *K*.

Y

Yield: The interest rate which can be earned on an investment, currently quoted by the market or implied by the current market price for the investment – as opposed to the **coupon** paid by an issuer on a security, which is based on the coupon rate and the face value. For a bond, generally the same as yield to maturity unless otherwise specified.

Yield curve: Graphical representation of the maturity structure of interest rates, plotting yields of bonds that are all of the same class or credit quality against the maturity of the bonds.

Yield-curve option: Option that allows purchasers to take a view on a yield curve without having to take a view about a market's direction.

Yield-curve swap: Swap in which the index rates of the two interest streams are at different points on the yield curve. Both payments are refixed with the same frequency whatever the index rate.

Yield to equivalent life: The same as **yield to maturity** for a bond with partial redemptions.

Yield to maturity: The **internal rate of return** of a bond – the yield necessary to discount all the bond's cashflows to an **NPV** equal to its current price. See **simple yield to maturity, current yield**.

YTM: See **yield to maturity**.

Z

Zero-cost collar: A **collar** where the premiums paid and received are equal, giving a net zero cost.

Zero-coupon: A zero-coupon security is one that does not pay a **coupon.** Its price is correspondingly less to compensate for this. A zero-coupon **yield** is the yield which a zero-coupon investment for that term would have if it were consistent with the **par yield curve**.

Zero-coupon bond: Bond on which no coupon is paid. It is either issued at a discount or redeemed at a premium to face value.

Zero-coupon swap: Swap converting the payment pattern of a zero-coupon bond, either to that of a normal, coupon-paying **fixed-rate** bond or to a **floating rate**.

Zero-premium option: Generic term for options for which there is no premium, either because the buyer undertakes to forgo a percentage of any gain or because he or she offsets the cost by **writing** other options.

JP Morgan Chase ITS 1st XI, September 2002
Back row, from left: the author, Michael Nicoll, Khurram Butt, Ben Burrell, Neil Lewis, Dean Annison, Chee Hau
Front row, from left: Stuart Medlen, Richard McCarthy, Graham Gooden, Rich Lynn, Alan Fulling, Rogerio Monaco, Jonathan Rossington

Index

Index prepared by Terry Halliday

Printed and bound by CPI Group (UK) Ltd, Croydon, CR0 4YY
08/05/2025
01864778-0003